Linguistics
and Literary History
Essays in Stylistics

Linguistics
and Literary History
Essays in Stylistics

By Leo Spitzer

NEW YORK
RUSSELL & RUSSELL · INC
1962

PUBLISHED, 1962, BY RUSSELL & RUSSELL, INC.
BY ARRANGEMENT WITH PRINCETON UNIVERSITY PRESS
L. C. CATALOG CARD NO: 62—10235

PRINTED IN THE UNITED STATES OF AMERICA

FOREWORD

THE following studies owe their birth to the kind invitation of the Department of Modern Languages and Literatures at Princeton University, extended to me at the behest of Professor Américo Castro, to give a lecture on the subject indicated by the title of the first essay, and to the further invitation of the Princeton University Press to expand the lecture (which is reproduced herein with the addition of some notes) into a book which would show some practical applications of my linguistic method to literature.

I dedicate this first book of mine printed in America, which is to continue the series of studies in stylistics previously published in Germany—*Aufsätze zur romanischen Syntax und Stilistik*, Halle (Niemeyer) 1918; *Stilstudien*, I-II, München (Hueber) 1928; *Romanische Stil- und Literaturstudien*, I-II, Marburg an der Lahn (Elwert) 1931—to Assistant Professor ANNA GRANVILLE HATCHER who is an outstanding American scholar in the too little cultivated field of syntax—which, in her case, is expanded into stylistic and cultural history—and who could thus teach me, not only the intricacies of English syntax and stylistics, but some of the more recondite features of American culture and of its particular moral, logical, and aesthetic aspirations: a knowledge without which all endeavors of the philologist to explain poetry to an American public must fail completely. For poetry has always been addressed to a public with which the poet felt himself to be united—so that the explanation of poetry, too, must needs be addressed to a public whose reactions the commentator is able to foresee. It is one of the benefits falling to the lot of the emigrant scholar that, however much his outward activity may be curtailed in the new country in comparison with his former situation, his inner activity is bound to be immensely enhanced and intensified: instead of writing as he pleases, after the usual fashion of the German scholar in particular (who is so well satisfied to live in the paradise of his ideas, whether this be accessible to his fellow men or not), he must, while trying to preserve his own idea of scholarship, continually count with his new audience, bearing in mind not only the conventional requirements but also those innermost strivings of the nation (inasmuch as it is given him to feel them) which, opposed to his nature as they may have seemed to him in the beginning, tend imperceptibly to become a second nature in him—indeed, to make shine by contrast his first nature in the clearest light. And, by so doing, he comes to feel enriched and to find that he has attained peace and happiness.

L.S.

THE JOHNS HOPKINS UNIVERSITY
SEPTEMBER 1945.

CONTENTS

Because the chapters listed above are intended to be read as articles one after the other, and consultation as a reference book is not envisaged, the author has decided that an index should not be included in the book.

I

LINGUISTICS AND LITERARY HISTORY[1]

THE title of this book is meant to suggest the ultimate unity of linguistics and literary history. Since my activity, throughout my scholarly life, has been largely devoted to the rapprochement of these two disciplines, I may be forgiven if I preface my remarks with an autobiographic sketch of my first academic experiences: What I propose to do is to tell you only my own story, how I made my way through the maze of linguistics, with which I started, toward the enchanted garden of literary history—and how I discovered that there is as well a paradise in linguistics as a labyrinth in literary history; that the methods and the degree of certainty in both are basically the same; and, that if today the humanities are under attack (and, as I believe, under an unwarranted attack, since it is not the humanities themselves that are at fault but only some so-called humanists who persist in imitating an obsolete approach to the natural sciences, which have themselves evolved toward the humanities)—if, then, the humanities are under attack, it would be pointless to exempt any one of them from the verdict: if it is true that there is no value to be derived from the study of language, we cannot pretend to preserve literary history, cultural history—or history.

I have chosen the autobiographical way because my personal situation in Europe forty years ago was not, I believe, essentially different from the one with which I see the young scholar of today (and in this country) generally faced. I chose to relate to you my own experiences also because the basic approach of the individual scholar, conditioned as it is by his first experiences, by his *Erlebnis*, as the Germans say, determines his method: *Methode ist Erlebnis*, Gundolf has said. In fact, I would advise every older scholar to tell his public the basic experiences underlying his methods, his *Mein Kampf*, as it were—without dictatorial connotations, of course.

I had decided, after college had given me a solid foundation in the classical languages, to study the Romance languages and particularly French philology, because, in my native Vienna, the gay and orderly, skeptic and sentimental, Catholic and pagan Vienna of yore was filled with adoration of the French way of life. I had always been surrounded by a French atmosphere and, at that juvenile stage of experience, had acquired a picture, perhaps overgeneralized, of French literature, which seemed to me definable by an Austrianlike mixture of sensuousness and reflection, of vitality and discipline, of sentimentality and critical wit. The moment when the curtain rose on a French play given by a French troupe, and the valet, in a knowing accent of psychological alertness, with his rich, poised voice, pronounced the words "Madame est servie," was a delight to my heart.

But when I attended the classes of French linguistics of my great teacher Meyer-Lübke no picture was offered us of the French people, or of the Frenchness of their language: in these classes we saw Latin *a* moving, according to relentless phonetic laws, toward French *e* (*pater* > *père*); there we saw a new system of declension spring up from nothingness, a system in which the six Latin cases came to be reduced to two, and later to one—while we learned that similar violence had been done to the other Romance languages and, in fact, to many modern languages. In all this, there were many facts and much rigor in the establishment of facts, but all was vague in regard to the general ideas underlying these facts. What was the mystery behind the refusal of Latin sounds or cases to stay put and behave themselves? We saw incessant change working in language—but why? I was a long while realizing that Meyer-Lübke was offering only the *pre*-history of French (as he established it by a comparison with the other Romance languages), not its history. And we were never allowed to contemplate a phenomenon in its quiet being, to look into its face: we always looked at its neighbors or at its predecessors—we were always looking over our shoulder. There were presented to us the relationships of phenomenon *a* and phenomenon *b*; but phenomenon *a* and phenomenon *b* did not exist in themselves, nor did the historical line *a* - *b*.

In reference to a given French form, Meyer-Lübke would quote Old Portuguese, Modern Bergamesque and Macedo-rumanian, German, Celtic, and paleo-Latin forms; but where was reflected in this teaching my sensuous, witty, disciplined Frenchman, in his presumably 1000 years of existence? He was left out in the cold while we talked about his language; indeed, French was not the language of the Frenchman, but an agglomeration of unconnected, separate, anecdotic, senseless evolutions: a French historical grammar, apart from the word-material, could as well have been a Germanic or a Slav grammar: the leveling of paradigms, the phonetic evolutions occur there just as in French.

When I changed over to the classes of the equally great literary historian Philipp August Becker, that ideal Frenchman seemed to show some faint signs of life—in the spirited analyses of the events in the *Pèlerinage de Charlemagne*, or of the plot of a Molière comedy; but it was as if the treatment of the contents were only subsidiary to the really scholarly work, which consisted in fixing the dates and historical data of these works of art, in assessing the amount of autobiographical elements and written sources which the poets had supposedly incorporated into their artistic productions. Had the *Pèlerinage* to do with the Xth crusade? Which was its original dialect? Was there any epic poetry, Merovingian or other, which preceded Old French epic poetry? Had Molière put his own matrimonial disillusionment into the *Ecole des femmes*? (While Becker did not insist on an affirmative conclusion, he considered such a question to be a part of legitimate literary criticism.) Did the medieval farce survive in the Molière comedy? The existing works of art were stepping-stones from which to proceed to other phenomena, contemporary or previous, which were in reality quite heterogeneous. It seemed indiscrete to ask what made them works of art, what was expressed in them, and why these expressions appeared in France, at that particular time. Again, it was prehistory, not history, that we were offered, and a kind of materialistic prehistory, at that. In this attitude of positivism, exterior events were taken thus seriously only to evade the more completely the real question: Why did the phenomena *Pèlerinage* and *Ecole des femmes* happen at all? And, I must admit, in full loyalty to Meyer-Lübke, that he taught more of reality than did Becker: it was unquestionable that Latin *a* had evolved to French *e*; it was untrue that Molière's experience with the possibly faithless Madeleine Béjart had evolved to the work of art *Ecole des femmes*. But, in both fields, that of linguistics as well as that of literary history (which were separated by an enormous gulf: Meyer-Lübke spoke only of language and Becker only of literature), a meaningless industriousness prevailed: not only was this kind of humanities not centered on a particular people in a particular time, but the subject matter itself had got lost: Man.[2] At the end of my first year of graduate studies, I had come to the conclusion, not that the science offered *ex cathedra* was worthless but that I was not fit for such studies as that of the irrational vowel *-i-* in Eastern French dialects, or of the *Subjektivismusstreit* in Molière: never would I get a Ph.D.! It was the benignity of Providence, exploiting my native Teutonic docility toward scholars who knew more than I, which kept me faithful to the study of Romance philology. By not abandoning prematurely this sham science, by seeking, instead, to appropriate it, I came to recognize its true value as well as my own possibilities of work—and to establish my life's goal. By using the tools of science offered me, I came to see under their dustiness the fingerprints of a Friedrich Diez and of the Romantics, who had created these tools; and henceforth they were not dusty any more, but ever radiant and ever new. And I had learned to handle many and manifold facts: training in handling facts, brutal facts, is perhaps the best education for a wavering, youthful mind.

And now let me take you, as I promised to do, on the path that leads from the most routinelike techniques of the linguist toward the work of the literary historian. The different fields will appear here in the ascending order, as I see them today, while the concrete examples, drawn from my own activity, will not respect the chronological order of their publication.

Meyer-Lübke, the author of the comprehensive and still final etymological dictionary of Romance languages, had taught me, among many other things, how to find etymologies; I shall now take the liberty of inflicting upon you a concrete example of this procedure—sparing you none of the petty drudgery involved. Since my coming to America, I have been curious about the etymology of two English words, characterized by the same "flavor": *conundrum* "a riddle the answer to which involves a pun; a puzzling question," and *quandary* "a puzzling situation." The NED attests conun-*drum* first in 1596; early variants are *conimbrum, quonundrum, quadrundum*. The meaning is "whim" or "pun." In the seventeenth century it was known as an Oxford term: preachers were wont to use in their sermons the baroque device of puns and conundrums, e.g. "Now all House is turned into an Alehouse, and a pair of dice is made a Paradice; was it thus in the days of Noah? Ah no." This baroque technique of interlarding sermons with puns is well known from the *Kapuziner-Predigt*, inspired by Abraham a Santa Clara, in Schiller's *Wallenstein's Lager*: "Der *Rheinstrom* ist worden zu einem *Peinstrom*," etc.

The extraordinary instability (reflecting the playfulness of the concept involved) of the phonetic structure: *conundrum - conimbrum - quadrundrum*, points to a foreign source, to a word which must have been (playfully) adapted in various ways. Since the English variants include among them a *-b-* and a *-d-* which are not easily reducible to any one basic sound, I propose to submit a French word-family which, in its different forms, contains both *-b-* and *-d-*: the French *calembour* is exactly synonymous with *conundrum* "pun." This *calembour* is evidently related to *calembredaine* "nonsensical or odd speech," and we can assume that *calembour*, too, had originally this same general reference. This word-family goes back probably to Fr. *bourde* "tall story" to which has been added the fanciful, semipejorative prefix *cali-*, that can be found in *à califourchon* "straddling" (from Latin *quadrifurcus*, French *carrefour* "crossroads": the *qu-* of the English variants points to this Latin etymon). The French ending *-aine* of *calembredaine* developed to *-um*: *n* becomes *m* as in *ransom* from French *rançon*; *ai* becomes *o* as in *mitten* (older *mitton*) from French *mitaine*. Thus *calembourdane*, as a result of various assimilations and shortenings which I will spare you, becomes **colundrum, *columbrum* and then *conundrum, conimbrum*, etc. Unfortunately, the French word-family is attested rather late, occurring for the first time in a comic opera of Vadé in 1754. We do find, however, an *équilbourdie* "whim" as early as 1658 in the *Muse normande*, a dialectal text. The fact is that popular words of this sort have, as a rule, little chance of turning up in the (predominantly idealistic) literature of the Middle Ages; it is, therefore, a mere accident that English *conundrum* is attested in 1596 and French *calembour* only in 1757; at least, the chance appearance of *équilbourdie* in the dialectal text of 1658 gives us an earlier attestation of the French word-family. That the evidently popular medieval words emerge so late in literature is a fact explainable by the currents prevalent in literature; the linguist must take his chances with what literature offers him in the way of attestation. In view of the absolute evidence of the equation *conundrum = calembredaine* we need not be intimidated by chronological divergencies—which the older school of etymologists (as represented by the editors of the NED) seem to have overrated.

After *conundrum* had ceased to be a riddle to me, I was emboldened to ask myself whether I could not now solve the etymology of the word *quandary*—which also suggested to me a French origin. And, lo and behold: this word, of unknown origin, which is attested from about 1580 on, revealed itself etymologically identical with *conundrum*! There are English dialect forms such as *quándorum quóndorum* which serve to establish an uninterrupted chain: *calembredaine* becomes *conimbrum conundrum quonundrum quandorum* and these give us *quandary*.[3]

Now what can be the humanistic, the spiritual value of this (as it may have seemed to you) juggling with word forms? The particular etymology of *conundrum* is an inconsequential fact; that an etymology can be found by man is a miracle. An etymology introduces meaning into the meaningless: in our case, the evolution of two words in time—that is, a piece of linguistic history—has been cleared up. What seemed an agglomeration of mere sounds now appears motivated. We feel the same "inner click" accompanying our comprehension of this evolution in time as when we have grasped the meaning of a sentence or a poem—which then become more than the sum total of their single words or sounds (*poem* and *sentence* are, in fact, the classical examples given by Augustine and Bergson in order to demonstrate the nature of a stretch of *durée réelle*: the parts aggregating to a whole, time filled with contents). In the problem which we chose, two words which seemed erratic and fantastic, with no definite relationships in English, have been unified among themselves and related to a French word-family.

The existence of such a loan-word is another testimony to the well-known cultural situation obtaining when medieval England was in the sway of French influence: the English and French word-families, although attested centuries after the Middle Ages, must have belonged to one Anglo-French word-family during that period, and their previous existence is precisely proved by proving their family relationship. And it is not by chance that English borrows words for "pun" or "whim" from the witty French, who have also given *carriwitchet* "quibble" and (perhaps: see the NED) *pun* itself to English. But, since a loan-word rarely feels completely at home in its new environment, we have the manifold variations of the word, which fell apart into two word-groups (clearly separated, today, by the current linguistic feeling): *conundrum-quandary*. The instability and disunity of the word-family is symptomatic of its position in the new environment.

But the instability apparent in our English words had already been characteristic of *calembredaine - calembour,* even in the home environment: this French word-family, as we have said, was a blend of at least two word-stems. Thus we must conclude that the instability is also connected with the semantic content: a word meaning "whim, pun" easily behaves whimsically—just as, in all languages throughout the world, the words for "butterfly" present a kaleidoscopic instability. The linguist who explains such fluttery words has to juggle, because the speaking community itself (in our case, the English as well as the French) has juggled. This juggling in itself is psychologically and culturally motivated: language is not, as the behavioristic, antimentalistic, mechanistic or materialistic school of linguists, rampant in some universities, would have it: a meaningless agglomeration of corpses: dead word-material, automatic "speech habits" unleased by a trigger motion. A certain automatism may be predicated of the use of *conundrum* and *quandary* in contemporary English, and of *calembour*, *calembredaine* in contemporary French (though, even today, this automatism is not absolute, since all these words have still a connotation of whimsicality or fancifulness and are, accordingly, somewhat motivated). But this is certainly not true for the history of the words: the linguistic creation is always meaningful and, yes, clear-minded: it was a feeling for the appositeness of nomenclature which prompted the communities to use, in our case, two-track words. They gave a playful expression to a playful concept, symbolizing in the word their attitude toward the concept. It was when the creative, the Renaissance, phase had passed that English let the words congeal, petrify, and split into two. This petrification is, itself, due to a decision of the community which, in eighteenth-century England, passed from the Renaissance attitude to the classicistic attitude toward language, which would replace creativity by standardization and regulation. Another cultural climate, another linguistic style. Out of the infinity of word-histories which could be imagined we have chosen only one, one which shows quite individual circumstances, such as the borrowing of a foreign word by English, the original French blend, the subsequent alterations and restrictions; every word has its own history, not to be confused with that of any other. But what repeats itself in all word-histories is the possibility of recognizing the signs of a people at work, culturally and psychologically. To speak in the language of the homeland of philology: *Wortwandel ist Kulturwandel und Seelenwandel*; this little etymological study has been humanistic in purpose.

If we accept the equation: *conundrum* and *quandary* = *calembredaine*—how has this been found? I may say, by quite an orthodox technique which would have been approved by Meyer-Lübke—though he would not, perhaps, have stopped to draw the inferences on which I have insisted. First, by collecting the material evidence about the English words, I was led to seek a French origin. I had also observed that the great portion of the English vocabulary which is derived from French has not been given sufficient attention by etymologists; and, of course, my familiarity with the particular behavior of "butterfly words" in language was such as to encourage a relative boldness in the reconstruction of the etymon. I had first followed the inductive method—or rather a quick intuition—in order to identify *conundrum* with *calembredaine*; later, I had to proceed deductively, to verify whether my assumed etymon concorded with all the known data, whether it really explained all the semantic and phonetic variations; while following this path I was able to see that *quandary* must also be a reflection of *calembredaine*. (This to-and-fro movement is a basic requirement in all humanistic studies, as we shall see later.) For example, since the French word-family is attested later than is the English, it seemed necessary to dismiss the chronological discrepancies; fortunately—or, as I would say, providentially—the Normandian *équilbourdie* of 1658 turned up! In this kind of gentle blending together of the words, of harmonizing them and smoothing out difficulties, the linguist undoubtedly indulges in a propensity to see things as shifting and melting into each other—an attitude to which you may object: I cannot contend more than that this change was *possible* in the way I have indicated, since it contradicts no previous experience; I can say only that two unsolved problems (the one concerning the prehistory of *conundrum*, the other that of *calembredaine*) have, when brought together, shed light on each other, thereby enabling us to see the common solution. I am reminded here of the story of the Pullman porter to whom a passenger complained in the morning that he had got back one black shoe and one tan; the porter replied that, curiously enough, a similar discovery had been made by another passenger. In the field of language, the porter who has mixed up the shoes belonging together is language itself, and the linguist is the passenger who must bring together what was once a historical unit. To place two phenomena within a framework adds something to the knowledge about their common nature. There is no mathematical demonstrability in such an equation, only a feeling of inner evidence; but this feeling, with the trained linguist, is the fruit of observation combined with experience, of precision supplemented by imagination—the dosage of which cannot be fixed a priori, but only in the concrete case. There is underlying such a procedure the belief that this is the way things happened; but there is always a belief underlying the humanist's work (similarly, it cannot be demonstrated that the Romance languages form a unity going back to Vulgar Latin; this basic assumption of the student in Romance languages, first stated by Diez, cannot be proved to the disbeliever).[4] And who says belief, says suasion: I have, deliberately and tendentiously, grouped the variants of *conundrum* in the most plausible order possible for the purpose of winning your assent. Of course, there are more easily believable etymologies, reached at the cost of less stretching and bending: no one in his senses would doubt that French *père* comes from Latin *pater*, or that this, along with English *father*, goes back to an Indo-European prototype. But we must not forget that these smooth, standard equations are relatively rare—for the reason that a word such as "father" is relatively immune to cultural revolutions or, in other words, that, in regard to the "father," a continuity of feeling, stretching over more than 4000 years, exists in Indo-European civilization.

Thus our etymological study has illuminated a stretch of linguistic history, which is connected with psychology and history of civilization; it has suggested a web of interrelations between language and the soul of the speaker. This web could have been as well revealed by a study of a syntactical, a morphological evolution—even a phonetic evolution of the type "*a* becomes *e*," wherein Meyer-Lübke had failed to see the *durée réelle*, exclusively concerned as he was with *l'heure de la montre*: his historical "clock time."

Now, since the best document of the soul of a nation is its literature, and since the latter is nothing but its language as this is written down by elect speakers, can we perhaps not hope to grasp the spirit of a nation in the language of its outstanding works of literature? Because it would have been rash to compare the whole of a national literature to the whole of a national language (as Karl Vossler has prematurely tried to do) I started, more modestly, with the question: "Can one distinguish the soul of a particular French writer in his particular language?" It is obvious that literary historians have held this conviction, since, after the inevitable quotation (or misquotation) of Buffon's saying: "*Le style c'est l'homme,*" they generally include in their monographs a chapter on the style of their author. But I had in mind the more rigorously scientific definition of an individual style, the definition of a linguist which should replace the casual, impressionistic remarks of literary critics. Stylistics, I thought, might bridge the gap between linguistics and literary history. On the other hand, I was warned by the scholastic adage: *individuum est ineffabile*; could it be that any attempt to define the individual writer by his style is doomed to failure? The individual stylistic deviation from the general norm must represent a historical step taken by the writer, I argued: it must reveal a shift of the soul of the epoch, a shift of which the writer has become conscious and which he would translate into a necessarily new linguistic form; perhaps it would be possible to determine the historical step, psychological as well as linguistic? To determine the beginning of a linguistic innovation would be easier, of course, in the case of contemporary writers, because their linguistic basis is better known to us than is that of past writers.

In my reading of modern French novels, I had acquired the habit of underlining expressions which struck me as aberrant from general usage, and it often happened that the underlined passages, taken together, seemed to offer a certain consistency. I wondered if it would not be possible to establish a common denominator for all or most of these deviations; could not the common spiritual etymon, the psychological root, of several individual "traits of style" in a writer be found, just as we have found an etymon common to various fanciful word formations?[5] I had, for example, noticed in the novel *Bubu de Montparnasse* of Charles-Louis Philippe (1905), which moves in the underworld of Parisian pimps and prostitutes, a particular use of *à cause de*, reflecting the spoken, the unliterary language: "Les réveils de midi sont lourds et poisseux. . . . On éprouve un sentiment de déchéance *à cause* des réveils d'autrefois." More academic writers would have said "en se rappelant des réveils d'autrefois. . . ," "à la suite du souvenir. . . ." This, at first glance, prosaic and commonplace *à cause de* has nevertheless a poetic flavor, because of the unexpected suggestion of a causality, where the average person would see only coincidence: it is, after all, not unanimously accepted that one awakes with a feeling of frustration from a noon siesta *because* other similar awakenings have preceded; we have here an assumed, a poetic reality, but one expressed by a prosaic phrase. We find this *à cause de* again in a description of a popular celebration of the 14th of July: "[le peuple], *à cause de* l'anniversaire de sa délivrance, laisse ses filles danser en liberté." Thus, one will not be surprised when the author lets this phrase come from the mouth of one of his characters: "Il y a dans mon coeur deux ou trois cent petites émotions qui brûlent *à cause de toi.*" Conventional poetry would have said "qui brûlent pour toi"; "qui brûlent *à cause de toi*" is both less and more: more, since the lover speaks his heart better in this sincere, though factual manner. The causal phrase, with all its semipoetic implications, suggests rather a commonplace speaker, whose speech and whose habits of thought the writer seems to endorse in his own narrative.

Our observation about *à cause de* gains strength if we compare the use, in the same novel, of other causal conjunctions, such as *parce que*: for example, it is said of the pimp's love for his sweetheart Berthe: "[il aimait] sa volupté particulière, quand elle appliquait son corps contre le sien. . . . Il aimait cela qui la distinguait de toutes les femmes qu'il avait connues *parce que* c'était plus doux, *parce que* c'était plus fin, et *parce que* c'était sa femme à lui, qu'il avait eue vierge. Il l'aimait *parce qu'*elle était honnête et qu'elle en avait l'air, et pour toutes les raisons qu'ont les bourgeois d'aimer leur femme." Here, the reasons why Maurice loved to embrace his sweetheart (*parce que c'était doux, fin, parce que c'était sa femme a lui*) are outspokenly classified or censored by the writer as being *bourgeois*; and yet, in Philippe's narrative, the *parce que* is used as if he considered these reasons to be objectively valid.

The same observation holds true for the causal conjunction *car*: in the following passage which describes Maurice as a being naturally loved by women: "Les femmes l'entouraient d'amour comme des oiseaux qui chantent le soleil et la force. Il était un de ceux que nul ne peut assujettir, *car* leur vie, plus forte et plus belle, comporte l'amour du danger."

Again, it can happen that a causal relationship is implied without the use of a conjunction, a relationship due to the gnomic character adherent, at least in that particular milieu, to a general statement—the truth of which is, perhaps, not so fully accepted elsewhere: "Elle l'embrassa à pleine bouche. *C'est une chose hygiénique* et bonne entre un homme et sa femme, qui vous amuse un petit quart d'heure avant de vous endormir." (Philippe could as well have written "car. . . ," "parce que c'est une chose hygiénique. . . .") Evidently this is the truth only in that particular world of sensuous realism which he is describing. At the same time, however, the writer, while half-endorsing these bourgeois platitudes of the underworld, is discreetly but surely suggesting his criticism of them.

Now I submit the hypothesis that all these expansions of causal usages in Philippe cannot be due to chance: there must be "something the matter" with his conception of causality. And now we must pass from Philippe's style to the psychological etymon, to the radix in his soul. I have called the phenomenon in question "pseudo-objective motivation": Philippe, when presenting causality as binding for his characters, seems to recognize a rather objective cogency in their sometimes awkward, sometimes platitudinous, sometimes semipoetic reasonings; his attitude shows a fatalistic, half-critical, half-understanding, humorous sympathy with the necessary errors and thwarted strivings of these underworld beings dwarfed by inexorable social forces. The pseudo-objective motivation, manifest in his style, is the clue to Philippe's *Weltanschauung*; he sees, as has also been observed by literary critics, without revolt but with deep grief and a Christian spirit of contemplativity, the world functioning wrongly with an appearance of rightness, of objective logic. The different word-usages, grouped together (just as was done with the different forms of *conundrum* and *quandary*) lead toward a psychological etymon, which is at the bottom of the linguistic as well as of the literary inspiration of Philippe.

Thus we have made the trip from language or style to the soul. And on this journey we may catch a glimpse into a historical evolution of the French soul in the twentieth century: first we are given insight into the soul of a writer who has become conscious of the fatalism weighing on the masses, then, into that of a section of the French nation itself, whose faint protest is voiced by our author. And in this procedure there is, I think, no longer the timeless, placeless philology of the older school, but an explanation of the concrete *hic et nunc* of a historical phenomenon. The to-and-fro movement we found to be basic with the humanist has been followed here, too: first we grouped together certain causal expressions, striking with Philippe, then hunted out their psychological explanation, and finally, sought to verify whether the element of "pseudo-objective motivation"[6] concorded with what we know, from other sources, about the elements of his inspiration. Again, a belief is involved—which is no less daring than is the belief that the Romance languages go back to one invisible, basic pattern manifest in them all: namely, the belief that the mind of an author is a kind of solar system into whose orbit all categories of things are attracted: language, motivation, plot, are only satellites of this mythological entity (as my antimentalistic adversaries would call it): *mens Philippina.* The linguist as well as his literary colleague must always ascend to the etymon which is behind all those particular so-called literary or stylistic devices which the literary historians are wont to list. And the individual *mens Philippina* is a reflection of the *mens Franco-gallica* of the twentieth century; its ineffability consists precisely in Philippe's anticipatory sensitivity for the spiritual needs of the nation.

Now, it is obvious that a modern writer such as Philippe, faced with the social disintegration of humanity in the twentieth century, must show more patent linguistic deviations, of which the philologist may take stock in order to build up his "psychogram" of the individual artist. But does Philippe, a stranded being broken loose from his moorings, transplanted, as it were, into a world from which he feels estranged—so that he must, perforce, indulge in arbitrary whimsicality—represent only a modern phenomenon? If we go back to writers of more remote times, must it not be that we will always find a balanced language, with no deviations from common usage?

It suffices to mention the names of such dynamic writers of older times as Dante or Quevedo or Rabelais to dispel such a notion. Whoever has thought strongly and felt strongly has innovated in his language; mental creativity immediately inscribes itself into the language, where it becomes linguistic creativity; the trite and petrified in language is never sufficient for the needs of expression felt by a strong personality. In my first publication, "Die Wortbildung als stilistisches Mittel" (a thesis written in 1910), I dealt with Rabelais' comic word-formations, a subject to which I was attracted because of certain affinities between Rabelaisian and Viennese (Nestroy!) comic writing, and which offered the opportunity of bridging the gap between linguistic and literary history. Be it said to the eternal credit of the scholarly integrity of Meyer-Lübke that he, in contrast to the antimentalists who would suppress all expressions of opposition to their theories, recommended for publication a book with an approach so aberrant from his own. In this work I sought to show, for example, that a neologism such as *pantagruélisme*, the name given by Rabelais to his stoic-epicurean philosophy ("certaine gayeté d'esprict, conficte en mépris des choses fortuites") is not only a playful outburst of a genuine gaiety, but a thrust from the realm of the real into that of the unreal and the unknown—as is true, in fact, of any nonce-word. On the one hand, a form with the suffix *-ism* evokes a school of serious philosophic thought (such as *Aristotelianism, scholasticism*, etc.); on the other, the stem, *Pantagruel*, is the name of a character created by Rabelais, the half-jocular, half-philosophical giant and patriarchal king. The coupling of the learned philosophical suffix with the fanciful name of a fanciful character amounts to positing a half-real, half-unreal entity: "the philosophy of an imaginary being." The contemporaries of Rabelais who first heard this coinage must have experienced the reactions provoked by any nonce-word: a moment of shock followed by a feeling of reassurance: to be swept toward the unknown frightens, but realization of the benignly fanciful result gives relief: laughter, our physiological reaction on such occasions, arises precisely out of a feeling of relief following upon a temporary breakdown of our assurance. Now, in a case such as that of the creation *pantagruélisme*, the designation of a hitherto unknown but, after all, innocuous philosophy, the menacing force of the neologism is relatively subdued. But what of such a list of names as that concocted by Rabelais for the benefit of his hated adversaries, the reactionaries of the Sorbonne: *sophistes, sorbillans, sorbonagres, sorbonigenes, sorbonicoles, sorboniformes, sorboniseques, niborcisans, sorbonisans, saniborsans.* Again, though differently, there is an element of realism present in these coinages: the Sorbonne is an existing reality, and the formations are explainable by well-known formative processes. The edition of Abel Lefranc, imbued with his positivistic approach, goes to the trouble of explaining each one of these formations: *sorboniforme* is after *uniforme*, *sorbonigene* after *homogène*, while *niborcisans, saniborsans* offer what, in the jargon of the linguists, is called a metathesis. But by explaining every coinage separately, by dissolving the forest into trees, the commentators lose sight of the whole phenomenon: they no longer see the forest—or rather the jungle which Rabelais must have had before his eyes, teeming with viperlike, hydralike, demonlike shapes. Nor is it enough to say that the scholarly Rabelais indulges in humanistic word lists with a view to enriching the vocabulary—in the spirit of an Erasmus who prescribed the principle of *copia verborum* to students of Latin—or that Rabelais' rich nature bade him make the French language rich; the aesthetics of richness is, in itself, a problem; and why should richness tend toward the frightening, the bottomless? Perhaps Rabelais' whole attitude toward language rests upon a vision of imaginary richness whose support is the bottomless. He creates word-families, representative of gruesome fantasy-beings, copulating and engendering before our eyes, which have reality only in the world of language, which are established in an intermediate world between reality and irreality, between the nowhere that frightens and the "here" that reassures. The *niborcisans* are as yet an entity vaguely connected with the *sorbonisans*, but at the same time so close to nothingness that we laugh—uneasily; it is *le comique grotesque* which skirts the abyss. And Rabelais will shape grotesque word-families (or families of word-demons) not only by altering what exists: he may leave intact the forms of his word material and create by juxtaposition: savagely piling epithet upon epithet to an ultimate effect of terror, so that, from the well known emerges the shape of the unknown—a phenomenon the more startling with the French, who are generally considered to inhabit an orderly, clearly regulated, well-policed language. Now, of a sudden, we no longer recognize this French language, which has become a chaotic word-world situated somewhere in the chill of cosmic space. Just listen to the inscription on the *abbaye de Thélème,* that Renaissance convent of his shaping, from which Rabelais excludes the hypocrites:

> Cy n'entrez pas, hypocrites, bigots,
> Vieux matagotz, marmiteux, borsoufles,
> Torcoulx, badaux, plus que n'estoient les Gotz,
> Ny Ostrogotz, precurseurs des magotz,
> Haires, cagotz, cafars empantouflez,
> Gueux mitoufles, frapars escorniflez,
> Befflez, enflez, fagoteurs de tabus;
> Tirez ailleurs pour vendre vos abus.

The prosaic commentators of the Lefranc edition would explain that this kind of rather mediocre poetry is derived from the popular genre of the *cry* (the harangue of a barker), and overloaded with devices of the *rhétoriqueur* school. But I can never read these lines without being frightened, and I am shaken in this very moment by the horror emanating from this accumulation of *-fl-* and *-got-* clusters—of sounds which, in themselves, and taken separately, are quite harmless, of words grouped together, bristling with Rabelais' hatred of hypocrisy—that greatest of all crimes against life. A *cry*, yes, but in a more extensive meaning of the word: it is the gigantic voice of Rabelais which cries to us directly across the gulf of the centuries, as shattering now as at the hour when Rabelais begot these word-monsters.

If, then, it is true that Rabelais' word-formation reflects an attitude somewhere between reality and irreality, with its shudders of horror and its comic relief, what of Lanson's famous statement on Rabelais in general, which is repeated in thousands of French schools and in most of the Lanson-imbued seminars of French throughout the world: "Jamais réalisme plus pur, plus puissant et plus triomphant ne s'est vu"? Well, it is simply wrong. I have not time to develop here the conclusions which would round out the utterly anti-realistic picture of Rabelais that stands out in his work; it could be shown that the whole plot of Rabelais' epic, the fantastic voyage of fantastic people to the oracle of the priestess Bacbuc (whose ambiguous response: "*Trinc!*" is just a nowhere word) as well as the invention of detail (e.g. Panurge's speech on debtors and lenders, in which the earthy Panurge drives forward, from his astute egoistic refusal to live without debts, to a cosmic, utopian vision of a paradoxical world resting on the universal law of indebtedness)—that everything in Rabelais' work tends toward the creation of a world of irreality.

Thus, what has been disclosed by the study of Rabelais' language, the literary study would corroborate; it could not be otherwise, since language is only one outward crystallization of the "inward form," or, to use another metaphor: the life-blood of the poetic creation[7] is everywhere the same, whether we tap the organism at "language" or "ideas," at "plot" or at "composition." As regards the last, I could as well have begun with a study of the rather loose literary composition of Rabelais' writings and only later have gone over to his ideas, his plot, his language. Because I happened to be a linguist it was from the linguistic angle that I started, to fight my way to his unity. Obviously, no fellow scholar must be required to do the same. What he must be asked to do, however, is, I believe, to work from the surface to the "inward life-center" of the work of art: first observing details about the superficial appearance of the particular work (and the "ideas" expressed by a poet are, also, only one of the superficial traits in a work of art);[8] then, grouping these details and seeking to integrate them into a creative principle which may have been present in the soul of the artist; and, finally, making the return trip to all the other groups of observations in order to find whether the "inward form" one has tentatively constructed gives an account of the whole. The scholar will surely be able to state, after three or four of these "fro voyages," whether he has found the life-giving center, the sun of the solar system (by then he will know whether he is really permanently installed in the center, or whether he finds himself in an "excentric" or peripheric position). There is no shadow of truth in the objection raised not long ago by one of the representatives of the mechanist Yale school of linguists against the "circularity of arguments" of the mentalists: against the "explanation of a linguistic fact by an assumed psychological process for which the only evidence is the fact to be explained."[9] I could immediately reply that my school is not satisfied with psychologizing one trait but bases its assumptions on several traits carefully grouped and integrated; one should, in fact, embrace *all* the linguistic traits observable with a given author (I myself have tried to come as close as possible to this requirement of completeness in my studies on Racine, Saint-Simon, Quevedo [in *RSL*]). And the circle of which the adversary just quoted speaks is not a vicious one; on the contrary, it is the basic operation in the humanities, the *Zirkel im Verstehen* as Dilthey has termed the discovery, made by the Romantic scholar and theologian Schleiermacher, that cognizance in philology is reached not only by the gradual progression from one detail to another detail, but by the anticipation or divination of the whole—because "the detail can be understood only by the whole and any explanation of detail presupposes the understanding of the whole."[10] Our to-and-fro voyage from certain outward details to the inner center and back again to other series of details is only an application of the principle of the "philological circle." After all, the concept of the Romance languages as based on one Vulgar Latin substratum, and reflected in them although identical with none—this has been reached by the founder of Romance philology, Diez, the pupil of the Romantics, precisely by means of this "philological circle," which allowed him to sit installed in the center of the phenomenon "Romance Languages," whereas Raynouard, his predecessor, by identifying one of the Romance varieties, Provençal, with Proto-Romance, found himself in an excentric position, from which point it was impossible to explain satisfactorily all the outward traits of Romance. To proceed from some exterior traits of Philippe's or Rabelais' language to the soul or mental center of Philippe and Rabelais, and back again to the rest of the exterior traits of Philippe's and Rabelais' works of art, is the same *modus operandi* as that which proceeds from some details of the Romance languages to a Vulgar Latin prototype and then, in reverse order, explains other details by this assumed prototype—or even, from that which infers from some of the outward, phonetic and semantic appearances of the English word *conundrum* to its medieval French soul, and back to all its phonetic and semantic traits.

To posit a soul of Rabelais which creates from the real in the direction of the unreal is, of course, not yet all that is desirable in order to understand the whole phenomenon: the Rabelaisian entity must be integrated into a greater unit and located somewhere on a historical line, as Diez, in a grandiose way, did with Romance—as we have tried to do, on a minor scale, with *calembredaine - conundrum.* Rabelais may be a solar system which, in its turn, forms part of a transcending system which embraces others as well as himself, others around, before, and after him; we must place him, as the literary historians would say, within the framework of the history of ideas, or *Geistesgeschichte*. The power of wielding the word as though it were a world of its own between reality and irreality, which exists to a unique degree with Rabelais, cannot have sprung out of nothingness, cannot have entirely ebbed after him. Before him there is, for example, Pulci, who, in his *Morgante Maggiore*, shows a predilection for word-lists, especially when he has his facetious knights indulge in name-calling. And, with Pulci, the Rabelaisian tendency to let language encroach on reality, is also to be found: when he retells, in half-facetious vein, the story immortalized by Turoldus of the battle of Roncevaux, we learn that the Saracens fell under the blows of the Christian knights in a trice: they stayed not upon the order of their dying but died at once: not tomorrow, or the day after tomorrow, nor the day after the day after tomorrow, nor the day after the day after the day after tomorrow: not *crai e poscrai, o poscrilla, o posquacchera.* In this sequel of gurgling and guttural sounds, the words *crai* and *poscrai* are genuine Italian reflections of the Latin words *cras* and *posteras*; but *poscrilla, posquacchera* are popular fantasy words.[11] The onomatopoeias with which popular language likes to juggle have here been used by a reflective poet for purposes of grotesque art: we can see here the exact point of transition of popular language into literature. Pulci believes in the ideals of Christian orthodox knighthood less full-heartedly than did Turoldus, for whom the heroic and religious values were real, and who must needs subordinate his language to the expression of these values. The word-world, admitted to a work of art by Pulci, was not yet available to Turoldus, or even to Dante (the "etymological puns" of the *Vita nuova* are quite another matter: they are only "illustrations," just as had been true of the puns of the Church Fathers).[12] The appearance of this intermediate world is conditioned by a belief in the reality of words, a belief which would have been condemned by the "realists" of the Middle Ages. The belief in such vicarious realities as words is possible only in an epoch whose belief in the *universalia realia* has been shaken. It is this phantasmagoric climate, casually evoked by Pulci, in which Rabelais will move easily and naturally, with a kind of cosmic independence. It is the belief in the autonomy of the word which made possible the whole movement of Humanism, in which so much importance was given to the word of the ancients and of the Biblical writers; it is this belief which will in part explain the extraordinary development of mathematics in the sixteenth and seventeenth centuries—i.e. of the most autonomous language that man has ever devised.

Now, who are the descendants of Rabelais? French classical literature, with its ideal of the *mot juste*, of the *mot mis à sa place*, broke away from the Renaissance tradition of the autonomy of the word. But undercurrents persisted, and I would say that Balzac, Flaubert (in his Letters), Théophile Gautier (in his *grotesqueries*), Victor Hugo (in his *William Shakespeare*), and Huysmans are, to a certain extent, descendants of Rabelais in the nineteenth century. In our own time, with Ferdinand Céline, who can build a whole book out of invectives against the Jews ("Bagatelles pour un massacre"), we may see language exceed its boundaries: this book, in the words of André Gide, is a "chevauchée de Don Quichotte en plein ciel . . ."; "ce n'est pas la réalité que peint Céline; c'est l'hallucination que la réalité provoque." The following sample of Celinian inspiration makes a pseudo-Rabelaisian effect, and can be compared with the apocalyptic inscription over the portal of Thélème: "Penser 'sozial!' cela veut dire dans la pratique, en termes bien crus: 'penser juif! pour les juifs! par les juifs, sous les juifs!' Rien d'autre! Tout le surplus immense des mots, le vrombissant verbiage socialitico-humanitaro-scientifique, tout le cosmique carafouillage de l'impératif despotique juif n'est que l'enrobage mirageux, le charabia fatras poussif, la sauce orientale pour ces encoulés d'aryens, la fricassée terminologique pour rire, pour l'adulation des 'aveulis blancs,' ivrognes rampants, intouchables, qui s'en foutrent, à bite que veux-tu, s'en mystifient, s'en baffrent à crever."

Here, evidently, the verbal creation, itself a *vrombissant verbiage* (to use the alliterative coinage of Céline), has implications more eschatological than cosmic: the word-world is really only a world of noisy words, clanking sounds, like so many engines senselessly hammering away, covering with their noise the fear and rage of man lonely in the doomed modern world. Words and reality fall apart. This is really a *voyage au bout du monde*: not to the oracle of Bacbuc but to chaos, to the end of language as an expression of thought.

The historical line we have drawn (we may call it the

evolution of an idea: the idea of "language become autonomous"), which is marked by the stages Pulci - Rabelais - Victor Hugo - Céline, is paralleled or crossed by other historical lines with other names located on the historical ladder. Victor Hugo is not Rabelais, although there may be Hugoesque traits in Rabelais, Rabelaisian traits in Hugo. We must not confuse a historical line with a solar system resting in itself: what appeared to us central in Rabelais may be peripheric in Victor Hugo, and the reverse. Every solar system, unique in itself, undefinable ("*ineffabile*") to a certain extent, is traversed by different historical lines of "ideas," whose intersection produces the particular climate in which the great literary work matures—just as the system of a language is made up of the intersections of different historical lines of the *calembredaine - conundrum* variety.

Thus we started with a particular historical line, the etymology of a particular word-family, and found therein evidences of a change of historical climate. Then we considered the change of a whole historical climate as expressed in the innovations, linguistic and literary, of writers of two different epochs (the twentieth and the sixteenth), finally to arrive at the point of positing theoretically self-sufficient systems: the great works of art, determined by different historical developments and reflecting in all their outward details, linguistic as well as literary, their respective central "sun." It is obvious that, in this paper, I have been able to give you only scattered samples, the conclusions from which I have loaded, and perhaps overloaded, with an experience resulting from hundreds of such to-and-fro voyages—all directed by the same principles, but each one bound for an unpredictable goal. My personal way has been from the observed detail to ever broadening units which rest, to an increasing degree, on speculation. It is, I think, the philological, the inductive way, which seeks to show significance in the apparently futile, in contrast to the deductive procedure which begins with units assumed as given—and which is rather the way followed by the theologians who start from on high, to take the downward path toward the earthly maze of detail, or by the mathematicians, who treat their axioms as if these were God-given.

In philology, which deals with the all-too-human, with the interrelated and the intertwined aspects of human affairs, the deductive method has its place only as a verification of the principle found by induction—which rests on observation.

But, of course, the attempt to discover significance in the detail,[13] the habit of taking a detail of language as seriously as the meaning of a work of art—or, in other words, the attitude which sees all manifestations of man as equally serious—this is an outgrowth of the preestablished firm conviction, the "axiom," of the philologian, that details are not an inchoate chance aggregation of dispersed material through which no light shines. The philologian must believe in the existence of some light from on high, of some *post nubila Phoebus*. If he did not know that at the end of his journey there would be awaiting him a life-giving draught from some *dive bouteille*, he would not have commenced it: "Tu ne me chercherais pas si tu ne m'avais pas déjà trouvé," says Pascal's God. Thus, humanistic thought, in spite of the methodological distinction just made, is not so completely divorced from that of the theologian as is generally believed; it is not by chance that the "philological circle" was discovered by a theologian, who was wont to harmonize the discordant, to retrace the beauty of God in this world. This attitude is reflected in the word coined by Schleiermacher: *Weltanschauung*:[14] "die Welt anschauen": "to see, to cognize the universe *in its sensuous detail*." The philologian will then continue the pursuit of the microscopic because he sees therein the microcosmic; he will practice that "*Andacht zum Kleinen*" which Jacob Grimm has prescribed; he will go on filling his little cards with dates and examples, in the hope that supernal light will shine over them and bring out the clear lines of truth. The Humanist believes in the power bestowed on the human mind of investigating the human mind. When, with scholars whose goal and whose tool are thus identical, the faith in the human mind, as a tool and as a goal, is broken, this can only mean a crisis in the humanities—or, should I say, in the *Divinities*? And this is the situation today. A man without belief in the human mind is a stunted human being—how can he be a Humanist? The humanities will be restored only when the Humanists shed their agnostic attitudes, when they become human again, and share the belief of Rabelais' humanistic and religious king: "sapience n'entre point en ame malivole; et science sans conscience n'est que ruine de l'ame"—or, to go back to the Augustinian wording: "Non intratur in veritatem nisi per charitatem."[15]

* *
*

In the essays to follow I have made an attempt to apply the principle of the "philological circle" to various authors of different nations and periods, applying it in varying degree and manner and in combination with other methods. But these articles are conceived not only as illustrations of my procedure, but as independent contributions to the understanding of the writers treated therein: contributions which should prove readable for any cultured person interested in the style of works of art.[16] For if my procedure should have any value, this must be revealed in the new results, the scholarly progress, attained by its means: the philological circle should not imply that one moves complacently in the circle of the already-known, in a *piétinement sur place*. Thus each single essay is intended to form a separate, independent unit: I hope that the repetitions of theoretical and historical statements which are the unavoidable consequence of this manner of presentation, will be felt by the reader rather as recurrent *leitmotifs* or *refrains* destined to emphasize a constancy and unity of approach.

Before putting to the test the method of the "philological circle" already delineated, I should like to warn the reader that he must not expect to find, in my demonstration of this method, the systematic step-by-step procedure which my own description of it may have seemed to promise.[17] For, when I spoke in terms of a series of back-and-forth movements (first the detail, then the whole, then another detail, etc.), I was using a linear and temporal figure in an attempt to describe states of apperception which, in the mind of the humanist, only too often co-exist. This gift, or vice (for it has its dangers), of seeing part and whole together, at any moment, and which, to some degree, is basic to the operation of the philological mind, is, perhaps, in my own case, developed to a particular degree, and has aroused objections from students and readers—in Germany, where the synthetic capacities of the public are, in general, superior to their analytic capacities, as well as in America where the opposite obtains. A very understanding but critical ex-student of mine, an American, once wrote me: "To establish a behavioristic technique which would reveal the application of your method is, it seems to me, beyond your possibilities. You know the principles that motivate you, rather than any 'technique' that you rigorously follow. Here, it may be a memory from boyhood, there an inspiration you got from another poem; here, there and everywhere it is an urge in you, an instinct backed up by your experience, that tells you immediately: 'this is not important; this is.' At every second you are making choices, but you hardly know that you make them: what seems right to you must be immediately right. And you can only show by doing; you see the meaning as a whole from the beginning; there are almost no steps in your mental processes; and, writing from the midst of your thoughts you take it for granted that the reader is with you and that what is self-evident to you as the next step (only, it's not the next step, even: it's already included, somehow) will also be so to him."

These words, obviously, offer a picture of the limitations of a particular individual temperament. But much of what my correspondent says is given with the operation of the circle—when this is applied, not to routine reading, on the one hand, or to the deductions of schematic linguistics on the other, but to a work of art: the solution attained by means of the circular operation cannot be subjected to a rigorous rationale because, at its most perfect, this is a negation of steps: once attained, it tends to obliterate the steps leading up to it (one may remember the lion of medieval bestiaries who, at every step forward, wiped out his footprints with his tail, in order to elude his pursuers!).

Why do I insist that it is impossible to offer the reader a step-by-step rationale to be applied to a work of art? For one reason, that the first step, on which all may hinge, can never be planned: it must already have taken place. This first step is the awareness of having been struck by a detail, followed by a conviction that this detail is connected basically with the work of art; it means that one has made an "observation,"—which is the starting point of a theory, that one has been prompted to raise a question—which must find an answer. To begin by omitting this first step must doom any attempt at interpretation—as was the case with the dissertation (mentioned in note 1 of my article on Diderot) devoted to the "imagery" of Diderot, in which the concept "imagery" was based on no preliminary observation but on a ready-made category applied from without to the work of art.

Unfortunately, I know of no way to guarantee either the "impression" or the conviction just described: they are the results of talent, experience, and faith. And, even then, the first step is not to be taken at our own volition: how often, with all the theoretical experience of method accumulated in me over the years, have I stared blankly, quite similar to one of my beginning students, at a page that would not yield its magic. The only way leading out of this state of unproductivity is to read and reread,[18] patiently and confidently, in an endeavor to become, as it were, soaked through and through with the atmosphere of the work. And suddenly, one word, one line, stands out, and we realize that, now, a relationship has been established between the poem and us. From this point on, I have usually found that, what with other observations adding themselves to the first, and with previous experiences of the circle intervening, and with associations given by previous education building up before me (all of this quickened, in my own case, by a quasi-metaphysical urge toward solution) it does not seem long until the characteristic "click" occurs, which is the indication that detail and whole have found a common denominator—which gives the etymology of the writing.[19] And looking back on this process (whose end, of course, marks only the conclusion of the *preliminary* stage of analysis), how can we say when exactly it began? (Even the "first step" was preconditioned.) We see, indeed, that to read is to have read, to understand is equivalent to having understood.[20]

I have just spoken of the importance of past experience in

the process of understanding the work of art—but as only one of the intervening factors. For experience with the "circle" is not, itself, enough to enable one to base thereupon a program applicable to all cases. For every poem the critic needs a separate inspiration, a separate light from above (it is this constant need which makes for humility, and it is the accumulation of past enlightenments that encourages a sort of pious confidence). Indeed, a Protean mutability is required of the critic, for the device which has proved successful for one work of art cannot be applied mechanically to another: I could not expect that the "trick of the five *grands*" (which I shall apply to an ode of Claudel's) would work for the "récit de Théramène," or that proper names, which will serve as a point of departure in my article on Cervantes, would play any part in the study on Diderot. It is, indeed, most trying for the experienced teacher to have to watch a beginner re-use and consequently mis-use, a particular clue that had served the teacher when he was treating a quite different writer—as though a young actor were to use the leer of Barrymore's Richard III for his performance of Othello. The mutability required of the critic can be gained only by repeated experiences with totally different writers; the "click" will come oftener and more quickly after several experiences of "clicks" have been realized by the critic. And, even then, it is not a foregone conclusion that it will inevitably come; nor can one ever foretell just when and where it will materialize ("The Spirit bloweth . . .").

The reason that the clues to understanding cannot be mechanically transferred from one work of art to another lies in the fact of artistic expressivity itself: the artist lends to an outward phenomenon of language an inner significance (thereby merely continuing and expanding the basic fact of human language: that a meaning is quite arbitrarily—arbitrarily, at least, from the point of view of the current usage of the language—associated with an acoustic phenomenon); just *which* phenomena the literary artist will choose for the embodiment of his meaning is arbitrary from the point of view of the "user" of the work of art. To overcome the impression of an arbitrary association in the work of art, the

reader must seek to place himself in the creative center of the artist himself—and re-create the artistic organism. A metaphor, an anaphora, a staccato rhythm may be found anywhere in literature; they may or may not be significant. What tells us that they are important is only the feeling, which we must have already acquired, for the whole of the particular work of art.

And the capacity for this feeling is, again, deeply anchored in the previous life and education of the critic, and not only in his scholarly education: in order to keep his soul ready for his scholarly task he must have already made choices, in ordering his life, of what I would call a moral nature; he must have chosen to cleanse his mind from distraction by the inconsequential, from the obsession of everyday small details—to keep it open to the synthetic apprehension of the "wholes" of life, to the symbolism in nature and art and language. I have sometimes wondered if my "explication de texte" in the university classroom, where I strive to create an atmosphere suitable for the appreciation of the work of art, would not have succeeded much better if that atmosphere had been present at the breakfast table of my students.

NOTES

1. Text of an address, originally entitled "Thinking in the Humanities," delivered to the Department of Modern Languages and Literatures of Princeton University, to which some notes and an epilogue have been added.

It is paradoxical that professors of literature who are too superficial to immerse themselves in a text and who are satisfied with stale phrases out of a manual, are precisely those who contend that it is superfluous to teach the aesthetic value of a text of Racine or Victor Hugo: the student will, in some way or another, come to grasp its beauty without any direction—or, if he is incapable of doing so, it is useless to talk about it. But there are hidden beauties which do not reveal themselves at the first exploratory attempts (as the apologetic theologians know) ; in fact, all beauty has some mysterious quality which does not appear at first glance. But there is no more reason for dodging the description of the aesthetic phenomenon than of any natural phenomenon. Those who oppose the aesthetic analysis of poetic works seem to affect at times the susceptibility of a sensitive plant: if one is to believe them, it is because they cherish so deeply the works of art, it is because they respect their chastity, that they would not deflower, by means of intellectual formulas, the virginal and ethereal quality of works of art, they would not brush off the shimmering dust from the wings of these poetic butterflies! I would maintain, on the contrary, that to formulate observations by means of words is not to cause the artistic beauty to evaporate in vain intellectualities; rather, it makes for a widening and a deepening of the aesthetic taste. Love, whether it be love for God, love for one's fellow men, or the love of art, can only gain by the effort of the human intellect to search for the reasons of its most sublime emotions, and to formulate them. It is only a frivolous love that cannot survive intellectual definition; great love prospers with understanding.

2. The presentation of so great a scholar as Meyer-Lübke from the only angle which concerns us here is necessarily one-sided; for a more complete evaluation of his scholarship, as well as for a picture of his personality, I may refer the reader to my paper, "Mes souvenirs sur Meyer-Lübke" in *Le français moderne*, VI, 213. As for Philipp August Becker, my few remarks have given no real idea of his exuberant personality—which seldom penetrated into his scholarship; his was an orgiastic nature which somehow did not fit into the traditional pattern of a scholar. A story told me by Walther von Wartburg may illustrate this: Becker, who was rather given to the worship of Bacchus-Dionysos, used to invite his colleagues at Leipzig to a certain popular inn for copious libations. One night, after many hours of merrymaking, he realized that the bourgeois patrons sitting around him were shocked by his exuberance; immediately turning to his colleagues, he remarked: "And now I want to tell you something about early Christian hymns!" For almost an hour he talked, to the delight, not only of his colleagues but also of the crowd of *Spiessbürger* who had gradually drawn closer to him, enthralled by the eloquence of this greybeard bard who was reviving the spirit of Saint Ambrosius in a tavern.

3. These etymologies have appeared in the *Journal of English and Germanic Philology,* XLII, 405; there I suggested also the possibility of a **calembourd-on* as etymon, but today I prefer *calembredaine* to that unattested formation.

4. In fact, Ernst Lewy would destroy the unity of "Romance Languages" by placing French and Spanish, along with Basque and Irish, in an Atlantic group of languages, and Rumanian within the Balkan group (see my discussion in *Anales de l'Inst. de lingüística de Cuyo*, II). Again, there is the Russian school of "Japhetists" who believe not in "families" but in "systems" of languages, and who make bold to discover in any given language certain primeval basic "elements" of the prelogical period in human speech (see Malkiel's article in *Language*, XX, 157).

5. Perhaps the transition from a particular historical line in language, as traced by an etymology, to the self-contained system of a work of literature, may seem violent to the reader: in the first case the "etymon" is the "soul of the nation" at the moment of the creation of the word; in the second, it is the "soul of one particular author." The difference, as Professor Singleton has pointed out to me, is that between the unconscious will of the nation that creates its language, and the conscious will of one member of the nation who creates wilfully and more or less systematically. But, apart from the fact that there are rational elements in popular linguistic creations, and irrational ones in those of the creative artist—what I would point out here is the relationship, common to both, between the linguistic detail and the soul of the speaker(s), and the necessity, in both cases, of the to-and-fro philological movement.

Perhaps a better parallel to the system of a work of art would be the system of a language at a definite moment of its evolution. I attempted just such a characterization of a linguistic system in my article on Spanish in *Stilstudien*, I.

6. This study has been published in *Stilstudien*, II.

The method I have been describing in the text is, of course, one that is followed by all of us when we must interpret the correspondence of someone with whom we are not well acquainted. For several years I had been in correspondence with a German emigrant in France whom I did not know personally and whose letters had given me the impression of a rather self-centered person who craved a cozy and congenial environment. When she was finally rescued to another country, she published a book of memoirs, a copy of which was sent me. On the cover of the book I saw pictured the window of the room she had occupied in Paris; behind this window, in the foreground, was a great cat looking out upon the Cathedral of Notre Dame. A great part of the book itself was taken up with this cat, and I had not read far before I found—without great surprise—several sentences such as "blottie dans un fauteuil, j'éprouvai un tel bonheur, je me sentis si bien à mon aise sous ce soleil doux qui me faisait ronronner à la manière des chats." Evidently a catlike existence was the deep-felt aspiration of this emigrant who, in the midst of world catastrophe, had lost the feeling of protectedness and had had to seek protection in herself.

7. We could here also be reminded of Goethe's simile (in *Die Wahlverwandtschaften*, II, 2): "We have learned about a special arrangement of the English Navy: all ropes of the Royal Fleet, from the strongest to the thinnest, have a red thread woven into them in such a way that it cannot be taken out without completely raveling the rope, so that even the smallest particle is stamped as the property of the Crown. Similarly, Ottilia's diary is pervaded by a thread of affection and attachment which connects every part and characterizes the whole of it." In this passage Goethe has formulated the principle of inner cohesion as it exists in a

sensitive writer. It is the recognition of this principle which enabled Freud to apply his psychoanalytical finds to works of literature. While I do not wish to disavow the Freudian influence in my earlier attempts at explaining literary texts, my aim today is to think, not so much in terms of the all-too-human "complexes" which, in Freud's opinion, are supposed to color the writing of the great figures of literature, but of "ideological patterns," as these are present in the history of the human mind.

Mr. Kenneth Burke, in his book *Philosophy of Literary Form* (Louisiana, 1940), has worked out a methodology of what he calls the "symbolic" or "strategic" approach to poetry—an approach which comes very close to the Freudian one (and to my own, as far as it was influenced by Freud), and which consists of establishing emotional clusters. When Mr. Burke finds such clusters in Coleridge, for example, and observes their constancy in the writings of this poet, he will claim to have found a factual, observable, irrefutable basis for the analysis of the structure of the work of art in general.

What I would object to in this method is that it can, obviously, be applied only to those poets who do, in fact, reveal such associational clusters —which is to say, only to those poets who do allow their phobias and idiosyncrasies to appear in their writing. But this must exclude all writers before the eighteenth century, the period in which the theory of the "original genius" was discovered and applied. Before this period, it is very difficult to discover, in any writer, "individual" associations, that is to say, associations not prompted by a literary tradition. Dante, Shakespeare, Racine are great literary "individuals," but they did not (or could not) allow their style to be permeated by their personal phobias and idiosyncrasies (even Montaigne, when portraying himself, thought of himself as "l'homme"). When a student of mine, working on the style of Agrippa d'Aubigné, was influenced by Professor Burke's book to apply the method of "emotional clusters" to that sixteenth-century epic poet, and was able, indeed, to find a series of antithetical associations, such as "milk - poison," "mother - serpent," "nature - unnatural" used in reference to pairs represented by the Catholic Catherine de Medicis and her Protestant opponents, I had to point out to him that these particular associational patterns (which had reminded him of Joyce) were all given by classical and Scriptural tradition: D'Aubigné merely gave powerful expression to age-old ideological motifs that transcended his personal, nervous temperament: the starting point for his "mère non-mère" was, obviously, the Greek *μήτηρ ἀμήτωρ*. Recently, I have had occasion also to point out the same truth in regard to the sixteenth-century poet Guevara, whose style has been explained by Freudian frustration.

8. Under the noble pretext of introducing "history of ideas" into literary criticism, there have appeared in recent times, with the approval of the departments of literary history, academic theses with such titles as "Money in Seventeenth-Century French (English, Spanish etc.) Comedy," "Political Tendencies in Nineteenth-Century French (English, Spanish etc.) Literature." Thus we have come to disregard the philological character of the discipline of literary history, which is concerned with ideas couched in linguistic and literary form, not with ideas in themselves (this is the field of history of philosophy) or with ideas as informing action (this is the field of history and the social sciences). Only in the linguistico-

literary field are we philologians competent qua scholars. The type of dissertations cited above reveals an unwarranted extension of the (in itself commendable) tendency toward breaking down departmental barriers, to such a degree that literary history becomes the gay sporting ground of incompetence. Students of the department of literature come to treat the complex subjects of a philosophical, political, or economic nature with the same self-assurance that once characterized those Positivists who wrote on "The Horse in Medieval Literature." But while it is possible for the average person to know "what a horse is" (if less so what "a horse in literature" is), it is much more difficult for a student of literature to know "what money is" (and still more so what "money in literature" is). In fact, this new type of thesis is only an avatar of the old positivistic thesis; but, while the original positivism was motivated by a sincere respect for competence, the neo-positivists now would administer the death-blow to scholarly competence.

9. Cf. my article in *Modern Philological Quarterly*: "Why Does Language Change?" and the polemics resulting therefrom in *Language*, xx, 45 and 245.

10. Cf. Schleiermacher, *Sämtl. Werke,* III, 3, p. 343. "Über den Begriff der Hermeneutik mit Bezug auf F. A. Wolfs Andeutungen und Arts Lehrbuch"—a speech delivered in 1829. Schleiermacher distinguishes between the "comparative" and the "divinatory" methods, the combination of which is necessary in "hermeneutics," and since hermeneutics falls into two parts, a "grammatical" and a "psychological" part, both methods must be used in both parts of hermeneutics. Of the two methods, it is the divinatory which requires the "Zirkelschluss." We have been dealing here with the *Zirkelschluss* in the "divination" of the psychology of authors; as for "grammatical divination," any college student who attempts to parse a Ciceronian period is constantly using it: he cannot grasp the construction except by passing continuously from the parts to the whole of the sentence and back again to its parts.

Dr. Ludwig Edelstein has called my attention to the Platonic origin of Schleiermacher's discovery: it is in *Phaedo* that Socrates states the importance of the whole for the cognition of the parts. Accordingly, it would appear that I err in adopting Schleiermacher's "theological" approach and that I am undiplomatic in asking for an approach so at variance with that which is traditional in the humanities (when Dewey reproved the Humanists for the residues of theology in their thinking, they made haste to disavow any theological preoccupation—while I take the stand of saying: "Yes, we Humanists are theologians!"); would it not, I am asked, be better to show the irrationalism inherent in any rational operation in the humanities, than to demand the overt irrationalism of religion which our secular universities must thoroughly abhor? My answer is that Socrates himself was a religious genius and that, through Plato, he is present in much of Christian thought. As concerns the necessity, for the scholar, of having recourse to religion, cf. the conclusive reasoning of Erich Frank in his book *Philosophical Understanding and Religious Truth* (1945).

The traditional view of the "viciousness" of the philological circle is unfortunately held in an otherwise brilliant attack against "the biographical fashion in literary criticism" (University of California Publications, in *Classical Philology,* XII, 288) by Professor Harold Cherniss: in his argument against the philologians of the Stefan George school who, though not dealing with the outward biography of artists, believe that the inner form of the artist's personality can be grasped in his works by a kind of intuition, Cherniss writes: "The intuition which discovers in the writings of an author the 'natural law' and 'inward form' of his personality, is proof against all objections, logical and philological; but, while one must admit that a certain native insight, call it direct intelligence or intuition as you please, is required for understanding any text, it is, all the same, a vicious circle to intuit the nature of the author's personality from his writings and then to interpret those writings in accordance with the 'inner necessity' of that intuited personality. Moreover, once the intuition of the individual critic is accepted as the ultimate basis of all interpretation, the comprehension of a literary work becomes a completely private affair, for the intuition of any one interpreter has no more objective validity than that of any other."

I believe that the word "intuition" with its deliberate implication of extraordinary mystic qualities on the part of the critic, vitiates not only the reasoning of the Stefan George school but also that of their opponents. The "circle" is vicious only when an uncontrolled intuition is allowed to exercise itself upon the literary works; the procedure from details to the inner core and back again is not in itself at all vicious; in fact, the "intelligent reading" which Professor Cherniss advocates without defining it (though he is forced to grant rather uncomfortably that it is "a certain native insight, call it direct intelligence or intuition as you please") is based precisely on that very philological circle. To understand a sentence, a work of art, or the inward form of an artistic mind involves, to an increasing degree, irrational moves—which must, also to an increasing degree, be controlled by reason.

Heidegger, in *Sein und Zeit*, I, 32 ("Verstehen und Auslegung"), shows that all "exegesis" is circular, i.e. is a catching up with the "understanding," which is nothing else than an anticipation of the whole that is "existentially" given to man: "Zuhandenes wird immer schon aus der Bewandtnisganzheit der verstanden. . . . Die Auslegung gründet jeweils in einer *Vorsicht*, die das in Vorhabe Genommene auf eine bestimmte Auslegbarkeit hin 'anschneidet.' . . . Auslegung ist nie ein voraussetzungsloses Erfassen eines Vorgegebenen. . . . Alle Auslegung, die Verständnis beistellen soll, muss schon das Auszulegende verstanden haben. . . . *Aber in diesem Zirkel ein vitiosum sehen und nach Wegen Ausschau halten, ihn zu vermeiden, ja ihn auch nur als unvermeidliche Unvollkommenheit 'empfinden,' heisst das Verstehen von Grund aus missverstehen* [the italics are the author's]. . . . Das Entscheidende ist nicht aus dem Zirkel heraus-, sondern in ihn nach der rechten Weise hineinzukommen. . . . In ihm verbirgt sich eine positive Möglichkeit ursprünglichsten Erkennens, die freilich in echter Weise nur dann ergriffen ist, wenn die Auslegung verstanden hat, dass ihre erste, ständige und letzte Aufgabe bleibt, sich jeweils Vorhabe, Vorsicht und Vorgriff nicht durch Einfälle und Volksbegriffe vorgeben zu lassen, sondern in deren Ausarbeitung aus den Sachen selbst her das wissenschaftliche Thema zu sichern. Der 'Zirkel' im Verstehen gehört zur Struktur des Sinnes, welches Phänomen in der existenzialen Verfassung des Daseins, im auslegenden Verstehen verwurzelt ist."

This "Vorsicht," this anticipation of the whole, is especially necessary for the understanding of philosophical writing. Franz Rosenzweig, "Das neue Denken" (in *Kleinere Schriften*, 1937) writes: "The first pages of philosophical books are held by the reader in special respect. . . . He thinks they [such books] ought to be 'especially logical,' and by this he means that each sentence depends on the one that precedes it, so that if the famous one stone is pulled, 'the whole tumbles.' Actually, this is nowhere less the case than in philosophical books. Here a sentence does not follow from its predecessor, but much more probably from its successor. . . . Philosophical books refuse such methodical ancien-régime strategy; they must be conquered à la Napoleon, in a bold thrust against the main body of the enemy; and after the victory at this point, the small fortresses will fall of themselves." (I owe this quotation to Kurt H. Wolf's article, "The Sociology of Knowledge" in *Philosophy of Science*, x; Wolf calls the anticipatory understanding of wholes a "central attitude": "In our everyday social interaction we constantly practice the central-attitude approach without which we could not 'know' how to behave toward other persons, or how to read a book, to see a picture, or to play or listen to a piece of music. . . .") What Heidegger, Rosenzweig, and Wolf describe is the method of the humanities which Pascal has called the "esprit de finesse" (as contrasted to the "esprit géométrique").

For the students in Romance Gröber formulated the idea of the philological circle (without mentioning the "circle" itself) in *Gröber's Grundriss* I/3 (1888): "Absichtslose Wahrnehmung, unscheinbare Anfänge gehen dem zielbewussten Suchen, dem allseitigen Erfassen des Gegenstandes voraus. Im sprungweisen Durchmessen des Raumes hascht dann der Suchende nach dem Ziel, Mit einem Schema unfertiger Ansichten über ähnliche Gegenstände scheint er das Ganze erfassen zu können, ehe Natur und Teile gekannt sind. Der vorschnellen Meinung folgt die Einsicht des Irrtums, nur langsam der Entschluss, dem Gegenstand in kleinen und kleinsten vorsichtigen Schritten nahe zu kommen, Teil und Teilchen zu beschauen und nicht zu ruhen, bis die Überzeugung gewonnen ist, dass sie nur so und nicht anders aufgefasst werden müssen."

It is also true of the comparative linguist who establishes his "phonetic laws" on the basis of "evident etymologies," which themselves are based on those "phonetic laws," that he moves in a circle, in the words of Zupitza, *Zeitschr. f. vergl. Sprachwissenschaft*, XXXVII (1904) p. 387: "Unsere wissenschaft kommt aus einem kreislauf nicht heraus: sie geht von evidenten gleichungen aus, entnimmt diesen ihre gesetze und prüft an diesen gesetzen jene gleichungen, die ihre grundlage bilden." And even elementary language teaching must move in a circle: R. A. Hall in *Bull. of the American University Professors*, XXXI, 6, advocating the modern "direct method" as preferable to the old "reading method," writes: "When he [the student] has learnt a sufficient number of examples, the linguistic analysis becomes simply a series of obvious deductions from what he has learned; it helps him to perceive the patterns inherent in what he already knows, and tells him how far he can go in extending these patterns to new material." The inference from "patterns" is nothing but an anticipation of a whole deduced from the known examples.

11. This point has been entirely overlooked in the treatment of the passage by an antimentalist; see my article in *Italica*, XXI, 154.

12. This is not to say that the puns and repetitions used by Rabelais do not historically develop from the same devices used by the Fathers and the medieval writers. Rabelais' facetious etymology *Beauce* = "[je trouve]

beau ce," and his repetition of words, such as *moine moinant de moinerie*, are scholastic devices—only that they are used by him in an antimedieval manner, informed by a worldly spirit and, most important of all, by the consciousness of the autonomy of a "word world."

13. I have often wondered how historians of literature could make such sweeping statements, as they are wont to do, on the whole of the literary work of a poet, or of a period, without descending into the detail of texts (and into the linguistic detail). Goethe speaks pertinently ("Einleitung in die Propyläen") of the "Anschauung" necessary for the concrete apperception of works of art: "Um von Kunstwerken eigentlich und mit wahrem Nutzen für sich und andere zu sprechen, sollte es freilich nur in Gegenwart derselben geschehen. Alles kommt aufs Anschauen an; es kommt darauf an, dass bei dem Worte, wodurch man ein Kunstwerk zu erläutern hofft, das Bestimmteste gedacht werde, weil sonst gar nichts gedacht wird. Daher geschieht es so oft, dass derjenige, der über Kunstwerke schreibt, bloss im Allgemeinen verweilt. . . ."

The same seems to have been felt by Santayana in regard to the field of philosophy; in *The Middle Span*, p. 155, he has the following to say about the habits of his Harvard students during the last decades of the nineteenth century: "I doubt that the texts were much studied directly in those days at Harvard. The undergraduates were thinking only of examinations and relied on summaries in the histories of philosophy and on lecture notes. . . . Philosophy can be communicated only by being evoked: the pupil's mind must be engaged dialectically in the discussion. Otherwise, all that can be taught is the literary history of philosophy, that is, the *phrases* that various philosophers have rendered famous. To conceive what those phrases meant or could mean would require a philosophical imagination in the public which cannot be demanded. All that usually exists is familiarity with current phrases, and a shock, perhaps of pleased curiosity but more often of alarm and repulsion, due to the heterodoxy of any different phrases." It is needless to add that a "literary history" which is satisfied with enumerating the "phrases" (whether famous or not) used by a writer (philosophical or otherwise), without establishing any connection between them and the mainspring of the writer's inspiration, is sham literary history.

14. According to Gundolf, in his essay on Schleiermacher. According to A. Götze, *Euphorion* 1924, however, the word was not previously coined by him, but is a creation of his period.

15. Even with philologians (who are not by nature apt to be insensitive to literary values, as are so many of the so-called "linguists") one can discern "unhumanistic" prejudices. For example, Professor Entwistle ("Idealistic Extensions of Linguistics" in *Miscel·lania Fabra*, Buenos Aires, 1943) maintains that the linguistic interpretation of poetry implies the crossing of an intellectual frontier: the philologian has to deal not with "science" which treats of things that can be measured and weighed, not with "unambiguous facts" which can be tested by anyone, but with "knowledge" irreducible to "scientific" treatment—to which belongs hermeneutics, the study of the poet's meaning: this meaning cannot be treated in the "old assertive language" of the positivistic linguist, and still less can be the elusive significance of a poetic text, which transcends the poet's conscious intention. By such distinctions Professor Entwistle is perpetuating the nineteenth-century rift between positivistic science

and wisdom. As concerns what Entwistle considers to be the purely scientific part of philology—such as the phonetic laws, which he ranks with the facts testable by everyone—I wonder if the formulation of a phonetic law is not as much of a speculation as is the attempt to discover the significance of a poetic passage; and is it really true that a phonetic law can be tested by anyone who has not had a preparation for this type of study? It can be done only to the same extent, I should think, which would hold true for the establishment of the meaning of a poetic passage. And as for the unconscious intentions of the poet, I simply would not advise the interpreter to concern himself with them. As a matter of fact, the example of "unconscious poetic intention" offered by Mr. Entwistle seems to me to show how little he has grasped the purpose of philological studies: of the passage from the *Aeneid* in which Aeneas sees depicted on the walls of Carthage the Trojan war and his father's deeds:

> En Priamus! Sunt hic etiam sua praemia laudi;
> sunt lacrimae rerum, et mentem mortalia tangunt.
> Solve metus; feret haec aliquam tibi fama salutem.

Entwistle writes: "The sense of the second last line, in its context, seems to be encouraging [he has translated it: "tears are shed for his misfortunes and his death moves men's minds to pity"]: it is better to be remembered sorrowfully than to be forgotten altogether. Yet *sunt lacrimae rerum* means something other and more moving than that. There is music and intensity in the line beyond anything Vergil may have consciously meant. . . . 'Nature's tears and the mortal sadness of mankind' has been discovered in that music by posterity, and, I think, justly so." But it can be *proved* by the philologist that Vergil *meant* (and it is only with conscious meaning that the philologian is concerned) the first, the "lesser" of the two meanings mentioned (as is indicated by the two anaphoric *sunt*'s which suggest a parallelism of arguments leading to the encouraging final line). The second meaning which has been attached to the line by posterity is an error due to its isolated consideration out of context (which led to the misinterpretation of *rerum* as "Nature" instead of "misfortunes," an error comparable to the famous misinterpretation of Buffon's "le style c'est l'homme même"—or even to many witty or punning misinterpretations of certain poetic lines (e.g. when the line of Schiller's Maid of Orleans: "Johanna geht und nimmer kehrt sie wieder" is facetiously interpreted to mean that never again will she sweep the floor). To the philologian this secondary graft or palimpsest imposed upon the original text may be historically quite interesting, but it has to be discarded from his interpretation of the given work of art. There is no music in Vergil's poetry but that which he put in it—but, by the same token, it is also necessary that this music be retained and not destroyed, as it is by such a translation as "tears are shed for *his* misfortunes and *his* death": the indefinite quality of "misfortune" and "death" should be preserved. Vergil's poetic music consists in the procedure of expanding the particular example of Priam's fate to that of man (and, similarly, *mortalia* should not be concretized to "death" but left as "the mortal fate"); it is the general gnome, so indissolubly linked by Vergil with the particular case, that posterity has arbitrarily detached (and, in addition to this antipoetic first move, has misinterpreted—this time poetically, in the manner mentioned above).

In this, as in the following studies, the reader will find me polemizing against the views of fellow scholars. I have sometimes been accused of raising up straw men just to knock them down, instead of being satisfied with offering my own picture of the phenomenon in question. My answer is that, in matters stylistic as well as in factual questions of literary history or linguistics, the *consensus omnium* is a desideratum, the only path to which is the discussion of the pros and cons of theories different from one's own, which enable us to vindicate the relative superiority of our own theory. The greater the objective certainty that a stylistic explanation can claim, the more we will have overcome that impressionism which, until recently, has seemed the only alternative to the positivistic treatment of literature.

16. The frequent occurrence, in my text, of quotations in the original foreign language (or languages) may prove a difficulty for the English reader. But since it is my purpose to take the word (and the wording) of the poets seriously, and since the convincingness and rigor of my stylistic conclusions depends entirely upon the minute linguistic detail of the original texts, it was impossible to offer translations.

17. Perhaps I should make it clear that I am using the word "method" in a manner somewhat aberrant from common American use: it is for me much more a "habitual procedure of the mind" (Lalande, *Vocabulaire de la philosophie*, s.v. *méthode* 1) than a "program regulating beforehand a series of operations . . . in view of reaching a well-defined result" (*ibid.* 2). As used by me it is nearly synonymous with *Erlebnis*, and consequently would correspond relatively to what is called in America "approach," were it not for the volitional and even "strategic" nuance, in this word, of military siege or of tracking down a quarry, by which it may be historically explained.

In this connection I may quote a passage from a letter of Descartes to Mersenne (*Oeuvres*, ed. Adam-Tannery, I, 347): "Mais ie n'ay sceu bien entendre ce que vous objectez touchant le titre [Discours de la Méthode]; car ie ne mets pas *Traité de la Methode*, mais *Discours de la Methode*, ce qui est le mesme que *Preface ou Advis touchant la Methode*, pour monstrer que ie n'ay pas dessein de l'enseigner, mais seulement d'en parler. Car comme on peut voir de ce que i'en dis, elle consiste plus en Pratique qu'en Theorie, & ie nomme les Traitez suivans des *Essais de cette Methode*, pource que ie pretens que les choses qu'ils contiennent n'ont pû estre trouvées sans elle, & qu'on peut connoistre par eux ce qu'elle vaut."

18. If I were to give one piece of advice to our students of literary history, it would be substantially the same as that which Lanson, touring the United States forty years ago, gave to the students of his time who were then, as they are now, only too eager to rush to their big libraries to find in the many books of "secondary literature" an alibi for getting away from the "primary" texts they should study: "*Read your texts*!" My "circular method" is, in fact, nothing but an expansion of the common practice of "reading books": reading at its best requires a strange cohabitation in the human mind of two opposite capacities: contemplativity on the one hand and, on the other, a Protean mimeticism. That is to say: an undeflected patience that "stays with" a book until the forces latent in it unleash in us the recreative process.

19. Sometimes it may happen that this "etymology" leads simply to a characterization of the author that has been long accepted by literary historians (who have not needed, apparently, to follow the winding path

I chose), and which can be summed up in a phrase which smacks of a college handbook. But, to make our own way to an old truth is not only to enrich our own understanding: it produces inevitably new evidence, of objective value, for this truth—which is thereby renewed. A *comédie-proverbe* of Musset is based, after all, on a commonplace saying: was it a waste of time to illustrate so wittily "il faut qu'une porte soit ouverte ou fermée"?

20. The requirement at St. John's for the Hundred Great Books is good, I believe, in so far as it may encourage the "click" to repeat itself in an accelerated manner—if, of course, it has come about in the first experiences: to have read these hundred books "without click" would be equivalent to not having read a single book.

2

LINGUISTIC PERSPECTIVISM IN THE *DON QUIJOTE*

Argumentum: Here, the procedure will be to start from a particular feature of Cervantes' novel which must strike any reader: the instability and variety of the names given to certain characters (and the variety of etymological explanations offered for these names), in order to find out what may be Cervantes' psychological motive behind this polyonomasia (and polyetymologia). I see this as a deliberate refusal on the part of the author to make a final choice of one name (and one etymology): in other words, a desire to show the different aspects under which the character in question may appear to others. If this be true, then such a relativistic attitude must tinge other linguistic details in the novel; and, indeed, it is surely such an attitude that is behind the frequent debates (particularly between Quijote and Sancho), which never end conclusively, over the relative superiority of this or that word or phrase. It is as if language in general was seen by Cervantes from the angle of perspectivism. With this much settled, it will not be difficult to see (what, in fact, has been recognized by Castro) that perspectivism informs the structure of the novel as a whole: we find it in Cervantes' treatment of the plot, of ideological themes as well as in his attitude of distantiation toward the reader.

And yet, beyond this perspectivism, we may sense the presence of something which is not subject to fluctuation: the immovable, immutable principle of the divine—which, perhaps, to some extent, is reflected in the earthly *artifex* himself: the novelist who assumes a near-divine power in his mastery of the material, in his own unshaken attitude toward the phenomena of his world (and even in his aloofness from the reader). And it is in this glorification of the artist that the main historical significance of the Spanish masterpiece is to be seen.

MUCH, though not too much, has been written about Cervantes' master novel. Yet, we are still far from understanding it in its general plan and in its details as well as we do, for instance, Dante's *Commedia* or Goethe's *Faust*—and we are relatively further from an understanding of the whole than of the details. The main critical works of recent years, which represent gigantic strides forward toward the understanding of the whole, are, in my opinion, Américo Castro's *El pensamiento de Cervantes* (Madrid, 1925), in which the themes of Cervantes' poetry of ideas are stated, and Joaquín Casalduero's article in *Revista de filología hispánica*, II, 323 "La composición de 'El Ingenioso Hidalgo Don Quijote de la Mancha,' " in which the artistic architecture of the novel, as based on the themes recognized by Castro, is pointed out. As for the style of the novel, Helmut Hatzfeld, in his book *Don Quijote als Wortkunstwerk* (Leipzig, 1927), has attempted to distinguish different "styles" determined by previous literary traditions (the pastoral or chivalric styles, the style of Boccaccio, etc.)—without, however, achieving what I should call an integration of the historical styles into one Cervantine style in which the personality of the writer would manifest itself. Perhaps it is better not to break up the unity of a work of art into historical units which, in any case, are extraneous to Cervantes and, instead, to proceed according to a method by which one would seek to move from the periphery toward the center of the artistic globe—thus remaining within the work of art. Any one outward feature, when sufficiently followed up to the center, must yield us insight into the artistic whole, whose unity will thus have been respected. The choice of the particular phenomenon, then, would appear to be of secondary importance: any single one must, according to my ideology, give final results.

Accordingly, I shall choose certain linguistic phenomena (of, at first glance, slight importance for Cervantes' artistic cosmos) which I shall attempt to reduce to a common denominator, later to bring this into relationship with the "pensamiento," the *Weltanschauung* of Cervantes.

Any reader of the *Quijote* is struck by the instability of the names of the main characters of the novel: in the first chapter we are told by Cervantes that the protagonist has been called, by the sources of "this so truthful story," alternatively Quixada, Quesada, or Quixana (this last, according to Cervantes, being the best "conjecture"); from this assortment the "ingenioso hidalgo" chose, before starting his knightly career, the name that he was to bear in the whole book: Quijote. When, at the end, he is cured of the fever of quixotism and repudiates *Amadis de Gaula* and the rest of the novels of chivalry, he recovers his unpretentious prosaic original name (II, 74): "ya no soy don Quixote de la Mancha, sino Alonso Quixano a quien mis buenas costumbres me dieron renombre de Bueno"; and the final scene of his Christian death and regeneration seems rounded out by a kind of rebaptism, as this "loco" becomes a "cuerdo" (the change of name is thrice mentioned in this final chapter, as if the author wanted to din it into our heads that the old Adam is dead); in his will, "Quixano" calls his niece Antonia by the name Quixana, as if to emphasize that he is now a "bourgeois rangé" to the extent of having a family bearing his own (everyday) name. The first-mentioned name Quixada is also used in recognition of the reasonable side of the protagonist's nature: earlier (I, 5) he was referred to, by an acquaintance who knew him in the days before his madness, as "Señor Quixada." Again, just as Quesada, Quixada, or Quixana became a Quijote when he fancied himself a knight, so, when his chivalric dreams seemed about to give way to those of pastoral life, he imagines himself to be called "el pastor Quijotiz" (and his companion, Sancho Panza, "el pastor Pancino").[1] In another episode, Dorotea, who plays the role of Princess Micomicona (I, 30), feigns that her presumptive rescuer is called "[si mal no me acuerdo,] don Azote o don Jigote." And the Countess Trifaldi jocundly endows him with the superlative for which she seems to have a predilection: "Quijotísimo." As for his epithet "de la Mancha," this is coined (I, 1) after Amadis de Gaula. Later, he will be called by the name, first given him by Sancho, "el caballero de la Triste Figura," still later by "el caballero de los Leones" (in II, 27-29, this change is strongly emphasized, and a certain character is rebuked by Sancho for having disregarded the distinction).[2]

It is obviously required by chivalric decorum that whoever enters the sphere of the knight Don Quijote must also change his or her name: Aldonza Lorenza > Dulcinea ("nombre a su parecer músico y peregrino y significativo"), Tolosa > doña Tolosa, la Molinera > doña Molinera (I, 3), and the anonymous nag receives the name of Rocinante ("nombre a su parecer alto, sonoro y significativo": note the parallel wording appearing in the justifications for the names given to Dulcinea and to the nag); incidentally, the ass from which Sancho is inseparable is not deemed worthy of a change of name that would be indicative of a change of rank. Although Sancho Panza, the peasant squire, undergoes no change of name similar to that of his master,[3] and is resolved always to remain (governor or no governor) plain Sancho without the addition of "don" (II, 4), there is some uncertainty in regard to his name, too, since, in the text of Cide Hamete Benengali, the Arabian chronicler whose manuscript Cervantes purports to have found at the moment when other sources gave out (I, 5), there is a picture of thick-set Sancho with "la barriga grande, el tallo corto, y las zancas largas," bearing the inscription: "Sancho Zancas."

It is, however, in regard to the name of Sancho's wife, that the greatest confusion obtains: Sancho calls her first "Juana Gutiérrez mi oislo" (I, 7); a few lines later, he ponders whether a crown would fit "la cabeza de Mari Gutiérrez"—which change the more intelligent commentators, seeking to avoid bringing the charge of inconsistency against Cervantes, rightly explain by the fact that *Mari* had come to represent simply a generic and interchangeable name for women. But in II, 5, Sancho's wife calls herself Teresa Cascajo; from then on she is either Teresa Panza or Teresa Sancho, "mujer de Sancho Panza"; of the name Teresa itself she says (II, 5): "Teresa me pusieron en el bautismo, nombre mondo y escueto. . . ." Evidently we have to do with a woman named Juana Teresa Gutiérrez, who becomes a Juana Panza or Teresa Panza when called after her husband, or . . . Cascajo when called after her father. Occasionally, however, according to the mood of the situation, she may be called "Teresaina" (II, 73) or "Teresona" (II, 67: because of her "gordura").[4]

There are other cases, slightly different from those enumerated so far, in which the ignorance and weak memory of Sancho seem to create a "polyonomasia": here we can hardly think in terms of different traditions offered by chroniclers (as in the case of the names of Quijote), or of popular variation (as in that of the names of Sancho's wife): Sancho must multiply names simply because all the forms of names that he retains are only approximations to the real ones; they are variable because he cannot take a firm hold on them; he indulges in what linguists call "popular etymologies," i.e. he alters names according to the associations most convenient to his intellectual horizon. Sometimes he offers several variations, but even when only one alteration is involved, the effect of polyonomasia still remains because of the fact that the real name is also present in the reader's mind. Mambrino (I, 19-21), of whose helmet he speaks, becomes "Malandrino" (a "moro"), "Malino" (=the Evil One), or "Martino" (a common first name); Fortinbras > feo Blas (I, 15), Cide Hamete Benengeli > ". . . Berengena" (II, 2; this Sancho justifies with the remark: ". . . los moros son amigos de berenjenas"[5]), Señora Rodriguez de Grijalva > Señora González (II, 31), Magalona > "la señora Magellanes o Magalona" (II, 41). A similar alteration of names is practiced by the *ama* who (I, 7) contends that the books which we know to have fallen prey to the *auto-da-fé* (I, 6) had been ravished by the sorcerer Muñaton: Don Quijote corrects this to "Frestón." "Never mind Frestón or Tritón," answers the *ama*, "provided it is a name ending in *-ton*": word forms that are unalterable for the learned Don Quijote are quite exchangeable in the mind of the uncultured *ama*.

The names of the Countess Trifaldi are in a class by themselves since, in addition to the instability of names conditioned by a masquerade, there are involved the alterations to which Sancho is prone: here there coexist polyonomasias of the first and second degrees. The Countess is first (II, 36) introduced to us (by her messenger Trifaldi de la Barba) as "la condesa Trifaldi, por otro nombre llamada la Dueña Dolorida"; one of the two names is her authentic one, the other her "name within the world of romance" (just as Don Quijote is also the "Caballero de la Triste Figura"). When she appears in the pageant (II, 38) of the *carro triunfal* her name "Trifaldi" is given the following explanation: "la cola, o falda, o como llamarla quisieren, era de tres colas"; the "mathematical" (geometrical) figure of her skirt with three flounces (or trains?) is so striking that every spectator must interpret her name as "la Condesa de las Tres Faldas." But the scrupulous chronicler Benengeli who, like Cervantes, seems to care about even the minor details of the fiction-within-the-fiction, is said by Cervantes to have stated that the character was really called "la Condesa *Lobuna*"—allegedly because of the presence of wolves in her domain (he adds that, according to onomastic traditions in princely houses she would have been called "la Condesa Zorruna" if foxes had been prevalent in her domain)—but that she had dropped this name in favor of the more novel one derived from the form of her skirt. Now, this etymology of the name "Trifaldi," as stated by the chronicler (and as made evident to the eye of the spectators who see the masquerade skirt), had been somewhat anticipated by Sancho's popular etymology in II, 37: "esta condesa Tres Faldas o Tres Colas (que en mi tierra faldas y colas, colas y faldas todo es uno)." Ultimately we are presented with an array of (possible) names for the same character: "la Condesa Trifaldi, de Tres Faldas, de Tres Colas (the latter name would be due to what the modern linguist in his jargon calls "synonymic derivation"), Lobuna ("Zorruna" again being a "synonymic derivate"[6]), Dueña Dolorida—a list as impressive as that of the names of Don Quijote.

Now those commentators who, in general, take the line of emphasizing the satiric intent of Cervantes, will point out that the variety of names attributed to the protagonist by Cervantes is simply an imitation of the pseudohistorical tendencies of the authors of chivalric novels who, in order to show their accurateness as historians, pretend to have resorted to different sources.[7] In the case of the names of Sancho's wife, some commentators point out, as we have seen, that the polyonomasia is due to the onomastic habits of the period; in the alterations of the name "Mambrino" they usually see a satire on Sancho's ignorance; in the case of the Condesa Trifaldi I have seen no explanation (Rodríguez Marín's edition points out possible "historical" sources for the costume itself of "tres colas o faldas"). But, evidently, there must be a common pattern of thought behind all these cases, which would explain (1) the importance given to a name or change of name, (2) the etymological concern with names, (3) the polyonomasia in itself.

Now it happens that just these three features are well known to the medievalist (less, perhaps, to students of Renaissance literature): they ultimately derive from Biblical studies and from ancient philology: one need only think of Saint Jerome's explanation of Hebrew names or of Isidore's "Etymologies"—and of the etymologizing habits of all great medieval poets. The names in the Bible were treated with seriousness; in the Old Testament the name, or rather the names of God were all-important (*Exodus* VI, 2-3: "I am *Iahve*, and I have appeared to Abraham, Isaak and Jacob as *El Schaddai*, under the name of Jahve I was not known to them," cf. *ibid.*, III, 14); the many *nomina sacra* revealed the many aspects through which the divine might make itself felt (cf. *PMLA*, LVI, 13 seq.). Nor does the importance of the name decrease with the New Testamentary divinity (Christ is Immanuel). And, in the New Testament, a tendency appears which will have great influence on medieval chivalry: the change of name subsequent to baptism will be imitated by the change of name undergone by the newly dubbed knight. In all these sacred (or sacramental) names or changes of names, etymology plays a large part, because the true meaning (the etymon) may reveal eternal verities latent in the words—indeed, it was possible for many etymologies to be proposed for the same word, since God may have deposited different meanings in a single term: polyonomasia and polyetymology. Both these techniques are generally applied to a greater degree to proper names than to common nouns—because the former, "untranslatable" as they are by their nature, participate more in the mysterious aspect of human language: they are less motivated. In proper names the medieval mind could see reflected more of the multivalence of the world full of arcana. The Middle Ages were characterized by an admiration as well for the correspondence between word and thing as for the mystery which makes this correspondence unstable.

By all this I do not mean to deny that Cervantes followed the models pointed out to us by the commentators: what I do say is that, in doing so, he was also following certain accepted medieval patterns (which, however, he submitted to a new interpretation: that of his critical intelligence). It is possible, for example, in the case of the name "Trifaldi," to see on the surface a medieval imagination at work: the name is given an interpretation (*Trifaldi* = *tres faldas*) which, from our modern linguistic or historical point of view, is evidently wrong but which would have delighted a medieval mind, ever ready to accept any interpretation offering a clarification of the mystery of words.[8] The ancient and medieval etymologies are indeed rarely those a modern linguist would offer, trained as he is to respect the formational procedures current in human language; the aim of those etymologies was to establish the connection between a given word and other existing words as an homage to God whose wisdom may have ordained these very relationships. The etymological connections that the medieval etymologist sees are direct relationships established between words vaguely associated because of their homonymic ring—not the relationships established by "historical grammar" or those obtained by decomposition of the word into its morphological elements.[9] In other words, we are offered edifying ideal possibilities, not deterministic historical realities; Isidore will connect *sol* and *solus* because of the ideological beauty of this relationship, not *sol* and ἥλιος as the comparative grammarian of today must do.

But, if the equation *Trifaldi* = *tres faldas* represents a "medieval" etymology, Cervantes himself did not take too seriously his own etymologizing: he must have been perfectly well aware of the historically real explanation—that which prompted him to coin the word. *Trifaldi* is evidently a regressive form from *Trifaldín*, which name, in turn, is the farcical

Italian *Truffaldino* "nome di personaggio ridicolo e basso di commedia" (Tomm.-Bellini); the reference to *truffare* "to cheat" is apposite, in our story, given the farcical episode intended to delude Don Quijote and Sancho. Thus the name of the messenger *Trifaldín* is (historically) not a diminutive of *Trifaldi*, as it might seem but, on the contrary, was preexistent, in Cervantes' mind, to the name of the mistress. The etymology of "tres faldas" is, historically speaking, entirely out of place. We have to face here the same para-etymological vein in which Rabelais (facetiously imitating medieval practice, while exemplifying the joyous freedom with which the Renaissance writer could play with words) explained the name *Gargantua* by *que grand tu as* [sc. *le gosier*]! and *Beauce* by [*je trouve*] *beau ce* [sc. *pays*]. In this story, the para-etymological play with names serves to underline the deceitfulness of outward evidence; what for Quijote and Sancho are wondrous events are, in reality, only *burlas* in a baroque world of histrionics and disingenuity.[10]

The disingenuous procedure of offering such "medieval" etymologies as would occur to his characters (for the simpleton Sancho as well as the learned Arab Benengeli are medieval primitives) is also exemplified in the case of the nag Rocinante, whose name is interpreted by Don Quijote[11] in the style of Isidore: the horse was a "rocín antes"—which may mean either "a nag before" ("previously a nag," "an erstwhile nag") or "a nag before all others": "antes de todos los rocines del mundo." Two explanations are given of one word, as was the general medieval practice[12]—not the *one* historically true significance according to which the name was actually coined: viz. *rocín* + the noble and "literary" participial ending *-ante*. Cervantes was perfectly aware of the correct etymology but he allowed his medieval Don Quijote to offer a more "significant" one. He knew also the explanation of the name *Quijote* (= *quij-* "jaw" + the comic suffix *-ote*, derived from *jigote* etc.), while his protagonist, who adopted this name, thought of it as patterned on *Lanzarote*.[13]

Thus we may conclude that, while, for the medieval world, the procedures of polyonomasia and polyetymologia amounted to a recognition of the working of the divine in the world,

Cervantes used the same devices in order to reveal the multivalence which words possess for different human minds: he who has coined the names put into them other meanings than those conceived of by the characters themselves: a *Trifaldín* who is for Cervantes a *truffatore,* a cheater or practical joker, is understood by Don Quijote and Sancho to be the servant of a Countess *Trifaldi* who wears a three-flounce skirt.

Perhaps this procedure is symptomatic of something basic to the texture of our novel; perhaps a linguistic analysis of the names can carry us further toward the center, allowing us to catch a glimpse of the general attitude of the creator of the novel toward his characters. This creator must see that the world, as it is offered to man, is susceptible of many explanations, just as names are susceptible of many etymologies; individuals may be deluded by the perspectives according to which they see the world as well as by the etymological connections which they establish. Consequently, we may assume that the linguistic perspectivism of Cervantes is reflected in his invention of plot and characters; and, just as, by means of polyonomasia and polyetymologia, Cervantes makes the world of words appear different to his different characters, while he himself may have his own, the coiner's, view of these names, similarly he watches the story he narrates from his own private vantage point: the way in which the characters conceive of the situations in which they are involved may be not at all the way in which Cervantes sees them—though this latter way is not always made clear to the reader. In other words, Cervantes' perspectivism, linguistic and otherwise,[14] would allow him qua artist to stand above, and sometimes aloof from, the misconceptions of his characters. Later we will have more to say about what lies behind this attitude of Cervantes; suffice it for us here, where we are given the first opportunity to look into the working of the (linguistic) imagination of the novelist, to have summarily indicated the relationship between his linguistic ambivalences and his general perspectivism.[14a]

If, now, we turn back for a moment to Sancho's mispronunciations of names—which, as we have seen, was one of the contributing factors to the polyonomasia of the novel—

we will recognize a particular application of Cervantes' linguistic perspectivism at work: to Sancho's uncultured mind, "Mambrino" must appear now as "Malino," now as "Martino," etc. In this, there is no suggestion of smugness on the part of Cervantes, as there might be with modern intellectual writers who would mock the linguistic "abuses" of ignorant characters; Cervantes presents "Malino," "Martino," etc., simply as the "linguistic appearances" of what, for Don Quijote, for example, can evidently be only Mambrino.[15] This lack of auctorial criticism in the face of so much linguistic relativity tends to shake the reader's confidence in established word usage. Of course, we are apt to rely on the correctness of Don Quijote's use of words and names; but who knows whether the knight, who is so often mistaken in his attempts to define reality (as he is precisely in his identification of the helmet of Mambrino), has hit this time upon the right name, whether this name is not as much of a dream as are the fantastic adventures he envisions (we are reminded of the baroque theme *par excellence* ". . . que los sueños sueños son")? Why should, then, "Mambrino" and not "Malino" or "Martino" be the name representing *reality*? The same insistence on "correctness" of word-usage, as applied to the nonexistent, occurs in the scene where Quijote listens to the *ama*'s cock-and-bull story of the theft of the books by "the sorcerer Muñaton," and finds nothing to correct therein but the name: not "Muñaton" but "Freston": Freston and Mambrino are names correct in irreality (in books), representing naught in reality. Evidently we are offered in Don Quijote a caricature of the humanist[16] who is versed in books and bookish names, but is unconcerned as to their valid relationship to reality (he has a pendant in the *licenciado*, to whom Don Quijote tells the fantastic story of his descent to the "cueva de Montesinos," and who is outspokenly qualified by Cervantes as a "humanista").[17]

In these two incidents we have a suggestion of a theme which informs our whole novel: the problem of the reality of literature. I belong with those critics who take seriously Cervantes' statement of purpose: "derribar la máquina mal fundada de los libros de caballería"; this statement, which indicts a particular literary genre, is, in fact, a recognition of the potential danger of "the book." And, in its larger sense, the *Quijote* is an indictment of the bookish side of Humanism,[18] a creed in which, seventy years earlier, Rabelais had so firmly believed, and an indictment of the "word-world" in which the Renaissance had delighted without qualms. Whereas the writers of the Renaissance were able to build up their word-worlds out of sheer exuberance, free to "play" linguistically because of their basic confidence in life—with the baroque artist Desengaño, disillusionment is allowed to color all things of the world, including books and their words, which possess only the reality of a *sueño*. Words are no longer, as they had been in the Middle Ages, depositories of truths nor, as they had been in the Renaissance, an expansion of life: they are, like the books in which they are contained, sources of hesitation, error, deception—"dreams."

The same linguistic perspectivism is present in Cervantes' treatment of common nouns. For the most part we have to do with the confusion, or the criticism, engendered by the clash of two linguistic standards determined mainly by social status.[19] Here, too, in this continuous give-and-take between cultured and uncultured speakers, there is given a suggestion of linguistic relativism that is willed by Cervantes. The opposition between two different ways of speech takes different forms: it may be Sancho who is interrupted and corrected by Don Quijote: in I, 32 [*hereje o*] *flemático* is corrected to *cismático*; in II, 7 *relucido* > *reducido*; II, 8 *sorbiese* > *asolviese*; II, 9 *cananeas* > *hacaneas*; II, 187 *friscal* > *fiscal.*[20] Particularly interesting are the cases in which the term used by Sancho and the correction offered by Quijote are in the relationship of etymological doublets (popular and learned developments of the same root): (I, 12): *cris - eclipse, estil - estéril* (how admirably has Cervantes anticipated the discoveries of nineteenth-century linguistics!). Again, it may be a question of Sancho's reaction to the language of the knight which the squire either misunderstands (in I, 8 Quijote's *homicidios* "murders" is transposed by Sancho into the more familiar, semipopular doublet *omecillos* "feuds") or fails to understand (in II, 29 Quijote must explain the meaning of *longincuos* ["por longincuos caminos"], which he "translates" by *apartados*). In general, Don Quijote shows more tolerance for linguistic ignorance (in regard to the *longincuos* just mentioned, he excuses Sancho with the words: "y no es maravilla que no lo entiendes, que no estás tu obligado a saber latín") than his uncultured associates (who seem more concerned with things than with words) do for linguistic pedantry: they often blame the knight for his *jerigonza* (I, 11), for his *griego* (I, 16). And, when Don Quijote reproves Sancho for his use of *abernuncio* instead of *abrenuncio*, the squire retorts: "Déjeme vuestra grandeza, que no estoy agora para mirar en sotilezas ni en letras mas o menos" (similarly, in II, 3, when the *bachiller* Sansón Carrasco corrects *presonajes* to *personajes*, Sancho remarks: "Otro reprochador de voquibles tenemos! Pues andense a eso y no acabaremos en toda la vida"). Sancho adopts the attitude of a Mathurin Régnier, opposing the "éplucheurs de mots"! It may happen that the same Sancho, the advocate of naturalness in language, turns purist for the moment[21] for the edification of his wife, and corrects her *revuelto* to *resuelto* (III, 5); but then he must hear from her lips—oh, relativity of human things!—the same reproach he was wont to administer to his master: "No os pongáis a disputar, marido, conmigo. Yo hablo como Dios es servido, y no me meto en más dibujos!" (here, she is referring to the language of God, Who, as Sancho himself had already claimed, is the great "Entendedor" of all kinds of speech).[22] Another example of the linguistic intolerance of the common people is the retort of the shepherd who has been corrected for having said *mas años que sarna* instead of . . . *que Sarra*: "Harto vive la sarna," he answers, "y si es, señor, que me habéis de andar zaheriendo [='éplucher'] a cada paso los vocablos no acabaremos en un año." In this case Don Quijote apologizes, and admits that there is as much sense to the one as to the other expression (in other words, he is brought to recognize the wisdom of "popular etymology"). Indeed, Don Quijote the humanist is made to learn new words, popular graphic expressions unknown to him—such as terms descriptive of *naturalia turpia* which the high-minded knight was wont to eschew in his conversation (I, 48: *hacer aguas* "to urinate"; Sancho is triumphant: "Es posible que no entienda vuestra merced hacer aguas mayores o menores?"), or low argot expressions (I, 22: *gurapas, canario*, from the language of galley-slaves). And—the acme of shame for a humanist!—it may even happen that he has to be instructed in Latinisms by Sancho (with whom they appear, of course, in garbled form), as when he fails to understand his squire's remark: "quien infierno tiene *nula es retencia*" (I, 25): it is significant that Sancho the Catholic Positivist is more familiar with ecclesiastical Latin terms than is his master, the idealistic humanist. Thus, Don Quijote is shown not only as a teacher but also as a student of language; his word-usage is by no means accepted as an ideal. And the reader is allowed to suppose that, to Cervantes himself, the language of the knight was not above reproach: when, in his solemn challenges or declarations of love, Quijote indulges in archaic phonetics (*f* - instead of *h* -) and morphology (uncontracted verb forms), this is not so different from the *a Dios prazca* of Sancho, or the *voacé* of one of the captives.

It seems to me that Cervantes means to present the problem of the Good Language in all its possibilities, without finally establishing an absolute: on the one hand, Sancho is allowed to state his ideal of linguistic tolerance (II, 19): "Pues sabe que no me he criado en la corte ni he estudiado en Salamanca para saber si añado o quito alguna letra a mis vocablos, no hay para qué obligar al sayagués a que hable como el toledano, y toledanos puede haber que no las cortan en el aire en esto del hablar polido." On the other, Don Quijote may assert his ideal of an "illustrated language" (in the sense of Du Bellay): when Sancho fails to understand the Latinism *erutar* (II, 43), Don Quijote remarks: "*Erutar*, Sancho, quiere decir 'regoldar,' y este es uno de los mas torpes vocablos que tiene la lengua castellana, aunque es mas significativo. La gente curiosa se ha acogido al latín, y al *regoldar* dice *erutar*, y a los *regüeldos, erutaciones*; y cuando algunos no entienden sus términos, importa poco, que el uso los irá introduciendo con el tiempo, que con facilidad se entiendan; y esto es enriquecer la lengua, sobre quien tiene poder el vulgo y el uso." Thus, Don Quijote would create a more refined word-usage—though, at the same time, he realizes that the ultimate decision as to the enrichment of the language rests with the people; and he does not deny the expressivity of the popular expressions. Sancho's principle of linguistic expressivity, which is in line with his advocacy of the natural, of that which is inborn in man, must be seen *together* with Quijote's principle of linguistic refinement—which is a reflection of his consistent advocacy of the ideal: by positing the two points of view, the one problem in question is dialectically developed. It is obvious that in the passage on *erutar* we have a plea for a cultured language—though the ratification by the common people is urged. But this is not the same as saying that Cervantes himself is here pleading for linguistic refinement: rather, I believe, he takes no final stand but is mainly interested in a dialectical play, in bringing out the manifold facets of the problem involved. Sancho has a way of deciding problems trenchantly; Don Quijote is more aware of complexities; Cervantes stands above them both: to him, the two expressions *regoldar* and *erutar* serve to reveal so many perspectives of language.[23]

Within the framework of linguistic perspectivism fits also Cervantes' attitude toward dialects and jargons. Whereas, to Dante, all dialects appeared as inferior (though inferior in different degrees) realizations of a Platonic-Christian ideal pattern of language, as embodied in the *vulgare illustre*, Cervantes saw them as ways of speech which exist as individual realities and which have their justification in themselves. The basic Cervantine conception of perspectivism did not allow for the Platonic or Christian ideal of language: according to the creator of Don Quijote, dialects are simply the different reflections of reality (they are "styles," as the equally tolerant linguist of today would say), among which no one can take precedence over the other. Borgese, in "Il senso della letteratura italiana" (*Quaderni di domani*, Buenos Aires, 1933), speaks definitively of Dante's conception of the *vulgare illustre*: "Si veda nel *De vulgari eloquentia* com' egli si costruisca una lingua italiana che abbia carattere di perfezione divina, che sia, diremmo, una lingua celestiale e di angeli, di religione e di ragione; tanto che questa lingua, illustre, antica, cardinale, cortegiana, non si trova per natura in nessun luogo, e il parlare nativo di questo o di quel luogo, il dialetto di questa o quella città, è tanto più o meno nobile quanto più o meno s'avvicina a quell' ideale, così come un colore è più o meno cospicuo, più o meno luminoso, secondo che somigli al bianco o gli contrasti. Il bianco, il puro, il tutto-luce, l'astratto . . . da Dante è considerato . . . come tipo supremo del bello." Cervantes, on the contrary, delights in the different shades, in the particular gradations and nuances, in the gamut of colors between white and black, in the transitions between the abstract and the concrete. Hence we may explain the frequent excursions of Cervantes into what today we would call "dialectal geography" (I, 2): "un pescado que en Castilla llaman *abadejo* y en Andalucía *bacallao* y en otras partes *curadillo*, y en otras *truchuela*" (in fact, a modern Catalonian linguist, Montoliu, has been able to base his study of the synonyms for "mackerel" on this passage) ; I, 41: "*Tagarinos* llaman en Berbería a los moros de Aragón, y a los de Granada *mudéjares*, y en el reino de Fez llaman a los mudéjares *elches*."[24] In these lexicological variants, Cervantes must have seen not a striving toward the approximation of an ideal, but only the variegated phantasmagoria of human approaches to reality: each variant has its own justification, but all of them alike reflect no more than human "dreams." Don Quijote is allowed to expose the inadequacy of such chance designations, as appear in any one dialect, by punning on the word *truchuela* "mackerel": "Como hay muchas truchuelas, podrán servir de una trucha," where he interprets (or pretends to interpret) *truchuela* as "little trout." What, ultimately, is offered here is a criticism of the arbitrariness of any fixed expression in human language (*Sprachkritik*): the criticism which underlies the unspoken question, "Why should a mackerel be called a small trout?" Again, when Don Quijote hears the expression *cantor* used in reference to the galley-slaves, he asks the candid question (I, 22): "Por músicos y cantores van también a galeras?" Thus the literal interpretation of the expression serves to put into relief the macabre and ironic flavor of its metaphorical use [*cantar* = *cantar en el ansia* "to 'sing' under torture"]. Here we witness the bewilderment of Don Quijote, who tries to hold words to a strict account; we may, perhaps, sense a criticism of Quijote's too-literal approach toward language—but this, in itself, would amount to a criticism of the ambiguity of human speech. Cervantes is satisfied, however, merely to suggest the linguistic problem, without any didactic expansion.

A masterpiece of linguistic perspectivism is offered in the transposition, by Sancho, of the high-flown jargon of love contained in Don Quijote's letter to Dulcinea, of which the squire has remembered the spirit, if not the exact words. Sancho, like most primitive persons, has an excellent acoustic memory, "toma de memoria" and "tiene en su memoria" (in line with medieval practice, he does not "memorize," cf. my article on *decorar* in *RHF*, VI, 176, 283) but, in attempting to cope with Don Quijote's florid language, he must necessarily "transpose," remembering what he *thinks* Quijote has said. In this way, "soberana y alta señora" becomes "alta y sobajada señora"—which the barber corrects to ". . . sobrehumana o soberana": for this single term of address we are presented with three versions, resulting in a polyonomasia, as in the case of the proper names. Again, "de punto de ausencia y el llagado de las telas del corazon" > "el llego y falto de sueño y el ferido" (it is as though Sancho, while indulging in Isidorian etymologies, is shrewdly diagnosing his master). In such linguistic exchanges we have a parallel to the numerous dialogues between the knight and the squire which, as is well known, are inserted into the novel in order to show the different perspectives under which the same events must appear to two persons of such different backgrounds. This means that, in our novel, things are represented, not for what they are in themselves but only as things spoken about or thought about; and this involves breaking the narrative presentation into two points of view. There can be no certainty about the "unbroken" reality of the events; the only unquestionable truth on which the reader may depend is the will of the artist who chose to break up a multivalent reality into different perspectives. In other words: perspectivism suggests an

Archimedean principle outside of the plot—and the Archimedes must be Cervantes himself.

In the second chapter, the nickname "los del rebuzno" is loaded with a double-entendre: the Spanish variants of Gothamites draw on the doubtful art of braying for their proud war slogan: their banner bears the verse "no rebuznaron en balde | el uno y otro alcalde" (the "regidores" have been promoted to "alcaldes" in the course of history and—evidently—thanks to the compulsion of rhyme). Here, Don Quijote is entrusted by Cervantes with exploding the vanity of such sectional patriotism: the humanistic knight, in a masterful speech which includes a series of Spanish ethnical nicknames (which take the modern philologian, Rodríguez Marín, over four full pages to explain): "los de la Reloja, los cazoleros, berenjeneros, ballenatos, jaboneros," shows the excessive vanity, originating in the flesh, not in the spirit, in the devil, not in true Catholicism, that is underlying the townspeople's attitude of resenting nicknames—i.e. of investing such trifling expressions of the language with disproportionate symbolic value. The Don Quijote who, on other occasions, is only too apt to introduce symbolism and general principles into everyday life, is here inspired by Cervantes to expose the vanity of misplaced symbolizing and generalization. The epithet "los del rebuzno" is thus made to shine with the double light of a stupidity—that wants to be taken seriously; of a local peculiarity—that aspires to "national" importance. The reader is free to go ahead and extend this criticism to other national slogans. That here Cervantes is endorsing Don Quijote seems beyond doubt since, when the novelist introduces this incident, he, speaking in his own right, attributes the adoption of the communal slogan to the activity of "the devil who never sleeps" and who is forever building "quimeras de no nada"—we might say: to a baroque devil who delights in deluding man. The chimeric and self-deluding quality of human vanity could hardly be illustrated more effectively than in this story, where the art of braying is first inflated and then deflated before our eyes, appearing as a "special language of human vanity."[25] And we may see in Cervantes' twofold treatment of the problem of nicknames another example of his baroque attitude (what is true, what is dream?)—this time, toward language. Is not human language, also, *vanitas vanitatum*, is it not sometimes a "braying" of a sort? Cervantes does not outspokenly say so.

The double point of view into which Cervantes is wont to break up the reality he describes may also appear in connection with one key-word, recurring throughout a given episode, upon which Cervantes casts two different lighting effects. We have a most successful example of this in the two chapters II, 25 and 27, where our interest is focused on the motif "braying like an ass." The connecting link between the two chapters is evidently "vanity": it is vanity that prompts the two *regidores* of the Mancha de Aragón to try to out-bray each other, as they search for the lost animal which they want to decoy and whose answering bray each seems to hear —only to learn, at the end, that the braying he heard was that of the other *regidor* (the ass, meanwhile, having died). It is vanity, again, that induces the townspeople—who, after this adventure, were called "los del rebuzno" by the inhabitants of neighboring villages—to sally forth to do battle with their deriders. And it is also due to vanity, on Sancho's part, that he, while deprecating, along with Don Quijote, the gift of imitating an ass, cannot refrain from showing off his own prowess in this regard before the townspeople—who straightway turn upon him in anger and beat him.

The vanity of "braying" shares with all other vanities the one characteristic that an inconsequential feature is invested with a symbolic value which it cannot, in the light of reason, deserve. Thus a duality (sham value vs. real value) offers itself to the artist for exploitation. In the first chapter, Cervantes has the two *regidores* address each other with doubtful compliments: "de vos a un asno, compadre, no hay alguna diferencia en cuanto toca al rebuznar" or "[you are the] más perito rebuznador del mundo." In the word *rebuznador*, there is a striving after the noble ring of *campeador, emperador*—which is drowned out by the blatant voice of the unregenerate animal: an ambivalence which exposes the hollow pretense.

There is one case in which Cervantes' perspectivism has

crystallized into a bifocal word-formation; in Don Quijote's remark: "eso que a ti te parece bacía de barbero me parece a mí el yelmo de Mambrino, y a otro le parecerá otra cosa" (I, 25),[26] there is contained a Weltanschauung which Américo Castro has, in a masterly fashion, recognized as a philosophical criticism (typical of the Renaissance) of the senses ("el engaño a los ojos"); and this vision finds its linguistic expression, highly daring for Cervantes' time, in the coinage *baciyelmo*, with which the tolerant Sancho concludes the debate about the identity of the shining object—as if he were reasoning: "if a thing appears to me as *a*, to you as *b*, it may be, in reality, neither *a* nor *b*, but *a* + *b*" (a similar tolerance is shown by Don Quijote a little later in the same episode, when he remarks, in the argument about the hypothetical nature of the hypothetical Mambrino: "Asi que, Sancho, deja ese caballo, o asno, o lo que quisieras que sea"; Quijote, however, does not go so far as to coin a **caballi-asno*). Now, it is evident to any linguist that, when shaping *baciyelmo*, Cervantes must have had in mind an existing formation of the same type; and his pattern must have been that which furnished designations of hybrid animals—i.e. of a fantastic deviation from Nature—so that this quality of the fantastic and the grotesque is automatically transferred to the coinage *baciyelmo*; such a form does not guarantee the "actual" existence of any such entity *a* + *b*. In most cases, Cervantes must obey language, though he questions it: a basin he can only call "bacía," a helmet, only "yelmo"; with the creation of *baciyelmo*, however, he frees himself from linguistic limitations.[27] Here, as elsewhere, I would emphasize, more than Castro (whose task it was to show us the conformity to Renaissance thinking of what Cervantes himself has called his "espíritu lego"), the artistic freedom conquered by Cervantes. In the predicament indicated by (the paradigmatic) ". . . o lo que quisieras que sea," the artist has asserted his own free will.

Now, from what has been said it would appear that the artist Cervantes uses linguistic perspectivism only in order to assert his own creative freedom; and this linguistic perspectivism, as I have already suggested, is only one facet of the general spirit of relativism which has been recognized by most critics as characteristic of our novel.[28] Such perspectivism, however, had, in the age of Cervantes, to acknowledge ultimately a realm of the absolute—which was, in his case, that of Spanish Catholicism. Cervantes, while glorying in his role of the artist who can stay aloof from the "engaños a los ojos," the "sueños" of this world, and create his own, always sees himself as overshadowed by supernal forces: the artist Cervantes never denies God, or His institutions, the King and the State. God, then, cannot be attracted into the artist's linguistic perspectivism; rather is Cervantes' God placed above the perspectives of language, he is said to be, as we have seen, the supreme "Entendedor" of the language He has created—just as Cervantes, from his lower vantage-point, seeks to be. Perhaps we may assume with Cervantes the old Neo-platonic belief in an artistic Maker who is enthroned above the manifold facets and perspectives of the world.

The story of the *Cautivo* (I, 37 *seq.*), one of the many tales interpolated into the main plot, exemplifies linguistic perspectivism made subservient to the divine. The maiden betrothed to the ex-captive, who enters the stage dressed and veiled in Moorish fashion and who, without speaking a word, bows to the company in Moorish fashion, gives from the beginning the impression "que . . . devia de ser mora y que no sabía hablar cristiano" (note the expression *hablar cristiano* [instead of *hablar castellano*] which, with its identification of "Spanish" and "Christian," anticipates the religious motif basic to the story). Dorotea is the one to ask the all-important question: "esta señora es mora o cristiana?"—to which the Cautivo answers that she is a Moor in her costume and in her body, but in her soul, a great Christian, although not yet baptized—but "Dios será servido que presto se bautice" (again, we may see in this mention of God not only a conventional form but a suggestion of the main problem, which is the working of Divine Grace). The Cautivo, speaking in Arabic, asks his betrothed to lift her veil in order to show forth her enchanting beauty; when asked about her name, he gives it in the Arabic form: *lela Zoraida.* And now the Moorish girl herself speaks for the first time: "No, no Zoraida: María, María"—repeating this statement twice more (the last time half in Arabic, half in Spanish: "Sí, sí, María: Zoraida *macange* ['not at all']." The change of name which she claims—evidently in anticipation of the change of name which will accompany her baptism—is of deep significance; it is a profession of faith, of conversion. We will learn later that she must become a María because, since her early childhood, she had been taken under the mantle of the Virgin.

After this first appearance of "Zoraida-María," whose two names are nothing but the linguistic reflection of her double nature, the episode is interrupted by Don Quijote's speech on *armas y letras*; thus, after the briefest of introductions, we must lose sight for a while of Zoraida-María, the puzzle of whose twofold name and Januslike personality remains suspended in midair. The interruption is significant: Cervantes, in the episodic short stories, follows for the most part a technique opposed to that of the main plot: in the latter we are always shown first the objective reality of events, so that when they later become distorted after having passed through the alembic of Don Quijote's mind (Sancho, in general, remains more true to the reality he has experienced) we, from the knowledge we have previously gained, are proof against the knight's folly. But, in the short stories, on the contrary, Cervantes' technique is to tantalize us with glimpses into what seems an incredible situation, worthy of Quijote's own imagination (in our own story there suddenly appears before the group of Don Quijote's friends assembled in an inn, an exotic-looking woman, dressed in outlandish gear, with her companion who has to talk for her) and with all the connotations of the unreal; and the author is careful to protract our suspense to the utmost before giving us the solution of the initial puzzle. Thus the interpolations of these episodic short stories, whose reality is at least as fantastic as the most daring dreams of the mad knight, offer another revelation of the perspectivism of Cervantes; we have to do not only with the opposition between prosaic reality and fantastic dreams: reality itself can be both prosaic and fantastic. If, in the main plot, Cervantes has carried out his program of "derribar la máquina mal fundada" of the fantastic, he has taken care to rebuild this machinery in the by-stories. And our tale of the *Captive* is an excellent illustration of this rule.

When, after Don Quijote's speech, the Captive tells his story *ab ovo*, explaining how the startling fact of a "Zoraida-María" came to pass, we are allowed a glimpse into the historic reality of that hybrid world of Mohammedans and Christians, which was the equivalent in Cervantes' time of the *fronterizo* milieu of the romances—only, a more complicated variant because of the two different groups representative of the Mohammedan faith then facing the Spaniards: the Turks and the Arabs, the former the more ruthless type, the latter (to which Lela Marién and her father belong) the type more amenable to the Christian way of life. Indeed, the Arabs themselves seem to feel more akin to the Christian civilization than to the Turkish (the girl's father calls the Turks *canes*; it is ironic that later, after he has been deeply wronged by the Christians, he must call them *perros*).

As the Captive tells the story of the tragic events that took place against the background of the warring Turkish Empire, he embellishes his (Spanish-language) narrative with words from Turkish and Arabic, offering a linguistic mosaic that adds to the local color of his story. If we compare the Turkish words with the Arabic, we will note the sharpest of contrasts: the former are of a factual reference, narrowly descriptive, with no transcendental connotations (for the Turks are excluded from the possibility of Enlightenment by Grace): *leventes, bagarinos,*.*baño* (wrongly offered as a Turkish word for "prison"), *pasamaques, zoltanís, gilecuelco*; we find also the pejorative epithet *Uchalí Fartax* "que quiere decir en lengua turquesca el renegado tiñoso, porque lo era" (again, the *convenientia* between names and objects!). The Arabic words, on the contrary, are nearly always connected with things religious and, more specifically, with things Christian—so that a kind of transposition (or perspectivism) is achieved: "Lela Marién" instead of "Nuestra Señora la Vírgen María"; "Alá" for the Christian God, and also the interjection "quelá" in the same reference; *nizarani* for "Christians"; *la zalá cristianesca* for "the Christian prayer," in which the adjective *cristianesco* (instead of *cristiano*), formed after *morisco, turquesco,* has something of the same transposed character, as if the Christian rites were seen from the outside. And, in addition to the linguistic medley offered the reader directly, there is a reference to the polyglot habits among the protagonists of the story. Zoraida, for example, chooses Arabic as the private language in which to talk and write to the Captive, but converses with the Christians (as also does her father) in the *lingua franca*—which language is characterized by the Captive as "lengua que en toda la Berberia, y aun en Constantinopla se habla entre cautivos y moros, que ni es morisca ni castellana ni de otra nacion alguna, sino una mezcla de todas las lenguas, con la cual todos nos entendemos," or "la bastarda lengua que . . . allí se usa": a characterization, it may be noted, which is not basically different from that offered in our times by Schuchardt ("Mischsprache," "Verkehrssprache"), the student of *lingua franca,* of the Creole languages etc., and the advocate of an international artificial language. Castilian, Turkish, Arabic, with reminiscences of *lingua franca*: why this Babelic confusion of tongues in our story? It does not suffice to appeal to the historical fact that these languages were actually spoken at the time in the Ottoman Empire, where Cervantes himself had lived as a captive: for, in addition to the foreign phrases that might serve simply for local color, we have to do evidently with an express concern for each individual language as such—to the extent that we are always informed in which language a certain speech, letter or dialogue was couched. It seems to me that Cervantes would point out that differences of language do not, by principle, hinder the working of Christian Grace—though he evidently grades the languages according to their penetrability by things Christian: Turkish is presented as on a lower level than Arabic—which lends itself so easily to the transposition of Christian concepts.[29] And this linguistic transposition of things Christian into things Moorish reflects only the transposed situation of a Moor who becomes a Christian; the story of the Captive and of Zoraida María shows Grace working toward the salvation of a disbeliever and toward the sacramental union, by a Christian marriage, of two beings of different races: above the divergence of race and language[30] God understands the Christian longing of Zoraida for the *Alá cristiano*. It was the Virgin Mary, of whom she had learned from a Christian nurse, who inspired her to rescue the Christian soldier and to flee with him to a Christian country in order there to be baptized and married. When Zoraida speaks of Alá, every one knows that the Christian God is meant—whose true nature shines through the linguistic disguise. The same symbol is carried out on another plane: when, from her window, Zoraida's white hand is seen, adorned with Moorish jewels (*ajorcas*), waving a Christian cross, the *ajorcas* are naturally overshadowed by the cross.[31] Again, in the case of Zoraida's letters to the prisoners, written in Arabic but adorned with the sign of the Cross, it is clear that these indications of different cultural climates clearly express only one thing: her will to be a Christian. It is not the language, the gesture, the costume, or the body that matter to Him, but the meaning behind all the exterior manifestations: the soul. God, Cervantes is telling us, can recognize behind the "perspective" of a disbeliever, His true faithful follower.

I cannot quite agree with Castro, who seems to see mainly the human side of the episode, when he says (*El pensamiento de Cervantes*, p. 147): "Amor y religión (ésta como envoltura de aquél) llevan a Zoraida tras su cautivo," and considers the story to be one of "armonía entre seres concordados." Rather, I should say that religion is the kernel, love the envelopment; we have here a drama of Divine Grace working against all possible handicaps and using the love between Moor and Christian as a means to an end: the conversion of Zoraida (and, incidentally, the return of a renegade[32] to the bosom of the Church); therefore Cervantes has devised his story against the background of the Spanish-Turkish wars, which ended with the victory of the Spaniards at Lepanto and in which, as Titian has represented it, Spain succors Christian faith. I concur absolutely with Castro, however, when he goes on to say that this story of abduction is the most violent and the most tragic of all the episodes in the novel: Zoraida, in her zeal to receive holy baptism and the sacrament of Christian marriage, must cheat her father, must see him subjected by her doings to the violence of the Christians who truss him up and finally leave him marooned on a desert island, where he cries out to his daughter, alternately cursing and beseeching her. Here is a good Arab, meek and truthful to Christians, who is thrown back to the Mohammedan god by the ruthless deed of his Christian daughter. That such sins may be committed for the rescue of a soul can only be explained, Cervantes seems to tell us, by the incalculable will of Providence. Why should these sins be made corollary to the salvation of the particular soul of Zoraida—while the soul of her father becomes thereby utterly lost to salvation? What whimsicality of God! I should say that this scene exhibits not so much the "abismos de lo humano," as Castro has it, but rather "abismos de lo divino." No harmonious earthly marriage could be concluded on the basis of such a terrifying violation of the Fourth Commandment; but God is able to put the laws of morality out of function in order to reach His own goal.

In our story, which is the story of a great deceit, the words referring to "deceit" take on a particularly subtle double-entendre. When, for example, Zoraida, in one of her letters to the Captive, says: "no te fies de ningun moro, porque son todos *marfuzes*" of her Moslem coreligionists, she is using an originally Arabic word for "treacherous" which had come to be borrowed by the Spaniards probably to refer, primarily, to the treachery of the Mohammedans (meaning something like "false as a Moor"); the choice of this word, which sounds rather strange when used by an Arab, must mean that Zoraida is judging the Arabs according to Christian prejudices (it is ironical that, in this story, it is the Arabs who are faithful and kind, and the Christians who are "marfuzes"—although working toward a goal presumably willed by Providence). Again, the accusation of cheating is reversed when Zoraida, speaking as a Moor to the Christian captive, in the presence of her father, remarks: ". . . vosotros cristianos siempre mentís en cuanto decís, y os hacéis pobres por engañar a los moros"; here, where her judgment is, indeed, factually justified, she is actually speaking disingenuously—in order to further the stratagem planned by the Christians. The discrepancy between words and meaning, between judgment and behavior, has reached such proportions that we can view only with perplexity the "abismo del divino" which makes it possible that such evil means are accepted to further a noble purpose; the story offers us no way out but to try to share Zoraida's belief in the beneficent intervention of Lela Marién, who has prompted the good-wicked enterprise ("plega a Alá, padre mio, que Lela Marién, que ha sido la causa de que yo sea cristiana, ella te consuele en tu tristeza"). When Zoraida, speaking to her father, states of her deed "que parece tan buena como tú, padre amado, la juzgas por mala," we are offered basically the same perspectivistic pattern that we have noted in the case of the *baciyelmo*: it is implied, evidently, that Lela Marién knows of no perspectivism. There can be no doubt that what Cervantes is dealing with here is the tortuous and Jesuitic divinity that he was able to see in his time —whose decisions he accepts, while bringing out all the complications involved. Along with the submission to the divine there is instituted a tragic trial against it, a trial on moral grounds, and, on these grounds, the condemnation is unmitigated; the sacramental force of a father's curse is not entirely counterbalanced by the sacramental force of the Christian rites, the desire for which on Zoraida's part brought about the father's plight. Perhaps no writer, remaining within the boundaries of orthodox religion, has revealed more of the perplexities inherent in the theocratic order (a Nietzsche might have called this story an example of the immorality of God and have advocated the overthrow of such a God— whereas Cervantes quietly stays within the boundaries of the Christian fold). And this acme of submissive daring has been achieved by placing the divine beyond the perspectives which appear to the human eye.

Zoraida herself, for all her religious fervor, innocence, and supernatural beauty is, at the same time, capable of great wickedness. And again linguistic perspectivism is invoked in order to bring this side of her nature into relief. There is a moment when the band of fugitives pass the promontory called, after the mistress of Roderick, the last of the Gothic

Kings, *cabo de la Cava Rumia* ". . . de la mala mujer cristiana"; they insist, however, that to them it is not the "abrigo de mala mujer, sino puerto seguro de nuestro remedio." Now, when the name of this infamous woman, who sinned for love, is brought before the reader, he cannot fail to think of Zoraida—though, in the comparison with the Arabic prostitute "por quien se perdió España," the betrothed of the Captive must appear as a pure woman, who refused to live in a state of sin before her marriage. At the same time, however, Cervantes may wish us to realize how close was Zoraida to the abyss, and to see the ward of the Virgin, for a moment, under the perspective of la Cava.

* *
*

If we look back now over the development of this essay, we will see that we have been led from a plethora of names, words, languages, from polynomasia, polyetymologia and polyglottism, to the linguistic perspectivism of the artist Cervantes who knows that the transparence of language is a fact for God alone. And, at this point, I may be allowed to repeat, as a kind of epitomizing epilogue, the final passages of a lecture on the *Quijote* which I have given at several universities —which, I trust, will serve to round out the linguistic details I have pointed out earlier and to put them into relationship with the whole of the novel: a relationship which, in the course of our linguistic discussion, has already been tentatively indicated. After explaining that the *Quijote* appeals as well to children as to adults because of its combination of imagination and criticism, and that the modern genre of the critical novel, which started with a criticism of books and of a bookish culture (a criticism of the romances of chivalry) and came to be expanded to a new integration of the critical and the imaginative, was the discovery of Cervantes, I continued thus:

It is one of the great miracles of history (which is generally regarded deterministically by professional historians, who present individual phenomena as enclosed within tight compartments), that the greatest deeds sometimes occur at a place and a time when the historian would least expect them.

It is a historical miracle that, in the Spain of the Counter-Reformation, when the trend was toward the reestablishment of authoritarian discipline, an artist should have arisen who, thirty-two years before Descartes' *Discours de la méthode* (that autobiography of an independent philosophical thought, as Lanson has called it), was to give us a narrative which is simply one exaltation of the independent mind of man—and of a particularly powerful type of man: of the artist. It is not Italy, with its Ariosto and Tasso, not France with its Rabelais and Ronsard, but Spain that gave us a narrative which is a monument to the narrator qua narrator, qua artist. For, let us not be mistaken: the real protagonist of this novel is not Quijote, with his continual misrepresentation of reality, or Sancho with his skeptical half-endorsement of quixotism—and surely not any of the central figures of the illusionistic by-stories: the hero is Cervantes, the artist himself, who combines a critical and illusionistic art according to his free will. From the moment we open the book[33] to the moment we put it down, we are given to understand that an almighty overlord is directing us, who leads us where he pleases. The prologue of the whole work shows us Cervantes in the perplexity of an author putting the final touches to his work, and we understand that the "friend" who seemingly came to his aid with a solution was only one voice within the freely fabricating poet. And, on the last page of the book when, after Quijote's Christian death, Cervantes has that Arabian historian Cide Hamete Benegeli lay away his pen, to rest forever, on the top of the cupboard in order to forestall any further spurious continuation (after the manner of Avellaneda) of the novel, we know that the reference to the Arabian pseudo-historian is only a pretext for Cervantes to reclaim for himself the relationship of real father (no longer the "step-father," as in the prologue) to his book. Then the pen delivers itself of a long speech, culminating in the words: "For me alone Don Quijote was born and I for him; his task was to act, mine to write. For we alone are made for each other" ("Para mí solo nació Don Quijote, y yo para él; él supo obrar, y yo escribir; solos los dos somos para en uno"). An imperious *alone* (*solo*[*s*]) which only Cervantes could have said and in which all the Renaissance pride of the poet asserts itself: the poet who was the traditional immortalizer of the great deeds of historical heroes and princes. An Ariosto could have said the same words about the Duke of Ferrara.

The function of eulogizing princes was, as is well known, the basis of the economical situation of the Renaissance artist: he was given sustenance by the prince in return for the immortal glory which he bestowed upon his benefactor (cf. Zilsel, *Die Entstehung des Geniebegriffs*). But Don Quijote is no prince from whom Cervantes could expect to receive a pension, no doer of great deeds in the outer world (his greatness lay only in his warm heart), and not even a being who could be attested in any historical source—however much Cervantes might pretend to such sources. Don Quijote acquired his immortality exclusively at the hands of Cervantes—as the latter well knows and admits. Obviously, Quijote wrought only what Cervantes wrote, and he was born for Cervantes as much as Cervantes was born for him! In the speech of the pen of the pseudo-chronicler we have the most discreet and the most powerful self-glorification of the artist which has ever been written. The artist Cervantes grows by the glory which his characters have attained; and in the novel we see the process by which the figures of Don Quijote and Sancho become living persons, stepping out of the novel, so to speak, to take their places in real life—finally to become immortal historical figures. Thomas Mann, in a recent essay on the *Quijote* (in "Leiden und Grösse der Meister"), has said: "This is quite unique. I know of no other hero of a novel in world literature who would equally, so to speak, live off the glory of his own glorification ("ein Held, der von seinem Ruhm, von seiner Besungenheit lebte"). In the second part of the novel, when the Duke and Duchess ask to see the by now historical figures of Quijote and Panza, the latter says to the Duchess: "I am Don Quijote's squire who is to be found also *in the story* and who is called Sancho Panza—unless they have changed me in the cradle—I mean to say, at the printer's." In such passages, Cervantes willingly destroys the artistic illusion: he, the puppeteer, lets us see the strings of his puppet-show: "see, reader, this is not life, but a stage, a book: art; recognize the life-giving power of the artist as a thing distinct from life!"[34] By multiplying his masks (the friend of the prologue, the Arabian historian, sometimes the characters who serve as his mouthpiece), Cervantes seems to strengthen his grip on that whole artistic cosmos. And the strength of the grip is enhanced by the very nature of the protagonists: Quijote is what we would call today a split personality, sometimes rational, sometimes foolish; Sancho, too, at times no less quixotic than his master, is at other times incalculably rational. In this way, the author makes it possible for himself to decide when his characters will act reasonably, when foolishly (no one is more unpredictable than a fool who pretends to wisdom). At the start of his journey with Sancho, Don Quijote promises his squire an island kingdom to be ruled over by him, just as was done in the case of numerous squires in literature. But, acting on his critical judgment (of which he is not devoid), Don Quijote promises to give it to him immediately after their conquest—instead of waiting until the squire has reached old age, as is the custom in the books of chivalry. The quixotic side of Sancho accepts this prospective kingship without questioning its possibility, but his more earthly nature visualizes—and criticizes—the actual scene of the coronation: how would his rustic spouse Juana Gutiérrez look with a crown on her head? Two examples of foolishness, two critical attitudes: none of them is the attitude of the writer, who remains above the two split personalities and the four attitudes.

With the Machiavellian principle "divide and conquer" applied to his characters, the author succeeds in making himself indispensable to the reader: while, in his Prologue, Cervantes calls for a critical attitude on our part, he makes us depend all the more on his guidance through the psychological intricacies of the narrative: here, at least, he leaves us no free will. We may even infer that Cervantes rules imperiously over his own self: it was he who felt this self to be split into a critical and an illusionistic part (*desengaño* and *engaño*); but in this baroque Ego he made order, a precarious order, it is true, which was reached only once by Cervantes in all his works—and which was reached in Spain only by Cervantes (for Calderón, Lope, Quevedo, Gracián decided that the world is only illusion and dreams, "que los sueños sueño son"). And indeed only once in world literature has this precarious order come into being: later thinkers and artists did not stop at proclaiming the inanity of the world: they went so far as to doubt the existence of any universal order and to deny a Creator, or at least, when imitating Cervantes' perspectivism (Gide, Proust, Conrad, Joyce, Virginia Woolf, Pirandello),[35] they have failed to sense the unity behind perspectivism—so that, in their hands, the personality of the author is allowed to disintegrate. Cervantes stands at the other pole from that modern dissolution of the personality of the narrator: what grandeur there is in his attempt—made in the last moment before the unified Christian vision of the world was to fall asunder—to restore this vision on the artistic plane, to hold before our eyes a cosmos split into two separate halves: disenchantment and illusion, which, nevertheless, by a miracle, do not fall apart! Modern anarchy checked by a classical will to equipoise (the baroque attitude)! We recognize now that it is not so much that Cervantes' nature is split in two (critic and narrator) because this is required by the nature of Don Quijote, but rather that Don Quijote is a split character because his creator was a critic-poet who felt with almost equal strength the urge of illusionary beauty and of pellucid clarity.

To modern readers the "schizophrenic" Don Quijote might seem to be a typical case of social frustration: a person whose madness is conditioned by the social insignificance into which the caste of the knights had fallen, with the beginnings of modern warfare—just as, in Flaubert's *Un coeur simple*, we are meant to see as socially conditioned the frustrations of Félicité, the domestic servant, which lead to the aberration of her imagination. I would, however, warn the reader against interpreting Cervantes in terms of Flaubert, since Cervantes himself has done nothing to encourage such a sociological approach. Don Qujote is able to recover his sanity, if only on his death-bed; and his erstwhile madness is but one reflection of that generally human lack of reason—above which the author has chosen to take his stand.[36]

High above this world-wide cosmos of his making, in which

hundreds of characters, situations, vistas, themes, plots and subplots are merged, Cervantes' artistic self is enthroned, an all-embracing creative self, Naturelike, Godlike, almighty, all-wise, all-good—and benign: this visibly omnipresent Maker reveals to us the secrets of his creation, he shows us the work of art in the making, and the laws to which it is necessarily subjected. For this artist is Godlike but not deified; far be it from us to conceive of Cervantes as attempting to dethrone God, replacing Him by the artist as a superman. On the contrary, Cervantes always bows before the supernal wisdom of God, as embodied in the teachings of the Catholic Church and the established order of the state and of society. *Qua* moralist, Cervantes is not at all "perspectivistic."[37] Nor can we expect to find in Cervantes any of that romantic revolt of the artist against society. But, on the other hand, the artist Cervantes has extended, by the mere art of his narrative, the Demiurge-like, almost cosmic independence of the artist. His humor, which admits of many strata, perspectives, masks—of relativization and dialectics—bears testimony to his high position above the world. His humor is the freedom of the heights, no fate-bound dionysiac dissolution of the individual into nothingness and night, as with Schopenhauer and Wagner, but a freedom beneath the dome of that religion which affirms the freedom of the will. There is, in the world of his creation, the bracing air with which we may fill our lungs and by which our individual senses and judgment are sharpened; and the crystalline lucidity of an artistic Maker in its manifold reflections and refractions.

NOTES

1. And in that same pastoral game (II, 67) Sansón Carrasco would become "el pastor Sansonino" or "el pastor Carrascón (two names!), the barber > "Nicolás Miculoso" (after *Nemoroso,* as Quijote explains), *el Cura* > "el pastor Curiambro" (reminiscence of the giant Caraculiambro?); as for the name of Sancho's wife, however, the squire, who always pays heed to the *convenientia* of words and objects, agrees only to "Teresona" as the pastoral name for his fat Teresa. We see why he cannot agree to "Teresaina": this name, proposed by Sansón Carrasco (II, 73) is so evocative of the ethereal music of the flute (*dulzaina*) that Don Quijote must laugh at "la aplicacion del nombre."

2. A pendant to Quijote, the believer in an unreal order of virtue, is Cardenio, the lover who cannot face that injustice which so often obtains in the reality of love. Thus we will not be astonished to find that the onomastic pattern, dear to the romances of chivalry, represented by *Caballero de la Triste Figura* is also applied to Cardenio: he is alternatively called (by the shepherds who tell his story) *Roto de la Mala Figura, Caballero de la Sierra, Caballero del Bosque*—before he himself is allowed to state his simple, real name: "Mi nombre es Cardenio."

The importance of the *name* for the Middle Ages appears here most clearly; any knight of romance, Amadis or Perceval or Yvain, is presented as undergoing an inner evolution, whose outward manifestations are the different "adventures" which mark his career; and it is by virtue of these adventures that he acquires different names, each of which is revelatory of the particular stage attained; in this way, the evolution is clearly labeled for the reader. Yvain acquires a new dignity, so to speak, when he becomes the "Chevalier au Lion"; "Orlando innamorato" is a different person from "Orlando furioso." Consequently, a mistake in names is no slight mistake: it is a sin against the law of inner evolution which presides over the events of a heroic life. It is significant that Don Quijote speaks (I, 28) of "la ventura aquella de Amadís [de Grecia], *cuando se llamaba el Caballero de la Ardiente Espada,* que fué una de las mejores espadas que tuvo caballero en el mundo." It is precisely because this extraordinary sword distinguishes objectively one of the exemplary phases of the evolution of the knight that the name under which he appears has a somewhat objective, temporally definable validity.

3. In II, 2, Sancho reports with pride that, though Don Quijote and his beloved are being celebrated by the historiographer Cide Hamete Berengena [sic], under their fanciful names ("El ingenioso hidalgo," "Dulcinea del Toboso"), his name has suffered no such treatment: "que me mientan . . . *con mi mesmo nombre de Sancho Panza.*"

4. Again, we have evidence of the importance of nomenclature: a change of suffix, in itself, may be equivalent to a change of linguistic perspective.

In another incident (I, 22), from one of the secondary episodes, we are told that, when the guard speaks of his prisoner, Ginés de Pasamonte, as "el famoso Ginés de Pasamonte, que por otro nombre llaman Ginesillo de Parapilla," the other retorts: "Señor Comisario, . . . no andemos ahora a deslindar nombres y sobrenombres. Ginés me llamo, y no Ginesillo, y Pasamonte es mi alcurnia, y no Parapilla, como voacé dice . . . algún día sabrá alguno si me llamo Ginesillo de Parapilla o no. . . . Yo haré que no me lo llamen." Again, just as in the case of Sancho's rebuke to the one who had altered Quijote's title, Cervantes takes occasion to show the natural indignation aroused by a violation of the "perspective" which the bearer of the name has chosen and under which he has a right to appear.

5. The same type of justification of a mispronunciation by the invention *ad hoc* of a (secondary) relationship is found in II, 3, when Sancho, in order to explain his version of the Arabic name *Benengeli* (i.e. Berengena), refers to the Moors' predilection for *berengenas.*

6. Sancho offers us another example of popular "synonymic derivation": *rata* "rate, installment of payment" has been understood by him as "rat," which, with him, must lead to *gata* "cat." As a matter of fact, the procedure by which developments take place in argot is not basically different from this: *dauphin* "dolphin" > "pimp" in French argot was interpreted as *dos fin* so that a *dos vert* could follow. The modern linguist would say that Sancho has the makings of an excellent subject for an inquirer such as Gilliéron, who wanted to seize, on the spot, the working of the popular imagination. When faced with the problem of language, Sancho is not lazy and passive, as he is in general (and in this incessant linguistic criticism and linguistic activity, side by side with inactivity in other realms of life, he is typically Spanish): he asks himself why the Spanish battlecry is *Santiago y cierra España!*: "Está por ventura España abierta, y de modo que es menester cerrarla, o qué ceremonia es esta?" Erroneously he seeks to interpret, by contemporary patterns, a way of speech obscured by historic development. While he does not know as much historical grammar as does Rodríguez Marín, the modern commentator of the *Don Quijote,* he shows himself to be aware of the basic problem of linguistics: the opaqueness of certain ways of speech.

7. Accordingly, this variety of names would be on one level with such pseudo-historical interruptions of the narrative as we have seen in I, 2, when Cervantes pretends to hesitate about which particular adventure of his protagonist to narrate first: it seems that there are some *autores* ("authors" or "authorities") who say that the adventure of Puerto Lápice was the first; others contend the same about that of the windmills, while Cervantes, himself, has ascertained, from the annals of La Mancha . . . etc.

We shall see later, however, that the pseudo-historical device has implications much more important than the parodying of chronicles.

8. It is in the medieval vein that Cervantes, in the Trifaldi episode (II, 39), has the name of the horse *Clavileño el Alígero* explained as follows: "cuyo nombre conviene con el ser de leño y con la clavija que trae en la frente y con la ligereza con que camina": *convenir, conveniencia* are the medieval (originally Ciceronian) expressions for "harmony"—as well as "grammatical accord," harmony between word and meaning, etc.

9. A characteristic trait of the ancient and medieval etymological procedures was to explain by compounds where the modern linguist would assume derivation: Thus Eng. *dismal* was explained by *dies mali* instead of as a derivative from OF *disme* "dime" (cf. *MLN,* LVII, 602). In the same vein is the decomposition of the derivative *Truff-ald-*[*ino*] into the two parts *tri* + *fald-*. Compare also Sancho's decomposition (II, 3) of *gramática* into *grama* (the herb) + *tica* (the meaning of the latter word has not yet been elucidated by commentators).

10. The trick intended for the protagonists is revealed in the midst of the pageant, when the majordomo, who plays the countess, corrects himself: "a este su criado, *digo, a esta su criada.*"

It may be stated that such baroque effects are on the increase in the second part of the *Quijote*, where pageants, *burlas* and *truffe* flourish (cf. "Las bodas de Camacho y Guiteria"). In Part I we are shown the aggressive Don Quijote and his grumbling but faithful follower Sancho challenging the outward world—meeting, in their adventures, with a flux of humanity in a series of chance encounters against the fluid background of roadsides and inns. In Part II, however, the couple appear rather as being challenged than as challenging the world—and this world, the world of the big city, the world of the aristocracy, is now more formidable, more firmly constituted. The resistance of the first environment was not sufficient to bring about the necessary cure of the knight: Quijote must be brought to face the criticism of the higher spheres of society, where he is victimized with sophisticated *burlas*. The aristocrats play theater for Don Quijote and Sancho (in a way that may remind us of Shakespeare's Sly—and the "governorship" of Sancho resembles Sly's temporary courtship). And theater, like *sueño*, is bound to end with an awakening from illusion. This is a baroque theme.

If Mr. Stephen Gilman (*RFH*, v, 148) is right in claiming for Avellaneda's continuation of the *Quijote* a baroque style, it might be apposite to add that Cervantes himself, whether prompted by his competitor or not (and I personally think, rather not), went the same path of "baroquization" in his own continuation of the story.

11. Don Quijote himself explains words according to an Isidorian scheme: e.g. when he takes it upon himself to explain *albogues* (II, 67), he begins by describing the "res" designated by the word ("albogues son unas chapas . . ."), and follows this with the etymon: it is originally Arabic, he says, as the prefix *al-* suggests. Don Quijote cannot stop here, however; giving full rein to his associative imagination, he goes on to mention other Arabic words in Spanish likewise characterized by *al-*, and ends by including certain loan-words with a termination in *-í*.

12. The same "twofold pattern" is followed for the etymology of the (legendary, medieval) island of which Sancho is to become the ruler (II, 45): "la ínsula Baratería, o ya porque el lugar se llamaba Baratario o ya por el barato con que se le había dado el gobierno"; here, the first etymology is the formal or tautological one which Cervantes slyly proposes (in order to remain faithful to the dichotomy) as an alternative to the second—which is the historically "real" etymology.

13. My reason for believing that the hidalgo had *Lanzarote* in mind when he changed his name, is found in the episode of I, 2, where Don Quijote adapts the text of the old *romance* to his own situation, substituting his own name for that of the protagonist: "Nunca fuera caballero/ De damas tan bien servido/ Como fuera don Quijote/ Cuando de su aldea vino." The suffix *-ote* (as in *monigote, machacote*) has a comic ring for the reader but not, evidently, for the coiner of the name.

We have a somewhat similar bivalence in the case of the name *Rocinante*—though here, of course, it is not the suffix but the radical which provides the comic effect. The noble connotation of *-ante*, that participial ending which had dropped out of current use in Old Romance languages, is to be found, with a nuance of high distinction, in such epic names as OF *Bali-*

gant, Tervagant, and in common nouns such as OF *aumirant* (Sp. *almirante*) and Sp. *emperante* (found along with *emperador* in the *Libro de buen amor*). Thus, our learned knight, with his "epic imagination," came naturally by his predilection for such a pattern of nomenclature.

As for the factual etymology of the word *quijote* (<OF *cuissot* "cuissart") this has been established by Malkiel, *Language*, XXI, 156. Mr. Malkiel, however, confuses historical linguistics with the study of a work of art when he writes: "The etymology of this word naturally aroused the curiosity of Cervantes." In reality, Cervantes has not shown himself interested in the etymology of the common noun *quijote*, but in that of the proper name *Quijote*; and the latter was not, for him, derived from OF *cuissot*, but from *Lanzarote*, and from the group *Quijada, Quijano* (whatever the origin of these may be).

14. As a non-linguistic example of such perspectivism, we may point to the passage made famous by Hume: two kinsmen of Sancho, called upon to give their opinion of a hogshead of wine, find it excellent, in the main, except for a peculiar flavor—on which they disagree. The one insists it has a leathery taste, the other, a metallic taste. When they have finally drunk their way to the bottom of the cask, they find a rusty iron key with a leather strap attached.

14a. It is not astonishing that Dostoievski, that great absolutist who delighted in showing up the relativity in human affairs, should have imitated the polyonomasia of Cervantes: In *Crime and Punishment*, the monomaniac Raskolnikov (whose name, related to *raskolnik* "heretic," suggests his monomania) has a friend named *Razumichin* (related to *razum* "reason"), who is the flexible, optimistic, helpful, and loquacious defender of reason: his flexibility of mind is mirrored in the alterations to which his name is subjected by other characters in the novel: *Vrazumichin* (to *vrazumlyaty* "to explain") and *Rassudkin* (to *rassudok* "judgment").

15. Sancho, who appears so often as the representative of that Catholic positivism which takes the world, as it is, as God-given, without envisaging the possibility of a more ideal order, expresses his linguistic doubts about the mysterious, significant, and musical names of Quijote's making, just as he usually (though not always) suspects the *arcana* of the world of enchantment that his master visualizes: (I, 28): ". . . no eran fantasmas ni hombres encantados, como vuestra merced dice, sino hombres de carne y de hueso *como nosotros*, y todos, según los oí nombrar . . . tenían sus nombres: que el uno se llamaba Pedro Martínez y el otro Tenorio Hernández, y el Ventero oí que se llamaba Juan Palomeque el Zurdo." When he hears from Quijote's lips the fantastic names of beings from a world he does not believe to exist, he tries to bring these names down to earth, to adapt them to his homely environment. And in I, 29, when it is explained to him that the princess Micomicona is called so after her estate Micomicón in Guiney, Sancho is happy only when he can find a parallel in the names of the common people he knows, such as Pedro de Alcalá, Juan de Úbeda, Diego de Valladolid, who are named after their birthplaces.

Evidently, the names in the world of Don Quijote must be, in opposition to the homespun names of Sancho's world, the more grandiloquent the less they cover of reality: they are of the grotesque, that is the comically frightening kind, that distinguishes the names of Pulci's and Rabelais' giants: we find (I, 18) Caraculiambro de Malindranía; el grande emperador Alifarfarón, señor de la grande isla Trapobana; Pentapolín del Arremangado Brazo; Espartafilando del Bosque, duque de Nestria; (I, 30) Pandafilando de la Fosca Vista—which last is transposed by Sancho (in accord with the feeling he has acquired for linguistic correspondences between his master's speech and his own: *f > h, -ando > -ado*) into *Pandahilado*; similarly, the poetic name *Fili* becomes, with Sancho, *hilo* (I, 23): Sancho's capacity of transposition is the linguistic equivalent of his capacity for adopting the fanciful schemes of Don Quijote. Another aspect of Sancho's positivistic approach is his lack of that symbolic feeling so characteristic of his master. He gauges symbolic actions according to their "positive" or pragmatic value in actual life: when Don Quijote invites him, in order to symbolize the Christian democracy of men, to sit at his table with him and the shepherds, Sancho refuses because of the inconvenience of having to be on his best behavior at the master's table. On the other hand (for Cervantes knows always an "on-the-other-hand"), Sancho's unmystical attitude is capable of producing good results: he is, during his governorship, able to uncover the swindle involving the money concealed in the staff, precisely because he disregards the symbolic value of the staff.

16. For us to apply this label to the knight striving to revive a medieval chivalric world, in the midst of his contemporary world of mass armies employing firearms, may seem surprising to the reader. But the humanistic world was a continuation of the medieval world: and what Don Quijote seeks to revive and reenact are humanistic dreams of antiquarians. The humanist tends to revive, by the strength of his imagination, a more beautiful past, regardless of how it may fit into his time; this is the ideal strength and the weakness of any humanist, and Cervantes has described both aspects.

17. It has not been sufficiently emphasized that Cervantes, as so often happens (e.g. in the case of the diptychs Marcela - Don Quijote, Cardenio - Don Quijote, el Cautivo - el Oidor; or in Don Quijote's speech on "armas y letras"), is proceeding by offering pendant pictures when he opposes to Don Quijote's vision in *la cueva de Montesinos* the speech of the *licenciado* on the humanistic books which he intends to write. Both turn to the past: the one seeks to relive it in the present, the other, to exhume it and transmit it through his books; both attempts, illustrating the same pattern of thought, are equally futile. Don Quijote's account of his visions is welcomed by the *licenciado* as a new "source" for his complication of fanciful lore—while these same visions have been inspired by that same sort of lore.

18. Cervantes himself must have been vulnerable to the humanistic "book-virus": he tells us that he used to pick up every printed scrap of paper—surely not, like Saint Francis, because some sacred words might be on it, but in order to live through the printed words a vicarious existence, in the fashion of his Don Quijote, i.e. as a "novel-reader."

Cervantes must also, like any humanist, have delighted in the deciphering of old documents: he tells us of the adventure of having Benengeli's Arabic deciphered for his benefit; in the story of the *Cautivo*, the Arabic letter of Lela Zoraida is puzzled out; and, in II, 39, a Syriac text is referred to: "escritas en lengua siríaca unas letras, que habiéndose declarada en la candayesca, y ahora en la castellana, encierran esta sentencia." To be polyglot is to delight in many perspectives.

19. It could be said, of nearly every character in the *Quijote*, that he appears located at his own particular linguistic level, somewhere along a hierarchic ladder. The duchess, for example, who is quite conscious of her social and linguistic superiority over Sancho, and who takes care to distinguish her speech from his (II, 32: "la flor de las ceremonias, o cirimonias, *como vos decís*") must be shown her inferiority, at least in matters linguistic, to Don Quijote: when the latter has occasion to speak of "la retórica ciceroniana y *demostina*," the duchess asks about the significance of the last word, remarking "que es vocablo que no he oido en todos los días de mi vida," and is taunted by her husband: "habéis andado deslumbrada en tal pregunta." Thus the same character has a chance to snub and be snubbed linguistically—as well as otherwise.

On the other hand we may ask ourselves: does Cervantes the superhumanist smile here at the reader over the head of the humanistic character Don Quijote? For the adjective *demostino* (an evidently popular haplology for *demostenino* "of Demosthenes") is incorrectly formed. Is Cervantes here revindicating again for himself a position above his protagonist by having Quijote the scholar make elementary mistakes?

Even when the characters lapse into a foreign language, there is a difference according to social classes—the standard "second language" in Cervantes' time being Italian. Don Quijote, being a Spanish humanist, must, of course, know Italian: he expressly states (II, 52) that he knows "somewhat" of Tuscan and can sing some stanzas of Ariosto; he examines a printer as to his knowledge of Italian vocabulary ("does he know that *pignatta* corresponds to Sp. *olla*?"); and he occasionally inserts Italian forms into his facetious speeches: II, 24: "Notable *espilorchería*, como dice el italiano"; II, 25: "Dígame vuestra merced, señor adivino: *que peje pillamo*?" Here we have rather far-fetched idioms by which the humanist Quijote shows how conversant he is with the nuances that are better expressed in Italian than in Spanish.

We also find, in our novel, Italianisms used in the speech of the lower strata of society, where they seem to suggest the language of conviviality: the Ventero says of Maese Pedro (II, 25): ". . . es hombre galante (como dicen in Italia) y bon compaño"; in the drinking scene between Sancho, his ex-companion Ricote, and the other pseudo-pilgrims, a *lingua franca* version of Italian is used at the height of their merriment (II, 44): "Español y Tudesqui tuto uno: bon compaño"—(Sancho:) "Bon compaño, juradí." Clemencín and Rodríguez Marín are therefore wrong when they object to a *caro patron mio* in the mouth of Sancho (II, 23); this is not humanistic Italian but the language of plain people indulging in exuberant gaiety.

Thus we have two types of Italianate Spanish, according to social strata.

20. Compare, for other mispronunciations of Sancho (II, 68): *trogloditas* > *tortolitas*, *bárbaros* > *barberos*, *antropófagos* > *astropajos*, *scitas* > *perritas a quien dicen cita cita*.

21. It was to be expected that when Sancho became governor he would establish a linguistic level of his own, above that of his subjects. And, in fact, he once satirizes the way of speaking of a peasant by ironically carrying further a grammatical mistake of the latter; the scene in question could not be better analyzed than in the words of Morel-Fatio (*Rom.*, XVI,

476): "Lorsque le paysan vient conter son cas au gouverneur de Barataria, il cherche dans sa mémoire le mot juridique qui exprime décemment l'acte qu'il a commis [that is, *yacer* 'to lie, sleep with'], et au lieu de 'hizo que *yoguiesemos*,' imparfait du subjonctif dont il n'avait conservé qu'un vague souvenir, il dit *yogasemos* . . . comme si l'infinitif était *yogar*. Sancho, qui, depuis qu'il est gouverneur, s'étudie à parler correctement, saisit avec joie l'occasion de souligner une grosse faute grammaticale chez un de ses semblables: 'Faites en sorte, mon brave homme, de ne plus *yogar* avec personne,' dit-il avec un sourire protecteur et appuyant sur le mot. Il y a là une finesse qu'ont dû sentir la plupart des lecteurs du *Don Quichotte*." Sancho, the perpetrator of so many linguistic sins, is not insensitive to those committed by his subjects; his linguistic personality varies according to his interlocutor.

22. This idea, which is a medieval one, is clearly expressed by Sancho when his wife contends that, since the time he became a member of the knight-errantry, she is no longer able to understand him (II, 5): "Basta que me entienda Dios, mujer, que el es el entendedor de todas cosas." The same reliance on God appears in II, 7, when Sancho, whose remark, "yo soy tan fócil" (*fócil* evidently representing a combination of *dócil* + *facil*) has not been understood by Quijote, explains: "soy tan así"; when this does not help, he exclaims: "Pues si no me puede entender, no sé como lo diga; no sé mas, y Dios sea conmigo." The coinage *fócil*, however nonexistent it may be in common language, covers the reality of Sancho's inner being, which is defined simply as "being as he is," and which he trusts God may recognize.

(Don Quijote, himself, must admit [II, 20] that Sancho, in spite of his "rústicos términos," would make a good preacher; and Sancho concurs boastfully, immediately introducing a solecism: "Bien predica quien bien vive, y no sé otras *tologías*.")

23. The attitude of Cervantes toward the popular adages is no different from that toward popular words: Sancho is given to piling up such stereotyped word material indiscriminately; Don Quijote, who is himself prone to quote adages, admires Sancho's spontaneity and fluency in this regard, as well as the original and natural wisdom which they reveal—though he advocates more restraint in their use; Cervantes does not commit himself one way or the other.

24. In the *entremés* "Los habladores" a character is made to accumulate synonyms in different languages: "Una criada se llama en Valencia *fadrina*, en Italia *masara*, en Francia *gaspirria*, en Alemania *filomiquia*, en la corte *sirvienta*, en Vizcaya *moscorra*, y entre pícaros *daifa*." Here we have the raw material (*copia verborum*) on which Cervantes will draw in the *Quijote*.

25. The raw material from which Cervantes drew the first episode is, according to Rodríguez Marín, a folk-tale (I would say, of the *Schildbürger*-tale variety). But, obviously, the introduction therein of the baroque element is a Cervantine touch. It is also in line with this element that the chimeric expedition of the townspeople, who are bent on conquering the whole countryside, should end in the beating administered to Sancho—a victory which, if they had been familiar with the ancient Greek custom, says Cervantes, they would have celebrated by raising a monument, a "trofeo."

26. The same pattern is evident in other passages: what is the *cueva*

de Montesinos for Quijote is a "pit of hell" for Sancho: "'Infierno le llamáis?' dijo Don Quijote," II, 22.

27. Linguistically speaking, *baciyelmo* fits into the group of *dvandva* formations designating hybrids in Spanish: *marimacho, serpihombre* (Góngora): an object, like an animate being, may present a hybrid aspect, and be represented by the same pattern: *arquibanco, catricofre* (and *baciyelmo*). As Miss Hatcher will show, in a forthcoming article, this Renaissance type in Spanish word-formation goes ultimately back to Greek: ἀνδρογύνης—τραγέλαφος, in Latinized form: *masculo-femina, hircocervus*—and *tunico-pallium.* Thus Cervantes has expressed his perspectivistic vision in a word-formational pattern of the Renaissance reserved for hybrids.

28. Interesting, in connection with Cervantes' linguistic perspectivism, are the many puns that appear in the *Quijote*: (I, 2) Don Quijote calls the innkeeper a *castellano* because the inn appears to him as a *castillo* in which he will be dubbed knight; but the innkeeper thinks that he has been called a "Castilian" "por haberle parecido de los sanos [the toughs] de Castilla." I, 3: "No se curó ['did not care'] el harriero destas razones (y fuera mejor que se curase porque fuera curarse ['be cured'] en salud)." II, 36 [Someone takes money] "no para tomar el mono ['because of having taken the donkey'] sino la mona ['in order to get tipsy']." II, 66: when the lackey says to Sancho, "tu amo debe de ser un loco," the squire answers: "Como debe? No debe nada a nadie; que todo lo paga, y más cuando la moneda es locura."

The pun is a bifocal manner of expression which relaxes and relativizes the firmness with which language usually appears to speaking man.

Sometimes the "word-world," in Renaissance fashion, encroaches on outward reality. The word *donas* in the phrase *ni dones ni donas* is an entirely fantastic formation, without any reality behind it (since the feminine of *don* is *doña* or *dueña*): it is to be explained as an extraction from *don(es)* and susceptible of usage in connection with this word alone —just as *ínsulos* is possible only in the phrase *ni ínsulas ni ínsulos.* Such formations are intended to exclude from consideration all possible varieties of the species denoted by the radical—a tendency to be found in many languages: cf. Turk. *šapka yok mapka yok* "[I have] no cap no nothing" (*mapka* being a nonce-word patterned on *šapka*). But by the very creation of a name for that which exists only at the moment it is denied, the non-existent entity is endowed with a certain (fantastic) reality.

29. In the story of Ana Félix, the Christian daughter of the Morisco Ricote, we see again how closely connected are language and faith: she explains (II, 53): "Tuve una madre cristiana . . . mamé la Fé catolica con la leche; criéme con buenas costumbres; ni en la lengua ni en ellas jamás, a mi parecer, di señales de ser morisca." The reader should note the expression *mamar la fé con la leche*: the same expression is used in Cervantes (II, 16) of the mother tongue: "todos los poetas antiguos escribieron en la lengua que mamaron con la leche"; and Castro has pointed out the origin of this metaphor (Bembo, *Della volgar lingua* 1525: ". . . nella latina [sc. *lingua*] essi [the Romans] tutti nascevano et quella insieme col latte dalle nutriei loro beeano. . ."). Here, we are at the bottom of the concept of *Muttersprache, langue maternelle, mother tongue,* which ultimately go back to an Augustinian concept: the Christian learns the name of God from his mother ("hoc nomen salvatoris mei . . . in ipso adhuc lacte matris

tenerum cor meum biberat") : the "name of God" is the most important and the most intimate linguistic knowledge the mother can impart to her child; thus (and this is in harmony with Christianity, which, in general, tends to present spiritual truths behind a human veil), the concept of "mother tongue" is vitally connected with that of maternal religion (cf. *Monatshefte für deutschen Unterricht*, XXXVI, 120).

30. In the other Moorish story in our novel, that of the expelled Ricote who, having fled to Germany, comes back in the disguise of a German pilgrim to Spain (II, 44) ; the exile mixes German (*Guelte! Guelte!*) into his Spanish—a language which he knows as well as does Sancho, whose "neighborhood shopkeeper" he had been. Cervantes describes Sancho's inability to understand the Germanate jargon of Ricote, whose identity he fails at first to recognize. Later, the pilgrim throws aside his incognito and hails Sancho "en voz alta y muy castellana"; "Ricote, sin tropezar nada en su lengua morisca, en la pura castellana le [to Sancho] dijo las siguientes palabras." In the ensuing drinking scene, Sancho, in his mellow tipsiness, finally ends up by speaking the esperanto of *lingua franca*. In this episode we must infer that the difficulties of linguistic understanding are all artificially contrived: here are *Ricote el morisco* and *Sancho el bueno*, who have lived side by side for many years and who are quite able to understand each other perfectly, who have the same habits of living, eating, and drinking—and are separated from each other only by the (arbitrary) fact of the Morisco's exile.

Ricote is as good a Spaniard as is Sancho (perhaps also a more gifted one: this comes out in his ironic question, so natural with emigrants who, returning to their mother country, see themselves in a position inferior to their merits: "Faltaban hombres más hábiles para gobernadores que tú eres?"), and his daughter is a perfect Christian; nevertheless, as exiles, they have been the victims of an arbitrary death-blow. But, by his exile, Ricote has not only learned to say *guelte* instead of *limosna*: he has come to know religious tolerance as he saw it practiced in Augsburg, in the heart of Protestantism. No bolder words could have been written, in Counter-Reformation Spain, about religious freedom, than are expressed here by Ricote. Nevertheless, the same Ricote bows submissively before the expulsion of the Moors by the Spanish King and his minister, which has plunged him and his family into despair and misery. Cervantes seems here more interested in the dialectic play of arguments, in the facets and perspectives of the problem, than in giving a decision on the moral issue. To the Spanish subject-matter of the novel, the stories of Moorish emigrants, renegades, and converts add a new perspective, that of Spain seen from the outside—a perspective of "spiritual geography."

31. The same double light is cast on the *caña*, that angling rod dropped by Zoraida to the captives, which is first only a utensil, an astute device, and then becomes a symbol of the miracle ("milagro") of a twofold salvation.

32. In this tale, the "renegade" develops before our eyes and gradually comes to take on stature; he shows his eagerness to help in the escape of the prisoners: after his repentance, when he swears by the cross to change from a "foul" member of the Church to a true member, the Christian fugitives put themselves "en las manos de Dios y en las del renegado" (as though God's hands used those of the renegade for His purposes). Later, it is true, his plan is abandoned for another one ("Dios, que lo ordenaba

de otra manera, no dió lugar al buen deseo que nuestro renegado tenía") but, nevertheless, he is saved along with the whole party and succeeds in his desire "a reducirse por medio de la santa Inquisición al gremio santísimo de la Iglesia."

33. In this connection, we should consider the famous opening sentence of the novel: "En un lugar de la Mancha de cuyo nombre no quiero acordarme." All the explanations hitherto offered (the silly autobiographical one: Cervantes had personal reasons for not wanting to remember the name); that based on literary history, proposed by Casalduero (Cervantes opposes his novel to the romances of chivalry, which claimed to know exactly wherefrom their heroes hailed); the folkloristic one of María Rosa Lida (the sentence is in line with the beginning of folk-tales) fail to take into sufficient consideration the functional value, for the novel, of the attitude of the author expressed therein—which, in my opinion, is the glorification of the freedom of the artist. Even if, for example, Mme. Lida should be right, the transfer of a sentence traditional in folk-tales into this particular novel of Cervantes could give the transferred sentence a new meaning, just as certain folklorisms adopted by Goethe or Heine become more than folklorisms in the lyrical poetry of these poets. By the deliberate assertion of his free will to choose the motifs of his plot, to emphasize or disregard what detail he pleases (and "no quiero" expresses deliberate disregard), Cervantes has founded that genre of "subjective story-telling" which, before him, is found at its incipient stage with Boccaccio and which, later, was to inspire Goethe (in the beginning of the *Wahlverwandtschaften*: "Eduard—so nennen wir einen reichen Baron im besten Mannesalter—Eduard hatte . . ."), Laurence Sterne, Fielding, Melville ("Call me Ishmael!").

In an address to the Baltimore Goethe Society, entitled "Laurence Sterne's *Tristram Shandy* and Thomas Mann's *Joseph the Provider*" (later published in *M.L.Qu.*, VIII, 101 *seq.*), Professor Oskar Seidlin pointed out the presence, in both these modern works, of some of the same comic devices (change of names, assumption of fictional sources, introduction of "relativizing dialogues," etc.) which I have been discussing as characteristic of Cervantine perspectivism. Since Thomas Mann himself had stated in 1942 that, during the composition of his *Joseph* he had had two books as his steady companions, *Tristram Shandy* and *Faust*, the stylistic congruences between the German and the English novel are easily explained. On the other hand, the devices of Sterne which reappear with Mann were, in turn, borrowed from Cervantes; and, in this connection, it is relevant to note that, in 1935, Thomas Mann had published his essay on the *Don Quijote*: thus the Cervantine climate may have acted doubly upon him: directly as well as indirectly. And, though the idea expressed in *Joseph the Provider* that the world is "Jehovah's Jest" would not have occurred to Cervantes, who glorified the "artist beneath the dome of God," the great *Entendedor*, the Spanish poet could have subscribed to Mann's idea of "artistic lightness" as man's consolation (*loc. cit.*, New York edition, p. 357): "For lightness, my friend, the artful jest, that is God's very best gift to man, the profoundest knowledge we have of this complex, questionable thing called life. God gave it to humanity so that life's terribly serious face might be forced to wear a smile. . . . Only in lightness can the spirit of men rise above them [the questions put to us by life]: with a laugh at being faced with the unanswerable, perhaps he can make even God Himself, the great Unanswering, to smile."

It is interesting that Thomas Mann who, in his *Buddenbrooks*, was still the pure representative of what Walzel has called "objective narration" (in the Spielhagen style), has from the time of his *Magic Mountain* developed consistently in the direction of Cervantine "story-telling" technique; this evolution must be due, not only to the general change in literary trends that has been taking place, but also to Mann's growing consciousness of the triumphant part the artist is called upon to play in modern society.

In this connection I may cite also the opening line of E. M. Forster's novel *Howard's End* (1910): "One may as well begin with Helen's letters to her sister," on which Lionel Trilling, *E. M. Forster* (1943) remarks: "Guiding his stories according to his serious whim . . . Forster takes full and conscious responsibility for his novels, refusing to share in the increasingly dull assumption of the contemporary novelist, that the writer has nothing to do with the story he tells, and that, *mirabile dictu*, through no intention of his own, the story has chosen to tell itself through him. Like Fielding, he shapes his prose for comment and explanation. He summarizes what he is going to show, introduces new themes when and as it suits him."

34. I realize that this is an opinion contrary to that of the writers of the Enlightenment who, in their treatment of the *Don Quijote*, made much of Cervantes' own classicistic pronouncement that art imitates nature. Locke, for example, has written: "Of all the books of fiction, I know none that equals Cervantes's 'History of Don Quijote,' in usefulness [!], pleasantry, and a constant decorum. And indeed no writings can be pleasant, which have not nature at the bottom, and are not drawn after copy." And Sydenham, the English Hippocrates and founder of modern clinical treatment, is reported to have advised young medical students to read the *Don Quijote* instead of books on medicine—because (as Professor Edelstein shows, in *Bulletin of the History of Medicine*, suppl. 3, 1944, p. 54) he evidently thought the Spanish novel offered a deterrent example of a person who views the world in the light of his preconceived ideas instead of that of facts—with which alone Dr. Sydenham was concerned.

Needless to say, my historical interpretation is also at the other pole from the poetic vision of an Unamuno who believes that this story was dictated to Cervantes' pen by the suprapersonal and perennial Spanish character, by the innate Spanish will to immortality by suffering and the "sentimiento trágico de la vida" as embodied in the figures of the quasi-saint Nuestro Señor Don Quijote de la Mancha and of his evangelical squire. In my opinion, it is Cervantes the "artistic dictator," who dictated the story to his pen, and Cervantes, no half-christian like Unamuno, knew how to distinguish the earthly plane from the transcendental. On the former plane he obeyed his own *sovereign reason*. He does, then, not belong to the family of Pascal and Kierkegaard, but to that of Descartes and Goethe.

35. Pirandello's perspectivism is in this respect different from that of Cervantes: with the latter, it is the *author* who looks for his characters, not the reverse.

I beg also to disagree with those critics who compare Cervantes with El Greco because of the novelist's "modern impressionism." We must be clear about the meaning of the term "impressionism." Cervantes never offers *his own* impressions of outward reality, as does the modern artist of the impressionistic school; he presents simply the impressions which his characters may have had—and, by juxtaposing these different impressions, he implicitly criticizes them all. The program of the modern impressionist, on the other hand, makes impossible the intervention of the critical sense into what he sees. As for the impressionism of El Greco, while this involves no criticism of reality as does that of Cervantes (since the ultimate reality he portrays is the divine), it does offer the evanescent reflections of the divine—which may, of course, have prepared the public for the perception of the evanescent in this world, i.e. for modern "impressionistic" perception.

36. Professor Auerbach, in his book *Mimesis* (Bern, 1946), p. 319, states the lack, in the *Don Quijote* (as in the whole literature of the *siglo de oro*) of any "problematische Erforschung der zeitgenössischen Wirklichkeit," of any "Bewegung in den Tiefen des Lebens," of any search into the social motivations of Don Quijote's madness, and of the life of his age—the underlying idea being that the "real" motivations of life are those of sociology, not of morality, on which Cervantes has based his novel (though, as we have said, he offers us the conflict between different moral standards). The attitude of this critic, which seems to abound in the sense of Carl Becker ("the historian has become the successor of the theologian") is, in my opinion, contingent on the presupposition that moral values are obsolete in a modern world given to the sociological explanation of history.

37. It should perhaps be pointed out here that "perspectivism" is inherent in Christian thought itself. The pair Don Quijote - Sancho Panza is, after all, a Cervantine replica of the medieval characters Solomon and Marcolf, in whom the wisdom of the sage and that of the common man are contrasted (we may also see in Sancho Panza's *refranes* a later version of the *proverbes au vilain*). Such an exemplary contrast is derived from the evangelic truth that the common man has access to wisdom, as well as the learned man; that the spirit, if not the letter, of the law can be understood by anyone. Here, we have an example of "medieval gradualism," according to which the social or mental level of Christ's followers is ultimately irrelevant. It is for this reason that, in medieval mystery plays, lofty scenes treating the life of Christ may alternate with scurrilous scenes in which shepherds or clowns are allowed to express their "point of view," on the august events in question, in their own unregenerate rustic speech. In this "gradualism," perspectivism is implied; and, to the perspectivism which Cervantes found in the medieval tradition, he added only the artistic aloofness of a Renaissance thinker.

3

THE "RÉCIT DE THÉRAMÈNE"*

Argumentum: This time I shall not, according to my usual procedure, start from a detail (of style) but shall first seek to establish the meaning of the whole (the tragedy) before coming to the *récit* itself, and to the linguistic details therein. Since, in this case, we are dealing with a division of a work of art, rather than with the work of art as a whole (as with Cervantes), it is obvious that this division must be first placed rightly within the whole before any treatment of linguistic detail can be considered. In some cases (compare the chapter on Claudel), it is possible to state this relationship in a single sentence, and then

* For the convenience of the reader, the text in question is here inserted:

THÉSÉE

Théramène, est-ce toi? Qu'as-tu fait de mon fils?
Je te l'ai confié dès l'âge le plus tendre.
Mais d'où naissent les pleurs que je te vois répandre?
Que fait mon fils?

THÉRAMÈNE

O soins tardifs et superflus!
Inutile tendresse! Hippolyte n'est plus.

THÉSÉE

Dieux!

THÉRAMÈNE

J'ai vu des mortels périr le plus aimable,
Et j'ose dire encor, seigneur, le moins coupable.

THÉSÉE

Mon fils n'est plus! Hé quoi! quand je lui tends les bras
Les dieux impatients ont hâté son trépas!
Quel coup me l'a ravi? quelle foudre soudaine?

THÉRAMÈNE

A peine nous sortions des portes de Trézène:
Il était sur son char; ses gardes affligés
Imitaient son silence, autour de lui rangés:
Il suivait tout pensif le chemin de Mycènes;
Sa main sur ses chevaux laissait flotter les rênes:
Ses superbes coursiers, qu'on voyait autrefois
Pleins d'une ardeur si noble obéir à sa voix,
L'oeil morne maintenant et la tête baissée,
Semblaient se conformer à sa triste pensée.
Un effroyable cri, sorti du fond des flots,
Des airs en ce moment a troublé le repos;
Et du sein de la terre une voix formidable

proceed to the linguistic detail. But in the present case, the relation of the "récit de Théramène" to *Phèdre* as a whole—and, indeed, the purpose of the play itself—have not, I feel, been clearly recognized in previous scholarship, so that the necessity of a "prestudy" seems to impose itself.

When we consider the play as a whole it will be seen that the terrible events in *Phèdre* are meant for the disillusionment of the only one of the main characters who survives: Thésée; it is on him that Phèdre's guilt and the death of the innocent Hippolyte produce their cumulative effect, by revealing to him the

---

Répond en gémissant à ce cri redoutable.
Jusqu'au fond de nos coeurs notre sang s'est glacé.
Des coursiers attentifs le crin s'est hérissé.
Cependant, sur le dos de la plaine liquide,
S'élève à gros bouillons une montagne humide:
L'onde approche, se brise, et vomit à nos yeux,
Parmi des flots d'écume, un monstre furieux.
Son front large est armé de cornes menaçantes;
Tout son corps est couvert d'écailles jaunissantes;
Indomptable taureau, dragon impétueux,
Sa croupe se recourbe en replis tortueux;
Ses longs mugissements font trembler le rivage.
Le ciel avec horreur voit ce monstre sauvage;
La terre s'en émeut, l'air en est infecté,
Le flot qui l'apporta recule épouvanté.
Tout fuit; et, sans s'armer d'un courage inutile,
Dans le temple voisin chacun cherche un asile.
Hippolyte lui seul, digne fils d'un héros,
Arrête ses coursiers, saisit ses javelots,
Pousse au monstre, et d'un dard lancé d'une main sûre
Il lui fait dans le flanc une large blessure.
De rage et de douleur le monstre bondissant
Vient aux pieds des chevaux tomber en mugissant,
Se roule, et leur présente une gueule enflammée
Qui les couvre de feu, de sang, et de fumée.
La frayeur les emporte; et, sourds à cette fois,
Ils ne connaissent plus ni le frein ni la voix;
En efforts impuissants leur maître se consume;
Ils rougissent le mors d'une sanglante écume.
On dit qu'on a vu même, en ce désordre affreux,
Un dieu qui d'aiguillons pressait leur flanc poudreux.
A travers les rochers la peur les précipite;
L'essieu crie et se rompt: l'intrépide Hippolyte
Voit voler en éclats tout son char fracassé;
Dans les rênes lui-même il tombe embarrassé.
Excusez ma douleur: cette image cruelle
Sera pour moi de pleurs une source éternelle.
J'ai vu, seigneur, j'ai vu votre malheureux fils
Traîné par les chevaux que sa main a nourris.

tragic truth that the gods persecute those they seem to protect. *Phèdre* is then a baroque tragedy of *desengaño*. The "récit de Théramène" in the fifth act, parallel to the "récit de Phèdre" in the second, but intended for the King himself, has the function of driving home at last the truth of divine perfidy and human helplessness.

In the properly linguistic part of the article I take up three stylistic features of the *récit* which I show to be characteristic of Racine's style in general: the frequency of the sense-word *voir*, with its intellectual connotation ("to see" = "to witness, to un-

---

Il veut les rappeler, et sa voix les effraie;
Ils courent: tout son corps n'est bientôt qu'une plaie.
De nos cris douloureux la plaine retentit.
Leur fougue impétueuse enfin se ralentit:
Ils s'arrêtent non loin de ces tombeaux antiques
Où des rois ses aïeux sont les froides reliques.
J'y cours en soupirant, et sa garde me suit;
De son généreux sang la trace nous conduit;
Les rochers en sont teints; les ronces dégouttantes
Portent de ses cheveux les dépouilles sanglantes.
J'arrive, je l'appelle; et, me tendant la main,
Il ouvre un oeil mourant qu'il referme soudain.
"Le ciel, dit-il, m'arrache une innocente vie.
"Prends soin après ma mort de la triste Aricie.
"Cher ami, si mon père un jour désabusé
"Plaint le malheur d'un fils faussement accusé,
"Pour apaiser mon sang et mon ombre plaintive,
"Dis-lui qu'avec douceur il traite sa captive:
"Qu'il lui rende. . ." A ce mot, ce héros expiré
N'a laissé dans mes bras qu'un corps défiguré:
Triste objet où des dieux triomphe la colère,
Et que méconnaîtrait l'oeil même de son père.

THÉSÉE

O mon fils! cher espoir que je me suis ravi!
Inexorables dieux, qui m'avez trop servi!
A quels mortels regrets ma vie est réservée!

THÉRAMÈNE

La timide Aricie est alors arrivée:
Elle venait, seigneur, fuyant votre courroux,
A la face des dieux l'accepter pour époux.
Elle approche; elle voit l'herbe rouge et fumante;
Elle voit (quel objet pour les yeux d'une amante!)
Hippolyte étendu, sans forme et sans couleur.
Elle veut quelque temps douter de son malheur;
Et, ne connaissant plus ce héros qu'elle adore,
Elle voit Hippolyte, et le demande encore,
Mais, trop sûre à la fin qu'il est devant ses yeux,
Par un triste regard elle accuse les dieux;

derstand"), the "klassische Dämpfung" by which the emotional stream of narrative is interrupted by intellectual evaluations (e.g. *digne fils d'un héros*), and the paradoxical mode of expression by which Racine is wont to formulate the unnatural in nature (e.g. *le flot qui l'apporta recule épouvanté*). These three traits belong to the baroque background of Racine, in whose imagination antagonistic polar forces play: senses and intellect, emotion and intellect, anarchy and order. In other words: Racine's vision of a world in which the gods counteract their own doings, repudiate their own creation, makes itself felt in a linguistic form which, although hovering precariously on the verge of anarchy, manages always to maintain its poise.

Et froide, gémissante, et presque inanimée,
Aux pieds de son amant elle tombe pâmée.
Ismène est auprès d'elle; Ismène tout en pleurs
La rappelle à la vie, ou plutôt aux douleurs.
Et moi, je suis venu, détestant la lumière,
Vous dire d'un héros la volonté dernière,
Et m'acquitter, seigneur, du malheureux emploi
Dont son coeur expirant s'est reposé sur moi. . . .

The two most recent contributions to criticism of the "récit de Théramène" are to be found in an article of Mr. Carlos Lynes Jr., "A Defense of the 'Récit de Théramène'" (*MLN*, LIX, 387), and a note of Professor Lancaster appended to this article. Mr. Lynes takes exception to the previous statement of Professor Lancaster's (in *A History of French Dramatic Literature in the Seventeenth Century*, IV, 199) that the lengthiness and ornateness of the *récit* is to be explained by Racine's overzealous admiration of the ancients. Mr. Lynes believes that these characteristics were intended to invite "aesthetic repose" on the part of the audience. Professor Lancaster, in his answer, seems to concede the effect of "aesthetic repose," but contends that this very repose rather enhances the poignant appeal of the poetry than gives emotional relief. The debate (which is taken up again in *MLN*, LIX, 584-586, each of the two opponents blaming the other for having shifted his attitude in the course of the discussion) seems, to this somewhat puzzled *tertius gaudens*, somewhat tangential.

SINCE the time of Racine himself, critics have discussed the great length and ornate style of the "récit de Théramène" in the Fifth Act of *Phèdre*, and generations of French schoolboys have had to struggle with the problems which this passage presents. If, in this book, I feel impelled to offer my own contribution to the famous scene, it is because two American critics have recently attempted explanations which seem to me to lead in wrong directions: on the one hand they have not been "microscopical," on the other they have not been "macroscopical" enough; it is the correct combination and dosage of both approaches which, alone, can yield an insight into Racine's artistic endeavors. To posit "correctness" as a criterion may seem like begging the question; and yet any method that is able to explain more of the features extant in a work of art must be held more correct.

I shall divide this study, which will, evidently, be determined by the "Zirkelschluss," into two parts. In the first, we will proceed from the macroscopic to the microscopic, in an attempt to answer the questions: what is the design of the whole play, and how does the "récit de Théramène" fit into this whole? In the second, the procedure will be the reverse, from the microscopic to the macroscopic; we shall ask: what stylistic features characterize the *récit*, and are these features also characteristic of the whole tragedy—and, possibly, of the art of Racine in general? In this way, I hope to be able to point out, incidentally, the reason for the ornateness and lengthiness of the "récit de Théramène."

What is the design of the play? Let us begin by considering the elementary fact that, of the six characters (which does not include Ismène and Panope) in *Phèdre*, three die and three survive. All who die are guilty: Phèdre, whose guilt is evident from the beginning; Oenone, the nurse, the accomplice in her mistress's crime; and Hippolyte, whose guilt is slight but, according to Racine himself, is none the less a guilt (it is against his father's will that he loves Aricie). Of those who survive, Théramène and Aricie are blameless, while Thésée, never a figure of virtue (divided as he has always been between the labors of a hero and his less glorious erotic adventures), commits the crime, though out of blindness, of sacrificing virtue in the person of his son Hippolyte, whom he curses and sends into exile. Why, then, it may be asked, is the criminal Thésée allowed to escape unscathed? He, too, however, is crushed in the double role of victim and perpetrator of a crime which has destroyed his whole family and which he is forced to acknowledge. My interpretation is that he is spared death in order to comprehend and to acknowledge—not only his own crime and its consequences but also the perversity of the world order. The king, to whom Théramène's récit is addressed, is on the stage before us, a bewildered spectator of what can befall a royal family; he is involved in the action only by his one act of blindness; for the most part he stays in his "private loge on the stage," witnessing a drama that unfolds before him. While his son Hippolyte is destroyed by the action of the play without understanding (no god appears to explain to him the reason for his death, as in the play of Euripides, who has Hippolyte brought back before his death to be enlightened and encouraged by Artemis), and while Phèdre is destroyed with the full understanding, from the beginning, that she and her family, especially the female branch, are persecuted by Venus, Thésée must witness the destruction of his son and his wife before he is brought to see the shape of his doom. He emerges from the play as the most important character, who will, grimly, knowingly, survive his torture, and will be the living example of the lesson he has learned "dramatically." What is this lesson? Perhaps, "timeo deos et dona ferentes": the gods crush those whom they favor most. He, the protégé of the god Neptune, has been made the instrument of doom; the denouement of the action elicits his final understanding that, when he thought himself to be protected by a loving god, he was, in reality, his victim. Two gods are responsible for the devastation wrought on the family of Thésée (the destruction of the family has not been sufficiently emphasized by critics—who were misled, no doubt, by the title of the play and by Racine's failure to mention Thésée in his preface). Unlike Euripides, who allows the vengeance of Aphrodite to be counteracted by the ever-loyal Artemis, Racine presents his two gods, though working separately and by different procedures, as contributing jointly to the destruction of the family: the one by direct persecution (Venus → Phèdre), the other by "loving protection" (Neptune → Thésée)—and both together by warring against each other in the breast of Hippolyte.[1] Faced by such a conjunction of forces there is no possibility that the characters may escape; the whole tragedy, as the most crushing, the most tragic of tragedies, amounts to an accusation of the world order, and invites man's revolt against the gods.

After the unprovoked wrath of the gods has been sated, there is left to Thésée only the one gesture which his dying son had asked of him: to be kind to the guiltless Aricie. The calm of the last lines spoken by Thésée is one of conscious desperation. He has finally become a *désabusé*, as Hippolyte had predicted in his dying words; he has tasted that *desengaño* which all the Spanish moralists of Racine's time knew so well.

Since Thésée is the one for whose benefit the disillusioning events of the play are staged, we must feel him present during the whole play (the first part of the drama is full of his name, and from the beginning we look forward with suspense to his entrance in Act III), and we must seek to observe the process of his disillusionment—which begins the moment he enters the stage. Those critics who have taken exception to his "undramatic" character have not pondered the drama of enlightenment which goes on within him; it starts, as we have said, when he crosses his threshold, once again victorious through Neptune, eager to greet his wife and son—and sees first one, then the other, withdraw from him on some pretext. His suspicions are aroused, are given a focus by Oenone, and finally vent themselves when he banishes his son. At this point, though disillusioned about human relationships, he still thinks Neptune to be his ally; moreover, his grief over his son is still endurable, because coupled with anger. The report of Théramène will give him his second, his greatest shock: he will learn that Neptune has listened only too well to his impulsive prayer for revenge, and boundless desperation will overwhelm him. The final blow will come when, in the last scene, he learns from Phèdre's lips that his son was blameless,[2] and had to perish as an innocent victim of his father's commerce with the gods. Now the utter chaos and perversity of the world order stand revealed. The "récit de Théramène," as the second step in this development, is intended exclusively for the enlightenment of the king as to man's relationship to the gods, and must be studied in this light.

The picture of Hippolyte's death, "cette image cruelle" (unforgettable to Théramène: l. 1545) becomes for Thésée a picture of universal destruction. In the scene which follows our récit, Thésée, who has had time to digest its awful import, succeeds in formulating the lesson he has learned: the dubious character of divine protection, and the perversity of the cosmic scheme:

> Confus, persécuté d'un mortel souvenir,
> De l'univers entier je voudrais me bannir.
> Tout semble s'élever contre mon injustice.
> L'éclat de mon nom même augmente mon supplice.
> Moins connu des mortels, je me cacherais mieux.
> Je hais jusqu'aux soins dont m'honorent les dieux:
> Et je m'en vais pleurer leurs faveurs meurtrières,
> Sans plus les fatiguer d'inutiles prières.
> Quoi qu'ils fissent pour moi, leur funeste bonté
> Ne me saurait payer de ce qu'ils m'ont ôté.

Since the allusions to the persecution of Phèdre and her kin by Venus ("C'est Vénus toute entière à sa proie attachée,") seem to have been better understood by critics than have those to the (equally destructive) protection of Thésée by Neptune, we must study the latter more closely. It will be seen how, throughout the play, the Neptune motif combines with the Venus motif; and how the "récit de Théramène" takes up the first, while the second is dealt with in other scenes. And, as we watch the interplay of these two motifs, we will see how carefully Racine has plotted the course of the "wrath of the gods" in this tragedy of a Greek royal family.

As the play opens, Hippolyte, in the course of his conversation with Théramène, distinguishes two modes of behavior observable in his father's career, corresponding to the works of Neptune and those of Venus: on the one hand, the slaying of monsters by the "héros intrépide," on the other, his less glorious love affairs (for which Théramène excuses him, saying: "Quels courages Vénus n'a-t-elle pas domptés?"). We learn that Hippolyte has not, to his regret, equaled his father in his feats of monster-slaying; he does, however, give involuntary signs of having fallen in love—that is, of having given himself up to the power of that Venus who shares with Neptune the ascendancy over his father and who exclusively dominates Phèdre—and, through her, the whole family. Théramène, reminding Hippolyte of his earlier prowess in the service of Neptune, indicates the shift in his allegiance which has taken place (129 *seq.*):

> Avouez-le, tout change; et depuis quelques jours
> On vous voit moins souvent, orgueilleux et sauvage,
> Tantôt faire voler un char sur le rivage,
> Tantôt, *savant dans l'art par Neptune inventé,*
> *Rendre docile au frein un coursier indompté.* . . .
> Chargés d'un feu secret, vos yeux s'appesantissent.
> Il n'en faut pas douter: vous aimez, vous brûlez.

(We may compare line 991: "Quel funeste poison / L'amour a répandu sur toute sa [of the king] maison!") Hippolyte, then, has inherited his father's double nature—if on a lesser scale. When we come to the "récit de Théramène," the reader will find a parallel to the verses above, underlined by me, in the lines:

> J'ai vu, seigneur, j'ai vu votre malheureux fils
> Traîné par les chevaux que sa main a nourris.
> Il veut les rappeler, et sa voix les effraie.

Hippolyte, once the worshiper of Neptune, will at the end of the tragedy be punished for his allegiance to Venus by the god of horse-taming (there is no doubt that, in line 1538: "On dit qu'on a vu même, en ce désordre affreux, / Un Dieu qui d'aiguillons pressait leur flanc poudreux," this Racine-invented God, to whom some critics take exception, is Neptune), and will no longer be able to "faire voler un char sur le rivage," or to "rendre docile au frein un coursier indompté."[3] Thus the *récit* is anticipated by the opening scene, with its reference to Neptune as the inspiration of Hippolyte's (former) accomplishments—a motif reiterated in identical terms in Act II, 559 *seq.*, when Hippolyte himself laments:

Mon arc, mes javelots, mon char, tout m'importune;
Je ne me souviens plus des leçons de Neptune;
Mes seuls gémissements font retentir les bois,
Et nos coursiers oisifs ont oublié ma voix.

As for the protection accorded by Neptune to Thésée (at least, to the "hero" Thésée), this is alluded to throughout the play. When, in Act II, we learn of rumors to the effect that Thésée is dead and has perished in the sea, in the element of Neptune ("Les flots ont englouti cet époux infidèle": 381), Hippolyte maintains stoutly: "Neptune le protège, et ce dieu tutélaire / Ne sera pas en vain imploré par mon père"; in the last words, tinged with filial pride, we can sense a tragic irony—since, later, Thésée's success with Neptune will be scored at the expense of Hippolyte's life:

Et toi, Neptune, et toi, si jadis mon courage
D'infâmes assassins nettoya ton rivage . . .
Je t'implore aujourd'hui. Venge un malheureux père:
J'abandonne ce traître à toute ta colère.

Here, it is on his prowess as a slayer of monsters that Thésée relies in his appeal to Neptune—an appeal which he is confident will be granted ("Neptune . . . M'a donné sa parole, et va l'exécuter": 1158 / ; "Neptune me la [sa perte] doit, et vous [Phèdre] serez vengée / . . . . Espérons de Neptune une prompte justice. / Je vais moi-même au pied de ses autels / Le presser d'accomplir ses serments immortels": 1178-1192). But this mood of confidence fed by desperation is shaken by the news of Oenone's suicide (I find it significant that it is in the element of Neptune that she meets her death: "Les flots pour jamais l'ont ravie à mes yeux": 1467), an event which seems to the messenger an inscrutable mystery ("On ne sait point d'où part ce dessein furieux": 1466). Has Neptune a "dessein furieux" against Thésée's household? Immediately afterwards, the king learns of Phèdre's collapse and of her desire for death, and his wrathful certitude of Hippolyte's guilt begins to crumble. With a new despair he revokes his prayer to Neptune (1483): "Ne précipite point tes funestes bienfaits, / Neptune, j'aime mieux n'être exaucé jamais" (the paradoxical phrase "funestes bienfaits" is echoed later by "faveurs meurtrières" [1693] and "funeste bonté" [1615], while the motif "j'aime mieux n'être exaucé jamais" will be strengthened at the close of the play by the line 1650 in which Thésée resolves to "expier la fureur d'un voeu que je déteste"). In the very moment when Thésée, wavering in his judgment of Hippolyte's guilt, and sensing the imminence of death which threatens his household, seeks to hold back Neptune's intervention, Théramène enters. The sight of Hippolyte's governor can only sharpen the anxiety of the father: "Théramène, est-ce toi? Qu'as tu fait de mon fils? / Je te l'ai confié dès l'âge le plus tendre"—a marvelous Racinian sentence, with its example of the "short-cut" which betrays the progress of the father's anguish and self-torture; he speaks as though he knows already what Théramène has come to tell him, and must blame the messenger for the sad news he brings. And Théramène's words confirm his darkest apprehensions: "O soins tardifs et superflus! Inutile tendresse! Hippolyte n'est plus!" Once more, *ce dieu tutélaire* has answered the prayer of his protégé. Thus we see how the Neptune motif fits into the development by which the scales are made to fall at last from Thésée's eyes.

There is a corollary motif which must be considered here, for this, also, leads up to and expands within the "récit de Théramène": the monster motif. The traditional Greek hero (a Theseus, a Heracles), aware of his divine extraction, distinguishes himself by "labors," by superhuman exploits which rid the world of monsters, that is from the infrahuman bestiality which infests it and which is liable to imperil the triumph of human reason and civilization. The motif of "monster-slaying," which, indeed, permeates our whole play, is to be seen in connection with that of "the hero agreeable to Neptune." In Thésée the two are perfectly reflected, and the same might have been expected of the hero's son: this implication is not lost upon Hippolyte, when he comes to ask permission of his father to embark upon heroic enterprises: "Souffrez, si quelque monstre a pu vous échapper, / Que j'apporte à vos pieds la dépouille honorable." And it is in just this light that Hippolyte is seen by Phèdre when she first falls in love with him—according to her own words (854); Racine, with a marvelous grasp of the psychology of love, anticipating modern experience, has Phèdre pretend to see in Hippolyte a younger Thésée (thus she remains faithful to the type represented by her husband, so true is it that love is "typologically monogamic" and that matrimonial infidelity, after the passage of years, can be a form of faithfulness to the original lover!)—not, of course, the impudent lover Thésée who sacrifices to a cheap Venus, but the hero who slew *le monstre de la Crète*:

> Tel qu'on dépeint nos dieux, ou tel que je vous voi.
> Il avait votre port, vos yeux, votre langage;
> Cette noble pudeur colorait son visage,
> Lorsque de notre Crète il traversa les flots . . .

—"flots," the element of Neptune. But irony demanded that Hippolyte should not conform entirely to type: as we know, and as Phèdre was later to learn to her hurt, he has ceased to give sole allegiance to Neptune. But at the moment the mirage is complete—as Phèdre betrays her illusion by the "short-cut" of the outburst: ". . . ou tel que je vous voi" (in which the fallacy rests in the "ou"). It is another irony that later, all hope and pretense abandoned, she must ask Hippolyte to resemble his father, the monster-slayer, by slaying the monster that *she* has become: "Délivre l'univers d'un monstre qui t'irrite. . . . / Crois-moi, ce monstre affreux ne doit point t'échapper." This use of "monstre" in reference to evil human beings whose destruction is urged as a heroic deed is most significant in our play, where it frequently recurs: Aricie herself applies the term to Phèdre, whom she implores Thésée to exterminate (1443 *seq.*):

> . . . vos invincibles mains
> Ont de monstres sans nombre affranchi les humains;
> Mais tout n'est pas détruit, et vous en laissez vivre
> Un . . .

(note the powerful enjambment, reminiscent of the famous "Moi!" of Corneille's *Médée*). To Thésée, whose soul is poisoned by Oenone's slander, the innocent Hippolyte appears as a "monstre, qu'a trop longtemps épargné le tonnerre, / Reste impur des brigands dont j'ai purgé la terre" (1045)—as he had, earlier, to the tortured mind of Phèdre (384). The idea of the human monster is also implicit in Thésée's reference to his most recent conquest: "D'un perfide ennemi j'ai purgé la nature. . . . A ses monstres lui-même a servi de pâture." And, into this network of motifs fits the death scene of Hippolyte. So far as I know, no critic has noted the new significance, in Racine's play, of the sea-monster as the instrument of death. In Euripides' drama this instrument was a bull emerging from the sea to avenge Venus; Racine's sea-monster has a closer relationship to Neptune, it has been created, by an unjust god, as a tool of senseless *contrappasso* against the family of monster-slayers.

If, then, we consider Thésée primarily as the hero, the monster-slayer agreeable to Neptune, we are better able to understand what his reactions must be when he listens to Théramène's recital. As he grasps the import of the words, we are allowed to guess the course of his thoughts by the occasional outbursts which interrupt the tragic tale, and which betray not so much regret for the son he has lost as consternation over the trickery of the gods: "Dieux!"—". . . Les Dieux impatients ont hâté son trépas?"—"Inexorables Dieux, qui m'avez trop servi!" It seems to me that the criticism of Mr. Lynes is far too much concerned with the probable reactions of the public to Théramène's report; it is Thésée's reaction which is all important here—and the public watches *this*! From the general conclusion of Théramène, "des Dieux triomphe la colère," Thésée can only draw the specific implication: the "un dieu" of Théramène is Neptune to Thésée. Later, Phèdre will enter the stage and, as the king hears her confess her guilt and Hippolyte's innocence, he will realize that her doom, too, has been willed by a god ("le ciel mit dans mon sein une flamme funeste"), that, in fact, all the sufferings endured by his family have their origin in the gods. The récit, far from being a negligible part of the tragedy, is highly important; it is a high plateau which invites us to a contemplative repose before the full vista of the doomedness of man. This contemplation of the condition of man as that of a "triste objet, où des Dieux triomphe la colère" can be called lacking in dramatic value only if drama be considered exclusively as outward action—a conception which is evidently much too narrow if one remembers the choral parts of the Greek drama, especially such hymns as Ἔρως ἀνίκατε μαχᾶν. The gradual dawning upon man of his own tragic condition is, in reality, the greatest drama imaginable.[4]

Thus, those critics are quite right who relate the ornateness and lengthiness of our récit to its contemplativity; what, perhaps, they have failed to grasp is the extent of the picture we are called upon to contemplate: the condition of man under the inexorable and unjust rule of the Gods. From the crudest possible vision of reality, of blood, disorder and debris, Racine extracts, as by a kind of supreme wager, the most intellectual and poetic formulation, a transposition into the language of a compassionate and detached philosopher. Théramène belongs to that ancient theater, of which Racine says, in a passage of his preface (where commentators are wont to see only the compromise made by an artist with the moralizing Jansenists, but which may well contain the true ethical direction ascribed to dramatic poetry by Racine and, after him, by Schiller): "Leur [the ancients'] théâtre était une école où la vertu n'était pas moins bien enseignée que dans les écoles des philosophes." Théramène is a scholar in philosophy on the stage; he is, in fact, the voice of Racine. And what Sainte-Beuve once said of Racine could be said of Hippolyte's tutor: "Il a le calme de l'âme supérieure et divine au travers et au-dessus de tous les pleurs et de toutes les tendresses." The whole of this tragedy consists of transposition and indirect rendition of reality; the "récit de Théramène" is a most concentrated precipitate in the dramatic alembic of Racine. Mr. Lynes was quite close to that truth when he wrote: "As a classical dramatist Racine does not wish actual tears at all, but only intense aesthetic contemplation." But he went astray, in my opinion, when, instead of seeing in the "récit de Théramène" a reduction *in nuce* of the general aesthetics of Racine, he attributes to the poet an intention to temper our indignation against Phèdre, whereas the truth seems to me to be that Racine's *main* purpose was to show us the collapse of the world order as revealed to Thésée.[5] For Hippolyte's death is not, as Mr. Lynes would have it, to be explained in terms of human responsibility: granted that Phèdre was responsible for Thésée's curse, it was Neptune who fulfilled it by sending his monster out of the blue ocean that lapped the shores of "aimable Trézène."[6] And why did Hippolyte's horses, a moment before so sensitive to their master's mood that they were sharing his taciturn sadness, refuse, at the critical moment, to obey the familiar hand of their master? The guilt of Hippolyte's death rests entirely on the gods, and the récit is not intended so much to lessen our anger against Phèdre as to lift us to that higher serenity in which the bitter lesson for humanity can be received. The dying Hippolyte himself, whose closing eyes are open to abiding truth, formulates most clearly this same bitter lesson: "*Le ciel* . . . m'arrache une innocente vie . . . / Cher ami, si mon père un jour désabusé / Plaint le malheur d'un fils faussement accusé. . . ." The victim places the responsibility for the calamity on the Heaven that permitted the calamity to happen.

Nor is the "récit de Théramène" the only passage that offers us an opportunity to contemplate the sorry condition of man: the other is what might be called the "récit de Phèdre" in Act I, Scene III, which seems to have escaped the censure of the critics because of its lesser length (though it is equally "ornate") and because, in this passage, it is the principal character who is exposing her own doomed situation, so that this can be no mere "hors-d'oeuvre." In this récit we are shown the devastation wrought by Venus upon her victim, which, evidently, offers a parallel to Théramène's account of Neptune's vengeance; we witness the physical dying, more painful than death, of a beautiful body ("Un reste de chaleur tout prêt à s'exhaler"), which is no less moving a spectacle of human decay than is that depicted by Théramène ("Tout son corps n'est bientôt qu'une plaie"). Phèdre has to divulge no sudden disastrous blow but a sequence of sufferings;

Neptune strikes swiftly, Venus works insidiously in the blood. Théramène is a messenger describing a sudden, violent incident, Phèdre is an autobiographer recounting years of suffering; she begins this biography with the words: "Mon mal vient de plus loin"—and, in fact, the malady whose course she traces had darkened the history of her family for generations. The récit of Phèdre, coming from a passionate woman who is at the same time a conscious witness of her own doomedness, excites us more; that of Théramène, who is a wise and ultimately dispassionate observer, is the more objective, making the effect of a final chorus which dismisses the audience with the truth for which they had been waiting. The two messages have converged in us. But we, the audience, must linger awhile longer, until our own understanding is echoed and corroborated by that of Thésée. When he first learns of Hippolyte's death, he may think Neptune's vengeance too violent, but not illegitimate; only in the following scene does he learn, from Phèdre, that Hippolyte was blameless. But we, whose suspicions of the gods had been aroused by Phèdre from the beginning, and who knew throughout of Hippolyte's innocence, are able to understand Théramène's reference to the accusing eyes of Aricie ("Par un triste regard elle accuse les dieux") before it is given to Thésée to grasp the full import of her accusation.

For, though we have called Phèdre's explanations to Oenone the "récit de Phèdre," she has stayed silent toward Thésée throughout the play; and this "éternel silence," which is emphasized in several passages, has served, by the intervention of the more active Oenone, to involve Hippolyte in his father's suspicions. In the paradoxical dramatic world of Racine, where the best intentions of man are hopelessly twisted by the Gods, this fatal silence had its origin in the noblest side of Phèdre's nature: it is the main instrument of the self-imposed tortures by which Racine has sought to redeem this character (we read in the preface: "Elle fait tous ses efforts pour la [la passion] surmonter. Elle aime mieux se laisser mourir que de la déclarer à personne"). The outcome is, as we know, that her pledge of silence is twice broken (Oenone, Hippolyte), with dire results in each case—

while the silence she maintains with Thésée until the final moment has equally dire results.[7] Thus, as we listen to Théramène give his passionate-dispassionate revelation of the doom weighing on man, we wonder how much longer Phèdre will be able to maintain the rule of silence toward Thésée. And when, after Théramène's recital, she finally cries out: "Non, Thésée, il faut rompre un injuste silence," we feel a vast relief to hear at last the long-repressed confession of a woman eaten up by worms of passion—a confession which testifies to the same unjust world order as that revealed by Théramène. The play can come to an end only when all the evidence of the workings of the Gods piles up before Thésée; it is Racine's procedure, motivated so skillfully, of retarding this confession that has made possible the gradual unfolding of the picture.

Before we close the chapter on the dramatic connections between the "récit de Théramène" and the play as a whole, let us stop to consider for a moment the relationship between this récit and Théramène himself; we will see that Théramène's role, in Act v, as well as the particular quality of his report, is dramatically prepared from the beginning. And, in this connection, I must question the procedure of my predecessors in criticism who are not enough "at home" in the play they discuss, who have not spent enough effort in visualizing the data and the relationships which Racine has placed at their disposal. The critic should be so familiar with the play he is studying as to be able to reconstitute the interplay between all the characters and situations, to release all the springs which the author has built into the structure of his play. To be at home in a play of Racine does not entail living in many mansions, for Racine is not Shakespeare; nevertheless, in his one-mansion edifices we must focus on many cross-relationships existing between the different characters and situations.[8] Racine has very few characters on the stage, but he exhausts all the possibilities of relationship between them; he restricts the field of vision, but he has filled it with manifold parallelograms of forces. The Théramène whom we hear speak in Act v is no mere "messenger" in the Euripidean sense; we have seen him, in the opening scene of our play, as the philosophical tutor of Hippolyte, who had the task of instructing him in the accomplishments of a ruler (among them, history with its noble or evil examples) and, at the same time, as the appointed historian of Thésée's family. We learn from Hippolyte himself how Théramène was wont to acquaint him with the events of the family history; the prince describes the eagerness with which he would listen as his tutor depicted the heroic exploits of Thésée (73 *seq.*):

> Attaché près de moi par un zèle sincère,
> Tu me contais alors l'histoire de mon père.
> Tu sais combien mon âme, attentive à ta voix,
> S'échauffait au récit de ses nobles exploits,
> Quand tu me dépeignais ce héros intrépide

—but also the regret and impatience aroused in him by the account of less glorious episodes: "Tu sais comme à regret écoutant ce discours [on Thésée's faithlessness as a lover] / Je te pressais souvent d'en abréger le cours." Here we have obvious analogies with the "récit de Théramène": in both, Théramène is the "family chronicler" and, in both, his picture of nobility is clouded by painful truths that the listener shrinks from hearing. In the récit he must tell the most tragic of truths: however much we might prefer to dwell on the beauty and heroism of the young prince, we must be made to face the wrath of the gods, and we must allow the long and ornate threnody, which has no equal on the French stage, to sink in. This is, perhaps, what Racine might have answered his critics who (in his own words) "le pressaient d'abréger le cours du récit de Théramène." It is as if Racine had anticipated, in the first scene, the criticism which his récit was to arouse.[9] The dramatist has conceived both scenes in relationship to each other, in relationship both to the character of Théramène and to the nature of his teaching. Théramène, like Racine himself, is a humanistic historiographer who can teach only in a lengthy and ornate fashion, because history is a solemn and sad spectacle which can be unveiled only by a sage who steps beyond it and speaks of it from a higher, "transposed" plane. Consequently, the question: "why did Racine make the 'récit de Théramène' so lengthy and ornate?" is asked from a point of view outside the tragedy: from the aprioristic prejudice that a play should not (evidently for the sake of *vraisemblance*) contain lengthy and ornate récits. (And, of course, the answer of Professor Lancaster: ". . . because Racine came to indulge more and more in descriptive writing from the period of *Iphigénie* on," has a slightly tautological flavor.)

We must be more modest when facing the great works of art; we must forget our critical attitudes which are, so often, only aesthetic prejudices abstracted from a routine reading which does not consider the meaning of the individual work of art. We would understand better a great masterpiece such as *Phèdre* by affirming the adage of which Professor Lancaster declares himself skeptical: "tout est au mieux dans la meilleure des tragédies." Why should we not, a priori, engage in a "critique des beautés,"[10] believing, as a working hypothesis, and until the contrary is proved, that a great masterpiece *is* perfect in all its parts? How can the average literary critic, who is so seldom a poet-critic (like Diderot or Hugo) justify his temerity in assuming as his working hypothesis: "tout n'est pas au mieux dans la meilleure des tragédies"? Does it give him comfort that he can find flaws in the masters? If, at least, these flaws were real—and not, rather, the critic's own flaws of aesthetic understanding projected back into the work he studies! To leave it to the taste of the individual reader to decide whether or not Racine was justified in inserting such a récit reveals an attitude of critical agnosticism which is at variance with the readiness to admit flaws, and which amounts to a renouncement of aesthetic canons: if there *are* flaws we must condemn them on aesthetic grounds; if the lengthy, ornate récit is out of place, it is no longer a matter of "taste" to find it so. The critic who goes so far as to raise up before us the possibility of a Racinian error, should not stop before dealing the lethal blow. If Racine has erred, we must prove it; if we cannot prove it, let us rather not suggest the possibility of error.

* * *

After having proceeded from the whole of the play to the part, to the "récit de Théramène," which we found to reflect microcosmically the whole and to have a definite place therein, we will now reverse the procedure, asking ourselves what stylistic traits are offered by this fragment that are necessarily characteristic of the whole of the play.

1. Let us begin by considering Racine's preoccupation with the act of "seeing," which cannot fail to strike any observer of Racinian style. Twice in the récit, Théramène stresses the visual apperception of the event he has experienced: once when he mentions his own reaction to the horrid spectacle:

> Excusez ma douleur. Cette image cruelle
> Sera pour moi de pleurs une source éternelle.
> *J'ai vu, Seigneur, j'ai vu* votre malheureux fils
> Traîné par les chevaux que sa main a nourris . . .

and again when he presents to us Aricie's grief on discovering the dead body of Hippolyte:

> . . . *elle voit* l'herbe rouge et fumante;
> *elle voit* (quel objet pour les yeux d'une amante!)
> Hippolyte étendu, sans forme et sans couleur . . .
> Et ne connaissant plus ce héros qu'elle adore,
> *Elle voit* Hippolyte et le demande encore.
> Mais trop sûre à la fin qu'il est devant ses yeux,
> Par un triste regard elle accuse les Dieux.

To Théramène the dead youth has already become a picture ("cette image cruelle"), and this crystallized image is transmitted to Thésée who, though he has not seen the "sad object" with the physical eye (and, as he is told, would have been unable to recognize it: "Triste objet . . . que méconnaîtrait l'oeil même de son père"), will be haunted evermore by what he has seen with the eyes of the soul ("De mon fils déchiré fuir la sanglante image"). This insistence on the act of seeing, whether physical or "transposed," which is not isolated in Racine, cannot fail to impress us with the importance of "sight" for Racine's *Weltanschauung* (in the literal sense of the German word): we cannot brush aside as "poetic formulae" such phrases as "l'oeil d'un père" = "un père," or the repetition of *voir* (although this is an imitation of the "anaphora" of the ancients, it must, like the many other ancient formulae borrowed by Racine, be granted a new meaning in Racine's poetic system). In the poetic world of Racine, all "things seen," all events in their matter-of-fact brutality are, for the most part, excluded: they appear only indirectly, as things spoken of. From the visible world an intellectual vision is extracted which is revealed to the public only through words: by conversation all the light of the intellect is cast upon brutal reality, so that its essence shines out before us. To present this vision, Racine must often introduce intermediate persons who lend us their eyes. In the "récit de Théramène" we are allowed to see things through the medium of a reporter who tells us "J'ai vu, j'ai vu . . . ," and who even goes so far as to impose upon us a secondary visualization: his seeing of what Aricie saw: here we have an extreme case of Racine's care in preventing the bloody scene itself from striking our senses too abruptly. Moreover, in addition to the "refraction" achieved by the use of such human intermediaries, Racine interposes still another element between us and crude reality, which is his particularly poetic and intellectual language (thus, in the case of Aricie we have two intermediary persons plus a tertiary medium: a multiplication of planes which may remind us of the baroque "mirror" technique of Velásquez).

If, now, we try to reconstruct the scene actually seen by Aricie, we will first notice that Racine, contrary to the practice of a modern naturalist,[11] does not depict directly the bloody corpse of the young hero. Even "blood" is not directly mentioned, only implied by the reference to the vestiges recognizable on the grass ("herbe rouge et fumante"). Physical blood, warm, human blood is absent—not only from the stage but from the picture in words. (Later, it is true, Thésée speaks of the "sanglante image," but the very word order shows that he has sensed not a "bloody picture" [an "image sanglante"] but a picture of carnage: the post-positional adjective does not describe physical facts but draws moral implications from the bloodshed, implying and transcending "blood."[12]) For, in this passage describing Aricie's discovery, Racine focuses our attention not on the sad object of physical vision, but on the act of seeing itself—which represents an attempt to recognize, to identify.[13] And this process of identification is presented in slow-motion: Racine prolongs for five lines Aricie's hesitancy about the identity of Hippolyte. She comes to realize that "this Hippolyte" is defined by the absence of the traits ("sans forme et sans couleur,")[14] which make him Hippolyte, "ce héros qu'elle adore." The continuity of her lover's being, which she would represent by "he" has become problematic: is this body "he"? ("elle voit Hippolyte et le demande encore"). The outer and the inner continuity are not congruous. When Aricie is finally forced to recognize that what she sees "is Hippolyte," she has cognized the destructive world order responsible for this discrepancy. And all this is to be read in her look accusing the gods.[15] Later, when the philosophical Théramène, at the close of his speech, declares that he has come to Thésée "détestant la lumière" (an expression which would, as we shall see, be appropriate also for Phèdre) we realize that his rejection of daylight[16] is equal in tragic weight to Aricie's accusing glance toward heaven.

The "récit de Phèdre" is no less "transposed" than is that of Théramène, since here Phèdre speaks of her bodily and psychological reactions, not only as a woman, but as a woman with the intellect and poetry of a Racine, capable of sifting and stylizing her emotions (incidentally, this blend with Racine is an inheritance from Seneca, whose emotional-philosophical Medea is Medea + Seneca: Medea + a philosophical poet). When Phèdre has "seen," there is involved a seeing of herself, a seeing sharpened by her critical self-judgment:

> Mon repos, mon bonheur semblait être affermi;
> Athènes me montra mon superbe ennemi.
> *Je le vis*, je rougis, je pâlis à sa vue.
> Un trouble s'éleva dans mon âme éperdue.
> *Mes yeux ne voyaient plus*, je ne pouvais parler.
> Je sentis tout mon corps et transir et brûler;
> *Je reconnus* (!) Vénus et ses feux redoutables
> J'adorais Hippolyte; et *le voyant* sans cesse . . .
> Je l'évitais partout. O comble de misère!
> *Mes yeux le retrouvaient* dans les traits de son père . . .
> *J'ai revu* l'ennemi que j'avais éloigné:
> Ma blessure trop vive aussitôt a saigné.

Ce n'est plus une ardeur dans mes veines cachée:
C'est Vénus tout entière à sa proie attachée.

Here, however, we are confronted with new implications of the act of seeing. In Phèdre's case, the "seeing" is, in a double sense, the tragic mainspring of her being: her sin is to have "seen" Hippolyte, to have experienced love for him, and her torture is to see (to cognize) that her sin is "having seen." Phèdre's *voir* is stained with sin and knowledge of sin. The fire of sin came through the eye (the covetous sense par excellence, according to Saint Augustine); it is for this reason that Phèdre wishes henceforth to shun the light of day ("ne plus voir le jour": note the ambiguity of *jour* = "life" and "light of day"[15a]), and flees into the darkness of death. In her final words she applies to herself the law of retaliation: "Déjà je ne vois plus qu'à travers un nuage / Et le ciel et l'époux que ma présence outrage; / Et la mort, à mes yeux dérobant la clarté, / Rend au jour qu'ils souillaient, toute sa pureté." Phèdre is the incarnation of God-willed self-destruction that comes through the eye: the eye that cognizes; Théramène, the spectator of tragedy, suffers only sympathetically the God-willed destruction in the objective world.

2. In the preceding paragraphs we have had occasion to speak of the reality-sifting quality inherent in Racine's "intellectual and poetic" language. The reader may have wondered whether the two terms are not mutually exclusive: is not Racine, moreover, the poet of pure emotion, untrammeled by fetters of the intellect? Is he not, better than any other poet of his time, able to let pure feeling breathe through words of incomparable evocatory power—"Que ces vains ornements, que ces voiles me pèsent," and "Ariane, ma soeur, de quel amour blessée / Vous mourûtes aux bords où vous fûtes laissée"? But such lines, with their great appeal to our emotional and acoustic imagination, have generally been isolated from the context by modern literary critics who have gone to school to the Romantics; when replaced in their original context, they appear neutralized by more intellectual expressions. For example, the first verse quoted is followed by the lines (159-

160): "Quelle importune main, en formant tous ces noeuds, / A pris soin sur mon front d'assembler mes cheveux?" Here the epithet *importune* implies an intellectual judgment, at variance with the rest, while the sad flute music of Phèdre's utterances is followed by the cool remark of Oenone: "Que faîtes-vous, Madame? et quel mortel ennui / Contre tout votre sang vous anime aujourd'hui?" where *mortel ennui* represents an evaluation, a diagnosis. But even when these two famous "emotional utterances" are considered in themselves, it is possible to see how the impact is softened by the expression of an intellectual judgment: in "ces vains ornements" *vains* is fraught with moral connotations (the Biblical "vanitas vanitatum"); the passage about Ariane contains a full-fledged logical demonstration underscored by repetition of the same syntactical pattern: it had been preceded by Phèdre's ejaculation: "O haine de Vénus! O fatale colère! / Dans quels égarements l'amour jeta ma mère!" (corresponding to "de quel amour blessée . . .!"), and ends with the conclusion "Puisque Vénus le veut, de ce sang déplorable / Je péris la dernière et la plus misérable." Here, underlying the exclamations, we find the logical pattern of a syllogism:

1. dans quels égarements . . . (Pasiphae was persecuted by Venus)
2. de quel amour blessée . . . (Ariane was persecuted by Venus)
3. *Consequently* (this is implied by the *puisque*), Venus persecutes all the women of the family: I am only a link in the chain.

This passage, in which the lyrical outburst is mitigated by ratiocination, is one example of what I have called, in an earlier article, "klassische Dämpfung": a continuous repression of the emotional by the intellectual. Indeed, it could be said that the alternation between these two conflicting tendencies is the most distinctive characteristic of Racine's style. As such it can be found in the speech of all his characters[17]: Racine has taught them all to speak with his voice. It is, understandably enough, especially frequent in the language of Phèdre, being a trait thoroughly consonant with her nature:

in her, boundless passion and severe analysis coincide to a remarkable degree. In Théramène's character, too, there is a comparable blend of the objective and intellectual (as historian and philosopher) with the subjective (as a compassionate friend of the God-stricken family)—though, with him, as we have said, objectivity must prevail.[18] Thus it will not be difficult to find in the "récit de Théramène" the same general tendency of tempering as that noted in the "récit de Phèdre." When, for example, he describes how he and his companions followed the bloody path that led them to the body of Hippolyte:

> De son généreux sang la trace nous conduit:
> Les rochers en sont teints; les ronces dégouttantes
> Portent de ses cheveux les dépouilles sanglantes

he offers vivid, concrete details appealing to our imagination. And yet the emotional effect is tempered by moral interpretations: the bloody hair, stuck to the thornbushes wet with blood, become "les dépouilles." The ghastly picture is ennobled: we are asked to contemplate the remains of a hero dead in battle. Still more characteristic is "son généreux sang": the actual blood as in similar cases pointed out above, is sublimated, transposed by the epithet *généreux* into the moral sphere. Again, in the passage:

> . . . A ce mot ce héros expiré
> N'a laissé dans mes bras qu'un corps défiguré,
> Triste objet où des Dieux triomphe la colère,
> Et que méconnaîtrait l'oeil même de son père

the expression "ce héros expiré," in which the defining phrase *héros expiré* is preceded by the demonstrative, has an oratorical ring, with Ciceronian overtones. It appeals to the emotion, if you will, but to the emotion of an intellectual person. One who was still under the impact of an affecting situation would not be so able to "define" and, instead of the demonstrative, would use, perhaps, the definite article which, by referring to something as already known, allows us to remain within the situation. The "distantiating demonstrative" (as I have called it), to the contrary, suggests a point of view from outside the situation; when we say, for example, *dans ce pays* "in this country," instead of *dans notre pays* "in our country," there is effected, at least for a split second, a disinterested comparison with other countries. Similarly, the *ce* of our passage is the expression of a dispassionate historian who feels the necessity of assuring his readers that he is still dealing with the same person.

Moreover, in this same phrase *ce héros expiré*, there is another trait of style to be observed, one which had been particularly favored by Roman historians and by the Roman playwrights who dealt with historical subjects (Seneca, for example) and which has existed in French since the time of the Renaissance (cf. Lerch's treatment of this construction under the title "C'est son rêve accompli," Beiheft 42 to *ZRPh*, 1912). *Ce héros expiré* stands for *l'expiration, la mort de ce héros*—or rather, we should say that *ce héros expiré / N'a laissé dans mes bras qu'un corps défiguré* is ambiguous by intent: is it the person of the hero (who happened to be dead), or his death, which left the sad vestiges? This type of expression, which ascribes to the agent what really belongs to the resulting action, and which remains on the borderline between the abstract and the concrete, gives an intellectual, sophisticated flavor ("can a dead hero act?") to a passage which otherwise speaks so directly to the heart. Finally, the personality of Hippolyte, of that "object," is further reduced by the use of the relative adverb *où*, which seems to refer not to a person but to a locality: the object has become a "place where" the Gods have sated their anger. This *où*, of which modern symbolistic poets might have been proud, immediately renders visualization impossible: we are in No Man's Land somewhere between an object and a place, between the visible and the abstract, the emotional and the intellectual, between a picture and a definition.

In the following passage, which contains a parenthetical remark, the tendency of "Dämpfung" has found another congruous form, and one which represents a characteristic and oft-repeated pattern in Racine's verse:

> Elle voit (quel objet pour les yeux d'une amante!)
> Hippolyte étendu, sans forme et sans couleur.

Here we are ready to identify ourselves with the sorrowing Aricie, to see with her eyes—and Théramène-Racine decides to postpone the picture we are eager to see, perhaps in order to prepare us for the horrifying sight: that is, in order to temper our emotions. Now this parenthesis is, in its syntactical form, an exclamation, an emotional outburst (like Phèdre's "*de quelle amour* blessée . . . !"), but its contents offer a rational appraisal of the object of vision. There is in the phrase *objet pour les yeux* something definitional and intellectual; the dead youth appears as a "visual unit," framed as it were, ready to be cognized by a scrutinizing eye. The effect is obviously to place us outside the range of Aricie's feelings —since these are defined. We feel for her but not with her; we have the attitude of a sympathetic but dispassionate witness—the attitude of Théramène-Racine. In addition, the presence of the indefinite article ("les yeux d'une amante") introduces a comparison of her plight with the normal lot of lovers in general; this projection of the particular case against a framework, this invocation of a general law, is a philosophical and intellectual device, particularly characteristic of Racine (which, with him, may take on a variety of nuances: entreaty, [self-] pity, self-assertion, protestation; the latter is found in Hippolyte's last words: "plaint le malheur d'*un* fils faussement accusé").

We have to do again with an interpolation, if not with a parenthesis, in the following example:

On dit qu'on a vu même, en ce désordre affreux,
Un Dieu qui d'aiguillons pressait leurs flancs poudreux.

Here, all is "poetic" and "seen"—and yet, in the interpolated *en ce désordre affreux*, the events narrated are judged, a rational diagnosis is given: by means of the term "extreme" the canon of normality is brought into play. And, simply by the act of calling something "extreme," we liberate ourselves from its impact; the impression of disorder or disharmony is not allowed to dominate the scene; on the contrary, the scene is gauged and defined for us. Here, too, however, the approach is not wholely rational: in the epithet *affreux* there is condensed, as it were, an emotional exclamation which sums up the whole scene: "c'était affreux!"—but, at the same time, this epithet is neutralized by the "diagnostic" noun *désordre*.[19] Again, we may consider the following passage, in which the description of factual events is interrupted by a moral judgment ("digne fils d'un héros"):

Hippolyte lui seul, digne fils d'un héros,
Arrête ses coursiers, saisît ses javelots,
Pousse au monstre, et d'un dard lancé d'une main sûre,
Il lui fait dans le flanc une large blessure.

The eye of the observer is also a moral eye: it moralizes while it observes. Not only is the heroism of Hippolyte shown by a description of his exploits: it is also verbally defined.

Such interpolations, which generally fill out the second hemistich of the first line of a couplet, are generally called "chevilles" (paddings), as if to suggest that the classical poets of the seventeenth century were in the habit of composing, in the original draft, the first hemistich of the first line, together with the whole second line, later to fill out the missing second hemistich of the first line. (According to this suggestion, Molière would have first written in his *Misanthrope*: "On sait que ce pied plat. . . . Par de sales emplois s'est poussé dans le monde," later to add "digne qu'on le confonde"). If this analysis, which assumes a "two-installment procedure" in poetic composition, were correct this would mean that the intellectual element must represent an extraneous addition to the emotional (of course, the question as to why such a prosaic phrase was added on second thought, would be only the more perplexing) whereas I contend that the rationalistic interpolation was conceived *along with* the emotionally flowing sentence, and is inseparable therefrom (it would evidently be impossible to separate the two elements in the insertion itself: *quel objet pour les yeux d'une amante*!). It is highly significant that, in the interpolations of Dämpfung, the classical poets put references to that stable world of moral values toward which they most insistently strove. These reminders of a moral and rational realm, in the midst of emotional turmoil, exert a steadying influence; over the waves of passion there shine forth, from these "lighthouses," the tranquil beams of reason and calm.

3. Now we are ready to consider an aspect of Racine's art, the failure to recognize which has led to misunderstanding on the part of many critics, from the seventeenth century to our own time. Students of Racine are familiar with the debate between Houdar de la Motte and Boileau, in which the former attacked, the latter defended, that line of our récit in which Théramène describes the reaction of Nature to the appearance of the sea-monster: "Le flot, qui l'apporta, recule épouvanté."

According to Houdar de la Motte: "Ce vers est excessif dans la bouche de Théramène. On est choqué de voir un homme accablé de douleur, si recherché dans ses termes et si attentif à sa description."[20] To this Boileau answers: "Pouvoit-il [Racine] employer la hardiesse de sa métaphore dans une circonstance plus considérable et plus sublime que dans l'effroyable arrivée de ce monstre, ni au milieu d'une passion plus vive que celle qu'il donne à cet infortuné gouverneur d'Hippolyte?" In other words, Houdar de la Motte bases his attack on the principle of "vraisemblance," while Boileau (the translator of Longinus!) invokes "sublimity" in his defense of the passage. What the one refers to as "excessif" and the other as "hardiesse de sa métaphore" is, more specifically, the interpretation of the physical fact of a wave's ebb and flow in a sophisticated and clever manner, whereby this natural process is ascribed to the ocean's fear. Since a "précieux" expression is usually defined as "une métaphore suivie jusqu'au bout" (the classical example being Théophile de Viau's "il [le poignard] en rougit, le traître!"), or an overextended intellectual interpretation of a physical fact, we may say that the "excess" to which the critic Houdar de la Motte objected was the preciosity of the metaphor.

But now let us place the incriminated line in its context (as the classical critics failed to do), and examine the dominant idea of the passage as a whole:

Un effroyable cri, sorti du fond des flots,
Des airs en ce moment a troublé le repos;
Et du sein de la terre une voix formidable
Répond en gémissant à ce cri redoutable.
Jusqu'au fond de nos coeurs notre sang s'est glacé.
Des coursiers attentifs le crin s'est hérissé.
Cependant, sur le dos de la plaine liquide,
S'élève à gros bouillons une montagne humide:
L'onde approche, se brise, et vomit à nos yeux,
Parmi des flots d'écume, un monstre furieux.
Son front large est armé de cornes menaçantes;
Tout son corps est couvert d'écailles jaunissantes;
Indomptable taureau, dragon impétueux,
Sa croupe se recourbe en replis tortueux;
Ses longs mugissements font trembler le rivage.
Le ciel avec horreur voit ce monstre sauvage;
La terre s'en émeut, l'air en est infecté,
Le flot qui l'apporta recule épouvanté.
Tout fuit; et, sans s'armer d'un courage inutile,
Dans le temple voisin chacun cherche un asile.

Here we are faced with the fact that Nature shrinks back from what she has given birth to, that the monster, though a part of Nature, is repudiated by the whole of Nature. As is well known, the classical procedure for evoking the whole of Nature is that of enumerating the four elements (note, in 1133, the evocation of Nature, when Hippolyte swears: "Que la terre, le ciel, que toute la nature . . .": here, Racine has added to the two elements mentioned by Euripides, the phrase "toute la nature"); in our passage the four elements (the sky, the seat of light, replaces the element of fire) respond with fright to the frightful product of Nature—the greatest fear being felt by the sea which gave birth to the sea-monster. Now, if we turn to the "récit de Phèdre," we find another example of Racinian baroque: Phèdre's address to the "soleil . . . qui . . . rougis"—and, indeed, of the same pattern of thought: the paradoxical fact of an ancestor who must blush at his own progeny is of the same sort as that of Nature rejecting what she has brought forth.[21] Where Houdar de la

Motte saw only a witty conceit, out of place in a tragedy, and unconvincing because of its excessive *invraisemblance*, there is a deeply felt expression of what was sensed as paradox in Nature.[22] In the cases where Racine allows himself to lend human emotions to Nature, this has a functional value for the play. Indeed, the play itself is based on the comparable paradox that the Gods repudiate their creatures; they send man into the world endowed with gifts which prove to be Danaïc, and abandon him to his doom. We may remember the lines of Goethe:

> Ihr führt ins Leben uns hinein
> Und lasst den Menschen schuldig werden,
> Dann überlasst ihr ihn der Pein,
> Denn alle Schuld rächt sich auf Erden.

Racine's sensitivity to such a paradox as that of "creation and repudiation" reveals a *Weltanschauung* which is essentially baroque.

That the baroque element in Racine's art was not recognized (as such) by his contemporaries is hardly surprising. During this period, the classical ideal of reason and simplicity was accepted so implicitly in France (where it was followed so much more faithfully than was the case in Spain, Italy, England, Germany) that any tendencies which appeared to be in opposition to pure classicism were considered, by the critics, as so many flaws: aberrations from the norm. They were unable to sense in their lifetime the positive nature of such tendencies, whenever these did appear, to see them as manifestations of another artistic ideal which were integral to the work of art; instead, they were viewed only as excesses, as excrescences which could and should be pruned off. Or, if they were condoned, this was apt to be due more to an inconsistent attitude than to critical understanding (Boileau, for example, defends the line of Racine mentioned above but stoutly condemns the "clinquant du Tasse"). But, while such confusion is understandable in the classical critics, who did not have at their disposal the conception of the "baroque" which modern historians of art and literature have developed,[23] the same excuse will not hold for those of our modern historians of French seventeenth-century literature, to whom this conception has not yet penetrated and who, even after the investigations into the baroque carried on by Wölfflin, Weisbach, Walzel, etc., insist on remaining faithful to the confusion which had its *raison d'être* in circumstances of the seventeenth century.[24] Brunetière, for example, sees such tendencies as "préciosité, le boursouflé, le grotesque" only as flaws contrary to the classical ideal. And he also makes the mistake of assuming too easily that, with the triumph of classicism in seventeenth-century literature, these unfortunate tendencies were vanquished. But who can overlook the "précieux" vein in Molière, that critic of the *précieuses*? And this preciosity, of course (as well as "le boursouflé," "le grotesque") is a manifestation of the baroque.

The baroque phenomenon in the seventeenth-century art and literature must be considered in contradistinction to the (purely) classical art which preceded it: while this follows the path of the golden mean between two extremes, in an atmosphere of calm and of an equipoise easily and inevitably reached, baroque art reveals the conflict of polarities which is so acute that the final equilibrium is achieved only by a violent effort and at the expense of our tranquillity. Even when balance is attained, the vestiges of the struggle remain indelible in the work of art, so that asymmetry prevails. The conflicting forces may be worldliness and religion, sensuousness and a disillusioning recognition of the vanity of the world, passion and intellect, anarchy and authority, but in every case the victory of the second force is hard won. In such a tense atmosphere, the three "stylistic diseases" mentioned by Brunetière—each of them a distinct trend in itself—can easily flourish. In Italy, Ariosto and Tasso, in Spain, Garcilaso and Góngora represent classic and baroque poetry respectively; among the artists, Raphael represents Renaissance art as opposed to the baroque of the later Michelangelo. In France, the baroque factor, whether in art or in literature, was much less conspicuous: what a tame variant of it is offered by the preciosity and the grotesque of Théophile! Nevertheless, there are baroque elements in Corneille and Racine as well as in Molière—and most of all, in Pascal and Bossuet (the same is true of Poussin, who appears to Gide as a mitigated Rubens).

To return to our play, it is evident that *Phèdre* is the ideal type of a baroque tragedy, not only by its style, but by its basic conception (though this the historians of French literature generally do not say) : we need only consider the heroine given over to a burning passion and, at the same time, to an intellectual awareness of it which multiplies her sufferings; Thésée, the heroic monster-slayer and happy lover, powerless against those gods who seem to protect him; kingly beings, enjoying a position far above common mankind, grope in the dark of their passion or their intellectual blindness. Here we have the typically baroque theme of the great of the earth who are creatures with all the frailty, the "Kreatürlichkeit" of such (cf. Shakespeare, *Henry V*: "I think the King is but a man as I . . . all his senses have but human conditions: his ceremonies laid by, in his nakedness he appears but a man") —together with the motif of the "dream of life," whose mystery man cannot unravel. Again and again, throughout the play, the characters are involved in a struggle between conflicting forces one of which will be allowed with great difficulty to subdue the other; a resolution is always achieved (by "klassische Dämpfung"), but one feels the revolt of the senses and of the emotions. The over-all impression remains that of a Pyrrhic victory.

In this connection, it is illuminating to consider the alterations which Racine introduced in the characters inherited from Euripides. Of Phèdre he says in his preface: "Phèdre n'est ni tout à fait coupable, ni tout à fait innocente. Elle est engagée par sa destinée, et par la colère des dieux dans une passion illégitime, dont elle a horreur toute la première. . . . Lorsqu'elle est forcée de la découvrir, elle en parle avec une confusion qui fait bien voir que son crime est plutôt une punition des dieux qu'un mouvement de sa volonté. J'ai même pris soin de la rendre moins odieuse qu'elle n'est dans les tragédies des anciens, où elle se résout d'elle-même à accuser Hippolyte. J'ai crue que la calomnie avoit quelque chose de trop bas et de trop noir pour la mettre dans la bouche d'une princesse qui a d'ailleurs des sentiments si nobles et si vertueux. Cette bassesse m'a paru plus convenable à une nourrice, qui pouvoit avoir des inclinations plus serviles."

This means to imply, when interpreted in terms of modern criticism, that Racine has made the character of Phèdre more baroque: the natural nobility of a great queen is in violent contrast with her debasing passion; the play consists of the *mise en jour* (to use Racine's own expression) of the all-too-human baseness of an exalted being. This basic structure of the character Phèdre is intended to show us how love, a gift of the Gods to mankind, can become poison and debasement; by love the mighty are cast down—indeed, dehumanized. To lead us toward the heights only to precipitate us into the abyss, this is the scheme of the Gods, and the baroque poet does his utmost to preserve the sharp contrast of the two extremes—as he exposes the shame of the exalted to the eyes of the world (we may be reminded of the line "Seht wie ein König kniet!" which closes the play of Grillparzer: a sentiment typical of baroque drama wherever and whenever found). Only death, which has been hovering over the five acts of the drama, brings a resolution of the conflict. No such thought of exposing the frailty of the mighty was uppermost in the mind of Euripides, whose Hippolyte was pure, an innocent victim of the anger of the Gods. And the reason for Racine's shift of emphasis from Hippolyte to Phèdre, a shift which has been pointed out by so enlightened a critic as Batteux, must have been that, by making Phèdre the protagonist, Racine was given the possibility of showing a princely being at its most frail ("frailty, thy name is woman" said the one who was the baroque hero par excellence): a woman in conflict between moral nobility and earthly passion.

And once the torn character of Phèdre had become the center of the play, once its theme had been changed from that of purity persecuted by the inexplicable cruelty of the Gods, to the baroque inner *Zerrissenheit* of a character within whom the God-sent monster rages, then the character of Hippolyte had to be transformed: he, too, must share in the baroque *Kreatürlichkeit* of Phèdre by assuming the role of a lover who loves against the will of his father—endowed, that is, with a flaw, however slight, in conformity with the law of the baroque stage where the limelight is cast not on ideality but on human frailty. Of Racine's innovations in this regard Batteux writes: "Phèdre criminelle, et Hippolyte vertueux, tous deux malheureux, sont mieux placés dans Euripide que dans Racine, parce qu'il est dans la nature et dans l'ordre que quand la vertu malheureuse se trouve en concurrence avec le crime malheureux, l'intérêt dominant et l'affection principale soient pour la vertu, qui n'a pas mérité son malheur, plutôt que pour le crime, qui a mérité le sien. L'objet naturel de la pitié, dit Aristote, est le malheur non mérité: d'où il suit qu'il est possible qu'Euripide ait mieux pris son sujet, relativement à l'effet de la tragédie, en subordonnant Phèdre à Hippolyte. . . . Phèdre est l'héroïne de la pièce de Racine; et c'est pour rendre son rôle plus beau et plus touchant qu'Hippolyte a été en quelque sorte dégradé. Euripide savait que les héros qu'on veut offrir à la pitié doivent être bons d'une bonté morale; Racine le savait aussi, puisqu'il donne partout l'amour de Phèdre comme l'effet de la colère de Vénus, pour la rendre moins odieuse; mais Euripide n'a eu qu'à suivre son plan simplement et sans aucun effort; Racine a eu besoin de beaucoup d'art pour suivre le sien. . . . Ne pouvant diminuer le malheur d'Hippolyte, il a fallu en diminuer la vertu, sans quoi il eût éclipsé Phèdre et emporté tout l'intérêt."[25]

Batteux has seen beautifully the dependence of Hippolyte's transformation on that of Phèdre but, imbued as he had to be with Aristotelian normative aesthetics, he could not recognize in that change the definite artistic will of Racine, so different from that of Euripides; the baroque poet who had conceived one character according to the pattern of conflict could not but shape the other accordingly. It was not apprehension lest an entirely virtuous Hippolyte eclipse Phèdre (an idea which seems to have left its imprint in Mr. Lynes' statements) which led Racine to depict Hippolyte as slightly less perfect: it was because, according to his baroque vision of the prince who is at the same time a human being, it was necessary that all the royal characters be shaken by ontologically conditioned conflicts. Phèdre "moins odieuse," Hippolyte less perfect: each represents a vision of man as a basically torn being; each of them is as baroque a creation as was Pascal's *roseau pensant*. Fénelon's and Arnauld's criticism of Racine's Hippolyte is quite beside the mark: they have failed to see the anthropological view underlying Racine's dramatic system. The lover's role assigned to Hippolyte represented no compromise with contemporary society (as has been suggested by the dubious anecdote of Racine's apology: "Qu'auraient dit nos petits-maîtres?"). In fact, Hippolyte is undermined by his pure passion for Aricie just as truly as is Phèdre by her impure passion. The gradual weakening of Hippolyte's power over his horses (which was to lead to his undoing) is parallel to the undermining of Phèdre's will-power by her consuming love. Hippolyte's love is Phèdre's passion on a minor scale; Racine presents his pessimistic judgment of love in a pure and an impure version: a total criticism which Proust will repeat.

Finally, the de-idealization of Hippolyte had to entail the creation of the ideal Aricie: this pure princess inherits the original role of Hippolyte in Euripides; and she inherits also his protecting deity, Diana. The character of Aricie was conceived not only in order to motivate the flaw in Hippolyte's character, a "super" on whom Racine could hang the label "loved by Hippolyte": it was also necessary that purity be represented in the drama. And Aricie, who stands beyond the reach of the curse which lies on the family of Thésée, is unstained by sin, unshadowed by doom.

We have begun this section by the consideration of a stylistic feature (*préciosité*) which revealed itself as a reflection of a characteristically baroque conception, and we have seen how the fabric of the play itself was shot through with baroque themes, involving the clash of polarities. Now, returning to stylistic questions, we will find, not only the feature of preciosity, which is one of the forms of the baroque in French literature, but a device which embodies the basic baroque pattern of contrasted polarities. When, for example, Phèdre's passion is described as a *flamme noire*, we are offered a paradoxical expression of the type to which the ancients gave the name *oxymoron*; such a phrase presents the impossible as possible. The flame that should bring light and life in the being called Phaedra, "the shining one," in reality brings darkness and death (Phèdre is the daughter not only of Pasiphaë, the "all-shining," but also of Minos, the god of hell, to whom, unable longer to bear the light of day, she will descend; thus she is herself an oxymoron incarnate). The fire that warms ends in the cold of death. No wonder that the poisoned love that Phèdre bears cannot warm the heart: "Je *goûtais en tremblant* ces *funèbres plaisirs*" (Act IV)—two oxymora are found in one sentence. And we may also remember the expression "funestes bienfaits" by which Thésée, filled with a presentiment of Hippolyte's death, characterizes the Danaïc gifts of the Gods. A less obvious type of oxymoron is to be seen in the line (which antagonized the unpoetic critics of Racine's time) from our récit: "Traîné par les chevaux que sa main a nourris."[26] This underscores beautifully the paradox, the *Widersinn* of life: the heroic horse-tamer is trampled by his horses. Here, just as with *flamme noire* and *funestes bienfaits*, there is the suggestion of an intolerable world order subject to the clash of polarities. And yet, by virtue of having been defined, the disharmonious is overcome: disharmony is conquered by the harmony of form.

As a final manifestation of baroque art in *Phèdre*, let us turn again to the description of the monster which is central to the récit. The motif itself was, evidently, given. What Racine has brought out most conspicuously is the element of the demoniac—if this may be defined as a death-bringing vital force. In the ancient world, the monster had its legitimate place, accepted as one of the forces of nature: in the world of Christian values, the monstrous must appear as a threat to the cosmos, sent by *natura parens* to inflict death. And this threat is felt in Racine's description, where nature, in its hideous beauty, is presented in a variety of novel forms worthy of a Baudelaire or a Flaubert:

> Cependant sur le dos de la plaine liquide
> S'élève à gros bouillons une montagne humide;
> L'onde approche, se brise, et vomit à nos yeux
> Parmi des flots d'écume, un monstre furieux.
> Son front large est armé de cornes menaçantes;
> Tout son corps est couvert d'écailles jaunissantes;

Indomptable taureau, dragon impétueux,
Sa croupe se recourbe en replis tortueux.

All in these lines is movement and action; in a momentary metamorphosis where the animate takes on the inanimate (*montagne humide*), and the reverse (*dos de la plaine*), strange shapes emerge as if painted by a Rubens or a Bosch. Those critics who have spoken of the "descriptive style" in the "récit de Théramène" should, more specifically, have spoken of the "baroque descriptive style," of the "description of the hideous and the demoniac." It is surely significant that this passage, which has always been recognized as one of the most highly descriptive to be found in Racine, is focused on the demoniac, the monstrous, the gruesome. For, what is a monster unless seen? A monster in the abstract! Since monster it had to be (because of the ancient model), it could be only a baroque monster: a monster presented in all its horrid sensuous reality.

But this anarchy of shapes and movement will be curbed by Racinian verse; the monster will be transposed into the realm of poetry. Since the matter of Théramène's story was the ugly and the destructive, the manner had to be ornate and weighty: the more exciting the events witnessed by Théramène, the more poised must be his description of it—the more of intellectual detachment, of aesthetic repose, of plastic beauty open to contemplation must we be offered. Firmly architectured alexandrines impose their measure on the ghastly vision; rhetorical patterns mold and purify crude reality. By the intellectual act of distinguishing these patterns, the emotions of the listener are held in check; while he is invited to visualize strangeness and horror, he is constantly reminded of the familiar and the traditional—for the devices used by Racine are, for the most part, highly conventional. Let us note just a few of these quite conventional features: the traditionally poetic vocabulary ("onde" for "mer," which involves the conventional device of synecdoche), chiasmus ("indomptable taureau" - "dragon furieux"), anaphoric prefixes ("se recourbe en replis"), onomatopoeia ("l'essieu *crie et* se rompt"), and finally (e.g. "monstre furieux") the classical use of "colorless" adjectives, so obnoxious to a modern critic who is apt to share the opinion of Jules Renard that " 'Ciel' dit plus que 'ciel bleu'; l'épithète tombe d'elle-même, comme une feuille morte." But the "dead" quality of such epithets is precisely what serves to establish calm and serenity. The ultimate effect of these devices is that the chaotic vital forces on the verge of explosion are stemmed, subjected to rule and form, to "klassische Dämpfung." For Racine, the baroque poet, is a French poet; he is not tempted, as a Quevedo might be, to overthrow all boundaries of form, but understands how to subject the baroque flow of vital forces to classical measure. It is true that the "récit de Théramène" is a "most baroque" piece of poetry, and its critics have been troubled by its close approach to the anarchic and the chaotic. None the less, the récit succeeds in taming the monster by style.

My three divisions devoted to the style of the "récit de Théramène" were intended to show how reality is sifted by the intellect, how the expression of emotion is attended with "klassische Dämpfung," how life is seen as a conflict between polar forces. We have also tried to show that former critics have failed to let themselves be guided by the words of the play toward its inner economy and coherence, preferring rather to establish relationships between certain unrelated details of the play and aprioristic criteria extraneous to the play. Since we have chosen to remain within the play, our procedure has been to penetrate from the periphery of the words toward the inner core. For the words of the poet are shafts leading to the innermost part of the mine, while extraneous rapprochements are dead alleys. Criticism must remain immanent to the work of art, and draw its categories therefrom.

NOTES

1. This crisscross design of divine influences is the invention of Racine: with Euripides, the chaste Hippolyte had, as his patron, the chaste Diana. Since, in Racine's version, he was not "entirely chaste," he had to be a worshiper of the patron God of his father: Neptune—and, to some extent, of Venus.

2. Blameless, of course, only insofar as concerns the pure nature of his love for Aricie (for the *fact* of this love is presented as a flaw). On the other hand, every precaution is taken by Racine to indicate that Hippolyte's listless mood, which may have caused his waning attention to the horses that he had trained, is due to this love; cf. the lines (551-552) in which Hippolyte complains that his love-longing has interfered with his once favorite sport of horse-taming (and which anticipate somewhat the lines of the "récit de Théramène": ". . . et sourds à cette fois,/Ils ne reconnaissent plus ni le frein ni la voix").

3. To these examples for the "chariot" motif there may be added lines 176-178 in Act I, when Phèdre depicts her tortured state of mind to Oenone (before giving her any explanation of her condition) by means of two images of the peace which is denied her; one of these contains precisely the motif of the chariot:

> Dieu! que ne suis-je assise à l'ombre des forêts!
> Quand pourrai-je, au travers d'une noble poussière,
> Suivre de l'oeil un char fuyant dans la carrière . . . ?

No sooner has she made this admission than she realizes that she is no longer mistress of her spirits:

> Insensée, où suis-je? et qu'ai-je dit?
> Où laissé-je égarer mes voeux et mon esprit?
> Je l'ai perdu: les Dieux m'en ont ravi l'usage.
> Oenone, la rougeur me couvre le visage.

Here we can discover the delicate working of Racine's psychology of love, of that love which restricts the field of vision and turns everything therein into a means of torture. Euripides had offered a list of possibilities which would refresh Phaedra's soul: a spring, poplars on a meadow, mountains, horseback-riding—a variety of pleasures in which to find recreation. These distractions Racine limits to one—toward which the tortured soul of Phèdre turns: she craves to be outside of turmoil, a spectator of life; she wants not to ride herself but to watch from the shadow the "noble dust" from a speeding chariot. Then, immediately, this very picture of peace is turned into poison: if she sees a race she must think of the youthful and gallant chariot-driver Hippolyte.

Here, we have been given an insight into the awakening of Phèdre's self-poisoning imagination. Racine has used restriction in the choice of the possibilities, but has intensified the efficacy of one element.

In a lecture given at the Johns Hopkins University by Dr. Richmond Lattimore of Bryn Mawr College, the speaker pointed out that the young, Amazonlike Phaedra of Euripides is presented throughout as an Outlander, ill-acclimated to Troezene: horseback-riding was not a "lady-like" activity in the eyes of Euripides' public. In Phaedra, according to Dr.

Lattimore, Euripides has created one of his numerous characters who are ill at ease and dissatisfied with the environment in which they must live. Thus, while in Euripides, Phaedra's desire for change and recreation shows mainly her nostalgia for the activities of her native climate, in Racine, Phèdre's same desire for equestrian feats—in which Hippolytus, not she, should figure—only serves to bind her the more to her passion.

4. Batteux has excellently realized that, in Racine's fifth act, the interest shifts from Phèdre to Thésée: "Phèdre, après la scène de la rivalité, n'intéresse plus; Thésée est le seul qui reste, ou du moins qui domine sur la scène. Cette translation de l'intérêt ne se trouve pas dans la pièce grecque. Hippolyte, donné pour point de vue dès la première scène, intéresse continuement et d'une façon dominante jusqu'à son dernier soupir." But the reason for this shift is not given by Batteux: that with Racine we see an almighty and heroic king blindly and desperately groping (like another King Lear, since he is close to madness) to find where truth lies, groping with the problem of the world order. Phèdre, at the end of the tragedy is less important than is the king, before whom the whole picture must be unrolled.

5. When Mauriac, in his *Vie de Jean Racine*, says of Phèdre: "Le soleil pour elle seule, contre elle seule. Les autres humains n'existent pas. Hippolyte même n'apparaît que dans la fulguration du désir de Phèdre," he is right insofar as he means only to characterize Phèdre's monomania. This certainly is not true of the architecture of the play from an objective point of view.

6. There is, in Phèdre, a particular motif of doom attached to a location (a motif not unknown to the ancients)—especially to Trézène. The anger of the Gods brings about the situations in which the family will be destroyed by making them go to that ill-omened Trézène which, on the surface, presents itself as the *aimable Trézène*: when Hippolyte says, near the beginning of the play (28): "Et je fuirai ces lieux que je n'ose plus voir" Théramène answers: "Hé! depuis quand, Seigneur, craignez-vous la présence / De ces paisibles lieux, si chers à votre enfance?" Hippolyte counters: "Tout a changé de face / Depuis que sur ces bords les Dieux ont envoyé / La fille de Minos et de Pasiphaë." Schlegel has indicted the expression *la présence de ces lieux* ("Have you ever heard that places have a presence?"). *Pace* Schlegel, it might be stated that in this tragedy places do have a presence: we must accept the clear indication of this artistic intention by Racine. The critic, instead of indicting a striking expression, should take therefrom the clue to his understanding: a striking expression in a masterpiece cannot be due to chance, it is rather a passkey! Consider, for example, some of the allusions to the doom by which Trézène is weighed down: (267, Oenone) "Voyage infortuné! Rivage malheureux, / Fallait-il approcher de tes bords dangereux!"; (302, Phèdre) "Vaines précautions! cruelle destinée! / Par mon époux lui-même à Trézène amenée, / J'ai revu l'ennemi que j'avais éloigné"; (929, Hippolyte) "Je ne la [Phèdre] cherchais pas: / C'est vous qui sur ces bords conduisîtes ses pas. / Vous daignâtes, Seigneur, aux rives de Trézène . . ."; (953, Thésée) "Que vois-je? Quelle horreur dans ces lieux répandue / Fait fuir devant mes yeux ma famille éperdue?" The temple of faith and purity, where the wedding of Hippolyte and Aricie should have taken place, is "aux portes de Trézène" near the ancient tombs of noble

ancestors (1392). But it is precisely there ("nous sortions des portes de Trézène," says Théramène—and he repeats the words of Hippolyte ["... ou ces tombeaux / Des princes de ma race antiques sépultures"] in a minor key: "ces tombeaux antiques, / Où des rois ses aïeux sont les tristes[!] reliques") that Hippolyte is destroyed; and there, consequently, Aricie will voice her accusation of the Gods. Little wonder that Thésée will, at the end, flee "loin de ce rivage / De mon fils déchiré fuir la sanglante image." His is a cursed race on a cursed soil.

7. Racine is careful not to allow Phèdre to act directly: he makes her guilty in her thought (it is, as R. A. Schröder has pointed out in *Racine und die Humanität*, the thought, not only the deed, which makes a Christian soul guilty) : just as no overt action is involved in Phèdre's love for Hippolyte, Phèdre being criminal only in her amorous thoughts, so she commits no act herself to bring about Hippolyte's death. But her evil thought ratifies Oenone's evil action.

Racine has squared the circle by making his unfortunate queen "act without acting" in the scene where she decides against her earlier impulse to reveal Hippolyte's innocence to Thésée—stung to jealousy by the king's reference to Aricie. By this act of decision she espouses, by her sin of omission, the evil adviser's sin of commission; this is the maximum of action granted her before she takes poison (her death, itself, being extremely undramatic, and the exact *contrappasso* to that insidious poison of love to which we have seen her subjected). The baroque princess, reduced to a suffering body and soul, a figure gagged and bound, as it were, must submit throughout the play to the fatality of guilt which has elected her as victim. Oenone is the evil thought of Phèdre become action; Phèdre is not allowed the outlet of direct evil action.

8. For example, in the case of Théramène and Oenone, both are mentors, both teach their royal pupils to yield to love; but Oenone encourages a criminal, Théramène a healthy, love—consequently, she must die while he is allowed to survive. Although Théramène and Oenone never meet on the stage they have been conceived in obvious parallelistic antagonism.

9. This careful preparation for an action which will develop only in the fifth act, reminds us of the parallel case in which the death of Oenone is foreshadowed in her words in Act I (229 *seq.*) :

> Quoiqu'il vous [Phèdre] reste à peine une faible lumière,
> Mon âme chez les morts descendra la première.
> Mille chemins ouverts y conduisent toujours:
> Et ma juste douleur choisira les plus courts.

The commentary of the *Grands écrivains* edition, with its predilection for information concerning things extraneous to the play, gives the ancient source for the third of these lines, but fails to explain the functional value of the lines within the play: to sound the note of tragic irony.

10. Indeed, any *explication de texte*, any philological study, must start with a *critique des beautés*, with the assumption on our part of the perfection of the work to be studied and with an entire willingness to sympathy; it must be an apologia, a theodicy in a nutshell. In fact, philology has its origin in the *apologia*—of the Bible or of the classics. For philology is born from Biblical criticism and humanistic endeavors, both of them attempts to justify the *So-sein*, the "being so and not otherwise" of exemplary texts. A criticism which insists on faults is justifiable only after the

purpose of the author has been thoroughly understood and followed up in detail. The glibness with which critics, especially great German critics (Lessing, Schiller, and Schlegel), have slandered French classical drama, is only to be explained on the basis of premature judgments drawn from a quite extraneous comparison with Shakespeare.

Professor Lancaster's partial acknowledgment of the "beauty" of *Phèdre* may remind us of the similar statement of Menéndez y Pelayo on Lope's masterpiece *Fuenteovejuna*: "Hay mucho que aplaudir en esta comedia, o más bien casi todo es excelente"—a statement which has elicited the protest of a scholar of the new generation, Joaquín Casalduero (*RFH*, v, 23) who, quoting Proust's allusion to "les oeuvres d'art achevées où il n'y a pas une seule touche qui soit isolée, où chaque partie tour à tour reçoit des autres sa raison d'être comme elle leur impose la sienne" (i.e. to the "circular" quality of works of art), opposes the relativism of his predecessor in violent terms: "En su día fué esto un descubrimiento que expresaba; hoy es un lugar común que, además de no querer decir nada, denota pereza intelectual excesiva o una rigidez mental grande en quien lo emplea. No: Lope ha producido obras perfectas. . . . *Fuenteovejuna* pertenece a la clase de obras en que todo es excelente." The time is past when the critic could read a masterpiece at his ease, feeling no obligation to relate parts to whole, here approving, there disapproving, as his eudaemonistic sensibility happened to be impressed.

11. Incidentally, it may be added that the intellectual nature of Aricie's perception in this scene is not at all "unrealistic": in moments when the most terrible sights strike our vision, there comes about a crystalline lucidity in which we are most clearly aware of our mental operations: if Aricie had been the one to report on her exact impressions at the moment, she would, perhaps, have been most true to reality in saying: "Je m'approche; je vois l'herbe . . . , je vois (quel objet . . .)" etc.

12. It is true that, in the words of the dying Hippolyte as reported by Théramène, we find the line "pour apaiser mon *sang* et mon ombre plaintive." Here, however, "blood" refers not only to physical blood: it is also a metonymical periphrase for "death"—with the Biblical implication that the blood of the murdered cries out for revenge. But this suggestion of a cry of vengeance immediately gives way to an appeased sigh of a softly plaintive Vergilian, or Dantean, shadow-soul.

In *Andromaque*, also, we are offered (as Miss Hatcher will point out in her forthcoming article) a picture of a bloody corpse: i.e. when the captive heroine describes the scene her eyes beheld the night of Troy's destruction:

> Seigneur, voyez l'état où vous me réduisez.
> J'ai vu mon père mort, et nos murs embrasés;
> J'ai vu trancher les jours de ma famille entière,
> Et mon époux sanglant traîné sur la poussière,
> Son fils seul avec moi, réservé pour les fers . . . (927-931)

But this reference to a bleeding form dragged in the dust does not offer a photographic reproduction of a mutilated body to our physical vision: we are not invited to visualize physiological details. It is the husband of Andromaque (*mon époux*) who has perished, it is the last of the Trojan heroes. And this figure is shown us against the background of the burning city; the framework of the whole is the destruction of Troy, the destruction of a civilization. Moreover, the description of Hector follows upon *trancher les jours* . . . ; this portentous reference to the death of a dynasty ennobles the blood-grimed figure in the dust—in the symbolic dust of defeat.

13. With Racine, the words for "seeing" are always fraught with connotations of intellectual clarification and cognizance, as Miss Hatcher will prove; in my previous study on Racine in *Rom. Stil u. Literaturstudien,* I had ventured some tentative remarks in this connection. The preferential place given to "sight" in comparison with the other senses, as we find it in Racine, is the continuation of an Augustinian and medieval trend of thought: cognizance, love, sin all come through the sense of senses, the eye.

14. We could also point out that, to the picture offered to Aricie ("[elle vit] Hippolyte étendu, sans forme et sans couleur"), a conceptual analysis has been added: since form and color are the elements of the (Thomistic) ideal definition of beauty, this sentence must mean that Aricie saw before her a Hippolyte bereft of beauty—and, consequently, was unable to recognize him ("et ne connaissant plus ce héros qu'elle adore"). The cultured listener is no doubt supposed to know this definition of beauty in order to be able to understand the meaning of these lines.

Just how much this insistence on "intellectual seeing," which seeks to identify the object seen, is in line with what I shall call later the "baroque" *desengaño*, can be shown by a German baroque play written earlier than *Phèdre*: Gryphius' *Cardenio und Celinde*. In a passage quoted by Ernst Feise, *Journal of Eng. and Germ. Phil.*, XLIV, 188, the protagonist tells of a vision in which he saw his daemonic beloved:

> Da sah ich / und erstarrt' in ungeheurem Schrecken
> Da sah ich / und erblast! da sah ich keine Zir!
> Da sah ich / und verging / Olympen nicht vor mir!
> Ich sah ein Totenbild! / ohn Aug / ohn Lipp und Wangen
> Ohn Ader / Haut und Fleisch / gehärt mit grünen Schlangen

The traits we observed in the passage on Aricie are also found here: not only the attempt to identify the dire sight, but also the hesitancy of the "seeing" person, who dreads to acknowledge the awful reality—as well as the total *desengaño* to which this seeing leads. There is surely no relationship of dependence between Racine and Gryphius: both write within the same climate; and both have studied Seneca and have adapted his anaphoric style to their baroque purposes.

15. That Aricie does not reappear on the stage at the moment of the denouement (we hear of her in the récit and in the final lines of the play), may be motivated by the dramatic reason that the bodily presence of such a figure of light as was Aricie would have distracted attention from the main victims of the Gods. She will always be to us "la triste Aricie" who indicts divinity.

15a. An ambiguity of classical origin: "to see the light," means "to live" in the *Iliad* (18, 442).

16. Compare Hippolyte's statement, "Le jour n'est pas plus pur que le fond de mon coeur," and the following passage (line 166 *seq.*):

> OENONE: Vous vouliez vous montrer et revoir la lumière.
> Vous l'avouez, Madame; et prête à vous cacher,

> Vous haïssez le jour que vous veniez chercher.
> PHÈDRE: Noble et brillant auteur d'une triste famille. . . .
> Qui peut-être rougis du trouble où tu me vois,
> Soleil, je te viens voir pour la dernière fois.

for the relationship between "daylight" and "purity."

17. The serenely intellectual atmosphere that permeates the last words of Hippolyte is remarkable; we have stressed above, in the text, his clear formulation of the meaning of his death, a formulation which admits of only a slight admixture of "poetry" ("mon ombre plaintive"). It is as though Hippolyte applied "classical restraint" to his last words, and to the last moments of his existence. Even when his words are interrupted by the agony of death ("qu'il lui rende . . .") this fits into the classical pattern of "aposiopesis": there is lacking, for example, the "naturalistic" effect, depending on the truncation of a single word, as we find it in Ariosto: "nè men ti raccomando la mia *Fiordi—* / Ma dir non potè *ligi*, e qui finío." Moreover, in the unfinished words of Hippolyte, what is interrupted is not the evocation of a name that embodies the personal happiness of the lover, but the expression of an altruistic thought concerning the welfare of the other being that should live on after her lover's death.

18. Diderot, in his "Paradoxe sur le comédien," has written immortal lines which seem almost to be meant to apply to the "récit de Théramène": "Avez-vous jamais réfléchi à la différence des larmes excitées *par un événement* tragique et des larmes excitées par un récit pathétique? On entend raconter une belle chose: peu à peu la tête s'embarrasse, les entrailles s'émeuvent, et les larmes coulent. Au contraire, à l'aspect d'un accident tragique, l'objet, la sensation et l'effet se touchent; en un instant les entrailles s'émeuvent, on pousse un cri, la tête se perd, et les larmes coulent; celles-ci viennent subitement; les autres sont amenées. Voilà l'avantage d'un coup de théâtre naturel et vrai sur une scène éloquente, il opère brusquement ce que la scène fait attendre; mais l'illusion en est beaucoup plus difficile à produire; un incident faux, mal rendu, la détruit. Les accents s'imitent mieux que les mouvements, mais les mouvements frappent plus violemment.

". . . C'est lorsque la grande douleur est passée, quand l'extrême sensibilité est amortie, que l'âme est calme, qu'on se rappelle son bonheur éclipsé qu'on est capable d'apprécier la perte qu'on a faite, que la mémoire se réunit à l'imagination, l'une pour retracer, l'autre pour exagérer la douceur d'un temps passé; qu'on se possède et qu'on parle bien." Théramène is self-controlled and speaks well.

19. The "klassische Dämpfung" of Racine may have been learned from Vergil, cf. e.g. *Aeneid*, VI, 274-281:

[in the vestibule of Hell]

> Luctus et ultrices posuere cubilia Curae;
> pallentes habitant Morbi tristisque Senectus,
> et Metus et malesuada Fames ac turpis Egestas,
> *terribiles visu formae*, Letumque Labosque;
> tum consanguineus Leti Sopor et mala mentis
> Gaudia, mortiferumque adverso in limine Bellum,
> ferreique Eumenidum thalami ex Discordia demens
> vipereum crinem vittis innexa cruentis.

The enumeration of the two groups of monsters is, as E. Norden has pointed out in his commentary on the Sixth Book, separated by v. 277 with the interpolation *terribiles visu formae* "die einen gewissen Ruhepunkt bildet. . . . Das alles zeugt von bedachter Kunst." It must be added to these words of Norden that, by this very interpolation, the frightening description of the monsters gives way, for a moment, to a quiet *judgment* in regard to the manner in which they must appear to the eye of the spectator—and this is in line with Racine's habits. That a whole poetic attitude (not only certain devices which are derivative thereof) has been adopted from the ancients (and, necessarily, transformed) by this French classical poet is not an isolated fact: La Fontaine has learned from Horace what I have called (in *PMLA*, LIII, 393) his *suavitas*.

20. In another passage of the récit, we find intellectual criticism expressed by a play on words:

> . . . Ismène, toute en pleurs,
> La rappelle à la vie, ou plutôt aux douleurs.

The last hemistich, which indicates a paradoxically pessimistic equation "life = sorrows," is clearly an extension on the trivial phrase *rappeler à la vie*—which becomes, thereby, didactically ("plutôt") transformed into something like "call back to the sorrows (in which life consists)": this is life judged from without, not lived from within. The very self-correction which Théramène purports to impose on himself is an intellectual procedure likely to be used by an observer calm enough to pay attention to his choice of words. But to this attitude we should not, like De la Motte, attach blame.

21. This is, in fact, the situation which obtains for Phèdre also: she, too, is a monster who has been given her monstrous nature (her incestuous love) by Nature (= Venus), but is rejected by her.

22. One could ask why De la Motte did not equally object to this metaphor used by Phèdre (169):

> Noble et brillant auteur d'une triste famille,
> Toi, dont ma mère osait se vanter d'être fille,
> Qui peut-être rougis du trouble où tu me vois,
> Soleil, je te viens voir pour la dernière fois!

It could be said that the concept of a "sun that blushes" is as daring a *précieux* deviation from the normal "the sun shines," as daring an intellectual interpretation of a physical fact, as is Théophile's conception of a dagger, red with blood, blushing over its treachery.

On the other hand, the "sun" in question is also a god, and an ancestor: if Phèdre were thinking of him exclusively in that guise, the reaction of blushing from shame would be wholly congruous. Perhaps we have here a deliberate ambiguity (symbolized by the epithet *brillant*); Phèdre sees the sun both as a shining orb and as a divine being.

23. The literary historians of today, in France and elsewhere, are too prone to repeat seventeenth-century French criticism on seventeenth-century French literature. Their confidence in this criticism is due to the illusion of a homogeneous "siècle de Louis XIV," brilliant in all fields; whereas the truth is that in that epoch literature alone, not literary criticism, was outstanding. I associate myself with J. Hadamard who writes in his article "Science et monde moderne" (in the journal *Renaissance*,

I, 550): "Le XVIIe siècle a été, et particulièrement en France, un âge de décadence. . . . Il semble même que le progrès des sciences positives ait, à ce moment-là, nui aux études historiques en en détournant les esprits que, d'autre part, l'éclat de la production littéraire à la même époque éblouissait. La critique littéraire elle-même, comme le note Renan (*L'Avenir de la science*, p. 144), témoigne de la même faiblesse."

24. H. Peyre, *Rom. Rev.*, XXXI, 297, has listed a number of points of difference between the theater of Racine and that of the Greeks, according to which the former appears as a quite original creation: he fails, however, to mention the magic word "baroque."

25. Still another character had to be changed in consequence of Racine's baroque approach: the nurse Oenone. Schlegel who, on moral grounds, condemned Phèdre for putting the burden of guilt on Oenone, has not understood what is brought out excellently by W. Benjamin in his book, *Ursprung des deutschen Trauerspiels* (Berlin, 1928): that the baroque drama, which shows the rulers and princes in all their earthly glory but also in their congenital depravity as human beings, must give a preponderant part to the evil counselors who exploit the earthly power of their masters, and thereby precipitate them into the abyss of their human depravity. The kingly character of a baroque drama is sometimes extremely weak (e.g. a Herod), a pawn in the hands of his advisers, "out-Heroded" by them. What Phèdre says to Oenone, who has served her not wisely but too well (1317):

> Va-t'en, monstre exécrable . . .
> Et puisse ton supplice à jamais effrayer
> Tous ceux qui comme toi, par de lâches adresses,
> Des princes malheureux nourrissent les faiblesses,
> Les poussant au penchant où leur coeur est enclin,
> Et leur osent du crime aplanir le chemin,
> Détestables flatteurs, présent le plus funeste
> Que puisse faire aux rois la colère céleste

has also been expressed by Shakespeare, when he has his King John berate those "slaves" who serve royal failings:

> It is the curse of Kings to be attended
> By slaves that take their humors for a warrant
> To break within the bloody house of life
> And on the winking of authority
> To understand a law, to know the meaning
> Of dangerous majesty, when perchance it frowns
> More upon humor than advised respect (*King John*, IV, l. 208)

Oenone works at the behest of that blind predestination which persecutes in the great of the earth their frail humanity, their *Kreatürlichkeit* (that the kingly being is held to be noble by nature, that the adviser could more easily have "des inclinations serviles" is due not to any contempt of Racine for the lower classes but to his belief in the theocratic order of the state—an order according to which the most exalted person in the state is a "Sun King," and consequently should be ideal). On the other hand, classical drama has also furnished famous examples of good counselors; whatever the moral quality of the counselor's advice, his role is always a crucial element of baroque drama. Cf. the statement of Luis Vives in his dialogue "Regia" (1539): "Istos quos in consilium adhibet princeps, prudentissimos esse oportet, magni rerum usus et in decernendo gravitatis et moderationis summae. . . . Quia sunt oculi et aures principis atque adeo regni universi. *Et eo magis si caecus aut surdus sit rex, captus suis sensibus*, vel ob ignorantiam vel ob delicias."

26. The topos of the "horse tamed with great effort," as we have it in the line: "Rendre docile au frein un coursier indompté," is another typical theme of baroque art (one immediately remembers its frequency with Velásquez). The role given to the horses in *Phèdre* is exceptional among seventeenth-century plays (especially tragedy), if we are to believe Professor Lancaster's erudite study in *Essays in Honor of Albert Feuillerat* (Yale, 1943), p. 106. However, Professor Lancaster has failed to inquire into the reason for the infrequency of such references in seventeenth-century French tragedy (as opposed to its frequency in Spanish drama)—which reason is precisely the anti-baroque tendency of French classical tragedy. As a matter of principle, studies of this type should, in my opinion, be subordinated to categories derived from history of art and history of ideas; we should no longer follow the positivistic manner of "catalogues" (inaugurated by the German dissertation of the Stengel school: "Das Ross in den altfranzösischen Artus- und Abenteuerromanen," 1888).

4

THE STYLE OF DIDEROT

Argumentum: I had often been struck, in reading Diderot, by a rhythmic pattern in which I seemed to hear the echo of Diderot's speaking voice: a self-accentuating rhythm, suggesting that the "speaker" is swept away by a wave of passion which tends to flood all limits. This pattern (which is a feature quite at variance with classical style) is apt to appear, with varied nuances, anywhere in Diderot's writings, didactic as well as narrative (or epistolary). The conclusion seemed obvious that this rhythm was conditioned by a certain nervous temperament which, instead of being tempered by style, was allowed to energize style. Now, the historians of philosophy have long recognized that Diderot is one of the chief exponents of the eighteenth-century philosophy of mobility: while his approach is strictly empirical, there is, with him, the perpetual desire to transcend the rationally graspable. It would then appear that, in this writer, nervous system, philosophical system, and "stylistic system" are exceptionally well attuned. Moreover, given this temperament and this philosophy, we may expect to find other indications of the tendency toward mobility and "self-potentiation"—as, for example, Diderot's predilection for characters who, mimetically gifted, strive to transcend their own nature—only to fall into a kind of automatism, a mental stuttering (which was not absent from Diderot personally). Ultimately, it is in the erotic *Erlebnis* of Diderot that this urge for self-potentiation—which informs his writings and which leads, sometimes, to automatism—is grounded.

This is the only one of the articles in this collection in which I have allowed myself to attempt to penetrate to the soul not only of the author but of the man; such an approach could be legitimate only in the case of a modern author: one who enjoys the freedom permitted by the conception of the "original genius."

"L'art d'écrire n'est que l'art d'allonger les bras."

Diderot himself has said of his writings (ed. Assézat, I, 177): "Les prétendus connoisseurs en fait de style chercheront vainement à me déchiffrer," a statement which implies his own consciousness of the uniqueness of his style. Perhaps a stylistician, who must modestly confess to be only a "prétendu connoisseur en fait de style diderotique" can still, and not in vain, attempt at least to clarify the reasons for this uniqueness.

In general, stylisticians have rather shied away from Diderot, and what pronouncements they have made have been inconsequential.[1] It is amazing to see how little Lanson has to say, in his *L'art de la prose,* about the essence of Diderot's style; he judges him only from the outside, aprioristically: "Voici la prose désordonnée, tumultueuse, tour à tour bravement encanaillée, ou lyrique éperdument de M. Diderot [one may note the ironic condescension of this 'Monsieur']. Il pratique le style sensible dans toute son horreur" etc. Lanson is here simply continuing the normative genre of criticism characteristic of Sainte-Beuve who, possessed as he thought himself to be of "*le* goût," believed he could cut Diderot in two, separating the good from the bad, Diderot's vivacity from his "exaggerations"—and who certainly did not practice, in regard to Diderot, what he declared to have learned from him: "Cette faculté de demi-métamorphose, qui est le jeu et le triomphe de la critique, et qui consiste à se mettre à la place de l'auteur et au point de vue du sujet qu'il examine, à lire tout écrit selon l'esprit qui l'a dicté" (*Causeries du Lundi,* II, 307). The critics of our day, too, fall into the a priori: H. Dieckmann, who has in recent times made the best contribution toward the unification of the seemingly contradictory opinions of Diderot (I must heartily subscribe to his statement, *Romanische Forsch.,* LII, 62: "Die fast unbestritten herrschende Auffassung von dem unbändigen und sprunghaften Denken Diderots ist einer der oberflächlichsten Irrtümer der Forschung") finds that in the majority of cases Diderot has expressed his ideas "inadequately" ("Diderot's Naturempfinden und Lebensgefühl," *Travaux du séminaire roman d'Istanbul,* I). But, surely, a judge of style, faced with what at first glance appears to him inadequate, should succeed in reaching finally a positive statement; "inadequately"[2] indicates an approach as aprioristic as is that of the dispensers of normative criticism (and, in fact, Dieckmann's is a type of normative criticism). The works of Folkierski, Gillot, and Luc list and discuss the aesthetic theories of Diderot, but what they have to say about his style is singularly shallow—witness such remarks (cited from Luc, p. 58) as: "Il écrit comme il parle. Trop mauvais artisan pour être un très grand artiste. . . . La facilité de la plume suffit. . . ." etc. Fritz Schalk, who has collected in his *Einleitung in die Encyclopädie der französischen Aufklärung* (Munich, 1936) Diderot's own programmatic utterances about his manner of writing (including his remark about its undecipherability), has refused to apply the technique of the philologian (direct observation of specific stylistic traits) by which this style could be made understandable. The best that has been written on Diderot is still, in my opinion, Groethuysen's article "La pensée de Diderot" in *La grande revue* (Nov. 15, 1913); later we shall see how our stylistic analysis squares with his interpretation of Diderot's ideas—after we shall have made some first-hand observations of our own.

Let us consider first, as a sample of Diderot's style, the (somewhat abridged) article "Jouissance," which he wrote for the *Encyclopédie* (Assézat, xv, 312):

JOUISSANCE, s.f. (Gram. et Morale). Jouir, c'est connaître, éprouver, sentir les avantages de posséder: on possède souvent sans jouir. A qui sont ces magnifiques palais? qui est-ce qui a planté ces jardins immenses? c'est le souverain: qui est-ce qui en jouit, c'est moi.

Mais laissons ces palais magnifiques que le souverain a construits pour d'autres que lui, ces jardins enchanteurs où il ne se promène jamais, et arrêtons-nous à la volupté qui perpétue la chaîne des êtres vivants, et à laquelle on a consacré le mot de *jouissance*.

Entre les objets que la nature offre de toutes parts à nos désirs, vous qui avez une âme, dites-moi, y en a-t-il un plus digne de notre poursuite, dont la possession et la *jouissance* puissent nous rendre aussi heureux que celles de l'être qui pense et sent comme vous, qui a les mêmes idées, qui éprouve la même chaleur, les mêmes transports, qui porte ses bras tendres et délicats vers les vôtres, qui vous enlace, et dont les caresses seront suivies de l'existence d'un nouvel être qui sera semblable à l'un de vous, qui dans ses premiers mouvements vous cherchera pour vous serrer, que vous élèverez à vos côtés, que vous aimerez ensemble, qui vous protégera dans votre vieillesse, qui vous respectera en tout temps, et dont la naissance heureuse a déjà fortifié le lien qui vous unissait? . . .

La propagation des êtres est le plus grand objet de la nature. Elle y sollicite impérieusement les deux sexes, aussitôt qu'ils en ont reçu ce qu'elle leur destinait de force et de beauté. Une inquiétude vague et mélancolique les avertit du moment; leur état est mêlé de peine et de plaisir. C'est alors qu'ils écoutent leurs sens, et qu'ils portent une attention réfléchie sur eux-mêmes. Un individu se présente-t-il à un individu de la même espèce et d'un sexe différent, le sentiment de tout autre besoin est suspendu; le coeur palpite; les membres tressaillent; des images voluptueuses errent dans le cerveau; des torrents d'esprits coulent dans les nerfs, les irritent, et vont se rendre au siège d'un nouveau sens qui se déclare et qui tourmente. La vue se trouble, le délire naît; la raison, esclave de l'instinct, se borne à le servir, et la nature est satisfaite.

C'est ainsi que les choses se passaient à la naissance du monde, et qu'elles se passent encore au fond de l'antre du sauvage adulte.

Mais lorsque la femme commença à discerner, lorsqu'elle parut mettre de l'attention dans son choix, et qu'entre plusieurs hommes sur lesquels la passion promenait ses regards, il y en eut un qui les arrêta, qui put se flatter d'être préféré, qui crut porter dans un coeur qu'il estimait l'estime qu'il faisait de lui-même, et qui regarda le plaisir comme la récompense de quelque mérite; lorsque les voiles que la pudeur jeta sur les charmes laissèrent à l'imagination enflammée le pouvoir d'en disposer à son gré, les illusions les plus délicates concoururent avec le sens le plus exquis pour exagérer le bonheur; l'âme fut saisie d'un enthousiasme presque divin; deux jeunes coeurs éperdus d'amour se vouèrent l'un à l'autre pour jamais, et le ciel entendit les premiers serments indiscrets.

Combien le jour n'eut-il pas d'instants heureux, avant celui où l'âme tout entière chercha à s'élancer et à se perdre dans l'âme de l'objet aimé! On eut des *jouissances* du moment où l'on espéra.

Cependant la confiance, le temps, la nature et la liberté des caresses, amenèrent l'oubli de soi-même; on jura, après avoir éprouvé la dernière ivresse, qu'il n'y en avait aucune autre qu'on pût lui comparer; et cela se trouva vrai toutes les fois qu'on y apporta des organes sensibles et jeunes, un coeur tendre et une âme innocente, qui ne connût ni la méfiance ni le remords.[2a]

After the initial definition of the word "jouissance," we find a description of one particular case of enjoyment, sexual enjoyment, as it acts on man, this psycho-physically conditioned being, and as it serves the purpose of Nature. Although the expressions used by Diderot belong to the technical terminology of the psychology and physiology current in his time (and, for the most part, also in ours): *sens, attention réfléchie, esprits, nerfs, instincts, passion, imagination, illusions, organes sensibles,* etc., we have here a poeticized picture of the factual reality of the sexual act. Dealing as he does with an act which is not easily describable in our civilization because of the feeling it arouses of the incongruity between the positive data and their implications, Diderot had to poeticize the positive facts; let us consider the way in which this transfiguration has been achieved.

In addition to several subsidiary devices (e.g. the apostrophe addressed to man) with which I shall deal later, there is one fundamental feature to be discerned in this passage: the symbolic rendering of the rhythm of feeling by the rhythm of language—an onomatopoeic rendering of feelings which one has been in the habit of dating from Flaubert. As we follow the development of the passage quoted, we note that the rhythmical correspondance begins only with the third paragraph; in the first and second brief paragraphs we are mainly conscious of Diderot's haste to arrive at the subject matter which is so congenial to him: that erotic *jouissance* which is for him the prototype of all enjoyment (here, he has no time to discuss the "enjoyment" of art or of Nature, about which he has shown himself elsewhere so competent to speak). And his mention, in the opening paragraph, of the magnificent gardens owned (but not enjoyed) by kings, serves to enforce, by contrast, the democratic principle: "all of you (who have a soul) have at your disposal an enchanted garden in which you may enjoy the most desirable gifts of Nature."[3] And, with the first words of the third paragraph, which deals with love at the primeval stage, there is a surge of forward movement, symbolizing the rush of young lovers toward a bodily union; the accelerating sentence is given constantly new impetus by the succession of relative clauses. In the next paragraph, which describes sexual love with greater precision, the sentences become shorter, more breathless; in the fifth paragraph, in which is depicted the union of beings at a more highly civilized level, the sentences flow again: the "divine enthusiasm" begotten by this union of souls is again (though in a calmer manner than in the preceding paragraph) figured by means of urgent clauses, in which the *lorsque*'s spur the sentence onward. And finally, in the closing lines, descriptive of that stable connubium with its possibility of periodic renewal, the tension of the sentence structure relaxes.

Within a framework devoted to the historical stages of mankind, with a development so reminiscent of Rousseau (natural stage: bodily union; advanced stage of civilization: union of souls; institutionalized stage: marriage), Diderot has managed to introduce a suggestion of the sexual act itself: the perturbation of the senses, consummation, and relaxation. Most of the passage could be read as a sober piece of historical prose; only the emotional ear of the reader perceives the inner vibrations which echo the surge of erotic emotions. But in paragraph four no reader can fail to sense immediately the physiological rhythm of an erotic moment, isolated from the historical flow. And if we compare the stylistic effectiveness of the different paragraphs it is not difficult to see where Diderot's artistic sensitivity vibrates most sympathetically; the calm of the final lines is due, in part at least, to a lag of emotional interest.

Let us consider more closely the third paragraph, where we have the first example of that stylistic correspondence we have described above; here, it is not only the union of the lovers, but also the fructification of this union, which is rendered by the rhythm of the sentences. Diderot begins by addressing to all men the rhetorical question (in so many words): "Tell me, is there any enjoyment [which means possession with full consciousness of possession] so beatifying as is the enjoyment derived from that being who is your mate?" He proceeds to define this mate, this counterpart of man, in a sentence consisting of a rhythmical sequence of anaphoras and parallelistic clauses which, while dwelling on the same basic motif (of the equality of the two beings—which I have pointed out by italics), mirrors the increasing intensity of feeling and intimacy:[4]

<table>
<tr><td>qui pense et sent comme vous,[5]</td><td></td></tr>
<tr><td>qui a les mêmes idées,</td><td></td></tr>
<tr><td>qui éprouve la même chaleur
les mêmes transports</td><td>[=sent comme vous
a physically]
b spiritually]</td></tr>
<tr><td>qui porte ses bras tendres et délicats vers les vôtres</td><td>[the epithets tendre, délicat have both a spiritual and a physical connotation]</td></tr>
<tr><td>qui vous enlace</td><td></td></tr>
</table>

And, with "et dont les caresses seront suivis de l'existence d'un nouvel être," this motif reaches its apex[6]—with which a new perspective is opened up: the existence of the new being. This being, which is dependent on the Beloved, figures now in another series of (secondary) relative clauses which are arranged in a temporal sequence depicting the growth and development of the child, and tending toward a new apex:

<table>
<tr><td>qui sera semblable à l'un de vous</td><td>[the motif "comme vous" continues now with the child]</td></tr>
<tr><td>qui dans ses premiers mouvements vous cherchera pour vous serrer</td><td>[the temporal sequence is indicated by "premiers"]</td></tr>
<tr><td>que vous élèverez à vos côtés</td><td></td></tr>
<tr><td>que vous aimerez ensemble</td><td>[cooperation of the two]</td></tr>
<tr><td>qui vous protégera dans votre vieillesse</td><td>[physically]</td></tr>
</table>

qui *vous* respectera en tout temps	[morally: *en tout temps* ends the temporal sequence and makes the time-bound relationship timeless]
et dont la naissance heureuse a déjà fortifié le lien qui *vous* unissait[7]	

With this last, we have a retrospective clause which suddenly refers us back to the moment of birth, at which the union (suggested by *enlacer*) of the lovers has been consolidated into a lasting bond (*lien*) ; with *déjà* and with the shift to the past tense (*a fortifié, unissait*), the line of temporal development is seen in reverse. The *dont la naissance* seals the clauses descriptive of the growing child, just as the *dont les caresses* had rounded off the lines dealing with the Beloved. And, in both sections, the repetition of the generic pronoun *vous* insists on the theme that the gift of Nature makes for an enrichment of the "vous (qui avez une âme)" : wife and children are both "known possessions," enrichments and aggrandizements of the Ego of man. The *vous*-motif is willed by Nature.

The diagram I have just outlined may make a painfully rationalistic and pedantic impression upon the reader, who could be tempted to argue that, if all the effects I have pointed out were deliberately intended by Diderot, he must have been absorbed in petty measurements of sentence members. But, obviously, all the devices I have discerned are assimilated only half-consciously by the reader, and we may surmise that Diderot himself found them half-consciously.

If we turn now to the physico-psychological picture of the act of sexual union as offered in the fourth paragraph, we will find that the symbolization of thought by sentence-structure is achieved in a quite different manner. In this passage, dealing as it does with man in the stage of pure sensuality, Nature appears at the beginning and at the end as a moving force: "La propagation des êtres est le plus grand objet de la Nature"; "et la Nature est satisfaite." The underlying idea is that Nature achieves her end, the propagation of the human species, by beclouding the reason of man before the act of procreation ("... le délire naît; la raison, esclave de l'instinct, se borne à le servir, et la nature est satisfaite").[8] And the paragraph as a whole is given up to a description of this state of perturbation—which is symbolized in the rhythm of the brief, breathless staccato sentences ("le coeur palpite, les membres tressaillent"); a suggestion of haste and impatience is given also by the temporal indications: "aussitôt que," "moment," "alors" (cf. also "un individu se présente-t-il" = "immediately when ..."). The poetic art of Diderot is the greater, the more factual and scientific is his description: he clearly distinguishes, within the state of perturbation ("inquiétude vague"), the flashes of intellectual clarity ("attention réfléchie"). Out of this alternation of emotional haze and mental clarity is born a "new sense," which has been the goal toward which the preliminary fluctuations tended—and this movement toward a goal is figured by the rhythm of the sentence "des torrents d'esprits coulent dans les nerfs, les irritent, et vont se rendre au siège d'un nouveau sens qui se déclare et tourmente."[9] The climax suggested by *tourmente* is maintained throughout the following sentence—until, with the final words "et la nature est satisfaite," the tension of the sentence relaxes. The closing phrase is fraught with a double meaning: from the point of view of the lovers, it is their nature, their animal nature, which is satiated; from the teleological point of view, the goal of Nature herself has been achieved. And the *et*, which introduces the announcement of the convergence of man's and Nature's urge, is a stylistic triumph; I would call it the "*et* of culmination," in which there is the reassuring echo of a beneficent world order.

Paragraph six, which is dedicated to the civilized stage of man, is arranged so as to form three groups, the first two of them being compound sentences containing temporal clauses introduced by *lorsque*, and the third consisting of three short separate independent clauses; the two clauses "l'âme fut saisie d'un enthousiasme[10] presque divin," and "deux jeunes coeurs éperdus d'amour se vouèrent l'un à l'autre pour jamais" lead to "et le ciel[11] entendit les premiers serments indiscrets"[12] (where again we find an example of the "*et* of culmination" equally insistent on a propitious world order). Nowhere in this paragraph do we find that fragmentary sentence structure which was used so felicitously in the preceding passage to render the state of emotional perturbation. The two compound sentences at the beginning are of the accelerating type we noted in paragraph three; in the last three clauses, the movement somewhat slackens, to suggest the calm, the lasting joy, of the quasi-mystic union. In reading this prose, which is addressed as well to the ear as to the mind, one will find one's voice rising steadily and uninterruptedly until the final terrace is reached—to correspond with the movement of the souls toward Heaven. For, in this paragraph, the divine emotion of the lovers inspires them to call upon Heaven as their witness and protector—in contrast to the preceding passage, in which the purely fleshly union was presided over by Nature. Indeed, the whole sixth paragraph appears as a transposition of the fourth on a higher plane. The development of monogamic marriage is a decisive step in the history of civilization: it is a mark of the progress from the state of Nature to the civilized state; and therefore, in this paragraph, the temporal aspect is stressed: by *lorsque*, and by the historical past tense; in paragraphs three and four we find the present: sexuality is an a-temporal phenomenon of man's nature. And it is also true that this decisive step of monogamy was taken when man became conscious of time: "deux jeunes coeurs se vouèrent l'un à l'autre *pour jamais*"; les *premiers* serments indiscrets . . ."; "combien le jour n'eut il pas d'*instants* heureux, avant celui où l'âme tout entière chercha à s'élancer et à se perdre. . . . On eut des jouissances *du moment* où l'on espèra." The time-consciousness which leads to the "mystic" union is itself a result of the development of man in time (we may assume that the Augustinian idea that time is engendered by the immortal divine soul of man is not quite absent from this passage).

And here, for the first time, Diderot deals with the stages leading up to the choice of a mate (indeed, only in the state of civilization can there be a question of individual choice), and with the additional factors by which love, on this higher level, is complicated (here, not before, we have a suggestion of what Stendhal was later to call "crystallization de l'amour") ; now, instead of the blindness and automatism of the pure sex urge, as pictured in paragraph four, mental deliberation is presented: the woman weighs the objective merits of her suitors—and it is important to note that, in the civilized stage, it is woman who takes the initiative (in this paragraph it is her mate who is described in dependent clauses). In this way the drama of hope and fear enters to complicate love. The second historical factor which Diderot mentions as contributing to the refinement of amorous sensibility is, interestingly enough, the clothed state of the lovers; by this avenue, not only suspense but illusion becomes possible. (The awkwardness of such a blunt juxtaposition of technical and spiritual cultural history: the weighing of individual merits — the wearing of clothes, cannot be denied). This reference to the illusionary effect of clothing is almost the only allusion to the bodily to be found in this paragraph; another may be seen in "après avoir éprouvé la dernière ivresse"—where, however, the erotic ecstasy is represented as a thing already past; in both cases the sensuous is brought in only indirectly.

But while there can be little doubt that the type of love described in this paragraph is presented as a higher form of the sexual relationship, it is indicative of Diderot's own natural preferences that it is here that, for the first time, a critical note enters; the note of disillusionment is unmistakable in Diderot's statement that the illusions made possible by civilization tend to "*exagérer* le bonheur" (must not "illusion" lead to disillusionment?) ; again, the delights of the "mystic" union are qualified as "un enthusiasme *presque* divin," while "l'âme tout entière *chercha* à s'élancer" suggests something quite different from the note of pure and uninhibited rapture which vibrates in the preceding paragraph.

And the rational element which had already been presented, in paragraph six, as a factor in the "love of two souls," becomes predominant in the last paragraph, dealing with the institutionalization of love: here the lovers are shown as rather soberly comparing the enjoyments of love with other pleasures, as calculating the possibilities of renewal within an established union—a union which will require some sacrifice of the individual's self, an "oubli de soi-même" which one cannot help contrasting with that concentration upon enjoyment ("attention réfléchie sur eux-mêmes"), upon the aggrandizement of the ego, which was stressed in paragraph four. And so it is fitting that the impersonal and gnomic *on* (which made its first appearance at the end of paragraph seven) should be used exclusively in the final paragraph. No longer are we given a picture of "les deux sexes" or of "deux jeunes coeurs" who rush to embrace: it is the colorless *on* which figures in the generalizations about marriage which Diderot offers. Indeed, here, it is the institution of marriage which is the protagonist, to which the individual must pay tribute; the *organes sensibles,* the *coeur tendre,* the *âme innocente* are now simply the preconditions for marriage which it is man's duty to fulfill.[13]

Throughout this article we have found an "innervation" of language by emotion, a translation into rhythm of emotions[14] —and the predominant emotion is that of a dynamic accelerating self-expansion, self-potentiation. This rhythmic translation, this innervation of language, seems to appear mainly in two forms: there is the breathless, tense, cramped "style coupé" which was prominent in paragraph four, and the freer flow of the longer periods, which was in evidence in the other passages. It was the first type, with its suggestion of automatism, which was used in the description of the most sensuous aspects of connubium: indeed, it is the rhythm of orgasm itself.[15] And, whenever it appears, it may be taken as a sure indication that the phenomenon described (or, the description itself!) is felt by Diderot as a physical, nervous experience.[16] In contrast, the more flowing rhythm seems to denote a state of enthusiasm in which body and soul are fused in a more harmonious expansion.

The passage we have just chosen for our first orientation in the style of Diderot describes, variously, the psychophysical harmony of a sexual relationship in which body and soul are in unison and which serves Nature, society, and Heaven. But Diderot, with his gift of psycho-physical innervation of language, was equally able to adapt his style to the description of disharmony. Let us choose, as an extreme case of disharmony, an example of perversion, as it is found in the scene of the homosexual Mother Superior in *La religieuse*, in whom emotional unsteadiness, hypocrisy, and natural kindness are inextricably mixed. After having finally succeeded in drawing out of the young nun, Suzanne, the account of the hardships and persecutions she had endured in the convent where she had previously been established, she gives vent to her mingled emotions in the following words (as reported by Suzanne in a memorandum addressed to a certain marquis before whom she wishes to justify herself): " 'Les méchantes créatures! Les horribles créatures! Il n'y a que dans les couvents où l'humanité puisse s'éteindre à ce point. . . . Heureusement je suis douce; j'aime toutes mes religieuses; elles ont pris, les unes plus, les autres moins, de mon caractère, et toutes elles s'aiment entre elles. Mais comment cette faible santé a-t-elle pu résister à tant de tourments? Comment tous ces petits membres n'ont-ils pas été brisés? Comment toute cette machine délicate n'a-t-elle pas été détruite? Comment l'éclat de ces yeux n'est-il pas éteint dans les larmes? Les cruelles! Serrer ces bras avec des cordes!' Et elle les baisait. 'Arracher la plainte et le gémissement à cette bouche!' Et elle la baisait. 'Condamner ce visage charmant et serein à se couvrir sans cesse des nuages de la tristesse!' Et elle le baisait. 'Faner les roses de ces joues!' Et elle les flattait de la main et les baisait. 'Déparer cette tête! arracher ces cheveux! charger ce front de souci!' Et elle baisait ma tête, mon front, mes cheveux. 'Oser entourer ce cou d'une corde, et déchirer ces épaules avec des pointes aigües!' Et elle écartait mon linge de cou et de tête; elle entr'ouvrait le haut de ma robe; mes cheveux tombaient épars sur mes épaules découvertes; ma poitrine était à demi-nue, et ses baisers se répandaient sur mon cou, sur mes épaules découvertes et sur ma poitrine à deminue."

This passage begins smoothly enough, with no hint of anything shocking or even startling. The Mother Superior's opening words have the lulling quality of platitudes; Diderot has prepared us for them by previous statements as to the conditions prevailing in convents ("Ah! monsieur, les méchantes créatures que des femmes recluses. . . !" had been said earlier by Suzanne herself [p. 75], while her former Mother Superior had remarked to her [p. 68]: "Entre toutes ces créatures que vous voyez autour de moi, si dociles, si innocentes, si douces, eh bien! mon enfant, il n'y en a presque pas une, non, presque pas une, dont je ne puisse faire une bête féroce"). And, as the Mother Superior begins her series of pitying exclamations over the violence visited upon the body of the nun, we seem to be following a familiar path: we had already been given Suzanne's own detailed account, which the Mother Superior is evidently here reproducing factually, if with embellishments. It is only gradually that we realize that what is unfolding before us is no repetition but a ghastly parody. Even the first caresses might be accepted as manifestations of genuine (if highly sentimental) compassion—but we soon become aware that this is the working of an automatism which cannot stop.

It is also evident that we are offered here the picture of a nature working on two planes simultaneously; we realize that we must constantly distinguish between words and deeds. The Mother Superior would convince Suzanne by her words that she is moved by a mellow Christian spirit, by an abhorrence of inhumane acts; but her own acts reveal themselves more and more clearly as manifestations of a selfish sexual love which would exploit the same young body that had been so cruelly tortured. At first, of course, there is only one track: in the opening lines (from "les cruelles! . . ." to ". . . les cruelles!") her reactions are purely verbal, as she recapitulates the total injury done to "cette machine délicate." But when she begins to list separately the details of Suzanne's torture, limb by limb, she accompanies this account with gestures—as if restaging the painful incidents in a "contrapasso" of love. But we sense with horror that we are witnessing, instead, a new assault on the nun's body. And surely Diderot means to stress the parallelism of the two criminal procedures: each limb that had been tortured is now violated by caresses (even the detail of the "cheveux épars" reappears), to the accompaniment of soft words of compassion.[17]

The double track which is so evident in the behavior of the Mother Superior bears witness, obviously, to a basic split in her personality: in one part of her being, as manifested in her speech, she desires to appear (and, perhaps, even to be) purely compassionate; in another part of her being, which reveals itself in her gestures, the covetous will of the body rules. In her acts she is moved from below, she behaves, that is "hypo-critically" (Gr. ὑπόκρισις "thinking from below"); Diderot knew that bodily perversion is necessarily linked with hypocrisy.

We spoke earlier of the suggestion of automatism in this passage. It is interesting to see to what pains Diderot goes to enforce this impression. The most obvious trait is the fact that each anatomical reference is accompanied, without fail, by a gesture. But the automatism is present not only in this mechanical coupling of speech and gesture: it can be seen also in the speech considered in itself, and in the gestures (and the manner in which they are reported). As for the words of the Mother Superior, these consist of a sequence of conventional, sentimental expressions—which constitute, as it were, a variant of the "blason," in which, according to tradition, each member of the beloved body is praised in turn; in her recital, accompanied by gestures, we have a grotesque reminder of the origin of this literary genre, which grew up out of the religious practice of the *exercitium spirituale* which requires the believer to visualize every stage of Christ's bodily suffering; with the perverted Mother Superior, this becomes an *exercitium corporale*, in which the visualization becomes enactment. And the law of this genre is the law of automatism: once the first step is taken the process must run its course. In our passage the monotony of the process is reflected in the invariability of construction: the sequence of infinitives, the anaphoric repetition, first of exclamatory questions (*comment* . . . .), then of demonstrative pronouns.

And the same dulling monotony of construction appears, to an extreme degree, in the refrain which announces each succeeding gesture (which is always the same: a kiss that becomes increasingly more revelatory and more menacing): "et elle le[s] baisait." The repetition of this formula has a hypnotic effect—which is enhanced by the fact that it is the victim herself who is speaking, and whose words thus seem to reflect the hypnotic state[18] induced in her by the evil automatism of the Mother Superior (earlier Diderot had referred to the "contagion" which had spread from the malady of this woman). An important stylistic element of the refrain is the conjunction *et*, which seems to me to represent a parody of the sublime "fiat lux *et* lux facta est."[19] In the Biblical expression we have the suggestion of a "divine automatism," as it were, according to which a wish is inevitably followed by its fulfillment; thus, by means of this pattern, a vicious realization of desire is presented as if it were a natural, a sanctioned consequence. In the case of "serrer ces bras. . . ! . . . et elle les baisait," obviously, the desire which is realized has not been expressed in words. But the accompanying gestures reveal the true meaning of the Mother Superior's words—which, in themselves, could be ambiguous. Little by little, it has become evident that her speech, in which she intended to convey a generous sympathy, has become infected with the selfish possessiveness of her physical acts. Words-and-gestures form an inseparable couple, and from the moment the sequence of these couples is begun, the physical dynamism of the gesture[20] endows them with a mechanical, accelerating movement, a movement toward the abyss—until, finally, words cease entirely and sensuality is rampant: "Ces baisers se répandaient. . . ."

Can we recognize in this passage, as we were able to do in the article on "jouissance," a rhythmical reproduction of the subject matter? It is evident that here we have to do with the mechanical repetition of two alternating rhythmical patterns: the high-flown, sentimentally poetic language of the exclamations ("faner les roses . . . !"), and the emotionless, factual refrain, "et elle le baisait"—which has obviously an ironical flavor. We have to do with two rhythms, one of which mocks the other. In each of the couples formed by these two jarring patterns, as in the passage as a whole, there is reflected the split personality of the hypocritical pervert.

At the same time it is true that this passage, with its description of words and gestures, is but one overflow of emotion, continuously increasing until the climax of uninhibited, overt, vicious love-making is reached—a stream of feelings which tend to flood all dams. And the words chosen by Diderot echo this urge of self-potentiation on the part of an individual who wants to break her chains and to experience unfettered exaltation; they also reveal the ominous presence of the mechanism behind the foolish enterprise. Recapitulating our finds in the two passages quoted from Diderot, we see in both the same motif of self-potentiation—though complicated and retarded in the second case by inhibition—a motif which we may state to be basic to Diderot's *Lebensgefühl.* His most effective or conspicuous passages, those in which one feels the vibrations of Diderot's own nature,[21] will always be those which describe the emotional movement of an individual "hors de lui-même."

In both examples above, the emotion has been one of sexual passion; our discussion so far may have given the impression that Diderot is given mainly to such descriptions. As a matter of fact, I am convinced that the sexual act, with its power of expanding the individual, is the *Grunderlebnis* for Diderot (from Diderot's time to our own, his critics have mentioned his overflowing sensuousness, his indulgence in the *graveleux*, etc.) and that he is at his best in achieving what we have called the "innervation of language by emotion" when he has to translate into language the vibration of the senses. But his "innervation" has a wider range: he is able to translate rhythmically the "vibrations" of imagination—though here, too, the sensuous origin, even the sexual origin, of the emotional pattern may be discerned. That it is not the reverse process which has taken place, I infer not only from the well-known sensualistic approach of Diderot's philosophy, but also from the more general consideration that, in linguistics, the concrete precedes the abstract: the "etymology" of a stylistic pattern must be found in that situation which is closest to concrete, to sensuous, reality. It was just such reality which prevailed in the two previous passages, where we have found the close congruity of style and reality; whatever of similarity we may find in other, less obviously sensuous, passages must be considered as a secondary application of patterns based primarily on the sexual.

I shall choose for comment here one from many comparable

passages in Diderot's *Le neveu de Rameau*; in my citation I have adopted a somewhat clearer distinction between narration and speech than is to be found in the Assézat edition (v, 399): "Puis il se remit à chanter l'ouverture des 'Indes galantes' et l'air 'Profonds abîmes' [of Rameau the uncle], et il ajoutait: Le quelque chose qui est là et qui me parle me dit: Rameau, tu voudrais bien avoir fait ces deux morceaux-là; si tu avais fait ces morceaux-là, tu en ferais bien deux autres; et quand tu en aurais fait un certain nombre, on te jouerait, on te chanterait partout. Quand tu marcherais, tu aurais la tête droite, ta conscience te rendrait témoignage à toi-même de ton propre mérite, les autres te désigneroient du doigt, on dirait: C'est lui qui a fait les jolies gavottes (et il chantait les gavottes: Puis avec l'air d'un homme touché qui nage dans la joie et qui en a les yeux humides, il ajoutait en se frottant les mains:) Tu aurais une bonne maison (il en mesurait l'étendue avec ses bras,) un bon lit (et il s'y étendait nonchalament,) de bons vins (qu'il goûtait en faisant claquer la langue contre son palais,) un bon équipage (et il levait le pied pour y monter), de jolies femmes (à qui il prenait déjà la gorge et qu'il regardait voluptueusement); cent faquins te viendraient encenser tous les jours (et il croyait les voir autour de lui: il voyait Pelissot, Poinsinet . . . il les entendait, il se rengorgeait, les approuvait, leur souriait, les dédaignait, les méprisait, les chassait, les rappelait; puis il continuait:) Et c'est ainsi que l'on te dirait le matin que tu es un grand homme; tu lirais dans l'histoire des Trois Siècles que tu es un grand homme, tu serais convaincu le soir que tu es un grand homme, et le grand homme Rameau s'endormirait au doux murmure de l'éloge qui retentirait dans son oreille même en dormant, il aurait l'air satisfait: sa poitrine se dilaterait, s'élèverait, s'abaisserait avec aisance, il ronflerait comme un grand homme . . . (Et en parlant ainsi, il se laissait aller mollement sur une banquette; il fermait les yeux, et il imitait le sommeil heureux qu'il imaginait. Après avoir goûté quelques instants la douceur de ce repos, il se réveillait, étendait les bras, bâillait, se frottait les yeux, et cherchait autour de lui ses adulateurs insipides)."

If, in the case of the Mother Superior of *La religieuse*, the intended significance of the words was given a lie by the gestures, which represented the peremptory will of the body, here, the gestures merely execute what the words outspokenly imply. But in both cases it is true that the words unleash gestures by which they are expanded, by which they are prolonged and multiplied, as it were: the gestures are the potentiation afforded by the body in reaction to the thoughts expressed by the words. Again, in the previous passage, we had occasion to point out the suggestion of automatism present in the description of the emotional development; this ended with a picture of the machine triumphant; we were not shown the moment after, when the machinery runs down—though it was only too obvious that such emotional tension must end in self-annihilation. In the paragraph just quoted from *Le neveu*, we are also given the picture of a machinery in accelerating motion, but this does finally break down before our eyes.[22] We see a character who starts with a hypothetical situation ("If I had composed the two arias of my uncle") which he elaborates upon at greater and greater length, accompanying each new fiction with appropriate, vivid gestures, until he is finally exhausted by the physical and emotional energy he has expended. These gestures, called into being by the vivacity of his imagination, begin by being only accessory embellishments,[23] whose meaning and whose validity is determined exactly by the meaning and validity of the words. In the course of the elaboration, however, to the extent that the words depart further and further from reality, the gestures become more and more impassioned and evocative, they come more and more to constitute a reality in themselves—and as such they react upon the speaker himself, who ends by being convinced by his own gestures: the passage ends with the nephew completely seduced by his own imaginative pantomime.

In this incident Diderot has summed up the character of the nephew—as in the nephew himself he has symbolized the paradox of artistic existence; this whole dialogue is a pendant to the *Paradoxe sur le comédien*. The nephew is gifted with extraordinary powers of expression which seek immediate form, but the very talents which enable him to find so easily and so quickly an appropriate form are ultimately responsible for his failure to embody his artistic gifts in a form that is permanent and has objective reality. The nephew is presented as a performer, an imitator, instead of as creator (he sings well the airs of his uncle, which he could never have composed). Diderot was well aware that every creative artist must be first of all an imitator—just as every imitator, every performer, has the possibility of being creative,[24] in his way, if he can distinguish between the two planes. The tragedy of the nephew lies in his inability to make this distinction: as he listens to himself singing the arias his uncle has composed, he has the sensation of being a creator like his uncle, of being a "grand homme" ready made, with all the practical consequences that would follow therefrom.[25]

The philosopher, who cares only to discern truth is, according to Diderot's statements in *Le neveu*, by nature unmimical, and is thereby preserved from the danger which threatens every artist. It could be said that, in this dialogue, Diderot the philosopher is instituting a trial against his own artistic sensitivity, with all its expressive, impersonating, pantomimic, caricaturing, satirical elements.

As we read this treatment of a being who becomes the victim of his heated imagination, we could be reminded of episodes in Rabelais where a fantastic spinner of tales has been duped by his own fabrications: for example, that of Picrochole and his advisers who conquer the world in their dreams and are henceforth able to speak of the conquest in the past tense. And yet, when we read Rabelais' account we are only amused; it makes no impact on our nervous system. But no one, I believe, can read this description of the nephew without sharing something of the nervous anguish of the author Diderot who, in this dialogue as a whole, is so deeply concerned with the problem of artistic activity: the paradox that the artist, by his enthusiasm for reproducing reality, may falsify all reality including his own, the paradox that hypervitality leads ultimately to self-destruction. And, indeed, it is a diminutive death that we witness in this passage. As we see the self-exhausted body slump before us in a half-fictitious sleep, there is a suggestion of physical decay.

And Diderot has been able to render by the rhythm of his

style the process by which hypervitality leads to self-destruction. In the first part of the passage we find the devices of gradation and increase and expansion, which are already familiar to us and which indicate a heightening of emotion (as the "machine" picks up speed) : as the nephew's fanciful construction is built higher and higher, the rhythm of his speech is accelerated until, with "le grand homme" the apex is reached and the decline sets in: at first "le grand homme," repeated, maintains the high point, but then, by virtue of this repetition, this "perseveration" of automatism,[26] what had been a stimulant becomes a soporific, as the dreamed-of state (expressed by a sequence of conditional tenses) yields to the reality of exhaustion. The same curve of movement is to be seen in the language describing the gestures: we may note the accelerating *déjà,* and the string of imperfects following upon each other pell-mell, depicting the progress of self-infatuation ("il croyait voir - il voyait . . . - il les entendait"), with all the contradictions of his momentary moods ("les chassait, les rappelait," etc.).[27] In the final gestures that accompany his awakening, the planes of reality and irreality are so confused that we hardly know whether it is the exhausted, bemused actor or the *grand homme* he thinks he has become, who is gesticulating. Here, just as in the passage describing the Mother Superior, the gestures "take over": in the first case they serve to reveal the true meaning latent in ambiguous words; in the second, they have the effect of establishing an artificial reality out of hypothetical words. In both cases alike the movement is generated by the dynamism of the gestures—the actual bodily force which Diderot has made us feel by language.

We have said that the self-destruction brought about by excessive expressivity was seen by Diderot as a danger to which any artistic nature is exposed, and about which he was particularly apprehensive in his own case. It is true that numerous passages can be found (as quoted in Schalk's article) in which Diderot praises his own "désordre toujours nouveau" and states with apparent nonchalance: "je jette mes idées sur le papier et elles deviennent ce qu'elles peuvent"; he also quotes appreciatively Montaigne's self-description: "ou par la résistance d'un aultre, ou par la propre chaleur de ma narration, je grossis et enfle mon subject par voix, mouvements, vigueur et force de paroles, et encore par extension et amplification, non sans interest de la vérité naifve. . . . La parole vifve et bruyante, comme est la mienne ordinaire, s'emporte volontiers à l'hyperbole." But it must not be overlooked that Diderot was aware of the threat to any true representation of reality inherent in the "realistic" gifts of "grossissement," "extension," "amplification." It is for this reason that, in the *Paradoxe sur le comédien*,[28] and in the *Rêve de D'Alembert*, he develops the thesis that the great artist (as well as the great scientist) should strive to be cool-minded and rational, instead of giving way to his emotions, and that he expresses his distrust of the tears coming from the nervous system, the "entrailles" of the actor—a distrust Montaigne would have calmly smiled away. Montaigne, who was as little nervous over the problem of reality as was Rabelais, never doubted that he was pursuing a positive course to the goal of the "vérité naifve"; and, though he may have harbored many doubts and even fears, he knew the nature of his feelings as unquestionable and precisely definable realities. With Diderot we have an existential doubt as to the reality of the artistic existence; he is torn between feverish enthusiasm and despair as he sees the consequences of artistic sensitivity in its contact with life. It is as if he has created the nephew out of the doubtful material of his own artistic nature, as a gesture of rejection and condemnation.[29]

In this scene, we must believe that Diderot's condemnation of expressivity is absolute: we are given a vivid picture of decomposition with no suggestion of any higher principle in whose service the enthusiasm is exerted—an enthusiasm inspired by self-infatuation and by a concern for worldly advantage. Later on in the dialogue, when he comes to talk of the new musical trends in contemporary opera, the nephew is again caught up in a rapture that leads to a collapse of his being. But, in this case, his enthusiasm serves the noble purpose of championing the cause of the new music; accordingly, the reactions of Diderot himself (which he did not trouble to express in the earlier scene) are mingled: "Admirais-je? Oui, j'admirais. Étais-je touché de pitié? j'étais touché de pitié; mais une teinte de ridicule était fondue dans ces sentiments et les dénaturait."[30]

It is in this same scene that Diderot, who figures in the dialogue as MOI, asks his own creation how it could be that a person of such taste and such powers of discrimination in music could be so lacking in moral sensitivity.[31] And he has the nephew answer that his musical sensitivity has necessarily entailed the underdevelopment of his moral fiber. In this answer, which Diderot, as MOI, does not contest, the amorality of an artist is presented as a necessary concomitant of the "sensitive," expressive, artistic temperament. Goethe, in the notes to his translation of *Le neveu*, sums up this figure as a characterless adulator, an opportunist capable of any crime and deserving our contempt and hatred (the only touch of stability and dignity being revealed in his serious, disinterested discussion of musicological problems).[32] What Goethe has failed to see is the fact that the characterlessness of the nephew is only a consequence of his artistic mutability[33]—which is the primary factor of his being. It is difficult to understand that Goethe the artist should have failed to discover in this dialogue Diderot's concern with the moral paradox involved in all artistry,[34] the amorality which stems from the artistic impulse itself, the shamelessness of the performer (which prompted, in our times, the tenor Gigli to offer himself immediately to the Allied authorities occupying Rome, with the words: "I have sung for Mussolini and for the Germans—and now I will sing for you"). But, at the same time, the easy espousal of the opportunities of the moment can also lead to actions which, in another person, would be accepted as evidence of great character. The nephew does not always act as a parasite, an opportunist: he is capable of at least an occasional outburst of generous indignation which will cost him an opportunity for easy living—and which he prefers to sacrifice rather than give up the opportunity of shaming his host by an appeal to standards of "un peu de goût, un peu d'esprit, un peu de raison." The nephew belongs to the line of the "grands vauriens" (to use the epithet which Diderot applies to him elsewhere in the dialogue) who enact "la pantomime des gueux" in French literature: Renard the Fox, Panurge, *Mascarillus fourbum imperator*, Sganarelle, Gil Blas, Figaro; he is of those who let themselves live "au jour le jour," giving evidence of intelligence and of a critical, skeptical spirit: near-artists, serving as catalytic agents in an inert society, virtuosos of intellectual mobility who can stir up thinking in their fellow men. In the nephew we have the *raw material* of an artist and we see the conflicts which his artistic nature must bring upon him in a bourgeois society: essentially bourgeois in the enjoyments he desires, he is able to criticize the narrowness of bourgeois society. Diderot has posited the problem of the bourgeois artist with a clarity unequaled by the Romantics.

I have found it necessary to expatiate at such length on the basic idea underlying the *Neveu de Rameau* because, in my opinion, this had not been fully understood by the critics, and also because it is this idea (i.e. the paradox involved in the enthusiasm of a "sensitive" musician) which determines the rhythmic patterns of the long monologues of the nephew which make up the main bulk of this work. Let us now return to the second of our two pendant scenes, to the one in which the nephew, as he impersonates his musical ideal, is shown moving on a higher level, and in which Diderot's language manages to record this change of altitude. Here the nephew's fury of enthusiasm is described as having the dimensions and the connotations of a cosmic upheaval. Here, too, traces of physical disintegration are portrayed: saliva drips from his mouth as he speaks and, at the end of a seizure of gesticulation, he falls into a coma of exhaustion, from which he awakens with a start, wild-eyed, staring at imaginary bystanders. As Diderot reports the scene: "Mais vous vous seriez échappé en éclats de rire à la manière dont il contrefaisait les différents instruments; avec des joues renflées et bouffies, et un son rauque et sombre, il rendait les cors et les bassons; il prenait un son éclatant et nasillard pour les hautbois; précipitant sa voix avec une rapidité incroyable pour les instruments à corde dont il cherchait les sons les plus approchés; il sifflait les petites flûtes, il roucoulait les traversières; criant, chantant, se démenant comme un forcené, faisant lui seul les danseurs, les danseuses, les chanteurs, les chanteuses, tout un orchestre, tout un théâtre lyrique, et se divisant en vingt rôles divers; courant, s'arrêtant avec l'air d'un énergumène, étincelant des yeux, écumant de la bouche.

"... Que ne lui vis-je pas faire? Il pleurait, il riait, il soupirait, il regardait ou attendri, ou tranquille, ou furieux; c'était une femme qui se pâme de douleur, c'était un malheureux livré à tout son désespoir; un temple qui s'élève; des oiseaux qui se taisent au soleil couchant; des eaux ou qui murmurent dans un lieu solitaire et frais, ou qui descendent en torrent du haut des montagnes; un orage, une tempête, la plainte de ceux qui vont périr, mêlée au sifflement des vents, au fracas du tonnerre. C'était la nuit avec ses ténèbres, c'était l'ombre et le silence, car le silence même se peint par des sons. Sa tête était tout à fait perdue.

"Épuisé de fatigue, tel qu'un homme qui sort d'un profond sommeil ou d'une longue distraction, il resta immobile, stupide, étonné; il tournait ses regards autour de lui comme un homme égaré qui cherche à reconnaître le lieu où il se trouve; il attendait le retour de ses forces et de ses esprits; il essuyait machinalement son visage. Semblable à celui qui verrait à son réveil son lit environné d'un grand nombre de personnes dans un entier oubli ou dans une profonde ignorance de ce qu'il a fait, il s'écria dans le premier moment: 'Eh bien, messieurs, qu'est-ce qu'il y a? . . . D'où viennent vos ris et votre surprise? Qu'est-ce qu'il y a? . . .' Ensuite il ajouta: 'Voilà ce qu'on doit appeler de la musique et un musicien!' "

Here, the self-potentiation of the nephew which leads to exhaustion is, as we have said before, in the service of the noble cause of true (that is, in his way of thinking, expressive) music and, consequently, Diderot has insisted more on the creative aspects of the enthusiast's cosmic expansion than on its mechanistic aspects. Here, no words are reported, no gesture is specifically described, so that we cannot follow any development of automatism in the nephew's emotional state. The narrative of Diderot falls into three parts: the first describes the strange sounds uttered by the nephew (with the corresponding postures) ; in the second, these are interpreted; and only in the third does Diderot concentrate our attention on the physical state of the nephew. The nephew, instead of speaking, lends his voice to imitating an orchestra, becoming himself a living vocal instrument, and impersonating a Wagnerian-like *Gesamtkunstwerk*; when the meaning of this (imitated) orchestra is revealed, we recognize it as a world orchestra, echoing the music of the universe. The corybantic rapture which seizes the nephew is comparable to that invasion of the priest of Dionysos by his god, to that self-identification of the imitator with the cosmic force invading him, which, according to Nietzsche, has led to the birth of tragedy.

In the first paragraph quoted, we witness in the movement of the period the self-acceleration and self-potentiation of language which corresponds to the expansion and self-multiplication of the protagonist himself ("faisant lui seul les danseurs, les danseuses, les chanteurs, les chanteuses; tout un orchestre, tout un théâtre lyrique . . .") ; in the second, the human and the natural forces unleashed by world harmony are given their full range and gradually subside, returning to that "music of silence" ("le silence même se peint par des sons") which already the Pythagoreans had discovered: the crescendo in which vague tumultuous forces make themselves heard ("une femme . . . un malheureux . . . un temple . . . des oiseaux . . . des eaux . . . un orage, une tempête") yields to a decrescendo in which quieter and more familiar elements emerge: "la nuit avec ses ténèbres . . . l'ombre et le silence"; this descent from the apex of "un temple qui s'élève" has been already suggested by "des eaux . . . qui descendent en torrent du haut des montagnes." The music of silence to which all music returns (as to the dominant in *Abt Vogler*) is the symbol of subsiding cosmic forces—and of the exhaustion of the "énergumène." In the third paragraph we witness the blankness of the nephew's mind as he awakens from his coma ("il resta immobile, stupide, étonné"—three epithets asyndetically juxtaposed, which sustain the mood of stupefaction). The idea of automatism is faintly suggested by *machinalement*;[35] but even in this description of collapse, the machine is not made to swallow up the man—who is able to conclude his "demonstration" with the words: "Voilà ce qu'on doit appeler de la musique et un musicien!" (here is stated the problematic connection between expressive music and expressive musicianship), and to proceed immediately to further discussion. Self-potentiation by music is allowed for a moment to dominate in the being of this Protean actor-of-himself. Later, the nephew will again turn to grimaces and become again a mechanical "pagodah" ("Quand elle [Nature] fagota son [Rameau the Elder's] neveu, elle fit la grimace, et puis la grimace, et puis la grimace encore. Et en disant ces mots, il faisait toutes sortes de grimaces du visage: c'était le mépris, le dédain, l'ironie, et il semblait pétrir entre ses doigts un morceau de pâte, et sourire aux formes qu'il lui donnait; cela fait, il jeta la pagode hétéroclite loin de lui et dit: 'C'est ainsi qu'elle me fit et qu'elle me jeta à côté d'autres pagodes. . . .' ").[36] But in our passage no mechanism is allowed to seize our attention; rhythm is lost in meaning.[37]

This passage of *Le neveu de Rameau*, which describes the invasion by creative enthusiasm, is not isolated in Diderot's work—where we can find depicted various degrees of creative exaltation. At a low rung of the ladder (not far above the place assignable to the first description of the nephew), we may place the following passage from *Sur les femmes*, in which is presented the hysteria of the visionary Karsch: "Lorsque la Prusienne Karsch lève son oeil vers le ciel enflammé d'éclairs, elle voit Dieu dans le nuage. . . . Cependant la recluse dans sa cellule se sent élever dans les airs; son âme se répand dans le sein de la Divinité; son essence se mêle à l'essence divine; elle se pâme; elle se meurt; sa poitrine s'élève et s'abaisse avec rapidité; ses compagnes, attroupées autour d'elle, coupent les lacets de son vêtement. . . . La nuit vient; elle entend les choeurs célestes; sa voix s'unit à leurs concerts. Ensuite elle redescend sur la terre; elle parle de joies ineffables; on l'écoute: elle est convaincue."

Here we have a development through a nervous state toward heavenly peace and a final return to the earth. It is particularly interesting that the "style coupé," the style of nervousness, prevails even when the mystic's heavenly vision is recorded: there is not the musical flow which would be consonant with the celestial concerts she is supposed to hear—probably because Diderot himself could not hear the heavenly concerts that Raphael's Saint Cecilia chanted in her heart as well as he was able to hear the music of the nephew's orchestra.

In the next example we have a description of the poet being visited by enthusiasm. While this has much in common with the second vision of the nephew, we are spared here the description of the state of physical collapse: that painful awakening of the creative poetic genius from his trance, from the Saturnine process of self-consumption: "L'enthousiasme naît d'un objet de la nature. Si l'esprit l'a vu sous des aspects frappants et divers, il en est occupé, agité, tourmenté. L'imagination s'échauffe; la passion s'émeute. On est successivement étonné, attendri, indigné, courroucé. . . . Le poète sent le moment de l'enthousiasme; c'est après qu'il a médité. Il s'annonce en lui par un frémissement qui part de sa poitrine, et qui passe, d'une manière délicieuse et rapide, jusqu'aux extrémités de son corps. Bientôt ce n'est plus un frémissement; c'est une chaleur forte et permanente qui l'embrasse, le fait haleter, qui le consume, qui le tue, mais qui donne l'âme, la vie à tout ce qu'il touche. Si cette chaleur s'accroissait encore, les spectres se multiplieraient devant lui. Sa passion s'élèverait presque au degré de la fureur. Il ne connaîtrait de soulagement qu'à verser au dehors un torrent d'idées qui se pressent, se heurtent et se chassent."

But, on the other hand, it is even more impregnated with that "physical rhythm" (as was also the description of the mystic's enthusiasm) which we noted in the article on "jouissance."[38] H. Dieckmann, in his article on "genius," has pointed out the importance for the history of ideas of this passage which, instead of giving, in the manner of the seventeenth century, a pompous, rhetorical definition of the genius, describes critically an inner experience of Diderot himself: "the nature, the origin, the importance of the genius find their congruous expression, because Diderot is capable of attaining the same degree of inner tension and intensity which he tries to describe." But Dieckmann has failed to note the stylistic kinship of the paragraph on the creative experience of genius with that on sexual experience—a kinship which allows us to recognize the inner parentage between Diderot's feeling of the creative in art and that of the creative in Nature. In this connection we may quote Rilke's remarks (*Briefe an einen jungen Dichter*, p. 20) on R. Dehmel (whose life program was "brünstig leben und dichten"), in which Rilke points out the identity of the artistic and the sexual act: "Und tatsächlich liegt ja künstlerisches Erleben so unglaublich nahe am geschlechtlichen, an seinem Weh und an seiner Lust, dass die beiden Erscheinungen eigentlich nur verschiedene Formen einer und derselben Sehnsucht und Seligkeit sind. Und wenn man statt Brunst Geschlecht sagen dürfte, Geschlecht im grossen, weiten, reinen, durch keinen Kirchenirrtum verdächtigten Sinne, so wäre seine Kunst sehr gross und unendlich wichtig. Seine dichterische Kraft ist gross und wie ein Urtrieb stark, sie hat eigene rücksichtslose Rhythmen in sich und bricht wie aus Bergen aus ihm heraus."

In all the preceding descriptions of "states of being," the subject described has been swept away by his emotions, the usual pattern (whether using the "style coupé" or the more flowing rhythm) being that of exaltation followed by deflation. In the following dialogue (from the *Rêve de D'Alembert*), too, the movements of rise and fall may be discerned:

MLLE. DE L'ESPINASSE: Il m'a semblé plusieurs fois en rêve—

BORDEU: Et aux malades dans une attaque de goutte—

MLLE. DE L'E.: Que je devenais immense.

B.: Que leur pied touchait au ciel de leur lit.

MLLE. DE L'E.: Que mes bras et mes jambes s'allongeaient à l'infini, que le reste de mon corps prenait un volume proportionné; que l'Encélade de la fable n'était qu'un pygmée; que l'Amphitrite d'Ovide, dont les longs bras allaient former une ceinture immense à la terre, n'était qu'une naine en comparaison de moi, et que j'escaladais le ciel et que j'enlaçais les deux hémisphères.

B.: Fort bien. Et moi j'ai connu une femme en qui le phénomène s'exécutait en sens contraire.

MLLE. DE L'E.: Quoi! elle se rapetissait par degrés, et rentrait en elle-même?

B.: Au point de se sentir aussi menue qu'une aiguille: elle

> voyait, elle entendait, elle raisonmait, elle jugeait; elle avait un effroi mortel de se perdre; elle frémissait à l'approche des moindres objets; elle n'osait bouger de sa place.

When the feeling of expansion prevails in the speakers, the sentences have a free, uninterrupted flow, both partners seeming to sing a duet on the theme of expansion into the infinite; when that of contraction prevails, the "style coupé" is used (*fort bien* and *quoi*! are jerky interruptions of the flow; the asyndetons depict the perturbation caused by the "contraction").

There is, however, an important difference between this passage and all the others which we have considered: the speakers (the physician Bordeu and the intellectual Mlle. de l'Espinasse) are not emotionally shaken; they are giving an objective description of certain psycho-physical states observable in cases of dreams and illness. In spite of the fact that extraordinarily morbid or fantastic experiences are being described, we may read the description without a feeling of strain, for it was not written by Diderot out of nervous tension. We see from this that Diderot was capable of objectivizing the finds to which his subjective, sensitive nature gave him the clue. And, in this way, it became possible to render in an artistic style the scientific data which, with specialists, would be treated in a dry, factual manner: the sciences are relieved of their compartmentalization and isolation and become accessible to the art of style. Diderot is, perhaps, a "demi-poète," as Sainte-Beuve has said; but, truer to truth seems to me the statement that he was a "thinker-poet," a thinker who felt in himself the urge to translate his thoughts into poetic prose. That capacity, which characterized Diderot, of giving "gesticulating" expression to everything he thinks, becomes a way of conquering the new realm of science for literature.

* *
*

And now, in order to round out the picture of Diderot and to place him in his time, I may quote here some comments from Groethuysen's article, which should not surprise us after the acquaintance we have made with Diderot's style. Groethuysen recognizes a drama going on in Diderot's mind, involving the clash of two antagonistic forces: Diderot's mobility and his respect for scientific data.

In regard to his mobility, Groethuysen remarks: "[Ce qu'on désigne au XVIIIe siècle comme esprit] Ce n'est plus cette vérité simple et ingénue du XVIIe siècle . . . , qui consiste à bien définir et à bien peindre, à mettre de l'ordre et de la clarté dans les idées que l'homme du XVIIIe siècle recherchera. . . . C'est une liberté nouvelle que l'homme acquiert . . . l'esprit au XVIIIe siècle restitue en quelque sorte à la pensée sa mobilité spontanée. Diderot est le philosophe de cette liberté nouvelle dont jouit l'esprit qui s'abandonne à son propre mouvement, à sa vie, sans être entravé par le souci d'une objectivité qui lui imposerait des formes déterminées. Voyez la marche d'une conversation, voyez les circuits qu'on y fait: les rêves d'un malade ne sont pas plus hétéroclites. Cependant comme il n'y a rien de décousu dans la tête d'un homme qui rêve, ni dans celle d'un fou, tout se tient aussi dans la conversation.[39] . . . Pour lui, la pensée vraiment comprise ne saurait être détachée du penseur. . . . Au XVIIe siècle la valeur de la pensée se mesurait sur l'objectivité qui en forme le contenu. . . . Au XVIIIe siècle, on insiste sur l'originalité de la pensée, sur les tournures d'esprit, sur les différentes manières d'envisager les choses. . . . Aussi Diderot n'ira-t-il plus à la recherche de l'expression finie et achevée. . . . Autour de l'idée qui n'est qu'esquissée se grouperont les idées accessoires flottantes et variables. . . . Le langage reflètera le jeu des pensées se cherchant, se retrouvant, se fuyant et ne pouvant jamais se saisir complètement. C'est ainsi que l'esprit, dans des formes nuancées et multiples, devient conscient de sa vie mobile. Si ensuite il se tourne vers le monde des phénomènes et des apparences, les aspects toujours changeants sous lesquels la vie se présente à lui paraissent comme une projection de sa propre mobilité. . . . Ainsi Diderot trouve en face de soi un monde qui, vu l'instabilité de ses changements, vu la multiplicité des interprétations possibles . . . , semble ne pouvoir opposer aucune résistance au libre essor des facultés de l'esprit."[40]

Groethuysen then proceeds to state that Diderot, this representative of instability, sought and found the counterbalance of a firmly resistant reality opposing him, in the exact scientific research of his century, which consisted in cataloguing and circumscribing facts, in observation and experimentation; in this way the philosopher of the "esprit de finesse" becomes the forerunner of modern positivism. Both aspects of Diderot's mind, his emotional mobility and his urge to assimilate the solid facts of science, appear in his articles written for the *Encyclopedia.* We are dealing here only with the artistic style of Diderot (a style whose origin we discovered in a sample article from the scientific *Encyclopedia*!) not with his scientific writing proper—with the exception, perhaps, of the passage from the *Rêve de D'Alembert*, where we were able to show the penetration of artistic style into scientific prose.

In the passage just quoted textually from Groethuysen, that critic suggests that Diderot, the philosopher of the mobility of the mind, was bound to have a style of mobility;[41] he seems, however, to think of Diderot's language rather as conveying to the reader the "jeux des idées," as reflecting patterns of thought; Diderot's style evidently appears to him as "intellectually conditioned," revealing the ballet of ideas in the costume of words. I have attempted to show by my demonstration in detail that the style of mobility found with Diderot consists in the close adherence of his language to his thought, by way of a sort of inborn mimicry—that his style is an irruption of the *physiological* rhythm of speech into writing. It is for this reason that Diderot must dialogize, monologize, harangue, taunt, apostrophize—apostrophize not only persons but even his own subject-matter. Thought converts itself immediately into the flesh of speech and, with Diderot, speech means "allonger les bras" in a desire to leave behind one's ego and to expand toward a fellow being; it means a conversation with a partner, in which the dialectic in Diderot's nature is brought out by dialogue. Even in the *Encyclopedia* he harangues when we might expect him only to inform (cf. the beginning of the article "jouissance"). For Diderot, there was no bookish teaching, there was only flexible, alive, mobile speech, functioning for the self-liberation of the individual. Not only did Diderot reveal the thinker behind the thought, he revealed the speaker behind the thinker—the speaker, in the main, being himself. What best survives in Diderot's works (in the field of belles-lettres) is the creation of that type of "homme sensible" which he was himself and which he has embodied in a series of characters: Jacques le fataliste, le neveu de Rameau, Hardouin (in "Est-il bon? est-il méchant?")—characters who are satisfied to "live their attitude" of mobility toward the world, to express the mobility of their thinking, and their craving to free themselves from the limitations imposed upon them by their own nature.[42] Thus we are able to see, in Diderot's writings, the speaker Diderot in life-size before us, with his *Neveu*-like verbal orchestra—the virtuoso, a very orchestrator of his thought:[43] it is out of the laws of his nature that, in the *Neveu,* he is able to describe the swelling orchestration of an idea, as a scene of self-annihilation.

The phenomenon of Diderot the energumen is ultimately the manifestation of the dynamism of the self-propelled motion, the self-ignition, of a frenzied mind.[44] In that parody of the nephew which was a parody of himself, Diderot has declared the autonomy of expressivity, the dionysiac delirium which enjoys no god but itself (not without reason did Diderot praise the "gourde sacrée" of Rabelais' priestess Bacbuc—in *Jacques le fataliste*). Diderot has experienced to the bitter end the self-annihilation of the self-igniting mind; but we must be grateful that he has written the satire of it, warning of the danger of expressivity when it severs its ties with Logos. It is the absence of the feeling for the divine (which Meister has already pointed out: Diderot's nature is "riche, fertile, abondante en germes de toute espèce, douce et sauvage, simple et majestueuse, bonne et sublime, mais sans aucun principe dominant, sans maître et sans Dieu") which has made possible that autonomy of expressivity and that bodily mimicry of thought by speech which leads to the disintegration of thought: when the Spirit of God no longer bloweth whither it listeth, man feels his thought autonomous, and speech, no longer subdued to Logos, becomes predominantly a matter of the body, subject to automatism: something felt in one's veins and nerves (Dante felt things in his veins—including the supernatural—but these obeyed the supernatural). Diderot has discovered and expressed most vividly the Charybdis of automatism to which the emotional human soul, which would avoid the Scylla of dry rationalism, may fall victim; with his deep respect for natural law, he had to realize the limits and the frustration which the natural organization of man ultimately imposes on man: the frenzied singer paralyzes his vocal cords.

The feverish staccato style was invented by Diderot because he was deaf to the legato of the divine melody. And, just as the recession of the divine made possible, in a manner unequaled before Diderot, the description of the sexual mechanism, so the description of the bodily, physiological, mechanical side of thought was a new achievement, bought at the price of firm canons imposed by the divine. But, by his self-excommunication, Diderot was enabled to discover new paths for poetry, which, in the nineteenth century, have been followed by great poets (regardless of their religious attitude). For example, the element of the dionysiac which Diderot could claim to have rediscovered, lives gloriously in Hugo's poem *Le Satyre* (in "Légende des Siècles").[45] To invert a line from this same poem ("On fait du ténébreux avec du radieux"), it could be said, in reference to Hugo's poetry which was prefigured by Diderot: "on fait du radieux avec du ténébreux."

The philosophy of mobility as well as its expression by bodily mobility, by "mimicry," was not possible before the eighteenth century:[46] not before this period of the "original genius" could we have the impersonation of language by way of the writer's biological nature—and the ensuing possibility for the reader or stylistician to penetrate into the biological web of the writer's nature by a study of his style. And, when we find in a writer the cohabitation of this philosophy of mobility with this mobile style, an insoluble problem arises: we will probably never be able to disentangle the manner of expression from the manner of thinking or to decide which of the two came first: whether Diderot's natural mimicry (and his stylistic orchestration of it) conditioned his philosophy or whether the philosophy of his period penetrated his bloodstream and colored his style. The nerves and the philosophy of a time appear here so inextricably intermingled in the person of one man that analysis must simply abdicate —at least in our present state of knowledge about man's dependence on Nature.

Having come to the end of this article, I ask myself, in all humility, why no previous critic, so far as I know, has been able to formulate clearly the particular Diderotian essence. We seem to have here an example of the situation described by Henry James in *The Figure in the Carpet*: clues to the writer's general artistic intention have been given the critics in "every page and line and letter. The thing's as concrete there as a bird in a cage, a bait on a hook, a piece of cheese in a mouse-trap. It's stuck into every volume as your foot is stuck into your shoe. It governs every line, it chooses every word, it dots every *i*, it places every comma"—and, nevertheless, the critics have not seen the figure in the carpet which repeats itself, with all its circumvolutions, in the work before their eyes! It may be that the very prodigality of the evidence has blinded the critics, who are accustomed to searching for hidden clues.

NOTES

1. A study such as *Diderot's Imagery* by Eric M. Steel (New York, 1941), which is patterned on similar works dealing with the imagery of Shakespeare or Donne, proceeds by applying to Diderot the ready-made concept of "imagery," illustrating this by means of quantitative comparisons (in the *Rêve de D'Alembert* the percentage of similes is greater than in the *Lettre sur les aveugles*) which entail an overevaluation of the raw material on which the author draws (do Diderot's similes involve more birds or more flowers?). I should like to set down as a rule for all the generations of dissertation-writers to come: *never start writing on a subject of literary history unless you have made a particular observation of your own on this subject*! If you have been struck by a certain quality of Diderot's imagery, then write on this imagery—but not if you have only thought coldly, in the abstract: "Diderot is missing from the list of those whose imagery has been covered; why not fill in the gap?"

Imagery should be considered not *per se*, but according to the particular function that the author ascribes to it in his different works. There is, for example, practically no imagery in *Le neveu de Rameau*, Mr. Steel tells us. But why? (I would explain this as due to the fact that, in this work, the central device chosen by Diderot to render the central theme [mental mobility] was that of rhythm.) Conversely, in the *Rêve de D'Alembert*, this device is quite frequent: the two basic images are those of the spider-web and the cluster of bees—the latter, as Dieckmann has shown, borrowed from the physician Bordeu, who is also the protagonist of the *Rêve*. It is because Diderot is concerned in this dialogue with the seemingly frail or loose, but none the less stable, configurations in Nature, that he has chosen these two similes (and no others).

Quite a different function is to be assigned to the imagery of Diderot's *Entretien d'un philosophe avec la Maréchale*, in which the rational, arithmetical mind of the Maréchale, that positivistic Catholic, expresses itself in numbers and quantities—as, for example:

"Que gagnez-vous donc à ne pas croire?"	[the philosopher counters: "Est-ce qu'on croit, parce qu'il y a quelque chose à gagner?"]
"La raison d'intérêt ne gâte rien aux affaires de ce monde ni de l'autre"	[the Assézat edition remarks correctly: "la raison d'intérêt, sur laquelle roule presque toute son argumentation"]
". . . le mal, ce sera ce qui a plus d'inconvénients que d'avantages; et le bien, au contraire, ce qui a plus d'avantages que d'inconvénients"	[in the utilitarian definition of moral concepts the quantity of usefulness is the dominant factor]

Thus, it is not surprising to find, in her conversation, images borrowed from the world of business:

"J'avoue que je prête à Dieu à la petite semaine"	[the philosopher counters: "Pour moi, je mets à fonds perdu"]
"Mais oui : on peut faire l'usure avec Dieu tant qu'on veut; on ne le ruine pas. Je sais bien que cela n'est pas délicat, mais qu'importe? Comme le point est d'attraper le ciel, ou d'adresse ou de force, il faut tout porter en ligne de compte, ne négliger aucun profit" "Hélas! nous aurons beau faire, notre mise sera toujours bien mesquine en comparaison de la rentrée que nous faisons. Et vous n'attendez rien, vous?" "petit à petit, cela fait somme"	[this is the reaction of the Maréchale to the concession by the philosopher of some minor bad actions prevented by religion—a reaction couched in the language of the French bourgeois who, all his lifetime, makes "de petites épargnes"]

Here, then, imagery has a characterizing value; the type of metaphor used by the Maréchale (and, incidentally, by the philosopher who would disprove her arguments) is congenital with her turn of mind. Diderot is here illustrating (to an excessive degree, perhaps) the truth of the Latin dictum: *oratio vultus animi.* (Unless I am mistaken, this dialogue is not mentioned in Mr. Steel's dissertation.)

We have again a different use of imagery in the *Regrets sur ma vieille robe de chambre,* in which the device is intended as a reflection of a playful arbitrary attempt on the part of the writer to endow with life the objects surrounding him, to treat them as human beings, as friends or sweethearts. The problem of this essay is concerned precisely with our attachment to the things of our environment, an attachment which tends to take on quasi-human value; it is a problem quite in line with the general eighteenth-century tendency which cherished the cozy intimacy of the "intérieur," in contrast to that of the seventeenth century, "le grand siècle," in which the abstract, the monumental, the "public" was so greatly appreciated. In this masterpiece of Diderot's, the varying intensity of the personifications corresponds to the hesitancy or boldness of the author to recognize the human character of things. At the beginning, Diderot plays upon the ambiguity of the personal pronoun *elle*—it is only in line 14 that we understand that it represents not an animated being (as would be suggested by *sa complainte, le flanc*) but Diderot's old dressing gown (a garment which, since the time of Descartes, has been suggestive of the bachelor philosopher) : "Pourquoi ne l'avoir pas gardée? Elle était faite à moi; j'étais fait à elle. . . . Il n'y avait aucun besoin auquel sa complaisance ne se prêtât. . . . L'encre épaissie refusait-elle de couler de ma plume, elle présentait le flanc. . . . Sous son abri, je ne redoutais ni la maladresse d'un valet, ni la mienne. . . . J'étais le maître absolu de ma vieille robe de chambre; je suis devenu l'esclave de la nouvelle." Then comes the simile: "Le vieillard passionné qui s'est livré, pieds et poings liés, aux caprices, à la merci d'une jeune folle, dit depuis le matin jusqu'au soir: Où est ma bonne, ma vieille gouvernante?"

A human relationship is further indicated in the following passage, in which a masculine variant to the simile is introduced: "Une nouvelle gouvernante stérile qui succède dans un presbytère, la femme qui entre dans la maison d'un veuf, le ministre qui remplace un ministre disgracié, ce prélat moliniste qui s'empare du diocèse d'un prélat janséniste, ne causent pas plus de trouble que l'écarlate intruse en a causé chez moi." (This "scarlet intruder" becomes later on an "impérieuse," a "somptueuse écarlate.")

At the end, Diderot reassures us that his acquisitive sense has not gotten the mastery over him: he is able to give away a prized possession; but when he speaks of giving up "Laïs," he refers to this painting as to a mistress: "Ne craignez pas que la fureur d'entasser de belles choses me prenne. Les amis que j'avais, je les ai; et le nombre n'en est pas augmenté. J'ai Laïs, mais Laïs ne m'a pas. Heureux entre ses bras, je suis prêt à la céder à celui que j'aimerai et qu'elle rendrait plus heureux que moi. Et pour vous dire mon secret à l'oreille, cette Laïs, qui se vend si cher aux autres, ne m'a rien coûté."

It is because Diderot wished to suggest the intimate, almost personal relationship which ties us to cherished objects, that he had recourse to the images just cited—which serve to illustrate a personal way of seeing which he has recognized in himself.

I must repeat that we should observe stylistic procedures by taking the concrete work of art as the point of departure, not some a priori standpoint outside of the work. We must decipher the "hieroglyphs," as Diderot has called the discoveries of poets (the "expressions énergiques," "le beau propos," etc.) in the *hic et nunc* of the works where they are found.

2. Dieckmann's term "inadequately" is surprising. According to him, there were different strata in Diderot's being, the deepest of which is rarely revealed in his style. As an example of a rare case in which the reader is allowed a glimpse into Diderot's *Seinsgefühl* (that is, in which Diderot expresses himself "adequately"), Dieckmann quotes a letter from Diderot's private correspondence in which ideas are expressed which are quite aberrant from the usual tendencies of the Encyclopedists: "Les sensations douces, lorsqu'elles sont continues, calment, sans qu'on s'en aperçoive, les mouvements les plus violents. On ne se défend pas de cette paix de la nature qui règne sans cesse autour de soi. On s'en défend d'autant moins qu'elle agit imperceptiblement. Ce n'est point une éloquence qu'on entende, c'est une persuasion qu'on respire; c'est un exemple auquel on se conforme par une pente naturelle à se mettre à l'unisson avec tout ce qu'on voit. L'immobilité des arbres nous arrête; l'étendue d'une plaine égare nos yeux et notre âme; le bruit égal et monotone des eaux nous endort. . . . Toutes les douleurs finissent par être lentes et mélancoliques. Les querelles dans les champs ont un aspect plus hideux que dans les carrefours des villes; c'est comme un cri perçant dans le silence et l'obscurité de la nuit; c'est un contraste de guerre avec l'image d'une paix générale. . . . Ici d'instinct, on s'assied, on se repose, on regarde sans voir, on abandonne son coeur, son âme, son esprit, ses sens à la liberté; c'est à dire qu'on ne fait rien pour être au ton de tous les êtres. Ils sont, et l'on est. Tout est utile, tout sert, tout concourt, tout est bon, on n'est rien sans y tâcher. Est bien mal né, est bien méchant, est profondément pervers, celui qui médite le mal au milieu des champs. Il lutte contre l'impulsion de la nature entière qui lui répète à voix basse et sans cesse, qui lui murmure à l'oreille: demeure en repos, demeure en repos, reste comme tout ce qui t'environne dure comme tout ce qui t'environne, jouis douce-

ment comme tout ce qui t'environne, laisse aller les heures, les journées, les années, comme tout ce qui t'environne, et passe comme tout ce qui t'environne; voilà la leçon continue de la nature."

Dieckmann considers as quite exceptional in attitude and expression, Diderot's remarks about harmony in Nature: "So wenig achtet Diderot auf die fasslichen Sinneseindrücke, dass er den Höreindruck mit dem Seheindruck vertauscht: in Einklang mit allem was man *sieht*? Auch die Wendung: 'pour être au ton de tous les êtres' ist nicht klanglich gemeint, sondern bezeichnet das Ineinsfühlen mit dem Sein der Dinge." I feel that Mr. Dieckmann would not have found this passage exceptional had he been able to locate it in the history of ideas. The definition of the "peace of Nature" here attempted is in exact accordance with Rousseau (e.g. in the *Nouvelle Héloïse*) and with other thinkers of the eighteenth century: "peace in Nature" with them was related (as I shall show elsewhere) to the idea of "world harmony" as elaborated by the ancients (Plato, Cicero, Plotinus, etc.), by Augustine, and by Renaissance and Baroque writers; that Diderot was familiar with the Renaissance idea of world harmony (as expressed by Marsilio Ficino, etc.) is proven by his frequent simile in which he compares the resonance which one thought awakens in another with the vibrations imparted to the other strings of an instrument when one string is plucked. Now, for the ancients, harmony was as well a term of psychology and moral teaching as of music and natural philosophy: thus, in the passage from Diderot, the acoustic expressions ("se mettre à l'unisson," "être au ton") are illustrative at the same time of moral peace and of the peace of Nature, just as was the case in ancient literature. "Peace" is "the good," it is "love" (in "tout sert, tout concourt, tout est bon," the reminiscence of *concurrere* belongs to a traditional pattern which also included *consonantia, concordia*, etc.); it is spontaneous achievement ("imperceptiblement," "sans y toucher"), it is "musical harmony" and "world harmony" ("tous les êtres . . ."). "Strife" is "the wicked," strife is "hatred" ("méchant," "pervers"); it is conscious machination ("méditer le mal"); it is musical disharmony ("un cri perçant"). The gentle fusion of the perceptions of the particular senses into one self-contained *Stimmung* is a manifestation of peace and harmony. Thus Diderot is here continuing a two-thousand-year-old Platonic-Augustinian tradition. He manages, however, to give this his own personal touch; and I feel that Dieckmann has failed to sense the Diderotian ring in this passage—by which the thought is translated into rhythm: the extinction of consciousness in man, as he is lulled to sleep by Nature, and the cradling silence of Nature, could not have been expressed more musically; the sentences (much more so than in the *Rêverie* of Rousseau, who is rather given to formulating definitions) have the "monotonous" effect of dulling all sharp discordances—until we come to the lullaby which Nature sings to man: "demeure en repos, demeure en repos," with the repetition of "comme tout ce qui t'environne." This lullaby of Nature, incidentally, is not basically different in its pattern from the lullaby with which the nephew of Rameau puts himself to sleep (the refrain "le grand homme Rameau"): so constant in Diderot is the acoustic rendering of feelings! Far from sharing Dieckmann's idea that Diderot "pays no heed" to the data of the particular senses, I must state that Diderot shows his sensitivity to the acoustic as such by his translation of feelings into rhythm.

2a. Diderot's analysis of eroticism has evidently influenced the passage in Friedrich Schlegel's *Lucinde* where the repetition of the sexual act is defined as a combination of the determined and the undetermined (*Bestimmtes-Unbestimmtes*). Cf. also *ibidem* the *reizende romantische Unordnung* ascribed to eroticism. With Schlegel as a link, we may see a continuous line extending from Diderot's sensualism to that of Heine and Nietzsche.

3. This feeling for the direct accessibility of the enchanted garden of natural love could be called the "rococo" element in Diderot's attitude toward love, a feeling which includes some elements of the Enlightenment together with a remnant of French *gauloiserie*: by the eighteenth century, Tasso's paradise of sensuous love, which had been the prerogative of princes, had passed to all men as a gift from Nature. This mixture of the rococo with features of the Enlightenment has not been taken into account by Sainte-Beuve, who quotes with disapproval the passages of Diderot's *Salon* (x, 365) on the young painter Loutherbourg: "Courage, jeune homme, tu as été plus loin qu'il ne l'est permis à ton âge. . . . Tu as une compagne charmante, qui doit te fixer. Ne quitte ton atelier que pour aller consulter la nature. Habite les champs avec elle. Va voir le ciel se lever et se coucher. . . . Vois les herbes brillantes des gouttes de la rosée. . . . Quitte ton lit de grand matin, malgré la femme jeune et charmante près de laquelle tu reposes. Devance le retour du soleil. . . . Cet astre commence à peine sa carrière; ta compagne charmante a les yeux encore fermés; bientôt un de ses bras te cherchera à son côté. Hâte-toi de revenir. La tendresse conjugale t'appelle. Le spectacle de la nature animée t'attend."

Sainte-Beuve, while appreciating the description of the landscape "tout humectée de rosée et de lumière," finds unwarranted and indecent the allusions to the *compagne*, of which he quotes only two. It is in the name of "le goût" that he disapproves of this picture of "ce coin entr'ouvert de l'alcôve maritale"; he finds in Diderot's style "un déshabillé libre et bourgeois." Thus Sainte-Beuve is content to apply the purely normative judgment of "taste" instead of attempting historically to understand the taste and the thought-behind-the-taste of Diderot and his time. The thought, indicated in the last sentence of the passage just quoted, is evidently the same as that of the article "Jouissance": woman is animated nature, she belongs to nature as truly as do the landscapes depicted by the young artist. The taste revealed by these lines is that of the rococo, that sense of the immediate accessibility to man of the enchanted garden of sensuous love, of that "action génitale, si naturelle, si nécessaire et si juste" (as Diderot says in an apologia for the verb *foutre*, vi, 222). Diderot, like Watteau or Fragonard, wants us to feel how close to man Nature has put the rosy-fingered Eos, how easy she has made the Embarcation for Cythera. The sensuous picture offered by Diderot of the marital alcove is indeed "bourgeois," but it is, strangely enough, also Homeric, since one of the tenets of Diderot's creed is that the sexual freedom of the Homeric gods should be accessible to every bourgeois. Sainte-Beuve's repugnance, which is easily shared by a modern reader, can be explained by the fact that we no longer feel the "pathos" of sexual emancipation.

4. This passage appears to be an enlargement of the statement contained in Diderot's essay *Sur les femmes*, in which he blames Thomas for

not having spoken (in his "Essai sur le caractère, les moeurs et l'esprit des femmes") ". . . avec plus d'intérêt et de chaleur du seul être de la nature qui nous rende sentiment pour sentiment, et qui soit heureux du bonheur qu'il nous fait." "Mais il a voulu que son livre ne fût d'aucun sexe; et il n'y a malheureusement que trop bien réussi. C'est un hermaphrodite qui n'a ni le nerf de l'homme ni la mollesse de la femme." Diderot has evidently brought to the article "Jouissance" that "warmth" of style which he found missing in Thomas and which seemed to him required by the subject matter; it is his general tendency to write of a subject in a style which corresponds to it artistically, in a style that not only explains but represents it: "Il ne suffit pas de parler des femmes, et d'en parler bien, monsieur Thomas, faites encore que j'en voie."

5. One sees that this *vous* is no longer the indefinite "vous qui avez une âme," addressed indiscriminately to all men with feeling, but a dual ("vous deux") descriptive of "the couple": a general dual, however, since all mankind falls into couples. It is significant that when Diderot taunts the "homme pervers" who might object to his description of sexuality, he addresses him as "tu" ("Tais-toi, malheureux . . .") as if in order to isolate him in his perversion from the loving community of men.

6. The same "ritornello" development may be seen in the sentence from the "Neveu de Rameau" which defines the triumph and downfall of the musician Rameau (the Elder):

ce musicien célèbre

> qui nous a délivrés du plain-chant de Lulli . . .
>
> qui a tant écrit de visions inintelligibles sur la théorie de la musique où lui ni personne n'entendait jamais rien,
>
> et de qui nous avons un certain nombre d'opéras où il y a de l'harmonie, des bouts de chants . . .
>
> et qui, après avoir enterré *le Florentin* [= Lully], sera enterré par les virtuoses florentins, ce qu'il pressentait. . . .

7. I foresee objections to my attempt to find an organic meaning in certain linguistic traits; one could argue that, since there are many cases of accumulated *qui*-sentences in Diderot which do not depict productivity and potentiation, I am consequently not justified in finding this meaning expressed by them when the passage happens to deal with productivity and potentiation. But whenever one deals with the problem of expressivity of language, "expression" can be stated only when meaning and linguistic form converge: Grammont has often explained that *tic-tac* is a "mot expressif" (an onomatopoeia) because, in it, sound and meaning are conjoined, while *tactique*, while offering the same sound clusters, is not expressive because nothing in the concept of "tactics" asks for imitation by sound.

In *Les bijoux indiscrets*, we have a similar sentence which depicts, by means of accelerated rhythm (here, it is noun clauses, not relative clauses, that are involved) the progress of (psychological) possession of the Beloved (IV, 310): "Je voudrais qu'elle approuvât mes soins, qu'elle ne m'éconduisît pas par des mines, qu'elle m'apprît une bonne fois si je lui plais; qu'elle m'instruisît elle-même du moyen de lui plaire davantage; qu'elle ne me celât point les progrès que je ferais dans son coeur; qu'elle n'écoutât que moi, n'eût des yeux que pour moi, ne pensât, ne rêvât que moi, ne fût occupée que de moi, ne fît rien qui ne tendît à m'en convaincre; et que cédant un jour à mes transports, je visse clairement que je dois tout à mon amour et au sien. Quel triomphe! et qu'un homme est heureux de posséder une telle femme!" Trahard remarks: "Quand Amisadar parle, on croit entendre déjà Diderot s'adressant à Sophie Vollard." And, indeed, we do hear the same note of "possessiveness" in the following lines from one of Diderot's letters to Sophie (Trahard, p. 113)—which should, incidentally, be added to the dossier of "jouissance": "Il se répand sur tout votre corps un frémissement délicieux, tout vous annonce un amour infiniment plus grand, tout vous y convie: et vous ne voulez pas mourir et faire mourir de plaisir! Vous vous refusez à un moment qui a bien aussi son délire: celui où cet homme, vain d'avoir possédé cet objet qu'il prise plus que l'univers entier, en répand un torrent de larmes!"

The same basic sentence pattern prevails when Diderot imagines his union with Sophie after death—which, owing to his atomistic ideas, becomes a meeting of molecules: "O ma Sophie, il me resterait donc un espoir de vous toucher, de vous sentir, de vous aimer, de vous chercher [acceleration, striving toward the union], de m'unir, de me confondre avec vous quand nous ne serons plus [apex of mystic union], s'il y avait pour nos principes une loi d'affinité, s'il nous était réservé de composer un être commun, si je devais dans la suite des siècles refaire un tout avec vous, si les molécules de votre amant dissous avaient à s'agiter, à s'émouvoir et à rechercher les vôtres éparses dans la nature [in the hypothetic sentences the same movement of union starts once more toward a broad apotheosis]."

8. Here, for the first time, we find a rhythm which will recur many times in our paper: this "style coupé" (the term Diderot himself applied, in a laudatory vein, to Seneca's writing), which is produced by a sequence of short sentences, gives a mechanical effect—which is never likely to be achieved with the longer periods, however artificially they may be contrived. And this must imply a correspondent automatism in the organic process described: Diderot seems to have been sensitive to the inherent mechanism of the body when it is left free to act on its own level.

9. Here we have a discreet formulation, in which factual details are avoided, of that narrowing of consciousness during the sexual act which Diderot felt no qualms about describing in his letter to Sophie (Ledieu, p. 95): "Mais n'est-ce pas une chose bien bizarre que le songe n'offre presque jamais à mon imagination que l'espace étroit et nécessaire à la volupté, rien autour de cela; un étui de chair et puis c'est tout." In the article on "jouissance" there can be no sudden stop like "et puis c'est tout," since, here, Diderot is concerned not only with the egotistic feelings of the individual, but the continuing ebb and flow of Nature. This "et puis c'est tout" is revelatory of Diderot's basically unregenerate nature, the absence of the divine in his sexual *Grunderlebnis*, which has made possible Diderot's revoltingly coarse descriptions of the mechanics of the

sexual, in which there is not the slightest attempt at poeticization (cf. the letter quoted by Ledieu, p. 116).

10. The word "enthusiasm," as used here of the sexual enjoyment—not, for example, of the exaltation of the poet, the philosopher—need not astonish the reader. It will become evident in the course of my article that Diderot shares the Platonic conception (of which he gives his own version) of that *θεία μανία* "divine fury" which is present alike in the prophet, the *mystes*, the poet, and the lover. It is characteristic of Diderot's sensualistic approach that, when he applies the word *enthusiasm* to love, it is to sexual love.

11. Here, where Diderot associates "le ciel" with monogamy, we must translate this as "Heaven"—in contrast to the passage in the "Supplément au voyage de Bougainville," where it is evidently "the sky" (i.e. Nature) that is meant: that ever-changing background which would seem to require the mutability of human relationships; it is this passage which has inspired Musset's "Souvenir": "[Marriage is] Contraire à la loi générale des êtres; rien en effet te paraît-il plus insensé qu'un précepte qui proscrit le changement qui est en nous, qui commande une constance qui n'y peut être, et qui viole la Nature et la liberté du mâle et de la femelle en les enchaînant pour jamais l'un à l'autre . . . ; qu'un serment d'immutabilité de deux êtres de chair, à la face d'un ciel qui n'est pas un instant le même?"

In fact, the variability of the natural background is the framework of the whole dialogue: this begins and ends with a discussion of the inconstant weather, which changes during the dialogue. This symbolism must have been deeply present to Diderot's mind, for (as Chinard points out in his Introduction to the "Supplément," p. 47), the same framework of variable Nature is used for his "Sur l'inconséquences du jugement publique et de nos actions particulières," written during the same period.

12. Autobiographical confirmation of this recollective moment of Diderot's thought may be found in a passage of his letter to Sophie, quoted by Ledieu, p. 76: "Ce fut une chose si douce que le premier aveu, qu'on ne se lassa point d'y revenir. Ce fut une chose si douce que le premier moment, qu'on alla toujours le recherchant. On serre toujours contre son sein celui qu'on aime, et l'art d'écrire n'est que l'art d'allonger les bras." The writing of a love letter becomes a caressing of the past.

But, when I chose the motto of this chapter, I wished to suggest a wider meaning for Diderot's statement: writing in general is an erotic act for Diderot, an act that tends to integrate him into what is creative and self-potentiating in Nature.

13. In the mention of the poisoning factors of mistrust and remorse (which have no power on young, healthy, innocent, Arcadian beings), we may see, without betraying Diderot's thought, an allusion to the influence of Christianity, which has injected these unwholesome elements into natural sexual life (compare Diderot's references, in the "Supplément au voyage de Bougainville," to "crainte," "châtiment," "remords," which reactions he attributes to the marital policy of the Church).

14. This does not mean that traditional elements are lacking in his style. For example, the aphorism, repeatedly used in our passage, is a centuries-old device; again, such a phrase as "les voiles que jeta la pudeur sur les charmes" derives from sensuous French poetry and represents a

style which had been current in prose from "Le grand Cyrus" to "Le temple de Gnide"; the superlatives "les illusions les plus délicates," "le sens le plus exquis" are a traditional encomiastic device in "ideal" descriptions of Arcadian idyls. But the sentence rhythm to which these traditional elements are subjected, is new.

That Diderot had a clear conception of "rhythm" as an artistic factor in poetry and prose, and in speech, is shown by his remarks (XI, 268): "Qu'est-ce donc que le rhythme? C'est un choix particulier d'expressions; c'est une certaine distribution de syllabes . . . ou un enchaînement de petites onomatopées analogues aux idées qu'on a, et dont on est fortement occupé . . . , à la nature, au caractère, au mouvement des actions qu'on se propose de rendre. . . . Il est inspiré par un goût naturel, par la mobilité de l'âme, par la sensibilité. C'est l'image même de l'âme rendue par les inflexions de la voix . . . sans la facilité de trouver ce chant, cette espèce de musique, on n'écrit ni en vers ni en prose: je doute même qu'on parle bien. Sans l'habitude de la sentir ou de la rendre, on ne sait pas lire; et qui est-ce qui sait lire? . . . C'est elle qui prête aux écrits une grâce toujours nouvelle. . . . Ce n'est pas à l'oreille seulement, c'est à l'âme d'où elle est émanée, que la véritable harmonie s'adresse. . . . Ce ne sont pas les idées qui coûtent; c'est le ton qui leur convient."

15. Though there is poeticization in Diderot's treatment of the sexual theme, there is no real poetry: the poeticization consists of an avoidance of mentioning technical facts—which are, only too obviously, uppermost in the mind of the author. Thibaudet, in his article "Langage, littérature et sensualité" (*Nouvelle revue française*, XXXVII, 716), remarks that the eighteenth century is "le siècle de la périphrase érotique," that it had lost the Racinian, the Vergilian power of poetic alchemy whereby brute reality is transmuted. He quotes a passage from the *Aeneid* descriptive of the love of Mars and Venus, and comments: "Chacun de ces mots, le long de ce vers *qui digitos habet* frappe une touche, et cette touche déclenche quelque chose dans une mémoire organique, dans un passé de la sensation. L'homme fait des fouilles dans cette mémoire, dans ce passé, dans cette culture de la sensation qui lui donne aussi une sensation de culture."

16. Compare his physiological description, containing expressions reminiscent of his sexual *Grunderlebnis*, of the way in which he reacts to a virtuous action (letter to Sophie Volland of the 18th of October, 1760): ". . . celui [le spectacle] de l'équité me remplit d'une douceur et d'un enthousiasme où la vie, s'il fallait la perdre, ne me tiendrait à rien; alors il me semble que mon coeur s'étend au dedans de moi, qu'il nage; je ne sais quelle sensation délicieuse et subite me parcourt partout; j'aime à respirer; il s'excite à toute la surface de mon corps comme un frémissement, c'est surtout au haut du front, à l'origine des cheveux, qu'il se fait sentir; et puis les symptômes de l'admiration et du plaisir viennent se mêler sur mon visage avec ceux de la joie, et mes yeux se remplissent de pleurs."

17. Anyone, when reading this description must experience a slight shudder of repulsion—which is surely not alone due to the perversity of the Mother Superior. We feel that the glance of the author himself lingers unduly on the "charmes" of the young nun, as he savors her Greuze-like décolleté ("à deminue"). There is some undigested, unrefined, unassuaged sensuality in Diderot that allows him to abuse the privilege

of an author. And if we think that we get this impression of Diderot's enjoyment through the words of the nun herself, we must realize that this creature of Diderot's is made to appear conscious of her own seductive powers; that she has been infected by her creator's sensuality.

18. If this interpretation is true, there is obviously a lack of realism to be noted: Diderot would be making the nun relive the moment of hypnotism, from which she must have recovered when she writes her account.

19. As another parodistic example of this *et*, compare the following passage from *La religieuse*, in which the archdeacon extracts a "renunciation of Satan" from the innocent nun:

Il me dit ensuite: "Faites un acte de foi" et je le fis.
"Faites un acte d'amour" et je le fis.
"Faites un acte d'espérance" et je le fis.
"Faites un acte de charité" et je le fis.

In the following example the original suggestion of miraculous creation is better preserved: "[l'esprit observateur] c'est une machine rare qui dit: 'cela réussira' et cela réussit; 'cela ne réussira pas' et cela ne réussit pas; 'cela est vrai' ou 'cela est faux' et cela se trouve comme il l'a dit. Il se remarque et dans les grandes choses et dans les petites. Cette sorte d'esprit prophétique [!] n'est pas le même dans toutes les conditions de la vie; chaque état a le sien."

20. The imposition of a pattern on a character's gestures has been anticipated in the scene of the young nun's ordination by her first Mother Superior. While, here, there is no suggestion of perversion, an ironical touch is given by paralleling the ritual gestures of the ordination with the steps of a dance: [the Mother Superior inspects the young nun after she has taken the veil] "Elle me composa la tête, les pieds, les mains, la taille, le bras; ce fut presque une leçon de Marcel [a famous dancing-master of the time] sur les grâces monastiques: car chaque état a les siennes."

21. That, quite against my usual approach, I am here justified in dragging into the discussion of a work of art the character of the artist, becomes clear from the fact that Diderot was given to depicting his characters according to himself. We may compare, for example, the following self-portrait, in which he shows the influence of his temperament on his way of speaking (it is this passage with which Lanson, after Sainte-Beuve, opens the chapter on Diderot): "La tête d'un Langrois est sur ses épaules comme un coq au haut d'une clocher; elle n'est jamais fixe dans un point; et si elle revient à celui qu'elle a quitté, ce n'est pas pour s'y arrêter. Avec une rapidité surprenante dans les mouvements, dans les désirs, dans les projets, dans les fantaisies, dans les idées, il a le parler lent. Pour moi, je suis de mon pays; seulement le séjour de la capitale et l'application assidue m'ont un peu corrigé" with the portrait of the Mother Superior in *La religieuse*: "C'est une petite femme toute ronde, cependant prompte et vive dans ses mouvements: sa tête n'est jamais assise sur ses épaules; . . . ses yeux, dont l'un, c'est le droit, est plus haut et plus grand que l'autre, sont pleins de feu et distraits; quand elle marche, elle jette ses bras en avant et arrière. Veut-elle parler? elle ouvre la bouche, avant que d'avoir arrangé ses idées; aussi bégaye-t-elle un peu . . . ; elle est alternativement compatissante et dure; sa figure décomposée marque tout le décousu de son esprit et toute l'inégalité de son caractère. . . ." It is from her creator

Diderot that she has taken her chameleonesque mobility and her speech which cannot keep up with the rapidity of her mind.

22. In other passages of our dialogue, the nephew's tirade will end in self-interruption, when he feels that he has reached the realm of the inexpressible: e.g. p. 396 (after offering many hypothetical enumerations): "vous riez? mais laissez-moi dire . . ."; p. 404 (after a sequence of *moi*'s that tend to glorify his personality): "moi! moi enfin! j'irais! . . . Tenez, monsieur, cela ne se peut. . . ." In such cases Diderot means to signify that hypervitality and hyperexpressivity are bound to end in inarticulateness.

23. That Diderot had an eye for the gesture that functions as a complement and a completion of words must be explained not only by the discovery, achieved in the psychology of his time, of the psycho-physical unity of the human body, but also by his own fundamental desire for self-fulfillment, for achievement of psycho-physical unity. This trait is rather extraordinary in a French thinker, since the French, in general, tend toward the subjugation of body and gesture to mind and word; it is more characteristic of the Mediterranean type, with whom word and gesture are one—if, indeed, the gesture does not take precedence over the words, which merely follow the acting. Given the function assigned by Diderot to gestures among other expressive means, it is not surprising that he should have chosen for his *Neveu* a protagonist who is a born actor, a "Schauspieler seiner selbst," as Nietzsche would have put it.

It is not only the foolish nephew whose gesticulations Diderot finds it interesting to describe; he does the same in the case of the scientist D'Alembert (in *Le rêve de D'Alembert*, II, 124): ". . . je suis bien un, je n'en saurais douter (en disant cela, il se tâtait partout)." Here we have a case of "penser avec les mains," a procedure which appealed instinctively to Diderot; to think about the unity of man would immediately have bodily consequences and bodily evidence. Again (*ibid.* 131): "Il avait imité avec sa main droite le tube d'un microscope, et avec sa gauche, je crois, l'orifice d'un vase. Il regardait dans le vase par ce tube, et il disait. . . ." D'Alembert, the intuitive scientist, being as "fou" as was the nephew, must be presented with gesticulations of his own.

24. It is no accident that the dionysiac nephew was a musician. That the dionysiac expresses itself directly in music was, incidentally, Diderot's own experience: compare his remark to Falconet, quoted by Trahard, that he and other creative minds often hear "flutes."

25. We may be reminded here of Diderot's definition of the "imitator" (quoted by Dieckmann): "La nature pousse l'homme de génie, l'homme de génie pousse l'imitateur. . . . Le génie attire fortement à lui tout ce qui se trouve dans la sphère de son activité, qui s'en exalte outre mesure. L'imitateur n'attire point, il est attiré; il s'aimante par le contact avec l'aimant, mais il n'est pas l'aimant."

26. Diderot has discovered the efficacy of the prose refrain in narrative; before him, there existed only the refrain in poetry—with the exception of its use in conversation, as in Molière's "Et Tartufe?" or "Que diable allait-il faire dans cette galère?" (which, likewise, indicate a mechanism prevailing in a character). The prose refrain is predicated on the reader's capacity to distinguish it from the poetic refrain, which suggests not the imposition of a mechanism upon reality that disturbs its natural flow,

but the recurrence of natural, of eternal laws: "Mais où sont les neiges d'antan?" (a cosmic mechanism, perhaps—as we have spoken of the "divine mechanism" of *Fiat lux. Et lux facta est*).

We find the same criticism of a mechanism by a mechanical refrain in the "lullaby" with which Diderot represents the timorous, conventional mind of a jurist as putting itself to sleep ("Entretien d'un père avec ses enfants") : "Les juges s'en tiennent strictement à la loi, comme mon père et le père Bouin; et font bien. Les juges ferment, en pareïls cas, les yeux sur les circonstances, comme mon père et le père Bouin, par l'effroi des inconvénients qui s'ensuivraient; et font bien. Ils sacrifient quelquefois contre le témoignage même de leur conscience, comme mon père et le père Bouin, l'intérêt du malheureux et du fripon . . . ; et font bien. Ils redoutent, comme mon père et le père Bouin, de prononcer un arrêt équitable dans un cas déterminé, mais funeste dans mille autres . . . ; et font bien."

With Diderot, the use of the "refrain" to suggest automatism seems to appear only in descriptions of heightened emotion, when the person concerned loses his mental balance and is caught up in the machinery of feeling.

But in our contemporary literature this device is quite often used to reproduce the mechanical aspect of quite routine thought processes of the "stream of consciousness." In the passage below from Marquand's *So Little Time* (p. 399), there is also to be found the suggestion that the character is obsessed by the automatic aspect of everyday life itself: "He [Jeffrey, the playwright] did not know why he should be sensitive about appearing financially before Milton Cooke. After all, he did not have implicit confidence in Milton's judgment, and yet he depended upon Milton because Milton was in the Standard Bank and knew about such things. What was more, Madge [Jeffrey's wife] always depended on Milton, because Milton was what she described as a 'man of business.' . . . Besides, Milton was a friend—they had been in the same class at Harvard. Jeffrey had never known about this until Milton had told him one day, shortly after he began looking at Madge's things, and shortly after that Milton had asked him to lunch at the Harvard Club. . . . Shortly after that, Milton had asked him to his apartment for a quiet little dinner, and while Madge and Laura, Milton's wife, talked in the other room, Milton had told Jeffrey what a headache everything was on Wall Street. There might have been a time, Milton said, when one man, with reasonable intelligence, could supervise his own savings, but now it was getting to be more and more of a science. . . . Milton was talking about the S.W.C., and about a scandal that had broken downtown, and Milton had known the man very well. No one had been as surprised as Milton. . . . Milton was always sure that nothing would come up, but, then, you never could tell. Milton seemed to have a dusty sort of immortality. He made Jeffrey feel that he might die, but that somehow Milton never would, since estates and investment lists must go on forever. Milton was reaching into the briefcase again, his fingers moving adroitly through the papers. . . . Jeffrey smiled. 'And if I die on the way,' he said, 'just call up Milton.' . . . Madge never liked to joke about death. But then, that was what Milton was there for, because Madge knew that Milton, or someone like Milton, would live forever."

In this passage, it is obvious that "Milton" has become a prose refrain (almost never is the pronoun "he" allowed to take the place of the name), representing the mechanical thinking of Jeffrey and Madge who are haunted by the thought of Milton-the-Institution with his "dusty sort of immortality," and of the precedence over individual life which financial arrangements have in their world. Since the passage is mainly given up to the "style indirect libre" ("Milton was always sure that nothing would come up, but then, you never could tell"), the oft-repeated "Milton" must be the magic name that the two money-impressed characters have continually on their lips or on their minds: such a sentence as "yet he depended upon Milton because Milton was in the Standard Bank" is only a transposition of Jeffrey's thought: "I must depend on Milton because Milton. . . ."

27. It is interesting to see how Diderot gives to stage-directions a stylistic movement, a literary flavor of their own. Indeed, we must not think of them simply as factual stage-directions; we should read the passage as a whole, as Diderot must have conceived it, giving to the description of gestures and the rendering of words, alike, their proper acoustic value. (For example, the repetitious rhyming flexional endings in *-ait* are no overdose of "style" on the part of Diderot, but the organic expression of his inner "mechanism of enthusiasm.")

28. There are critics, such as J. Reinach, for example, who are astonished that Diderot should champion the cause of cool reason against turbulent sensitivity: this means that they have recognized only one pole in Diderot's basically paradoxical or dialectical nature: the man who could weep about an artistic creation of his own (*La religieuse*)—as later Balzac was to do—sensed the danger of absorption by his capacities of impersonation, and felt keenly the advantages of calm and economy of effort. Mr. Dieckmann has rightly written: "The *Paradoxe sur le comédien* is, in truth, a polemic of Diderot's against himself, an antagonism between his extremely sensitive and his rationalistic tendencies."

29. How close, in Diderot's opinion, the nephew is to the real genius is shown by the following passage in which a famous mathematician is described (quoted by Dieckmann from XI, 125): "Celui-ci est un imitateur sublime de nature; voyez ce qu'il sait exécuter . . . admirez son ouvrage étonnant; eh bien, il n'a pas sitôt déposé l'instrument de son métier, qu'il est fou. Ce poète que la sagesse paraît inspirer et dont les écrits sont remplis de sentences à graver en lettres d'or, dans un instant ne sait plus ce qu'il fait; il est fou. Cet orateur qui s'empare de nos âmes et de nos esprits, qui en dispose à son gré, descendu de la chaire, il n'est plus maître de lui; il est fou. . . . Heureux, cent fois heureux, m'écriai-je encore, M. Baliveau, capitoul de Toulouse! C'est M. Baliveau qui boit bien, qui mange bien, qui digère bien, qui dort bien. . . . M. Baliveau est un homme fait pour son bonheur et pour le malheur des autres. Son neveu, M. de l'Empirée, tout au contraire." (Baliveau and M. de l'Empirée are characters in Piron's *La métromanie*.)

30. To express it in the words of Diderot himself, as found elsewhere in the dialogue: "Je n'estime pas ces originaux-là. . . . Ils m'arrêtent une fois l'an parce . . . qu'ils rompent cette fastidieuse uniformité que notre éducation, nos conventions de société, nos bienséances d'usages ont introduite . . . c'est un grain de levain qui fermente. . . . Il secoue, agite, il fait

approuver ou blâmer; il fait sortir la vérité, il fait connaître les gens de bien, il démasque les coquins, . . . c'est alors que l'homme de bon sens écoute et démêle son monde."

Or, in the absolutely concordant observations on "sensibilité" to be found in the *Paradoxe sur le comédien,* which sound like a description of the nephew (and which Trahard was right in placing at the beginning of his discussion of this character) : "La sensibilité . . . est, ce me semble, cette disposition compagne de la faiblesse des organes, suite de la mobilité du diaphragme, de la vivacité de l'imagination, de la délicatesse des nerfs qui incline à compatir, à frissonner, à admirer, à craindre, à secourir, à fuir, à crier, à perdre la raison, à exagérer, à mépriser, à dédaigner, à n'avoir aucune idée précise du vrai, du bon et du beau, à être injuste, à être fou."

Diderot, that "homme de bon sens," may perhaps have listened oftener than he would admit to the stimulating fool that existed in himself. The union of the stimulating fool with the epicurean and opportunistic "average man" ("je suis l'apôtre de la familiarité et de l'aisance," says the nephew) in all these *vauriens* is a typically French blend: the German type (e.g. Michael Kohlhaus) and the Spanish (e.g. Don Quijote) are not epicureans but stoics. Falstaff, perhaps, comes very close to the French figures, only that his belly does not make him fit for dynamicism. It would appear that the period of the French bourgeois, whose desires tend toward the preservation of an unquestioned, mediocre, material welfare, has engendered a revolutionary type which is critical of this same bourgeoisie.

31. In fact, the nephew's self-characterization: "Vous savez que je suis un ignorant, un sot, un fou, un impertinent, un paresseux, ce que nos Bourguignons appellent un fieffé truand, un escroc, un gourmand . . ."; "j'étais leur petit Rameau, leur joli Rameau, leur Rameau le fou, l'impertinent, l'ignorant, le paresseux, le gourmand, le bouffon, la grosse bête" is derived from Marot's enumeration of derogatory epithets (in his characterization of the "valet de Gascogne," another in the series of the French "grands vauriens")—which culminates in the indulgent conclusion "au demourant le meilleur fils du monde." This same indulgent attitude was also characteristic of the milieu in which the nephew moved.

It is interesting to read the description of Diderot himself, drawn up according to Marot's pattern, as given by a contemporary: cf. Trahard, II, 60.

32. When Goethe calls the nephew a "nicht ganz talentloser, phantastisch-praktischer Musikus" he has blurred the real paradox in this character: it is of no great moment whether he has talent or not, whether he is fantastic or practical; what truly matters is the basic paradox which he consistently illustrates. In the portion of the dialogue which has pleased Goethe the most, the nephew makes himself the advocate of that new music of Duni and the Bouffons, which Diderot himself felt to be the right music (as is shown by the approving remarks of MOI), the music which characterizes and expresses human nature, instead of stylizing it into a uniform, evenly flowing *bel canto.* But, while the nephew, as musical critic, knows true values—as a performer of this expressive music he is shown to be utterly lacking in restraint and coordination. Here Diderot has the nephew become the mouthpiece of his own (musical) ideals, while

behaving like a clown as he enacts these ideals. Thus the reactions of Diderot the philosopher, who watches, along with us, the ridiculous spectacle of this performer playing an orchestra of imaginary instruments, who finally collapses under the stress of emotion, are divided between admiration and derisive pity. Expressive art must not be performed expressively: this truth, which is expounded in the *Paradoxe sur le comédien*, is here illustrated by the deterrent example of the nephew, who is chosen because, unlike his uncle the creative artist, he is only performer and imitator. He is the uncreative musician; we see him beat his brains, knock his forehead, searching for a creative idea; when none is forthcoming, he finds a new gesture: with his hand over his heart he exclaims: "je sens, oui, je sens." He is an embodiment of "le paradoxe du musicien sensible."

33. Nor is there lacking autobiographical confirmation of Diderot's fear of being unable to cope with reality and of being overpowered by his imitative mobility (Ledieu, p. 139): "Grimm m'a dit plusieurs fois que j'avais été fait pour un autre monde. . . . ce qu'il y a de certain, c'est qu'il y a bientôt cinquante ans que je suis étranger dans celui-ci, que je vis d'une vie imitative, qui n'est pas la mienne, et que je suis comme un chien qui apprend à marcher sur deux pattes. De là une démarche tantôt originale, tantôt gauche."

34. This failure may be explained, perhaps, by the fact that Diderot, in the nephew has presented the artistic nature *in corpore vili*; and Goethe, the translator and interpreter of Cellini, was wont to predicate the artistic nature only on genuine artistic achievements. Sainte-Beuve remains even further behind understanding, since he confesses that he can see in the dialogue only less than Goethe. And he does what un-understanding critics will always do: blame the author for what they have not understood: "Ce sont des idées qui se sont enivrées et qui se sont mises à courir les unes après les autres." But these ideas originated in a potent brain which Sainte-Beuve has failed to understand.

Daniel Mornet in his article "La véritable signification du Neveu de Rameau" (*Revue des deux mondes* [1927], p. 889), distinguishes three elements in our dialogue: (1) a realistic element, the description of the "physiognomy" and "pantomime" of Jean-François Rameau, who was a historical personage; (2) a polemic or satire against the moral prostitution prevalent among writers of the time; (3) a forceful demonstration of the moral consequences of Diderot's own philosophy—which, according to Mornet, was a materialistic one. Accordingly, to begin with (1), the description of the nephew's pantomime would be relegated to the biographical datum of the historical Rameau (while, according to Mornet, the actual features and behavior of the historical Rameau have been greatly embellished, this represents a "dramatic and poetic realism" on the part of Diderot, who sees this figure "à travers son imagination échauffée"). To this I would answer that what Mornet considers as artistic embellishments added by Diderot onto the historical features of Jean-François Rameau ("rehaussées, diversifiées, amusées d'une vie frénétique et sans aucun doute surnaturelle") are rather the core of the artistic character: it is the "vie frénétique" that Diderot has embodied in a person whom he borrowed from contemporary history for illustrative purposes. And one must wonder at the psychological awkwardness of the critic which can conceive of supernatural gifts as an "amusing" embellishment!

As for the two morals of this dialogue (points 2 and 3), neither is basic, it seems to me: there is really only one problem, that of the "vie frénétique": a problem which unfolds before us dialectically and dramatically—and which is never solved (as little as the problem of "Est-il bon, est-il méchant?" is solved). By Mornet's three-fold classification, the unity of the problem is dissolved and its poignancy diluted.

Moreover, though Mornet makes much of the satirical intention of this dialogue (he stresses the fact that *Le neveu de Rameau* has the subtitle "Satire"), that is, in my opinion, only secondary: the nephew is not exclusively the butt of satire; admiration forms part of the medley of feelings with which Diderot views him (and he is declared by his creator to be "better than most; for he is, at least, no hypocrite"). As for the satiric light cast on contemporary (especially on literary) mores, it could be said that this gives us, so to speak, only a by-pleasure—as we listen to the nephew fulminate against the bourgeois world, whose pleasures he does not disdain.

According to G. Rohlfs, who was kind enough to send me an offprint of a short note of his in *Arch. f. neuere Sprachen*, CLXXXII, 137, E. R. Curtius has published an article on *Le neveu de Rameau* in which he seeks to refute the thesis of Mornet, and sees in the work of Diderot a satire patterned on Horace's Seventh—that paraphrase of the Stoic teaching "only the wise man is free; the fool is a slave." I am quite willing to agree that this Stoic and Horatian idea is present in Diderot's "satire"; I am not in a position to state whether Curtius is satisfied with thus cataloguing our work or whether he has pointed out the relationship of the *Neveu* with the inner rhythm of Diderot himself.

The idea of the *corpus vile* of the artist will be taken up later by Nietzsche who, when portraying the artist—that "über alle Massen sinnlicher und eitler Affe"—was wont to exemplify with the actor (and saw the "Schauspieler seiner selbst" in the artist Wagner). Again, Thomas Mann insists that the raw material of the actor is apishness ("affisch - komödiantisch") and that of the epic narrator, swaggering ("das Aufschneiderische"): cf. his speech on Wassermann in "Die Forderung des Tages." And Thomas Mann's character Felix Krull, the "confidence man," is only another version of Diderot's nephew with all his eagerness to act, to simulate, to masquerade, to consider himself an artist superior to the rest of mankind, and with his profession of anti-bourgeois feelings and immoralism: Thomas Mann's protagonist has imbibed in early youth the teaching of his god-father that Phidias was a thief: "Eine auffallende Mischung. Aber so sind die Leute. Sie wollen wohl das Talent, welches doch an und für sich eine Sonderbarkeit ist. Aber die Sonderbarkeiten, die sonst noch damit verbunden—und vielleicht notwendig damit verbunden—sind, die wollen sie nicht und verweigern ihnen jedes Verständnis."

35. We must stress here the word "machinalement" which is a neologism for Diderot's time: *machinal* is first attested with Voltaire in 1731, when he speaks of Peter the Great's phobia against water. While the seventeenth century reader (because of Descartes' celestial mechanics) had held such terms as *machine* (du monde), used in reference to the cosmic structure, in high esteem, the use of this word in a human reference, had no such lofty reference (Mme. de Sévigné: "Nos pauvres machines sont sujettes à bien des misères"). The texts cited by Littré concerning *machinal* for the

eighteenth century mention, for example, those "terreurs machinales" stemming from our human nature (from which education should free us), or express uneasiness over the "accord machinal" characteristic of the regimented Swiss army.

With Diderot, on the contrary, the best actions of man may sometimes be "automatic": it is "machinalement" that one of the two "Amis de Bourbonne" receives the blow intended for the other. The "spirit of observation" characteristic of the genius able to prophesy results without having to calculate them (IV, 26) is a "machine rare." In the *Paradoxe sur le comédien* the perfect comedian appears as the one who subjects himself to the automatism of a "mannequin" (the famous actress Clairon espouses in her acting "l'âme d'un grand mannequin qui l'enveloppe"). The great actor in general makes use of the "grimace pathétique," the "singerie sublime." The great comedian, the courtesan, the "flatterer by profession" (here, Diderot must have thought of the nephew) are "pantins" moved by the thread of their master. The very fact that Diderot can see automatism in the highest and in the lowest activities alike, shows that he is not, in principle, suspicious of automatism; it becomes alarming (though none the less a fascinating phenomenon for the observation of a scientist) only when the machinery is uncontrolled, with no engineer at the throttle.

36. The nephew whom Diderot describes as given to automatism has himself a keen eye for the automatism of others: the hypochondriac to whom he has hired himself as entertainer is described (p. 430) as a *pagodah* with a thread attached to his chin, who moves his jaws like an automaton; a "bégueule" who poses as an intellectual is described (p. 431) by a sequence of *item . . . item* which give the effect of a mechanism. The person who sees comic automatism everywhere must needs have something of the automaton in himself—as was, of course, the case with Diderot.

37. It is remarkable that, with Diderot, speech never deteriorates into psittacism or inarticulateness, as is the case with some modern writers—for example, Céline. Diderot describes the dionysiac in a language which renders it faithfully, but by means of an always grammatically correct French: indeed, a quite formal order may sometimes be observed, as, in our passage, the use of *ou . . . ou*: "il regardait *ou* attendri, *ou* tranquille, *ou* furieux . . . des eaux *ou* qui murmurent . . . *ou* qui descendent." This pattern, by means of which the contradictory parts of the subject matter are organized into the logical form of the alternative, has come (along with *et . . . et*) to be considered pedantic in modern French.

It is true that there can be found in Diderot's writings one type of "incoherent" syntax: the syncope represented by such examples as the following, where parallel actions are involved: (letter to Sophie of November 10, 1760) ". . . mon marivaudage, car je marivaude, Marivaux sans le savoir, *et moi le sachant*"; (*La religieuse*, v, 157): "Il acheva de me confier de sa vie, *moi de la mienne*, une infinité de circonstances qui formaient entre lui et moi autant de points de contact et de ressemblance." Compare also, from *Le neveu* (v, 391): "Je serais mieux entre Diogène et Phryne. Je suis affronté comme l'un, et je fréquente volontiers chez les autres" [*les autres*] = Phryne and the other courtesans?]; this example is the only one of the three which has been commented upon by the editors of the Assézat edition.

38. It must not, however, be forgotten that when Diderot insists on the bodily manifestations of the enthusiasm of the genius he is only reviving the bodily experience of the θεία μανία which had already been defined by antiquity (according to the Aristotelians, the poetic frenzy was even conditioned by bodily illness) and which the theoreticians of the Renaissance had taken pleasure in describing: "deus, ecce deus jam corpora fatigat, / altius insinuat venis, penitusque per artus / deditur atque faces saevas sub pectore versat. / Nec se jam capit acer agens calor igneaque intus / vis saevit totoque agitat se corpore numen" (Vida, cf. R. Meissner, *Festschrift f. Oskar Walzel*, p. 37). Shakespeare's line "the poet's eye, in a fine frenzy rolling" is a well-known bodily description of the *furor poeticus*. Diderot has transferred the traditional description of the θεία μανία to his own, characteristically eighteenth-century conception of the genius, and has made this description graphic by his personal gift of "innervation of style." Also in line with ancient thought is the equality of treatment which Diderot gives to "the lunatic, the lover, and the poet."

39. This statement is very important for the understanding of the conduct of the dialogue in Diderot's writings. Since, for Diderot, the conversation of a fool is no more and no less coherent than is any human conversation, and reflects the totality of life—why not depict conversation (and life) in general by that of a fool? With this theory, all the tricks and ticks of the nephew which Diderot brings into such relief are justified: not only his extravagant style and gestures, but also, for example, his habit of carrying on a conversation with himself, of interpolating a speech, and even a dialogue, within a speech (pp. 405, 446); here we witness a multiplication of levels and a demonstration of the power and vitality of human speech. Even genuine artists, in Diderot's opinion, can permit themselves a like freedom of interpolation; in his *Paradoxe sur le comédien*, Diderot's partner in the dialogue relates admiringly how two comedians playing Molière's *Dépit amoureux* interpolated a domestic quarrel between the lines of the play (in such a case we would have a tertiary interpolation: quarrel between the actors - their playing of Molière - the dialogue with Diderot). Again, in the *Rêve de D'Alembert*, Mlle. de l'Espinasse reads to Dr. Bordeu the notes she has taken down of the delirious words of her friend D'Alembert, who evidently was under the illusion of speaking to a fellow philosopher; the primary dialogue (between D'Alembert and the philosopher) is fitted into that between l'Espinasse and Bordeu. In *Jacques le fataliste* we have the innkeeper who speaks alternately as a story-teller and as an innkeeper. And the same *dédoublement* can be discerned with Diderot himself: he may introduce the public as speaker (e.g. in his "Ceci n'est pas un conte"), or he may address his own subject matter or the protagonists of his tale: the first takes place in his *Regrets sur ma vieille robe de chambre* (on which Sainte-Beuve has frowned: "l'apostrophe me gâte le naturel"), the second, in the article "Jouissance" and in the essay *Sur les femmes.*

Again, since a dream, like the conversation of a fool, is no more and no less coherent than conversation in general, and reflects the totality of life, Diderot can, in *Le rêve de D'Alembert,*" entrust a discussion of the totality of life to a conversation on a dream—the conversation and the dream having equal validity. We learn in this dialogue how a discovery has come to the scientist in his sleep: to D'Alembert, who had recently noticed a spider in the center of its web, the same pattern reappears in his dream, where he sees the organization of the unit called man as a network of sensations centered around one point. The conclusions which Bordeu and Mlle. de l'Espinasse develop logically from the incoherent words spoken by D'Alembert in his sleep, the latter has discovered as a consequence of his physiologically conditioned state of mind. After he has waked up, he listens rather passively to the logical exposition of the two partners who now tell him what he had already elaborated, subconsciously. We have here a bifurcation of the scientist's nature: the instinctive, intuitive (physiological) part of D'Alembert speaks out of his dream; the rational, theoretical part is expressed by the two partners. Here, Diderot has given dramatic expression to a saying of his (quoted by Schalk, p. 135, from the *Encyclopédie*): "Le génie porte naturellement son flambeau, et l'esprit qui ne suit pas avec la même vitesse reste en arrière et tâtonne dans les ténèbres"; we may also compare the sentiment expressed in a letter to Sophie (Ledieu, p. 91) which must have been written at the time of the *Rêve*: "Heureux celui qui a reçu de la nature une âme sensible et mobile! . . . C'est son coeur qui lie ses idées. . . . Cela tient du délire et ce n'est point du délire; cela tient du rêve et ce n'est point le rêve; ce sont les fils du réseau [the simile of the spider] qui commandent à leur origine; le maître se résout à la condition d'interprète."

Thus D'Alembert the theoretician must go to school to his intuition.

40. Paul Valéry, in his article on Montesquieu (in *Variété*, II) has come to approximately the same conclusions regarding the characteristics of the eighteenth century: this was, for him, the period of "the beginning of the end of a social arrangement," when the existing order was still enjoyed though, at the same time, there was a longing for freedom and disorder—which was afforded by the criticism of the existing order: "Alors, entre l'ordre et le désordre, règne un moment délicieux. . . . C'est l'heure de la jouissance et de la consommation générale. . . . Une flamme encore féerique, qui se développera en incendie, s'élève et court sur la face du monde. Elle éclaire bizarrement la danse des principes et des ressources. Les moeurs, les patrimoines fondent. Les mystères et les trésors se font vapeurs. Le respect se dissipe, et toutes les chaînes s'ammollissent dans cette ardeur de vie et de mort qui va croître jusqu'au délire."

41. Since it is true that the mobility we have observed in Diderot's writing belongs to a general tendency of eighteenth-century philosophy, it might be wondered if what has been pointed out as peculiar to Diderot may not also be observed in the writings of his contemporaries. And yet, even with a writer who was so akin intellectually and temperamentally to Diderot as was La Mettrie (the two were not friends, perhaps because of this very similarity), it is possible to see how "mobility" takes on an aspect quite different from that which we have noted with Diderot. For example, in La Mettrie's writing, nowhere have I found any indication that the rhythm of his periods is informed by his basic concept of the mechanical in man. What seems to me most conspicuous in his style is a certain "spirit of rapidity," the self-enjoyment of an imagination which delights in darting ahead unhampered; in the "exaggerations" of his descriptions there is a lightness of touch, a freedom of movement, which contrasts with the tension and exhaustion which Diderot's efforts so often seem to cost him. This "freedom" of expression is well illustrated in the two examples

below dealing with the play of the imagination: "Par elle [imagination], par son pinceau flatteur, le froid squelette de la raison prend des chairs vives et vermeilles; par elle, les sciences fleurissent, les arts s'embellissent, les bois parlent, les échos soupirent, tout prend vie par les corps inanimés . . . elle ne marche pas seulement à la suite des grâces et des beaux arts, elle ne peint pas seulement la nature, elle peut aussi la mesurer. Elle raisonne, juge, pénètre, compare . . . approfondit. . . . Plus on exerce l'imagination ou le plus maigre génie, plus il prend pour ainsi dire d'embonpoint; plus il s'agrandit, devient nerveux, robuste, vaste et capable de penser."

In this continuous, effortless crescendo, the phrase "prend des chairs vives" is immediately expanded to ". . . vermeilles," and a little later to "prendre de l'embonpoint"; the imagination of the author himself delights in immediate expansion. La Mettrie must have been describing his own imagination when, a little farther on, he remarks: "Voyez cet *oiseau sur la branche*[!], il semble toujours prêt à s'envoler; l'imagination est de même. Toujours emportée par le tourbillon du sang et des esprits; une onde fait une trace, effacée par celle qui suit; l'âme court après, souvent en vain: il faut qu'elle s'attende à regretter ce qu'elle n'a pas assez vite saisi et fixé: et c'est ainsi que l'imagination, véritable image du temps, se détruit et se renouvelle sans cesse."

It is true that, in the following passage, he recommends the bridling of imagination; but he seems to have experienced none of Diderot's anguish over the destructive power of a too fertile imagination. There was a basic gaiety in his nature which preserved him from the existential fear by which Diderot was haunted; as Frederick the Great wrote at La Mettrie's death: "M. de La Mettrie était né avec un fond de gaîté naturelle intarissable; il avait l'esprit vif et l'imagination si féconde, qu'elle faisait croître des fleurs dans le terrain aride de la médecine."

42. It is by reference to Diderot's conception of the necessity of mobility, when the human mind is faced with reality, that we can best explain *Jacques le fataliste*, this replica of the *Don Quijote* novel, whose basic plot is built upon the principle of the interruption and correction which reality forces upon minds which have rigid convictions (e.g. the fatalistic Jacques) or proclivities (e.g. Jacques' master who, with his craving for "stories," would subject life to the fixed experiences of the past). In this book, the speeches of the characters are regularly interrupted by situations which ask for appropriate deeds; human speech, with its "fixing function," is shown as a factor which prevents man from coping with reality. The basic narrative device used by Diderot in this work is that of interruption of the speaker: the innkeeper, at the most dramatic stages of her story of the Marquis des Arcis and Mme. de La Pommeraye finds herself beset by trivial solicitations ("Madame? Madame? Madame?" - ". . . je vous ai défendu de m'appeler; appelez mon mari" - "Il est absent" - "Messieurs, je vous demande pardon, je suis à vous dans un moment")—a graphic demonstration of the exactingness of life that breaks up crystallized speech.

43. Needless to say, the critics who complain about the fragmentariness of Diderot's work (e.g. Sainte-Beuve, Reinach, etc.) forget that this fragmentariness is conditioned by the style of mobility which made Diderot see things in flashes and, also, was responsible for his indifference to publishing his writings—which he may have dismissed as momentary out-

bursts. Diderot was more interested in performance than in achievement, more interested in activity than in acts.

Another fallacy of the critics is to judge Diderot contradictory and inconclusive because of this same mobility of mind and style. It is true that the movement of Diderot's writing seems to follow no straight line, but moves in circles. Nevertheless, this gyration takes place around the same set of problems. And the problem of the mobility of the mind can be made understandable only by an artistic process in which it is reflected. The nature of the problem treated by Diderot has unfortunately led the critics to see inconsistency in his apperceptive mind.

It is also easy to answer the objections about the absence of "creative imagination" in Diderot ("creative imagination" being identified with the invention of plots) and to justify those digressions in Diderot's "novels" which arouse Reinach, for example, to such impatience. In order to illustrate the mobility of the mind, Diderot multiplies anecdotes and digressions; a ready-made plot would have subordinated the freedom of the mind to an external inorganic order. Reinach states of *Le neveu de Rameau* that it is a fireworks of which nothing remains but a momentary impression. But since the dialogue in question is concerned with the fireworks of the human mind, how could this be depicted save by "momentary impressions"?

44. That human speech in itself has a self-igniting force (we say in common speech that a person "warms up" to his own words) is well known. But Diderot has found a "linguistic mechanism" whereby to render it: the use of the accelerating noun-clauses introduced by an anaphoric *que*. The following passage pictures the increasing firmness of speech and of conviction on the part of the speaker ("Entretiens d'un père avec ses enfants"): "Le docteur Bissei, après un moment d'incertitude, répondit ferme qu'il le [a murderer] guérirait; *qu*'il oublierait le nom du malade, pour ne s'occuper que du caractère de la maladie; *que* c'était la seule chose dont il fût permis de connaître; *qu*'il faisait un pas au delà, bientôt il ne saurait plus où s'arrêter; *que* ce serait abandonner la vie des hommes à la merci de l'ignorance, des passions, du préjugé, si l'ordonnance devait être précédée de l'examen de la vie et des moeurs du malade."

Or, again, the speech may become more heated and vivacious the less truth there is to the words ("Entretien d'un philosophe avec la Maréchale"): "Elle me répondit que c'était une chose d'usage [to show one's décolleté] . . . *qu*'il ne fallait pas se vêtir ridiculement. . . ; *qu*'elle se laissait habiller pas sa couturière. . . ; *que* c'était la fantaisie de son mari. . . ." Or when the words describe idle dreams (*La religieuse*) "[the hopes of a nun are:] qu'on trouvera les portes ouvertes, un jour; *que* les hommes reviendront de l'extravagance d'enfermer dans des sépulcres de jeunes créatures toutes vivants, et *que* les couvents seront abolis; *que* le feu prendra à la maison; *que* les murs de la clôture tomberont; *que* quelqu'un les secourra. Toutes ces suppositions roulent par la tête."

Finally, the speech may consist "only of words," of gossip (and it is this variant of the *que*-clause which has led, in certain Romance dialects, to a fixed form suggesting rumor, gossip, etc.). In the following example the gossipy nature of the Mother Superior's conversation is also indicated by zeugma (*demander* is out of place after the first clause; the Mother Superior may not have distinguished, by her voice, between question and statement: she simply wants to rattle away): "Elle [la supérieure] me demande comment je me portais; *que* l'office avait été bien long aujourd'hui; *que* j'avais un peu toussé; *que* je lui paraissais indisposée. . . ."

45. I have nowhere seen any reference to this rapprochement—which seems obvious to me. Mornet only remarks, by way of illustrating the opinion of the realistic school of commentators: "Jean-François Rameau—serait [sic] une sorte de faune non point mythologique, mais bien 'vivant.'"

46. The contagious quality of Diderot's mimicking style can be seen in its influence on Goethe, the translator of *Le neveu de Rameau*: in a note appended to this translation, in which he sums up the ideal characteristics of the French writer as embodied in Voltaire, we find a long list of qualities from which I detach only the following enumeration: "Leichtigkeit, Lebhaftigkeit, Feinheit, Brillantes, Saillantes, Petillantes, Pikantes, Delikates, Ingeniöses"—which surely sounds like an imitation of the prose of Diderot.

And the same stylistic contagion acts on Hofmannsthal when he defines Diderot's *Neveu* as an impersonation of life with all its contradictions (*Gesamm. Werke* III, 133): "Diderot, für den die Welt existierte, Diderot, der den Narziss Rameau schrieb, der die Gestalt schuf, die von Leben trieft und von Wirklichkeit strotzt und von mehr als Wirklichkeit funkelt, diesen Schwätzer Narziss Rameau, diesen Denker, diesen Schmarotzer, diesen im Innern unbestechlichen Richter der Menschen, diesen Lumpen, diese verführerische Seele von einem Menschen . . . für einige . . . spaziert er noch immer umher . . . und redet, redet, redet, und indem er redet, und klatscht und philosophiert und Komödie spielt und einen dicken Bankier kopiert und eine kleine Dirne kopiert und bellt wie ein Hund und dazwischen das Menschliche schmerzlich höhnt wie Hamlet und darüber lächelt wie ein Weiser Griechenlands—unter diesem strömt von seinen wulstigen feuchten Lippen, strömt von seiner nicht sonderlich edlen Stirn ein Etwas, das die Luft erfüllt, das Fetzen von Lebensmöglichkeiten herumstreut in allen Ecken, Fetzen von Liebe, Hass, Verachtung, Zärtlichkeit, Glanz, Jammer, Dirnenhaftigkeit, Reinheit, Gottähnlichkeit, jammervoller Verlassenheit . . . Leben, Leben, Leben. Welch eine französische Kreatur, welch eine menschliche Kreatur, welch eine zeitlose Kreatur, welch eine nicht wieder zu vergessende Kreatur!" It is as though the German poet could not speak of the *Neveu* without falling into Diderot's "automatism of enthusiasm."

5

INTERPRETATION OF AN ODE BY PAUL CLAUDEL

Argumentum: One stanza (the first) from one poem ("La Muse qui est la Grâce"), belonging to a series of six "Grandes Odes," is singled out from the whole work of Claudel for stylistic interpretation—a stanza of unusual length (covering several pages) in which the author seems to set forth the purpose of the ode(s), and which, at first sight, appears oppressively dense and opaque. The linguistic detail which, here, served as the point of departure was the repetition of the epithet "grand," found five times in the selection. The five lines in which it occurs were found, when analyzed logically, to offer a skeleton outline of the author's program; when observed from the lyrical point of view, they revealed an ever-increasing intensity and breadth. This suggested that theme and rhythm must be considered together: the theme is that of gradual ascension and triumph (a two-fold triumph: that of man over Nature, and that of the poet struggling to conquer his subject), and this forward and onward movement is incarnated in the ever-ascending waves of the rhythm—as in the verbal motif-work. But, as one begins to follow the course of the poem, one sees that this ascending movement makes its way against an adverse current: the poet's expressions of determination and confidence in his solemn purpose are counterbalanced in the first part of the poem: we find successive outbursts (gradually diminishing) of petulance, which reveal a conflict in the poet (such devices as the repetition of "Laisse-moi . . ." !), as well as occasional shifts of tone from the lofty to the trivial and jocular. Both of these are due to the influence (from which the poet has not yet been able quite to free himself) of the pagan Muse, to whom he had formerly paid allegiance. Thus the whole stanza reveals itself as expressing a struggle between pagan and Christian forces in the breast of the poet—a struggle which informs also the other odes of the collection, and which is inherent in any attempt on the part of a modern Christian poet who would write in the form of an ancient ode. And, with this, we are brought to a comparison of

Claudel's Christian ode with the paganistic ode of Ronsard: where the latter failed, Claudel has succeeded in resolving the ever-present paradox underlying the reception by a modern artist of an ancient form. Whereas a literary historian, interested in his categories, may easily speak of "Christian vs. pagan poetry," this *versus,* this sign of a historical struggle of cultures, is reenacted in Claudel's soul and is embodied in the linguistic form of his poem.

"O grammarien dans mes vers!
Ne cherche point le chemin, cherche le centre!"
(Cinq Grandes Odes, I*)*

THE passage below is taken from the fourth ode in the collection *Cinq grandes odes suivies d'un processional pour saluer le siècle nouveau* (Paris, 1913), which deals, with variations, with the task of the Catholic poet in our modern world. Ode IV "La Muse qui est la Grâce" was written at Tientsin in 1907. The passage we shall consider is Strophe I of the ode, which is constructed according to a Ronsardian or Pindaric scheme: after an introduction there follow three "strophes" with their respective "antistrophes" (the first containing the words of the poet, the latter those of the Muse), and the poem ends with an "epode" which, like the introduction, reveals to us the feelings of the poet.[1] To this ode Claudel has prefixed the following "argument" (in which I have introduced references to the metrical divisions): "[introduction] Invasion de l'ivresse poétique. [strophes and antistrophes I-III]. Dialogue du poète avec la Muse qui devient peu à peu la Grâce. Il essaye de la refouler, il lui demande de la laisser à son devoir humain, à la place de son âme il lui offre l'univers entier qu'il va recréer par l'intelligence et la parole. En vain, c'est à lui personnellement que la Muse qui est la Grâce ne cesse de s'adresser! C'est la joie divine qu'elle lui rappelle et son devoir de sanctification personnelle.—[epode] Mais le poète se bouche les oreilles et se retourne vers la terre. Suprême évocation de l'amour charnel et humain."

Here follows the text of Strophe I:

—O Muse, il sera temps de dormir un autre jour! Mais puisque cette grande nuit tout entière est à nous,
Et que je suis un peu ivre en sorte qu'un autre mot parfois
Vient à la place du vrai, à la façon que tu aimes,
Laisse-moi avoir explication avec toi,
Laisse-moi te refouler dans cette strophe; avant que tu ne reviennes sur moi comme une vague avec un cri félin!
Va-t-en de moi un peu! laisse-moi faire ce que je veux un peu!
Car, quoique je fasse et si que je le fasse de mon mieux,
Bientôt je vois un oeil se lever sur moi en silence comme vers quelqu'un qui feint.
Laisse-moi être nécessaire! laisse-moi remplir fortement une place reconnue et approuvée,
Comme un constructeur de chemins de fer, on sait qu'il ne sert pas à rien, comme un fondateur de syndicats!
Qu'un jeune homme avec son menton orné d'un flocon jaunâtre,
Fasse des vers, on sourit seulement.
J'attendais que l'âge me délivrât des fureurs de cet esprit bachique.
Mais, loin que j'immole le bouc, à ce rire qui gagne des couches plus profondes
Il me faut trouver que je ne fais plus sa part.
Du moins laisse-moi faire de ce papier ce que je veux et le remplir avec un art studieux,
Ma tâche, comme ceux-là qui en ont une.
Ainsi le scribe égyptien recensait de sa pointe minutieuse les tributs, et les parts de butin, et les files de dix captifs attachés,
Et les mesures de blé que l'on porte à la meule banale, et les barques à la douane.
Ainsi l'antique sculpteur avec sa tignasse rougie à la chaux attrapé à sa borne de basalte noir avec la massette et le ciseau,
Et de temps en temps il souffle sur ses caractères pareils à des clous entrecroisés pour ôter la poussière et se recule avec contentement.
Et je voudrais compasser un grand poème plus clair que la

lune qui brille avec sérénité sur la campagne dans la semaine de la moisson,
Et tracer une grande Voie triomphale au travers de la Terre,
Au lieu de courir comme je peux la main sur l'échine de ce quadrupède ailé qui m'entraîne, dans sa course cassée qui est à moitié aile et bond!
Laisse-moi chanter les oeuvres des hommes et que chacun retrouve dans mes vers ces choses qui lui sont connues,
Comme de haut on a plaisir à reconnaître sa maison, et la gare, et la mairie, et ce bonhomme avec son chapeau de paille, mais l'espace autour de soi est immense!
Car à quoi sert l'écrivain, si ce n'est à tenir des comptes?
Que ce soit les siens ou d'un magasin de chaussures, ou de l'humanité tout entière.
Ne t'indigne pas! ô soeur de la noire Pythie qui broie la feuille de laurier entre ses mâchoires resserrées par le trisme prophétique et un filet de salive verte coule du coin de sa bouche!
Ne me blesse point avec ce trait de tes yeux!
O géante! ne te lève pas avec cet air de liberté sublime!
O vent sur le désert! ô ma bien aimée pareille aux quadriges de Pharaon!
Comme l'antique poète parlait de la part des dieux privés de présence,
Et moi je dis qu'il n'est rien dans la nature qui soit fait sans dessein et propos à l'homme adressé,
Et comme lumière pour l'oeil et le son pour l'oreille, ainsi toute chose pour l'analyse de l'intelligence,
Continuée avec l'intelligence qui la
Refait de l'élément qu'elle récupère,
Que ce soit la pioche qui le dégage, ou le pan du prospecteur et l'amalgame de mercure,
Ou le savant, la plume à la main, ou le tricot des métiers, ou la charrue.
Et je puis parler, continu avec toute chose muette,
Parole qui est à sa place intelligence et volonté.
Je chanterai le grand poème de l'homme soustrait au hasard!
Ce que les gens ont fait autour de moi avec le canon qui ouvre les vieux Empires,

Avec le canot démontable qui remonte l'Aruwhimi, avec l'expédition polaire qui prend des observations magnétiques,
Avec les batteries de hauts-fourneaux qui digèrent le minerai, avec les frénétiques villes haletantes et tricotantes, (et ça et là une anse bleue de la rivière dans la campagne solennelle),
Avec les ports tout bordés intérieurement de pinces et d'antennes et le transatlantique qui signale au loin dans le brouillard,
Avec la locomotive qu'on attelle à son convoi, et le canal qui se remplit quand la fille de l'Ingénieur-en-chef du bout de son doigt sur le coup-de-poing fait sauter à la fois la double digue,
Je le ferai avec un poème qui ne sera plus l'aventure d'Ulysse parmi les Lestrygons et les Cyclopes, mais la connaissance de la Terre,
Le grand poème de l'homme enfin par delà les causes secondes réconcilié aux forces éternelles,
La grande Voie triomphale au travers de la Terre réconciliée pour que l'homme soustrait au hasard s'y avance!

Strophe I opens after the poet has already been invaded by the poetic frenzy, and when he is ready to formulate the task he feels to be incumbent upon him; this strophe, in which this formulation is developed, is addressed to the Muse, whose answer, given only in Antistrophe I, sets up a conflict which rages throughout the poem: viz. the question of the estrangement of the poet from the earth. Though we isolate this one strophe of one ode, the notes will provide the connections with the other parts of the ode and the other odes of the collection.

An artistic unit such as this, startling as it must have appeared when first printed, is hardly less baffling to us today: it offers the form of a sphere, whose unbroken surface seems to yield no likely point of attack. For, whatever particular part we may choose to concentrate upon, we are intimidated from the start by the thought that this will always be only a particular part, and that such concentration may impair our understanding of the unity and cohesiveness of the work of art. But, if we think of this globe as a sun-ball, and of the particular points as sunbeams, we may be sure that, just as from any particular sunbeam we may infer the live force which sends forth all the sunbeams, so we will be able to penetrate from any peripheral point of the work of art to its core. It is my firm belief, corroborated by the experience of many exercises practiced in seminars with my students, where I chose to start from any particular point suggested by one of the group, that any one good observation will, when sufficiently deepened, infallibly lead to the center of the work of art. There are no preferential vantage points (such as the "ideas," the structure, of the poem, etc.) with which we are obliged to start: any well-observed item can become a vantage-point and, however arbitrarily chosen, must, if rightly developed, ultimately lose its arbitrariness.

Let us decide to start with the language of the poem—which, in itself, offers various aspects: the poet's syntactical license, his blend of popular and learned words,[2] etc. I shall deal first with Claudel's technique of "word-motifs," where the possibilities are still greater: I could start from any single one of the leading words indicated in the title of this collection, or in the title of our ode ("Muse," "Grâce," "odes," "saluer," "siècle nouveau")—all of which are repeated or paraphrased in our strophe. I choose to start with the epithet "grand" in the title "Cinq grandes odes . . . ," an epithet which suggests that level of poetic sublimity which is traditionally associated with the ode, and which distinguishes Claudel's ode from the lighter Anacreontic variety with which in France the genre has traditionally been confused since the time of the Pléïade. The epithet "grand" occurs six times:[3]

(1) O Muse! . . . puisque cette grande nuit tout entière est à nous

(22) Et je voudrai compasser un grand poème

(23) Et tracer une grande Voie triomphale au travers de la Terre

(42) Je chanterai le grand poème de l'homme soustrait au hasard!

(49) Le grand poème de l'homme enfin par delà les causes secondes réconcilié aux forces éternelles
(50) La grande Voie triomphale au travers de la Terre réconciliée pour que l'homme soustrait au hasard s'y avance!

Three things are great: the night of inspiration (1), the poem envisaged (22, 42, 49), and the progress of man (23, 49, 50)—which shall be the subject of this poem. The purposefulness and precision of Claudel's use of "grand," as illustrated by these six passages,[4] is evident and could suggest that the passages themselves have prominence in the architecture of our strophe; and, upon examination, this turns out to be the case. The first passage sets the background of the composition of our strophe (while also connected with the Introduction descriptive of the invasion of poetic frenzy); in the last (which is the final line of the strophe) we are offered the program of Claudel's poem—his *arma virumque cano*, which he builds up for us piecemeal in the preceding four lines: we see first a triumphal way traversing the earth, then man freed from the accidental and, finally, the convergence of both motifs in a triumphant apotheosis.[5] We could also speak of five motifs contained in this program and which are basic to the strophe: "homme" (11), "voie triomphale," "terre" (23), "l'homme," "soustrait au hasard" (42)—several of which we find repeated or paraphrased in these same six passages.

These six versets can be immediately reduced to four (1; 22-23; 42; 49-50), giving us three subdivisions of the strophe which we may be allowed to call "stanzas"—although no such indication is given by the printed arrangement. In the upward progression of this strophe the lines we have isolated represent plateaux breaking our climb toward the peak whence we can envisage the final panorama of Claudel's vision. Or if, remembering the surging flow of our poem, which from the start engulfs us like an ocean, we may be allowed to change our metaphor, these high ridges which loom above the rest of the lines are so many crests of onrushing waves, the last of which seems to prolong itself beyond the limits of our strophe—whose final word is "avance!"[6] We may, perhaps, conjecture that by this rolling upward and onward of word-floods and word-waves, Claudel means to figure the progression and ascension of man in his conquest of Nature; not only will the poem tell of progress, it will, itself, vibrate with the rhythm of a progress which carries us along in its forward movement—an idea become poetic activity. Here we are reminded of the poetry of Péguy in which we find the same process of gradual expansion toward a climax (though with Péguy each climax leads immediately, without recession, to a new height). What Claudel and Péguy have in common is the Bergsonian sensitivity to the *élan vital* and to the flow of time; the theme of Progress is essentially a theme of Time. By both poets the work of art is offered not as something "tout fait," but as "se faisant" before our eyes.[7]

Who says rhythm says metrics. We will not find in Claudel any regular system of rhyme or meter. Language, with him, is not subjected to the coercion from without of preordained metrics, as is the case with orthodox French poetry; it is conditioned by an inner motivation and impulsion whose intensity and direction may vary at any moment. And the divisions which the poet usually indicates by metrical devices are here suggested by the recurrence of word-motifs—what we have called the flood-and-wave technique. Within the expanse of the strophe, which is like a sea sending forth its floods, there cannot be the sharp division of fixed stanzas—only the tenuous limits we have been able to discern by following the wave-movement to its crest: indeed, it is possible to find double or triple crests, as in 22-23 and 48-49-50. As for the "stanzas" so discerned, we may observe the diminishing size of the three units: the poem starts slowly, with a gradual acceleration of its course until the end is reached—which prolongs itself into the infinite. The corresponding efforts of understanding called for from the reader must be given a chance to gain sufficient strength for the final synthesis or apotheosis. And, to the progressive intensification of the reader's effort, corresponds a growing firmness on the part of the poet; the stiffening of his will is reflected in the variation of tenses suggestive of three stages of decision: (1) "Et je voudrais compasser un poème" (still wavering); (42) "Je chanterai le grand poème . . ." (prediction of a firm decision); (48) "Je le ferai avec un poème" (*faire* emphasizes the practical realization of this purpose).

Up to now we have followed the verbal-metrical scheme of the strophe only insofar as it throws light upon the ideological purpose of this proem. But in a proem there is generally present a second topos: in order to fulfill his purpose the poet calls upon the Muse for inspiration. In our strophe the Muse is mentioned in the title and in the opening line (as in Homer's Ἄνδρα μοι ἔννεπε, Μοῦσα, πολύτροπον) but, as the poem proceeds, her influence seems to fade; she is mentioned for the last time in lines 31-32, where the vocatives and imperatives addressed to her come to an end. It is as though the "flood" of the Muse-motif had completely receded at this point. But in our strophe Claudel's Muse is a force, not invoked for his help but, on the contrary, rejected by him; this attitude, strange enough on the part of a poet, takes definite shape as early as the fifth line: "Laisse-moi te refouler[8] dans cette strophe; avant que tu ne reviennes sur moi comme une vague . . ."[9] (here Claudel himself uses the "wave" metaphor —which, I may say, was not suggested to me by this line but occurred to me independently when I was attempting to define his technique). And the recession of the Muse-flood forms a movement contrary to the movement by which the program of the poet gradually takes shape: she is an antagonistic power in whom is incarnated all that he would shun, that he fears or loathes; the inebriation caused by the gods of pleasure, of licentiousness, of casualness (her animality is emphasized by *cri félin*,[10] line 5, and *le bouc*, line 14). Now, if we seek to discover a "Muse" word-motif comparable to that descriptive of the poetic program, we shall find signs of this only in the series of vocatives and imperatives (which suggest the presence of an influenceable being and which must cease when the poet's new-found determination releases him from dependence on the Muse); this being, who must be "refoulée," is distinguished by no motif as graphic as that which was used in allusion to the positive purpose of the poet. The presence of the Muse as it acts on the poet is indicated only indirectly by allusions to his attitude toward her, and this attitude expresses itself in words with a climate of their own. First, we find humorously slighting expressions and a particularly flippant tone, as though the poet, in a gesture of withdrawal, sought to taunt her and make light of his previous inclination toward her.[11] The particular flavor of this vocabulary, fickle, wavering, unprecise, is, perhaps, primarily due to the poet's state of mild intoxication inspired by the capricious pagan Muse—against whose influence he is on guard (". . . en sorte qu'un autre mot parfois / Vient à la place du vrai, à la façon que tu aimes").[12]

The poet is only "un peu ivre," not drunken (as he must have been earlier, since he fears being invaded again by the Muse: "que tu ne reviennes sur moi . . .")—not drunken, that is, with the heavenly enthusiasm and sweet frenzy celebrated by the pagan poets from Plato to Ronsard.[13] One of the first of the expressions used about the Muse has a popular, even a vulgar ring: "Laisse-moi avoir explication avec toi" ("thrash things out with you"), as if tipsiness encouraged vulgarity, freeing the poet from the obligation of using the vocabulary of a cultured man. The teasing tone continues: "Va-t-en de moi *un peu*!" "laisse-moi faire ce que je veux *un peu*"; a pouting child that wants to be left alone would indulge in such stubborn, monotonous phrases.[14] Again, "quoique je fasse et *si que* je le fasse de mon mieux" has the deranged syntax that is to be heard in any French *bistro*. These humorous[15] expressions may seem at first glance strangely aberrant from the sublime tone characteristic of the ode. And indeed, the very fact that they are transplanted into an exalted environment serves to bring out in strong relief the lack of harmony and poise in the poet's attitude at this point: not yet having attained finality of decision, he can show his aversion only through (a humorous assumption of) childish petulance.

But humor recedes as a more serious guide makes an appearance—an anonymous force which bans the casual: "Bientôt je vois un oeil se lever *sur moi en silence* comme vers quelqu'un qui feint. Laisse-moi être nécessaire . . ." (as opposed to "avant que tu ne reviennes *sur moi . . . avec un cri félin*"). This silent being whose gaze he feels—and which may remind us of Hugo's silent eye of conscience—is evidently Christian grace, which will ultimately assume the role of the poet's true Muse and which now, mutely, within his conscience, rebukes him for his infidelity with the pagan Muse. And, with "nécessaire," the motif of "l'homme soustrait au hasard" appears for the first time; the poem, which will sing of man freeing himself from the casual, must not be casual. For what Claudel censures most in the pagan Muse is not sensuality itself so much as the arbitrariness of a spirit not oriented on Christian, on "necessary" principles. It would be a betrayal of his own nature to indulge in the irrelevancy of Bacchic frenzy or dionysiac corybantism (13-14); there is an insidious danger to the Christian soul in the laughter of Bacchus, "ce rire qui gagne des couches plus profondes"; laughter *per se* is, for Claudel, not "le propre de l'homme" (as Rabelais has declared); it is not "nécessaire," it is juvenile, worthy of a "jeune homme, avec son menton orné de. . . ."[16]

And now that the poet feels more free to follow his true and necessary nature, we will find again that technique associated with his positive purpose: word-repetition; "nécessaire" is the first wave which will ultimately lead to the "crests" of "Et je voudrais compasser un grand poème," "Je chanterai le grand poème de l'homme soustrait au hasard"—which can be achieved only after pagan enthusiasm has completely subsided. It is only gradually that this intoxication recedes: even after the poet has expressed his desire to write "un grand poème plus clair que la lune," the frivolous note reappears (though here, as always, he uses frivolity to exorcise the pagan world of frivolity): in verset 24 he describes Pegasus in words which limp, as if to mimic the erratic gait of this absurd beast (for, with Claudel, the heavenly courser of the Greeks, limps): "dans sa course cassée qui est à moitié aile et bond."[17] Here, the whimsicality of pagan poetry appears in the form of hybridism. And Claudel spurns the hybrid, which had been exalted in pagan poetry; like the medieval poets in their treatment of classical demigods, he (cynically) pretends to see in such blends only the imperfect and incongruous.

Now, after following the poet in his excursion into frivolity and animality, let us return to the line (9) where the motif "nécessaire" first appears. This impressive line is followed by a hemistich which may astonish many readers: after the poet has proclaimed inner necessity to be his moving force, we hear the request: "laisse-moi remplir fortement une place reconnue et approuvée, / Comme un constructeur de chemins de fer, on sait qu'il ne sert pas à rien, comme un fondateur de syndicats." The poet asks to play a role in society! This premium placed on *fama*, this acceptance of the "ut in pluribus" principle is evidence of the Thomist trend in Claudel; the inner necessity which guides him in his poetic activity asks for the complement of a necessary role among his fellow men. In Claudel's opinion, the poet should not be a peripheral phenomenon: he should occupy a place in society,[18] he should be necessary as a modern railroad executive is necessary, or a trade-union leader. And, since Claudel would like to join the ranks of the workingmen (to be himself a "writing-man"), he must adopt their language; his words have the bluff, hearty flavor of the speech of a Parisian workingman who talks straight from the shoulder ("on sait qu'il ne sert pas à rien")[19]—as "one sensible person to another." With this shift into the practical, commercial and political world of today, we are given the first indication in this strophe of the complex of ideas represented by the "siècle nouveau"[20] mentioned in the title of the collection: it is the material progress of our world which Claudel hails. The poet must not despise the world of his day, as Vigny did in *La Maison du Berger*, as Duhamel does in *Scènes de la vie future*."[21] But this gigantic program is not presented in one piece, a manifesto "tout fait"; it emerges only gradually out of conflicting tendencies; and the solemn resolve is first expressed childishly, almost petulantly ("laisse-moi *du moins*")—though it is immediately recast in accents of dignity: "remplir fortement une place reconnue et approuvée." The expression "art studieux" joins the ideological complex of "nécessaire" in its reminder of that laboriousness necessary to one who would be a workingman. The best examples which Claudel gives of the "art studieux" are drawn not from ancient Greece and Rome but from Egypt and Assyria: the Egyptian "scribe"[22] (which word is an etymological pun on *écrivain*, 27)[23], who was a tabulator, and the Assyrian engraver of cuneiform, bring to mind not the reverie of a poet withdrawn from the world but a technical skill which is socially useful (Claudel would share the professional pride of the Assyrian workman who rejoices in his skill), as well as precision of craftsmanship; from "pointe minutieuse," "attrapé avec la massette et le ciseau"[24] there is a smooth transition to "compasser (un poème plus clair que la lune)"[25] and "tracer (une grande voie au travers de la terre)"—which brings us to that main artery we have distinguished before. This vastest of enterprises which the poet envisages must be worked out with the greatest minuteness of detail, and this he proposes in lines which themselves have been chiseled with a painstaking precision that retards for the moment the oceanic sweep of the verse. The poet, then, must be an *écrivain*, a scribe—a simple "writing man." What Dante-like modesty (coupled with Dante's ambition) on the part of one of the greatest poets of all times![26]

With line 25, which is situated exactly in the middle of the poem, man makes his first appearance, in the phrase "l'oeuvre des hommes" (anticipatory of "l'homme," in 42)—as if to imply that man is the center of a universe created for him; this idea (which, for all of Claudel's disregard of serious pagan thought, is a Thomist derivate of the ancient πάντων μέτρον ἄνθρωπος will be outspokenly stated in line 34. In this same line, where the program motif "chanter" appears, we also find the last of Claudel's defensive "laisse-moi's" addressed to the Muse—whose "wave" must recede as his assurance gains in strength. His "chanter" is immediately followed by "et que chacun retrouve dans mes vers ces choses qui lui sont connues";[27] this is an echo of the motif "une place reconnue" wherein was suggested the poet's association with the practical things of modern everyday life—of which he will act as tabulator: "tenir des comptes" (27) may remind us of the duties of the Egyptian scribe. Thus, in Claudel's modest-ambitious definition of the role of the modern poet, there is no suggestion of a *poeta vates* on the scale of a Tyrtaeus or a Victor Hugo. Because the universe God has created is finite, the task of the poet can be only to recreate what has been created—or, better, to "take stock of" (*re-*

censer) things already existing. The ποιητής of Claudel is no divine artifex or Maker, but an artisan or recording-clerk, gathering together the work of God (drawing up a *summa* in medieval fashion); his public should not seek for novelty in his poetry but should recognize therein old familiar things.

But, though a tabulator rather than a creator, the modern poet must not abandon his lofty vantage-point, his eyrie, from which his gaze embraces infinite space, within which he can descry the single points. The poet is equally at home in the micro- and in the macrocosmos (26-28). In order to express this fusion of the macro- and the microcosmic, which is basic to Claudel's vision of the world, he uses a particular stylistic device discovered by Walt Whitman (after the way had been prepared by Gautier and Balzac): this is a presentative device which I have called, in a study published in Buenos Aires (1945), "chaotic enumeration," and which bespeaks the same inspiration, on another plane, as the modern department-store with its agglomeration of wares brought from the four corners of the globe. While the exuberant enumerations, the lists, the "catalogues" to be found with Rabelais or Quevedo still respected the distinctions between the different realms of Nature, the post-Whitmanian writer can enumerate things and thoughts detached from their frames, in order to evoke the plenitude of the world. Thus Claudel will list, among "ces choses qui lui sont connues" (note this pleonastic demonstrative, incorrect according to school grammars, which takes for granted our close association with "these" familiar objects): "sa maison," "la gare," "la mairie," "ce bonhomme avec son chapeau de paille," "l'espace," for he must keep "les comptes" (and here again there is an indiscriminate listing: "les siens," ". . . d'un magasin de chaussures," ". . . de l'humanité tout entière.") The whole and the part, the far and the near, the concrete and the abstract, the important and the inconsequential, can all appear side by side because they are fused in Claudel's vision. The more confusing and inchoate our civilization appears, the firmer seems to become the poet's grip on the essentials. But Claudel does not meet the confusion of our world by imposing thereupon a rigid orderliness of his own making: he is able to *accept* it without letting himself be distracted from the essentials: he can calmly depict the apparent disorder, for he sees it in a higher order. His faith remains unshaken. Evidences of this same faith that can so easily accept the juxtaposition of part and whole can be found in any Catholic church, where a painting presenting a single scene from the life of Christ, or of one of his saints, may hang side by side with one which represents the totality of God (the Trinity). And the juxtaposition of the sublime and the trivial ("ce bonhomme avec son chapeau de paille") is paralleled by the arrangement of those medieval towns in which, from out the midst of booths and shops and sheds, there emerges the Gothic spire—or, perhaps by the medieval mysteries in which comic and solemn scenes are made to alternate. By adducing such parallels I would seem to be assuming a religious inspiration for a passage which speaks only of the "choses connues" of everyday life and where the "Gothic spire" is missing. But I contend that it is indeed Claudel's religious nature which has enabled him to see together the trivial and the transcendental.[28] It is true that in our strophe the religious note is greatly subdued; but, later, it will sound forth gloriously in the poem.

But there is still another justification for the device of "chaotic enumerations" in our poem. According to the pattern fixed by Pindar, an ode must be rhapsodic, since this genre in contrast to others calls for the perpetuation, by the work of art, of the poet's original fervor: that "first fine careless rapture." In order to achieve this effect of enthusiasm, Ronsard, in his Pindaric odes, went to great pains to introduce drastic breaks (change of thought or of scenery) within his balanced stanzas; Claudel, having banned prophetic frenzy and Pythian obscurity from his poem, could not follow the Pindaric trend which Ronsard tried to imitate. It is the "disorderliness" of the chaotic enumerations, reflecting the diversity and fullness of the world, which offered the best approximation to the rhapsodic style of the ode. Thus Claudel does not, in the manner of the classicist André Chénier, seek, to make new poetry with ancient devices but, rather, to reach the effects of ancient poetry by means of new devices. His attempt is comparable with that of the modernist architect who designed the Catholic cathedral in Barcelona.

But now that he has defined the activity of the modern poet by inclusion of the trivial and the practical, Claudel cannot but think back to the idealism and sublimity of the ancient art which he has left behind him. In his last address to the pagan Muse (29-32), a new note informs his imperatives: behind him are the half-hearted, nervously joking maneuverings of self-defense ("laisse-moi," "laisse-moi"); now that he has decided to cut old ties, he is free squarely to appraise the totality of the being he abandons; for the first time he forces himself to contemplate her bitter beauty and sublimity; now he can call the Greek Muse his "bien-aimée," of whom he has loved the prophetic spirit ("ô soeur de la noire Pythie!")[29]—though admitting the bodily ugliness which must accompany prophetic frenzy ("et un filet de salive verte coule du coin de sa bouche");[30] the great Nike-like wings of freedom ("ô géante!"); and the winds of spaciousness that blow about her ("ô vent sur le désert!")—though he extends the background of the Greek goddess to include Egypt ("les quadriges de Pharaon").

But now the poet finds the strength and clarity of vision to oppose to the majesty, the enthusiasm, the propheticism, the freedom and spaciousness of Greek art, the fundamental objection of the Christian poet: Greek poetry cannot be ours because the Greek gods it praises have no "presence" (similarly, Lucretius had imagined the pagan gods as envious of man's reality), they have, that is, no action on man.[31] But, in the Christian conception of "natura rerum," all things are addressed to man's intelligence. And at this point the word-floods "man" and "earth" ("earth" = "Nature," "things") again coalesce; "les oeuvres des hommes," "au travers de la terre" are revealed in their full dimensions: it is to man that the works of Nature have been addressed[32] (we remember the Biblical account of Adam completing creation by giving things created their names). Nature, that is, is as purposeful in her workings ("rien . . . qui soit fait sans dessein et propos") as is man in his—and as the poet, a simple workingman, must be, according to Claudel who opposes the dionysiac and the enthusiastic. Nature addresses herself to man through the mediation of the senses (Claudel shares the Thomist, the non-Kantian [originally Greek] trust in the senses, the belief that "nihil est in intellectu quod non fuerit in sensu"); the observations carried out by means of the senses contain the results of an intellectual admixture of a "continued" intelligence, penetrate to the elements of Nature.[33] It is characteristic of the Thomist Claudel that he sees religious belief as based not on emotional and mystical fervor, not on a feeling of union with the divine which is realized in moments of rapture, but on the workings of human intelligence in the practical everyday world—progress promoted by intelligence is seen by Claudel as working to the glory of God. In the line "pour l'analyse de l'intelligence continuée avec l'intelligence qui la / Refait de l'élément qu'elle récupère," Claudel means to emphasize the motif of the continuity of the exercise of intelligence by his anaphoric repetition of *re-* in *refait* and *récupère*; the *re-* suggests the re-creation by man of what God has first created.[34] The continuity which, according to Christian belief, is established between the sense-data (Nature), the senses, and the intelligence of man, is precisely the opposite of the pagan presencelessness of the Gods. Nature's presence is manifested in her continuous "address" to man's mind. The versets "Et je puis parler, continu avec toute chose, / Parole qui est à sa place intelligence et volonté" follow up the motif of "lumière continuée" (i.e. the poet continues the work of Nature), of "moi je dis . . ." (a motif which is soon to reappear in the "crest" verse 42: "Je chanterai le grand poème de l'homme soustrait au hasard": when Claudel says "je puis parler" we realize how completely he has become disenthralled from the pagan Muse), of "nécessaire" ("à sa place": this anticipates "l'homme soustrait au hasard"), and of "natura rerum" ("toute chose muette": this, taken together with "moi je dis," "je puis parler," suggests that the poet is the voice of silent Nature). Nowhere in our strophe is there any word of the Christian divinity; apparently we are offered only the operation of Nature (as in Lucretius' poem). But when Claudel opposes to the presencelessness of pagan gods the workings of a Nature present at every moment to man's intelligence, the Christian reader knows that this Nature is the creation of the omnipresent God. We realize that there has been taking place in the strophe a psychomachy in which silent, intelligence-directed Nature has calmly defeated the winged, majestic and prophetic pagan Muse.

The crest line 42 is surrounded on both sides by new chaotic enumerations of the achievements of modern progress, wherein the plan of Nature is revealed. We shall not be surprised to find that in these lists man-made instruments, rather than man himself, occupy the foreground: the pen of the scholar is on the same level as the prospector's instrument; the Ingénieur-en-chef is dwarfed by "le canal qui remplit": indeed, he is made superfluous by the automatism of his creation which can be released at the touch of a child. Man can retire from the stage which he has set, to allow the drama to unfold: the drama between the stage-properties themselves. And this "play" is, in fact, that of Nature: we do not find in Claudel's poetry, as so often in modern indictments of the machine age, engines opposed to "natura rerum": rather, engines, which are the creations of man's intelligence, represent the continuation of "natura rerum" which addresses itself to man's intelligence.

The first of the two enumerations is concerned with the rudimentary tools with which man first learned to extend his range of influence over Nature; in the second are mentioned the more complicated modern machines, along with the vast achievements which are due to these instruments and which serve, in their turn, to produce new achievements. And just as, in Claudel's vision, "rerum natura" and machines are reconciled so, too, are man and Nature: it is Nature who encourages man to regroup its elements into new combinations, whereby he is enabled to free himself from the given in Nature—while remaining true to her essential designs. Claudel can sing, not only ἔργα καὶ ἡμέραι as did Hesiod in primitive times, not only "Georgica," as did Vergil in a primitivistic mood: with his face turned toward the future he joyfully hails the progress of industry, and is able to see in the industrial achievements of our age the modern variant of the primitive industries hallowed by traditional poetry: all human industry, all "industriousness" bespeaks the continuous communion between man and Nature. And so Claudel, by regrouping the elements and the fabricants of Nature, is working in accord with this great design. He need have no fear of scientific positivism since man, as he sees him, has never lost contact with the supernal forces.

It is in the second "chaotic enumeration" (43-47) that Claudel's imagination is given fullest expansion: his eye roves near and far[35] ("ce que les gens ont fait autour de moi . . ."—"le canot démontable qui remonte l'Aruwhimi"; "les ports tout bordés intérieurement . . ."—"le transatlantique qui signale au loin . . ."), embracing panoramas and single concrete details ("les frénétiques villes haletantes et tricotantes"—"quand la fille de l'Ingénieur-en-chef du bout de son doigt . . ."), the perennial or archaic, and the modern which invades them ("le canon qui ouvre les vieux empires" or again "le canot démontable qui remonte l'Aruwhimi"), technical civilization and Nature ("avec les frénétiques villes . . . et ça et là une anse bleue de la rivière dans la campagne solennelle": a blue patch of river glimpsed in the midst of the industrialized area),[36] the prosaic and the poetic ("le transatlantique qui signale—au loin dans le brouillard"). Claudel dominates the chaos of the modern world, not by reducing its confusing manifoldness and concreteness to a regularized, abstract, skeletal design (which has been attempted with greater success in painting than in poetry) but by subordinating this confusion to established poetic patterns—which, precisely because of their modern content, are difficult to recognize at first glance. But we may recognize in his chaotic or rhapsodic enumeration of modern industrial achievements, the old, the Biblical patterns of anaphoric repetition ("avec . . . , avec . . .") and of "parallelismus membrorum" (44-47); and, grafted thereupon, the more modern device of successive expansion of versets: in 43-47 the versets grow in size in proportion to the increase of the achievements of modern technics.

This whole enumeration is contained within the framework of the simple statement: "ce que les gens ont fait autour de moi avec le canon . . . je le ferai avec un poème." How revelatory is the phrase: "je le ferai avec un poème": by means of the preposition *avec* a parallel is offered between the poem Claudel is to write and the cannon, the collapsible boat, the blast-furnaces, the harbors, the ocean liner, the locomotive. We have already accepted that these industrial achievements are "necessary" fulfillments; now the full measure of their sublime and grandiose nature is brought out. How great, then, will have to be the poem which shall equal these achievements of modern civilization! And indeed, in the closing versets of this tremendous sentence, Claudel reveals in its final form a poetic program fit for a Conquistador.

And Claudel the Conquistador aims at nothing less than a poem of a Lucretian scope: he will treat "la connaissance de la terre"—in which phrase we recognize the combined motifs of intelligence (cognizance) and of things (Earth, Nature). He spurns the Homeric model of "unnecessary" adventurings in exotic lands; he will not celebrate a hero in his casual rovings over the earth: indeed, he will praise not a single man, but man himself and his cognizance of Nature.[37] The temporal indication given in his rejection of the Odyssean theme ("ne sera plus . . .") is followed up in 49 by the "enfin" (conspicuous by its unexpected position in the verse): "finally" is said from the point of view of the poet's inner struggle with the Muse which has come to an end, and also from the point of view of world history: Claudel feels strongly that the reconciliation of man with the laws of Nature has, in our day at least, become possible—and his affective "enfin" bespeaks the intensity of his desire to ally himself with this great cause.[38] Claudel does not use the expression "[réconcilié avec] les lois de la nature"; he speaks instead of "les forces éternelles," which, of course, stand for Nature. But at the same time, these are more than Nature. For the eternal forces are "above" the "causae secundae": they can be only the "causa primaria," or God. And again, just as we have noticed in the passage above dealing with the pagan gods "privés de presence," the Christian divinity has been evoked indirectly: simply by mentioning one member of a binomial he forces us to think in terms of the other: "force éternelle" in itself could be interpreted in a purely naturalistic manner, but once it is opposed to "causes secondes,"[39] it serves inevitably to suggest the supernatural. By using a term so suggestive of medieval Scholasticism, Claudel has been able to evoke the atmosphere of centuries of Christian philosophy.

And only now, "finally," does the full implication of the title of our ode "La Muse qui est la Grâce" stand revealed: the poem, which treats of man's secular progress, is a polemic against heathendom and an apologia of Christianity—the poem of glorification of Christian Grace has assumed the form of a Greek proem only in order to reject the core of pagan poetry—an apologia which points to the reconciliation of science and religion.[40] The progress of the twentieth century is welcomed in this new "carmen seculare" which traces the *via triumphalis* of man who is about to enter upon a new Augustan age of *pax christiana* (we remember that our poem was written in 1907!). "Reconciliation" is the final word-wave lifted up in the surge of the last crest line (50), in which, as we have seen, all the motifs of the strophe have been integrated. And the working of Christian Grace has been shown as well in the liberation of cognizant mankind from chance as in the poet's inner liberation from pagan seduction: the "Muse qui est la Grâce" has worked within the poem without ever having been mentioned by name (though from the ninth line on her silent gaze has rested on the poet). She can have worked only through the inner development of the poet who was brought from the petulant "laisse-moi" 's addressed to the pagan goddess, through "je voudrais," "je puis parler," to the confident "je chanterai," and finally to "[ce que les gens ont fait . . .] je le ferai," in which his poetic activity is aligned with the good works of his fellow men.

This strophe, which reveals the activity of Grace, is entirely given up to praise of man's activity; and this can be so because, to Claudel, human achievements (of which poetic achievements form only one branch) represent the intramundane workings of Grace. It is as if Claudel would have us recognize the divine in what is close at hand, familiar to us all; he will not encourage us to look away from the things of the earth toward heaven. The very fact that Grace is here not explicitly mentioned can be taken as proof of Claudel's deep belief that man is the field in which Grace silently and efficaciously works—this Grace who is Claudel's true Muse.[41] (Thus, in contrast to the procedure of conventional poetry, according to which the Muse is invoked at the beginning, our poem opens with a rejection of the traditional pagan Muse—without, however, following this up by an invocation of the Muse which is Grace. For Grace does not come at our bidding; we must abide the miracle of its coming.)[42]

This poem, which is so strongly opposed to ancient enthusiasm is intellectual rather than mystical—it has, that is, the orthodox-Catholic approach to the divine. To Claudel, whose motto seems to be "intellige ut credas," science and technics are intramundane "ancillae theologiae." It is possible to speak here of a miracle: the miracle by which Claudel becomes more and more aware of the necessity and nature of the poem that asks to be written. But the "miraculous" revelation that unfolds before our eyes implies no deviation from the intellectual, consisting as it does in the very working of intelligence for the glorification of intelligence.

Among the attempts made in the last century to reconcile aspects of modern civilization with values of the past, we may remember Renan's *Prière sur l'Acropole*, in which he offers the tortured image of modern man wavering between a Christian faith sentimentally retained and Greek clarity which his reason affirms, and the *Invocation à Minerva* of Maurras, who harmonizes French classical *raison* with Greco-Roman *ratio* and order—while Giraudoux, in his *Prière sur la Tour Eiffel* (in *Juliette au pays des Hommes*, 1924), simply ignores any such conflict and speaks only in terms of the general preeminence of *French* reason and taste. Claudel, for his part, without any similar symbolical localization, spreads before us the panorama of a pan-Christian harmony of reason and belief, offering us, in this panorama, the most "total" vision of our modern civilization I know of. Indeed, this is Claudel's *summa*, it ranks with such poems as the *Commedia*, as *Faust* and *Lear*; it is a "Weltgedicht," a world-ode. Such a *summa* must contain all the main strivings of the epoch it reflects and, if we survey the whole range of our strophe, we will see that no essential is missing here: we find references to art, to religion, technics, science, nature, society (and the relationship of these with art); the professions are fully represented, including that of the poet; the wide sweep and intricate nature of our civilization is revealed, its history and that of mankind (Egypt, Assyria, Greece, Japan; Rome is mentioned later in the ode); the spirit of Christianity blends with that of the Enlightenment, of the Industrial Revolution and of imperialism. This strophe, which purports to offer the prospectus of a poem to be written, is in itself "le grand poème de l'homme enfin par delà les causes secondes réconcilié aux forces éternelles." A complete factual commentary would have to extend over many pages if it were to clarify all the allusions to historical and technical details which the strophe furnishes; this poetry rivals in factual density that of Dante, while the French poet loses sight as little as the Italian of things eternal. One might say that it is just because these poets have their eyes calmly fixed on eternity that they can portray so well the "man of the world" and the things of their own century: for them (as Auerbach has pointed out in regard to Dante) the fullness of God radiates through the manifoldness of this earth. Dante, and Claudel, too (in spite of his polemics against the Greeks), cast a Greek eye on this world; in fact, it seems to me that Catholicism has been the most faithful continuator of things Greek, particularly that vivid pictorial sensitivity of the ancients to things seen in our world. This continuation is really symbolized, as Santayana has suggested, in the significant name of that Roman church *Santa Maria sopra Minerva* (and perhaps Claudel cannot be exempted from blame for his failure to see fully his indebtedness, as a Catholic thinker, to the θεία κόρη Pallas Athene-Minerva).[43]

In this poem Claudel has offered Frenchmen an example of the "Christian Ode," a genre which, properly speaking, was only to be found in England with Milton, in Germany with Klopstock, in Italy with Manzoni. In France, Ronsard had succeeded in re-creating the antique ode characterized necessarily by "enthusiasm" (Claudel suggests his opposition to the Pléïade in the words "loin d'immoler le bouc"), while Victor Hugo had shown his complete misunderstanding of the nature of the ode by mixing this with the ballad. Claudel has been able to renew an ancient genre[44] and to retain its main ingredient, mythology, by substituting a Christian mythology concerned with the intramundane working of Grace. And, what is still more important, he has (as certain critics have stated), made poetry sing of Christian subjects more than one hundred years after Chateaubriand had made the same attempt in his poetic prose. The difference between the two procedures is that between pious speech and pious work: Claudel's ποίησις is a doing, the doing of a workingman (perhaps he had in mind this revelatory etymological pun when he made the comparison between the poet and the worker); and its pious incentive is blessed by Grace, whose presence we feel in the poem. Chateaubriand, with much documentation couched in aesthetic language, is forever advocating piety, but his pages of magic and sweetness cannot achieve the simple evidence of the presence of Grace. It is interesting to inquire into the reasons why the two apologists of Christianity had to come so late, and why it was necessary that their two undertakings were separated from each other by a century. We must remember that, since the time of Classical Humanism, French poetry had teemed with pagan themes; this was possible, in a Catholic country, precisely because it represented simply a literary practice which subsisted quite apart from religious belief—and this tolerance of pagan themes could continue so long as faith remained unshaken (even today, in a Jesuit school, the inclusion of classical studies in the curriculum—though they are rigidly separated from Christian studies—is held to be without danger to religion—just as, in Catholic circles, there has never been any fear of scientific Positivism: "render unto Caesar those things which are Caesar's, and unto God those things which are God's"). But, with the period of the Enlightenment and the development of positivistic science, Christian beliefs were shattered: it was against this background that Chateaubriand reacted, as, later, Claudel had to react against the period of laicism in which the state (and its schools) were separated from the Church (our ode was written two years after the laws of separation were enacted): both poets voiced a reaction and helped bring about a "renouveau catholique." Claudel had to revive the program of Chateaubriand one hundred years later, because the Romantics had deflected poetry from the path laid out by Chateaubriand and had continued certain eighteenth-century (scientific or pantheistic) trends, which they endowed with a new poetic halo. Claudel sings of Christian values to a laicized world, but his attack on laicism disarms the opposing forces by declaring them ultimately God-willed: this lay-science, which had been so proudly hailed ever since the Enlightenment as an arm against religion, is accepted by Claudel as the preordained instrument of Christian divinity! Instead of impugning the scientific tendencies of our age he suggests another inspiration behind them; he does not, like Chateaubriand, preach the aesthetic values of Catholicism as offering a supererogatory beauty to earthly life: he discloses to us the continuous presence of the "cathedral" in the midst of the secular beauty of the workshops. What the lay institutions of the state have purported to protect, the labor of the common man, is now revealed as under the protection of divine powers. Thus, that scientific positivism in whose name the cudgels had been taken up against religion is revealed to be an intramundane form of religion: science and faith are reconciled.

Turning from the aspect of practical policy which must have been underlying Claudel's poem, to its purely literary significance, it may be observed that Claudel has restored in our time that "poetry of ideas" once practiced by Lucretius, Dante, and Rabelais; in this, he joins forces with Valéry, who considers the true subject matter of poetry to be not the "poetic" or the emotional but the "intellectual": that which offers most resistance to the alchemy of poetry. Claudel, however, while endorsing Valéry's program of extracting poetry from the shock and integration of ideas ("faire chanter les idées"), opposes the arrant agnosticism of Valéry by stressing the harmony of intelligence and faith.

A world-poem of today must evidently find a new form, evenly balanced between the conservative and the progressive, reflecting our own time while reminding us of the past. The old alexandrine[45] and the old stanza-forms were inadequate for this task; the first, Claudel replaced by the Biblical and Whitmanian verset, which offered the possibility of retaining the parallelism of Biblical style and the caesura characteristic of the alexandrine; the second was replaced by the "flood and wave" technique: a system of metrics in which the fixed forms of earlier literature give way to a Bergsonian flow; the language of such a poem must find a place somewhere between prose and poetry, since it is to show the integration of the prosaic and the poetic of modern life. The hymnic and the sublime characteristic of our ode had to emerge from the trivial; the totality of the vista implies the representation of a diversity of styles within the poem.

In our analysis we have sought to show the ascending movement in language; the network of the forces which determine the "waves and floods" was the task of this study[46]—which becomes superfluous once we have performed the mental activity imposed on us by the poet's words. Once the architecture of the work of art has been laid bare, the scaffolding, which the critic had to erect provisionally for this purpose, can be scrapped. Stylistics, as I conceive it, is an exclusively auxiliary science. Just as, according to Pascal, for him who knows truth no style, no "art de persuader" is needed, so stylistics (and the devices of suasion) must abdicate once the true nature of the work of art has been apperceived. A study of the kind we have attempted could have been made entirely unnecessary from the start by a simple recital of the poem, if the performer were able, by various pauses and intonations, to suggest the main motifs we have taken pains to distinguish, and to show, within the crystalline ball of the work of art, the play of the conflicting forces in the equilibrium which Claudel has been able to establish. For Claudel's poetry is, above all, an invitation to the listener to "reconcile," to harmonize its *idées-forces*—and to rest harmoniously in contemplation of harmony.

NOTES

1. It must be borne in mind that, in our ode, Claudel changes the tripartite scheme of the Pindaric-Ronsardian form in two ways: he replaces the sequence, repeatable at will, of strophe, antistrophe, and epode (the first two of which are equal in structure) by three sequences of strophe and antistrophe of unequal length and structure, followed, only at the end, by an epode and preceded by an introductory stanza; in addition, only in the dialogue between the Muse and the poet is there any alternation of strophe and antistrophe (in this way, the dialogue finds a form reflecting the to-and-fro movement of dialectics). This tight cohesive pattern may be contrasted with the leisurely air of Ronsard's "Ode à Michel de l'Hôpital"—at the end of which the author confesses that "the law of the song" bids him stop: he could have continued indefinitely with his system of loosely connected stanzas.

In the other odes the tripartite scheme is completely abandoned in all its original length, thereby improving the error of Ronsard who, misled by the contemporary editions of Pindar, thought to respect the Pindaric scheme by using shorter lines.

2. This was the starting-point I took in my explanation of Claudel's *Ballade*, the subject of an address at the convention of the Modern Language Association in 1937, which could not be published in its *Publications*—although the secretary had asked to have the manuscript submitted for publication—because the editorial committee deemed it "school-room work," not "scholarship." As though school-room work should not imply scholarship, and as though "scholars" are not tempted to err often in delimiting scholarship arbitrarily! The article ultimately appeared in the December 1942 issue of *The French Review*.

3. The epithet *grand* appears, in fact (together with the initial reference in Strophe I), in the introductory lines (before Strophe I): "Ah, ce soir est à moi! ah, cette *grande* nuit est à moi! . . . Voici le dépliement de la *grande* aile poétique!" (the last line suggests an allusion to the Greek Nike of the Louvre).

4. The epithet "grand" applied to our poem will, in later strophes, be expanded to "entier" (in Strophe II we find: "Et cependant quand tu m'appelles ce n'est pas avec moi seulement qu'il faut répondre, mais avec tous les êtres qui m'entourent, / Un poème tout entier comme un seul mot tel qu'une cité dans son enceinte pareille au rond de la bouche, / . . . Et moi c'est le monde tout entier qu'il me faut conduire à sa fin avec une hécatombe de paroles!"), and, in Ode V (as well as in the "Processional"), to "catholique" in the two meanings of the word: "Je vois devant moi l'Eglise catholique qui est de tout l'univers! . . . Tout est à moi, catholique, et je ne suis privé d'aucun de vous" "Voici l'immensité de tous mes frères vivants et morts, l'unanimité du peuple catholique, les douze tribus d'Israël réunies et les trois Eglises en une seule basilique."

The progression "great" > "complete" > "catholic" is a progression, to some extent, from dimension to integration and finally to the signification informing the integrated whole: Claudel considers himself a husbander of this vast, finite universe (Ode V: "Mon désir est d'être le rassembleur de la terre de Dieu! Comme Christophe Colomb quand il mit à la voile, / Sa pensée n'était pas de trouver une terre nouvelle, / Mais dans ce coeur plein de sagesse la passion de la limite et de la sphère calculée de parfaire l'éternel horizon." (This is also the main idea of Claudel's Spanish Catholic world-drama *Le soulier de satin.*) Claudel subjects this plenary universe to the limits of Catholicity. The "grande ode" is thus an annunciation of the Catholic Ode. There is a willful violence in this procedure of setting limits to the boundless universe and of making it Catholic in the narrower sense of the word: it is inspired by that same "passion de la limite" which the poet recognizes in Columbus (and which explains better, perhaps, than do the epithets "stubborn and obstinate" of the modern historian S. E. Morison, the reason for Columbus' misinterpretation of his own discovery).

5. Here we could use as well the metaphor of the path hewn through the forest: "la grande voie tromphale au travers de la Terre" comes to view only after the reader has fought his way through the underbrush of wildly luxuriant verse-vegetation.

6. Anyone who has watched the energetic consistency with which, at high-tide, the assault on the beaches is carried forward by the irregular succession of master-waves, while the weaker and less far-reaching currents provide *intermezzi* of relaxation, will realize how well this simile fits the rhythm of our poem, with its bold forward dashes, alternating with spells of calm, during which the poem rests for a moment, before undertaking a new attack.

7. In fact, we may state here that Claudel's collection of odes constitutes an *ars poetica* dramatically enacted. It is no didactic work like those of Boileau and Verlaine—or like Claudel's own treatise *Art poétique*—but an *art poétique* "se faisant," which develops before our eyes while the poet is wrestling with all the contradictory strivings which he feels in himself.

8. This "refouler" in Strophe I must not be confused with the "refouler" of the *argument*—though there may be a relationship of motif between the two cases: in Strophe I Claudel rejects the pagan muse, in Strophe II (which is resumed in the *argument*) he rejects the poetic muse as such because she distracts him from his earthly communion with human beings.

9. The "wave" motif has been prepared by numerous references, in the introductory lines, to the "sea," with which the poetic frenzy was compared: "Encore! encore la mer qui revient me rechercher comme une barque . . ." etc. And it is, as we have said, an oceanic impression that we receive from the opening lines of the poem.

10. This motif recurs in Strophe II, where the poet rejects the inspiration of the pagan Muse who receives no light from the Gospel: "les ténèbres et le chaos qui n'a point reçu l'évangile. / Ténèbres de la privation de Dieu! ténèbres actives qui *sautent sur vous comme la panthère*" (= the *incursiones daemonum* of the Scriptures).

11. If we were to state a literary model for the inclusion of the teasing tone into a serious poem, we could think of Victor Hugo's "Le satyre" (in *Légende des siècles*)—especially of its first part where the satyr, who later is to become Pan and thus mightier than the Gods, is facetiously introduced as though seen from the point of view of the Gods before they have realized his power.

But nothing could be further from Claudel than the state of mind of a

Hugo who seems to suggest (though without full conviction or convincingness) that a satyr-like animality is the source of art, science, political freedom. *Pace* Thibaudet, Victor Hugo was not as "intelligent" a poet as is Claudel: his vague humanitarianism and his pantheism did not integrate. To use Claudel's terminology, Victor Hugo did not create the "necessary" poem.

12. Distrust of "enthusiasm" does not imply a lack of those qualities normally associated with enthusiasm: exuberance, power of expression, revolutionary striving for new forms. In Ode I Claudel declines to follow in the footsteps of Homer, Vergil (and Dante), when he says: "Rien de tout cela! *toute route à suivre nous ennuie*! toute échelle à escalader! . . . / O mon âme, il *ne faut concerter aucun plan*, ô mon âme sauvage, il faut nous tenir libres et prêts . . . / O mon âme impatiente, pareille à l'aigle sans art! . . . / Que mon vers ne soit rien d'esclave! mais tel que l'aigle marin qui s'est jeté sur un grand poisson, / Et l'on ne voit rien qu'un éclatant tourbillon d'ailes et l'éclaboussement de l'écume!" He hastens, however, to add: "Mais vous ne m'abandonnerez point, ô Muses modératrices"; that is to say, Claudel's poetic revolution amounts not to anarchy but to a new order. It is a revolution, nonetheless: Boileau's precept concerning the ode: "Son style impétueux souvent marche au hasard, / Chez elle un beau désordre est un effet de l'art" (which is concerned only with an "*effect* of disorder" given by a poem which should be, in reality, most well-ordered), is timid in comparison.

13. With this stipulation Claudel shows himself opposed to the "furor poeticus"—and this in an ode, the very genre for which poetic frenzy had been held indispensable ever since the rediscovery of Pindar by the humanists. We can see in these lines a direct rebuke intended for Ronsard (who has his Jupiter tell the Muse: "Votre métier, race gentille, / *Les autres métiers passera,* / D'autant qu'esclave il ne sera / De l'art [= technical skill] aux Muses inutile, / Par art le navigateur / Dans la mer manie et vire . . . / Par art se font les ouvriers. / *Vous n'aurez de tel erreur;* / Sans plus, une sainte fureur / Polira votre science") and ultimately a criticism of Plato, who had put enthusiasm above *sophia* and *techne*. Claudel, by his theory (so at variance with his own practice and with the law of the genre of the ode he cultivates) that the poet should strive to be comprehensible to the average man, dissociates himself from the aristocratic poets of Humanism who despised the common people for their failure to grasp poetic enthusiasm (cf. also Strophe XV of Ronsard's "Ode à Michel de l'Hôpital").

14. In Strophe II, where the poet rejects the Muse still more violently, the same childish *un peu* is repeated:

> Ah! quoique mon coeur se brise, non! Je ne veux point! va-t-en
> de moi un peu! ne me tente pas ainsi cruellement!

and in the epode, where the poet finally turns away from the Muse, the *va-t-en* appears without the childish *un peu*:

> Va-t-en! Je me retourne désespérément vers la terre! Va-t-en! tu
> n'ôteras point ce froid goût de la terre . . .

15. In other words, humor, with Claudel as with the medieval poets, appears subordinated to the sacred, whereas the paganistic Ronsard was able to introduce burlesque among the Olympians: in the "Ode à Michel

de l'Hôpital" he shows us an assembly of the Gods listening to the song of the Muses, with Jupiter laughing at Mars "qui tenait l'oeil fermé, / Ronflant sur sa lance guerrière, / Tant la chanson l'avait charmé."

16. We can sense here the paraphrase of a colloquial word (such as *béjaune, blanc-bec,* for example) as well as a transposition into Homeric style ("orné de . . ."!). We remember Claudel's words: "Pas aucune de vos phrases que je ne sache reprendre!"

The motif of the "jeune homme" recurs in Strophe II: "Alors ne permettez pas [ô Seigneur] à celle-ci [à la Muse] qu'elle vienne me tenter comme un jeune homme . . ." (here, without the epithet equivalent to "béjaune"); cf. the parallel sublimation "va-t-en un peu" > "va-t-en" mentioned in note 14.

17. This motif of the "hybrid" nature of the paganistic poet is emphasized again in Antistrophe II, when the Muse, encouraging the poet to follow his path with the pride of a god, says:

> Afin que je te regarde et rie, et que j'imite, moi, la déesse, ton avancement mutilé!
> Je ne t'ai point permis de marcher comme les autres hommes d'un pied plan,
> Car tu es trop lourd pour voler
> Et le pied que tu poses à terre est blessé!

18. Here, Claudel is in accord with Péguy, the son of the *rempailleuse de chaises,* who always expressed pride in the craftmanship of the *homme de lettres* and who saw in Christ, the carpenter's son who did "de la bonne ouvrage," the patron of the intellectual.

19. It must also be remarked that the inclusion, in large periods, of such brief main clauses as though they were incidental clauses (a sentence-unification made possible by the breath), belongs to oral speech: this is one of the cases in which a great writer is able to conquer new areas of oral speech for artistic writing—which has a tendency to drift away from the spoken form. This incorporation of the spoken into the written is the great secret of innovation in writing. Compare in Antistrophe III: ". . . Jusque tu aies appris la mesure que je veux, à quoi ne sert point de compter un et deux, *tu l'apprendras,* serait-ce avec le hoquet de l'agonie!" where the interpolation is one of those benignly consoling sentences with which the Muse mocks the poet.

20. Claudel is writing a twentieth-century *carmen saeculare* as he will state later:

> Salut aurore de ce siècle qui commence!
> Que d'autres te maudissent, mais moi je te consacre sans frayeur ce chant pareil à celui qu'Horace confia à des choeurs de jeunes garçons et de jeunes filles quand Auguste fonda Rome pour la seconde fois.

Claudel's *carmen saeculare* will, of course, be a Christian and a Catholic one, in which progress and religion are reconciled: "un temple nouveau" will rise in the place of the French sanctuaries destroyed by "la pioche qui ne sait ce qu'elle fait"; "Je vois devant moi l'Eglise catholique qui est de tout l'univers" (to entertain such a hope in 1907, only two years after the laws separating Church and State had been enacted and when venerable sanctuaries were being desecrated, was most courageous). And he states in the "Processional":

> Je crois que Dieu est ici bien qu'il me soit caché.
> Comme il est au ciel avec tous ses anges et dans le coeur de la Vierge sans péché,
> Il est mêmement ici, dans la gare de chemin de fer et l'usine, dans la crêche, dans l'aire et dans le chais.

21. If, for a moment, I may step out of my role of linguistic-literary commentator of poetry, I may venture to say that this seems to me the most sensible view for a critic of our epoch to take. I have never understood the attitude of those critics of the mechanization of our world and of supposedly mechanized America, who see an unbridgeable gap between faith and technics. Duhamel, e.g. in his *Scènes de la vie future*, speaks with derision of the church he saw in Chicago which was located on the top floor of a skyscraper. What matters is that people preserve their faith and that they are not swallowed up by the machines: if the community *can* pray in that Chicago church, it is of little importance that they must use an elevator to enter the church instead of walking in through the front door. The moral significance of technics depends entirely on the moral purpose to which it is put: war or peace, irreligion or faith.

22. It may be noted that the two anaphoric *ainsi*'s in verses 18 and 20, introducing carefully developed "Homeric similes," correspond to the usage of ancient poets who compare (by means of sentences introduced e.g. by *sic . . . sic . . .*) the situation they are describing with parallels from the mythic or the historic past. But Claudel takes care also to vary the expression of the parallels by devices more modern: the "census" taken by the Egyptian scribe assumes the form of a Claudelian "chaotic enumeration" (*vide* later in our text); the picture of the Assyrian engraver is given in a *raccourci* by a participial construction ("l'antique sculpteur . . . attrapé") followed by an anacoluthon ("Et de temps en temps il souffle . . .") with the Biblical ring which will be described in note 30).

One would expect Claudel to mention the Greek and Roman epigraphists, who certainly did not lack a "pointe minutieuse," instead of the Egyptians and Assyrians; but we must face the fact that, in this context, the poet was forced to exclude a positive appraisal of the Greco-Roman civilization.

23. This is a medieval device, amply represented in St. Bernard and in Dante (cf. Schiaffini's book *Tradizione e prosa*), which Claudel has revived most felicitously. His equation *connaître - co-naître* is well known.

We may think that in this passage Claudel had another etymological pun in his mind: Lat. *ratio* means "accountancy" and "reason," hence Fr. *raisonable* "accountant" and "reasonable." Thus "tenir des comptes" can also evoke the ideas of "being rational, reasonable, using reason."

One may be reminded here of the words of the French historian Gabriel Hanotaux who asked to be no more than "le greffier de l'histoire." In Ode I Claudel defines the Muse of history as "Clio, le greffier de l'âme, pareille à celle qui tient les comptes." We may see in this idea the explanation for the outward biography of the poet: he can reconcile a bureaucratic job with his poetic métier. I, personally, am of the conviction that the idea was preexistent to his outward biography: celle-ci s'est mise à imiter celle-là. . . .

24. The motif of "massette et ciseau," a suggestion of technical precision, recurs in the following strophe containing the rejection by the Muse of Claudel's poetic program:

> Que m'importent toutes vos machines et toutes vos oeuvres d'esclaves et vos livres et vos écritures? . . .
> Ce n'est point avec *le tour et le ciseau* que l'on fait un homme vivant . . .

And, in Antistrophe III:

> Ce n'est pas *l'auge et la truelle* qui rassemble et qui construit,
> C'est le feu pur et simple qui fait de plusieurs choses une seule.

In Ode V ("La maison fermée"), the idea of the "necessity" of the poet, as well as the theme of the "accountant," recurs:

> Je sais que c'est moi qui vous [*sc.* aux grandes forces célestes] suis nécessaire . . .
> Et toutes vous êtes en ma possession, *comme un banquier* qui de son bureau de Paris fait argent avec l'écriture des gommes de la Sénégambie . . .

(Note the colloquialism *faire argent* and the bureaucratic flavor of *écriture*!) In *Positions et propositions,* I, 19, Claudel explains the French aversion to excess and superfluity, as a "besoin de nécessité," deeply rooted in the French national character: "Le Français a horreur du hasard, de l'accidentel et de l'imprévu. . . . Il a le besoin de justifier devant luimême chacun de ces actes, et, avisé d'ailleurs des regards acérés que chacun de ses voisins dirige sur lui, il s'arrange comme s'il avait à répondre à une accusation continuelle de détournement et de gaspillage. Le Français s'est toujours senti actionnaire d'une société dont chaque membre *doit des comptes* à tous les autres. Il ne veut rien laisser perdre. Un bien inutile et gâché, un agrément qu'on se donne, lui paraissent de mauvaises actions." What he is describing here is the Jansenist streak in the French national character.

25. Why should Claudel's poem be "clear like the moon," not "like the sun"? Evidently, not only because the Muse traditionally appears at night (a fact which troubled so greatly Alfred de Musset, who wished us to visualize in his *Nuits* the rebirth of Nature and his own nature-like spiritual rebirth—at night!), but mainly because the moonlight is clearly defined, cool and calm, not diffused, and not dazzling like that of the sun; and because the *via triumphalis* Claudel wants to draw must be coolly, calmly designed, must be clear-cut and sharply visible in the midst of the maze of the earth.

The simile of the "scribe" may have been prompted by Scriptural passages such as Ps. XLIV: "Lingua mea calamus scribae, velociter scribentis" which is interpreted by St. Jerome in Ep. LXV (Migne, *Patr. lat.*, XXII, 627): "Debeo ergo et linguam meam quasi stilum et calamum preparare, ut per illam in corde et auribus audientium scribat Spiritus Sanctus." Claudel, however, with his aversion to enthusiasm will not be the "stenographer writing (*velociter*!) under the dictation of the Holy Spirit": he will adopt only the skill and meticulousness of the scribe.

Claudel's poetry admits of no ambiguity behind which the poet may hide: he addresses himself to the whole of the nation and of humanity, and takes pride in being understood. His is not the "Mes-vers-ont-le-sens-qu'on-leur-prête" attitude of the esoteric Valéry, who could smile as he sat in the balcony of that Sorbonne amphitheater listening to Gustave Cohen explaining one of his poems. Claudel's poetry can be clearly, unambiguously explained—as we are trying to do here.

26. Similarly, Claudel's contemporary, Valéry, also insists on the ideal of "craftsmanship" for the modern artist, as opposed to the ideals of the enthusiastic romantic poetry of yore. And, today, one hears that the great and original Stravinski asks to be considered as a "craftsman," to the indignation of the lesser and more conventional Malipiero who retains the name of "musician."

27. In the introductory lines (before Strophe I) Claudel himself says:

> Les mots que j'emploie, ce sont les mots de tous les jours, et ce ne sont point les mêmes
>
> Vous ne trouverez point de rimes dans mes vers ni aucun sortilège. Ce sont vos phrases mêmes. Pas aucune de vos phrases que je ne sache reprendre! [note the vulgarism *pas aucune!*]
>
> Ces fleurs sont vos fleurs et vous dites que vous ne les reconnaissez pas?

In Antistrophe I the public is shown in its incapacity to understand, i.e. to recognize the things presented by the poet who is, at the moment of writing, under the impact of enthusiastic frenzy: he sees "Les choses comme elles sont et comme elles ne sont pas et les gens commencent à ne pas comprendre ce qu'il dit." In Ode V the public, recalcitrant to Claudel's esoteric poetry, is presented as saying: "Est-ce langage d'un homme ou de quelque bête? / Car nous ne reconnaissons plus avec toi, ces choses que nous t'avons apportées."

If we should attempt to define, in terms of the Roman tradition, the position claimed by Claudel for the poet, it would be neither that of the poets in archaic Rome (of whom it was said "in quibus nulla solida utilitas omnisque puerilis delectatio"), nor that of the *vates*, who is above society, claimed by Horace ("odi profanum vulgus et arceo"). Claudei looks upon his poetic activity as a *negotium* exercised in the interests of the people (cf., for these oppositions, Dag Norberg, *L'Olympionique, le poète et leur renom éternel*, Uppsala 1945). Thus the words of Claudel's poems will be those of Everyman.

One could also define Claudel's intention in Christian terms, if we remember the Church Fathers who ascribed to the Scriptures a style that "condescendit . . . ad eorum inscitias qui non intelligunt, et *simplici atque planiore atque usitato sermone* utitur, ut possit intelligi" (Ambrose); this is a language which, because of its clarity, wields all the more authority the more widely it is read: "et omnibus ad legendum esset in promptu . . . *verbis apertissimis et humillimo genere loquendi* se cunctis praebens . . . *ut exciperet omnes populari sinu* . . . multo . . . plures quam si non tanto epice auctoritatis emineret nec turbas gremio sanctae humilitatis hauriret" (Augustine: cf. Auerbach, "Sacrae scripturae sermo humilis" in *Istanbuler Schriften* no. 5, 1944)—terms which have been echoed by hundreds of medieval poets (e.g. Berceo: "Quiero fer una prosa en roman paladino, / en cual suele el pueblo hablar con su vecino"; "quiero fer la pasion de Sant Laurent / en romanz, que la pueda saber toda la gent").

28. Evidence that the chaotic enumeration is in Claudel a development of the conception of the omnipresence of God in creation can easily be seen from this stanza of the "Processional":

> Je crois que Dieu est *ici* bien qu'il me soit caché,
> Comme il est au ciel avec tous ses anges et dans le coeur de la Vierge sans pêché,
> Il est mêmement ici, dans la gare de chemin de fer, et l'usine, dans la crèche, dans l'aire et le chais.

It is significant that here the manger is referred to, not together with Heaven or the heart of the Virgin, but with the railway station and the wine-cellar. And the *ici* is most striking, which conjures up a momentary proximity, here, now, of all these disparate things which are inhabited by God.

Again, we find, in the "Processional," an enumeration of the saints:

> Voici tous les Saints du calendrier, répartis sur les quatres Saisons,
> Les saints de glace et de braise, et ceux qui annoncent la sortie des bêtes et la fenaison,
> Saint Médard et Saint Barnabé, Saints Crépin et Crépinien de Soissons,
> Saint Martin et Saint Vincent des vignerons, Sainte Macre de Fère-en-Tardenois où est la fête de ce bourg,
> Et Sainte Luce en décembre où le jour est plus court.

Though the choice of these saints is evidently determined by a definite pattern (the four seasons are represented, and the saints named are all patrons of labor), still the immediate impression is one of disorder and arbitrary selection—which serves impressively to evoke the richness of the Catholic calendar, able to furnish every day of the year with its saint, so that the menial can be continuously pervaded by the transcendental. (The patriotic note is inescapable in this list of exclusively French saints; we may also discern a parochial sentiment in "Sainte Macre de Fère-en-Tardenois où est la fête de ce bourg": Claudel, writing these words in China, visualizes, in immediate proximity, the annual feast-day in "ce bourg.")

For Claudel, no barrier between the two realms of the transcendental and the trivial is allowed to stand; the most daring example of barriers annihilated may be seen in the lines below from Ode v, in which he is depicting the solitary and silent immersion of his soul in Christ: "Moi tout seul, tout en bas, éclairant la face du grand Christ de bronze *avec un cierge de 25 centimes.*"

29. In this allusion Claudel has coupled the prophetic with the poetic enthusiasm. Plato, in addition to these, speaks of two other enthusiasms, those of the *mystes* and of the lover (and the same four are to be found, listed rather inorganically by Ronsard in his "Ode à Michel de l'Hôpital"). The enthusiasm of the *mystes* is also found in our strophe where it is represented by the dionysiac element—which Claudel wishes to repress. And the enthusiasm of love is embodied in the Muse who tempts the poet as a woman (Antistrophe I: "Et moi, je suis une femme entre les femmes").

"La Muse" in our strophe (i.e. the pagan Muse) is evidently Erato, the muse of love songs, who had earlier (Ode I) abducted the poet to her ship.

30. The anacoluthon in "ô soeur de la noire Pythie qui broie . . . *et* un filet de salive verte coule . . ." is figurative of disharmony: it is as though, in the phenomenon of prophetic enthusiasm, the bodily declares itself anarchically independent. Again, in the anacoluthon of line 26: "Comme de haut on a plaisir à reconnaître sa maison, . . . mais l'espace autour de soi est immense!" the syntactical yoke is shaken off by the exclamatory phrase: it is as though there is no easy transition from the pettiness of small-town existence to the immensity of space. Thus intellectual objections are figuratively mirrored by an anarchic syntax.

The most remarkable case of anacoluthon is offered by "Comme l'antique poète parlait de la part des dieux privés de présence, / Et moi je dis qu'il n'est rien dans la nature . . ." (33-34), where the flow of the sentence alluding to Lucretius is broken up by the impact of the phraseology of Jesus ("but I say unto you"). The anacoluthon, as found in Claudel, usually represents the deliberate introduction of the oral style into the written—though, at the same time, Claudel exploits the patterns hallowed by Biblical and Homeric traditions.

31. Cf. Lucretius, III, 18 *seq.*: "apparet divum numen sedesque quietae, / quas neque concutiunt venti nec nubila nimbis / aspergunt . . ."; II, 1039 *seq.* "nam pro sancta deum tranquilla pectora pace, / quae placidum degunt aevom vitamque serenam"—it is well-known that Lucretius, like his teacher Epicurus, sought not "to put the Greek gods into retirement as ex-service rulers, but to establish them as the images and prototypes of the Epicurean sage" (P. Friedländer, *Transact. of the Am. Phil. Ass.*, LXX, 373). This very life of the gods in the *intermundia*, without influence on the universe, but also without its griefs, must evidently have appeared to Claudel, who is conversant with the Judeo-Christian omnipresent God in whose "face" (= presence) everything on earth and in Heaven happens, as a "lack of presence." (Paradoxically enough Claudel uses, in denying real, spiritual presence to the pagan gods, the very word which for the ancients denoted their helpfulness: cf. such Latin phrases as *numina praesentia, praesentes divi*, etc.)

The reference to Lucretius as to a pagan poet superseded by Christianity, is quite outspoken in the following lines of Ode V:

> Maintenant je puis dire, mieux que le vieux Lucrèce: Vous n'êtes plus, ô terreurs de la nuit!
> Ou plutôt comme votre saint Prophète: "Et la nuit est mon exaltation dans mes délices!
> Réjouis-toi, mon âme, dans ces vers ambrosiens!"
> Je ne vous crains point, ô grandes créatures célestes! Je sais que c'est moi qui vous suis nécessaire . . .

This idea of a Nature who needs Man complements that of Nature addressed to Man.

32. The wording "il n'est rien dans la nature qui soit fait sans dessein et propos à l'homme adressé" is resumed in Antistrophe II when the Muse who has become Grace says: "Entre tous les êtres qui vivent, je suis la parole de grâce qui est adressée à toi seul" (and in the *argument*: "c'est à lui [au poète] personnellement que la Muse qui est la Grâce ne

cesse de s'adresser"). It is significant that what was the action of Nature has, in the progress of the poem, become that of Grace.

33. When Claudel presents the visual and acoustic senses as "intelligent" senses, he must have had in mind the Thomist hierarchy of senses in which the highest are those which involve material alteration of the sensing organ by the things sensed, the accuracy of the eye being the closest to the operation of the intellect (cf. E. Gilson, *Le Thomisme*, p. 201).

It may be assumed that here Claudel offers a paraphrase of the Thomist *vis cogitativa*, an "internal sense" (on one level with imagination, memory, etc.), and therefore superior to the external senses, but still a sense and, accordingly, inferior to the operations of the intellect and separated therefrom by an unbridgeable gulf because it is directed toward the individual and the material, whereas the intellect is directed toward the universal and the immaterial. In the following lines, we see how a modern psychologist versed in Thomism defines one of the activities of the *vis cogitativa* (Rudolf Allers, "Intellectual Cognition" in *Essays in Thomism*, New York, 1942): "Whenever the value-aspect of a thing is emphasized it is the *vis cogitativa* which is operative. To act upon something, the psychological power must have got hold of this value-content . . . [St. Thomas] frequently refers to the *vis cogitativa* as a *ratio particularis* and assigns it the task of co-operating with the rational faculties in the formation of judgments pertaining to action. Action by its very nature is destined to realize some value and, accordingly, presupposes an awareness of the value as well as a capacity of referring the will to the particular good in question." Thus man, acting with his will upon material and individual sensorial reality (that is, isolating and regrouping the elements thereof, as Claudel speaks of doing in our strophe), is still operating on the level of the senses, with his *ratio particularis* or *vis cogitativa*: he has not yet lifted himself up to the spheres of intellectual cognition of the immaterial and the universal. And Claudel, in our collection, reaches only in Ode v the stage of cognizing the universal and the immaterial. In our strophe the most important words are "at their place"—where we have to do with the pattern of medieval gradualism which stabilizes things at the "right place." The "word of the poet," on one level with the element isolated by the scientist, is the field for the *vis cogitativa* which, as Allers has said, "co-operates" with reason, but is not identical therewith.

34. It is time for us to recapitulate what the prefix *re-* means to our poet, who is so "prefix-conscious" (cf. his well-known puns on *connaître - co-naître*, on *com-poser*, etc.). The words with *re-* which Claudel uses are apt to be words quite current in French but, by repetition or groupment and by semantic expansion, he is able to create a *re*-cluster which reflects a group of ideas dear to him. Any single formation may be unobtrusive but, when all are taken together, they have an impressive power.

First, the poet declares himself to be simply a "recenseur" (similar to the Egyptian scribe, 18), a garnerer of things existing and already created in a finite world. In Ode II he will say: "J'ai recensé l'armée des cieux et j'en ai dressé l'état . . . J'ai tendu l'immense rets de ma connaissance" (note the reference to a net, which, with its clear lines, delimits the catch). When he speaks of the martyrs of whom he will sing (in "Processional"), it is of those "dont les noms sont recensés au ciel et sur nos diptyques."

Secondly, since the poet is not a creator but a re-creator, the public that listens to him must "recognize" the things already created: "et que chacun dans mes vers retrouve ces choses qui lui sont connues" (25)—a variant of the passage, in the Introduction of our ode: "Pas aucune de vos phrases que je ne sache *re*prendre! Ces fleurs sont vos fleurs et vous dites que vous ne les *re*connaissez pas!"

Thirdly, the "recognition" as a procedure that repeats the process of original creation is in the nature of our human intelligence, which only continues the "intelligence of the senses" (36-37): "[l'intelligence] continuée avec l'intelligence qui la / *Re*fait de l'élément qu'elle *ré*cupère." God's creation was the creation of the intelligent senses.

Fourthly, poetic activity is nothing but the continuation and repetition of the God-given human intelligence: to integrate, in the catholic manner, things garnered and catalogued ("recensées") brings unity into the poet's own mind and into the universe as cognized by it: contrary to Corneille's Auguste ("Je suis maître de moi comme de l'univers; / Je le suis, je veux l'être . . ."), the poet Claudel gives freedom, the freedom of cognition, to himself and to the universe. In Antistrophe III of Ode V he announces his intention "De connaître Dieu dans sa fixité et d'acquérir la vérité par l'attention et chaque chose qui est toutes les autres en la *re-créant* avec son nom intelligible dans la pensée"; and he glorifies "cette énergie divine de l'esprit qui ouvre les yeux, *Recommençant* sa journée et qui trouve chaque chose à sa place dans l'immense atelier de la connaissance." He wants to be "le *rassembleur* de la terre de Dieu" (this is the theme of Claudel's baroque drama, *Le soulier de satin*, in which he portrays the conquest, at the hands of the Spanish Conquistadores, of the whole world by the Catholic God); "et moi aussi, toutes les figures de la nature m'ont été données, . . . pour que je les *rassemble* dans mon esprit." Thus the poet is only a copyist (another variant of the accountant or the surveyor), comparable to the monk (of whom Claudel tells us in Ode V) whose task it was to copy the Gospel and who, returning to his devastated monastery, takes up once more his work where he had stopped: "*Recommence* l'initiale d'or sur le diplôme de pourpre."

And finally, since all activity of human (and poetic) intelligence consists in continuing, repeating, retracing God's creation, the poet is a "reconciliator" of what seems discordant ("le grand poème de l'homme . . . *ré*concilié"). "*Re-*" is, so to speak, the principle by which, in the medieval system of thought of an Alanus ab Insulis, the God-created universe is kept functioning by Nature.

As for the metrical break: "qui la / Refait de l'élément qu'elle récupère," this is introduced to make us draw breath before the important word *refait*, which stands out before us in relief; in "qui la / refait" Claudel would have us pronounce *re-fait* with a distinct separation of the two syllables, the stress being laid on the first—as is the practice of a Frenchman in oral speech when special emphasis is called for. Thus, by means of this metrical break, Claudel is able to indicate the intonation of oral speech (in a way that is generally impossible with the usual system of printing): oral speech and a technique of breathing. Here, indeed, metrics does reflect the measure of human breathing, but the modulation here indicated is due, not to the limitations of human nature but to its "intelligence et volonté."

Compare the separation of the versets in the lines of the introduction to Ode IV: "Ce n'est pas pour eux [les hommes] que je suis fait, mais pour le / Transport de cette mesure sacrée." The words of the last verset are isolated from the rest and are held up above earthly contamination like a pyx. Again, the poet must pause for breath—which is a pause of reverence before the transcendental revelation. Compare also the lines in Ode v: "Faites que je sois entre les hommes comme une personne sans visage et ma / Parole sur eux sans aucun son comme un semeur de silence . . ."—the phrase "parole sur eux" seems to hover aloft over the believers. In Ode I, when Claudel imagines himself on the bark with the muse Erato, he exclaims: "Toujours / Plus avant, jusqu'au coeur de la mer luisante"—the quest "plus ultra!" adapted here to his own state of mind, must detach itself from the rest: it is "quoted" reverently.

35. We may note here a variant of the chaotic enumeration which is particularly Claudelian and, at the same time, characteristic of our time, in which distances are annihilated: the device of the "geographically chaotic enumeration": "le canon qui ouvre les vieux Empires" is evidently the artillery of Admiral Perry in Japan, the "Aruwhimi" represents Africa, the blast-furnaces are Pittsburgh, while, in the transatlantic steamboat we have an allusion to the ocean separating continents. Compare, in Ode v:

> Et toutes [choses] vous êtes en ma possession, comme un banquier qui de son bureau de *Paris* fait argent avec l'écriture des gommes de la *Sénégambie*,
> Et de la pelletée de minerai sur le carreau de la mine *antarctique*, et de la perle des *Pomoton*, et du grand tas de laine *Mongol*

(here Claudel adopts the capitalization of the ethnic adjective as in English, in order to make the geographic entities stand out more independently). And, in Ode II:

> . . . je tire, j'appelle sur toutes mes racines, le Gange, le Mississippi,
> L'épaisse touffe de l'Orénoque, le long fil du Rhin, le Nil avec sa double vessie. . . .

Again, from his *Art poétique* (1907): "Cependant à toute heure de la Terre il est toutes les heures à la fois. Pendant que l'ouvrière en plumes voit qu'il est Midi au cadran de la Pointe-Saint-Eustache, le soleil de son premier rayon ras troue la feuille Virginienne, l'escadre des cachalots se joue sous la lune australe. Il pleut à Londres, il neige sur la Poméranie, pendant que le Paraguay n'est que roses, pendant que Melbourne grille." (This passage is probably influenced by *Purgatorio*, XXVII, I *seq.*, where Dante states that when it is sunset in Purgatory it is sunrise at Jerusalem, midnight in Spain, noon in India; but Dante admits of no chaotic disorder: he merely points out the synchronic relationships of the four fixed cardinal points.)

36. How touching is this parenthesis which suggests a "parenthetical interpolation" of Nature and which seems somehow related to the main effect of the poem intended by Claudel; we were told that this poem should be "plus clair que la lune qui brille avec sérénité sur la campagne dans la semaine de la moisson"—the moonlight and the patch of blue river combine to the same color sensation of clarity and linearity, serenity and solemnity. Claudel sees the cities framed by Nature: in his vision the two

are not opposed to each other, but are fused—a fusion which is so characteristic of our modern landscape (I think I shall never forget the impression made on me by the noisy streets of Istanbul teeming with gesticulating and screaming Southerners and the solemn quiet of the Bosporus and the mountains of Asia—boundless beyond man's gaze). A still further step would be to see the landscape character of our modern cities themselves: for example the "canyon" of Wall Street.

Should "et ça et là une anse bleue" be constructed grammatically together with "avec les frénétiques villes"? That is, should we understand: "ce que les gens ont fait avec les villes . . . et avec . . . une anse bleue"? Evidently not. We have here to do with a quite independent expression "et ça et là une anse . . . !" and this syntactical break is indicative of the cleavage man has forced between civilization and Nature. The brusqueness of the break, however, is mitigated by the inclusion of the exclamation within the sentence structure.

37. It must be noted that Claudel's *carmen saeculare* is a glorification of his century, not of any one august personality of the times, as was the case with the poem of Horace, and with those of the court poets of the baroque age (Ronsard and Boileau) who had accepted this limitation. It is true that Claudel, in more recent times, seems to have descended to the obsequious level in his "Ode to Marshal Pétain" (which I have not seen).

38. Grammatically speaking, "enfin" is an *ἀπὸ κοινοῦ*: you may construct "le grand poème de l'homme enfin" (*finally* the great poem comes into being) or "le grand poème de l'homme / enfin . . . réconcilié" (of mankind finally reconciled . . .). Sometimes Claudel places an *ἀπὸ κοινοῦ* in a clause to which it would not seem to belong naturally, thereby suggesting two contrasting forces which draw, as it were, the adverbial phrase toward themselves with equal force—compare the *dans mes vers* in the motto of this chapter.

39. In order to realize the full impact of this line, we must remember that Thomist philosophy, while centering all activity of creation in God, recognizes, at the same time, that things created act out of their own impulse: this is the so-called efficacy of the *causae secundae*; it is a gift of God's love just as creation is the act of His power. Etienne Gilson (*Le Thomisme*, p. 174), represents the convergence of God's activity (that is, the activity of the *causa principalis*) and the activity of things created, by the simile of a hatchet swung by a carpenter: although the hatchet has been made and is wielded by the carpenter, it is undeniably true that the hatchet, the *causa secunda*, does the chopping. Claudel, faithful to Thomism, seems to share the belief that "detrahere actiones proprias rebus est divinae bonitati derogare." And, accordingly, he puts the *causae secundae* in the foreground; he feels, nevertheless, the estrangement which has taken place in the modern world between the *causae secundae* (our material civilization) and the Prime Cause. Claudel offers no complaint against the "evil" modern world; he simply works by means of his harmonizing poetry toward the necessary "reconciliation": "oportet omnes causas inferiores agentes *reduci* in causas superiores sicut instrumentales in primarias."

40. At the celebration of the 400th anniversary of the University of Marburg in 1929, I heard a Catholic delegate quote a sentence he had heard from the mouth of the Pope: "Gaudet ecclesia studio veritatis." Or, as Claudel would say: "Gaudet Deus studio veritatis."

41. It is worthy of note that Claudel does not use the Ovidian technique of metamorphosis: he states suddenly the achieved transformation of "la Muse qui est la Grâce." In the *argument* Claudel speaks of (a gradual) "devenir," but in the poem there is only stage A followed by stage B—and declared identical therewith. A Christian miracle does not admit of gradual transformation: Segismundo, in "La vida es sueño" *is,* suddenly, from a particular scene on, enlightened.

Has not the idea of "la Muse qui est la Grâce" been suggested to Claudel by Ronsard's "Ode à Michel de l'Hôpital," which opens with the line: "Errant par les champs de la grâce" (where the particular "grace, or gift of poetry" is meant), and which contains such passages as: "C'est lui [Michel de l'Hôpital] dont les grâces infuses) / Ont ramené par l'univers / Le choeur des Piérides Muses" (where the wording seems to suggest the fusion of "grace - gift" and Divine Grace)? But with Ronsard there is rather an unconscious shift from the pagan to the Christian meaning, whereas Claudel maintains the opposition between the two extremes.

42. One could doubt whether I have not overstated the facts as far as our strophe is concerned: is Christian Grace really the Muse of the poet, *by the end of the first strophe*? It is true that, in the answer given by the Muse in Antistrophe I, we find only ideas which are quite at variance with Christianity and which can only be intended as a temptation to the poet—a temptation to which he almost succumbs (Strophe II); again, in Antistrophe II, the Muse presents creation as an amoral fire and appeals to the flamelike in the poet's nature. In Strophe III, where the poet reaffirms the inner necessity he feels of representing the whole world in his limited poetic activity, there is no word to indicate that he appeals to the Muse as to Grace. Only in Antistrophe III do we find the words, spoken by the Muse: "Tu m'appelles la Muse et mon autre nom est la Grâce," and later she explains her personal message to him: "je suis la parole de grâce qui est adressée à toi seul." And yet it is this envoy of Heaven that the poet, in the epode, rejects in his desire to cling to the earth and to his sainted earthly love: "Va-t-en! Je me retourne désespérément vers la terre." And we are asked to suppose that in the interval between the composition of Odes IV and V the poet has found happiness with his love, the "épouse nocturne." It is only in Ode V that the poet is fully ready to reconcile his private and circumscribed family-life ("la maison fermée") with the task of "collecting" the whole world for God. Thus it would appear that the moment when he was able to formulate his program in Strophe I of Ode IV was only an anticipation of that state of Grace-given inner freedom reached in Ode V. "La Muse qui devient peu à peu la Grace" (as she is called in the "argument") has only in Ode V truly become "la Muse qui est la Grâce." Ode IV ends on a desperate note: the poet had already understood, in our strophe, his superhuman task, but could not reconcile it with his earthly love; only in Ode V does he gain the strength necessary both for his superhuman and his earthly task. Still, our strophe remains a first and interimistic stage on the long and wavering road toward the final conquest of Grace. The miracle of the revelation of his task to the poet takes place, in fact, in our strophe, but it finds him yet not quite prepared to accept it. Grace is a gift coming to those who are not yet great enough fully to deserve it.

And now we are in a position to recognize the development of form, and the inner connection, in the sequence of the odes. Whereas, in Ode I, the Muses (and particularly the muse Erato) are invoked without any response on their part, we have, in Ode IV, a dialogue between the poet and the Muse. Such a dialogue is meant, with all modern poets (we may remember Musset) to symbolize the conflict between the creative forces of the poet and the rest of his being. This comes to an end in our ode: in Ode V the dialogue takes place only with the public. From this we may infer that the poet no longer has need of communication with his creative forces, since the latter have been integrated into his being. We can also understand now the alternation, in our collection, between paganistic and Christian odes: Ode I, "Les Muses"; II, "L'Esprit et l'eau"; III, "Magnificat"; IV, "La Muse qui est la Grâce"; V, "La maison fermée; VI, "Processional"—of which III and VI, the liturgical pieces, show two fairly clear stages in the gradual process by which the pagan element in the poet's soul is absorbed into Christianity. Ode III ends in the meditative serenity and confident peace of a vesper service, at a time of day when sharp contours are blurred "avant que la nuit ne commence et la pluie, avant que la longue pluie dans la nuit sur la terre ensemencée ne commence." The setting of our Ode IV is the night—a night in which the poet, after his triumphant wrestling with the pagan muse is, at the end, brought to a temporary defection from poetry altogether, and seeks happiness with his wife. In V, he is able to reconcile his avocation of poet with earthly happiness in "La maison fermée," where he finds the ultimate peace which sets the tone of the Processional: "Procedamus in pace in nomine Domini." Thus our collection of six odes embodies the whole drama of the separation and reintegration of the spiritual forces of the poet—a psychomachy.

There is still another development underlying the sequence of odes: the unfolding of the autobiographical element. It is as if the development by which the Muse becomes Grace is paralleled by the settlement of the practical existence of the poet in his house and his family—as if the abstract suffering due to his position between earth and heaven gave way in proportion as he took firmer roots in the concrete and necessarily narrower life: the more protected by God he is, the more "la maison fermée" comes into its own, and the more concrete becomes "la Muse qui est la Grâce." Whereas the "je" of the Introduction and of Strophe I of Ode IV is a quite general "poetic I," it tends, in the following stanzas, to become more and more the particular "Claudelian I" who identifies himself not only with the universe but with his family. In Strophe II of Ode IV Claudel will still complain to God: "Mais vous m'avez placé dans la terre, afin que j'endure la gêne et l'étroitesse et l'obscurité"; in Strophe III he will formulate his own situation in this narrow world in general terms: "Celui qui a acheté une femme à l'âge juste, ayant mis l'argent de côté peu à peu, / Il est avec elle comme un cercle fermé et comme une cité indissoluble. / Et leurs enfants entre eux deux comme de tendres grains mûrissants"—the motif of the "maison fermée" appears here for the first time, but the Biblical "acheter une femme" still veils the existence of his particular wife. In Ode V, however, she appears as "la gardienne du poète," to explain to the public (in the words of the *argument*): "Je sais que la clôture lui est nécessaire; il est temps que toute sa vie soit ordonnée vers l'intérieur; et par moi il a cet intérieur." Claudel includes the autobiographical element not at all moments but "chemin faisant," as his being is allowed to affirm itself in life: the autobiographical matter is not a fixed quantity, and nothing would be more contrary to the spirit of this poetry than for pragmatistic literary critics to operate with that matter as if it were something primordially given. Much earlier, Claudel had disclosed that he was writing from exile; only after he has, helped by Grace, made his peace with the world and heaven does he write the lines (reminiscent of Ovid's *Tristia ex Ponto*): "Mon Dieu qui m'avez conduit à cette extrémité du monde . . . , / Ne permettez point que parmi ce peuple dont je n'entends point la langue, / Je perde mémoire de mes frères qui sont *tous les hommes, pareils à ma femme et à mon enfant.*" When the biographical makes its appearance, it is fused with the ecumenic or Catholic concern of the poet; it has no exhibitionist purpose, as with some of the Romantic poets.

Our remarks about the gradual recession of the pagan theme and the final enthronement of the intramundane Christian element, as embedded in the practical biography of the poet, lead to another observation: the extension of the "poetic I." Claudel has beautifully exploited the wide range that is inherent in the personal pronoun. This type of pronoun is a kind of proper name that stands for a human person in his unquestionable evidence: "I" speaks of a human being as *existing*, as imposing his evidence on the interlocutor; we may use it before being "introduced" to someone: by means of "I" we introduce ourselves sufficiently without giving our name, presenting ourselves as "this human being before you, whatever his name." When the interlocutor becomes better acquainted with the person calling himself "I," he is in a position to fill out the empty framework of the being indicated only as "I," without sensing any interruption of continuity: "I" becomes not only an unquestionable existence as such, but a filled-out ("étoffée") existence. In Odes I-IV Claudel furnished us only the "poetic I," accepted in its vagueness by the reader; in Ode V, the "poetic I" has truly become that "Paul Claudel, the French ambassador who is living in China with his family." The autobiographical filling-out of the pronoun is meant for the reader (the interlocutor of the poet) and surely gives him the feeling of having come closer to the poet; at the same time, however, the poet has gained confidence in his "I"—that is, in the relevance of his autobiography—ever since the moment when Grace has affirmed him in life. The struggles whereby the "poetic I" is enabled to take root in life are the content of this sequence of odes. We have here a paradigmatic example of the poet's capacity of widening and deepening, in an individual manner, the meaning of a simple grammatical tool which is given to any individual speaker, quite matter-of-factly, by his mother-tongue. Or, in other words, the poet shows us the inner, the human struggle hidden behind the screen of the word "I"—that word on which rests all poetic and all human activity.

A last question remains to be solved: Why does Claudel write *five* odes ("followed by a processional")? And why are there *50* versets in the strophe we have here selected? The symbolism of numbers is in line with medieval practice (Dante), but why is Claudel's symbolism based on the number 5 (or 6)? One may think immediately of Manzoni's five *Inni sacri* (though these five odes simply happen to be the only ones preserved of the greater number Manzoni originally intended to write). But such literary parallels are less instructive than are Claudel's own words: in Ode v, on the cardinal virtues, we find the following lines on "Justice":

> Elle considère la terminaison de toutes choses et le jour quand il se consomme . . . ,
> Ce jour qui est le sixième, celui qui précède le sabbat et qui suit les cinq premiers.
> Elle acquitte mes comptes; elle règle pour moi ce qui est dû....
> D'autre part je sais que toute chose est bénie en elle-même et que je suis béni en elle.
> Car l'homme, héritier des cinq jours, qui l'ont précédé, reçoit sur sa tête leurs bénédictions accumulées.

In this passage which shows the workings of Providence-in-Time (or, Justice), a Providence which was at work in the creation of man at an appointed time (the sixth day) and which still works in bringing things to their just ends and in settling human accounts, Claudel figures the week (as a division of time) as divided into the Sabbath, the day before the Sabbath, and the remaining five, relatively undistinguished workdays. Perhaps this division can serve as a clue to the arrangement and the theme of the collection as a whole: the block of the five odes corresponds to the block of five days (the five working days); the sixth ode ("Processional") corresponds to the day preceding the Sabbath, and treats of the ritual of purification in view of the heavenly Sabbath—a theme which Claudel (unlike Dante) makes no attempt to treat: his poem takes us only to the threshold of Heaven (Ode v ends with the lines: "Le custode seulement et non point la coupe, car nous ne goûterons point de ce fruit de la vigne avant que nous le buvions nouveau dans le Royaume de Dieu"). The idea of the whole collection, then, is to prepare us for the heavenly Sabbath and to lead us, by way of everyday chores, through the particular purification of the Sabbath, to the threshold of eternal joy.

43. As an exception I venture here to voice criticism and not to apply only the *critique des beautés*. I feel justified in so doing because I have tried to understand Claudel's world of thought from within, and only after my apperception of his art was (in a manner of speaking) completed have I found a flaw which is inherent to the very conception of his poem. This "historical" flaw is conditioned by the basic idea of having Grace replace the Muse, or of having pious rationality replace secular enthusiasm: since there had to be the Muse (who was also made necessary by the invocation in the proem) she had to become the *repoussoir*: the personification of the Greek culture which had to be rejected. Claudel could then not admit in his poem a Pallas Athene as a prefiguration of the numerous Catholic patron saints of skills and technics.

My objection cannot be met by the argument that a poet is free to alter historical facts in accord with the laws of poetry: since Claudel's poem implies a historical picture of our civilization, this picture must be in harmony with at least that historical picture which our civilization calls its own, and which forms a part of it. When Dante alters history he is in accord with what his civilization taught him about history: Vergil could be his *duca e maestro*. When Villon makes of the Greek Alcibiades a lovely woman Archipiada, this was in accordance with what his civilization thought of Alcibiades. But when Claudel willingly shuts his eyes to *his own knowledge* that Greek philosophy and religion anticipate Christian philosophy and religion, he puts himself in opposition to himself, and the rift makes itself felt within the poem (the Egyptians and the Assyrians must replace the Greeks and Romans!).

44. According to Karl Viëtor, who (in *Geschichte der deutschen Ode* [1923]) seeks to define the ode on the basis of all the examples of this genre from antiquity to our day, the ode is characterized by its position between the *lied* and the hymn: its style ends toward the sublime and the elaborately poetic, its mood is that of heightened feeling coupled with reflection —Herder's definition "die poetische Ausbildung eines lebhaften Gedankens" can, according to Viëtor, be maintained if we grant to the terms used their full range of significance (*poetisch* - "elaborately poetic"; *lebhaft* - "animated by heightened feeling"; *Gedanken* - "mood of reflection"). From these basic characteristics Professor Viëtor derives other features: the mythical element must be in evidence and there must be that "beau désordre" which Boileau posited; the poem must have been inspired by a solemn occasion; rhyme must be absent (according to the Horatian model). Professor Viëtor states that the pure type of the ode which would contain all those elements together in perfect harmony is rarely to be found in the actually existing historical representatives of the genre; I would venture to claim for Claudel's odes the harmonious presence of *all* these essential features (in spite of the fact that the French poet was not able to read Viëtor's treatise!). And, when we read Viëtor's lament over the inability of contemporary German poets to breathe into their odes a new spirit uniting "Freiheit und Gesetz" (the freedom of artistic creativity and the law of form), we Romance philologists can point with pride to Claudel.

45. As if out of a feeling of pique against the alexandrine—which he has criticized in his treatise on French versification ("Positions et propositions," 1)—Claudel carefully avoids giving his shorter lines (generally descriptive of energetic decision, of concentration of forces, etc.) the correct form of an alexandrine:

lines:		
	3 . . 7 + 7	(with two hiatuses)
	4 . . 12	(without a caesura; one hiatus)
	15 . . 5 + 7	
	17 . . 3 + 9	(one hiatus)
	27 . . 7 + 8	
	etc.	

46. The reader may have noticed that, from the moment I had pointed out, with the help of the word-motif, the main structure of the poem, my study shifted more and more away from Claudel's words.

I have sought to obey the Claudelian motto of this study by first disobeying it: by starting with the attempt to cut a path through the poetic labyrinth in order to reach the "center." In clearing my path, it was necessary to brush away, for the moment, much of the underbrush—which later on had to be properly accounted for: hence the thicket of notes which could not be avoided if we were to respect the labyrinthine aspect of the poem willed by the poet. Thus it was necessary, for the purpose of exposition, to split into two (text and notes) what appears in the poem as a unit.

CALAMUS

CALAMUS

MALE HOMOSEXUALITY IN TWENTIETH-CENTURY LITERATURE

AN INTERNATIONAL ANTHOLOGY

Edited by

David Galloway and
Christian Sabisch

WILLIAM MORROW AND COMPANY, INC.
New York *1982*

Library of Congress Cataloging in Publication Data
Main entry under title:

Calamus : male homosexuality in twentieth-century literature.

1. Homosexuality, Male—Literary collections.
2. Literature, Modern—20th century. I. Galloway, David D. II. Sabisch, Christian.
PN6071.H724C3 1982 808.8′0353 81-13836
ISBN 0-688-00797-X AACR2
ISBN 0-688-00606-X (pbk.)

Printed in the United States of America

First U.S. Edition

1 2 3 4 5 6 7 8 9 10

BOOK DESIGN BY MICHAEL MAUCERI

For permission to reprint copyrighted material, we should like to make the following grateful acknowledgments:

B.V. Uitgeverij De Arbeiderspers: pages 175-186 from *Ik had een Wapenbroeder* by Maarten 't Hart. Copyright © 1973, 1978 by Maarten 't Hart. Originally published by B.V. Uitgeverij De Arbeiderspers, Amsterdam.

Ardis Publishers: "Aunt Sonja's Sofa" by Mikhail Kuzmin. Reprinted from *Wings: Prose & Poetry of Mikhail Kuzmin.* Copyright © 1972 by Ardis.

Giorgio Bassani and Erich Linder, Agenzia Letteraria Internazionale: pages 58-91 from *The Gold-Rimmed Spectacles* by Giorgio Bassani. Copyright © 1960 by Atheneum House, Inc., and Faber & Faber, Ltd. Originally published in Italian under the title *Gli Occiali D'Oro.* Copyright © 1958 by Giulio Einaudi Editore, S.p.A., Turin.

Marion Boyars Publishers, Ltd.: a selection from *Trans-Atlantyk* by Witold Gombrowicz. Originally published in Polish under the title *Trans-Atlantyk.*

John Calder (Publishers) Ltd. and Riverrun Press, Inc.: a selection from the pages 139-167 from *Sweet Tooth* by Yves Navarre. English translation copyright © 1976 by Donald Watson, Ltd. Originally published under the title *Les Loukoums.* Copyright © 1973 by Editions Flammarion.

Ronald Christ: "A Sinner's Guidebook" by Eduardo Gudiño Kieffer. Copyright © 1975 by Ronald Christ. Reprinted from *New Directions in Prose and Poetry,* 36. Originally published in Spanish under the title *Guía de pecadores* by Editorial Losada S.A., Buenos Aires.

City Lights Books: "A Supermarket in California" by Allen Ginsberg. Reprinted from *Howl* by Allen Ginsberg. Copyright © 1956, 1959 by Allen Ginsberg. "Please Master," "Rain-wet asphalt" by Allen Ginsberg. Reprinted from *The Fall of America* by Allen Ginsberg. Copyright © 1971 by Allen Ginsberg.

Lonnie Coleman and Curtis Brown, Ltd.: "Theban Warriors" by Lonnie Coleman. Copyright © 1955 by Lonnie Coleman. Reprinted from *Ship's Company,* published by Little, Brown & Co.

Candida Donadio & Assoc., Inc.: "On Ruegen Island" by Christopher Isherwood. Reprinted from *Goodbye to Berlin* by Christopher Isherwood. Copyright 1945 by New Directions, renewed © 1973 by Christopher Isherwood.

Gleerup Publishers and Anne-Marie Ekelund: "Nothing, Nothing Else in the World," "October" by Vilhelm Ekelund. Originally published in Swedish in

Elegier by Vilhelm Ekelund. Copyright 1903 by Vilhelm Ekelund. "The Friends," "Symposium" by Vilhelm Ekelund. Originally published in Swedish in *Hafvets stjärna* by Vilhelm Ekelund. Copyright 1906 by Vilhelm Ekelund.

Grove Press, Inc.: "Hassan's Rumpus Room" by William Burroughs. Reprinted from *The Naked Lunch.* Copyright © 1959 by William Burroughs. Originally published by Olympia Press, Paris. A selection from the pages 227-255 from *Funeral Rites* by Jean Genet. Copyright © 1969 by Grove Press, Inc. Originally published in French as *Pompes Funèbres* by Jean Genet, *Oeuvres Complètes.* Copyright 1953 by Editions Gallimard, Paris.

Thom Gunn: "The Miracle" by Thom Gunn. Copyright © 1980 by Thom Gunn. Originally published by Gay News, London. "Song: San Francisco Street" by Thom Gunn. Copyright © 1980 by Thom Gunn. Originally published by *Christopher Street,* New York.

Thom Gunn and Faber & Faber, Ltd.: "Modes of Pleasure" by Thom Gunn. Reprinted from *My Sad Captains* by Thom Gunn. Copyright © 1961 by Thom Gunn. Thom Gunn and Faber & Faber, Ltd. and Farrar, Straus & Giroux, Inc.: "Fever" by Thom Gunn. Reprinted from *Jack Straw's Castle* by Thom Gunn. Copyright © 1976 by Thom Gunn.

Gyldendal Publishers: a selection from the pages 32-53 from *Fornemmelser* by Christian Kampmann. Copyright © 1977 by Christian Kampmann.

Harcourt Brace Jovanovich, Inc.: "Body Remember" by Constantin Cavafy Copyright 1949 by Rea Dalven. Reprinted from *The Complete Poems of Cavafy* translated by Rea Dalven. "Gray," "The Tobacco-Shop Window," "The Next Table," "Their Beginning," "In an Old Book," "Before Time Changes Them" by Constantin Cavafy. Copyright © 1961 by Rea Dalven. Reprinted from *The Complete Poems of Cavafy,* translated by Rea Dalven.

The Hogarth Press, Ltd.: "On Ruegen Island" by Christopher Isherwood. Reprinted from *Goodbye to Berlin* by Christopher Isherwood. Copyright 1935 by Christopher Isherwood.

Stanley Kauffmann and Brandt & Brandt Literary Agents, Inc.: "Fulvous Yellow" by Stanley Kauffmann. Copyright 1949 by *Story* magazine.

King's College, Cambridge and The Society of Authors Ltd. as the literary representative of the Estate of E.M. Forster: "The Obelisk" by E.M. Forster. Reprinted from *The Life to Come, And Other Stories* by E.M. Forster. Copyright © 1972 by The Provost and the Scholars of King's College, Cambridge.

Verlag Gudula Lorez: "Visiting" by Anna Rheinsberg. Originally published under the German title "Zu Besuch" in *Wo die Nacht den Tag umarmt.* Copyright © 1979 by Verlag Gudula Lorez, West Berlin.

New Directions Publishing Corporation: "The Sailor's Son" by William Carlos Williams, *The Farmer's Daughters.* Copyright 1932 by William

Viking Penguin, Inc.: "Hands" by Sherwood Anderson. Reprinted from *Winesburg, Ohio.* Copyright 1919 by B.W. Huebsch, renewed 1947 by Eleanor C. Anderson. Originally published by Random House, Inc., New York. "The Prussian Officer" by D.H. Lawrence. Copyright © 1955 by The Estate of the late Mrs. Frieda Lawrence Ravagli.

The Estate of the late Louis Wilkinson: "The Better End" by Louis Wilkinson. Privately printed in 1959.

This volume is dedicated
to
Douglas Johnson and Derek Yeld

FOREWORD

The scope of this volume can only begin to suggest the immense complexity of homosexual experience and the rich variety of its literary expression. The designation "homosexual literature" cannot be avoided in these pages, but it is a thematic description that should not be automatically equated with the sexual preferences of an individual author. Heterosexual writers have sometimes addressed the theme of homosexual love with insight and compassion; many known homosexuals, on the other hand, have rigorously avoided the subject. Women have frequently portrayed the love of man for man in their writings—in part, no doubt, for the light it sheds on the entire problem of sexual role-playing. Thus, without reference to the author's biography, we have sought works of literary consequence that focus on the problems, the stereotypes, the poetry and psychology of homosexual relationships between men.

Our focus is on work produced in the twentieth century, when many writers have enjoyed a new freedom to explore sexuality in a direct, explicit manner. The development of this freedom is neither constant nor universal, but its tendency has been to reject the "coding" and the circumventions many earlier writers adapted in order to screen their real intentions. We have, in addition, limited ourselves to the theme of male homosexuality, despite persuasive arguments from the Gay Liberation Movement that male and female homosexuals must unite in a common front. For the purposes of this work, however, both social and legal actualities argue for the separation. However cruelly censored and suppressed they may have been, Lesbian relationships have seldom been actively, systematically persecuted by church or state. The particular institutionalized discrimination against male homosexuality has, inevitably, left a deep stamp on the manner of its literary expression; this reality demands a volume of its own. In making our selections we have sought to reflect a broad range of cultural backgrounds, though there is an inevitable concentration on the Western hemisphere—in particular, on Europe and the Americas. There, thanks to the growing consciousness and self-confidence produced by various homosexual and libertarian movements, the theme has been handled with particular frequency and assurance.

Every anthology is the product of numerous compromises. Often it was necessary to exclude works because of their excessive length, and some texts appear only in extracts; other selections were eliminated by problems of copyright, or because they were otherwise readily available to the interested reader. Certain well-known texts had to be included in order to establish the necessary historical dimension, but we have sought to complement these with a number of lesser-known pieces—works formerly suppressed, long out of print, or never before translated into English. We regret that, in the end, so little space could be apportioned for younger writers, but we have seen our primary obligation as establishing a foundation on which further work can be done. If our choices prompt the reader to compose his own, alternative table of contents, our goal has been achieved.

We hope that *Calamus* can make some contribution to restoring the blighted and obscured heritage of the homosexual, and that it can simultaneously offer the heterosexual a deeper insight. But above all we would welcome an audience that could approach the works presented here without recourse to labels and stereotypes, but as significant achievements of the literary imagination.

—David Galloway

—Christian Sabisch

ACKNOWLEDGMENTS

For their generous advice and assistance in the making of this book, we should like to thank:

Zoltán Abádi-Nagy
Vincent Balitas
Margret Büscher
John Calder
Ann Carter
Ronald Christ
Javier Coy
Louis Crompton
Jonathan Cutbill
S.M. Daly
Henriette Dornenberg
Lit Fischer
Armand de Fluvià
Hans-Peter Förding
Warren French
Jonathan Fryer
Stephen Gray
Page F. Grubb
Richard Hall
Ute Henneberg
Alison Hennegan
Michael Holm
Francis Howard
Joachim S. Hohmann
Raoul Hübner
Dieter Ingenschay
Josef Jarab
Douglas James Johnson
Jerzy Kutnik
Denis Lemon
Winston Leyland
Jürgen Loos
Franek Lyra
Ross McGregor

Julian Meldrum
Barbara Shelby Merello
Norbert Messler
Ron Mooser
Zdzisaw Najder
Bruno Peterson
Walter J. Phillips
Angela Praesent
James Purdy
Antonio Jorge Consalves Rodrigues
Georges-Michel Sarotte
Klaus Scherpe
Ed Schraepen
Richard Senate
Sven Sponberg
Bill Swainson
James Wootton
Derek Yeld
Ian Young
Thekla Zachrau

CONTENTS

Contents

CALAMUS

FULL OF LIFE NOW

Full of life now, compact, visible,
I, forty years old the eighty-third year of the States,
To one a century hence or any number of centuries hence,
To you yet unborn these, seeking you.

When you read these I that was visible am become invisible,
Now it is you, compact, visible, realizing my poems, seeking me,
Fancying how happy you were if I could be with you and become your comrade;
Be it as if I were with you. (Be not too certain but I am now with you.)

—Walt Whitman, Calamus

INTRODUCTION

The right to speak frankly and approvingly of homosexual love is still denied to many writers, but remarkable progress has been made in reversing the effects of centuries of suppression and hypocrisy, and in giving voice to a persecuted minority. Though pioneering work had in fact been accomplished three decades before, the beginnings can be symbolically dated from 1895, when the Brazilian writer Adolfo Caminha published the first sympathetic and accomplished novel of homosexual love. *Bon-Crioulo* (*Good Nigger*) explored the passionate sexual relationship between a mature black sailor and a fifteen-year-old ship's boy, "a beautiful little sailor with blue eyes, much liked by all, about whom 'certain things' were said." The novel concludes with the violence that would become obligatory for countless later works, but its descriptions of the love of an older man for a cherished boy are presented with tender compassion.

In 1895 the courageous German pioneer of homosexual liberation, Karl Heinrich Ulrichs, died in self-imposed Italian exile; Havelock Ellis began to publish in American periodicals the studies of homosexual and bisexual conduct that would form part of *The Psychology of Sex*; and Edward Carpenter completed the manuscript of *Love's Coming of Age.* The English poet, socialist and reformer championed women's rights and sex education; he also called, in "The Intermediate Sex," for a new, important role for the homosexual in society. Arguing in the manner of Walt Whitman—whom he had met and devoutly admired—that homosexuals can best rise above mere sex to spiritual comradeship, Carpenter insisted that they were thus especially well fitted for leadership in a progressive, democratic society.

In the history of homosexual literature, however, the most sensational and consequential event of 1895 was the trial of Oscar Wilde. Wilde was a married man and the father of two children; his writings had been internationally acclaimed, and two of his plays were enjoying successful runs in London theaters. He was also a well-known public figure, notorious for his wit, aesthetics and dandyism. For some years he had freely indulged in homosexual liaisons, including a romantic affair with his beloved "Bosie," Lord Alfred Douglas. A few days after the triumphant premiere of *The Importance of Being Earnest,* Wilde received an insulting card from Bosie's father, Lord Queensberry, accusing him of sodomy. At the insistence of his young lover, Wilde sued Queensberry for criminal libel. When the court ruled against Oscar Wilde, the spectators broke into cheers of approval. Wilde's books immediately disappeared from libraries and shops, his plays were closed, and the author bankrupted. A second trial, in which soiled bedsheets were entered as evidence and a professional blackmailer testified against Wilde, resulted in a maximum prison sentence of two years at hard labor.

There had been such scandals before—as when the Unitarian minister Horatio Alger, who went on to become the most influential writer of boys' books in America, was dismissed from the church for "the abominable and revolting crime of unnatural familiarity with *boys* . . ." Other, more publicized scandals would follow—the Krupp and Eulenberg-Moltke affairs in Germany, the purges of Senator Joseph McCarthy in the United States, the indictment of Liberal Party leader Jeremy Thorpe in England. The Wilde affair remains almost unique, however, in the depth of the shock waves it produced. Spotlighted in the international press, it provoked people to speak about the "unspeakable," and to debate the possible relationship between sexual preference and artistic temperament.

Reaction to the Wilde affair delayed publication of Edward Carpenter's *Love's Coming of Age* until 1896, the year in which Adolf Brand began to publish the German magazine *Der Eigene*, devoted to "art and masculine culture." In 1897 the world's first homosexual liberation organization was formed in Germany, under the leadership of Magnus Hirschfeld, and a petition campaign was launched to amend the notorious paragraph 175 of the German penal code, which made all sexual acts between males a criminal offense. More than 6,000 prominent Germans signed the petition—including Hermann Hesse, George Grosz, Krafft-Ebing, Martin Buber, Käthe Kollwitz, Thomas Mann, Stefan Zweig and Rainer Maria Rilke. Hirschfeld's work with the Scientific Humanitarian Committee further eroded the code of silence surrounding the problem of homosexuality, and gradually won major support from members of the Reichstag.

In 1929 the Committee on Criminal Law of the German Parliament recommended abolition of anti-homosexual legislation, but before that recommendation could become law, the nation was plunged into the economic and political chaos that brought about the rise of Adolf Hitler. On a May morning in 1933, Nazi youths sacked the Institute for Sexual Research where Hirschfeld's Scientific Humanitarian Committee was housed. A few days later, more than 10,000 volumes from the Institute's library, as well as extensive files, charts and photographs, fed an enormous bonfire on Opera Square. The bust of Hirschfeld, carried in a torchlight procession through the streets, was thrown into the flames. It was the beginning of a horror story that continued with the bloody Röhm-Putsch and the deaths of tens of thousands of homosexuals in Nazi concentration camps. In post-war, democratic Germany, those homosexuals who survived the barbarities of Auschwitz and Dachau would be repeatedly denied restitution for their sufferings on the grounds that they had been criminal and not political prisoners. Such events make tragically clear that homosexual emancipation cannot be charted on a simple curve. Furthermore, if progress in reform movements becomes too visible, the victors too jubilant, it may well trigger reactionary impulses—as in the self-righteous campaign of Anita Bryant. Nonetheless, the homosexual imagination has gradually won rights of self-expression that would have been unthinkable in the nineteenth century.

The selections included in this volume can only hint at the immense range of technique and thematic concern that characterize the literature of male homosexuality. To be sure, certain patterns recur: adolescent sexual initiation, transvestism, voyeurism, the fantasy figure of the handsome sailor, sexuality as religious ritual and as revolt. Particular settings are also archetypal: the prison, the ship at sea, the gay bar, the boarding school, the theater. In part, such patterns derive from the ghetto existence to which many homosexuals have been tacitly condemned; in part, they are reflections (or inversions) of behavior sanctioned by the dominant heterosexual culture. To this degree, at least, homosexual writing fits the basic patterns of minority literature, though with the important qualification that unlike other minorities, which are tolerated somewhere at least, homosexuals suffer a discrimination that is absolutely international.

Despite yawning differences in the legal status and social recognition of homosexuals themselves, their literature reveals numerous configurations that cut across political and cultural boundaries. Comparative anthropology suggests that some of these may be rooted in ancient rites of adolescent initiation and the all-male rituals of warrior societies. The image of the supermale may be embodied in Samurai warrior, Prussian officer, booted cowboy or black-jacketed motorcyclist. The female ideal takes romantic or comic or tragic form in the cherished "wife" of a German nobleman, a Brooklyn drag-queen, a Kabuki actor, a Brazilian soda-jerk, a confused Dutch soldier on holiday leave. Such recurrent prototypes, far from suggesting some implicit limitation of the homosexual imagination, underscore its universality; furthermore, the patterns implied here all have their counterparts in the established literatures of the heterosexual majorities. If Chekhov and Ibsen and Simone de Beauvoir offer alternative views of woman's role in society, so too do the transvestites portrayed by Kieffer, Genet and Selby. As Robert Duncan has argued about fellow-poet and fellow-homosexual Hart Crane, "Crane's suffering, his rebellion, and his love are sources of poetry for him not because they are different to, superior to, mankind, but because he saw in them a link with man; he saw in them his sharing in universal human experience."

A minority has the opportunity to develop a radical perspective on the dominant society, and this perspective has, in turn, allowed homosexuals to address certain themes with particular authority. Western literature in the twentieth century has repeatedly anatomized the figure of the lonely individual, alienated from his own culture—the impotent Fisher King of T.S. Eliot's *The Waste Land*, the aimless wanderers portrayed by Borges and Beckett, the estranged heroes of Albert Camus' *The Stranger*, Saul Bellow's *Dangling Man*, Ralph Ellison's *Invisible Man*—titles symbolic of a fundamental existentialist dread. The homosexual, so often compelled to cultivate invisibility, to live in what novelist John Rechy terms a *City of Night*, has been able to express the search for a viable identity with particular insight.

It is also frequently argued that homosexuals possess unique artistic gifts, that something in the presumed blending of male and female temperaments broadens their creative vision. Such arguments are commonly accompanied by a list of accomplished homosexuals, from Socrates through Michelangelo and DaVinci, to Proust, Gide and an encyclopedic company of actors, composers, painters and dancers. If one subscribes to the neurosis theory of art, it is, of course, entirely plausible that the friction and frustration of his life might encourage the homosexual to seek expression through aesthetic forms. It is also true that in many cultures the performing arts and Bohemian circles of the big cities have frequently been unusually tolerant of sexual difference, encouraging homosexual expression and rewarding it. But all such arguments are highly speculative. More persuasive is the contention of the American psychiatrist Colin J. Williams that "homosexuals are usually marginal to society and this marginality . . . seems to have something to do with a creative person's ability to tolerate ambiguity, project varying points of view, and strike out in new directions."

One thing remains certain: the homosexual sensibility has made a vital contribution to the arts, despite the efforts of prudery, religious dogmatism and official censorship to mask those achievements. For generations, American Blacks suffered from a similar conspiracy to conceal their unique cultural heritage. Such repression cruelly diminishes the self-identity of a group, but it is also a deprivation for the entire literate community. Male homosexuality has an ancient and accomplished literary tradition which is gradually being redeemed from centuries of suppression and outright falsification. Censorship has not always been so perverse as in the case of John Benson, the first important editor of Shakespeare's sonnets, who replaced the pronoun "he" with "she" in those sonnets addressed to the mysterious "Mr. W.H." On the other hand, generations of literary historians have ransacked the cupboards of metaphor to prove that these impassioned love poems were merely a courtly Renaissance tradition, utterly devoid of sexual implication. Conveniently, they ignore the entire pastoral tradition of homoerotic love elaborated by Theocritus and Virgil from which such Elizabethan conventions derived.

In 1684 an erotic play entitled *Sodom, or the Quintessence of Debauchery,* attributed to the satirist John Wilmot, Earl of Rochester, won the distinction of being the first work censored by the English government for obscenity and pornography. It was symbolic that this enraptured paean to the joys of homosexual love should be thus singled out. From the Middle Ages until the early twentieth century, the writer who wished to give positive expression to the love of men for their own sex was repeatedly compelled to disguise his intention with metaphor and encoded allusion, or to publish his works privately or anonymously. Perhaps more sinister than official censorship was the implicit censorship of publishers and public which frequently led the writer to falsify or deny his own art. Even Walt Whitman, so joyfully bold in projecting an entire politics of homosexual experience, felt compelled to modify later editions of *The Leaves of Grass* to blunt the poem's erotic content. Similarly, the "fair slim boy" who inspired Oscar Wilde's "Wasted Days" (1877) was heterosexualized into the inferior tribute to "a lily girl" in "Madonna Mia."

Jean Cocteau's remarkably graceful little novella, *The White Paper*, was published anonymously in 1928, and even today its authorship is rarely acknowledged in official literary histories. This lyric study of homosexual passion contained such transparently autobiographical references that its authorship was scarcely disguised, and the elegantly simplified line-drawings for the second edition bore Cocteau's unmistakable stamp. In fashionable Parisian circles, neither Cocteau's homosexuality nor his experiments with opium were secret; indeed, they helped establish his glamorous credentials as inheritor of the *fin de siècle* Decadents. On the other hand, it was neither fashionable nor wise to advertise such exotic preferences too blatantly. Cocteau may, as well, have enjoyed the private joke of this transparent anonymity. Far more extreme was E.M. Forster's unhappy decision to withhold his own homosexual short stories and the novel *Maurice*, which only appeared in print after the author's death. In our own time the English poet Stephen Spender has included in the official collected edition of his verse a poem concluding with the lines, "Whatever happens, I shall never be alone. I shall always have an affair, a railway fare, or a revolution." It is doubtful that the revision is a genuine improvement over the poem's original wording: "I shall always have a boy, a railway fare, or a revolution."

Even such self-censorship was not always sufficient to pacify audiences. Although Oscar Wilde never specified the "vices" of his decadent hero Dorian Gray, enough readers were scandalized by the mere implication of sexual waywardness for the bookseller W.H. Smith to withdraw from their newsstands the June, 1890, issue of *Lippincott's Monthly Magazine* in which *The Portrait of Dorian Gray* first appeared. Not coincidentally, and with unintentional prophecy, in the same year Wilde composed a short story centering on the riddle of the identity of Shakespeare's beloved "W.H." For two of the three characters involved, solution of the puzzle brings death. Oscar Wilde himself would soon stand trial for gross offenses against nature; dissolute, impoverished and abandoned by most of his friends, Wilde died in 1900 in Paris, where he lived after his release from prison under the pseudonym of Sebastian Melmoth. The allusion to the martyred St. Sebastian, later an idol of Japanese novelist Yukio Mishima, was suggested by arrows on the prison uniform Wilde wore in Reading Gaol. "Melmoth" was borrowed from a famous nineteenth-century novel, *Melmoth the Wanderer*, whose tormented hero has made a Faustian pact with the devil in order to gain eternal life, and who wanders the earth as an outcast, seeking someone who will relieve him from his painful bargain.

Wilde's affair with Lord Alfred Douglas and the legal persecution it provoked form the subject of Eric Bentley's historical drama, *Lord Alfred's Lover* (1978). In the opening of the play, the author tells his children the story of Dr. Jekyll and Mr. Hyde, converting it into a psychodrama of the tormented secret life of the homosexual:

> Dr. Hyde must have an alter ego. . . . A second personality. Called Mr. Jekyll. We'll simply keep Dr. Hyde from public view. He must live only at night, and have his nice times then. By day, coming out at his front door, only Mr. Jekyll will be seen, and he won't be nice and have a nice time, he will be respectable and have a respectable time. Now, all the crimes of London, all the vices, can be imputed to Dr. Hyde!

Bentley's parable neatly describes the double life countless homosexuals have been compelled to lead, and it is hardly surprising that motifs of disguise, impersonation and transformation should recur throughout homosexual literature. Often this takes the form of literal transvestism, recalling the pastoral tradition in which such disguises were a common device, as they were in Shakespeare's comedies and romances, and in the entire tradition of boy-actors playing female roles on the

Elizabethan stage. A writer may also subsume a male within a female character—as Proust shaped Albert into Albertine, or as Tennessee Williams has incorporated much of his own homosexual yearning into portraits of neurotic women, or as Edward Albee, according to some critics, presented a study of homosexual marriage in *Who's Afraid of Virginia Woolf?*

It would be naive to presume that such techniques of inversion automatically undermine the authority of the work of art. Blanche Dubois, the emotionally scarred and fragile heroine of Tennessee Williams' *Streetcar Named Desire,* may express the author's feeling of vulnerable isolation as a homosexual, but she is also an entirely credible female character. And to rewrite Proust by changing the name Albertine to Albert and *elle* to *il* would entirely falsify the aesthetic structure of *À la recherche du temps perdu.* Homosexual writers, furthermore, are hardly unique in having to resort to nuance and symbol and artful substitutions in their work. Political pressures and social conventions, the fear of censors or the guillotine or jealous wives, may give rise to similar techniques; it is necessary, always, to distinguish between transformation of the "real" subject—as in Swift's *Gulliver's Travels* or Alexander Solzhenitsyn's *Cancer Ward*—and evasion or conscious falsification.

Erotic subject matter was long under an equal ban for both heterosexual and homosexual authors; the explicit description of genital sex gave notoriety to John Cleland's *The Adventures of Fanny Hill,* D.H. Lawrence's *Lady Chatterley's Lover* and James Joyce's *Ulysses.* The right to depict the full sexual dimension of human relationships had to be won as part of a far broader struggle against the iniquities of censorship. Until the early twentieth century, deviations from the norm of sexual propriety could be portrayed only if the offender eventually underwent miraculous conversion, was murdered, or committed suicide. Stephen Crane's Maggie drowns herself, Tolstoy's adulterous Anna Karenina throws herself in front of a train, Flaubert's Madame Bovary drinks arsenic, and generations of confused homosexuals drown or poison or hang or shoot themselves in order to confirm the superior social order.

Nonetheless, the proscriptions on homosexual literature have had a particularly sinister quality. Readers, for example, take it for granted that the relationship between a man and a woman can be rendered in an infinite variety of ways, and that the given elements in a character's situation—gender, class or heredity—are diversely tempered by personal experience. But this assumption of uniqueness is rarely extended to those individuals who happen to make emotional and sexual attachments to members of their own sex. One does not find it necessary to classify *Othello* or *Buddenbrooks* as "heterosexual" literature, but the frank treatment of intimacy between members of the same sex guarantees such labeling. So long as the homosexual is isolated from the mainstream of his society, the label is perhaps necessary; he or she belongs to a sub-culture that has no option but to develop its own life-styles and codes. Minority literature itself has become a favorite theme of modern criticism, but there is no implicit moral judgment in a study of the working-class novel in Britain, Black or Jewish writing in the United States, Zulu poetry in South Africa, or French-Canadian drama. In marked contrast to such objectivity, in her provocative and influential study of "camp" as a homosexual style, Susan Sontag asserts that the homosexual viewpoint is incompatible with moral seriousness. And the gifted critic Philip Thody remarks that "Genet's homosexuals are unfaithful to one another because homosexuality is, of itself, a disappointing form of sexual activity." The same critics would quite rightly be resourceful in identifying extenuating circumstances to account, say, for the high illegitimacy rate among American Blacks, but homosexuality can be summed up in tired and untested clichés.

The presumption that the intimate attachment of male to male (or female to female) can only be viewed in sexual terms is, of course, a patent absurdity. It is another simplification of what Christopher Isherwood terms "the heterosexual dictatorship," and its pervasiveness has often had the unfortunate effect of determining the self-image of the homosexual himself. So long as he accepts this discriminating definition, he is unlikely to develop the crucial implications of sexual choice as they manifest themselves in the orientation to friendship, tradition, social mores, authority and the imagination. The homoerotic rituals of the football field and of all-male bands of spectators are sanctioned as part of the masculine role, but homogenital contact remains taboo. Thus, the homosexual is repeatedly told that his unacceptable difference is entirely and indelibly defined by his sexual performance. If he accepts that judgment, the homosexual artist who struggles to express his own identity may be compelled to place unreasonable stress on the sexual act itself. To the extent that this limits or trivializes his art, he is once more a victim of the heterosexual dictatorship.

Rather than speaking of homosexuality in literature, it would be more appropriate to examine "homosexualities," for homosexuals in fact express their relationships in infinitely variable and subtle ways. In the sixteenth century the essayist Montaigne reasoned that if a truly intimate bond could be established between men, "where not only the souls might have entire fruition, but the bodies also might share in this alliance, and a man be engaged throughout, the friendship would certainly be more full and perfect." What Walt Whitman termed "adhesiveness," the devotion of man to man, was the central emotional fact of his life; it was also the basis of his philosophical, political and spiritual beliefs, the cornerstone of his faith in a new human partnership. For a number of contemporary poets—including Allen Ginsberg, Robert Duncan and Thom Gunn—the physical love of men promises the way back to spiritual values that have gone out of modern industrialized cultures. Orgasm becomes the equivalent of religious ecstasy. For Jean Genet, homosexuality is a cherished expression of revolt against the state, for defining the individual in a mass culture. Consequently, he has argued that "I would like the world not to change so that I can be against the world." More characteristic of contemporary writers, particularly those influenced by the Gay Liberation Movement, is the desire to bring about fundamental alterations in law, social custom and popular attitudes. Feminists have often supported such arguments because they, too, have suffered the tyranny of traditional roles. To reduce that spectrum of homosexual attitudes to the motions a person performs in bed is blatant sophistry.

One way to curtail pernicious stereotyping is to restore to the homosexual his lost cultural heritage—and with it, his pride. The task is hardly simple, for so much of the ancient literary tradition has been bowdlerized, lost or destroyed by prudent guardians of heterosexual supremacy. The compass of these introductory remarks is not sufficient to explore the intricate implications of that heritage, but certain recurrent motifs should be underscored for the insight they offer into twentieth-century literary conventions. Warrior-lovers, for example, were frequently celebrated in ancient literature, as in the Babylonian epic of Gilgamesh, who with his lover Enbidu roamed the earth in search of the herb of immortality. Their counterparts include not only Achilles and Patroclus, Damon and Pythias or David and Jonathan, but the entire Sacred Band of Thebes, a Greek army consisting of 150 pairs of warriors, who remained invincible in battle until their defeat by Philip of Macedon. In Sparta, according to Xenophon's short essay *The Lacedaemonian Constitution,* the homosexual relationship between such comrades was treated as a conjugal union. Far from being regarded as "unmanly," male couples were widely believed to make exceptionally good citizens and soldiers. "Once Eros has entered into the souls of a pair of lovers," Plutarch argued, "no enemy ever succeeds in separating them. They display their ardor and risk their lives even when there is no need of it."

Frequently, the soldierly bond was not between equals but between officer and underling, as in the case of Achilles and Patroclus, or the Knights Templar and their body servants. Strabo, in his *Geography,* records that in nearly all the Celtic tribes of early England, the warriors not only slept with their squires, but valued them more highly than their wives. Such comradeship is praised as *comitatus* in the Anglo-Saxon world of *Beowulf;* and in the medieval period every knight had his squire. Wrestling ceremonies like those recorded by Pindar are an integral part of male education and the rituals of bonding; in its Greek root *gymnasium* means, literally, "to train naked," and described an institution where such manly arts as wrestling could be mastered. In *Men in Groups* Lionel Tiger argues that for primitive societies wrestling-initiation and homoerotic love were part of the intimate bond necessary to make the activities of all-male hunting tribes more efficient. Transformed, those contacts re-emerge in the complex rites, secret rituals and diverse all-male activities that constitute "blood brotherhood" (*Blutsbrüderschaft*).

An awareness of this traditional background enriches the implication of the powerful scene in Thomas Mann's *Death in Venice* when Jaschin and Tadzio wrestle, semi-naked, on the beach of the Lido. It also illuminates the wrestling match between Gerald and Birkin in D.H. Lawrence's *Women in Love,* restoring the explicit homoerotic dimension which Lawrence obscured by suppressing the novel's original introductory chapter. The love of warriors is repeatedly evoked in modern homosexual literature—obliquely and somewhat abstractly in the First World War poetry of Wilfred Owen and Siegfrid Sassoon, explicitly in Simon Raven's *Feathers of Death* (1959), Susan Hill's *Strange Meeting* (1971), Maarten 't Hart's *I Had a Brother in Arms* (1973) and Jennifer Johnston's *How Many Miles to Babylon?* (1974). It is raised to a point of religious ecstasy in the Samurai code elaborated by Yukio Mishima, and has provided the focus for numerous novels by Mary Renault.

As the legends of Achilles and Patroclus or Alexander and the slave-boy Bagoas make clear, differences in rank or in social standing were once no barrier to love. In early Rome, on the other hand, the first attempts to regulate homosexual conduct were specifically designed to promote a caste system; homosexual acts were not condemned, but the *Lex Scautinia* strictly prohibited freeborn men to have intercourse with slaves. As one consequence of the Hebraic-Christian campaign against homosexuality, the metaphor of class or caste taboo also attaches to the warrior bond as a further barrier to so-called sins against nature. In D.H. Lawrence's violent, compelling story "The Prussian Officer," a class struggle underlines the unspoken sexual conflict. Lawrence's neurotic, aggressive officer is a direct if distorted descendent of the Spartan ideal; his unwitting orderly, sensual and instinctive, is described as having "strong, heavy limbs, was swarthy, with a soft, black, young moustache." Similarly, Hemingway's "A Simple Enquiry" creates tension in the opposition of an elegant, disciplined, but somewhat effete officer with his "dark-faced" peasant orderly. The terms "swarthy" and "dark-faced" imply an ethnic difference as well as one of rank—thus adding yet another taboo to the classical warrior bond. From very different viewpoints, racial and sexual discrimination would be seen as corollaries by writers like LeRoi Jones and James Baldwin. Meanwhile, the "primitive" dark man and the working-class boy would become special objects of desire in the eyes of many homosexuals.

In Norman Mailer's *Why Are We in Viet Nam?* two American adolescents undergo ceremonial preparation for war; alone in the Alaskan wilderness they discover deep homosexual longings, but sublimate them into the mentality of the killer. In a score of other novels, repression of the sexual dimension between comrades at arms brings about senseless violence—in Mailer's *The Naked and the Dead*, Carson McCullers' *Reflections in a Golden Eye* and, most savagely, in James Purdy's *Eustace Chisolm and the Works*. Purdy's novel concludes with a grotesque scene in which an enlisted man and an officer, maddened by guilt, self-hatred and repressed love, enact a cruel parody of the blood-letting ceremony of *Blutsbrüderschaft*.

Even more pervasive than the soldier as a prototype in the literature of male homosexuality is the figure of the sailor, though he, too, has a complex classical inheritance. The sailor is often, as in Cocteau's *The White Paper*, a source of erotic fantasy; frequently, too, he evokes myths of the sea's boundless fertility, and of freedom from the strictures of land-bound society. In Lonnie Coleman's *Ship's Company* (1955), a collection of stories set on board a battleship during World War II, a young seaman is dazzled and intrigued by Montgomery, a new, athletically masculine crew member who openly indicates his sexual preference for other men. At the conclusion of the story, the narrator yields to Montgomery's pleading:

> Don't you know that most women hate men and use their sex to insult them and dominate them? I'm offering you something better than that, you damned fool. I'm offering you myself, and I promise you that I'll take you and hold you and keep you as long as such promises last. I love you, Barney.

With a nod to classical predecessors, Coleman entitled his story "The Theban Warriors." The tempestuous love of two sailors also forms the subject of "Divorce in Naples," a surprisingly tender and sympathetic story by William Faulkner.

In *The Enchafèd Flood* the English poet W.H. Auden remarked that:

> It is not an accident that many homosexuals should show a special preference for sailors, for the sailor on shore is symbolically the innocent god from the sea who is not bound by the law of the land and therefore can do anything without guilt. Indeed, in a book like *Querelle de Brest,* the hero is at once god and the devil. He is adored because, though he is a murderer and a police informer and sexually promiscuous in every sense, though, that is, he loves no one but himself, is in fact Judas, yet he remains Billy Budd, the beautiful god who feels neither guilt nor remorse, and whose very crimes, therefore, are a proof of his divinity.

Genet has more than once hymned the mysterious and sensuous charm, the sadomasochistic virility of "those shoulders, profiles, mouths, those sinuous, turbulent rumps, those strong and supple boys," but the definitive image of the handsome sailor is indeed Melville's Billy Budd.

The blond and innocent seaman, whose "rustic beauty" is universally admired, is executed to reaffirm and renew the existing social order; his death recalls innumerable primitive rituals of the sacrifice of surrogates representing kings or gods. Behind his agony are the rites of Osiris and Adonis, the sea voyages and trials of Hercules and Odysseus, and of spiritual leaders like Moses symbolically resurrected from the water. He is related to Hylas, the boy-lover of Hercules drowned by water-nymphs, and to the near-universal harvest ritual described in Sir James Frazer's *The Golden Bough,* in which the young corn god is sacrificed. His literary peers include the character in William Burroughs' *The Soft Machine* identified as "young Corn God" and the various adolescents put to violent death in *The Naked Lunch.* They also include the young homosexual anthropologist murdered and eaten by cannibals in Tennessee Williams' *Suddenly Last Summer,* and the executed Maurice Pilorge whose beauty is celebrated in Jean Genet's poem *Le Condamné a Mort.*

Though *Billy Budd* never alludes directly to physical contact between men, Melville was more explicit in other writings of the sea—referring to sailing ships in *White Jacket* as the "wooden-walled Gomorrahs of the deep," the setting of "sins for which the cities of the plains were overthrown." Like other military figures, the sailor wears a uniform whose cut stresses classically masculine dimensions, and even more than the soldier, he inhabits a predominantly male world in which homoerotic contacts are not uncommon. In their letters and journals, both Walt Whitman and Hart Crane revealed the powerful attraction sailors had for them; in *Howl* Allen Ginsberg hymns men "who let themselves be . . . . . . in the . . . by saintly motorcyclists,/and screamed with joy,/who blew and were blown by those human seraphim, the sailors,/caresses of Atlantic and Caribbean love."

"The Obelisk," E.M. Forster's wryly comic tale of marital infidelity, shows a husband and wife equally incapable of resisting the appeal of a common seaman. In a short story by William Carlos Williams, the homosexual theme is signaled by the very title—"The Sailor's Son," and the visiting lover is a motorcyclist, another figure whose uniform and masculine control frequently associate him with the Spartan ideal. When the hero of James Baldwin's *Giovanni's Room* finally abandons his heterosexual charade, he spends three days with a sailor picked up in a bar on the the Côte d'Azur. Yukio Mishima explores the recurrent and seemingly universal ideal in *The Sailor Who Fell from Grace with the Sea,* and the Colombian poet Porfirio Barba-Jacob concluded his moving "Elegy to an Imaginary Sailor" with the lyric plea, "Give me your honey, child of the perfumed mouth!" It is thus particularly fitting that the first serious homosexual novel, Adolfo Caminha's *Bon-Crioulo,* is the story of the love between a sailor and a ship's boy.

In Caminha's novel, as in a number of the writings referred to above, there is a marked discrepancy between the ages of the lovers—a variation on the pederastic tradition commemorated in Greek mythology but practiced, in fact, in numerous ancient cultures as an established, integrated aspect of adolescent education. As in the ritual sacrifice of the young corn god, the conventions of pedagogic pederasty may well derive from primitive rituals in which a boy-surrogate was sacrificially murdered to renew the life of the king. This, in turn, takes the form of ceremonial rape of the boy-surrogate in a forcible rite of initiation. Later, when the use of force is forbidden, certain theatrical elements of the earlier rites still remain. According to Strabo's *Geography,* after the mock capture of a pubescent boy by an older man in Crete, the two spent sixty days together in the wilderness, hunting, fishing and making love—but always with the tacit approval of the boy's family. On their return from this "honeymoon," the older man was required to present his boy-lover with three gifts—a military outfit, an ox and a drinking cup. Cretan and Dorian homosexuality thus created the essential link between pedagogy and pederasty elaborated in Plato's *Symposium.* Comparative anthropology indicates that similar relationships played a part in the ancient civilizations of Egypt and Babylon, in South America, much of the Orient, and among numerous Indian tribes of North America. A homosexual bond of deep and consequential intimacy may not always have been homogenital, but it is difficult to read the praises of the Persian poet Hafiz for his smooth-cheeked cupbearers or descriptions of the *siang kong* academies for boy-actors in China without acknowledging their implicit sexuality.

The Virgilian *formosus puer*, the archetypal beautiful boy, figures prominently in Greek and early Roman mythology. Zeus had innumerable boy-lovers, all of whom coalesce in the enchanting person of Ganymede. Hercules, the ideal manly figure of the Greek imagination, was famed not only for his strength, but for transvestism and pederastic amours; according to Plutarch, he had so many male lovers that it would be impossible to name them all, but the favorites were Iolas and Hylas. Hylas accompanied Hercules on his voyages with the Argonauts, and is repeatedly referred to as his "squire" and "minion." Drawing on numerous ancient accounts, including those of Theocritus and Herodotus, Robert Graves summarizes the circumstances of Hylas' death in *The Greek Myths*. During a rowing contest, Hercules broke his oar, and the Argo had to be beached while he fashioned a new one. Leaving the crew to prepare the evening meal, Hercules went in search of a suitable tree, uprooted it, and dragged it back to the camp. Hylas, meanwhile, had set out to fetch water from a nearby pool and had not returned. Frantically crying, "Hylas! Hylas!", Hercules plunged into the wood where he encountered Polyphemus, who reported, "Alas, I heard Hylas shouting for help; and ran towards his voice. But when I reached Pegae I found no signs of a struggle . . . There was only his water-pitcher lying abandoned by the pool side." Hylas had been drowned by water-nymphs who, entranced by his beauty, persuaded him to live with them in an underwater grotto. Hercules' grief was so extreme that cults were established to honor the lamented water-bearer; they closely resemble the cults of Bormus, an extraordinarily beautiful youth who at harvest time went to fetch water for the reapers and was dragged into the well by water-nymphs. Once more, the young corn god, the idealized lover, the sacrificial youth draw together, as in the story of *Billy Budd*.

Both the praise for a young lover and the lament for his death become central elements of the pastoral tradition; the love of two youthful shepherds was also a common device. Theocritus, in the third century B.C., composed a series of sentimental *Idylls* that showed boy-love as a natural, healthy expression of virility. Virgil's second "Ecologue" commemorated the love of Corydon and Alexis, and André Gide would recall their devotion in giving his fictionalized dialogue on homosexuality the title *Corydon*. Eventually, such motifs made their way into the literature of the Renaissance—in Daphnis' love for Ganymede in Richard Barnfield's *The*

Affectionate Shephearde (1594) and in the more muted devotion of Hobbinol and Colin in Edmund Spenser's *The Sheppheardes Calender* (1579). In *Hero and Leander* (1598), Christopher Marlowe compares Leander—another drowned hero—to both Ganymede and Adonis. And in his play about the fall of the homosexual Edward II, when the nobles accuse the king's minion of wearing a jewel in his cap worth more than the crown, Queen Isabella complains, "Never doted Jove on Ganymede/So much as he on cursèd Gaveston." In the early years of our own century, the Dutch poet Willem de Merode languished in something very like house-arrest on the isolated farm to which his family removed him when his preference for adolescents threatened to cause scandal. His repressed tenderness and yearning flowed out in a poem entitled "Ganymede."

Though pastoral conventions were often heterosexualized, presenting exclusively the adoration of shepherd and shepherdess, the homosexual dimension would never be entirely suppressed. It emerges in the modern period in poems by Whitman and Gerard Manley Hopkins on boys bathing, in Proust's lyric explorations of "Bee and Orchid," and in such semi-pornographic classics as Richard Amory's *Loon Trilogy,* subtitled "a gay pastoral." García Lorca's "Ode to Walt Whitman" creates erotic beauty in the image of "the sun singing in the navels of boys playing baseball under the bridges." The sexual initiation of the narrator of Cocteau's *The White Paper* occurs in the sylvan park surrounding his father's château; significantly, his first awareness of homosexuality comes through the love-making of two dark-skinned gypsy boys; equally significantly, his own adored Dargello dies after swimming in the Seine. The idealized sexual memory of Gore Vidal's *The City and the Pillar* is set in a woodland retreat, on the bank of a river, where "the air was gold." In James Baldwin's *Giovanni's Room* the hero's most fulfilling sexual encounters occur in a room whose wallpaper recalls a dream of Eden, and where life "seemed to be occurring beneath the sea"; after murdering a wealthy homosexual, Giovanni is captured hiding under one of the bridges of the Seine.

Thus, as with the motif of warrior-lovers, classical elements persist—though metamorphosed, sometimes corrupted or tainted by taboos—in the literature of male homosexuality. The initiation of a boy by an older man (often of darker race) is central to such works as James Fenimore Cooper's "Leatherstocking" novels, Herman Melville's *Moby Dick*, Mark Twain's *The Adventures of Huckleberry Finn* and William Faulkner's *The Bear*—an element which led critic Leslie Fiedler to assert that classic American literature contains a deep strain of latent homosexuality. The pederastic theme becomes overt in Thomas Mann's *Death in Venice*, Giorgio Bassani's *The Gold-Rimmed Spectacles* and many of the writings of Christopher Isherwood. It also emerges with nightmarish irony in Paul Bowles' story, "Pages from Cold Point." In William Inge's crude but powerful short play, "The Boy in the Basement" (1950), the cherished youth is a corpse awaiting the embalmer's art, and a ghastly symbol of the repression of homosexual desire.

Taking various form as the relationship between tyro and initiate, priest and acolyte, teacher and pupil, the ancient pederastic-pedagogic tradition yields such modern psychological studies as Stefan Zweig's *Episode in the Early Life of Privy Councillor D.* or Fritz Peters' *Finistere.* Peters' novel, which caused a sensation when it appeared in 1951, tells the story of a lonely American teenager who falls in love with the ruggedly handsome athletic director at his French boarding school. Their sexual affair begins soon after the teacher saves his pupil from drowning; emotionally, intellectually and physically, their intense relationship is a model of the Hellenic ideal. When the affair is revealed, the tormented boy drowns himself off the Brittany coast, thus once more re-enacting the death of Hylas, companion to the super-athlete Hercules. Vastly trivialized, the relationship of an athletic coach and a brilliant young track star becomes the subject of Patricia Nell Warren's *The Front Runner* (1974), commercially one of the most successful novels published in the wake of the Gay Liberation Movement in the United States. Numerous other novels and autobiographies have dealt with the prevalence of homosexuality among athletes, but few if any have the canny persuasiveness of "The Zenner Trophy," a story published by Gore Vidal in 1956.

Boy-love remains, meanwhile, the most heavily tabooed form of homosexual expression, and its defenders almost invariably point to the Hellenic ideal—as in the ingenuously "literary" photographs of semi-naked Greek and Sicilian boys made by the Baron von Glöden. Both Jean Genet and Allen Ginsberg have given impassioned arguments for intimate relations between men and boys, the latter stressing psychic renewal for the man and education for the young lover. But twentieth-century reality is better represented by Alexander Ziegler's documentary novel, *The Consequence* (1975), in which the Swiss author describes his own persecution for love of a teenager, and the far more grotesque sufferings of the boy himself.

It would, however, be naive to counter such contemporary realities with images of the Greek world as an untroubled paradise for men who loved youths or other men. The exclusively homosexual male was often pictured as laughable and despicable by the ancients. Solon condemned to death men who sneaked into gymnasiums in Athens; in Sparta, Lycurgus made sexual relations with a youth punishable by exile. Aristophanes anticipated numberless modern critics in arguing that the homosexual lacked the "spunk" to produce great poetry, and even Plato in his later writings became increasingly critical of homosexual conduct. No doubt much homosexual activity then, as now, took place in secret and with a brand of shame, but in certain institutionalized forms it was not only permissible but, often, fully integrated into contemporary social and ethical standards.

In the modern period Freudian psychology called special attention to the "transitory" homosexual phase common to adolescent boys, and consequently provoked fears that outright indulgence of such passions might curb the later evolution into heterosexuality. In fact, adolescent sexual ambiguity —often reminiscent of the androgynous traditions of Greek mythology and Renaissance poetry and drama—proved a relatively safe theme for writers who would have felt intimidated by the portrayal of adult homosexuality. It was thus responsible for the creation of an entire sub-genre of homosexual fiction. The boarding school has been particularly important in the English literary tradition, but an early example—*Bertram Cope's Year* (1919) by Henry Blake Fuller—was published in the United States, and Robert Musil's tense scenes of sexual initiation in *Young Törless* (1906) have rarely been surpassed. Like Lawrence, Genet and the English playwright Joe Orton, Musil was acutely sensitive to the relationships between sexuality and power. A similar pathology is observable in much homosexual prison literature, including John Herbert's play *Fortune and Men's Eyes* (1967). But the confined environment of prison, school or army barracks may also offer alternatives to the conformist values of the outside world—as it does in Genet's *Thief's Journal* (1949), Manuel Puig's *Kiss of the Spider Woman* (1976) or Martin Sherman's drama *Bent* (1979), set in a Nazi concentration camp.

Nearly all the archetypes discussed in these pages flow together immediately beneath the surface of John Knowles' school novel, *A Separate Peace* (1959), which describes the adoration of a fellow pupil for the school athletic star. Overt sexuality is never described, since friendship is transformed into hatred before it can manifest itself as corporal love. The narrator proposes a "test" for his athletic friend, and in conforming to it the handsome and virile idol is mutilated and dies. Like countless other works, the novel illustrates the perils that beset the homosexual's pursuit of identity in a society that brands his intuitive longings as perverse and degraded.

The homosexual impulse turns inward, becomes neurotic, violent and self-destructive under the burden of guilt heaped on it by the Hebraic-Christian tradition. It was not homosexuality itself that the early Hebrews condemned, but the particular form of homosexual practice—including temple prostitution—they had known during their captivity in Babylon. Sexual acts between men were not regarded as a crime or a perversion or sickness, but as heresy—adherence to an unorthodox religious institution associated with the mystical cult of the Canaanite priests. Throughout the Old Testament the homosexual lover is excommunicated as a practitioner of the pagan rituals of the city of Sodom and the cult of Artemis. In early Rome homosexuality was not condemned but regulated; in 249 A.D., for example, the Emperor Philip attempted with limited success to outlaw the *exsoleti*, mercenary catamites who followed the legions. But when Christianity was adopted as the official state religion, heresy immediately became treason. During the fourth-century reign of Emperor Constantine, homosexuals were beheaded; under the fifth-century Emperor Valentinian, they were burned at the stake—supposedly by fire and brimstone. Such acts of "purification" would reach a frenzy during the Inquisition, when fully one-quarter of those burned at the stake were condemned for sodomy. Centuries later, the enlightened democrat Thomas Jefferson recommended substituting castration for capital punishment. It is noteworthy that in the long, grim history of torture, banishment and execution, it was almost exclusively homosexual acts between men that were officially condemned; the fact suggests that homosexual love itself was not initially the "abomination" in question, but the heresy of male temple prostitutes.

By the end of the twelfth century anti-homosexual prejudice had almost entirely usurped the humanistic tradition of Greek love. In Canto XV of the *Inferno,* Dante meets his former cherished comrade Brunetto Latine, condemned to eternal suffering for his "violence against nature." When questioned about his homosexual companions in the underworld, Latine responds that "all were clerks, and great scholars, and of great renown; by the same crime on earth defiled." Their number includes a distinguished grammarian, Priscian, whose position as a teacher of youth made him particularly liable to such vice. Boccaccio's *Decameron* offers a similar image in the ghost of Prince Lycidas, damned for thievery and homosexual affairs. The most repulsive characters in Chaucer's *Canterbury Tales* are the Summoner and the Pardoner—the one with scruffy hair, scabs and pimples on his face, the other effeminate in voice and manner. Riding together, they form a parody of knight and squire, and they sing an obscene love-song that almost certainly has homosexual implications. The Summoner is sexually promiscuous, and perhaps likes boys as well as girls; the Pardoner is described as a ''gelding,'' but the charge of unmanliness may have to do with perversity rather than literal castration. While elements of an earlier tradition would persist in the sonnet and the pastoral lament, the homosexual as villain had now moved to center-stage. Even Christopher Marlowe's sympathetic portrayal of Edward II's homosexuality could not reverse the pattern. Based on Holinshed's *Chronicles,* from which Shakespeare drew many of his plots, it demonstrates how the king so doted on his French minion Gaveston that the court was corrupted, the land despoiled, and the people brought to the brink of civil war. In the centuries to follow—including our own—the homosexual would be acceptable in literature only as villain, corrupter of youth, effeminate clown, criminal or corpse.

A further consequence of Judeo-Christian prohibitions is that homosexual practice (and particularly sodomy) is increasingly associated with the decadence and exoticism of an imaginary Orient. By the mid-nineteenth century this never-never land had become a highly elaborated cultural abstraction, of such potency that its distortions persist to the present day. The publishing sensation of 1885 in England was the appearance of the first ten volumes of the *Book of the Thousand and One Nights,* translated by Sir Richard Burton. An inveterate traveler and anthropological scholar, his early researches had included an official report on male bordellos in Karachi. Burton's amazing adventures made him the most famous travel writer of all time, and wherever he went, he gathered information on local sexual customs. His translation of what was popularly known as *The Arabian Nights* included entire erotic passages omitted by previous translators—including those dealing with pederasty, bestiality and female orgasm. Even more sensational, however, was the rambling ''Terminal Essay'' summarizing his observations on sexual customs. One part of the essay was devoted to homosexual practices, and out of the jumble of gossip, genuine scholarship and wild hypothesis emerged the influential theory of the ''Sotadic Zone." Homosexuality, Burton argued, was "geographic and climatic," located approximately between the latitudes of 43 and 30 degrees, within which homosexuality flourished without social restraint. Including southern Spain, France and Italy, the zone stretched from Greece across Turkey and Afghanistan and ultimately took in not only most of the Near and Far East, but by some geographical *reductio ad absurdam,* the entire hemisphere of pre-Columbian America. Burton insisted that:

> Within the Sotadic Zone, the vice is popular and endemic, held at the worst to be a mere peccadillo, while the races to the north and south of the limits here defined practise it only sporadically amid the opprobrium of their fellows who, as a rule, are physically incapable of performing the operation and look upon it with the liveliest disgust.

Even Burton sensed that what he was actually describing was not a geographic distinction but a theological boundary erected by Christendom.

Sir Richard Burton was scarcely alone in forming the popular concept of homosexuality as a "vice" of heathen and hot-blooded men, but his "Terminal Essay" unintentionally served to authenticate a superstition that had theological origins. The Arab became a common symbol of pederastic excess, but it was Italy that became the Sotadic "capital" in the Occidental imagination, and above all Venice, with its trading ties to the East. In *The Unfortunate Traveler* (1594), Thomas Nashe called Venice "the Sodom of Italy," and Byron termed it "the sea-Sodom of Italy." For countless homosexuals, Italy was an ideal; significantly, when Karl Heinrich Ulrichs fled Germany, he went directly to Naples, and then to Aquila, where he spent the last twelve years of his life. Baron Corvo's "disguised" idyll of the love of an English traveler for an Italian boy, *The Desire and Pursuit of the Whole,* composed shortly before the author's death in 1913, is subtitled "A Romance of Modern Venice." In Donald Windham's *Two People* (1965) a young American businessman, estranged from his wife, falls in love with an Italian boy during a visit to Rome. The definitive link between Italy and homosexual awakening is, of course, to be found on every page of Thomas Mann's *Death in Venice*. The explicit homosexual scenes in John Horne Burns' *The Gallery* (1946) take place in Naples, and the expatriated American hero of *Giovanni's Room* has his first adult homosexual experience with a handsome, sensuous Italian. In linking homosexuality, death and the Italian setting, Wolfgang Koeppen's *Death in Rome* (1954) pointedly echoes the dominant motifs of *Death in Venice*. As a comic variation on the theme, in Bernard Malamud's *Pictures of Fidelman* (1969), the American schlemiel is sodomized by a lusty Venetian glass-blower.

Homosexual literature is, indeed, filled with characters who might in this context be regarded as "symbolic Italians," congenital representatives of the Sotadic temperament. The men of darker skin who so frequently appear as objects of erotic fantasy or sexual experimentation add racial taboo to religious proscription; the taboo of class compounds the forbidden aspect of homosexual love, and as Christopher Isherwood has pointed out, it was almost a fetish for upper-class Englishmen to pursue working-class boys—between the wars, in Germany and Austria, but most frequently in France, Italy and North Africa. Implicit in such obsessions is the myth of the superior virility of "primitive" or working-class men. The guilt produced by the violation of multiple taboos frequently produces grotesque and tragic results, as the earlier rites of initiation become savage rites of exorcism. In Tennessee Williams' "Desire and the Black Masseur," a timid, frail, middle-aged man submits to sadomasochistic tortures at the hands of a massive Negro who ultimately kills and eats him. In the final scenes, the voice of a neighborhood preacher is heard shouting, "Suffer, suffer, suffer!" The beautiful Luc, a French visitor to New York in Yves Navarre's *Sweet Tooth* (1973), undergoes an even more brutal death at the hands of a handsome Negro. When Andrew first strikes him, Luc remembers a book he had read as a child in which a black man dies in the arms of a Missionary Priest: "Luc tries to sit up. Andrew clobbers him with a good resounding slap. Luc falls back on the Missionary's lap. The Missionary blesses him. . . .

Ceremonial." In a room that "smells like hell," two potential lovers—one black, the other white—beat each other into unconsciousness in Le Roi Jones' *The Toilet* (1967).

The cherished "dark companion" of earlier initiation rites thus becomes the dark avenger, often satanic in his manifestations. Corrupted and faded, the beautiful Hylas becomes the fop, the hustler, the agonized adolescent driven to suicide, or the anarchic "angels" of Genet's twilight world. Similarly, and though many transvestites are exclusively heterosexual, transvestism degenerates into a parody of the effeminate and ineffectual male, a subject for cheap farce, burlesque comedies of errors and "safe" glimpses of homosexual waywardness. It becomes, as well, a cherished cinematic device, as in Billy Wilder's *Some Like It Hot*, whose title recalls Shakespeare's *As You Like It*, in which Rosalind appears disguised as the celebrated Ganymede.

In an essay entitled "The Homosexual Villain" written in 1954, Norman Mailer sought to analyze the unpleasant, often sinister presentation of homosexual characters in his own early writings. "At the time I wrote these novels," he remarked, "I was consciously sincere. I did believe—as so many heterosexuals believe—that there was an intrinsic relation between homosexuality and 'evil,' and it seemed perfectly natural to me, as well as *symbolically* just, to treat the subject in such a way." In attempting to come to terms with these clichés, the author himself achieved a new awareness of the sinister correlations between sexual repression and political oppression: "I suppose I can say that for the first time I understood homosexual persecution to be a political act and a reactionary act, and I was properly ashamed of myself." Unhappily, even the most committed defenders of homosexuality are likely to embrace similar stereotypes. Mart Crowley's *The Boys in the Band*, which opened in New York in 1968, became the first play dealing exclusively with a homosexual milieu to achieve broad popular success; it was acclaimed as "the frankest and funniest homosexual play ever put on a stage," and enjoyed similar esteem as a popular motion picture. Yet *Boys in the Band* parades the very clichés of vicious queen, closet-case, brainless hustler, promiscuity and insecurity under which homosexuals have suffered for centuries. That such types and such patterns of behavior "really" exist is unquestionable, as do the heterosexual sterotypes of the jealous husband, absentminded professor, overbearing mother and power-hungry tycoon. The difference between soap opera and art, however, is that the latter probes sterotypes to reveal the depth and uniqueness of the individual character. This is what Tennessee Williams achieves with the figure of the hustler in "One Arm" or the study of promiscuity in "Two on a Party." In Ernest Hemingway's "Mother of a Queen" the effeminate male is a vicious, one-dimensional caricature, but in Yukio Mishima's "Onnagata" transvestism is depicted as an art of ultimate grace and refinement, and in Hubert Selby's "The Queen is Dead," from *Last Exit to Brooklyn* (1964), Georgette's monologue moves from shrill hysteria to genuinely tragic passion.

A rich body of literature has been created on the theme of the "tragic queen," a figure whose wit and superficial gaiety are often the mask for profound despair. Here one is not concerned with simple transvestism, which may be a passing fancy or a carnival joke, but a man in flight from his own virility—in flight, often, from the coarse, insensitive image that the heterosexual majority approves as "a man's man." Such persons may not, literally, want to *be* women; in fact, few homosexual transvestites are actually transsexuals. But they embrace a feminine ideal and, with it, notions of delicacy and tenderness and vulnerability that are typically labeled as "feminine" by societies that insist only women should be sexually attracted to men. In Nathanael West's novel of Hollywood sham and imposture, *The Day of the Locust* (1939), the only convincingly womanly character is a female-impersonator who sings in a night-club; this compassionate portrayal by a heterosexual writer is worth quoting for its rare insight:

> He had a soft, throbbing voice and his gestures were matronly, tender and aborted, a series of unconscious caresses. What he was doing was in no sense parody; it was

> too simple and restrained. It wasn't even theatrical. This dark young man with his thin, hairless arms and soft, rounded shoulders, who rocked an imaginary cradle as he crooned, was really a woman.

John Rechy's *City of Night* (1963) presents two queens who are equally successful in presenting womanliness rather than a parody of woman. One is the celebrated "Miss Destiny," whose Hollywood wedding, complete with flowing white gown and veil, becomes a legend for the other characters in the novel. The second is Trudi, who "has most accurately been able to duplicate the female stance so that, unlike most other queens, she has not become the parody of a woman." But parody is often present in the figure of the bitchy queen who consciously cultivates the coarseness of a fishwife as well as the possessive and mercenary qualities that are part of an accepted heterosexual stereotype of the wife's negative attributes. Again, whether as "evil queen" or "tragic queen," the homosexual is reflecting or inverting patterns imposed by the heterosexual dictatorship. The full range of transvestite responses is examined in the films of Andy Warhol.

The despair felt by Selby's Georgette or by the nameless narrator of Eduardo Gudiño Kieffer's "A Sinner's Notebook" at belonging to neither sex is a moving symbol of the identity-crisis suffered by countless homosexuals. Rarely is a male able to embrace a female identity without guilt or anxiety; Mishima's Onnagata is an exception because his "impersonation" is within a respected tradition, and in "Snow White Revisited," a short story by Brazilian writer Darcy Penteado, the transvestite hero finally succeeds in being "enshrined" as a princess only after decades of persecution and rejection. More typical of the transvestite's dilemma is the anonymous tale of "The Marquis de Saint-Brissac," in which the impersonation ends in suicide. The universality of the phenomenon symbolized by such figures is underscored in "Miss Knight," one of the stories Robert McAlmon published in *Distinguished Air* in 1925, and which presents a compulsive, cocaine-sniffing, vulgar American tourist in Berlin; despite burly shoulders and the repeated boast that "I'm so glad I'm a real man,"

Charlie Knight has a particular fondness for elegant evening dresses. Miss Knight disappears unexpectedly from Berlin, but a few weeks later sends her friends a postcard from Paris. "That one!" a character remarks. "If she was run over by a truck or a steam roller she'd turn up, about to appear in Paris, or London, or Madrid, or Singapore. She's just that international."

In the selections that follow, numerous other figures emerge as "international." They highlight common elements in homosexual experience, but they also suggest an even more universal dimension: the search for self, the hunger for love and recognition, the conflict between instinct and convention, the need for ritual. These motifs occur and reoccur in all literatures. Centuries of persecution and misrepresentation give the homosexual writer a particular mandate, but that must not obscure his ties and his obligations to a larger community of suffering and joy and aspiration. The relatively new liberties of expression available to many writers sometimes obscure that wider dimension; intoxicated by the freedom to explore sexual experience, homosexual and heterosexual alike may end by reducing human relationships to genital contacts. And the recent mode of creating homosexual versions of such cookie-cutter clichés of popular literature as the western, science fiction, the detective story and the sentimental romance does no service either to literature or to sexual liberation. The right openly to embrace a homosexual life-style can paradoxically end by creating self-styled ghettos as isolating as the old conspiracies of repression and silence. There is a danger, too, that homosexuality becomes merely another "fashion" in liberal societies; indeed, the feminist Kate Millett has described the homosexual as "our current nigger of love."

The new freedoms clearly bring new dangers and responsibilities in their wake. Prophetically, Norman Mailer concluded his essay on "The Homosexual as Villain" with the following paragraph:

> If the homosexual is ever to achieve real social equality and acceptance, he too will have to work the hard row of

> shedding his own prejudices. Driven into defiance, it is natural if regrettable, that many homosexuals go to the direction of assuming that there is something intrinsically superior in homosexuality, and carried far enough it is a viewpoint which is as stultifying, as ridiculous, and as anti-human as the heterosexual's prejudice. Finally, heterosexuals are people too, and the hope of acceptance, tolerance and sympathy must rest on this mutual appreciation.

The challenge implicit in Mailer's remarks is immense, but homosexuals know only too well what it means to struggle against seemingly impossible odds. Many have been broken by the struggle; but the survivors have often developed a remarkable muscularity of spirit. This volume commemorates both the victims and the victors.

VILHELM EKELUND

THE FRIENDS

O auch mir ist das Andenken an unsere
Spaziergänge das heiligste das ich kenne.

—Heinrich Wackenroder
Briefe an L. Tieck

O hour of melancholy in the great city
when the pale sun sinks below the dull gliding edge
of dark blue hanging smoke—
no lights have been turned on yet. In coal blue July evening
Berlin hides.
A horse lies dead on the street, a white and gray skeleton.
Completely deafening
minute after minute
like a clap of thunder
train on the elevated:
Hallesches Thor

Every evening when I wander home
I go here.

But in the middle of the confused roar,
over the scream and din
it can happen sometimes
that a holy silence
falls over my soul:
a picture appears.

In the summer first
it is a morning—
here lay small quiet houses
behind garden plots and hedges and trees
going back a hundred years.
Two figures approach, catch a glimpse of each other,
and the soul itself lifts, blessedly enlarged,
an infinite space
trembling with
light
shaking with tenderness.

Out in the sunny space
they step quietly—
and now—silent . . .
stay,
two hands
bend over
the book,
cheeks meet
softly radiating
warmth to each other,
caressing arms
lay themselves
on young smooth shoulders,
eyes darken
with faithfulness,
glance up and
meet in radiant
embrace of love.

From the dust and noise
into the dimness of the trees along the quay I wander
where homeless ones sleep

on the benches—
heads sunk in their hands
children cry softly in the darkness . . .

SYMPOSIUM

Yes, you are our beautiful land,
the spirit in living blood;
yes, you bear in your figure's liveliness,
in your fine limbs' noble construction,
in your cheeks' flushed sheen,
in the strength of your deeply glancing eyes
all the light of this beautiful land.

But of your forehead's purity:

music
of clear gentle verse.

Yes, a song to you should bear
in words newly minted,
words warmly beaming
words of fragrance and fine air
all the beauty of our land:

clear land, southerly,
caressed by mild light
and the reflecting sea's softly shimmering blue veil:

land where laurels bloom,
the soft plantains endure the winter
and Zeus's beautiful tree
on strong, lifted trunk
light embracing powerful
lifts the arching of the noble crown
and Hyacinthus, lily above lilies,
bears in purpureal sign
the lament of the God.

OCTOBER

When will I see you again,
dear one?

The last time:
evening dark with autumn rain.
Then you came there in the pale lantern light
beneath the large spacious leaves of the walnut trees—
soon soon my heart said to me . . .

Around your mouth,
precociously serious,
playfully subdued jesting,
yet to me you hardly seemed happy
your arm on the neck of your friend,
and your hand fell
with its fine, tired fingers
over his shoulder.
So you walked away.
Ah your walk,
where shall I find
words soaring
words light enough
for your knees' soft bending,
slight round thighs,
light submissive line of your delicate calves?

NOTHING, NOTHING ELSE IN THE WORLD. . .

Nothing, nothing else in the world can warm my soul now
except to write poems about you.
I want to search out words that cool and burn like the
caress of your skin,

words with the shimmer of your blood's smooth light
and the luster of your eyes' deep, hard glance,
shining there under the marble whiteness of your forehead.
I want to seize the stride and stretch of your limbs,
the languid smoothness of your movements,
in verses of consuming voluptuousness.

—Translated by Sam Charters

ROBERT MUSIL

YOUNG TÖRLESS

There came two public holidays; and since they fell on a Monday and Tuesday, the headmaster gave the boys Saturday off as well, so that they had four days free. For Törless this was still too short a time to make the long journey home worth while; and he had therefore hoped that at any rate his parents would come and see him. However, his father was kept by urgent affairs at his government office, and his mother did not feel well enough to face the strain of travelling alone.

But when Törless received his parents' letter, in which they told him they could not come and added many affectionate words of comfort, he suddenly realised that this actually suited him very well. He knew now that it would have been almost an interruption—at least it would have embarrassed him considerably—if he had had to face his parents just at this stage.

Many of the boys had invitations to estates in the district. Dschjusch, whose parents owned a fine property at the distance of a day's drive from the little town, was one of those who went away, and with him went Beineberg, Reiting, and Hofmeier. Basini had also been asked, but Reiting had bidden him refuse. Törless excused himself on the grounds that he did not know for certain whether his parents might not come after all; he felt totally disinclined for innocent, cheerful frolics and amusements.

By noon on Saturday the great building was silent and almost quite deserted.

When Törless walked through the empty corridors, they echoed from end to end. There was nobody to bother about him, for most of the masters had also gone away for a few days' shooting or the like. It was only at meals, which were now served in a small room next to the deserted refectory, that the few remaining boys saw each other. When they left the table they once more took their separate ways through the many corridors and class-rooms; it was as if the silence of the building had swallowed them up, and whatever life they led in these intervals seemed to be of no more interest to anyone than that of the spiders and centipedes in the cellars and attics.

Of Törless's class the only two left were himself and Basini, with the exception of a few boys in the sick-bay. When leaving, Reiting had exchanged a few words in private with Törless in the matter of Basini, for he was afraid that Basini might make use of the opportunity to seek protection from one of the masters; he had therefore impressed it on Törless to keep a sharp eye on him.

However, there was no need of that to concentrate Törless's attention on Basini.

Scarcely had the uproar faded away—the carriages driving to the door, the servants carrying valises, the boys joking and shouting good-bye to each other—when the consciousness of being alone with Basini took complete possession of Törless's mind.

It was after the first midday meal. Basini sat in his place in front, writing a letter. Törless had gone to a corner right at the back of the room and was trying to read.

It was for the first time again the volume of Kant, and the situation was just as he had pictured it: in front there sat Basini, at the back himself, holding Basini with his gaze, boring holes into him with his eyes. And it was like this that he wanted to read: penetrating deeper into Basini at the end of every page. That was how it must be; in this way he must find the truth without losing grip on life, living, complicated, ambiguous life....

But it would not work. This was what always happened when he had thought something out all too carefully in advance. It was too unspontaneous, and his mood swiftly lapsed into a dense, gluey boredom, which stuck odiously to every one of his all too deliberate attempts to get on with his reading.

In a fury, Törless threw the book on the floor. Basini looked round with a start, but at once turned away again and hurriedly went on writing.

So the hours crept on towards dusk. Törless sat there in a stupor. The only thing that struck clearly into his awareness —out of a muffled, buzzing, whirring state of generalised sensation—was the ticking of his pocket-watch. It was like a little tail wagging on the sluggish body of the creeping hours. The room became blurred . . . Surely Basini could no longer be writing . . . 'Aha, he probably doesn't dare to light a lamp,' Törless thought to himself. But was he still sitting over there in his place at all? Törless had been gazing out into the bleak, twilit landscape and now had to accustom his eyes again to the darkness of the room. Oh yes, there he was. There, that motionless shadow, that would be Basini all right. And now he even heaved a sigh—once, twice. He hadn't gone to sleep, had he?

A servant came in and lit the lamps. Basini started up and rubbed his eyes. Then he took a book out of his desk and began to apply himself to it.

Törless could hardly prevent himself from speaking to him, and in order to avoid that he hurried out of the room.

In the night Törless was not far from falling upon Basini, such a murderous lust had awakened in him after the anguish of that senseless, stupefying day. By good fortune sleep overtook him just in time.

The next day passed. It brought nothing but the same bleak

and barren quietness. The silence and suspense worked on Törless's overwrought nerves; the ceaseless strain on his attention consumed all his mental powers, so that he was incapable of framing any thought at all.

Disappointed, dissatisfied with himself to the point of the most extreme doubt, he felt utterly mangled. He went to bed early.

He had for a long time been lying in an uneasy, feverishly hot half-sleep when he heard Basini coming.

Lying motionless, with his eyes he followed the dark figure walking past the end of his bed. He heard the other undressing, and then the rustling of the blankets being pulled over the body.

He held his breath, but he could not manage to hear any more. Nevertheless he did not lose the feeling that Basini was not asleep either, but was straining to hear through the darkness, just like himself.

So the quarter-hours passed . . . hours passed. Only now and then the stillness was broken by the faint sound of the bodies stirring, each in its bed.

Törless was in a queer state that kept him awake. Yesterday it had been sensual pictures in his imagination that had made him feverish. Only right at the end had they taken a turn towards Basini, as it were rearing up under the inexorable hand of sleep, which then blotted them out; and it was precisely of this that he had the vaguest and most shadowy memory. But tonight it had from the very beginning been nothing other than an impelling urge to get up and go over to Basini. So long as he had had the feeling that Basini was awake and listening for whatever sounds he might make, it had been scarcely endurable; and now that Basini was apparently asleep, it was even worse, for there was a cruel excitement in the thought of falling upon the sleeper as upon a prey.

Törless could already feel the movements of rising up and getting out of bed twitching in all his muscles. But still he could not yet shake off his immobility.

'And what am I going to do, anyway, if I do go over to him?' he wondered, in his panic almost speaking the words aloud. And he had to admit to himself that the cruelty and lust in him had no real object. He would have been at a loss if he had now really set upon Basini. Surely he did not want to beat him? God forbid! Well then, in what way was his wild sensual excitement to get fulfillment from Basini? Instinctively he revolted at the thought of the various little vices that boys went in for. Expose himself to another person like that? Never!

But in the same measure as this revulsion grew the urge to go over to Basini also became stronger. Finally Törless was completely penetrated with the sense of how absurd such an act was, and yet a positively physical compulsion seemed to be drawing him out of bed as on a rope. And while his mind grew blank and he merely kept on telling himself, over and over again, that it would be best to go to sleep now if he could, he was mechanically rising up in the bed. Very slowly—and he could feel how the emotional urge was gaining, inch by inch, over the resistance in him—he began to sit up. First one arm moved . . . then he propped himself on one elbow, then pushed one knee out from under the bed-clothes . . . and then . . . suddenly he was racing, barefoot, on tip-toe, over to Basini, and sat down on the edge of Basini's bed.

Basini was asleep.

He looked as if he were having pleasant dreams.

Törless was still not in control of his actions. For a moment he sat still, staring into the sleeper's face. Through his brain there jerked those short, ragged thoughts which do no more, it seems, than record what a situation is, those flashes of thought one has when losing one's balance, or falling from a height, or when some object is torn from one's grasp. And without knowing what he was doing he gripped Basini by the shoulder and shook him out of his sleep.

Basini stretched indolently a few times. Then he started up and gazed at Törless with sleepy, stupefied eyes.

A shock went through Törless. He was utterly confused; now all at once he realised what he had done, and he did not know what he was to do next. He was frightfully ashamed. His heart thudded loudly. Words of explanation and excuse hovered on the tip of his tongue. He would ask Basini if he had any matches, if he could tell him the time . . .

Basini was still goggling at him with uncomprehending eyes.

Now, without having uttered a word, Törless withdrew his arm, now he slid off the bed and was about to creep back soundlessly into his own bed—and at this moment Basini seemed to grasp the situation and sat bolt upright.

Törless stopped irresolutely at the foot of the bed.

Basini glanced at him once more, questioningly, searchingly, and then got out of bed, slipped into coat and slippers and went padding off towards the door. And in a flash Törless became sure of what he had long suspected: that his had happened to Basini many times before.

In passing his bed, Törless took the key to the cubby-hole, which he had been keeping hidden under his pillow.

Basini walked straight on ahead of him, up to the attics. He seemed in the meantime to have become thoroughly familiar with the way that had once been kept so secret from him. He steadied the crate while Törless stepped down on to it, he cleared the scenery to one side, carefully, with gingerly movements, like a well-trained flunkey.

Törless unlocked the door, and they went in. With his back to Basini, he lit the little lamp.

When he turned round, Basini was standing there naked.

Involuntarily Törless fell back a step. The sudden sight of this naked snow-white body, with the red of the walls dark as blood behind it, dazzled and bewildered him. Basini was beautifully built; his body, lacking almost any sign of male development, was of a chaste, slender willowyness, like that of a young girl. And Törless felt this nakedness lighting up in his nerves, like hot white flames. He could not shake off the spell of this beauty. He had never known before what beauty was. For what was art to him at his age, what—after all—did he know of that? Up to a certain age, if one has grown up in the open air, art is simply unintelligible, a bore!

And here now it had come to him on the paths of sexuality . . . secretly, ambushing him . . . There was an infatuating warm exhalation coming from the bare skin, a soft, lecherous cajolery. And yet there was something about it that was so solemn and compelling as to make one almost clasp one's hands in awe.

But after the first shock Törless was as ashamed of the one reaction as of the other. 'It's a man, damn it!' The thought enraged him, and yet it seemed to him as though a girl could not be different.

In his shame he spoke hectoringly to Basini: "What on earth d'you think you're doing? Get back into your things this minute!"

Now it was Basini who seemed taken aback. Hesitantly, and without shifting his gaze from Törless, he picked up his coat from the floor.

"Sit down—there!" Törless ordered. Basini obeyed. Törless leaned against the wall, with his arms crossed behind his back.

"Why did you undress? What did you want of me?"

"Well, I thought..."

He paused hesitantly.

"What did you think?"

"The others..."

"What about the others?"

"Beineberg and Reiting..."

"What about Beineberg and Reiting? What did they do? You've got to tell me everything! That's what I want. See? Although I've heard about it from them, of course." At this clumsy lie Törless blushed.

Basini bit his lips.

"Well? Get on with it!"

"No, don't make me tell! Please don't make me! I'll do anything you want me to. But don't make me tell about it. . . . Oh, you have such a special way of tormenting me . . . !" Hatred, fear, and an imploring plea for mercy were all mingled in Basini's gaze.

Törless involuntarily modified his attitude. "I don't want to torment you at all. I only mean to make you tell the whole truth yourself. Perhaps for your own good."

"But, look, I haven't done anything specially worth telling about."

"Oh, haven't you? So why did you undress, then?"

"That's what they wanted."

"And why did you do what they wanted? So you're a coward, eh? A miserable coward?"

"No, I'm not a coward! Don't say that!"

"Shut up! If you're afraid of being beaten by them, you might find being beaten by me was something to remember!"

"But it's not the beatings they give me that I'm afraid of!"

"Oh? What is it then?"

By now Törless was speaking calmly again. He was already annoyed at his crude threat. But it had escaped him involuntarily, solely because it seemed to him that Basini stood up to him more than to the others.

"Well, if you're not afraid. as you say, what's the matter with you?"

"They say if I do whatever they tell me to, after some time I shall be forgiven everything."

"By the two of them?"

"No, altogether."

"How can they promise that? *I* have to be considered too!"

"They say they'll manage that all right."

This gave Törless a shock. Beineberg's words about Reiting's dealing with him, if he got the chance, in exactly the same way as with Basini now came back to him. And if it really came to a plot against him, how was he to cope with it? He was no match for the two of them in that sort of thing. How far would they go? The same as with Basini? . . . Everything in him revolted at the perfidious idea.

Minutes passed between him and Basini. He knew that he lacked the daring and endurance necessary for such intrigues, though of course only because he was too little interested in that sort of thing, only because he never felt his whole personality involved. He had always had more to lose than to gain there. But if it should ever happen to be the other way, there would, he felt, be quite a different kind of toughness and courage in him. Only one must know when it was time to stake everything.

"Did they say anything more about it—how they think they can do it? I mean, that about me."

"More? No. They only said they'd see to it all right."

And yet . . . there was danger now . . . somewhere lying in wait . . . lying in ambush for Törless . . . every step could run him into a gin-trap, every night might be the last before the fight. There was tremendous insecurity in this thought. Here was no more idle drifting along, no more toying with enigmatic visions—this had hard corners and was tangible reality.

Törless spoke again.

"And what do they do with you?"

Basini was silent.

"If you're serious about reforming, you have to tell me everything."

"They make me undress."

"Yes, yes, I see that for myself . . . And then?"

A little time passed, and then suddenly Basini said: "Various things." He said it with an effeminate, coy expression.

"So you're their—mi—mistress?"

"Oh no, I'm their friend!"

"How can you have the nerve to say that!"

"They say so themselves."

"What!"

"Yes, Reiting does."

"Oh, Reiting does?"

"Yes, he's very nice to me. Mostly I have to undress and read him something out of history-books—about Rome and the emperors, or the Borgias, or Timur Khan . . . oh well, you know, all that sort of big, bloody stuff. Then he's even affectionate to me. . . . And then afterwards he generally beats me."

"After what? Oh, I see!"

"Yes. He says, if he didn't beat me, he wouldn't be able to help thinking I was a man, and then he couldn't let himself be so soft and affectionate to me. But like that, he says, I'm his chattel, and so then he doesn't mind."

"And Beineberg?"

"Oh, Beineberg's beastly. Don't you think too his breath smells bad?"

"Shut up! What I think is no business of yours! Tell me what Beineberg does with you!"

"Well, the same as Reiting, only . . . But you mustn't go yelling at me again. . . ."

"Get on with it."

"Only . . . he goes about it differently. First of all he gives me long talks about my soul. He says I've sullied it, but so to speak only the outermost forecourt of it. In relation to the innermost, he says, this is something that doesn't matter at all, it's only external. But one must kill it. In that way many people have stopped being sinners and become saints. So from a higher point of view sin isn't so bad, only one must carry it to the extreme, so that it breaks off of its own accord, he says. He makes me sit and stare into a prism. . . ."

"He hypnotises you?"

"No, he says it's just that he must make all the things floating about on the surface of my soul go to sleep and become powerless. It's only then he can have intercourse with my soul itself."

"And how, may I ask, does he have intercourse with it?"

"That's an experiment he hasn't ever brought off yet. He sits there, and I have to get quite dull and drowsy from staring into the glass. Then suddenly he orders me to bark. He tells me exactly how to do it—quietly, more whimpering—the way a dog whines in its sleep."

"What's that good for?"

"Nobody knows what it's good for. And he also makes me grunt like a pig and keeps on and on telling me there's something of a pig about me, in me. But he doesn't mean it offensively, he just keeps on repeating it quite softly and nicely, in order—this is what he says—in order to imprint it firmly on my nerves. You see, he says it's possible one of my former lives was that of a pig and it must be lured out so as to render it harmless."

"And you believe all that stuff?"

"Good lord, no! I don't think he believes it himself. And then in the end he's always quite different, anyway. How on earth should I believe such things? Who believes in a soul these days anyway? And as for transmigration of souls———! I know quite well I slipped. But I've always hoped I'd be able to make up for it again. There isn't any hocus-pocus needed for that. Not that I spend any time racking my brains about how I ever came to go wrong. A thing like that comes on you so quickly, all by itself. It's only afterwards you notice that you've done something silly. But if he gets his fun out of looking for something supernatural behind it, let him, for all I care. For the present, after all, I've got to do what he wants. Only I wish he'd leave off sticking pins in me. . . ."

"What?"

"Pricking me with a pin—not hard, you know, only just to see how I react—to see if something doesn't manifest itself at some point or other on the body. But it does *hurt*. The fact is, he says the doctors don't understand anything about it. I don't remember now how he proves all this, all I remember is he talks a lot about fakirs and how when they see their souls they're supposed to be insensitive to physical pain."

"Oh yes, I know those ideas. But you yourself say that's not all."

"No, it certainly isn't all. But I also said I think this is just a way of going about it. Afterwards there are always long times—as much as a quarter of an hour—when he doesn't say anything and I don't know what's going on in him. But after that he suddenly breaks out and demands services from me—as if he were possessed—much worse than Reiting."

"And you do everything that's demanded of you?"

"What else can I do? I want to become a decent person again and be left in peace."

"But whatever happens in the meantime won't matter to you at all?"

"Well, I can't help it, can I?"

"Now pay attention to me and answer my questions. How could you steal?"

"How? Look, it's like this, I needed money urgently. I was in debt to the tuck-shop man, and he wouldn't wait any longer. Then I really did believe there was money coming for me just at that time. None of the other fellows would lend me any. Some of them hadn't got any themselves, and the saving ones are always just glad if someone who isn't like that gets short towards the end of the month. Honestly, I didn't want to cheat anyone. I only wanted to borrow it secretly. . . ."

"That's not what I mean," Törless said impatiently, interrupting this story, which it was obviously a relief for Basini to tell. "What I'm asking is *how*—how were you able to do it, what did you feel like? What went on in you at that moment?"

"Oh well—nothing, really. After all, it was only a moment, I didn't feel anything, I didn't think about anything, simply it had suddenly happened."

"But the first time with Reiting? The first time he demanded those things of you? You know what I mean. . . ."

"Oh, I didn't like it, of course. Because it had to be done just like that, being ordered to. Otherwise—well, just how many of the fellows do such things of their own accord, for the fun of it, without the others knowing anything? I dare say it's not so bad then."

"But you did it on being ordered to. You debased yourself. Just as if you had crawled into the muck because someone else wanted you to."

"Oh, I grant that. But I had to."

"No, you didn't have to."

"They would have beaten me and reported me. Think how I would have got into disgrace."

"All right then, let's leave that. There's something else I want to know. Listen. I know you've spent a lot of money with Božena. You've boasted to her and thrown your weight about and made out what a man you are. So you want to be a man? Not just boasting and pretending to be—but with your whole soul? Now look, then suddenly someone demands such a humiliating service from you, and in the same moment you feel you're too cowardly to say no—doesn't it make a split go through your whole being? A horror—something you can't describe—as though something unutterable had happened inside you?"

"Lord! I don't know what you mean. I don't know what you're getting at. I can't tell you anything—anything at all—about that."

"Now attend. I'm going to order you to get undressed again."

Basini smiled.

"And to lie down flat on the floor there in front of me. Don't laugh! I'm really ordering you to! D'you *hear* me? If you don't obey instantly, you'll see what you're in for when Reiting comes back! . . . That's right. So now you're lying naked on the ground in front of me. You're trembling, too. Are you cold? I could spit on your naked body now if I wanted to. Just press your head right on to the floor. Doesn't the dust on the boards look queer? Like a landscape full of clouds and lumps of rock as big as houses? I could stick pins into you. There are still some over there in the corner, by the lamp. D'you feel them in your skin even now? . . . But I don't mean to do that. I could make you bark, the way Beineberg does, and make you eat dust like a pig. I could make you do movements—oh, you know—and at the same time you would have to sigh: 'Oh, my dear Moth———!'" But Törless broke off abruptly in the midst of this sacrilege. "But I don't mean to—don't mean to —do you understand?"

Basini wept. "You're tormenting me . . ."

"Yes, I'm tormenting you. But that's not what I'm after. There's just one thing I want to know: when I drive all that into you like knives, what goes on in you? What happens inside you? Does something burst in you? Tell me! Does it smash like a glass that suddenly flies into thousands of splinters before there's been even a little crack in it? Doesn't the picture you've made of yourself go out like a candle? Doesn't something else leap into its place, the way the pictures in the magic-lantern leap out of the darkness? Don't you *understand* what I mean? I can't explain it for you any better. You must tell me yourself . . .!"

Basini wept without stopping. His girlish shoulders jerked. All he could get out was to the same effect: "I don't know what you're after, I can't explain anything to you, it happens just in a moment, and then nothing different can happen, you'd do just the same as me."

Törless was silent. He remained leaning against the wall, exhausted, motionless, blankly staring straight in front of him.

'If you were in my situation, you would do just the same,' Basini had said. Seen thus, what had happened appeared a simple necessity, straightforward and uncomplicated.

Törless's self-awareness rebelled in blazing contempt

against the mere suggestion. And yet this rebellion on the part of his whole being seemed to offer him no satisfactory guarantee . . . '. . . yes, *I* should have more character than he has, *I* shouldn't put up with such outrageous demands—but does it really matter? Does it matter that I should act differently, from firmness, from decency, from—oh, for all sorts of reasons that at the moment don't interest me in the least? No, what counts is not how I should act, but the fact that if I were ever really to act as Basini has done, I should have just as little sense of anything extraordinary about it as he has. This is the heart of the matter: my feeling about myself would be exactly as simple and clear of ambiguity as his feeling about himself . . .'

This thought—flashing through his mind in half-coherent snatches of sentences that ran over into each other and kept beginning all over again—added to his contempt for Basini a very private, quiet pain that touched his inmost balance at a much deeper point than any moral consideration could. It came from his awareness of a sensation he had briefly had before and which he could not get rid of. The fact was that when Basini's words revealed to him the danger potentially menacing him from Reiting and Beineberg, he had simply been startled. He had been startled as by a sudden assault, and without stopping to think had in a flash looked round for cover and a way of parrying the attack. That had been in the moment of a real danger; and the sensation it had caused him—those swift, unthinking impulses—exasperated and stimulated him. He tried, all in vain, to set them off again. But he knew they had immediately deprived the danger of all its peculiarity and ambiguity.

And yet it had been the same danger that he had had a foreboding of only some weeks previously, in this same place—that time when he had felt so oddly startled by the lair itself, which was like some forgotten scrap of the Middle Ages lying remote from the warm, bright-lit life of the class-rooms, and by Beineberg and Reiting, because they seemed to have changed from the people they were down there, suddenly turning into something else, something sinister, blood-thirsty, figures in some quite different sort of life. That had been a transformation, a leap for Törless, as though the picture of his surroundings had suddenly loomed up before other eyes—eyes just awakened out of a hundred years of sleep.

And yet it had been the same danger. . . . He kept on repeating this to himself. And ever and again he tried to compare the memories of the two different sensations. . . .

Meanwhile Basini had got up. Observing his companion's blank, absent gaze, he quietly took his clothes and slipped away.

Törless saw it happening—as though through a mist—but he uttered no word and let it go at that.

His attention was wholly concentrated on this straining to rediscover the point in himself where the change of inner perspective had suddenly occurred.

But every time he came anywhere near it the same thing happened to him as happens to someone trying to compare the close-at-hand with the remote: he could never seize the memory images of the two feelings together. For each time something came in between. It was like a faint click in the mind, corresponding more or less to something that occurs in the physical realm—that scarcely perceptible muscular sensation which is associated with the focusing of the gaze. And each time, precisely in the decisive moment, this would claim all his attention: the activity of making the comparison thrust itself before the objects to be compared, there was an almost unnoticeable jerk—and everything stopped.

So Törless kept on beginning all over again.

This mechanically regular operation lulled him into a rigid, waking, ice-cold sleep, holding him transfixed where he was—and for an indefinite period.

Then an idea wakened him like the light touch of a warm hand. It was an idea apparently so obvious and natural that he marvelled at its not having occurred to him long ago.

It was an idea that did nothing at all beyond generalising the experience he had just had: what in the distance seems so great and mysterious comes up to us always as something plain and undistorted, in natural, everyday proportions. It is as if there were an invisible frontier round every man . . . What originates outside and approaches from a long way off is like a misty sea full of gigantic, ever-changing forms; what comes right up to any man, and becomes action, and collides with his life, is clear and small, human in its dimensions and human in its outlines. And between the life one lives and the life one feels, the life one only has inklings and glimpses of, seeing it only from afar, there lies that invisible frontier, and in it the narrow gateway where all that ever happens, the images of things, must throng together and shrink so that they can enter into a man . . .

And yet, closely though this corresponded to his experience, Törless let his head sink, deep in thought.

It seemed a queer idea . . .

At last he was back in bed. He was not thinking of anything at all any more, for thinking came so hard and was so futile. What he had discovered about the secret contrivings of his friends did, it was true, go through his mind, but now as indifferently and lifelessly as an item of foreign news read in a newspaper.

There was nothing more to be hoped from Basini. Oh, there was still his problem! But that was so dubious, and he was so tired and mangled. An illusion perhaps—the whole thing.

Only the vision of Basini, of his bare, glimmering skin, left a fragrance, as of lilac, in that twilight of the sensations which comes just before sleep. Even the moral revulsion faded away. And at last Törless fell asleep.

No dream disturbed him. There was only an infinitely pleasant warmth spreading soft carpets under his body. After a while he woke out of it. And then he almost screamed. There, sitting on his bed, was Basini! And in the next instant, with crazy speed, Basini had flung off his night-clothes and slid under the blankets and was pressing his naked, trembling body against Törless.

As soon as Törless recovered from the shock, he pushed Basini away from him.

"What do you think you're doing———?"

But Basini pleaded. "Oh, don't start being like that again! Nobody's the way you are! They don't despise me the way you do. They only pretend they do, so as to be different then afterwards. But you—you of all people! You're even younger than me, even if you are stronger. We're both younger than the others. You don't boast and bully the way they do . . . You're gentle . . . I love you . . ."

"Here, I say! I don't know what you're talking about! I don't know what you want! Go away! Oh, go *away*!" And in anguish Törless pushed his arm against Basini's shoulder, holding him off. But the hot proximity of the soft skin, this other person's skin, haunted him, enclosing him, suffocating him. And Basini kept on whispering: "Oh yes . . . oh yes . . . please . . . oh, I should so gladly do whatever you want!"

Törless could find nothing to say to this. While Basini went on whispering and he himself was lost in doubt and consideration, something had sunk over his senses again like a deep green sea. Only Basini's flickering words shone out in it like the glint of little silvery fishes.

He was still holding Basini off with his arms. But something made them heavy, like a moist, torpid warmth; the muscles in them were slackening . . . he forgot them. . . . Only when another of those darting words touched him did he start awake again, all at once feeling—like something fearful and incomprehensible—that this very instant, as in a dream, his hands had drawn Basini closer.

Then he wanted to shake himself into wakefulness, wanted to shout at himself: Basini's tricking you, he's just trying to drag you down to where he is, so that you can't despise him any more! But the cry was never uttered, nor was there any sound anywhere in the whole huge building; throughout the corridors the dark tides of silence seemed to lie motionless in sleep.

He struggled to get back to himself. But those tides were like black sentinels at all the doors.

Then Törless abandoned his search for words. Lust, which had been slowly seeping into him, emanating from every single moment of desperation, had now grown to its full stature. It lay naked at his side and covered his head with its soft black cloak. And into his ear it whispered sweet words of resignation, while its warm fingers thrust all questionings and obligations aside as futile. And it whispered: In solitude you can do what you will.

Only in the moment when he was swept away he woke fleetingly, frantically clutching at the one thought: This is not myself! It's not me! . . . But tomorrow it will be me again! . . . Tomorrow . . .

—Translated by
Eithne Wilkins and
Ernst Kaiser

MIKHAIL KUZMIN

AUNT SONYA'S SOFA

I dedicate this true story to my sister

It's so long that I've been standing in the storeroom, surrounded by all kinds of junk, that I have only the dimmest recollections of my young days, when the Turk with a pipe and the shepherdess with a little dog scratching itself for fleas, hind leg raised, all of them embroidered on my spine, gleamed in bright hues—yellow, pink and sky-blue—as yet unfaded and undimmed by dust; and so what occupies my thoughts now more than anything else are the events to which I was witness before once more being consigned to oblivion, this time, I fear, for ever. They had me covered in a wine-colored silken material, stood me in the passageway and threw over my arm a shawl with a pattern of bright roses, as if some beauty from the days of my youth, disturbed at a tender tryst, had left it behind in her flight. I should add that this shawl was always carefully draped in exactly the same way, and if the General, or his sister, Aunt Pavla, happened to disturb it, Kostya, who had arranged this part of the house to his own taste, would restore the folds of the soft, gaily-colored stuff to their former exquisite casualness. Aunt Pavla protested against my disinterment from the storeroom, saying that poor Sophie had died on me, that someone or other's wedding had been upset because of me, that I brought the family misfortune; however, not only was I defended by Kostya, his student friends and the other young people, but even the General himself said:

"That's all prejudice, Pavla Petrovna! If that old monstrosity ever had any magic power in it, sixty years in the storeroom should have taken care of that; besides, it's standing in the passageway—no one's likely to die or propose on it there!"

Although I wasn't very flattered to be called a "monstrosity," and the General proved to be less than a prophet, I did at any rate establish myself as part of the passageway with the greenish wallpaper, where I stood faced by a china cabinet, over which hung an old round mirror, dimly reflecting my occasional visitors. There lived in General Gambakov's house, in addition to his sister Pavla and his son, Kostya, his daughter Nastya, a student at the institute for young ladies.

The next room had a westerly outlook, and so admitted into my passageway the long rays of the evening sun; they would strike the rose-patterned shawl, making it glint and shimmer more enchantingly than ever. At this moment, these rays were falling across the face and dress of Nastya, who was sitting on me; she seemed so fragile that I almost thought it strange that the ruddy light did not pass through her body, which hardly seemed a sufficient obstacle to it, and fall on her companion. She was talking to her brother about the Christmas theatricals, as part of which they were planning to put on an act from "Esther"; it seemed, however, that the girl's thoughts were far from the subject of the conversation. Kostya remarked:

"I think we could use Seryozha too—his accent is pretty good."

"Are you suggesting that Sergey Pavlovich should play a young Israelite girl—one of my handmaidens?"

"Why that? I can't bear *travesti* roles—not that he wouldn't look good in a woman's costume."

"Well, what other part is there for him to play?"

I knew at once that they were talking about Sergey Pavlovich Pavilikin, young Gambakov's friend. To me he had always seemed an insignificant boy, in spite of his striking good looks. His close-cropped dark hair emphasized the fullness of his round, strangely bloodless face; he had a pleasing mouth and large, pale-gray eyes. His height enabled him to carry off an inclination to plumpness, but he was certainly very heavy, always collapsing onto me and scattering me with ash from the *papirosy* with very long mouthpieces which he smoked one after another; and nothing could have been more empty-headed than his conversation. He came to the house almost every day, notwithstanding the displeasure of Pavla Petrovna, who could not abide him.

After a silence the young lady began hesitantly:

"Do you know Pavilikin well, Kostya?"

"What a question! He's my best friend!"

"Is he . . . But you haven't been friends all that long, have you?"

"Ever since I began attending university this year. But what difference does that make?"

"None, of course. I just asked because I wanted to know. . . ."

"Why do you find our friendship so interesting?"

"I would like to know whether one can trust him. . . . I'd like to. . . ."

Kostya's laughter interrupted her.

"It depends what with! In monetary affairs I wouldn't advise it! . . . All the same, he's a good friend, and no skinflint when he's in funds—but you know he's poor. . . ."

Nastya said after a pause:

"No, I didn't mean that at all—I meant in matters of feeling, affection."

"What nonsense! What on earth do they put into your heads at those institutes? How should I know?! . . . Have you fallen for Seryozha or something?"

The young lady continued without answering:

"I want you to do something for me. Will you?"

"Is it to do with Sergey Pavlovich?"

"Perhaps."

"Well, all right—though you'd better not forget that he's not much of a one for wasting time on young ladies."

"No, Kostya, you have to promise me! . . ."

"I've said I'll do it, haven't I? Well?"

"I'll tell you this evening," announced Nastya solemnly, looking into her brother's uneasily shifting eyes, eyes which, like hers, were hazel flecked with gold.

"Whenever you like—now, this evening," said the young man unconcernedly, as he got up and readjusted the rose-patterned shawl which the girl had released as she too rose.

But no ray of the evening sun gleamed on the tender roses because Nastya had gone into the next room and taken up a position at the window, as impenetrable to the ruddy light as before; she stood there gazing at the snow-covered street until the electric lights were lit.

Today I simply haven't had a moment's quiet—such comings and goings all day, and all through my passageway! And what's the point of all these amateur theatricals—that's what I'd like to know. A swarm of young misses and young men—lord knows who they all are—bustling about, yelling, running, calling for some peasants or other to saw through something or other, dragging about furniture, cushions, lengths of cloth; it's a mercy they didn't start taking things from the passage—why, they might even have carried off my shawl! At last things quieted down and a piano began to play somewhere far off. The General and Pavla Petrovna emerged cautiously and sat down beside each other; the old maid was saying:

"If she falls in love with him, it will be a family misfortune. Just think of it—a mere boy, and worse than that—with no name, no fortune, absolutely nothing to offer! . . ."

"It seems to me you're very much exaggerating all this—I haven't noticed anything. . . ."

"When did men ever notice such things? But I, for one, will fight against it to the bitter end."

"I shouldn't think things will ever reach the point where you have to be for or against."

"And he has absolutely no morals at all: do you know what they say about him? I'm convinced that he's corrupting Kostya too. Nastya's a child, she doesn't understand anything," fulminated the old lady.

"Well, my dear, and whom don't they talk about? You should hear the gossip about Kostya! And it wouldn't surprise me if some of these fairy tales didn't have a grain of truth in them. Only age can protect you from gossip—as the two of us ought to know! . . ."

Pavla Petrovna blushed crimson and said curtly:

"You do as you wish; at least I've warned you. And *I* shall certainly be on my guard—Nastya is my blood too, you know!"

At this moment Nastya herself entered, already dressed in her costume for the play—pale blue with yellow stripes, with a yellow turban.

"Papa," she began breathlessly, turning to the General, "why aren't you watching the rehearsals?"—and without waiting for a reply she rushed on, "What about lending our emperor your ring? It has such a huge emerald!"

"You mean this one?" asked the old man in surprise, showing an antique ring of rare workmanship, set with a dark emerald the size of a large gooseberry.

"Yes, that one!" answered the young lady, not at all disconcerted.

"Nastya, you don't know what you're asking!" her aunt intervened. "A family heirloom which Maksim never parts with, and you want him to let you take it to that madhouse of yours where you'll lose it in no time? You know your father never takes it off his finger!"

"Well, it's only once or twice, and even if someone does drop it, it's sure to be somewhere in the room. . . ."

"No, Maskim, I absolutely forbid you to take it off!"

"You see, Aunt Pavla won't let me!" said the old General with an embarrassed laugh.

Nastya stalked out crossly without the ring, and Pavla Petrovna set about comforting her brother, who was upset to see his daughter disappointed.

And again there was hubbub, rushing about, changing of clothes, leavetaking.

Mr. Pavilikin remained in the house a long time. When he and Kostya came into my passageway it was nearly four o'clock in the morning. Coming to a standstill, they kissed each other good-bye. Sergey Pavlovich said in an embarrassed voice:

"You don't know how happy I am, Kostya! But I feel so uncomfortable that this should have happened today of all days, after you had let me have that money! Lord knows what awful things you might think. . . .'"

Kostya, pale, his eyes shining with happiness, his hair rumpled, again kissed his friend, and said:

"I won't think anything at all, you idiot! It's simply coincidence, chance—something that could happen to anyone."

"Yes, but I feel awkward, so awkward. . . ."

"Don't say another word about it, please—you can let me have it back in the spring. . . ."

"It was just that I needed those six hundred roubles desperately. . . ."

Kostya made no rejoinder. After a little while he said:

"Good-bye, then. Don't forget you're going to 'Manon' with me tomorrow."

"Yes, of course! . . ."

"And not with Petya Klimov?"

"O, *tempi passati!* Good-bye!"

"Close the door gently, and tread softly when you go past Aunt Pavla's bedroom: she didn't see you come back, and you know she doesn't much care for you. Good-bye!"

The young men embraced once more; as I said before, it was nearly four o'clock in the morning.

Without taking off her rose-trimmed fur hat after the ride, Nastya sat down on the edge of the chair, while her escort kept pacing up and down the room, his cheeks faintly pink from the frost. The girl was chattering gaily away, but underneath the bird-like twitter there lurked a certain unease.

"Wasn't that a glorious ride! Frost and sunshine—that's so nice! I adore the embankment! . . ."

"Yes."

"I love to go horseriding—in the summer I disappear for days on end. You've never visited our place at Svyataya Krucha, have you?"

"No. I prefer to ride in a car."

"You do have bad taste. . . . You know, don't you, that Svyataya Krucha, Alekseyevskoye and Lgovka are all my personal property—I'm a very good match. And then Auntie Pavla Petrovna is going to leave me everything. You see—I'm advising you to think things over."

"The likes of us mustn't be getting ideas above our station!"

"Where do you pick up these germs of shop-assistants' wisdom?"

Seryozha shrugged and continued his steady pacing back and forth. The young lady made one or two more attempts to start up her twittering, but each time more halfheartedly, like a broken toy, until she at last fell silent; when she spoke again, it was in a sad, gentle voice. Without taking off her hat, she sank back in the chair; as she spoke in the darkened room, she seemed to be addressing a plaint to herself:

"How long it's been since we put on our play! Do you remember? Your entrance. . . . What a lot has changed since then! You've changed too—I have, everyone has. . . . I didn't really know you then. You've no idea how much better I understand you than Kostya does! You don't believe it? Why do you pretend to be so slow on the uptake? Would it give you pleasure if I came out and said what is considered humiliating for a woman to say first? You're tormenting me, Sergey Pavlovich!"

"How dreadfully you exaggerate everything, Nastasya Maksimovna—my dimness of wit, my pride, and even, perhaps, your feelings for me. . . ."

She stood up and said almost soundlessly:

"Do I? Perhaps. . . ."

"Are you going?"—he was suddenly alert.

"Yes, I have to change for dinner. You're not dining with us?"

"No, I'm invited somewhere."

"With Kostya?"

"No. Why do you ask that?"

She was standing by the table with the magazines, reluctant to leave the room.

"Are you going to him now?"

"No, I'm leaving straight away."

"Are you? Good-bye, then! And I love you—there!" she added suddenly, turning away. No word came from him in the darkness which hid his face from her, and she threw in laughingly (or that was the effect she intended), "Well, are you satisfied now?"

"Surely you don't think that's the word I would choose?" he said, bending over her hand.

"Good-bye. Go now,"—the words came from her as she left the room.

Seryozha turned on the light and began walking in the direction of Kostya's room, whistling cheerfully.

The General was pacing about holding a newspaper; he seemed very upset about something. Pavla Petrovna was following him about the room in a rustle of black silk.

"You mustn't let it upset you, Maksim! It happens so often these days that you almost get used to it. Of course, it's dreadful, but what can we do about it? It's no good kicking against the pricks, as they say."

"It's no good, Pavla, I just can't reconcile myself to the thought of it: all that was left was his cap and a mess of blood and brains on the wall. Poor Lev Ivanovich!"

"Don't think about it, brother! Tomorrow we'll have a funeral mass said for him at Udely. Put it out of your mind, think of your own well-being—you have a son and daughter of your own to worry about."

The General, red in the face, sank down onto me, letting fall his newspaper; the old lady, nimbly picking it up and placing it out of her brother's reach, made haste to change the subject:

"Well, did you find the ring?"

The General again displayed signs of uneasiness:

"No, no, I haven't. That's another thing I'm terribly worried about."

"When do you last remember having it?"

"I showed it to Sergey Pavlovich this morning on this very sofa; he seemed most interested. . . . Then I dozed off—when I woke up it had gone, I remember that. . . ."

"Did you take it off?"

"Yes. . . ."

"That was ill-advised of you. Quite apart from its cash value, as a family heirloom it's priceless."

"I'm sure it means some misfortune is in store for us."

"Let's hope that Lev Ivanovich's death is misfortune enough for the time being."

The General heaved a deep sigh. Pavla Petrovna pressed on relentlessly:

"Did Pavilikin take it with him, I wonder. That's just the sort of thing I'd expect of him."

"Why should he have? He had such a good look at it—and he asked how much a dealer would give for it and all that."

"Well, perhaps he just took it."

"Stole it—is that what you're trying to say?"

Pavla Petrovna had no chance to reply: the conversation was interrupted by Nastya, who came rushing excitedly into the room.

"Papa!" she cried, "Sergey Pavlovich has proposed to me; I hope you're not opposed to the idea?"

"Not now, not now!"—the General waved her away.

"And why not? Why put it off? You know him pretty well by now," said Nastya, reddening.

Pavla Petrovna rose to her feet:

"I have a voice in this matter too, and I am opposed to the match under any circumstances; at the very least I demand that we postpone this discussion until Maksim's ring is found."

"What has papa's ring to do with my fiancé?" asked the girl haughtily.

"We think Sergey Pavlovich has the ring."

"You think he has committed a theft?"

"You could put it like that."

Nastya turned to the General without answering her aunt, and said:

"And do you believe this fairy tale?"

Her father said nothing, redder in the face than ever.

The girl again turned to Pavla:

"Why are you standing between us? You hate Seryozha—

Sergey Pavlovich—and you invent all sorts of nonsense! And you're trying to set father against Kostya too. What is it you want from us?"

"Nastya, don't you dare, I forbid you! . . ." said her father, gasping for breath.

Nastya paid him no attention.

"What are you getting in such a rage about? Why can't you wait until the matter is cleared up? Can't you see that it's a matter of principle?"

"I can see that where my fiancé is concerned no one should dare even to suspect such a thing!" shouted Nastya. The General sat in silence, turning redder and redder.

"You're afraid—that's the truth isn't it?"

"There can only be one truth, and I know what it is. And I advise you not to oppose our marriage—or it'll be the worse for you!"

"You think so?"

"I know!"

Pavla gave her a searching look.

"Is there any reason for this hurry?"

"What a nasty mind you have! Kostya!"—Nastya threw herself toward her brother, who had just entered, "Kostya darling, you be the judge! Sergey Pavlovich has proposed to me, and father—Aunt Pavla has him completely under her thumb—won't give his consent until we clear up this business about his ring."

"What the devil is all this?! Do you mean to tell me you're accusing Pavilikin of theft?"

"Yes!" hissed the old lady. "Of course you'll stand up for him, you'll even redeem the ring. There are a few things I could tell about you too! I can hear the doors squeaking from my room when your friend leaves and what you say to each other. Be grateful for my silence!"

Never in all my life have I heard such an uproar, such a scandal, such a torrent of abuse. Kostya banged with his fist and shouted; Pavla appealed for respect to be shown to years; Nastya screamed hysterically. . . . But all at once everyone fell silent: all the voices, the noise and the shouting, were pierced by the strange animal-like sound emitted by the General, who, silent to this moment, had suddenly risen to his feet. Then he sank back heavily, his face between red and blue, and began to wheeze. Pavla threw herself toward him:

"What's the matter? Maksim, Maksim?"

The General only wheezed and rolled the whites of his eyes, now completely blue in the face.

"Water! Water! He's dying—it's a stroke!" whispered the aunt, but Nastya pushed her aside with the words:

"Let me see to him—I'll undo his collar!" and sank down on her knees before me.

Even the passageway was not free of the pervasive smell of incense from the old General's funeral mass; the sound of chanting too could be faintly heard. More than once I had the feeling that they were singing a farewell to me. Ah, how close I was to the truth!

The young men came in, deep in conversation; Pavilikin was saying:

"And then today I received the following note from Pavla Petrovna"—and taking a letter from his pocket, he read it aloud:

"Dear Sir, for reasons which I trust there is no need to go into here, I find your visits at this time, a time so painful to our family, to be undesirable, and I hope that you will not refuse to comport yourself in accordance with our general wish. The future will show whether former relations can be resumed, but in the meantime, I can assure you that Anastasia Maksimovna, my niece, is fully in agreement with me on this matter. Yours, etc."

He looked inquiringly at Kostya, who remarked:

"You know, from her point of view my aunt is right, and I really don't know what my sister will have to say to you."

"But, I mean to say, all because of such a little thing! . . ."

"Is that what you call papa's death?"

"But it wasn't my fault!"

"Of course it wasn't. . . . You know, not long ago I read a story in the 'Thousand and One Nights': a man is throwing date stones—a perfectly harmless occupation—and happens to hit a Genii's son in the eye, thus bringing down on his head a whole series of misfortunes. Who can predict the results of our most trivial actions?"

"But the two of us will still see each other, won't we?"

"Oh certainly! I shan't be living with the family any more, and I'm always delighted to see you. What's between us is a bit more permanent than a schoolgirl crush."

"And doesn't have to be afraid of date stones?"

"Precisely. . . ."

Seryozha put his arm round young Gambakov, and they went out of the room together. I was never to see Pavilikin again, as I was to see little of any of the people I had grown familiar with during my final period of grace.

Early next morning some peasants came tramping in; "This one here?" they asked Pavla Petrovna, and set about lifting me. The oldest of them lingered, trying to find out if there was anything else to be sold, but on being assured that there wasn't, he went out after the others.

When they turned me on my side to get me through the doorway, something struck the floor (the carpets having already been taken up in anticipation of summer). One of my bearers picked up the fallen object and handed it to the old lady, saying:

"Now there's a fine ring for you, ma'am. Someone must have dropped it on this here couch, and it must have gone and rolled down inside the covers."

"Good. I'm very much obliged to you!" said Aunt Pavla, turning pale; hastily dropping into her reticule a ring with an emerald like a large gooseberry, she left the room.

JUNE, 1907

—Translated by
Neil Granoien and
Michael Green

CONSTANTIN CAVAFY

GRAY

Looking at a half-gray opal
I remembered two beautiful gray eyes
I had seen; it must have been twenty years ago . . .

For a month we loved each other.
Then he went away, I believe to Smyrna,
to work there, and we never saw each other after that.

The gray eyes—if he is alive—must have grown ugly;
the handsome face must have spoiled.

Dear Memory, preserve them as they used to be.
And, Memory, bring back to me tonight all that you can,
of this love of mine, all that you can.

THE TOBACCO-SHOP WINDOW

They stood among many others
near a lighted tobacco-shop window.

CALAMUS

Their glances chanced to meet,
and they timidly, haltingly expressed
the deviate desire of their flesh.
Then, a few steps uneasily taken on the sidewalk—
until they smiled, and gently nodded.

And after that the closed carriage . . .
the carnal closeness of their bodies;
the clasped hands, the met lips.

BODY, REMEMBER . . .

Body, remember not only how much you were loved,
not only the beds on which you lay,
but also those desires for you
that glowed plainly in the eyes,
and trembled in the voice—and some
chance obstacle made futile.
Now that all of them belong to the past,
it almost seems as if you had yielded
to those desires—how they glowed,
remember, in the eyes gazing at you;
how they trembled in the voice, for you, remember, body.

THE NEXT TABLE

He must be scarcely twenty-two years old.
And yet I am certain that nearly as many
years ago, I enjoyed the very same body.

It isn't at all infatuation of love.
I entered the casino only a little while ago;
I didn't even have time to drink much.
I have enjoyed the same body.

If I can't recall where—one lapse of memory means nothing.

Ah see, now that he is sitting down at the next table
I know every movement he makes—and beneath his clothes,
once more I see the beloved bare limbs.

THEIR BEGINNING

The fulfillment of their deviate, sensual delight
is done. They rise from the mattress,
and they dress hurriedly without speaking.
They leave the house separately, furtively; and as
they walk somewhat uneasily on the street, it seems
as if they suspect that something about them betrays
into what kind of bed they fell a little while back.

But how the life of the artist has gained.
Tomorrow, the next day, years later, the vigorous verses
will be composed that had their beginning here.

IN AN OLD BOOK

In an old book—about a hundred years old—
forgotten among its pages,
I found a water color unsigned.
It must have been the work of a very able artist.
It had as its title, "A Presentation of Love."

But more fitting would have been, "Of Utter Sensual Love."

For it was evident when you looked at the work
(the artist's idea was easily understood)
that the young man in the painting was not destined
to be one of those who loves more or less healthily,
remaining within the limits of the more or less
permissible—with chestnut, deep-coloured eyes;
with the exquisite beauty of his face,
the beauty of deviate attractions;

with his ideal lips that offer
sensual delight to a beloved body;
with his ideal limbs created for beds which
current morality brands as shameless.

BEFORE TIME CHANGES THEM

They were both deeply grieved   at their separation.
They did not desire it;   it was circumstances.
The needs of a living   obliged one of them
to go to a distant place—   New York or Canada.
Their love certainly   was not what it had been before;
for the attraction   had gradually waned,
for love's attraction   had considerably waned.
But they did not desire   to be separated.
It was circumstances.—   Or perhaps Destiny
had appeared as an artist   separating them now
before their feeling should fade,   before Time had changed them;
so each for the other will   remain forever as he had been,
a handsome young man   of twenty-four years.

—*Translated by Rae Dalven*

SHERWOOD ANDERSON

HANDS

Upon the half decayed veranda of a small frame house that stood near the edge of a ravine near the town of Winesburg, Ohio, a fat little old man walked nervously up and down. Across a long field that had been seeded for clover but that had produced only a dense crop of yellow mustard weeds, he could see the public highway along which went a wagon filled with berry pickers returning from the fields. The berry pickers, youths and maidens, laughed and shouted boisterously. A boy clad in a blue shirt leaped from the wagon and attempted to drag after him one of the maidens who screamed and protested shrilly. The feet of the boy in the road kicked up a cloud of dust that floated across the face of the departing sun. Over the long field came a thin girlish voice. "Oh, you Wing Biddlebaum, comb your hair, it's falling into your eyes," commanded the voice to the man, who was bald and whose nervous little hands fiddled about the bare white forehead as though arranging a mass of tangled locks.

Wing Biddlebaum, forever frightened and beset by a ghostly band of doubts, did not think of himself as in any way a part of the life of the town where he had lived for twenty years. Among all the people of Winesburg but one had come close to him. With George Willard, son of Tom Willard, the proprietor of the new Willard House, he had formed something like a friendship. George Willard was the reporter on the *Winesburg Eagle* and sometimes in the evenings he walked out along the highway to Wing Biddlebaum's house. Now as the old man walked up and down on the veranda, his hands moving nervously about, he was hoping that George Willard would come and spend the evening with him. After the wagon containing the berry pickers had passed, he went across the field through the tall mustard weeds and climbing a rail fence peered anxiously along the road to the town. For a moment he stood thus, rubbing his hands together and looking up and down the road, and then, fear overcoming him, ran back to walk again upon the porch on his own house.

In the presence of George Willard, Wing Biddlebaum, who for twenty years had been the town mystery, lost something of his timidity, and his shadowy personality, submerged in a sea of doubts, came forth to look at the world. With the young reporter at his side, he ventured in the light of day into Main Street or strode up and down on the rickety front porch of his own house, talking excitedly. The voice that had been low and trembling became shrill and loud. The bent figure straightened. With a kind of wriggle, like a fish returned to the brook by the fisherman, Biddlebaum the silent began to talk, striving to put into words the ideas that had been accumulated by his mind during long years of silence.

Wing Biddlebaum talked much with his hands. The slender expressive fingers, forever active, forever striving to conceal themselves in his pockets or behind his back, came forth and became the piston rods of his machinery of expression.

The story of Wing Biddlebaum is a story of hands. Their restless activity, like unto the beating of the wings of an imprisoned bird, had given him his name. Some obscure poet of the town had thought of it. The hands alarmed their owner. He wanted to keep them hidden away and looked with amazement at the quiet inexpressive hands of other men who worked beside him in the fields, or passed driving sleepy teams on country roads.

When he talked to George Willard, Wing Biddlebaum closed his fists and beat with them upon a table or on the walls of his house. The action made him more comfortable. If the desire to talk came to him when the two were walking in the fields, he sought out a stump or the top board of a fence and with his hands pounding busily talked with renewed ease.

The story of Wing Biddlebaum's hands is worth a book in itself. Sympathetically set forth it would tap many strange, beautiful qualities in obscure men. It is a job for a poet. In Winesburg the hands had attracted attention merely because of their activity. With them Wing Biddlebaum had picked as high as a hundred and forty quarts of strawberries in a day. They became his distinguishing feature, the source of his fame. Also they made more grotesque an already grotesque and elusive individuality. Winesburg was proud of the hands of Wing Biddlebaum in the same spirit in which it was proud of Banker White's new stone house and Wesley Moyer's bay stallion, Tony Tip, that had won the two-fifteen trot at the fall races in Cleveland.

As for George Willard, he had many times wanted to ask about the hands. At times an almost overwhelming curiosity had taken hold of him. He felt that there must be a reason for their strange activity and their inclination to keep hidden away and only a growing respect for Wing Biddlebaum kept him from blurting out the questions that were often in his mind.

Once he had been on the point of asking. The two were walking in the fields on a summer afternoon and had stopped to sit upon a grassy bank. All afternoon Wing Biddlebaum had talked as one inspired. By a fence he had stopped and beating like a giant woodpecker upon the top board had shouted at George Willard, condemning his tendency to be too much influenced by the people about him. "You are destroying yourself," he cried. "You have the inclination to be alone and to dream and you are afraid of dreams. You want to be like others in town here. You hear them talk and you try to imitate them."

On the grassy bank Wing Biddlebaum had tried again to

drive his point home. His voice became soft and reminiscent, and with a sigh of contentment he launched into a long rambling talk, speaking as one lost in a dream.

Out of the dream Wing Biddlebaum made a picture for George Willard. In the picture men lived again in a kind of pastoral golden age. Across a green open country came clean-limbed young men, some afoot, some mounted upon horses. In crowds the young men came to gather about the feet of an old man who sat beneath a tree in a tiny garden and who talked to them.

Wing Biddlebaum became wholly inspired. For once he forgot the hands. Slowly they stole forth and lay upon George Willard's shoulders. Something new and bold came into the voice that talked. "You must try to forget all you have learned," said the old man. "You must begin to dream. From this time on you must shut your ears to the roaring of the voices."

Pausing in his speech, Wing Biddlebaum looked long and earnestly at George Willard. His eyes glowed. Again he raised the hands to caress the boy and then a look of horror swept over his face.

With a convulsive movement of his body, Wing Biddlebaum sprang to his feet and thrust his hands deep into his trousers pockets. Tears came to his eyes. "I must be getting along home. I can talk no more with you," he said nervously.

Without looking back, the old man had hurried down the hillside and across a meadow, leaving George Willard perplexed and frightened upon the grassy slope. With a shiver of dread the boy arose and went along the road toward town. "I'll not ask him about his hands," he thought, touched by the memory of the terror he had seen in the man's eyes. "There's something wrong, but I don't want to know what it is. His hands have something to do with his fear of me and of everyone."

And George Willard was right. Let us look briefly into the story of the hands. Perhaps our talking of them will arouse the poet who will tell the hidden wonder story of the influence for which the hands were but fluttering pennants of promise.

In his youth Wing Biddlebaum had been a school teacher in

a town in Pennsylvania. He was not then known as Wing Biddlebaum, but went by the less euphonic name of Adolph Myers. As Adolph Myers he was much loved by the boys of his school.

Adolph Myers was meant by nature to be a teacher of youth. He was one of those rare, little-understood men who rule by a power so gentle that it passes as a lovable weakness. In their feeling for the boys under their charge such men are not unlike the finer sort of women in their love of men.

And yet that is but crudely stated. It needs the poet there. With the boys of his school, Adolph Myers had walked in the evening or had sat talking until dusk upon the schoolhouse steps lost in a kind of dream. Here and there went his hands, caressing the shoulders of the boys, playing about the tousled heads. As he talked his voice became soft and musical. There was a caress in that also. In a way the voice and the hands, the stroking of the shoulders and the touching of the hair was a part of the schoolmaster's effort to carry a dream into the young minds. By the caress that was in his fingers he expressed himself. He was one of those men in whom the force that creates life is diffused, not centralized. Under the caress of his hands doubt and disbelief went out of the minds of the boys and they began also to dream.

And then the tragedy. A half-witted boy of the school became enamored of the young master. In his bed at night he imagined unspeakable things and in the morning went forth to tell his dreams as facts. Strange, hideous accusations fell from his loose-hung lips. Through the Pennsylvania town went a shiver. Hidden, shadowy doubts that had been in men's minds concerning Adolph Myers were galvanized into beliefs.

The tragedy did not linger. Trembling lads were jerked out of bed and questioned. "He put his arms about me," said one. "His fingers were always playing in my hair," said another.

One afternoon a man of the town, Henry Bradford, who kept a saloon, came to the schoolhouse door. Calling Adolph Myers into the school yard he began to beat him with his fists. As his hard knuckles beat down into the frightened face of the schoolmaster, his wrath became more and more terrible. Screaming with dismay, the children ran here and there like disturbed insects. "I'll teach you to put your hands on my boy, you beast," roared the saloon keeper, who, tired of beating the master, had begun to kick him about the yard.

Adolph Myers was driven from the Pennsylvania town in the night. With lanterns in their hands a dozen men came to the door of the house where he lived alone and commanded that he dress and come forth. It was raining and one of the men had a rope in his hands. They had intended to hang the schoolmaster, but something in his figure, so small, white, and pitiful, touched their hearts and they let him escape. As he ran away into the darkness they repented of their weakness and ran after him, swearing and throwing sticks and great balls of soft mud at the figure that screamed and ran faster and faster into the darkness.

For twenty years Adolph Myers had lived alone in Winesburg. He was but forty but looked sixty-five. The name of Biddlebaum he got from a box of goods seen at a freight station as he hurried through an eastern Ohio town. He had an aunt in Winesburg, a black-toothed old woman who raised chickens, and with her he lived until she died. He had been ill for a year after the experience in Pennsylvania, and after his recovery worked as a day laborer in the fields, going timidly about and striving to conceal his hands. Although he did not understand what had happened he felt that the hands must be to blame. Again and again the fathers of the boys had talked of the hands. "Keep your hands to yourself," the saloon keeper had roared, dancing with fury in the schoolhouse yard.

Upon the veranda of his house by the ravine, Wing Biddlebaum continued to walk up and down until the sun had disappeared and the road beyond the field was lost in the grey shadows. Going into his house he cut slices of bread and spread honey upon them. When the rumble of the evening train that took away the express cars loaded with the day's harvest of berries had passed and restored the silence of the summer night, he went again to walk upon the veranda. In the darkness he could not see the hands and they became quiet. Although he still hungered for the presence of the boy, who was the medium through which he expressed his love of man, the hunger became again a part of his loneliness and his waiting. Lighting a lamp, Wing Biddlebaum washed the few dishes soiled by his simple meal and, setting up a folding cot by the screen door that led to the porch, prepared to undress for the night. A few stray white bread crumbs lay on the cleanly washed floor by the table; putting the lamp upon a low stool he began to pick up the crumbs, carrying them to his mouth one by one with unbelievable rapidity. In the dense blotch of light beneath the table, the kneeling figure looked like a priest engaged in some service of his church. The nervous expressive fingers, flashing in and out of the light, might well have been mistaken for the fingers of the devotee going swiftly through decade after decade of his rosary.

MATEI CARAGIALE

REMEMBER

This is a dreadful incident.
—Memoirs of the Bal-Mabille

There are dreams which we imagine ourselves to have lived through somehow, somewhere, just as there are actual experiences of which we ask ourselves whether they were not in fact dreams. I was thinking of this the other evening as I browsed through my papers to see which of them could be burned—paper is such a bother!—and thereby came across a letter which awakened in me the memory of an extraordinary incident, one so strange that were it not seven years since it occurred, doubts would beset me, and I should believe myself in reality only to have dreamed it, or a long time before to have read or heard of it.

It was in the year 1907. Having withstood a severe illness in Bucharest, I had returned to Berlin. My convalescence made slow progress and required careful nursing. Before my departure the doctor enjoined me to avoid the slightest emotional shock. The poor dear! Smiling, I shrugged my shoulders and told him he need trouble himself no further.

After a two-year banishment I saw Berlin once more. For

Berlin I have such a great weakness that even the saddest circumstances could not alter my pleasure in returning. I found the city just as I had left it: wherever once glanced, there were cascades of flowers. But it had never appeared to me as beautiful as in those first days of June.

Still, it was no longer possible to roam, to wander through the city as before. I tired rapidly, and exhaustion could easily have led to a relapse of my illness. I thus surrendered to the necessity of remaining at home for a time—a sacrifice partially compensated by the lovely baroque music sounding through the house from morning until night. Drifting in this sweet narcosis, billowed by miraculous harmonies, I let my dream freely ascend and then melt away, while with half-closed eyes I watched rainbows flutter through the fine mist of the fountain in the broad, gardenlike square. The gentle breath of sunset swayed the purpled clusters of rambling roses that twined about the front terrace of the house, drifting their scent toward me. As evening lent the shadows life, a shudder glided mysteriously across the mirror. This was the hour I awaited in order to delight in the loveliest corner of the garden, a little wooded area that had remained untouched in the middle of the city—a few ancient, dark trees with dense foliage that were worthy of serving as models to the most celebrated masters of the painterly arts.

And indeed I encountered them again in the Kaiser-Friedrich Museum, in a painting by Ruysdael: the same bushy crowns shadowed a ruined castle beside a waterfall. Never was I able to pass it without pausing a while. As I gazed at the painting, my thoughts were irresistibly drawn to a small section of blue-gray sky. I was born with the dregs of ancient superstition, a heathenish-pious love for old trees. To them I owe noble and earnest impulses, for I scarcely believe that in the entire world there is a human voice or an artful melody which could move me more deeply than the mysterious rustling the evening wind awakens in their leaves. And yet the painted tree enchanted me even more than the real ones, for this little melancholy landscape seemed a reflection of my soul.

I used to go to the museum quite frequently. However

deeply engaged I might be in viewing the pictures, the other visitors, often so interesting, by no means escaped notice, and among them a young man drew my particular attention; he never failed to appear or to catch people's eyes, for one could well think that with the aid of a magician he had stepped out of one of the antique frames. Could there be anything more delightful for someone who partakes devoutly in the mystery of the past than to encounter an image from the past in actual flesh and blood? Two years before, in the French gallery of the museum, I had seen a lady in the process of copying Mignard's portrait of Maria Mancini, and she so conspicuously resembled the model one could have thought she painted her own face while gazing into a mirror, to which she merely added the appropriate coiffure.

Just so did the young man resemble some of those youthful lords whose glances, hands and smiles have been made immortal by Van Dyck and, after him, by Van der Faes—"some" of those lords, I say, because they are almost all alike. In times past each epoch stamped with the same bearing if not precisely the same appearance those who were so closely and multiply related, dwelling side by side in crowded castles, wearing the same clothing, and practicing the same customs. But it also happens, in turn, that where one least expects it, beings appear whose true resemblance one must seek elsewhere, in other countries, among other peoples, in other centuries, without conjecturing the slightest kinship with those from whom they are so separated by the chasms of time and ancestry.

Every surmise about the young man's origin was thus futile; nonetheless, I made all sorts of reflections about his person, which in manner was truly extraordinary, peculiar, so that it invited particular attention. I was intrigued by his cool, haughty bearing; handsome as a god, he moved solitarily through life, imperturbable, his head held proudly. From the beginning I took him to be one of those exceptional creatures, one of those oddities of nature, which have always attracted me. And I saw him almost daily, for the museum was not the only place I encountered him. During my strolls through the town, which I had taken up again, I used to rest for a while in a certain tavern, in order not to become fatigued; and there one could sample the finest wares of an old Dutch distillery. After Ruysdael, then, a little Van Brouwer and Van der Hooch. Nowhere else did I recuperate better than in that narrow, rather dark room, which would have done honor to any bourgeois household, richly clad with fumed oak half-way up the wall, where the projecting panels formed a continuous shelf on which Delft pots and pitchers stood. What marvelous moments have I passed there!

Beside me, on the sole bench in this inviting but by day rather lonely tavern, the youth with the face that seemed cut from an old portrait calmly sipped the sweetest and most aromatic drinks; they resembled liquified jewels, and through their pungent spices from Java or the Antilles conjured up exotic dream images, awakened wanderlust. There, so I fancied, we were no longer strangers; and remarkably, after we had become acquainted, we admitted to each other that it seemed to us both as though we had sat together in a room similar to this long before.

It would not have seemed plausible to me that we should precisely befriend each other, for I felt I was not unjustified in assigning him to a thoroughly different world than my own. It sprang to one's eyes: the difference between a simple wildflower and an exotic greenhouse blossom. Whether it had taken centuries for a noble race, before its final decline, to produce such a radiant flowering, in some proud, blue-blooded revival of the ideal type, or whether it was only a happy accident—more could not in any case have been achieved. Granted, it also required certain daily exertions for this ornament of mankind to present himself in utmost beauty, for I had not had the privilege of seeing so much make-up even on a woman. Should I therefore have taken him for one of those buffoons with unnatural preferences whose numbers seem everywhere to have increased of late in such deplorable proportions? No, that I could not believe, for even as a disturbing smile flitted across the lips of this painted doll, the eyes under their severe, penciled brows had that innocent clarity which gleams only beneath the lids of children and heroes.

He was also very young—twenty years old at most. What doesn't one close his eyes to at this age—particularly among the rich? The fact that it need not provide for the dawning day alters the human mind, since the feeling of responsibility is crippled; wealth makes soft and brings about a continuous state of pleasant delirium that insists on extraordinary pleasures and new, stimulating experiences. To this sort of passionless and blasé mortal, free of petty prejudice, belonged my new acquaintance, who doubtlessly had quite sufficient means at his disposal. Yet he seemed to live apart from the social whirl—indeed, completely outside society. There were yet more individuals like him in Berlin, but one rarely caught sight of them—by chance, perhaps, on a gallop through the morning mist, or in the evening as they hurried to their glittering amusements. I could only imagine him to be a resident of one of the stately avenues to the west, bordering on the royal Tiergarten and lined with magnificent villas, where money has succeeded to a notable degree in re-creating paradise on earth. So I imagined him, leafing with slender fingers through luxuriously bound books, in the voluptuous solitude of chambers with heavy mirrors and a wilting profusion of exotic flowers. Did not the very vision of such decor recall the stimulating fragrance that he used to diffuse about himself, so intoxicating that even while awake one glided into a dream?

Aubrey de Vere. When I think of him . . . One day we conversed with each other as though we were old acquaintances. His Norman name—to this day I do not know if it was the real one—did not seem strange to me, as it was the family title of the dissolute Earls of Oxford, which after they died out was assumed by the Stuarts of collateral descent, the Dukes of Saint-Albans, and joined to that of Beauclerk. Should he be descended from such ancestors, they could not have done him more honor than he to them. Though English to the marrow of his bones, in conversation he availed himself of French, and a French so perfect as has seldom been granted me to hear. His clear, supple voice with its rich *timbre* permitted the French language to become more than a means of communication; it was an accessory of seduction. When I heard who he was, I understood him at once in all matters. The bearing to which Beau Brummel had given the stamp of his name lived on in

Aubrey de Vere in full splendor. Even the fact that he found such pleasure in painting his face could now be explained. Were not the first inhabitants of Albion, as history records, painted blue from head to foot? This color was particularly dear to my new friend, who wore it in his very body, in his eyes and under the transparent skin of his hands, on which seven rings glittered, as alike as brothers—seven Ceylon sapphires. Together with an ornate bracelet and that unforgettable perfume with the fragrance of red carnations, these were the sole things to which he remained constant; otherwise, so far as his clothing was concerned, I hardly know if I saw him in the same suit twice. But this entire meticulous outfit was in his case only part of a whole of utmost perfection and noblest harmony. Aubrey de Vere possessed a wonderfully organized mind and a scintillating spirit; he would have done honor to the most exclusive club and would not have felt ill at ease in the company of scholars, for when he admitted having his linen washed in London, he appended that in the Eighteenth Century the young noblemen of Paris dispatched theirs to Flanders to be washed, and those of Bordeaux to Curaçao. He chatted in this way about everything, with analogies from the past, with allusions and enchanting details, and it often happened that he related his voyages in the ancient landscapes of the East, or to the lost islands of the Pacific Ocean, where spring reigns eternally. This much I could ascertain about his life: that in traveling continents and oceans he had seen much, that he had read even more—if not perhaps too much for his age, for it was entirely possible that he mingled what he had witnessed with what he had read, or that he regarded what he had truly seen through the distorting lenses of his books; this, combined with his wealth, had turned his head, although by nature his judgment seemed clear and cool. Thus, for example, I believed him to be occupied with daring occult researches, for which quite apart from a unique congenital inclination, he was also qualified through the most astonishing training. He seemed to have had even more connection with the spirits than with the living, for in his discourses human beings were never mentioned.

The occasions and the circumstances of undertaking such

wonderful journeys at such an early age were never explained, no more than who or what he was, where he came from, whether he had parents, relatives or friends, where he lived, at least—nothing, absolutely nothing. What self-control for a young man, to withhold everything in this manner without ever betraying himself! Since he revealed nothing, I inquired even less, and I assumed that precisely this was the reason for our forming a friendship. And even if we had continued to meet for an eternity, sooner would a remark have escaped from him than a question from me. Basically it was not important to me to learn anything. What concern was it of mine? By chance I saw him once—without his becoming aware of me—choosing flowers for four- or five-hundred marks, carnations and rare orchids; it seemed to me a dreadful extravagance. As I knew the saleswoman, it would only have been necessary to step in after he had left and purchase a *boutonnière* in order to ascertain where he had sent them, and in such a way, following the track, to make further inquiries. But to what purpose? It might well have been that the single-minded insistence with which he screened his brief past and his daily life served a particular purpose. There was (and I repeat it) such pride in his eyes; indifferent to everything that occurred on this earth, lost in the depths of a dream world, they would have dispersed the faintest shadows of mistrust or accusation. Still, it did not escape me that he was sometimes about to add something, but instantly thought better of it and swallowed his words. Did he then actually blush under his make-up, did his eyes become wreathed in sadness, as it appeared to me then, when he seemed for a brief instant to reveal some concealed misery? I cannot swear to it; however, what I know is that while he talked his deepening glance fixed itself long and wistfully on the ever-present rings, as though the jewels enclosed the secret of his life and mirrored in their clear blue ice all his thoughts and all his memories.

After some time, without our friendly relations taking intimate shape, we saw each other more frequently—sometimes in the morning, most often in the afternoon, never at night—never. Because it was hot, we had given up the Dutch tavern, and met in the Gruenwald on the terrace of a café near a little pine grove; it was an idyllic terrace, overgrown with roses of all sorts and colors, whose petals whirled into our glasses with the merest breath of wind. He always arrived without haste and without delay. Once, however, I awaited him without avail until five o'clock. When I returned home I found a letter in which he briefly excused himself for his absence, and which was signed *Sir* Aubrey de Vere. I carefully examined the commanding handwriting with its bold letters, as well as the blue seal: it showed a reclining sphinx in the center of a sash like that which adorns the British coat of arms. On the sash I read the word *Remember.*

As heraldist I was not satisfied; I had expected a proper coat of arms, not a simple emblem. After this letter Sir Aubrey gave no further sign of life. This was not to be wondered at: steaming, humid air pressed upon the city, making it seem a vast spawning-ground of indignity and baseness. One could only go out in the evening, when Sir Aubrey was unaccustomed to show himself. And yet the nights were so lovely that I could only with difficulty make the decision to return home. It was my custom to wander the city until quite late in the evening, and on one such occasion, around midnight, I had a remarkable encounter in a lonely *allée* of the Tiergarten.

Past me there moved a stately woman in a slim black sequined dress, with red hair cascading from beneath her feathered hat—a slender, bony woman with narrow hips and flat bosom. She strode along stiff as a corpse commanded by some strange power alien to its own will and driven or drawn to a mysterious nocturnal rendezvous. I scarcely know why, but from the very beginning I did not believe this to be a woman like every other, even before I seemed to recognize something familiar in her great, staring eyes, that gazed so intensely inward, and in the features of her heavily painted face. But still I had doubts. Could it be mere imagination that led me to see seven Ceylon sapphires smirking on the long-fingered hand? Stunned, I remained there, overpowered by an unclear feeling in which astonishment, disgust and fear played equal roles; then, drinking in the familiar perfume, the scent of red carnations, I resolved to follow. But it was too late; I had lost her. At the end of the *allée* hansom cabs waited; apparently the figure had entered one of them and departed.

As an old Berliner it would have been childish to permit myself to be overwhelmed by astonishment. After all, I had seen everything already! On the other hand, a vulgar curiosity drove me to lie in wait for several evenings. To no purpose. Meanwhile, the heat became ever more unbearable. On the day before the evening of which I shall now speak, people dropped in the street like flies.

It was a velvety and leaden night in which the sluggish breath of a hot wind unavailingly sought to disperse the clouds of steam that thickened the air. On the horizon flashed brief summer lightning, the woods and the joyless gardens kept silence as though an evil magic had caused them to petrify; it stank of the clandestine, of sin and despair. I proceeded only with great difficulty into the darkness which had stuffed the *allées* as with cotton-wadding, for again and again, overwhelmed by faintness, I had to halt. At the intersection where Berlin's Fountain of Roland is situated, in the glaring light that blinded me as I emerged from the darkness, I suddenly stood before Sir Aubrey—a fact which, as I observed him more closely, did not entirely give me pleasure.

Not so much because this time he had overstepped all bounds. One may think as he pleases: a man does not leave the house adorned in such a manner. The powder with which he had veneered his face was blue, the lips and the holes in his nose were tinted violet, his hair powdered with gold dust, and broad, blue-black circles were drawn around his eyes, giving him the appearance of a *chanteuse* or a dance-hall girl. Otherwise, he was faultlessly dressed, wearing a blue frock-coat under a light summer cape and with an orchid in his buttonhole; neither the bracelet nor the rings on his fingers were missing. But he seemed changed, appeared just as agitated and restless as I was sluggish and fatigued. Contrary to custom, he spoke precipitantly and insecurely, entreating me to remain with him—he, who belonged to those people who, despite their politeness, let it be understood that it requires immense sacrifice to bring themselves to be together with someone. Further still, he actually took my arm and demanded I reverse my steps. I felt his entire body trembling as in a chill and saw that his eyes, glassy as those of the red-haired woman, either stared vacantly into space or watered with exhaustion and desperation. Just as unbelievable as it had seemed to me that the passing apparition was a woman, so now I was incapable of believing that this creature dragging me into the darkness was a man. We walked silently along the edge of the wood, I depressed and concerned not to look peevish, he with a smile on his lips, gazing in the dim light at his blue jewels, to which, perhaps, clandestine memories were coupled, and to which he seemed to dedicate his final thoughts, passionately and yearningly. We moved along in silence until we reached the bridge over the canal where the Kurfürstendamm begins. There he stopped and detached himself from my arm.

Now I had quite another person facing me, one completely different than before. Could it be that his gems possessed secret powers? Slowly he had come to himself once more, had straightened his shoulders, held his head high again, and stood there stiff, cold and proud—very, very proud. The features of his elongated face now seemed pointed, the delicate blue of his eyes were transformed with the hard, sparkling glints of steel, and the smile on his narrow lips had become ghastly. With his chalky pallor and golden hair Sir Aubrey at that moment no longer looked earthly, more closely resembling a seraph or an archangel than a human being. He remained there a while as if turned to stone and his eyes bored inquisitively into the darkness, through which he suddenly slashed with his white gloves as though he wished to drive away a ghost.

"Such a strange night," he said earnestly. "Such nights are more to be feared than drunkenness; the warm wind permits dangerous fevers to spread. Stendhal writes that when a certain wind blows in Trastevere, murders occur in Rome.

"You too must feel exhausted by this humidity," he continued. "You will hopefully do me the pleasure of having something to eat with me, a trout or two and a bottle of Rhine wine, so that we may regain a little of our strength. However, you must permit that I leave you for a short while alone . . ." And he drew out his watch, a platinum blossom sprinkled with a dew of minute blue gems. "You will wait for me, won't you? It may take a little while, perhaps longer than a quarter of an hour, certainly less than half. Meanwhile, have a bit of a stroll, we shall meet here at the bridge, and whoever comes first will wait for the other." He extended me his hand, which was ice-cold, tipped his hat and turned away. I did as I was told and moved again in the direction of the woods; nearby stand the most beautiful trees one can imagine, giants from the age of the Druids, so tall and densely foliaged that at first glance one might think he were in another world. After the passage of a quarter-hour and before a half-hour had passed, I returned to the bridge but did not find my companion there. Since a delay, like all deficiencies, initially seemed unbearable, I dawdled again along the embankment, without distancing myself too far from our meeting place.

The embankment was empty of people, the houses blind. Everywhere the windows were black, yet some stood open so that inside one made out a somber glint of quicksilver leering through the darkness from the faces of mirrors. A sole upper window was illuminated as though by a mesh of faint beams, the window of a gorgeously ostentatious room in which a lamp glowed on the corner of an armoire—a lamp whose shade of green enamel permitted only a dim and poisonous light to shimmer through, the sort of light that, according to ancient accounts of witches, is favorable to the evil spirits that haunt at midnight.

I remained standing there, and my gaze remained fixed for a long while on this window. Oh, the magic of lighted windows by night. Who would dare seek to express this mystery after having read the novellas of Barbey d'Aurevilly! But in his immortal story *Le rideau cramoisi* it is a carmine-red drapery, in other, later, and so quickly forgotten works it is windows of I no longer know which colors; at my window there were neither draperies nor panes of glass, and yet through the greenish haze one could make out nothing but exquisite ornaments and mirrors that seemed hung with black crepe.

Whether some connection existed between that window which—I need only close my eyes—appears to me exactly as it was then, and what occurred on that evening, I can only surmise, not know. I returned to the bridge with as little success as the first time: of my friend, not a trace. Prepared for a longer wait than before, I leaned against the cast-iron railing close to the bank, removed the hat from my aching head, and surrendered totally to the wondrous beauty of the night.

I shall never forget it. And I must say that I have never experienced one lovelier—I who appreciate the night as no other, and who have loved it as one cannot love the day, with ardor and inexorable desire. My timid spirit, victim of an undefined discord, typically appears to be dozing off, trembling, and does not awaken to full life before the last flames of the departing day are extinguished; as the veils of night gather more and more thickly, I feel myself newborn, feel more deeply my own being, belong more to myself. Had my pecuniary means permitted me to fashion my living conditions differently, I would possibly not have caught sight of the sunlight for years. Oh, had it not been night, I would not have waited for Sir Aubrey—no! Basically it was of no consequence to me to see him ever again. I remained because I should not in any case have returned home, because I would have lingered there, roving about in the shadows under the tall, rustling trees, where one can imagine solitude to be boundless. Yet I could not forgive Sir Aubrey for keeping me awaiting, that I should wait for him while he partook of who knows what pleasures in this warm, stimulating night—perhaps, even, by that hazy greenish light, in the arms of some woman whose beauty might have seemed to him the counterpart to his own. Also, I entertained another suspicion: perhaps he had gone in order to prepare for a later hour the meeting of some occult circle, and had thereby forgotten the world of the living. However it might have been, I need not aggravate myself. With elbows propped against the railing, head cradled in my hands, I gave myself over to my meditations. Beneath me glided the broad, oily planes of the sluggish water, above which vapors mingled together like transparent gauze. The canal was somber. What a difference! By day this district presents a most charming appearance: the branches of the trees lean their crowns together in sisterly affection across the canal, which mirrors the delicate, fresh green of the light and restless foliage. Along this course glide the corpses of the drowned. I recall that on a brilliant April morning in the year 1905, the water bore a bride in her wedding dress. Moreover, in Berlin one sings a jolly song that begins, "A corpse is swimming in the Landwehr canal."

A fresh breeze cooled my forehead and awakened me from my daze. How much time had passed since I had been standing there I could not judge—I had, all undisturbed, dozed off—and could not remember having heard the Kaiser Wilhelm Memorial Church sound the time, and yet it must have sounded more than once. As I lifted my head from my hands, drunk with sleep, and rubbed my eyes, the row of houses took shape against the sky, which had become ash gray. The wind blew chilly, and the trees had commenced to sigh. I put on my hat, which I found lying on the pavement where it had fallen from my head, and again took a few steps along the embankment, in order to view once more the mysterious light. But it was extinguished. At last I determined to return home, for large drops of rain had begun to fall, and the day was dawning.

As a true night-owl I hate the dawn. Without considering that a chill could be harmful to me, I hurried through the empty streets without seeking shelter, pursued by the diffuse light that, weaving together with the rain, trickled from the gloomy sky, while from time to time a grim north wind assailed me. When I reached home, soaked to the skin, I was terribly angry, but that did not hinder my sleeping dreamlessly until noon.

Outside, the rainy weather had set in with a vengeance, and persisted for an entire week, only now and then pausing briefly in order to stream down with renewed force. Somehow I passed the time, and my thoughts often reverted to the events of that curious night. Whenever the postman came, I rushed out to see if he had anything for me. Obviously, I awaited a few lines from Sir Aubrey—which would have been only proper on his part, and I found no explanation for the fact that neither his commanding handwriting nor the seal with the sphinx was to be seen on the dampened envelopes.

On the eve of a holiday the bad weather decided to make peace. Not entirely trusting it, I began my promenade somewhat later. The diffuse light on the horizon signaled more rain. That sweet, mild evening was flooded with blue—such a deep, liquid blue that one might have imagined the city to be sunk in the mysterious depths of the sea. The streets teemed with people. The zest for life, the enchanting awareness of being able to relish the fruits of existence, was mirrored in every face, beamed from the lively, excited eyes, and lent the beauty of the women a particular gloss. The fantasy transported me to the most distant past, and I sought to picture how it might have been on such evenings in the great cities of antiquity, in Babylon, Palmyra, Alexandria, Byzantium. Thus, mingling dream and reality, I was carried along by the stream of people to the bridge over the canal where I had awaited Sir Aubrey for so many hours.

The charm of the place seemed heightened and perfected by the snow-white feathering of swans which, as though purposely, sailed the water in this blue hour. I did not cross the bridge, but entered a beer-garden nearby. As I waited for my food, my glance fell on a newspaper, and thus I learned only then what the whole town had been talking about for two full days.

In Charlottenburg, where the waters churn together as the River Spree reclaims the canal, a corpse had been fished out tightly buttoned up in a coat; it was that of a blond, slender, elegantly dressed young man in evening clothes with all the customary accessories, including gloves on his hands, but barefooted.

The young man had been murdered only a short time before. He bore a deep wound on the left side of his chest. The blow was delivered with such force that the weapon—a thin, flexible blade—had broken off and a piece remained lodged in the wound.

A small fortune in bank notes and gold had been found on the victim, separate and apart from the value of his jewelry, which he wore in wild profusion, each piece richly inlaid with Ceylon sapphires—exclusively with Ceylon sapphires. Otherwise, nothing printed or written which could have thrown light on the murder victim—nothing, absolutely nothing. The label with the tailor's name had been torn out of the suit and the lid of the pocketwatch with the goldsmith's monogram had been removed. The face of the corpse was no longer recognizable, for it had been drenched with acid, which had eaten the flesh away to the very bone.

Such was the end to which Sir Aubrey was destined. It should have been a better or at least a later end, one that occurred after my departure, for I am really not certain which one of us in that moment was the more pitiable. What I endured from the moment I grasped the identity of the corpse, what I suffered—that I hardly need say. And yet it was nothing in comparison to that which might have happened to me. *Remember?*—yes, I believe so. One says that fear is blue; I have experienced it in all colors, have passed through hell; have descended into its bottomless depths, have scaled its jagged heights, the peaks of horror lost in the clouds of madness, and it is a miracle that I did not succumb completely to insanity. I was the sole being in whose company Sir Aubrey had let himself be seen by the light of day; in the Dutch tavern, on the Grunewald terrace, we must have passed for inseparable friends; to be sure, no one would have believed that I—poor I—who seemed so attached to the young man, was the one who knew least of all—indeed, less than nothing. Must this not have aroused the suspicion that I was involved in the violent death of the unknown man? I perceived how the tightly woven net of the rigorous police closed secretly around me, saw myself seized, innocently indicted, hopelessly lost like the pitiable Joseph Lesurques, paying the penalty for another's crime. In the end, I held myself for guilty—and was I not really so, since I had made friends with a person like Sir Aubrey? At that moment it became absolutely clear to me how difficult life is in a strange country, among strangers. Thus, my first thought was to leave Berlin at once and flee to my native land. At night I could not close my eyes, the darkness now depressed me, and I greeted the dawn like a redemption. When it became light, calm and confidence returned. I cast away thoughts of departure, unpacked my things, packed them again in the evening, and swore to myself by all means to depart on the following morning—and in this manner passed many days, black days, and whenever I think back on them, even now, the distant reflection of the hideous fear of that time flares up in brief shudders, and then at the slightest provocation my heart begins to flutter like a wounded bird. But like all human feelings—with the exception of hatred—fear pales and evaporates with time. At this point I should mention that my deep agitation could not be observed externally; my everyday life had altered in no respect, and I sensed no desire to take anyone into my confidence about these consuming agonies, just as I held it to be inappropriate to report to the responsible authorities what I knew of Sir Aubrey or, better, what I did not know. Later I visited the Dutch tavern, and no one inquired after my former companion, no more than at the Grunewald terrace. Everywhere the same reticence. I read each and every newspaper and became almost annoyed—not a single line in which the grisly discovery was mentioned. Apparently nothing had been ascertained. The secret was preserved intact by the sphinx.

Otherwise, from my point of view Sir Aubrey's gruesome end bore no more significance than an everyday occurrence. What would have been the point of pressing my respectful regret so far that I mourned the unknown friend like a Marcellus? Because he was young and handsome? Perhaps he was not so young as he appeared. There are people whose appearance deceives with respect to age, and so far as beauty is concerned, a special explanation does not seem superfluous. I had not found Sir Aubrey's appearance in itself so beautiful as his resemblance to figures long since buried in the dust of centuries; I found him handsome because an image of bygone times found life again in him, because the cherished past was resurrected for me—the forever vanished past. Therefore, I also resisted the temptation to visit the morgue and view under glass that which had been Aubrey de Vere; since the appearance death lends frequently extinguishes that of life, it would have been a pity to permit the image of my memory to be destroyed—that which, animated, seemed cut from an old picture frame. It was important to me that he remain as I had known him, so much resembling those handsome lords at Whitehall Palace who indulged in the wildest pleasures with Killigrew and Rochester, with Barbara Villiers and Nell Gwynn, and who, enveloped in velvet and silk, adorned with lace and ribbons, clutching roses or stroking noble hounds, smiling and striking a proud pose, were captured on canvas by Sir Lely. Still, even more than his outer appearance I treasured irrepressibly certain inner impulses and ideas that suddenly flashed in his conversation, the equal of which I have never witnessed from others or ever found in writing. On his distant voyages this unique creature had developed the capacity to perceive the coming of a storm at sea through the shuddering of the leaves of the date palm; he was able to progress into unexplored distances, which were reflected in his clear, sapphire-colored eyes; he could unriddle mysteries that were revealed only to the chosen, and never penetrated by those who out of mere vocation vainly dedicate their lives, their eye-sight and their minds to dead letters. And all that—youth, beauty and intelligence—must end in the murky waters of a canal.

At last came the day of my departure. Autumn had begun, but not the russet autumn of the south, like a Bacchus draped with a leopard-skin, grapes and fruit in his coppery hair, but the pallid autumn of the lands of rye and beer, with faded sky and a low-hanging sun that drags itself feebly to the horizon. Recently I had cocooned myself in the house; I read voraciously, I read because music was no longer being played and because there was nothing more to see through the window, though it remained open until late in the evening. The fountain no longer flung crystal sprays into the air, the roses on the terrace before the house had lost their petals, and the pretty grove of old trees that might have been painted by Ruysdael had fallen to the axe.

Seven years have passed since then. As if it were yesterday, as if it had never been at all. As if it were yesterday because I have a good memory; as if it had never been, because I make no cult of my memories. I have often thought back on the hideous drama whose blind and invisible witness I may have been on that night of terror and agitation. What actually happened; what really took place there, I have never inquired, for it was no longer important to know—quite the contrary. And the proof of that: recently, when I could have learned the truth, I refused.

Bad weather had caught me in a nightclub in Bucharest, and an acquaintance from my schooldays joined my table; I had also had a distant glimpse of him in Berlin, where apparently he had been studying something or other. Endlessly garrulous, with his droll manner he set my head spinning with all kinds of trivialities, stories from the newspapers, anecdotes about landladies' daughters and chambermaids—all quite elevating themes. What a difference between the way in which I experienced Berlin and the way it had been seen by this man who sat facing me and who took not a little pride in his cheap vulgarity. But for what reason did there awaken on this evening, vivid as never before, the memory of Sir Aubrey, why did the features of Berlin nights with their strange encounters rise so persistently before me? Were the bitter vapors of schnapps to blame, which came from that old and celebrated distillery? No, it was something other. More intoxicating than the drink was the spicy scent of carnations which drifted toward me from the woman at the adjoining table. The same scent that had wafted from the young man with the blue jewels, the scent that once had trailed behind a red-haired woman in a lonely *allée* of the Tiergarten. And I saw her and him and the window with the diffused light once more before me, everything magically vivid. And I surrendered to a hitherto unconscious urge to relate the story of Sir Aubrey de Vere.

I was listened to attentively. I only noted how, from time to time, a slight smile played over the lips of my acquaintance. When I closed with the finding of the corpse, he asked me whether this was the entire story. I nodded. "Then I will tell you the sequel," he went on, "there was a great fuss, the whole matter was immediately covered up, but one could not prevent the truth leaking out. You'll hear the most unbelievable things, just listen . . ."

I cut him off: "I want to know nothing, nothing." And while

he looked at me in astonishment, scarcely knowing what to think, I gave the last word particular emphasis by repeating it several times. "It may seem strange to you," I explained, "but to my mind the beauty of a story consists only in that which remains mysterious; when this is revealed, I find it deprived of all its magic. Circumstances desired that I encounter in my life the fragment of a novel that satisfied my yearning for an endless mystery. Why should I let you spoil that?"

Expressing myself in such a way, I was not precisely lying; and yet behind this method of regarding things—somewhat frivolous, rather literary—something higher was concealed, a noble thought that determined me to silence my acquaintance, and I doubt whether, if I had divulged the same to him, he would have been capable of grasping it. Just as I had not desired to destroy for myself the fair image of his outer appearance by viewing the disfigured face of the poor young man, so I also wished to learn nothing about him, out of fear there might be something that could affect the memory of his rare spiritual essence. May this too remain beautiful, unblemished by the shadows of secrecy and arrogance; may Sir Aubrey de Vere in all things so remain as it pleased me to see him, just so—what concern is it of mine how he really was? The sole proof that I actually knew him has now been destroyed; I burned the letter on whose seal the smiling sphinx was encircled by the word *Remember*. Remember?—yes, of course, I shall not forget; but since the years dim certain old memories and permit them to float on the boundary between reality and fancy, if I should reach an advanced age, it may later seem that this entire occurrence was merely a dream, or a story I read somewhere, or that someone told me a long while ago.

—Translated by
David Galloway and
Christian Sabisch

WILLEM de MERODE

GANYMEDE

His beauty had reached its fullest bloom.
One more day and the timidity of youth
Would grow into the dark daring of the man,
His taut limbs on fire with yearning.
But not yet: a quivering glow
Now silver, then a tint of gold,
Then clear and pure, then deep and purple-red,
When he turned and walked, or danced or lay,
Matched the rhythmic quiver of his breathing,
Flowing softly or drawn in quickened gasps,
When hot desire with painful throb made audible
His trembling heart's vibration and with its pulse
His seething blood was swelled to soothing sleep.
And all the tenderness of awaking youth,
Shy and fleeting as the morning dew
Destroyed by the sun in adoration,
Shone dazzingly in Zeus's brilliant light.
The gods hold dear that class of mortal boys;
Their splendor loves to pair with such dark nakedness.
So Zeus—He saw the sweet secrecy
With which the boy each day, body and soul,

Offered sacrifice, as he swept from his clear brow
The dark overflow of hair, as his eye
Lingered dreamily on the sky's blue brightness,
Or (the evening mist veiling his light limbs)
He, become flesh, desirous, quite alone,
Walked through the sadness of a shimmering field.

—Translated by
Ross McGregor

H. H. von W.

THE MARQUIS de SAINT-BRISSAC

One of the most remarkable phenomena that I was shown on Capri was a male personage of indeterminate age who each day precisely at noon ascended all alone the street from the Hotel Quisisana to the piazza, crossed the square with its gleaming white facades, and mounted the great terrace that faces out to sea. Totally muffled up, regardless of the weather, and never without slouch hat and ascot, the singular man stared intensely into the distance through blue-tinted glasses, as though seeking a sailing ship, perhaps a steamer, or a long-awaited fishing bark that was reluctant to show itself. The stranger (for no native could have such an appearance) had something stiff in his bearing, if not to say something lifeless, corpse-like. The glimpse of a grey face that one caught as he moved past resembled the porous stone often used by artists to fake the weathered texture of antique busts. I asked my English friends the name of this extraordinary gentleman and learned to my astonishment that it was the Marquis de Saint-Brissac, a close acquaintance of mine from years before, whom I had lost sight of as a result of an appalling incident. Noting this astonishment, my friends hastened to remark that the Marquis had been resident on the island since the death of his spouse. With this remark their anglo-saxon features hardened somewhat; I knew such was their manner of cutting the conversation short whenever unwelcome questions threatened. I was not to inquire further. As diversion I turned the conversation to the blue spectacles the stranger wore. I surmised that the Marquis had ruined his eyesight in the glaring sunshine. "One says," my friends replied, "he wears glasses in order that no one see that his eyes are almost always filled with tears." Deeply touched, I turned away. I divined the pain of a human being for whom the years signify only an agonizing test—not of his love, but of his patience to bear this existence further.

In the evening, before falling asleep, I recalled that moment of the past which linked me to the Marquis de Saint-Brissac. For the first time, now that the death of the Marquise was actuality, I dared set things to rights whose tragic secret had obliged me to silence. Once more I saw the Marquise in her pale silk robe, as she appeared at one of the last receptions of the late Madame de Vaugirard. I gazed into her wide, gentian-blue eyes, so reminiscent of drawings by Fidus, thickly fringed by delicate lashes. One could only adore and marvel at this exquisite, slender, dark-haired creature who bore the ancient name of Marquise de Saint-Brissac. Her conspicuous reserve only added to her charm; the Marquis was everywhere envied for this treasure. It was rumored that no other woman could approach her for marital virtue and devotion—none, at least, with such spirit and taste. To be sure, it was said that the Marquise derived from humble bourgeois origins, that she came from Alsace. However, she did not precisely live in the world of high society. She frequently accompanied her husband on extended voyages, or assisted him in his scholarly pursuits. A renowned composer and misogynist confessed on his deathbed that she was the only woman he had ever loved, and bequeathed her a priceless collection of original scores by the most famous masters.

I myself was then scarcely more than a boy. Paris seemed to me the radiant center of the European world, and Maria de Saint-Brissac dominated, reigned over this center like an enchantress. Her madonna-like name seemed significant; must she not be mother to all of us, though childless herself? But to an even greater degree she was a comrade; she had an incomparable manner of placing herself at our level, we were smitten by her androgynous appearance, which joined the delicacy of classic beauty (in the sense of the art of the last century) with that almost boyish matter-of-factness common to modern women and to adolescents of both sexes. Now I comprehend her deportment with greater knowledge: I recognize it as the necessary expression of a clandestine arrangement hidden from us all. At the same time, I see in it the tragic prerequisite to the calamitous event in which I was destined to play a part.

We found ourselves at the charming country estate of the Saint-Brissacs, the little Château Monjoie near Reims. The company was not particularly numerous, for the buildings could accommodate only a few guests. The roses blossomed, the grain deepened in color as it ripened. We admired in the distance the Gothic ornamentation that twined about the beautiful towers of the cathedral; these towers ushered in the tranquility of evening, as they sent the rich greeting of their bells resounding through the landscape. Then we normally strolled a little beyond the gate, to breathe deeply the spicy odors of meadow and field. Crickets chirped, the trumpet flowers had already cautiously closed their white and rosy-red blossoms, and the path was bordered with wild sage. The last fleeting farewell of the departing day threw a blush across cloud and sky. The sun had long disappeared. At such an hour I was accustomed to stroll beside Frau von Ebersheide. I was much taken by this young German woman with the noble head of a chevalier, an Italian heart and a Russian temperament. It is not as though I loved her as one perhaps could love a young and tender woman. But her spirit charmed me, her grace enraptured me, her personality enchanted me beyond the possibility of mere physical desire. She was fulfilled by a great friendship, and this friendship had led her here. In her heart she bore a glowing, almost irrepressible attachment to Maria de Saint-Brissac. Such is not a rare occurrence with young maidens, and one also encounters it from time to time among more mature women. The Marquise shrank from the intensity of such feelings, or so it appeared. Her husband could only with difficulty persuade her to extend an invitation to Frau von Ebersheide; it would not have happened at all were it not for certain commercial considerations which were owed Herr von Ebersheide, an influential banker. Under such circumstances it was not surprising that the Marquise shunned the unwanted guest. Who knows but that perhaps she had a subconscious apprehension of the horrors that were to come from this woman.

During the evening stroll my companion often dallied a little behind and confided in me her thoughts, her hopes and wishes. We frequently spoke of the Marquise, and I exhausted myself with advice about how Maria de Saint-Brissac might be converted to friendship. The more Frau von Ebersheide encountered rejection, the more indomitable became her desire to be near her beloved creature, to envelop her in affection. One evening, as the disc of the moon already hung over the dewy fields, my companion told me she had the irresistible urge to see Maria sleeping. "Just think, simply imagine," she said, "Maria's face without eye-shadow, it would be a completely new look—the closed lids framed by curving brows, the dark tresses of hair against her white skin, shifting with each slight movement of her head. It must be an absolute festival when she sleeps!" I tried to talk Frau von Ebersheide out of such ideas, for I found her plan incompatible with the laws of social deportment; but she was not to be influenced and remained firm by her intention. Even my reference to the fact that the Marquise was in the habit of locking her room (often enough had I heard the sound of the key), even this made no impression. "Ah, well, we shall see what fortune brings me," Frau von Ebersheide countered.

A few hours later I sat across from the Marquis at a green baize table in the library. We were both bent over our books and paid no heed to the time. It might have been midnight as we suddenly heard such frightful, desperate screaming that we both blanched and with the greatest haste climbed to the first floor to determine the cause. In the yellow salon adjoining the bed-chamber of the Marquise, we found Frau von Ebersheide lying on the floor in a dreadful state, her body distorted, flinging her hands and feet about and, as it appeared, the victim of nervous hysteria. One of the guests, a medical student at the Sorbonne, was giving her attention, while other members of our small group stood about perplexed, beside themselves; their fantastic nightgowns, the forgotten chignons, dentures and spectacles transformed them into truly fantastic apparitions. Only the Marquise was missing; her door, as we all observed, remained shut, and she might well be lying in a deep sleep. There were numerous conjectures about the condition of the sick woman; it was said that she might be epileptic. Some spoke of hysteria and somnambulation, but no one could say anything more precise about the source of the attack. Before one had the chance to discuss the alarming event properly, the Marquis sent the guests back to their rooms with a few polite but firm words. Nor could I exclude myself therefrom, and thus had to leave Frau von Ebersheide to the medical student and to her fate. Naturally, I pondered over this bizarre incident; my supposition grew increasingly strong that there was some connection between the intended visit of my friend to the Marquise and her inexplicable seizure.

The following day was to confirm this. Frau von Ebersheide kept to her room, the lady of the house remained invisible, and the guests roamed bewilderedly about the park. The Marquis sent for me. I shall never forget his eyes, how they gazed at me in that tragic hour as I entered through the lacquered folding doors into his study. Those eyes disclosed the most indescribable pain, a passionate despair which his bearing sought to conceal. He gestured to a Louis XVI chair (how I still see it, this chair!), we both took our seats and he began: "I have sent for you because I need your assistance. I can, of course, rely on your discretion?" I wordlessly extended him my hand. During the following exchange he endeavored to suppress the trembling in his voice by continuously clearing his throat. "I presume," he said, "that I have your word of honor." I nodded. "Then," he continued, "you shall come to know my secret, and . . ." he hesitated a moment, "the riddle of the preceding night. Frau von Ebersheide is in love with the Marquise, but my wife has always had an aversion to her. Yesterday, if you can imagine such a thing, the lady forces her way into Maria's bed-chamber and there . . ." Here his voice broke, the blood shot to his head. Pearls of sweat stood out on his forehead, and I feared an attack of apoplexy. He gasped for breath, arching out of his chair. I had arisen, stood close beside him, attempted to support him. "Don't trouble yourself," said the Marquis, "it must be said. Oh," and with this he raised his clenched hands, "render me your assistance in this dark hour. You shall learn something which I had sworn would never cross my lips. Frau von Ebersheide looked on Maria, and on such a summer night she was lying naked on her divan, unclothed, only her body . . ."

He fixed me with burning eyes; I was agitated by these remarks but did not grasp their true meaning. In fact, it seemed to me the modesty and decorum of his own feelings had led him to exaggerate. I was about to speak up in order to utter some word of comfort, but a lordly gesture forbade it. "Say nothing," insisted the Marquis, "until you know all! Frau von Ebersheide, the wretch, looked upon that miraculous creature known to the world as the Marquise de Saint-Brissac. She saw that body,"—the Marquis righted himself with the strength, the courage of a wounded general on the field of battle—"that body which is the body of a youth, and not that of a woman." He sank back. Unconsciously, I had raised my hands to ward off the sudden shock. "Do not judge me," said the Marquis, and his voice had lost all melody. "Perhaps you would be right. But I cannot repent. I have loved, and I shall never love again. I owe you the explanation that this young man was named Eugen Maria Krancz, that I made his acquaintance in Germany and that after some initial reluctance he determined to live at my side under the ideal disguise of a *grande dame*—not as a companion, not as a friend, but as a lover. There dwelled in him the soul of a woman, and this soul could have fulfilled itself in no other guise. We were very happy. You know it and the whole world knows it. But now," —his voice broke into sobs—"now Eugen Maria has fled, in order to die. He left a letter for me. 'Poor friend,' he wrote, 'I must fulfill my destiny, as you yours. Now that my secret is broken, I can no longer remain by your side; but without your love I would scarcely know how and where I should live. I choose death, for it is the most dignified course, and a death which will totally obliterate my body and permit no investigation.' In this way Eugen Maria wanted to save me from the venom of evil tongues, and he wanted to spare the name Saint-Brissac this disgrace. Frau Ebersheide will and must remain silent—that is the most important thing—but then, but then," and the Marquis stretched his arms toward me in anguish, "how do we overtake Eugen Maria, how deter him, what can we do? You know the Foreign Minister . . . couldn't you through diplomatic channels . . . he has certainly fled abroad . . ."

I interrupted his agitated outpouring. "Such a course is not possible. It would lead to nothing."

"But you will speak with Frau von Ebersheide?" I promised to do so. We considered many a plan for rescuing Eugen Maria; not one seemed suitable. I was nonetheless so fortunate as to be able to persuade Frau von Ebersheide that the beautiful, naked, boyish form she had seen was merely an hallucination produced by nervous illness. The broken and desperate Marquis was unspeakably grateful to me. We let it be known that the Marquise had suddenly been taken seriously ill; the guests departed the house within hours. Furthermore, almost no one appeared for the unavoidable comedy of a burial without a corpse, for all feared the hideously contagious sickness which had apparently spirited its victim away so speedily. These circumstances, combined with the genuine grief of the chatelain, prevented discovery. The family doctor had been taken somewhat into confidence, without really telling him anything beyond the fact that the Marquise had departed this life in the most ghastly manner. In the interest of the family, as little attention as possible must be drawn, and the funeral had to take place without the untraceable corpse. Immediately after the last rites I left Monjoie. Circumstances in my own family required my presence in Russia, and I saw the Marquis no more. Years later I heard in Paris that he had departed France.

Now in the tranquility of this evening hour on Capri, by the glow of a friendly lamp, I felt deeply shaken that the lonely, broken man staring out to sea each day waits still for his loved one. His weary spirit cannot believe that the exquisite, peerless body is no more, that at best the beloved soul wanders somewhere, somehow in the unknown; his own sick being dreams only of the return of the past.

As I dressed on the following morning, haggard and depressed, it almost seemed a duty to seek out the Marquis de Saint-Brissac and to assure him of my sympathy. But I quickly put the thought aside. For such deep grief human contact itself is almost a sacrilege; for mourning of this kind words are desecration. The world knew of a great love whose commemoration had robbed this singular man of his senses, but none could surmise the dimension and the secret of this love. Eugen Maria Krancz has no more become an object of hateful jokes than the Marquise de Saint-Brissac was. When Krancz terminated his narrow life in the provinces, his flight was the gateway to a life of love and beauty. When the Marquise ceased to belong to the world, she passed through a similar gateway, and once more through flight, but this time a flight into death.

Before I sailed from Capri, I selected the finest rose that I could find and through one of those dark-skinned idlers lolling about everywhere, I sent the deep red blossom to the Marquis' residence. "A greeting," I wrote in accompaniment, "in memory of Maria."

—Translated by
David Galloway and
Christian Sabisch

ERNEST HEMINGWAY

A SIMPLE ENQUIRY

Outside, the snow was higher than the window. The sunlight came in through the window and shone on a map on the pine-board wall of the hut. The sun was high and the light came in over the top of the snow. A trench had been cut along the open side of the hut, and each clear day the sun, shining on the wall, reflected heat against the snow and widened the trench. It was late March. The major sat at a table against the wall. His adjutant sat at another table.

Around the major's eyes were two white circles where his snow glasses had protected his face from the sun on the snow. The rest of his face had been burned and then tanned and then burned through the tan. His nose was swollen and there were edges of loose skin where blisters had been. While he worked at the papers he put the fingers of his left hand into a saucer of oil and then spread the oil over his face, touching it very gently with the tips of his fingers. He was very careful to drain his fingers on the edge of the saucer so there was only a film of oil on them, and after he had stroked his forehead and his cheeks, he stroked his nose very delicately between his fingers. When he had finished he stood up, took the saucer of oil and went into the small room of the hut where he slept.

"I'm going to take a little sleep," he said to the adjutant. In that army an adjutant is not a commissioned officer. "You'll finish up."

"Yes, signore maggiore," the adjutant answered. He leaned back in his chair and yawned. He took a paper-covered book out of the pocket of his coat and opened it; then laid it down on the table and lit his pipe. He leaned forward on the table to read and puffed at his pipe. Then he closed the book and put it back in his pocket. He had too much paper work to get through. He could not enjoy reading until it was done. Outside, the sun went behind a mountain and there was no more light on the wall of the hut. A soldier came in and put some pine branches, chopped into irregular lengths, into the stove. "Be soft, Pinin," the adjutant said to him. "The major is sleeping."

Pinin was the major's orderly. He was a dark-faced boy, and he fixed the stove, putting the pine wood in carefully, shut the door, and went into the back of the hut again. The adjutant went on with his papers.

"Tonani," the major called.

"Signor maggiore?"

"Send Pinin in to me."

"Pinin!" the adjutant called. Pinin came into the room. "The major wants you," the adjutant said.

Pinin walked across the main room of the hut towards the major's door. He knocked on the half-opened door. "Signor maggiore?"

"Come in," the adjutant heard the major say, "and shut the door."

Inside the room the major lay on his bunk. Pinin stood beside the bunk. The major lay with his head on the rucksack that he had stuffed with spare clothing to make a pillow. His long, burned, oiled face looked at Pinin. His hands lay on the blankets.

"You are nineteen?" he asked.

"Yes, signor maggiore."

"You have ever been in love?"

"How do you mean, signor maggiore?"

"In love—with a girl?"

"I have been with girls."

"I did not ask that. I asked if you had been in love—with a girl."

"Yes, signor maggiore."

"You are in love with this girl now? You don't write her. I read all your letters."

"I am in love with her," Pinin said, "but I do not write her."

"You are sure of this?"

"I am sure."

"Tonani," the major said in the same tone of voice, "can you hear me talking?"

There was no answer from the next room.

"He cannot hear," the major said. "And you are quite sure that you love a girl?"

"I am sure."

"And," the major looked at him quickly, "that you are not corrupt?"

"I don't know what you mean, corrupt."

"All right," the major said. "You needn't be superior."

Pinin looked at the floor. The major looked at his brown face, down and up him, and at his hands. Then he went on, not smiling. "And you don't really want—" the major paused. Pinin looked at the floor. "That your great desire isn't really —" Pinin looked at the floor. The major leaned his head back on the rucksack and smiled. He was really relieved: life in the army was too complicated. "You're a good boy," he said. "You're a good boy, Pinin. But don't be superior and be careful someone else doesn't come along and take you."

Pinin stood still beside the bunk.

"Don't be afraid," the major said. His hands were folded on the blanket. "I won't touch you. You can go back to your platoon if you like. But you had better stay on as my servant. You've less chance of being killed."

"Do you want anything of me, signor maggiore?"

"No," the major said. "Go on and get on with whatever you were doing. Leave the door open when you go out."

Pinin went out, leaving the door open. The adjutant looked up at him as he walked awkwardly across the room and out of the door. Pinin was flushed and moved differently than he had moved when he brought in the wood for the fire. The adjutant looked after him and smiled. Pinin came in with more wood for the stove. The major, lying on his bunk, looking at his cloth-covered helmet and his snow glasses that hung from a nail on the wall, heard him walk across the floor. The little devil, he thought, I wonder if he lied to me.

JEAN COCTEAU

THE WHITE PAPER

As long ago as I can remember, and even looking all the way back to that age when the senses have still to come under the influence of the mind, I find traces of my love for boys.

I have always loved the stronger sex, the one I consider it legitimate to call the fairer sex. The misfortunes I have had at the hands of a society which views the unusual as the fit object of condemnation and obliges us, if they be rare, to reform our natural inclinations.

I recall three critical, three decisive incidents. My father lived in a little château near S***. Attached to that château was a park. At the further limit of the park, beyond where the château property stopped, were a farm and a watering-place. In return for some daily milk and butter and eggs, my father enabled the farmer to avoid the cost of fencing his animals off our land.

One August morning, I was prowling about the park with a toy rifle that fired caps and, playing at hunting, using a hedge for a blind, I was waiting for some animal to pass, when from my hiding-place I spied a young farm-boy leading a draft horse down to water. Wishing to ride out into the pond and knowing that people never ventured to the far end of the park, he peeled off his clothes, sprang upon the horse and guided it into the water a few yards from where, concealed, I was watching. The sunburn on his face, on his neck, his arms, his feet, contrasting with the whiteness of the rest of his skin, made me think of chestnuts bursting out of their husks; but those were not the only dark patches on his body. My gaze was drawn to another, from whose midst an enigma and every one of its details rose into the plainest view.

My ears rang. The blood rushed to my head, my face turned scarlet. The strength drained out of my legs. My heart beat like the heart of a murderer preparing to kill. Without realizing what was happening, I stood up, reeled, and fainted dead away, and it was only after a four-hour search that they found me. When I'd recovered my wits and was on my feet again, I took instinctive care not to disclose what had caused my weakness and at the risk of sounding ridiculous, I declared that I'd been frightened by a hare that had bolted from a thicket.

The second incident occurred the following year. My father had given some gypsies permission to camp in that same remote spot in the park where I had lost consciousness. I was taking a walk with my maid. All of a sudden, letting out a great shriek, she grabbed my hand and began to drag me after her, ordering me under no circumstances to look back. The weather was sparkling clear and hot. Two young gypsy lads had undressed and were climbing in a tree. A spectacle rendered unforgettable by my maid's shock and as though permanently framed by my disobedience: even if I live to be a hundred, thanks to that shriek and that mad dash I shall always see a covered wagon, a woman rocking a new-born infant, a smoking fire, a white horse grazing and, climbing a tree, two bronzed bodies each thrice-spotted with patches of black.

The third time it had to do with a young hired man whose name, if I'm not mistaken, was Gustave, who waited on the table. Aware of my glances, it would be all he could do to keep a straight face while serving. From returning again and again to dwell upon those memories of the farm-boy and of the gypsies, I'd come to have the keenest wish to touch my hand to what my eye had seen.

My scheme was wonderfully naive. I'd make a drawing of a woman, I'd take the picture and show it to Gustave, I'd make him laugh, once I'd encouraged him I'd ask him to let me touch the mystery which, seated at the dining table, I'd been trying to visualize behind the prominent bulge in his trousers. Now, the only woman I had ever seen wearing a shift was my nursemaid; I supposed that artists invented the firm breasts they put on women, and that in reality all women had flabby ones. My sketch was realistic. Gustave burst out laughing, asked who my model was; taking advantage of a new fit of mirth, with breathtaking courage I had proceeded halfway to the mark when he turned very red, batted my hand aside, pinched my ear, by way of excuse saying he was ticklish and, deathly afraid of losing his job, conducted me to the door.

Several days later Gustave stole some wine. My father dismissed him. I interceded, I wept, I tried everything, and failed. I accompanied Gustave to the railroad station, carrying the checker set and checkerboard I'd given him as a present for his little boy whose photograph he had often showed me.

My mother died in giving birth to me and I had always lived alone with my father, a sad and charming man. His sadness preceded the loss of his wife. Even when contented he had been sad and that is why, in an effort to understand his sadness, I sought beyond his bereavement for its deeper-lying roots.

The homosexual recognizes the homosexual as infallibly as the Jew recognizes the Jew. He detects him behind whatever the mask, and I guarantee my ability to detect him between the lines of the most innocent books. This passion is less simple than moralists are wont to maintain. For just as homosexual women exist, women with the outward aspect of Lesbians but who seek after men in the special way men seek after women, so homosexual men exist who do not know what they are and who live out the whole of their lives in a restlessness, in an uneasiness they ascribe to some lack of vitality, or to a sickly or retiring nature.

It has always seemed to me that my father and I too closely

resembled each other not to have this essential feature in common. He was probably unaware of his true bent; at any rate, instead of pursuing it, he struggled along another path without knowing what it was that made the way so dreary and life to hang so heavy upon him. Had he discovered the tastes he never had the chance to cultivate and which his phrases, his gestures, certain of his movements, a thousand details about his person revealed to me, he would have been thunderstruck. In his day, a man would kill himself for slighter cause. But no; he lived, living in ignorance of himself, and he accepted his burden.

To this exceeding blindness it may be that I owe the fact that I was brought into the world. Well, I deplore it, for it would have been to the benefit of us both had my father known the delights which would have spared me so much sorrow.

I entered the Lycée Condorcet in the third form. There the boys' senses awakened and, uncontrolled, grew like a baneful weed. It was nothing but holes poked in pockets and soiled handkerchiefs. Drawingboards on their laps, the pupils went particularly wild in art class. Sometimes, during an ordinary class, an ironical teacher would suddenly call upon a pupil on the verge of orgasm. The pupil, his cheeks aflame, would slouch to his feet and stammering whatever came to his head, endeavor to transform his dictionary into a fig-leaf. Our hilarity would increase his embarrassment.

The classroom smelled of gas, chalk, sperm. That mixture turned my stomach. I must say this: that which was a vice in the eyes of all my classmates, not being one in mine or, to be more exact, being the base parody of a form of love my instinct was to respect, I was the only one who appeared to disapprove of the situation. The result was perpetual sarcasm and assaults upon what the others took to be my prudery.

But Condorcet was a day-school. These practices never led as far as love affairs; they seldom got beyond the confines of a routine, clandestine sport.

One of the pupils, whose name was Dargelos, enjoyed a great prestige because of a virility considerably in advance of his years. He exhibited himself cynically and made a business of putting on a show which he even presented to pupils in other forms in exchange for rare stamps and tobacco. The seats surrounding his desk were at a premium. I still have an image of his brown skin. By the extremely short trousers he wore and the socks dragging around his ankles one could tell that he was proud of his legs. We all wore short pants, but thanks to his man's legs, only Dargelos was *barelegged.* Unbuttoned at the throat, his open shirt revealed a strong neck. A thick lock of hair hung over his forehead. That face—with its somewhat heavy lips, its somewhat slitted eyes, its somewhat snub nose—had every last one of the features of the type that was to be my undoing. Oh, it is cunning, the fatality that disguises itself, and gives us the illusion of being free and, when all is said and done, each time lures us straight into the same trap.

Dargelos's presence drove me out of my mind. I avoided him. I lay in wait for him. I dreamt of some miracle which would bring his attention to bear on me, disencumber him of his vainglory, reveal to him the real meaning of my attitude which, as things stood, he had necessarily to view as some sort of preposterous prudishness and which was nothing short of an insane desire to please him.

My sentiments were vague. I could not manage to specify them. They caused me either extreme discomfort or extreme delight. The only thing I was sure of was that they were in no way comparable to those my comrades experienced.

One day, unable to bear it any longer, I declared my problem to a pupil whose parents knew my father, and whom I saw on and off outside of school hours.

"But you're a complete idiot," said he, "there's nothing to it. Invite Dargelos to your place some Sunday, get him out there in the park, and the trick's done. It's automatic."

What trick? I'd not been plotting any trick. I mumbled something about this not having any connection with the sort of pleasure anyone could take right there in class and, unsuccessfully, I endeavored to clad my dream in the form of words. My friend shrugged his shoulders. "Why go looking for difficulties where there aren't any?" he asked. "Dargelos is bigger than we are"—he employed other terms—"but all you have to do is flatter him and you've got him wrapped around your little finger. If you like him, all you need to do is let him pitch it at you."

The crudeness of this recommendation stunned me. I realized that it was impossible to make myself understood. Supposing that Dargelos agreed to a rendezvous, what, I wondered, would I say to him, what would I do? I was not interested in fiddling around for five minutes, what I wanted was to live with him for the rest of my life. In short, I adored him, and resigned myself to suffer in silence, for, without giving my malady the name of love, I fully sensed that a whole world lay between it and our classroom exercises and that, in the class, it would evoke no response.

This adventure had no beginning but it did have an end. Urged on by the pupil in whom I had confided, I asked Dargelos to meet me in a vacant classroom after the five o'clock study hall. He turned up. I'd counted on some godsent inspiration that would dictate to me what to do. Face to face with him, I lost my bearings completely. All I saw were his sturdy legs and his scraped knees blazoned with scabs, mud and ink.

"What do you want?" he asked me, smiling cruelly. I surmised what he was imagining and that, insofar as he was concerned, my request could have no other meaning. I tried to invent some answer.

"I wanted to tell you," I mumbled, "to look out for the vice-principal, he's got it in for you."

The lie was absurd, for Dargelos's charm and bewitched our masters too. The privileges of beauty are immense. It gains its way even with those who seem the least responsive to it.

Dargelos leaned his head a little to one side and grinned. "The vice-principal?"

"Yes," I persevered, from my terror deriving the strength to continue, "the vice-principal. 'I'm watching Dargelos. He's going just a bit too far. I've got my eye on him'—I heard him say that to the headmaster."

"Ah. So I'm going just a bit too far, am I," he replied. "Well, old man, I'll give him an eyeful. And as for you, if all you want is to worry me with crap like that, I can warn you right now that the next time you do I'll plant a foot in your ass."

He disappeared.

For the space of a week I complained of cramps so as not to have to go to school and endure a glance from Dargelos. When I returned I learned that he was sick in bed. I didn't dare ask how he was getting on. There were rumors. He was a Boy Scout. They referred to an unwise dip in the mid-winter Seine, mentioned pneumonia. One afternoon during the geography lesson we were informed of his death. My tears forced me to leave the room. Youth is not the age of compassion. For a good number of pupils, this announcement, which the teacher rose to his feet to make, was simply a tacit authorization to do nothing for the rest of the day. And on the next day the renewed practice of their habits closed over their mourning.

Nevertheless, the *coup de grâce* had just been delivered to eroticism. Too many little pleasures were spoiled by the troubling phantom of the superb animal of delights whose figure had moved even death itself.

Summer vacation over, and now, having advanced into the second form, a radical change seemed to have occurred in my classmates. Their voices were different, they were smoking. They were shaving a hint of beard, they went out bareheaded, were wearing knickers or long trousers. Onanism yielded to braggadocio. Dirty post cards were circulating. *En masse,* all these lads were turning towards women as plants turn towards the sun. It was then that, in order to keep in step with the rest, I began to play out of tune with my nature, and to warp it.

Rushing headlong towards their own truth, they swirled me towards falsehood. What interested them repelled me; I blamed that upon my ignorance. I admired their dash, their composure, their unselfconsciousness. I forced myself to follow their example and to share their enthusiasms. I had continually to vanquish my disgust and my shame. This discipline finally bore fruit and made the task fairly easy. When things were at their worst, I'd tell myself that debauchery was rough going for everyone, but that the others faced up to the job with a better grace than I.

On Sunday, if the weather was fair, the whole band of us would set off with our rackets, giving it out as our intention that we were off for an afternoon of tennis at Auteuil. The rackets were stowed along the way with the concierge of one of the boys whose family lived in Marseille, and from there we hastened in the direction of the brothels in the rue de Provence. Halting before the leather drape at the entrance, the timidity proper to our youth would reassert itself. We'd pace to and fro, up and down, deliberating whether to enter that doorway as bathers hesitate about plunging into cold water. We'd toss coins to decide who was to lead the way. I'd be in a panic over the possibility that fate might designate me. Whoever was chosen to go first finally sneaked along the wall, slunk inside, the rest of us on his heels and in single file.

Nothing has a greater power to intimidate than children and whores. Too many things go into composing the gap dividing us from them. One doesn't know how to break the silence and attune one's outlook to theirs. In the rue de Provence, the only terrain of mutual understanding was the bed upon which I would lie down with the whore and the jointly accomplished act which gave neither of us the slightest pleasure.

Those visits emboldened us, we accosted streetwalkers and thus made the acquaintance of a little individual who was known as Alice de Pilbrac. She lived on the rue La Bruyère in a modest apartment which smelled of coffee. If I remember rightly, Alice de Pilbrac while she did receive us, allowed us to do no more than admire her in a sordid dressing-gown and with her thin drab hair hanging down her back. This regimen made my comrades pine or fidget, but it suited me handsomely. In the end, they grew tired of waiting and took off on a new tack. This time it was to pool our money, rent the front row for the Sunday matinee at the Eldorado, throw bouquets of violets at the vocalists and then go to the stagedoor and wait for them in the savage cold.

If I recount these trifling episodes it is to indicate the appalling fatigue and stricken feeling of utter hollowness with which our Sunday outings would reward us, and my amazement to witness my comrades feast the whole week long on the details of the miserable nothings we accomplished.

One of my friends knew the actress Berthe, through whom I met Jeanne. They were in the theatre. I took a liking to Jeanne; I asked Berthe to do me the favor of finding out if she would be willing to become my mistress. Berthe brought back word that I had been turned down and suggested that I deceive my comrade by sleeping with her. Shortly afterward, learning from him that Jeanne was disappointed at not having heard anything from me, I went to see her. We discovered that my message had never been transmitted and decided to take our revenge by reserving for Berthe the surprise of our happiness.

That adventure left such an imprint upon my sixteenth, seventeenth and eighteenth years that today, whenever I see Jeanne's name in a newspaper or her picture on a billboard, I still experience a shock. And for all that, it is still possible to say nothing at all in relating this banal affair which measured itself out in long waits in dress-shops and in playing a pretty disagreeable dual role, for the Armenian who kept Jeanne thought highly of me and made me his confidant.

It was in the second year that the scenes began. After the most lively one, which transpired at five in the afternoon on the place de la Concorde, I abandoned Jeanne on a traffic island and fled home. I was not halfway through dinner, and was already planning a telephone call, when I was told that a lady was waiting downstairs in a taxi.

It was Jeanne.

"I'm not hurt," she said, "on account of having been left stranded in the middle of the place de la Concorde, but you haven't got the guts to play the game all the way through to the end. Two months ago you'd have crossed the whole square. Don't let yourself think you proved yourself able to act like a man. All you proved is that your love is as weak as soda pop."

This poignant analysis enlightened me: it advised me that I was no longer enslaved.

In order that my love revive, I had to discover that Jeanne was unfaithful to me. She was, with Berthe. Today, this element in the story lays bare the basis of my love for her. Jeanne was a boy; she was fond of women, and I loved her with what my nature contained of the feminine. I came upon them in bed tangled up like an octopus. Administer a beating, that was what the situation called for; and instead I pleaded. They laughed at me, consoled me, and that was the bedraggled conclusion to an affair which, although it died of its own accord, nevertheless wreaked sufficient havoc upon me to alarm my father and force him to emerge from the reserve he always maintained in regard to me.

As I was returning to my father's house one evening at a later than usual hour, a woman approached me in the place de la Madeleine. She had a gentle voice. I peered at her, found her lovely, young, fresh as a rose. She said her name was Rose, she liked to talk and we strolled hither and yon until that time of night when the market-gardeners, asleep over the vegetables in their cart, drop the reins and permit their horses to wend their way through a deserted Paris.

I was to leave the next day for Switzerland. I gave Rose my name and address. She sent me letters written on lined paper and enclosed stamps for the reply postage. Back again in Paris, happier than Thomas de Quincey, I found Rose at the very same spot where we'd met the first time. She invited me to come to her hotel in Pigalle.

The Hotel M*** was lugubrious. The stairway stank of ether, which provides consolation for whores who come home without having bagged a client. The room was the prototype of rooms that are never tidied. Rose smoked in bed. I complimented her on how well she looked.

"That's because I'm made up. You should see me when I'm not," she said. "I haven't got any eyelashes. I look like a jackrabbit."

I became her lover. She would take nothing from me, not even the smallest gift. Ah, yes, she did accept a dress since, as she claimed, it was of absolutely no commercial value to her, was too elegant for the business, and would go into the closet to be preserved as a souvenir.

One Sunday there came a knock on the door. I jumped up.

Rose told me to take it easy and get back into bed. "It's just my brother. He'll be delighted to see you."

This brother resembled the farm-boy and the Gustave of my childhood. He was nineteen and blessed with the worst sort of style. His name was Alfred or Alfredo and he talked a queer kind of French, but I was indifferent to the question of his nationality; he struck me as belonging to the country of prostitution which has its own patriotism and this language of his may have been its idiom.

If I had to wage a somewhat uphill struggle to keep my interest in the sister alive, one may imagine how precipitous was the slope down which I was carried by a tremendous interest in the brother. He, as his countrymen put it, dug me perfectly, and we were soon employing all the craft and stealth of a pair of Apaches to contrive get-togethers and to prevent Rose from finding out about them.

Alfred's body was more the body my dreams had possessed than the powerfully outfitted body of some adolescent or other. A faultless body, rigged with muscles like a schooner with ropes, whose limbs seemed to radiate out like the rays of a star from a nuclear fleece whence would rear the one thing in a man that is incapable of lying and which is absent in women, who are constructed for feigning.

I realized I'd started off on the wrong road. I swore to myself never to go astray again, and now that I was on the right one, to follow it instead of getting sidetracked into the ways of others, and to pay much more attention to what my senses demanded than to what morality advised.

Alfred reciprocated my caresses. He confessed that he wasn't Rose's brother. He was her business manager.

Rose continued to play her role and we ours. Alfred would wink at me, give me the high sign and sometimes go off into gales of wild laughter. Puzzled, Rose would frown uncomprehendingly, never suspecting that we were in a conspiracy and that between us existed ties which guile consolidated.

The hotel porter came in one day and found us wallowing to right and left of Rose. "There you are, Jules," she exclaimed, "my brother on one side of me and my sweetie-pie on the other. They're all I love in the world."

The lies began to tire the lazy Alfred. He declared that he couldn't go on living this way, working one side of the street while Rose worked the other, tramping up and down this open-air market where the vendors are the merchandise. In other words, he was asking me to get him out of there.

I assured him that nothing would give me greater pleasure. We decided that I'd reserve a room in a place des Ternes hotel where Alfred would install himself permanently, that after dinner I'd join him there for the night, that with Rose I'd pretend to think he'd disappeared and say that I was starting out to search for him, which would leave me free and net us plenty of good times.

I arranged for the room, settled Alfred in it, and dined at my father's. The meal over, I rushed to the hotel. No Alfred. I waited from nine until one in the morning. Still no Alfred; and so I went home, my heart as heavy as lead.

The next morning towards eleven I went back to the place des Ternes to see what was what; Alfred was in his room, asleep. He woke up, whimpered, whined and told me it wasn't any use trying, he didn't have the necessary self-control to break his old habits, he couldn't ever possibly do without Rose. He'd hunted for her all night long, first at her hotel at which she'd checked out, then on sidewalk after sidewalk, in every brasserie in Montmartre and in all the rue de Lappe dance halls.

"Sure," I told him, "Rose is crazy. So what? She's got a fever. She's staying with a friend of hers who lives on the rue de Budapest."

He begged me to take him there without a moment's delay.

Rose's former room at the Hotel M**** was a little palace next to this one belonging to her friend. We had to fight to keep afloat in a practically paste-like atmosphere of odors, clothing and doubtful sentiments. The women were in their slips. Alfred was on the floor, moaning and hugging Rose's knees. I was pale. Rose turned a face smeared with cosmetics and tears in my direction, she stretched her arms towards me: "Oh," she cried, "let's all go back to Pigalle and live together for ever and ever. I'm sure that's what Alfred wants. It is, isn't it, Alfred?" she added, yanking his hair. He remained silent.

I had to accompany my father to Toulon for the wedding of my cousin, the daughter of Vice-Admiral G***-F***. The future looked enormously unsure, bleak. I announced this family trip to Rose, left them—Rose and the still mute Alfred—at the Pigalle hotel, and promised I'd visit them as soon as I got back.

At Toulon I noticed that Alfred hadn't returned a little gold chain of mine. It was my fetish. I'd looped it around his wrist, forgotten about it, and he'd not remembered to remind me.

Home again in Paris, I went to the hotel and when I entered the room, Rose welcomed me with a big kiss. There wasn't much light to see by. I didn't recognize Alfred at first. What was there unrecognizable about him?

The police were scouring Montmartre. Alfred and Rose were worried sick because of their questionable nationality. They'd fixed themselves up with a set of false passports, were ready to take off at the drop of a hat, and Alfred, full of the lore he'd picked up at the movies, had dyed his hair. It was with an anthropometric precision that his little blond face contradicted the jet-black mop surmounting it. I asked him for my chain. He denied having it. Rose declared he did indeed have it. He said it wasn't true, swore it wasn't. She fished it out from under the pillow, he swore he hadn't put it there, threatened her, threatened me and pulled a pistol out of his pocket.

I made it into the hallway in one leap and went down the stairs four at a time, Alfred hot on my trail.

Outside, I hailed a taxi. I shouted my address, jumped in, and as the taxi started off, I turned and peered through the rear window.

Alfred was standing motionless outside the door of the hotel. Great tears were flowing down his cheeks. He extended his arms imploringly; he called to me. Under his badly dyed hair he was heartbreakingly pale.

I wanted to rap on the glass partition, to tell the driver to stop. I could not simply turn my back upon that solitary distress and run off like a coward to take sanctuary in family comfort; but, on the other hand, there was the chain to consider, the pistol, I thought of the false passports and of this flight in which Rose would certainly ask me to join them. And now, whenever I ride in one of those old red Paris taxis, I have only to close my eyes to conjure up the little silhouette of Alfred, and to see the tears streaming down his face under that Chicago racketeer's hairdo.

The Admiral being ill and my cousin off on her honeymoon, I had to return to Toulon. It would be tedious to describe that charming Sodom smitten by wrathful heavenly fires in the form of a caressing sun. In the evening a still sweeter indulgence inundates the city and, as in Naples, as in Venice, a holiday-making crowd saunters in slow circles through the squares where fountains play, where there are trinket and tinsel stalls, waffle-sellers, and street hawkers. From the four corners of the earth men whose hearts go out to masculine beauty come to admire the sailors who hang about singly or drift in groups, smile in reply to longing's stare, and never refuse the offer of love. Some salt or nocturnal potion transforms the most uncouth ex-convict, the toughest Breton, the wildest Corsican into these tall, flower-decked girls with their low-necked jumpers, their swaying hips, their pompoms, these lithely graceful, colorful whores who like to dance and who, without the least sign of awkwardness, lead their partners into the obscure little hotels down by the port.

One of the cafés where you can dance is owned by a former café-concert singer who has the voice of a girl and who used to do a strip-tease, starting it off as a woman. These days he wears a turtle-neck sweater and rings on his fingers. Flanked by the seafaring giants who idolize him and whose devotion he repays with mistreatment. In a large, childish hand and with his tongue stuck out he jots down the prices of the drinks his wife announces to him in a tone of naive asperity.

One evening, pushing open the door to the place run by that astonishing creature who ever basks in the midst of the respect and deferential gestures of a wife and several husbands, I stopped abruptly, rooted to the spot. I'd just caught sight, caught a profile view, of Dargelos's ghost. Leaning one elbow upon the mechanical piano, it was Dargelos in a sailor-suit.

Of the original Dargelos this facsimile had above all the barefaced arrogance, the insolent and casual manner. *Tapageuse* was spelled out in letters of gold on the flat hat tilted over his left eyebrow, his tie was knotted up over his Adam's apple and he was wearing those amply bell-bottomed pants which sailors used once upon a time to roll to the thigh and which nowadays the regulations find some moral excuse or other for outlawing.

In another place I'd never have dared put myself within range of that lofty stare. But Toulon is Toulon; dancing eliminates uncomfortable preambles, it throws strangers into each other's arms and sets the stage for love.

They were playing dipsy-doodly music full of sauciness and winning smiles; we danced a waltz. The arched bodies are riveted together at the groin; grave profiles cast thoughtful downward glances, turn less quickly than the tripping and now and then plodding feet. Free hands assume the gracious attitudes affected by common folk when they take a cup of tea or piss it out again. A springtime exhilaration transports the bodies. Those bodies bud, push forth shoots, branches, hard members bump, squeeze, sweats commingle, and there's another couple heading for one of the rooms with the globe lights overhead and the eiderdowns on the bed.

Despoiled of the accessories which intimidate civilians and of the manner sailors adopt to screw up their courage, *Tapageuse* became a meek animal. He had got his nose broken by a syphon-bottle in the course of a brawl. Without that crooked nose his face might well have been uninteresting. A syphon-bottle had put the finishing touch to a masterpiece.

Upon his naked torso, this lad, who represented pure luck to me, had *Lousy Luck* tattooed in blue capital letters. He told me his story. It was brief. That afflicting tattoo condensed it in a nutshell. He'd emerged from the brig. After the *Ernest-Renan* mutiny there'd been the inquest; they'd confused him with a colleague; that was why his hair was only half an inch long; he deplored a tonsure which wonderfully became him.

"I've never had anything but lousy luck," he repeated, shaking that bald little head reminiscent of a classical bust, "and it ain't never going to change."

I slipped my fetish-chain around his neck. "I'm not giving it to you," I explained, "it's a charm, but not much of one, I guess, for it hasn't done much for me and won't for you either. Just wear it tonight."

Then I uncapped my fountain pen and crossed out the ominous tattoo. I drew a star and a heart above it. He smiled. He understood, more with his skin than with the rest, that he was in safe hands, that our encounter wasn't like the ones he'd grown accustomed to: hasty encounters in which selfishness satisfies itself.

Lousy luck! Incredible—with that mouth, those teeth, those eyes, that belly, those shoulders and cast-iron muscles, those legs, how was it possible? Lousy luck, with that fabulous little undersea plant, forlorn, inert, shipwrecked on the frothy fleece, which then stirs, unwrinkles, develops, rouses itself and hurls its sap afar when once it is restored to its element of love. Lousy luck? I couldn't believe it; and to resolve the problem I drowned myself in a vigilant sleep.

Lousy Luck remained very still beside me. Little by little, I felt him undertaking the delicate maneuver of extricating his arm from under my elbow. I didn't for a single instant think he was meditating a dirty trick. It would have been to demonstrate my ignorance of the code of the fleet. "Gentlemanliness," "semper fidelis" and the strict up-and-up embellish the mariners' vocabulary.

I watched him out of the corner of one eye. First, several times, he fingered the chain, seemed to be weighing it, kissed it, rubbed it against his tattoo. Then, with the dreadful deliberation of a player in the act of cheating, he tested to see if I was asleep, coughed, touched me, listened to my breathing, approached his face to my open right hand lying by my face and gently pressed his cheek to my palm.

Indiscreet witness of this attempt by an unlucky child who, in the midst of the sea's wilderness, felt a life-saver coming within reach, I had to make a major effort not to lose my wits, feign a sudden awakening and demolish my life.

Day had scarcely dawned when I left him. My eyes avoided his, which were laden with all the great expectations surging up in him and the hopes to which he couldn't give expression. He returned my chain. I kissed him, I edged past him and switched off the lamp by the bed.

Downstairs, I had to write the hour—5:00—when sailors are to be waked. On a slate opposite the room numbers were quantities of similar instructions. As I picked up the chalk I noticed I'd forgotten my gloves. I went back up. A sliver of light showed under the door. The lamp by the bed must have been turned on again. I was unable to resist peeping through the keyhole. It supplied the baroque frame to a little head upon which sprouted about half an inch of hair.

Lousy Luck, his face buried in my gloves, was weeping bitterly.

Ten long minutes I hesitated before that door. I was about to knock when Alfred's visage superimposed itself in the most exact manner upon *Lousy Luck's.* I stole on tiptoe down the stairs, pushed the button opening the door and slammed the door behind me. In the center of an empty square a fountain was pronouncing a solemn soliloquy.

"No," I thought to myself, "we aren't of the same species. It's wonderful—it's enough—to move a flower, a tree, a beast. But you can't live with one."

Now the sun had risen. Cocks crowed out over the sea. The sea lay cool and dark. A man came around a corner with a shotgun on his shoulder. Hauling an enormous weight, I trudged towards my hotel.

Fed up with sentimental adventures, incapable of responding to them, I limped about, weary in body and soul. I looked for some underworld atmosphere. I found it in a public bath. The place recalled the *Satyricon,* with its little cubicles, the central inner court, the low-ceilinged room where, seated on Turkish hassocks, young men were playing cards. When the owner gave the signal they stood and lined up against the wall. He then fingered their biceps, palpated their thighs, brought their less visible and most intimate charms into view and passed them out like tickets.

The clientele knew exactly what it was after, wasted few words and less time getting down to brass tacks. I must have been a mystery to those young men who were used to clear-cut requirements and to fulfilling them speedily. They gave me the blankest of bewildered looks; for I preferred conversation to action.

In me, heart and senses are so inextricably combined that I don't know quite how to involve the one without committing the others too. It's this that leads me to overstep the limits of friendship and makes me fear a summary contact from which I run the danger of catching the germ of love. I finally came to envy those who, not suffering vaguely in the presence of beauty, knowing what they want, have everything tabbed and filed, specialize in a vice, perfect it, pay and satisfy it.

One of them issued instructions that he be insulted, another that he be draped in chains. To reach his crisis, still another (a moralist) needed the spectacle of a young Hercules slaying a rat with a red-hot needle.

I saw them come and go, it was one long procession of those sage individuals who know the exact recipe for their pleasure and for whom it's all smooth sailing because, no nonsense about it, they pay punctually and the marked price to have a respectable bourgeois complication treated. The majority were wealthy industrialists who came down from the North to exercise their penchants and then went home to their wives and children.

After a while I began to space out my visits, for my almost continual presence was beginning to arouse suspicions. In France you're apt to run into difficulties if the role you're enacting isn't all of one piece. The miser had better be miserly all the time, the jealous man always jealous. That accounts for Molière's success. The proprietor thought me in league with the police. He gave me to understand that you are either a client or merchandise. And that you can't combine the two.

This warning shook me out of my lethargy and obliged me to abandon my unworthy habits. I took to the great outdoors again, where I saw the remembrance of Alfred floating on the faces of a thousand young apprentice bakers, butchers, cyclists, errand-boys, zouaves, sailors, acrobats and other professional travesties.

One of my few regrets was the transparent mirror. You get into a dark booth and pull aside a curtain. Now you are looking through a fine metallic screen, your view commands a small bathroom. On the other side, the screen was a mirror so highly polished and so smooth that no one could possibly suspect that it was honeycombed with spyholes.

When my budget could afford it, I'd pass entire Sundays at my post. There were twelve bathrooms, and of the twelve mirrors there was only one of this kind. It had cost a lot of money, and the proprietor had had to import it from Germany. His personnel didn't know about the observatory. Young members of the working class provided the show.

They all followed the same program. They undressed and carefully hung up their new suits. Rid of their finery, charming vocational deformations allowed you to guess the sort of work they were employed in. Standing in the tub, they would gaze at their reflection (at me) pensively and start with a Parisian grin which exposes the gums. Next, they'd scratch a shoulder, pick up the soap and, handling it slowly, make it bubble into a lather. Then they'd soap themselves. The soaping would gradually turn into a caress. All of a sudden their eyes would wander out of this world, their heads would tilt back and their bodies would spit like furious animals.

Some, exhausted, would subside into the steaming bathwater, others would box a second round; the youngest distinguished themselves by climbing out of the tub and, off in a corner, wiping the tiles clean of the sap their careless stems had hurled blindly towards love.

Once, a Narcissus who was pleasuring himself brought his mouth to the mirror, pressed his lips to it and pressed his adventure with himself all the way through to the end. Invisible like the Greek gods, I put my lips to his and imitated his gestures. Never was he to know that instead of reflecting him, the mirror had acted, had lived and loved him.

Fortune steered me towards a new life. I emerged from a

bad dream. I had sunk into an unwholesome indolence which is to the love of men what assignation houses and sidewalk pick-ups are to the love of women.

I knew and admired the Right Reverend Father X***. His deftness, his light-heartedness bordered on the miraculous. Wherever he went, like some magician he alleviated burdens, lightened whatever was heavy. He knew nothing of my intimate life, he simply sensed that I was unhappy. He spoke to me, comforted me and put me in touch with high Catholic intelligences.

I have always been a believer. My belief was confused. Thanks to frequenting an unsullied company, to reading so much peace in so many serene brows, to understanding the foolishness of unbelievers, I advanced along the path towards God. To be sure, dogma consorted ill with my decision to give a free rein to my impulses, but this recent period had left me with a bitterness, with a satiety which I was in a great hurry to interpret as evidence that I'd been pursuing the wrong course. After so much imbibing of wicked brews, all this water, all this milk revealed to me a future of limpid excellence and pureness of heart. If scruples assailed me, I beat off the attack by thinking of Jeanne and Rose. I'm not barred from having normal affairs, I told myself. Nothing prevents me from founding a family and resuming honest ways. I have, in a word, been ceding to my bent through fear of making an effort. Without an effort nothing good or fine exists. I'll pit myself against the devil and I'll be victorious.

A divine period! The Church cradled me in her arms. I felt myself the adopted son of a divine family. Holy communion, yes, the sanctified bread turns all to new-driven snow, and sets the tranquil soul deliciously aglow. I soared heavenward like a little balloon. At mass when the star of sacrifice dominates the altar and all the heads are bowed, I would pray ardently to the Virgin, beseeching her to take me under her holy protection: "I greet You, Mary," I'd murmur, "gladly I welcome You unto my heart, for are You not purity itself? What to You can be our ephemeral fancies, our humble follies? 'Tis all mere chaff, is it not? Can You be swayed by an exposed bosom? That which mortals behold as indecent, in Your sanctity must You not regard all this as we regard the amorous commerce between pistil and stamen, amongst the atoms? I shall obey the directives of Your Son's ministers upon earth, but I know very well that His goodness extends further than the chicanery of a Father Sinistrarius and the stringencies of an antiquated criminal code. So be it and Amen."

Following a fit of religiosity, the soul cools down again. That's the crucial instant. Man's unsupple and angular frame is not as easily rid as the gartersnake of this fragile sheath caught in the rose-briars. It's first of all love at first sight like a bolt out of the blue, betrothal to the Beloved, marriage and austere dedication.

At the outset, everything transpires in a sort of ecstasy. A wondrous zeal lays hold of the neophyte. Later, in cold blood, he steels himself to get up from a warm bed and go to church. Fasts, prayers, orisons monopolize him. The devil, who'd been banished out of the door, comes back in by the window, disguised as a ray of sunshine.

One's salvation cannot possibly be achieved in Paris; the soul is too distracted. I decided to go to the seaside. There, I'd divide my life between church and a rowboat. Far from all distractions, I'd pray upon the waves.

I took my old hotel room at T***.

From the very first day at T*** the heat's injunctions were to undress and enjoy myself. In order to get to the church one had to take evil-smelling streets and climb steps. This church was deserted. The fishermen never entered it. I admired God's unsuccess; masterpieces ought never to be popular. Which does not however prevent them from being illustrious and awe-inspiring.

Alas! I reasoned in vain, that emptiness exerted its influence upon me. I preferred my rowboat. I rowed as far out as possible, then I dropped the oars, removed my trousers and my undershorts, and sprawled out, limbs in disorder.

The sun is a veteran lover who knows his job. He starts by laying firm hands all over you. He attacks simultaneously from every angle. There's no getting away, he has a potent grip, he pins you and before you know it, you discover, as always happens to me, that your belly is covered with liquid drops resembling mistletoe berries.

Things weren't taking at all the right direction. I contracted a low opinion of myself. I sought to turn over a new leaf and try again. Finally, my prayers were reduced to succinct requests for God's forgiveness: "My God, You pardon me, for You understand me. You understand everything. For haven't You willed everything, created everything: bodies, sexes, waves, the blue heaven and the bright sun which, enamored of Hyacinth, metamorphosed him into a flower."

I'd located an isolated little beach for my sun-bathing. I would pull my boat up onto the shingle and dry myself in the kelp. On that beach one morning I came upon a young man who was swimming without a suit and who asked me if I minded. My reply was sufficiently frank to enlighten him as to my tastes. We were soon stretched out side by side. I learned that he lived in the neighboring village and was here for his health, he was convalescing from a faint threat of tuberculosis.

The sun accelerates the growth of sentiments. We cut a good number of corners and, thanks to a series of meetings in a state of nature and removed from the objects which divert the heart from prompt action, we arrived at the stage of being in love without ever having mentioned the word. H*** left his inn and set himself up in my hotel. He wrote. He believed in God, but displayed a puerile indifference towards dogma. The Church, that amiable heretic would declare, demands of us a moral prosody equivalent to the prosody of Alexander Pope. To want to stand with one foot planted alongside the Church on the reputedly unmovable rock of Saint Peter, and with the other foot mired in modern life, is to want to live the drawn-and-quartered existence of Saint Hippolytus. They ask for passive obedience from you, he said, and I give them active obedience. God loves love. In loving one another we demonstrate to Christ that we know how to read between the lines of a lawmaker's unavoidable severity. When you address the masses you're obliged not to allude to what distinguishes the common from the extraordinary.

He scoffed at my misgivings, at my pangs of conscience, he

called them weakness. He reprobated my doubts. "I love you," said he, "and I congratulate myself upon loving you."

Our dream might perhaps have been able to last under a sky where we lived half on land, half in the water, like mythological divinities; but his mother was calling him back to Paris, and we made up our minds to go there together.

That mother lived in Versailles, and as I was staying at my father's place, we rented a hotel room where we saw each other every day. He had a good many female acquaintances. They didn't particularly alarm me, for I'd often observed the great delight inverts take in the company of women, whilst women-loving men tend to scorn them and, apart from what is incidental to making use of women, prefer to pass the time with men.

One morning when he telephoned me from Versailles I noticed that this instrument, such a fine vehicle for falsehoods, was bringing me a voice I'd not heard hitherto. I asked him if he was really calling from Versailles. He stammered, talked faster, proposed we meet at the hotel at four that same afternoon, and hung up. Chilled to the marrow, gnawed by a frightful desire to know the truth, I gave the operator his mother's number. She told me that he'd not been home for several days and that, because of extra work which was keeping him till late every day in the city, he was sleeping at the home of a friend.

Passing the time until four o'clock amounted to an ordeal. A thousand circumstances only awaiting the signal to issue forth from shadow became instruments of torture and fastened their teeth upon me. The truth rose and smote my eyes. Madame V***, whom I'd taken for his friend, was in actuality his mistress. He returned to her in the evening and spent the night with her. This certitude pierced my breast like an executioner's bullet, it raked me like a tiger's claw. But despite my having realized the truth and despite the suffering it caused me, I still hoped he'd find an excuse and manage to furnish proof of his innocence.

At four he confessed that in the past he'd loved women and that, helpless before an insuperable force, he was resuming old ways and habits; this, he went on, ought not to distress me; it had nothing to do with us, was something quite different; he loved me, was disgusted with himself, couldn't do anything about it; every sanatorium was filled with similar cases. Credit for this ambivalence should be ascribed to tuberculosis.

I invited him to choose between women and me. I thought he was going to choose me and that he'd strive to renounce them. I was in error. "I risk making a promise," he replied, "and not keeping it. That would pain you. I don't want you to be in pain. Breaking off would hurt you less than false promises and lies."

I was leaning against the door and I was so pale that he was frightened. "Good bye," I murmured in a dead voice, "good bye. You gave my existence a meaning and an orientation and I had nothing else to do but lead it with you. What's to become of me? Where am I to go now? How shall I ever endure waiting for night to fall and after it has fallen, for day to come, and tomorrow, and the tomorrow after that? How shall I pass the weeks?" I saw nothing but a room swimming on the other side of my tears, and I was counting on my fingers like an idiot.

Suddenly he came to himself, waking as though from an hypnotic spell. He sprang from the bed upon which he'd been biting his nails, he clasped me in his arms, begged me to forgive him and swore he'd send women to the devil.

He wrote a letter to Madame V***, informing her that it was all over. She feigned suicide by absorbing the contents of a tube of sleeping pills, and we lived for three weeks in the country, having given no one our address. Two months went by, and I was happy.

It was the eve of an important religious holiday. Before repairing to the Holy Repast my custom was to go to have my confession heard by Father X***. He was virtually expecting my arrival. Crossing the threshold, I warned him that I'd come not to confess but to relate; and that, alas! I knew in advance what his verdict was going to be.

"Reverend Father," I enquired of him, "do you love me?"

"I love you."

"Would you be happy to hear that I find myself happy at last?"

"I'd be delighted."

"Well then, rejoice, for I am happy, but my happiness is of a variety the Church and society disapprove, for it is friendship that causes my happiness and, with me, friendship knows neither boundary nor restraint."

Father X*** interrupted me. "I believe," said he, "that you are the victim of scruples."

"Reverend Father," I rejoined, "I'd not insult the Church by supposing that she negotiates compromises or omits to cross the t's and dot the i's. I am familiar with the doctrine of *excessive friendships*. Whom can I deceive? God sees me. Why reckon the distance in fractions of an inch? I am on the downgrade. Sin lies ahead of me."

"My dear child," Father X*** told me in the vestibule, "were it but a question of jeopardizing my situation in heaven, the danger would be slight, for I believe that the goodness and mercy of God exceed all that we can imagine. But there is also the question of my situation here on earth. The Jesuits watch me very closely."

We embraced. Walking home beside the walls over which poured the scent of gardens, I considered God's economy and deemed it admirable. According to the divine scheme, love is granted when to one love is lacking and, to avoid a pleonasm of the heart, denied to those who possess it.

I received a telegram one morning: "Don't be alarmed. Off on a trip with Marcel. Will wire the date of our return."

This message left me stupified. There'd been no hint of a trip the evening before. Marcel was a friend from whom I had nothing underhanded to fear, but whom I knew to be wild enough to head for the moon on the spur of the moment, and never once to take into account the fact that his travelling companion's frail health might well buckle under an impromptu lark.

I was about to go to where Marcel lived to obtain further information from his servant when the doorbell rang and the next moment Mlle R*** appeared, disheveled, haggard and out of breath. "Marcel has robbed us!" she cried. "Marcel has taken him away from us! Something's got to be done!

Quick, let's get going! What are you doing, standing there like a blockhead? Act! Hurry! Avenge us! The wretch!" She waved her arms, was striding up and down the room, blowing her nose, tucking stray wisps of hair in place, knocking against furniture, catching her skirt on drawer-pulls, tearing her dress to ribbons.

My worry lest my father overhear the commotion and enter prevented me from understanding right away. Then the truth hove through the clouds and, concealing my distress, I herded the madwoman towards the entry, explaining to her that for my part I'd not been robbed of anything, that H*** was simply my friend, that I knew nothing whatsoever of the liaison she'd just got through sketching so clamorously.

"What!" she continued at the top of her lungs, "what! You are unaware that that child worships me and spends most of every night in my arms? He comes in from Versailles and returns there before dawn! I've had horrible operations! My stomach is one mass of scars! Well, there's something you ought to know about those scars. He kisses them and lays his cheek upon them in order to go to sleep."

It goes without saying that this visit plunged me into an ocean of dread. I received telegrams: "Hurrah for Marseille!" and "Leaving for Tunis."

The return was terrible. H*** thought he was in for the kind of scolding a child gets after playing a prank. I requested Marcel to leave us alone. Then I threw Mlle R*** in his face. He laughed it off. I told him it wasn't funny. He denied everything. I persisted. He denied. I bullied him, he admitted everything, and I cut loose. My pain maddened me. I lashed out like a brute. I grabbed him by the ears and beat his head against the wall. Blood trickled from the corner of his mouth. In a flash I recovered my senses. Tears streaming down my face, I tried to kiss that poor mauled face. But I encountered nothing but a flash of light blue eyes over which lids closed dolorously.

I fell upon my knees in one corner of the room. A scene like that taxes one's profoundest resources. One breaks down like a puppet whose strings have been snipped.

All of a sudden I felt a hand on my shoulder. I raised my head and saw my victim gaze at me, sink to the floor, kiss my fingers, my knees, choke, sputter, groan: "Forgive me, forgive me. I am your slave. Do what you like with me."

There was a month of truce. A weary truce, a blessed calm after the storm. We resembled those water-logged dahlias which hang their heads after a heavy rain. H*** didn't look well. He was wan, drawn, and often remained at Versailles.

Whereas I feel no awkwardness in talking about sexual relations, some modesty checks me whenever I think to describe the torments I am capable of experiencing. I'll devote a few lines to them and be done with it. Love ravages me. Even when calm, I tremble lest this calm cease, and the trembling anxiety is great enough to prevent me from tasting any sweetness in calm. The least setback wrecks everything. Impossible not to have constantly to foresee the worst, to have to cope with its latent threat. One *faux pas* and I inevitably wind up in a heap on the ground. Waiting is a torture, so is possessing by dint of dreading having taken away from me what I have been given.

Doubt made me pass sleepless nights in pacing the floor, in lying down on the floor, in wishing the floor would collapse and go on collapsing forever. I made myself the promise not to betray my fears. Immediately I was face to face with H***, I'd start plying him with questions. He kept still. That silence would either touch off my rage or my tears. I accused him of hating me, of wanting to destroy me. He knew only too well that there was no use answering and that, in spite of anything he could say, I'd start in again the next day.

That was all in September. But the 12th of November is the date I'll never forget as long as I live. We were to meet at the hotel at six. As I entered, the hotel manager stopped me and, visibly embarrassed by what he had to tell me, said that the police had been there and that H***, along with a bulky suitcase, had been taken to headquarters in a car containing the chief of the vice squad and some plainclothesmen.

"The police!" I cried. "What for?" I telephoned to influential people. They made enquiries and I found out the truth which, a little before eight that evening, a woebegone H***, released after his interrogation, confirmed to me.

He had been sleeping with a Russian woman who drugged him. Tipped off that a raid was likely, she'd asked him to remove her smoking equipment and supplies to the hotel. Some tough character he'd taken up with and confided in hadn't wasted much time in betraying him. It was a professional stool-pigeon. Thus, at one fell swoop, I discovered he'd deceived me not once again but twice. He'd tried to bluff it at the police station and, assuring them all that he was used to it, had sat down cross-legged on the floor and smoked during the questioning, much to the amazement of the onlookers. By now he was done for. I couldn't reproach him. I begged him to give up drugs. He told me he'd like to, but that he was addicted, done for, that it was too late.

I received a call the following day from Versailles. He'd spat blood and been rushed to the rue B*** hospital.

He was in Room 55 on the third floor. When I entered he had scarcely enough strength to look around to see who it was. His nose had become slightly thinner, pinched. His dull eyes rested on his waxen hands.

When the nurse left and we were by ourselves, he said: "I'm going to tell you my secret. In me there was a woman and there was a man. The woman was yours, and submissive; the man used to rebel against that submissiveness. Women displeased me, but I went after them to give myself a change and to show myself that I was free. The conceited, stupid man in me was the enemy of our love. I am sorry about that. I miss that love. I don't love anyone but you. When I'm all well again, I'll be different. I'll obey you willingly, without rebelling, and I'll do everything I can to make up for the way I've wronged you."

I couldn't sleep that night either. Towards morning, I dozed off for a few minutes and had a dream. I was at the circus with H***. The circus became a restaurant divided into two little rooms. In one of them, at the piano, a singer announced he was going to sing a new song. Its title was the name of a woman who had been extremely fashionable in 1900. After his opening remarks this title was an insolence in 1926. Here is the song:

The lettuces of Paris
Go walking in Paris.
There's even an endive
And who'd ever believe
They've got endive,
In Paris?

The magnifying quality of the dream inflated this absurd song into something celestial and extraordinarily funny.

I woke up. I was still laughing. That laughter seemed to augur well. I'd not have had so ridiculous a dream, I said to myself, if the situation were grave. I'd forgot that the weariness caused by pain somethimes gives rise to ridiculous dreams.

At the rue B*** hospital I was about to open the door to the room when a nurse came up and, in a cool voice, advised me that "Fifty-five isn't in his room anymore. He's in the chapel."

Where did I find the strength necessary to turn on my heels and walk down the stairs? In the chapel a woman was praying by a casket. In it was the corpse of my friend.

How serene it was, the dear face I'd struck! But what difference now could the memory of blows and caresses make to him? He no longer loved his mother, or women, or me, or anyone. For the only thing that interests the dead is death.

Horribly alone, I rejected all notions of returning to the Church; it would be too easy to employ the Host like an aspirin tablet or to fill up on negative vitamins at the Holy Table, too simple to turn towards heaven every time I become disenchanted with things on earth.

Marriage remained as a last resort. But had I not hoped to marry out of love, I'd have thought it dishonest to dupe a girl. At the Sorbonne I'd known a Mademoiselle de S*** whose boyishness had caught my fancy and I'd often told myself that if I were to have to take a wife someday, I'd prefer her to any other. I renewed our acquaintance, frequented the house in Auteuil where she lived with her mother, and we gradually came round to considering marriage a possibility. She liked me. Her mother feared seeing her daughter become a spinster. Our engagement was effortless.

She had a younger brother whom I didn't know, for he was finishing his studies at a Jesuit college in London. He came home. How had I failed to anticipate this newest wickedness on the part of a fate which yet persecutes me and which, donning all sorts of guises, masks nothing but an unalterable destiny? What had attracted me to the sister shone like a beacon in the brother. At the very first glance I beheld the drama in its entirety and understood that a mild and peaceful existence would be denied me. It was not long before I learned that, on his side, this brother, a good product of the English school, had fallen head over heels in love with me the moment we'd met. That young man adored himself. In loving me he cuckolded himself. We met in secrecy and matters progressed relentlessly to the fatal stage.

The atmosphere in the house was charged with an evil electricity. We skillfully camouflaged our crime, but my fiancée's nerves were set on edge by what she scented in the air, and all the more so because she had no suspicion of what was causing the tension. In the end, her brother's love for me moved into an intense passion. Could this passion have hidden a secret destructive impulse or need? Maybe so. He hated his sister. He pleaded with me to break our engagement, to take back my plighted word. I did all I could to slow things down. I tried to obtain a relative calm, and succeeded, succeeded simply in delaying the catastrophe.

One evening when I'd come to pay his sister a visit I heard sounds of weeping on the other side of the door. The poor girl was lying flat on the floor, a handkerchief in her mouth and her hair all askew. Standing over her, her brother was shouting: "He's mine! Mine! Mine! Since he's too much of a coward to tell you the truth, you can hear it from me!"

I couldn't bear this scene. His voice and his eyes were so ferociously cruel that I struck him in the face.

"Ah," he cried, "you'll always regret having done that," and he shut himself in his room.

While trying to bring our victim back to life, I heard a shot. I leapt up, dashed to the door of his room, tore it open. Too late. He lay beside a wardrobe. On its mirror, at the height of one's head, one could still make out the oily imprint of a kiss and the moist smudge left by breathing.

I could no longer live in these surroundings where misfortune and mourning dogged my footsteps. Suicide was out of the question because of my faith. This faith and the unending trouble of spirit and flesh I'd been in since quitting my religious exercises led me to the idea of a monastery.

Father X***, whom I consulted for advice, told me that one could not come to these very major decisions in haste, that the rule was very austere and that, for a start, I ought to test my strength by putting in a season of retirement at M*** Abbey. He furnished me with a letter of introduction to the Superior, setting forth the reasons why this retreat I was contemplating was something other than a dilettante's caprice.

When I reached the Abbey the temperature was hovering just above freezing. The falling snow was changing into freezing rain, the earth into mud. The gatekeeper summoned a monk at whose side I walked in silence under the arcades. I questioned him upon the schedules of the masses, and when he replied a shiver ran through me. I'd just heard one of those voices which, more surely, more amply than faces or bodies, inform me as to a young man's age and beauty.

He pushed back his cowl. His profile etched itself against the stone wall. It was the profile of Alfred, of H***, of Rose, of Jeanne, of Dargelos, of Lousy Luck, of Gustave and of the farm-boy.

I arrived limp before the door to the office of Dom Z***.

Dom Z*** greeted me cordially. He already had a letter from Father X*** on his desk. He dismissed the young monk. "Are you aware," he asked, "that our house can offer few comforts and that the rule here is very austere?"

"My Father," I replied, "I have reasons for believing that, austere as it may be, the rule here is not austere enough for me. I will confine myself to this visit and shall always preserve a fond memory of the welcome I have been shown today."

Yes, the monastery drove me away like everything else. The

only thing left was to leave, to imitate those Carmelite Fathers who consume themselves in the desert and for whom love is a pious suicide. But does God allow one to cherish Him in this manner?

Never mind, I'll leave—and behind me I'll leave this book. If anyone finds it, let him publish it. It may perhaps help to explain that, in exiling myself, I am exiling not a monster but a man society doesn't permit to live since society views as an error one of the mysterious quirks in the way the divine masterpiece operates.

Instead of taking unto itself the gospel according to Rimbaud: *Lo, we are come unto the age of assassins,* contemporary youth would have been better advised to have adopted *Love is to be reinvented* for its motto. Risky experiments—the world accepts them in the realm of art because the world does not take art seriously, but it condemns them in life.

I perfectly well understand that an anthill ideal like the Russians', aiming at the plural, condemns the singular to exist in one of the highest forms. But you cannot prevent certain flowers and certain fruits from being inhaled and eaten by the rich alone.

A social vice makes a vice of my outspokenness. I have no more to say, and so I withdraw. In France, this vice does not lead to the penitentiary, thanks to the longevity of the Code Napoléon and the morals of Cambacérès. But I am not willing merely to be tolerated. That wounds my love of love and of liberty.

JAMES T. FARRELL

A CASUAL INCIDENT

The kid stood at the edge of a small, nondescript crowd at State and Quincy Streets, listening while a sleek Greek conducted a Come-to-Jesus meeting. With appropriate showmanship, the fellow introduced presentable females who stood on a soap box and gave testimony. One of them was a mother, and after she had luridly described her sinful past and the joys and satisfactions of being washed from sin in the Blood of the Lamb, she put her seven-year-old girl on the box, because the girl had been living with Jesus inside of her for two years. The mother and the Greek tenderly instructed the girl to explain just how Jesus had come to her, as quick as a snap of the fingers, and just how nice and good and holy and happy it felt when you had kindly Jesus right inside of your breast. The child stood on the soap box, fidgeting, shyly dropping her eyes, saying nothing. The crowd laughed good-naturedly at her cute gestures. All coaxing failed, and the Greek lifted her down. He declared that anyway she loved Jesus, and loving Jesus was all that counted in this dark world of sin.

"Jesus got tongue-tied that time," the kid said to a burly Pole on his right.

"Dey all queer here," the stolid Pole answered, pursing his lips.

"Yeh, and it's funny the way Jesus got tongue-tied that time," the kid said.

"Yeh," the Pole said, smiling.

"I think it's damn funny. Here they say Jesus has been inside the kid for a couple of years, and then when they ask Him to speak, He gets tongue-tied."

The meeting concluded in song and the crowd dispersed. The kid and the Pole leaned against the window of an Owl Drug Store that was jumbled and confusedly decorated and placarded. They talked, and the kid noted that the Pole was a giant, with a heavy, planed face, and a deep bass voice. He had ox eyes, and looked very masculine.

"You know, dese religious people, dey all a little queer in de head," the Pole said.

"They're nuts. But it was funny, the way Jesus got tongue-tied," the kid said.

The Pole surveyed the kid. He was about twenty, with cleanly carved features, and he was carrying several books.

"Religious guys always like de ladies, doh," said the Pole.

"Yeh, they get themselves hooked up with a skirt every time."

"I was in Seattle one time, and dey had a big big place. It was a great big tent, and dere were crowds evry night. It was dat religion, what you callum? You know? Dat religion oh, gee, I know de name well. Dat religion, you know, where dey all roll round, all crazy in de head?"

"Holy Rollers."

"Yeh, dat's it, de Holy Rollers."

"Yeh," the kid said.

"Dey had a big big tent, and so big a place, and dey had big crowds evry night, and dey made all kindsa money, too. Well, de guy what was de preacher, he liked de wimmin . . . you know what I mean?"

The Pole smiled, and pursed his lips. He described how the preacher had seduced the choir master's wife and several girls in the congregation. He had finally eloped with the former, taking along the congregation funds. There had been a story about it on the front pages of the papers. The kid considered the account to be pointless, but listened, because he had nothing to do.

"Wimmin, dey all dangerous," the Pole said, pursing his lips.

He talked on, describing his life. At the age of twelve, he had run away from his native Polish village because of the poverty of his family. He had followed the sea, going to all parts of the world, and he had had adventures on many a waterfront.

"When a young fellow goes on his own, tings happen to him. You know . . . well, tings happen to him," the Pole said.

"I know."

"A young fellow, he goes on his own, and he don't know nottin', and well . . . tings happen to him."

"You have to take your chances, and if you can't swim, you sink. It's just your tough tiddy, then," the kid said.

"Yes, but tings happen."

The Pole recounted more of his experiences, interrupting his tales to remark:

"I got a nice place now, wid a fren. We have nice big place 'n' we bring anyone we want dere. No one to bodder us."

"That's pretty nice. You can bring your women there."

"Wimmin. . . . No, dey're dangerous," the Pole said, pursing his lips.

"Yes, I guess they can get to be a nuisance."

"Where you live? . . . At home?"

"Me, I live in an undertaking parlor."

The Pole laughed. The kid explained that he was paid three dollars a week, and received a bed for hanging around, answering telephone calls and sometimes going out on the ambulance. This was his evening off. The Pole again laughed, pursing his lips and exclaiming that it was funny.

"You bring girls dere, too?"

"Hell, no! We got six religious Irishmen there, and if I brought a girl around, sure as hell there would be a gang rape."

"Well, wimmin, dey're dangerous," the Pole said, laughing.

The kid leaned back against the window, and watched the

sleepy-eyed parade of people along State Street. He heard the traffic sounds and sudden jets of conversation.

"Wanna see my place?"

"Not tonight, thanks. I feel pretty tired," the kid answered.

The Pole seemed to become confused, and, to mask his confusion, he quickly asked the kid about the books he had under his arm. The kid casually answered that they were story books. The Pole talked about the sea, and then asked the kid if he had ever been on the road. The kid nodded, and told about how he had once gotten blind drunk in Hoboken.

"Well, as I say, tings happen to young fellows."

"Yeh," the kid yawned.

"You out now, lookin' for girls?"

"Not particularly. I feel pretty tired."

"I was just wonderin'," the Pole said, shrugging his broad shoulders; he pursed his lips.

"I don't like cat houses," the kid said.

"A young fellow, he got a have girls."

"Yeh, I guess he does," the kid said.

The kid yawned, said he was getting pretty tired, and guessed that he would be getting back to the undertaking parlor.

"Come up 'n' see my place?" the Pole said.

"No, thanks, I feel too tired."

The Pole smiled, and gave the kid his address. He told him that any time he was broke, or needed a place to sleep, to come up. He pursed his lips, and looked at the kid.

"Come up 'n' see my place," he said, his voice suddenly strained.

"I feel too tired. . . . Say, there's a saloon called Reilley's in Hoboken, right off the Fourteenth Street ferry. Ever been there?"

The Pole eyed the kid queerly as the kid went on to talk about the beer at Reilley's, fifteen cents a glass with the headache guaranteed. The Pole said he guessed he would be going home.

"And I guess I'll be blowing this town again pretty damn quick," the kid said.

"Chicago's a nice town. Lotsa girls here," the Pole said.

He pursed his lips.

"Nice girls are everywhere. They grow like apples on trees."

The Pole laughed, and said nice girls were very dangerous. The kid said anyway the idea about life was to live dangerously, on a volcano.

"Girls dat are nice, sometimes dey give you . . . you know . . . dose," the Pole said.

"Well, you got to take your chances," the kid said.

"But dere's a way ob not taking chances," the Pole said in a tense voice.

"What do you think of Cleveland as a town?" the kid asked.

The Pole was uninterested while the kid talked of Cleveland, comparing it with Chicago and New York.

"You got nice girl, ob your own?" asked the Pole.

"No, I don't believe in dragging nuisances around with me."

"But you like de girls?"

"Yeh, sometimes."

"Tonight?"

"No."

"You goin' back to de undertaker's and read?"

"Yes."

"Oh, gee, ain't it spooky?" the Pole asked, laughing; he pursed his lips, and he concentrated his ox eyes intensely on the kid.

"I got nice place. You come on up?"

"I'm pretty busy. I'm writing a book," the kid said.

"About de girls?"

"Not particularly."

"It must be nice to write books?"

He told the kid if he'd visit him, that he would tell him lots of things to put into the book, things about geisha girls, and Asiatic beachcombers, and sailors, and towns in all parts of the world.

"I'm pretty tired. Guess I'll blow," the kid said.

"Got my address?"

"Yes, but I'm pretty busy," the kid said.

"But ain't it spooky, out dere wid de corpses?"

"I don't mind it."

"It's funny," the Pole said, laughing hoarsely.

"Yep, I guess I'll be blowing," the kid said.

"Dat's funny, livin' at de undertaker's."

"It's better than sleeping in the parks," the kid said.

"You sure you wouldn't like to come to my place a little while?" the Pole asked, pursing his lips.

"No thanks," the kid answered, yawning.

"Sure?"

"Yes."

"But you got to be careful ob de girls. Dere dangerous."

"Yeh," the kid said yawning, again stating that he was going.

"So long," the kid said.

"So long, kid . . ."

"I'm going to the I. C. station at Van Buren Street."

"So long, kid . . . but I got a nice place."

D.H. LAWRENCE

THE PRUSSIAN OFFICER

They had marched more than thirty kilometres since dawn, along the white, hot road where occasional thickets of trees threw a moment of shade, then out into the glare again. On either hand, the valley, wide and shallow, glittered with heat; dark-green patches of rye, pale young corn, fallow and meadow and black pine woods spread in a dull, hot diagram under a glistening sky. But right in front the mountains ranged across, pale blue and very still, snow gleaming gently out of the deep atmosphere. And towards the mountains, on and on, the regiment marched between the rye-fields and the meadows, between the scraggy fruit trees set regularly on either side the high road. The burnished, dark-green rye threw off a suffocating heat, the mountains drew gradually nearer and more distinct. While the feet of the soldiers grew hotter, sweat ran through their hair under their helmets, and their knapsacks could burn no more in contact with their shoulders, but seemed instead to give off a cold, prickly sensation.

He walked on and on in silence, staring at the mountains ahead, that rose sheer out of the land, and stood fold behind fold, half earth, half heaven, the heaven, the barrier with slits of soft snow, in the pale, bluish peaks.

He could now walk almost without pain. At the start, he had determined not to limp. It had made him sick to take the first steps, and during the first mile or so, he had compressed his breath, and the cold drops of sweat had stood on his forehead. But he had walked it off. What were they after all but bruises! He had looked at them, as he was getting up: deep bruises on the backs of his thighs. And since he had made his first step in the morning, he had been conscious of them, till now he had a tight, hot place in his chest, with suppressing the pain, and holding himself in. There seemed no air when he breathed. But he walked almost lightly.

The Captain's hand had trembled at taking his coffee at dawn: his orderly saw it again. And he saw the fine figure of the Captain wheeling on horseback at the farmhouse ahead, a handsome figure in pale-blue uniform with facings of scarlet, and the metal gleaming on the black helmet and the sword-scabbard, and dark streaks of sweat coming on the silky bay horse. The orderly felt he was connected with that figure moving so suddenly on horseback: he followed it like a shadow, mute and inevitable and damned by it. And the officer was always aware of the tramp of the company behind, the march of his orderly among the men.

The Captain was a tall man of about forty, grey at the temples. He had a handsome, finely-knit figure, and was one of the best horsemen in the West. His orderly, having to rub him down, admired the amazing riding-muscles of his loins.

For the rest, the orderly scarcely noticed the officer any more than he noticed himself. It was rarely he saw his master's face: he did not look at it. The Captain had reddish-brown, stiff hair, that he wore short upon his skull. His moustache was also cut short and bristly over a full, brutal mouth. His face was rather rugged, the cheeks thin. Perhaps the man was the more handsome for the deep lines in his face, the irritable tension of his brow, which gave him the look of a man who fights with life. His fair eyebrows stood bushy over light-blue eyes that were always flashing with cold fire.

He was a Prussian aristocrat, haughty and overbearing. But his mother had been a Polish countess. Having made too many gambling debts when he was young, he had ruined his prospects in the Army, and remained an infantry captain. He had never married: his position did not allow of it, and no woman had ever moved him to it. His time he spent riding—occasionally he rode one of his own horses at the races—and at the officers' club. Now and then he took himself a mistress. But after such an event, he returned to duty with his brow still more tense, his eyes still more hostile and irritable. With the men, however, he was merely impersonal, though a devil when roused; so that, on the whole, they feared him, but had no great aversion from him. They accepted him as the inevitable.

To his orderly he was at first cold and just and indifferent: he did not fuss over trifles. So that his servant knew practically nothing about him, except just what orders he would give, and how he wanted them obeyed. That was quite simple. Then the change gradually came.

The orderly was a youth of about twenty-two, of medium height, and well built. He had strong, heavy limbs, was swarthy, with a soft, black, young moustache. There was something altogether warm and young about him. He had firmly marked eyebrows over dark, expressionless eyes, that seemed never to have thought, only to have received life direct through his senses, and acted straight from instinct.

Gradually the officer had become aware of his servant's young vigorous, unconscious presence about him. He could not get away from the sense of the youth's person, while he was in attendance. It was like a warm flame upon the older man's tense, rigid body, that had become almost unliving, fixed. There was something so free and self-contained about him, and something in the young fellow's movement, that made the officer aware of him. And this irritated the Prussian. He did not choose to be touched into life by his servant. He might easily have changed his man, but he did not. He now very rarely looked direct at his orderly, but kept his face averted, as if to avoid seeing him. And yet as the young soldier moved unthinking about the apartment, the elder watched him, and would notice the movement of his strong young shoulders under the blue cloth, the bend of his neck. And it irritated him. To see the soldier's young, brown, shapely peasant's hand grasp the loaf or the wine-bottle sent a flash of hate or of anger through the elder man's blood. It was not that the youth was clumsy: it was rather the blind, instinctive sureness of movement of an unhampered young animal that irritated the officer to such a degree.

Once, when a bottle of wine had gone over, and the red gushed out on to the tablecloth, the officer had started up with an oath, and his eyes, bluey like fire, had held those of the confused youth for a moment. It was a shock for the young soldier. He felt something sink deeper, deeper into his soul, where nothing had ever gone before. It left him rather blank and wondering. Some of his natural completeness in himself was gone, a little uneasiness took its place. And from that time an undiscovered feeling had held between the two men.

Henceforward the orderly was afraid of really meeting his master. His subconsciousness remembered those steely blue eyes and the harsh brows, and did not intend to meet them again. So he always stared past his master, and avoided him. Also, in a little anxiety, he waited for the three months to have gone, when his time would be up. He began to feel a constraint in the Captain's presence, and the soldier even more than the officer wanted to be left alone, in his neutrality as servant.

He had served the Captain for more than a year, and knew his duty. This he performed easily, as if it were natural to him. The officer and his commands he took for granted, as he took the sun and the rain, and he served as a matter of course. It did not implicate him personally.

But now if he were going to be forced into a personal interchange with his master he would be like a wild thing caught, he felt he must get away.

But the influence of the young soldier's being had penetrated through the officer's stiffened discipline, and perturbed the man in him. He, however, was a gentleman, with long, fine hands and cultivated movements, and was not going to allow such a thing as the stirring of his innate self. He was a man of passionate temper, who had always kept himself suppressed. Occasionally there had been a duel, an outburst before the soldiers. He knew himself to be always on the point of breaking out. But he kept himself hard to the idea of the Service. Whereas the young soldier seemed to live out his warm, full nature, to give it off in his very movements, which had a certain zest, such as wild animals have in free movement. And this irritated the officer more and more.

In spite of himself, the Captain could not regain his neutrality of feeling towards his orderly. Nor could he leave the man alone. In spite of himself, he watched him, gave him sharp orders, tried to take up as much of his time as possible. Sometimes he flew into a rage with the young soldier, and bullied him. Then the orderly shut himself off, as it were out of earshot, and waited, with sullen, flushed face, for the end of the noise. The words never pierced to his intelligence, he made himself, protectively, impervious to the feelings of his master.

He had a scar on his left thumb, a deep seam going across the knuckle. The officer had long suffered from it, and wanted to do something to it. Still it was there, ugly and brutal on the young, brown hand. At last the Captain's reserve gave way. One day, as the orderly was smoothing out the tablecloth, the officer pinned down his thumb with a pencil, asking:

"How did you come by that?"

The young man winced and drew back at attention.

"A wood axe, Herr Hauptmann," he answered.

The officer waited for further explanation. None came. The orderly went about his duties. The elder man was sullenly angry. His servant avoided him. And the next day he had to use all his will-power to avoid seeing the scarred thumb. He wanted to get hold of it and——A hot flame ran in his blood.

He knew his servant would soon be free, and would be glad. As yet, the soldier had held himself off from the elder man. The Captain grew madly irritable. He could not rest when the soldier was away, and when he was present, he glared at him with tormented eyes. He hated those fine, black brows over the unmeaning, dark eyes, he was infuriated by the free movement of the handsome limbs, which no military discipline could make stiff. And he became harsh and cruelly bullying, using contempt and satire. The young soldier only grew more mute and expressionless.

"What cattle were you bred by, that you can't keep straight eyes? Look me in the eyes when I speak to you."

And the soldier turned his dark eyes to the other's face, but there was no sight in them: he stared with the slightest possible cast, holding back his sight, perceiving the blue of his master's eyes, but receiving no look from them. And the elder man went pale, and his reddish eyebrows twitched. He gave his order, barrenly.

Once he flung a heavy military glove into the young soldier's face. Then he had the satisfaction of seeing the black eyes flare up into his own, like a blaze when straw is thrown on a fire. And he had laughed with a little tremor and a sneer.

But there were only two months more. The youth instinctively tried to keep himself intact: he tried to serve the officer as if the latter were an abstract authority and not a man. All his instinct was to avoid personal contact, even definite hate. But in spite of himself the hate grew, responsive to the officer's passion. However, he put it in the background. When he had left the Army he could dare acknowledge it. By nature he was active, and had many friends. He thought what amazing good fellows they were. But, without knowing it, he was alone. Now this solitariness was intensified. It would carry him through his term. But the officer seemed to be going irritably insane, and the youth was deeply frightened.

The soldier had a sweetheart, a girl from the mountains, independent and primitive. The two walked together, rather silently. He went with her, not to talk, but to have his arm round her, and for the physical contact. This eased him, made it easier for him to ignore the Captain; for he could rest with her held fast against his chest. And she, in some unspoken fashion, was there for him. They loved each other.

The Captain perceived it, and was mad with irritation. He kept the young man engaged all the evenings long, and took pleasure in the dark look that came on his face. Occasionally, the eyes of the two men met, those of the younger sullen and dark, doggedly unalterable, those of the elder sneering with restless contempt.

The officer tried hard not to admit the passion that had got hold of him. He would not know that his feeling for his orderly was anything but that of a man incensed by his stupid, perverse servant. So, keeping quite justified and conventional in his consciousness, he let the other thing run on. His nerves, however, were suffering. At last he slung the end of a belt in his servant's face. When he saw the youth start back, the pain-tears in his eyes and the blood on his mouth, he had felt at once a thrill of deep pleasure and of shame.

But this, he acknowledged to himself, was a thing he had never done before. The fellow was too exasperating. His own nerves must be going to pieces. He went away for some days with a woman.

It was a mockery of pleasure. He simply did not want the woman. But he stayed on for his time. At the end of it, he came back in an agony of irritation, torment, and misery. He rode all the evening, then came straight in to supper. His orderly was out. The officer sat with his long, fine hands lying on the table, perfectly still, and all his blood seemed to be corroding.

At last his servant entered. He watched the strong, easy young figure, the fine eyebrows, the thick black hair. In a week's time the youth had got back his old well-being. The hands of the officer twitched and seemed to be full of mad flame. The young man stood at attention, unmoving, shut off.

The meal went in silence. But the orderly seemed eager. He made a clatter with the dishes.

"Are you in a hurry?" asked the officer, watching the intent, warm face of his servant. The other did not reply.

"Will you answer my question?" said the Captain.

"Yes, sir," replied the orderly, standing with his pile of deep Army plates. The Captain waited, looked at him, then asked again:

"Are you in a hurry?"

"Yes, sir," came the answer, that sent a flash through the listener.

"For what?"

"I was going out, sir."

"I want you this evening."

There was a moment's hesitation. The officer had a curious stiffness of countenance.

"Yes sir," replied the servant, in his throat.

"I want you to-morrow evening also—in fact you may consider your evenings occupied, unless I give you leave."

The mouth with the young moustache set close.

"Yes, sir," answered the orderly, loosening his lips for a moment.

He again turned to the door.

"And why have you a piece of pencil in your ear?"

The orderly hesitated, then continued on his way without answering. He set the plates in a pile outside the door, took the stump of pencil from his ear, and put it in his pocket. He had been copying a verse for his sweetheart's birthday card. He returned to finish clearing the table. The officer's eyes were dancing, he had a little, eager smile.

"Why have you a piece of pencil in your ear?" he asked.

The orderly took his hands full of dishes. His master was standing near the great green stove, a little smile on his face, his chin thrust forward. When the young soldier saw him his heart suddenly ran hot. He felt blind. Instead of answering, he turned dazedly to the door. As he was crouching to set down the dishes, he was pitched forward by a kick from behind. The pots went in a stream down the stairs, he clung to the pillar of the banisters. And as he was rising he was kicked heavily again and again, so that he clung sickly to the post for some moments. His master had gone swiftly into the room and closed the door. The maid-servant downstairs looked up the staircase and made a mocking face at the crockery disaster.

The officer's heart was plunging. He poured himself a glass of wine, part of which he spilled on the floor, and gulped the remainder, leaning against the cool, green stove. He heard his man collecting the dishes from the stairs. Pale, as if intoxicated, he waited. The servant entered again. The Captain's heart gave a pang, as of pleasure, seeing the young fellow bewildered and uncertain on his feet with pain.

"Schöner!" he said.

The soldier was a little slower in coming to attention.

"Yes sir!"

The youth stood before him, with pathetic young moustache, and fine eyebrows very distinct on his forehead of dark marble.

"I asked you a question."

"Yes, sir."

The officer's tone bit like acid.

"Why had you a pencil in your ear?"

Again the servant's heart ran hot, and he could not breathe. With dark, strained eyes, he looked at the officer, as if fascinated. And he stood there sturdily planted, unconscious. The withering smile came into the Captain's eyes, and he lifted his foot.

"I forgot it—sir," panted the soldier, his dark eyes fixed on the other man's dancing blue ones.

"What was it doing there?"

He saw the young man's breast heaving as he made an effort for words.

"I had been writing."

"Writing what?"

Again the soldier looked him up and down. The officer could hear him panting. The smile came into the blue eyes. The soldier worked his dry throat, but could not speak. Suddenly the smile lit like a flame on the officer's face, and a kick came heavily against the orderly's thigh. The youth moved sideways. His face went dead, with two black, staring eyes.

"Well?" said the officer.

The orderly's mouth had gone dry, and his tongue rubbed in it as on dry brown-paper. He worked his throat. The officer raised his foot. The servant went stiff.

"Some poetry, sir," came the crackling, unrecognisable sound of his voice.

"Poetry, what poetry?" asked the Captain, with a sickly smile.

Again there was the working in the throat. The Captain's heart had suddenly gone down heavily, and he stood sick and tired.

"For my girl, sir," he heard the dry, inhuman sound.

"Oh!" he said, turning away. "Clear the table."

"Click!" went the soldier's throat; then again, "click!" and then the half-articulate:

"Yes, sir."

The young soldier was gone, looking old, and walking heavily.

The officer, left alone, held himself rigid, to prevent himself from thinking. His instinct warned him that he must not think. Deep inside him was the intense gratification of his passion, still working powerfully. Then there was a counteraction, a horrible breaking down of something inside him, a whole agony of reaction. He stood there for an hour motionless, a chaos of sensations, but rigid with a will to keep blank his consciousness, to prevent his mind grasping. And he held himself so until the worst of the stress had passed, when he began to drink, drank himself to an intoxication, till he slept obliterated. When he woke in the morning he was shaken to the base of his nature. But he had fought off the realisation of what he had done. He had prevented his mind from taking it in, had suppressed it along with his instincts, and the conscious man had nothing to do with it. He felt only as after a bout of intoxication, weak, but the affair itself all dim and not to be recovered. Of the drunkenness of his passion he successfully refused remembrance. And when his orderly appeared with coffee, the officer assumed the same self he had had the morning before. He refused the event of the past night—denied it had ever been—and was successful in his denial. He had not done any such thing—not he himself. Whatever there might be lay at the door of a stupid insubordinate servant.

The orderly had gone about in a stupor all the evening. He drank some beer because he was parched, but not much, the alcohol made his feeling come back, and he could not bear it. He was dulled, as if nine-tenths of the ordinary man in him were inert. He crawled about disfigured. Still, when he thought of the kicks, he went sick, and when he thought of the threat of more kicking, in the room afterwards, his heart went hot and faint, and he panted, remembering the one that had come. He had been forced to say: "For my girl." He was much too done even to want to cry. His mouth hung slightly open, like an idiot's. He felt vacant, and wasted. So, he wandered at his work, painfully, and very slowly and clumsily, fumbling blindly with the brushes, and finding it difficult, when he sat down, to summon the energy to move again. His limbs, his jaw, were slack and nerveless. But he was very tired. He got to bed at last, and slept inert, relaxed, in a sleep that was rather stupor than slumber, a dead night of stupefaction shot through with gleams of anguish.

In the morning were the manoeuvres. But he woke even before the bugle sounded. The painful ache in his chest, the dryness of his throat, the awful steady feeling of misery made his eyes come awake and dreary at once. He knew, without thinking, what had happened. And he knew that the day had come again, when he must go on with his round. The last bit of darkness was being pushed out of the room. He would have to move his inert body and go on. He was so young, and had known so little trouble, that he was bewildered. He only wished it would stay night, so that he could lie still, covered up by the darkness. And yet nothing would prevent the day from coming, nothing would save him from having to get up and saddle the Captain's horse, and make the Captain's coffee. It was there, inevitable. And then, he thought, it was impossible. Yet they would not leave him free. He must go and take the coffee to the Captain. He was too stunned to understand it. He only knew it was inevitable—inevitable, however long he lay inert.

At last, after heaving at himself, for he seemed to be a mass of inertia, he got up. But he had to force every one of his movements from behind, with his will. He felt lost, and dazed, and helpless. Then he clutched hold of the bed, the pain was so keen. And looking at his thighs he saw the darker bruises on his swarthy flesh, and he knew that if he pressed one of his fingers on one of the bruises, he should faint. But he did not want to faint—he did not want anybody to know. No one should ever know. It was between him and the Captain. There were only the two people in the world now—himself and the Captain.

Slowly, economically, he got dressed and forced himself to walk. Everything was obscure, except just what he had his hands on. But he managed to get through his work. The very pain revived his dull senses. The worst remained yet. He took the tray and went up to the Captain's room. The officer, pale and heavy, sat at the table. The orderly, as he saluted, felt himself put out of existence. He stood still for a moment submitting to his own nullification—then he gathered himself, seemed to regain himself, and then the Captain began to grow vague, unreal, and the younger soldier's heart beat up. He clung to this situation—that the Captain did not exist—so that he himself might live. But when he saw his officer's hand tremble as he took the coffee, he felt everything falling shattered. And he went away, feeling as if he himself were coming to pieces, disintegrated. And when the Captain was there on horseback, giving orders, while he himself stood, with rifle and knapsack, sick with pain, he felt as if he must shut his eyes—as if he must shut his eyes on everything. It was only the long agony of marching with a parched throat that filled him with one single, sleep-heavy intention: to save himself.

II

He was getting used even to his parched throat. That the snowy peaks were radiant among the sky, that the whity-green glacier-river twisted through its pale shoals, in the valley below, seemed almost supernatural. But he was going mad with fever and thirst. He plodded on uncomplaining. He did not want to speak, not to anybody. There were two gulls, like flakes of water and snow, over the river. The scent of green rye soaked in sunshine came like a sickness. And the march continued, monotonously, almost like a bad sleep.

At the next farmhouse, which stood low and broad near the high road, tubs of water had been put out. The soldiers clustered round to drink. They took off their helmets, and the steam mounted from their wet hair. The Captain sat on horseback, watching. He needed to see his orderly. His helmet threw a dark shadow over his light, fierce eyes, but his moustache and mouth and chin were distinct in the sunshine. The orderly must move under the presence of the figure of the horseman. It was not that he was afraid, or cowed. It was as if he was disembowelled, made empty, like an empty shell. He felt himself as nothing, a shadow creeping under the sunshine. And, thirsty as he was, he could scarcely drink, feeling the Captain near him. He would not take off his helmet to wipe his wet hair. He wanted to stay in shadow, not to be forced into consciousness. Starting, he saw the light heel of the officer prick the belly of the horse; the Captain cantered away, and he himself could relapse into vacancy.

Nothing, however, could give him back his living place in the hot, bright morning. He felt like a gap among it all. Whereas the Captain was prouder, overriding. A hot flash went through the young servant's body. The Captain was firmer and prouder with life, he himself was empty as a shadow. Again the flash went through him, dazing him out. But his heart ran a little firmer.

The company turned up the hill, to make a loop for the return. Below, from among the trees, the farm-bell clanged. He saw the labourers, mowing bare-foot at the thick grass, leave off their work and go downhill, their scythes hanging over their shoulders, like long, bright claws curving down behind them. They seemed like dream-people, as if they had no relation to himself. He felt as in a blackish dream: as if all the other things were there and had form, but he himself was only a consciousness, a gap that could think and perceive.

The soldiers were tramping silently up the glaring hill-side. Gradually his head began to revolve, slowly, rhythmically. Sometimes it was dark before his eyes, as if he saw this world through a smoked glass, frail shadows and unreal. It gave him a pain in his head to walk.

The air was too scented, it gave no breath. All the lush green-stuff seemed to be issuing its sap, till the air was deathly, sickly with the smell of greenness. There was the perfume of clover, like pure honey and bees. Then there grew a faint acrid tang—they were near the beeches; and then a queer clattering noise, and a suffocating, hideous smell; they were passing a flock of sheep, a shepherd in a black smock, holding his crook. Why should the sheep huddle together under this fierce sun? He felt that the shepherd would not see him, though he could see the shepherd.

At last there was the halt. They stacked rifles in a conical stack, put down their kit in a scattered circle around it, and dispersed a little, sitting on a small knoll high on the hill-side. The chatter began. The soldiers were steaming with heat, but were lively. He sat still, seeing the blue mountains rising upon the land, twenty kilometres away. There was a blue fold in the ranges, then out of that, at the foot, the broad, pale bed of the river, stretches of whity-green water between pinkish-gray shoals among the dark pine woods. There it was, spread out a long way off. And it seemed to come downhill, the river. There was a raft being steered, a mile away. It was a strange country. Nearer, a red-roofed, broad farm with white base and square dots of windows crouched beside the wall of beech foliage on the wood's edge. There were long strips of rye and clover and pale green corn. And just at his feet, below the knoll, was a darkish bog, where globe flowers stood breathless still on their slim stalks. And some of the pale gold bubbles were burst, and a broken fragment hung in the air. He thought he was going to sleep.

Suddenly something moved into this coloured mirage before his eyes. The Captain, a small, light-blue and scarlet figure, was trotting evenly between the strips of corn, along the level brow of the hill. And the man making flag-signals was coming on. Proud and sure moved the horseman's figure, the quick, bright thing, in which was concentrated all the light of this morning, which for the rest lay fragile, shining shadow. Submissive, apathetic, the young soldier sat and stared. But as the horse slowed to a walk, coming up the last steep path, the great flash flared over the body and soul of the orderly. He sat waiting. The back of his head felt as if it were weighted with a heavy piece of fire. He did not want to eat. His hands trembled slightly as he moved them. Meanwhile the officer on horseback was approaching slowly and proudly. The tension grew in the orderly's soul. Then again, seeing the Captain ease himself on the saddle, the flash blazed through him.

The Captain looked at the patch of light blue and scarlet, and dark head, scattered closely on the hill-side. It pleased him. The command pleased him. And he was feeling proud. His orderly was among them in common subjection. The officer rose a little on his stirrups to look. The young soldier sat with averted, dumb face. The Captain relaxed on his seat. His slim-legged, beautiful horse, brown as a beech nut, walked proudly uphill. The Captain passed into the zone of the company's atmosphere: a hot smell of men, of sweat, of leather. He knew it very well. After a word with the lieutenant, he went a few paces higher, and sat there, a dominant figure, his sweat-marked horse swishing its tail, while he looked down on his men, on his orderly, a nonentity among the crowd.

The young soldier's heart was like fire in his chest, and he breathed with difficulty. The officer, looking downhill, saw three of the young soldiers, two pails of water between them, staggering across a sunny green field. A table had been set up under a tree, and there the slim lieutenant stood, importantly busy. Then the Captain summoned himself to an act of courage. He called his orderly.

The flame leapt into the young soldier's throat as he heard the command, and he rose blindly, stifled. He saluted, standing below the officer. He did not look up. But there was the flicker in the Captain's voice.

"Go to the inn and fetch me . . ." the officer gave his commands. "Quick!" he added.

At the last word, the heart of the servant leapt with a flash, and he felt the strength come over his body. But he turned in mechanical obedience, and set off at a heavy run downhill, looking almost like a bear, his trousers bagging over his military boots. And the officer watched this blind, plunging run all the way.

But it was only the outside of the orderly's body that was obeying so humbly and mechanically. Inside had gradually accumulated a core into which all the energy of that young life was compact and concentrated. He executed his commission, and plodded quickly back uphill. There was a pain in his head as he walked that made him twist his features unknowingly. But hard there in the centre of his chest was himself, himself, firm, and not to be plucked to pieces.

The Captain had gone up into the wood. The orderly plodded through the hot, powerfully smelling zone of the company's atmosphere. He had a curious mass of energy inside him now. The Captain was less real than himself. He approached the green entrance to the wood. There, in the half-shade, he saw the horse standing, the sunshine and the flickering shadow of leaves dancing over his brown body. There was a clearing where timber had lately been felled. Here, in the gold-green shade beside the brilliant cup of sunshine, stood two figures, blue and pink, the bits of pink showing out plainly. The Captain was talking to his lieutenant.

The orderly stood on the edge of the bright clearing, where great trunks of trees, stripped and glistening, lay stretched like naked, brown-skinned bodies. Chips of wood littered the trampled floor, like splashed light, and the bases of the felled trees stood here and there, with their raw, level tops. Beyond was the brilliant, sunlit green of a beech.

"Then I will ride forward," the orderly heard his Captain say. The lieutenant saluted and strode away. He himself went forward. A hot flash passed through his belly, as he tramped towards his officer.

The Captain watched the rather heavy figure of the young soldier stumble forward, and his veins, too, ran hot. This was to be man to man between them. He yielded before the solid, stumbling figure with bent head. The orderly stooped and put the food on a level-sawn tree-base. The Captain watched the glistening, sun-inflamed, naked hands. He wanted to speak to the young soldier, but could not. The servant propped a bottle against his thigh, pressed open the cork, and poured out the beer into the mug. He kept his head bent. The Captain accepted the mug.

"Hot!" he said, as if amiably.

The flame sprang out of the orderly's heart, nearly suffocating him.

"Yes, sir," he replied, between shut teeth.

And he heard the sound of the Captain's drinking, and he clenched his fists, such a strong torment came into his wrists. Then came the faint clang of the closing of the pot-lid. He looked up. The Captain was watching him. He glanced swiftly away. Then he saw the officer stoop and take a piece of bread from the tree-base. Again the flash of flame went through the young soldier, seeing the stiff body stoop beneath him, and his hands jerked. He looked away. He could feel the officer was nervous. The bread fell as it was being broken. The officer ate the other piece. The two men stood tense and still, the master laboriously chewing his bread, the servant staring with averted face, his fist clenched.

Then the young soldier started. The officer had pressed open the lid of the mug again. The orderly watched the lip of the mug, and the white hand that clenched the handle, as if he were fascinated. It was raised. The young followed it with his eyes. And then he saw the thin, strong throat of the elder man moving up and down as he drank, the strong jaw working. And the instinct which had been jerking at the young man's wrists suddenly jerked free. He jumped, feeling as if it were rent in two by a strong flame.

The spur of the officer caught in a tree root, he went down backwards with a crash, the middle of his back thudding sickeningly against a sharp-edged tree-base, the pot flying away. And in a second the orderly, with serious, earnest young face, and underlip between his teeth, had got his knee in the officer's chest and was pressing the chin backward over the farther edge of the tree-stump, pressing, with all his heart behind in a passion of relief, the tension of his wrists exquisite with relief. And with the base of his palms he shoved at the chin, with all his might. And it was pleasant, too, to have that chin, that hard jaw already slightly rough with beard, in his hands. He did not relax one hair's breadth, but, all the force of all his blood exulting in his thrust, he shoved back the head of the other man, till there was a little "cluck" and a crunching sensation. Then he felt as if his head went to vapour. Heavy convulsions shook the body of the officer, frightening and horrifying the young soldier. Yet it pleased him, too, to repress them. It pleased him to keep his hands pressing back the chin, to feel the chest of the other man yield in expiration to the weight of his strong, young knees, to feel the hard twitchings of the prostrate body jerking his own whole frame, which was pressed down on it.

But it went still. He could look into the nostrils of the other man, the eyes he could scarcely see. How curiously the mouth was pushed out, exaggerating the full lips, and the moustache bristling up from them. Then, with a start, he noticed the nostrils gradually filled with blood. The red brimmed, hesitated, ran over, and went in a thin trickle down the face to the eyes.

It shocked and distressed him. Slowly, he got up. The body twitched and sprawled there, inert. He stood and looked at it in silence. It was a pity *it* was broken. It represented more than the thing which had kicked and bullied him. He was afraid to look at the eyes. They were hideous now, only the whites showing, and the blood running to them. The face of the orderly was drawn with horror at the sight. Well, it was so. In his heart he was satisfied. He had hated the face of the Captain. It was extinguished now. There was a heavy relief in the orderly's soul. That was as it should be. But he could not bear to see the long, military body lying broken over the tree-base, the fine fingers crisped. He wanted to hide it away.

Quickly, busily, he gathered it up and pushed it under the felled tree trunks, which rested their beautiful, smooth length either end on the logs. The face was horrible with blood. He covered it with the helmet. Then he pushed the limbs straight and decent, and brushed the dead leaves off the fine cloth of the uniform. So, it lay quite still in the shadow under there. A little strip of sunshine ran along the breast, from a chink between the logs. The orderly sat by it for a few moments. Here his own life also ended.

Then, through his daze, he heard the lieutenant, in a loud voice, explaining to the men outside the wood, that they were to suppose the bridge on the river below was held by the enemy. Now they were to march to the attack in such and such a manner. The lieutenant had no gift of expression. The orderly, listening from habit, got muddled. And when the lieutenant began it all again he ceased to hear.

He knew he must go. He stood up. It surprised him that the leaves were glittering in the sun, and the chips of wood reflecting white from the ground. For him a change had come over the world. But for the rest it had not—all seemed the same. Only he had left it. And he could not go back. It was his duty to return with the beer-pot and the bottle. He could not. He had left all that. The lieutenant was still hoarsely explaining. He must go, or they would overtake him. And he could not bear contact with anyone now.

He drew his fingers over his eyes, trying to find out where he was. Then he turned away. He saw the horse standing in the path. He went up to it and mounted. It hurt him to sit in the saddle. The pain of keeping his seat occupied him as they cantered through the wood. He would not have minded anything, but he could not get away from the sense of being divided from the others. The path led out of the trees. On the edge of the wood he pulled up and stood watching. There in the spacious sunshine of the valley soldiers were moving in a little swarm. Every now and then, a man harrowing on a strip of fallow shouted to his oxen, at the turn. The village and the white-towered church was small in the sunshine. And he no longer belonged to it—he sat there, beyond, like a man outside in the dark. He had gone out from everyday life into the unknown and he could not, he even did not want to go back.

Turning from the sun-blazing valley, he rode deep into the wood. Tree trunks, like people standing grey and still, took no notice as he went. A doe, herself a moving bit of sunshine and shadow, went running through the flecked shade. There were bright green rents in the foliage. Then it was all pine wood, dark and cool. And he was sick with pain, and had an intolerable great pulse in his head, and he was sick. He had never been ill in his life. He felt lost, quite dazed with all this.

Trying to get down from the horse, he fell, astonished at the pain and his lack of balance. The horse shifted uneasily. He jerked its bridle and sent it cantering jerkily away. It was his last connection with the rest of things.

But he only wanted to lie down and not be disturbed. Stumbling through the trees, he came on a quiet place where beeches and pine trees grew on a slope. Immediately he had lain down and closed his eyes, his consciousness went racing on without him. A big pulse of sickness beat in him as if it throbbed through the whole earth. He was burning with dry heat. But he was too busy, too tearingly active in the incoherent race of delirium to observe.

III

He came to with a start. His mouth was dry and hard, his heart beat heavily, but he had not the energy to get up. His heart beat heavily. Where was he?—the barracks—at home? There was something knocking. And, making an effort, he looked round—trees, and litter of greenery, and reddish, bright, still pieces of sunshine on the floor. He did not believe he was himself, he did not believe what he saw. Something was knocking. He made a struggle towards consciousness, but relapsed. Then he struggled again. And gradually his surroundings fell into relationship with himself. He knew, and a great pang of fear went through his heart. Somebody was knocking. He could see the heavy, black rags of a fir tree overhead. Then everything went black. Yet he did not believe he had closed his eyes. He had not. Out of the blackness sight slowly emerged again. And someone was knocking. Quickly, he saw the blood-disfigured face of his Captain, which he hated. And he held himself still with horror. Yet, deep inside him, he knew that it was so, the Captain should be dead. But the physical delirium got hold of him. Someone was knocking. He lay perfectly still, as if dead, with fear. And he went unconscious.

When he opened his eyes again he started, seeing something creeping swiftly up a tree trunk. It was a little bird. And the bird was whistling overhead. Tap-tap-tap—it was the small, quick bird rapping the tree trunk with its beak, as if its head were a little round hammer. He watched it curiously. It shifted sharply, in its creeping fashion. Then, like a mouse, it slid down the bare trunk. Its swift creeping sent a flash of revulsion through him. He raised his head. It felt a great weight. Then, the little bird ran out of the shadow across a still patch of sunshine, its little head bobbing swiftly, its white build, so compact, with piece of white on its wings. There were several of them. They were so pretty—but they crept like swift, erratic mice, running here and there among the beech-mast.

He lay down again exhausted, and his consciousness lapsed. He had a horror of the little creeping birds. All his blood seemed to be darting and creeping in his head. And yet he could not move.

He came to with a further ache of exhaustion. There was the pain in his head, and the horrible sickness, and his inability to move. He had never been ill in his life. He did not know where he was or what he was. Probably he had got sunstroke. Or what else?—he had silenced the Captain for ever—some time ago—oh, a long time ago. There had been blood on his face, and his eyes had turned upwards. It was all right, somehow. It was peace. But now he had got beyond himself. He had never been here before. Was it life, or not life? He was by himself. They were in a big, bright place, those others, and he was outside. The town, all the country, a big bright place of light: and he was outside, here, in the darkened open beyond, where each thing existed alone. But they would all have to come there sometime, those others. Little, and left behind him, they all were. There had been father and mother and sweetheart. What did they all matter? This was the open land.

He sat up. Something scuffled. It was a little brown squirrel running in lovely undulating bounds over the floor, its red tail completing the undulation of its body—and then, as it sat up, furling and unfurling. He watched it, pleased. It ran on again, friskily, enjoying itself. It flew wildly at another squirrel, and they were chasing each other, and making little scolding, chattering noises. The soldier wanted to speak to them. But only a hoarse sound came out of his throat. The squirrels burst away—they flew up the trees. And then he saw the one peeping around at him, half-way up a tree trunk. A start of fear went through him, though in so far as he was conscious, he was amused. It still stayed, its little keen face staring at him halfway up the tree trunk, its little ears pricked up, its clawey little hands clinging to the bark, its white breast reared. He started from it in panic.

Struggling to his feet, he lurched away. He went on walking, walking, looking for something—for a drink. His brain felt hot and inflamed for want of water. He stumbled on. Then he did not know anything. He went unconscious as he walked. Yet he stumbled on, his mouth open.

When, to his dumb wonder, he opened his eyes on the world

again, he no longer tried to remember what it was. There was thick, golden light behind golden-green glitterings, and tall, grey-purple shafts, and darknesses farther off, surrounding him, growing deeper. He was conscious of a sense of arrival. He was amid the reality, on the real, dark bottom. But there was the thirst burning in his brain. He felt lighter, not so heavy. He supposed it was newness. The air was muttering with thunder. He thought he was walking wonderfully swiftly and was coming straight to relief—or was it to water?

Suddenly he stood still with fear. There was a tremendous flare of gold, immense—just a few dark trunks like bars between him and it. All the young level wheat was burnished gold glaring on its silky green. A woman, full-skirted, a black cloth on her head for head-dress, was passing like a block of shadow through the glistening, green corn, into the full glare. There was a farm, too, pale blue in shadow, and the timber black. And there was a church spire, nearly fused away in the gold. The woman moved on, away from him. He had no language with which to speak to her. She was the bright, solid unreality. She would make a noise of words that would confuse him, and her eyes would look at him without seeing him. She was crossing there to the other side. He stood against a tree.

When at last he turned, looking down the long, bare grove whose flat bed was already filling dark, he saw the mountains in a wonder-light, not far away, and radiant. Behind the soft, grey ridge of the nearest range the farther mountains stood golden and pale grey, the snow all radiant like pure, soft gold. So still, gleaming in the sky, fashioned pure out of the ore of the sky, they shone in their silence. He stood and looked at them, his face illuminated. And like the golden, lustrous gleaming of the snow he felt his own thirst bright in him. He stood and gazed, leaning against a tree. And then everything slid away into space.

During the night the lightning fluttered perpetually, making the whole sky white. He must have walked again. The world hung livid round him for moments, fields a level sheen of grey-green light, trees in dark bulk, and the range of clouds black across a white sky. Then the darkness fell like a shutter, and the night was whole. A faint flutter of a half-revealed world, that could not quite leap out of the darkness!—Then there again stood a sweep of pallor for the land, dark shapes looming, a range of clouds hanging overhead. The world was a ghostly shadow, thrown for a moment upon the pure darkness, which returned ever whole and complete.

And the mere delirium of sickness and fever went on inside him—his brain opening and shutting like the night—then sometimes convulsions of terror from something with great eyes that stared round a tree—then the long agony of the march, and the sun decomposing his blood—then the pang of hate for the Captain, followed by a pang of tenderness and ease. But everything was distorted, born of an ache and resolving into an ache.

In the morning he came definitely awake. Then his brain flamed with the sole horror of thirstiness! The sun was on his face, the dew was steaming from his wet clothes. Like one possessed, he got up. There, straight in front of him, blue and cool and tender, the mountains ranged across the pale edge of the morning sky. He wanted them—he wanted them alone—he wanted to leave himself and be identified with them. They did not move, they were still and soft, with white, gentle markings of snow. He stood still, mad with suffering, his hands crisping and clutching. Then he was twisting in a paroxysm on the grass.

He lay still, in a kind of dream of anguish. His thirst seemed to have separated itself from him, and to stand apart, a single demand. Then the pain he felt was another single self. Then there was the clog of his body, another separate thing. He was divided among all kinds of separate things. There was some strange, agonised connection between them, but they were drawing farther apart. Then they would all split. The sun, drilling down on him, was drilling through the bond. Then they would all fall, fall through the everlasting lapse of space. Then again, his consciousness reasserted itself. He roused on to his elbow and stared at the gleaming mountains. There they ranked, all still and wonderful between earth and heaven. He stared till his eyes went black, and the mountains, as they stood in their beauty, so clean and cool, seemed to have it, that which was lost in him.

IV

When the soldiers found him, three hours later, he was lying with his face over his arm, his black hair giving off heat under the sun. But he was still alive. Seeing the open, black mouth the young soldiers dropped him in horror.

He died in the hospital at night, without having seen again.

The doctors saw the bruises on his legs, behind, and were silent.

The bodies of the two men lay together, side by side, in the mortuary, the one white and slender, but laid rigidly at rest, the other looking as if every moment it must rouse into life again, so young and unused, from a slumber.

WILLIAM CARLOS WILLIAMS

THE SAILOR'S SON

As the ferry came into the slip, there was a pause, then a young fellow on a motorcycle shot out of the exit, looked right and left, sighted the hill, opened her up and took the grade at top speed. Right behind him came three others bunched and went roaring by, and behind them, a youngster travelling in fast company, his eyes fastened on the others. Behind him an older guy sitting firm and with a face on him like a piece of wood, ripped by without a quiver.

That day Manuel waited in vain for his friend to visit him on the farm where he had taken a job for the summer. It came on to rain about eleven in the morning. The cows had been put to pasture, the chickens fed, the eggs collected. It was Sunday. He had been down for the papers and had taken them up to the big house. What the hell? He might as well go up to his room and write to Margy.

Lousy weather, he said to himself cutting across the lawn uphill through the slippery, wet grass. I suppose he guessed it and didn't want to risk the bad roads. But that boy is there, all right, he certainly is there.

In his room, on the third floor of the dignified country house where he was employed that year, he got out the ruled pad and a pencil and proceeded to write.

Dear Marge: Where have you been keeping yourself? I'm starting on the third month up here and you haven't been up to see me in six weeks. Why don't you come up some week-end sometime?

Then he stopped and thought a minute during which he tapped the butt of the long pencil against his closed lips, tap, tap, tap, tap, thinking; going on after a moment:

Drop me a line when to expect you. There's not much news except I'm pretty much alone here. I don't mind it though as long as I can earn something until I can get a job in the city. Not much chance for that now, I guess. I often think how good you are to me, giving me money and keeping me this spring while I was hunting for work. I'll never forget it. As soon as I can get back to New York and make what I ought to be getting, we can make our dream come true. I can just see a little apartment all neat and pretty. At first, I suppose, we'd both better work so we can save up a few dollars but after a year I like to think you'll quit that office for good. Christian didn't show up today. I suppose it's the rain. If you run into him, tell him I wanted to know why he didn't show up. I hope you can get up here sometime. I'm crazy to see you. This is a good place though, good food and all that but I've got to see my friends. So long, dearie, Yours, Manuel.

He put the letter in an envelope, addressed it and stuck it into his coat pocket. He took out his pipe and started to smoke. The rain beat down on the roof over his head with a drumming as of fingers tapping with their soft pads. He felt nervous and oppressed. He put his pipe aside, it didn't have the taste he expected of it and lay down on the bed wondering. What the hell? He felt lonesome and neglected.

But downstairs Mrs. Cuthbertson felt relieved. She liked Manuel, his work was satisfactory, he drove the car excellently and was docile and obedient. He was a real good boy. But she didn't have much use for the bozo who drove up from the city each week-end on a motorcycle for a visit to stay over till Sunday.

It's an old friend, Manuel explained to her, I've known him from the other side. I don't mind paying for his meals if that's what you mean, Mrs. Cuthbertson. Or he can ride down to the town for them.

Now, I've told you, Manuel, said Mrs. C., that I like you and I want you to stay here and help me. You are not so strong, you look twice as well as when you came up here this spring. But I don't think that young man is a good influence on you. I can't find you anywhere when he is here. I tell you if you want to stay here, you had better tell him not to come up so often. Once a month is all right but not every week-end. That is not what we hired you for. I do not like his looks. He has a fresh look in his eyes. You are not the same nice boy when he is here.

It was Mrs. Cuthbertson's habit to talk this way to the young men she hired to do the work for her in summer. She picked out boys that she liked and then looked after them. She talked their talk and most of them liked her. But this time she had not been quite frank with Manuel. She did not tell him that what she really objected to was his friend's air of proprietorship over Manuel, and the whole farm for that matter, when he was there. He drove up on his motorcycle; put the machine anywhere at all in the garage and proceeded to eat fruit, wander about the lawns and enjoy himself as if he owned the place. Manuel shared his meals with him and at night his bed. This was the point on which Mrs. C. stuck. Yet she didn't quite feel that she wanted to come out with it—just yet.

Mrs. Cuthbertson knew that Manuel was engaged to be married. Why didn't his girl come up to visit him more often if he was lonely? It would have been much better. But this young man was a nuisance. Manuel was a different person when he was there, silly, excited and worth nothing. At first she thought it would only last a few times, but every Saturday it had been the same. Mrs. C. was determined it should not continue longer.

But the following Saturday being fine, sure enough about four in the afternoon you could hear the chug chug of the motor as it took the steep hill, up the dirt road leading to the farm entrance. And there was the boy himself, the same cocky youngster who had shot out of the ferry entrance the week before. He honked his horn.

As Mrs. C. heard this, she called to Manuel to warn him. But he was already out the back door. She called to him from the kitchen window but though he must have heard her, he kept right on going at a run to meet his friend.

Hello, kid, Gees' I'm glad to see you. I almost passed out last week. Why didn't you come up? Did the rain keep you?

Sure, what the hell, he lied, don't you think I'd a been here if I could a made it? How are you, Baby? Feelin' your oats?"

You said it.

And with that, Manuel swung open the garage doors and the kid rolled his cycle into the space, standing it over against the wall, on one side.

Mrs. Cuthbertson was watching from the kitchen window, her jaw set, and a determined look in her eyes. Pretty soon she saw the men come out of the garage and after hanging around the corner of the building, talking a minute, she saw Manuel cast a quick look up at the house, then the two disappeared behind the stonework.

Mrs. C. waited a few minutes and went out. The hay barn lay directly behind the big stone garage building, its entrance concealed from view as far as the house on the hill was concerned. Mrs. Cuthbertson walked slowly along on the grass avoiding the cinder roadway and approached the barn. She saw no one about so she went further and listened. She thought she heard voices in the barn but listen as she would, she could not make out what they were saying.

With that she boldly walked up to the big doors and, being a powerful woman, she swung one of them open and walked in. The men were lying in the hay. She looked, felt her stomach rise into her throat and then she let her tongue go. The visitor she ordered off the farm at once. He laughed and walked past her out of the door without a quiver. But with Manuel it was different.

After rearranging his clothes, he sat down in the hay where he was and cried like a child. Then he got up and came to her begging her not to send him away. She felt sorry for the boy and after a few strong words ordered him up to his room to pack.

But there she was. The work had to be done. She had no one to take his place. So after an hour, she called the fellow down again and told him exactly what was on her mind. You may stay this week out, she said, until I get someone to take your place, but then you go.

He begged, he pleaded, in vain. Then he went upstairs, wrote another letter to his girl and the following morning when he had gone down with the milk he mailed it.

The next Sunday the girl, or woman rather, appeared. Why had Manuel been fired? Was he not good enough for the job? Mrs. Cuthbertson told the woman as much as she had the words for—but, to her surprise, it made no great impression.

The boy is lonesome up here, said the woman. Why do you keep his friends away? I am engaged to marry him, I don't care what he does. Why should you worry? Well, that was a hot one. Manuel begged to be kept on. He had nowhere else to go. He could not get a recommendation. What should he do? Tears came to his eyes. Finally the fiancée grew abusive and Mrs. Cuthbertson losing her temper very nearly struck her. It was a wild moment. But in the end Manuel was fired. And the woman took him back to the city with her where she told him she would pay for a room until she could find work for him elsewhere.

FEDERICO GARCÍA LORCA

ODE TO WALT WHITMAN

Along East River and the Bronx
the young men were singing, baring their waists,
with the wheel and the leather, the hammer, the oil.
Ninety thousand miners whittled silver from the rocks
and the boys traced ladders and perspectives.

But nobody slept
or wished to be: river;
none loved the big leaves
or the beach's blue tongue.

Along East River and Queensborough,
the young men were grappling with Industry.
The Jews sold the faun of the river
circumcision's rosette;
and the sky, over bridges and rooftops
emptied its buffalo herds to the push of the wind.

But nobody dawdled,
or wished to be: cloud;
none looked for the fern
or the drum's yellow wheel.

At moon-rise,
the block and the tackle will veer and startle the sky;
a zenith of needles will circle all memory in
and the coffins move off with the jobless.

Ah, filthy New York,
New York of cables and death.
What angel do you carry, concealed in your cheek?
What ineffable voice will speak the truths of the wheat?
Who, the terrible dream of your tainted anemones?

Not for one moment, Walt Whitman, comely old man,
have I ceased to envision your beard full of butterflies,
your corduroy shoulders, worn thin by the moon,
your chaste, Apollonian thighs,
your voice like a pillar of ashes;
patriarch, comely as mist,
you cried like a bird
whose sex is transfixed by a needle;
satyr's antagonist,
grapevine's antagonist,
and lover of bodies under the nap of the cloth.
Not for a moment, manly and comely one,
on mountains of railroads and coal and advertisements,
but you dreamed yourself river, and slept like a river,
with that comrade who took to your heart
the little complaint of the ignorant leopard.

Not a moment, blood-brother, Adam, and masculine,
lone man in a sea, Walt Whitman, comely old man—
for look!—on the rooftops,
or huddled in bars,
or leaping in packs from the gutters,
or held between legs of the motorist, shuddering,
or whirling on platforms of absinthe,
the perverts, Walt Whitman, all pointing you!

This one—and this one! They fall
on your decent and luminous beard,
the blond-headed northerners, the blacks from the sanddunes,
a legion of gestures and outcries,

catlike and serpentine—
perverts—the pack of them perverts, Walt Whitman—
grimy with tears, so much meat for the whiplash,
for the boot or the bite of the animal-tamers.

And this one! And this one! The taint of their fingernails points
to the brink of your dream
where the playfellow munches your apple
with a faint taste of gasoline,
and the sunlight sings out on the navels
of the boys at their games under bridges.

But you never went looking for the scar on the eye,
or the overcast swamp where the boys are submerged,
or the freezing saliva
or the contours, split open, like the sac of the toad,
that the perverts in taxis and terraces carry
as the moon whips them on into terrified corners.

You looked for a nude that could be like a river,
the bull and the dream that could merge, like seaweed and wheel,
sire of your agony, your mortality's camellia,
to cry in the flames of your secret equator.

It is fitting that no man should seek
in another day's thickets of blood for his pleasure.
Heaven has shores for our flights out of life,
and the corpse need not make itself over at dawn.

Agony, agony, dream, ferment and dream.
It is the world's way, my friend: agony, agony.
Under the town-clock the dead decompose.
War takes its course with a million gray sewer-rats, sobbing.
The well-to-do will to their darlings
little candle-lit death-beds,
and life is not noble, or wholesome, or holy.

Yet we might, if we would, lead our appetite on
through the vein of the coral or the heaven-sent nude.

Tomorrow our passion is rock, and Time,
a wind come to sleep in the branches.

Wherefore my voice is not raised
to admonish the boy who inscribes
a girl's name on his pillow, Walt Whitman, old friend;
not to shame the young man who dresses himself like a bride
in the dark of the clothes-closet,
or the stags of the dance-hall
who drink at the waters of whoredom and sicken,
or the green apparition of men
who cherish mankind and burn out their lips in the silence.
But you! against all of you, perverts of the cities,
immodest of thought and tumescent of flesh,
mothers of filthiness, harpies, sleeplessly thwarting
the Love that apportions us garlands of pleasure.

Always against you, whosoever bestow upon boys
the foul drop of death with wormwood of venom.
Against you to the end!
North American *fairies,*
Pájaros of Havana,
Jotos of Mexico,
Sarasas of Cádiz,
Apios of Seville,
Cancos of Madrid,
Floras of Alicante,
Adelaidas of Portugal.

Perverts of the world, dove-killers!
Toadies of women, dressing-room bitches,
brazen in squares in a fever of fans
or ambushed in motionless landscapes of hemlock.

No quarter! Death
oozes out of your eyes
and clusters gray flowers at the edge of a dog.
No quarter! Beware!
Let the pure, the bewildered,
the illustrious, classic, and suppliant
shut the festival doors in your face.

And you, on the shores of the Hudson, handsome Walt Whitman, asleep
with your beard to the pole, open-handed.
In the delicate marl or the snow, your tongue always summoning
the comrades to watch your gazelle, disembodied in air.
Sleep on; for nothing abides.

A dancing of walls rocks the meadows
and America drowns under engines and tears.
I could wish for a stirring of wind from the deepest abyss of the night
to undo all the letters and flowers from the arch where you drowse,
while a black boy declares to the gold-getting white
kingdom come in a tassel of corn.

—Translated by
Ben Belitt

CHRISTOPHER ISHERWOOD

ON RUEGEN ISLAND

(SUMMER 1931)

I wake early and go out to sit on the veranda in my pyjamas. The wood casts long shadows over the fields. Birds call with sudden uncanny violence, like alarm-clocks going off. The birch-trees hang down laden over the rutted, sandy earth of the country road. A soft bar of cloud is moving up from the line of trees along the lake. A man with a bicycle is watching his horse graze on a patch of grass by the path; he wants to disentangle the horse's hoof from its tether-rope. He pushes the horse with both hands, but it won't budge. And now an old woman in a shawl comes walking with a little boy. The boy wears a dark sailor suit; he is very pale and his neck is bandaged. They soon turn back. A man passes on a bicycle and shouts something to the man with the horse. His voice rings out, quite clear yet unintelligible, in the morning stillness. A cock crows. The creak of the bicycle going past. The dew on the white table and chairs in the garden arbour, and dripping from the heavy lilac. Another cock crows, much louder and nearer. And I think I can hear the sea, or very distant bells.

The village is hidden in the wood, away up to the left. It

consists almost entirely of boarding-houses, in various styles of seaside architecture—sham Moorish, old Bavarian, Taj Mahal, and the rococo doll's house, with white fretwork balconies. Behind the woods is the sea. You can reach it without going through the village, by a zig-zag path, which brings you out abruptly to the edge of some sandy cliffs, with the beach below you, and the tepid shallow Baltic lying almost at your feet. This end of the bay is quite deserted; the official bathing-beach is round the corner of the headland. The white onion-domes of the Strand Restaurant at Baabe wobble in the distance, behind fluid waves of heat, a kilometre away.

In the wood are rabbits and adders and deer. Yesterday morning I saw a roe being chased by a Borzoi dog, right across the fields and in amongst the trees. The dog couldn't catch the roe, although it seemed to be going much the faster of the two, moving in long graceful bounds, while the roe went bucketing over the earth with wild rigid jerks, like a grand piano bewitched.

There are two people staying in this house, besides myself. One of them is an Englishman, named Peter Wilkinson, about my own age. The other is a German working-class boy from Berlin, named Otto Nowak. He is sixteen or seventeen years old.

Peter—as I already call him; we got rather tight the first evening, and quickly made friends—is thin and dark and nervous. He wears horn-rimmed glasses. When he gets excited, he digs his hands down between his knees and clenches them together. Thick veins stand out at the sides of his temples. He trembles all over with suppressed, nervous laughter, until Otto, rather irritated, exclaims: '*Mensch, reg' Dich bloss nicht so auf!*'

Otto has a face like a very ripe peach. His hair is fair and thick, growing low on his forehead. He has small sparkling eyes, full of naughtiness, and a wide, disarming grin, which is much too innocent to be true. When he grins, two large dimples appear in his peach-bloom cheeks. At present, he makes up to me assiduously, flattering me, laughing at my jokes, never missing an opportunity of giving me a crafty, understanding wink. I think he looks upon me as a potential ally in his dealings with Peter.

This morning we all bathed together. Peter and Otto are busy building a large sand fort. I lay and watched Peter as he worked furiously, enjoying the glare, digging away savagely with his child's spade, like a chain-gang convict under the eyes of an armed warder. Throughout the long, hot morning, he never sat still for a moment. He and Otto swam, dug, wrestled, ran races or played with a rubber football, up and down the sands. Peter is skinny but wiry. In his games with Otto, he holds his own, it seems, only by an immense, furious effort of will. It is Peter's will against Otto's body. Otto is his whole body; Peter is only his head. Otto moves fluidly, effortlessly; his gestures have the savage, unconscious grace of a cruel, elegant animal. Peter drives himself about, lashing his stiff, ungraceful body with the whip of his merciless will.

Otto is outrageously conceited. Peter has bought him a chest-expander, and, with this, he exercises solemnly at all hours of the day. Coming into their bedroom, after lunch, to look for Peter, I found Otto wrestling with the expander like Laocoön, in front of the looking-glass, all alone: 'Look, Christoph!' he gasped. 'You see, I can do it! All five strands!' Otto certainly has a superb pair of shoulders and chest for a boy of his age—but his body is nevertheless somehow slightly ridiculous. The beautiful ripe lines of the torso taper away too suddenly to his rather absurd little buttocks and spindly, immature legs. And these struggles with the chest-expander are daily making him more and more top-heavy.

This evening Otto had a touch of sunstroke, and went to bed early, with a headache. Peter and I walked up to the village, alone. In the Bavarian café, where the band makes a noise like Hell unchained, Peter bawled into my ear the story of his life.

Peter is the youngest of a family of four. He has two sisters, both married. One of the sisters lives in the country and hunts. The other is what the newspapers call 'a popular society hostess.' Peter's elder brother is a scientist and explorer. He has been on expeditions to the Congo, the New Hebrides, and the Great Barrier Reef. He plays chess, speaks with the voice of a man of sixty, and has never, to the best of Peter's belief, performed the sexual act. The only member of the family with whom Peter is at present on speaking terms is his hunting sister, but they seldom meet, because Peter hates his brother-in-law.

Peter was delicate, as a boy. He did not go to a preparatory school but, when he was thirteen, his father sent him to a public school. His father and mother had a row about this which lasted until Peter, with his mother's encouragement, developed heart trouble and had to be removed at the end of his second term. Once escaped, Peter began to hate his mother for having petted and coddled him into a funk. She saw that he could not forgive her and so, as Peter was the only one of her children whom she cared for, she got ill herself and soon afterwards died.

It was too late to send Peter back to school again, so Mr Wilkinson engaged a tutor. The tutor was a very high-church young man who intended to become a priest. He took cold baths in winter and had crimpy hair and a Grecian jaw. Mr Wilkinson disliked him from the first, and the elder brother made satirical remarks, so Peter threw himself passionately on to the tutor's side. The two of them went for walking-tours in the Lake District and discussed the meaning of the Sacrament amidst austere moorland scenery. This kind of talk got them, inevitably, into a complicated emotional tangle which was abruptly unravelled, one evening, during a fearful row in a barn. Next morning, the tutor left, leaving a ten-page letter behind him. Peter meditated suicide. He heard later indirectly that the tutor had grown a moustache and gone out to Australia. So Peter got another tutor, and finally went up to Oxford.

Hating his father's business and his brother's science, he made music and literature into a religious cult. For the first year, he liked Oxford very much indeed. He went out to tea-parties and ventured to talk. To his pleasure and surprise, people appeared to be listening to what he said. It wasn't until he had done this often that he began to notice their air of slight embarrassment. 'Somehow or other,' said Peter, 'I always struck the wrong note.'

Meanwhile, at home, in the big Mayfair house, with its four bath-rooms and garage for three cars, where there was always too much to eat, the Wilkinson family was slowly falling to pieces, like something gone rotten. Mr Wilkinson with his diseased kidneys, his whisky, and his knowledge of 'handling men', was angry and confused and a bit pathetic. He snapped and growled at his children when they passed near him, like a surly old dog. At meals nobody ever spoke. They avoided each other's eyes, and hurried upstairs afterwards to write letters, full of hatred and satire, to their intimate friends. Only Peter had no friend to write to. He shut himself up in his tasteless, expensive bedroom and read and read.

And now it was the same at Oxford. Peter no longer went to tea-parties. He worked all day, and, just before the examinations, he had a nervous breakdown. The doctor advised a complete change of scene, other interests. Peter's father let him play at farming for six months in Devonshire, then he began to talk of the business. Mr Wilkinson had been unable to persuade any of his other children to take even a polite interest in the source of their incomes. They were all unassailable in their different worlds. One of his daughters was about to marry into the peerage, the other frequently hunted with the Prince of Wales. His elder son read papers to the Royal Geographical Society. Only Peter hadn't any justification for his existence. The other children behaved selfishly, but knew what they wanted. Peter also behaved selfishly, and didn't know.

However, at the critical moment, Peter's uncle, his mother's brother, died. This uncle lived in Canada. He had seen Peter once as a child and had taken a fancy to him, so he left him all his money, not very much, but enough to live on, comfortably.

Peter went to Paris and began studying music. His teacher told him that he would never be more than a good second-rate amateur, but he only worked all the harder. He worked merely to avoid thinking, and had another nervous breakdown, less serious than at first. At this time, he was convinced that he would soon go mad. He paid a visit to London and found only his father at home. They had a furious quarrel on the first evening; thereafter, they hardly exchanged a word. After a week of silence and huge meals, Peter had a mild attack of homicidal mania. All through breakfast, he couldn't take his eyes off a pimple on his father's throat. He was fingering the bread-knife. Suddenly the left side of his face began to twitch. It twitched and twitched, so that he had to cover his cheek with his hand. He felt certain that his father had noticed this, and was intentionally refusing to remark on it—was, in fact, deliberately torturing him. At last, Peter could stand it no longer. He jumped up and rushed out of the room, out of the house, into the garden, where he flung himself face downwards on the wet lawn. There he lay, too frightened to move. After a quarter of an hour, the twitching stopped.

That evening Peter walked along Regent Street and picked up a whore. They went back together to the girl's room, and talked for hours. He told her the whole story of his life at home, gave her ten pounds and left her without even kissing her. Next morning a mysterious rash appeared on his left thigh. The doctor seemed at a loss to explain its origin, but prescribed some ointment. The rash became fainter, but did not altogether disappear until last month. Soon after the Regent Street episode, Peter also began to have trouble with his left eye.

For some time already, he had played with the idea of consulting a psycho-analyst. His final choice was an orthodox Freudian with a sleepy, ill-tempered voice and very large feet. Peter took an immediate dislike to him, and told him so. The Freudian made notes on a piece of paper, but did not seem offended. Peter later discovered that he was quite uninterested in anything except Chinese art. They met three times a week, and each visit cost two guineas.

After six months Peter abandoned the Freudian, and started going to a new analyst, a Finnish lady with white hair and a bright conversational manner. Peter found her easy to talk to. He told her, to the best of his ability, everything he had ever done, ever said, ever thought, or ever dreamed. Sometimes, in moments of discouragement, he told her stories which were absolutely untrue, or anecdotes collected from case-books. Afterwards, he would confess to these lies, and they would discuss his motives for telling them, and agree that they were very interesting. On red-letter nights Peter would have a dream, and this gave them a topic of conversation for the next few weeks. The analysis lasted nearly two years, and was never completed.

This year Peter got bored with the Finnish lady. He heard of a good man in Berlin. Well, why not? At any rate, it would be a change. It was also an economy. The Berlin man only cost fifteen marks a visit.

'And you're still going to him?' I asked.

'No . . .' Peter smiled. 'I can't afford to, you see.'

Last month, a day or two after his arrival, Peter went out to Wannsee, to bathe. The water was still chilly, and there were not many people about. Peter had noticed a boy who was turning somersaults by himself, on the sand. Later the boy came up and asked him for a match. They got into conversation. It was Otto Nowak.

'Otto was quite horrified when I told him about the analyst. "What!" he said, "you give that man fifteen marks a day just for letting you talk to him! You give me ten marks and I'll talk to you all day, and all night as well!"' Peter began to shake all over with laughter, flushing scarlet and wringing his hands.

Curiously enough, Otto wasn't being altogether preposterous when he offered to take the analyst's place. Like many very animal people, he has considerable instinctive powers of healing—when he chooses to use them. At such times, his treatment of Peter is unerringly correct. Peter will be sitting at the table, hunched up, his downward-curving mouth lined with childhood fears: a perfect case-picture of his twisted, expensive upbringing. Then in comes Otto, grins, dimples, knocks over a chair, slaps Peter on the back, rubs his hands and exclaims fatuously: '*Ja, ja . . . so ist die Sache!*' And, in a moment, Peter is transformed. He relaxes, begins to hold himself naturally; the tightness disappears from his mouth, his eyes lose their hunted look. As long as the spell lasts, he is just like an ordinary person.

Peter tells me that, before he met Otto, he was so terrified of infection that he would wash his hands with carbolic after picking up a cat. Nowadays, he often drinks out of the same glass as Otto, uses his sponge, and will share the same plate.

Dancing has begun at the Kurhaus and the café on the lake. We saw the announcements of the first dance two days ago, while we were taking our evening walk up the main street of the village. I noticed that Otto glanced at the poster wistfully, and that Peter had seen him do this. Neither of them, however, made any comment.

Yesterday was chilly and wet. Otto suggested that we should hire a boat and go fishing on the lake: Peter was pleased with this plan, and agreed at once. But when we had waited three quarters of an hour in the drizzle for a catch, he began to get irritable. On the way back to the shore, Otto kept splashing with his oars—at first because he couldn't row properly, later merely to annoy Peter. Peter got very angry indeed, and swore at Otto, who sulked.

After supper, Otto announced that he was going to dance at the Kurhaus. Peter took this without a word, in ominous silence, the corners of his mouth beginning to drop; and Otto, either genuinely unconscious of his disapproval or deliberately overlooking it, assumed that the matter was settled.

After he had gone out, Peter and I sat upstairs in my cold room, listening to the pattering of the rain on the window.

'I thought it couldn't last,' said Peter gloomily. 'This is the beginning. You'll see.'

'Nonsense, Peter. The beginning of what? It's quite natural that Otto should want to dance sometimes. You mustn't be so possessive.'

'Oh, I know, I know. As usual, I'm being utterly unreasonable . . . All the same, this is the beginning . . .'

Rather to my own surprise the event proved me right. Otto arrived back from the Kurhaus before ten o'clock. He had been disappointed. There had been very few people there, and the band was poor.

'I'll never go again,' he added, with a languishing smile at me. 'From now on I'll stay every evening with you and Christoph. It's much more fun when we're all three together, isn't it?'

Yesterday morning, while we were lying in our fort on the beach, a little fair-haired man with ferrety blue eyes and a small moustache came up to us and asked us to join in a game with him. Otto, always over-enthusiastic about strangers, accepted at once, so that Peter and I had either to be rude or follow his example.

The little man, after introducing himself as a surgeon from a Berlin hospital, at once took command, assigning to us the places where we were to stand. He was very firm about this—instantly ordering me back when I attempted to edge a little nearer, so as not to have such a long distance to throw. Then it appeared that Peter was throwing in quite the wrong way: the little doctor stopped the game in order to demonstrate this. Peter was amused at first, and then rather annoyed. He retorted with considerable rudeness, but the doctor's skin wasn't pierced. 'You hold yourself so stiff,' he explained, smiling. 'That is an error. You try again, and I will keep my hand on your shoulder-blade to see whether you really relax . . . No. Again you do not!'

He seemed delighted, as if this failure of Peter's were a special triumph for his own methods of teaching. His eye met Otto's. Otto grinned understandingly.

Our meeting with the doctor put Peter in a bad temper for the rest of the day. In order to tease him, Otto pretended to like the doctor very much: 'That's the sort of chap I'd like to have for a friend,' he said with a spiteful smile. 'A real sportsman! You ought to take up sport, Peter! Then you'd have a figure like he has!'

Had Peter been in another mood, this remark would probably have made him smile. As it was, he got very angry: 'You'd better go off with your doctor now, if you like him so much!'

Otto grinned teasingly. 'He hasn't asked me to—yet!'

Yesterday evening, Otto went out to dance at the Kurhaus and didn't return till late.

* * *

There are now a good many summer visitors to the village. The bathing-beach by the pier, with its array of banners, begins to look like a medieval camp. Each family has its own enormous hooded wicker beach-chair, and each chair flies a little flag. There are the German city flags—Hamburg, Hanover, Dresden, Rostock and Berlin, as well as the National, Republic and Nazi colours. Each chair is encircled by a low sand bulwark upon which the occupants have set inscriptions in fir-cones: *Waldesruh. Familie Walter. Stahlhelm. Heil Hitler!* Many of the forts are also decorated with the Nazi swastika. The other morning I saw a child of about five years old, stark naked, marching along all by himself with a swastika flag over his shoulder and singing '*Deutschland über alles*'.

The little doctor fairly revels in this atmosphere. Nearly every morning he arrives, on a missionary visit, to our fort. 'You really ought to come round to the other beach,' he tells us. 'It's much more amusing there. I'd introduce you to some nice girls. The young people here are a magnificent lot! I, as a doctor, know how to appreciate them. The other day I was over at Hiddensee. Nothing but Jews! It's a pleasure to get back here and see real Nordic types!'

'Let's go to the other beach,' urged Otto. 'It's so dull here. There's hardly anyone about.'

'You can go if you like,' Peter retorted with angry sarcasm: 'I'm afraid I should be rather out of place. I had a grandmother who was partly Spanish.'

But the little doctor won't let us alone. Our opposition and more or less openly expressed dislike seem actually to fascinate him. Otto is always betraying us into his hands. One day, when the doctor was speaking enthusiastically about Hitler, Otto said, 'It's no good your talking like that to Christoph, Herr Doktor. He's a communist!'

This seemed positively to delight the doctor. His ferrety blue eyes gleamed with triumph. He laid his hand affectionately on my shoulder.

'But you *can't* be a communist! You *can't!*'

'Why can't I?' I asked coldly, moving away. I hate him to touch me.

'Because there isn't any such thing as communism. It's just

an hallucination. A mental disease. People only imagine that they're communists. They aren't really.'

'What are they, then?'

But he wasn't listening. He fixed me with his triumphant, ferrety smile.

'Five years ago I used to think as you do. But my work at the clinic has convinced me that communism is a mere hallucination. What people need is discipline, self-control. I can tell you this as a doctor. I know it from my own experience.'

This morning we were all together in my room, ready to start out to bathe. The atmosphere was electric, because Peter and Otto were still carrying on an obscure quarrel which they had begun before breakfast, in their own bedroom. I was turning over the pages of a book, not paying much attention to them. Suddenly Peter slapped Otto hard on both cheeks. They closed immediately and staggered grappling about the room, knocking over the chairs. I looked on, getting out of their way as well as I could. It was funny, and, at the same time, unpleasant, because rage made their faces strange and ugly. Presently Otto got Peter down on the ground and began twisting his arm: 'Have you had enough?' he kept asking. He grinned: at that moment he was really hideous, positively deformed with malice. I knew that Otto was glad to have me there, because my presence was an extra humiliation for Peter. So I laughed, as though the whole thing were a joke, and went out of the room. I walked through the woods to Baabe, and bathed from the beach beyond. I felt I didn't want to see either of them again for several hours.

If Otto wishes to humiliate Peter, Peter in his different way also wishes to humiliate Otto. He wants to force Otto into making a certain kind of submission to his will, and this submission Otto refuses instinctively to make. Otto is naturally and healthily selfish, like an animal. If there are two chairs in a room, he will take the more comfortable one without hesitation, because it never even occurs to him to consider Peter's comfort. Peter's selfishness is much less honest, more civilized, more perverse. Appealed to in the right way, he will make any sacrifice, however unreasonable and unnecessary.

But when Otto takes the better chair as if by right, then Peter immediately sees a challenge which he dare not refuse to accept. I suppose that—given their two natures—there is no possible escape from this situation. Peter is bound to go on fighting to win Otto's submission. When, at last, he ceases to do so, it will merely mean that he has lost interest in Otto altogether.

The really destructive feature of their relationship is its inherent quality of boredom. It is quite natural for Peter often to feel bored with Otto—they have scarcely a single interest in common—but Peter, for sentimental reasons, will never admit that this is so. When Otto, who has no such motives for pretending, says, 'It's so dull here!' I invariably see Peter wince and look pained. Yet Otto is actually far less often bored than Peter himself; he finds Peter's company genuinely amusing, and is quite glad to be with him most of the day. Often, when Otto has been chattering rubbish for an hour without stopping, I can see that Peter really longs for him to be quiet and go away. But to admit this would be, in Peter's eyes, a total defeat, so he only laughs and rubs his hands, tacitly appealing to me to support him in his pretence of finding Otto inexhaustibly delightful and funny.

On our way back through the woods, after my bathe, I saw the ferrety little blond doctor advancing to meet me. It was too late to turn back. I said 'Good morning' as politely and coldly as possible. The doctor was dressed in running-shorts and a sweater; he explained that he had been taking a '*Waldlauf*'. 'But I think I shall turn back now,' he added. 'Wouldn't you like to run with me a little?'

'I'm afraid I can't,' I said rashly. 'You see, I twisted my ankle a bit yesterday.'

I could have bitten my tongue out as I saw the gleam of triumph in his eyes. 'Ah, you've sprained your ankle? Please let me look at it!' Squirming with dislike, I had to submit to his prodding fingers. 'But it is nothing, I assure you. You have no cause for alarm.'

As we walked the doctor began to question me about Peter

and Otto, twisting his head to look up at me, as he delivered each sharp, inquisitive little thrust. He was fairly consumed with curiosity.

'My work in the clinic has taught me that it is no use trying to help this type of boy. Your friend is very generous and very well meaning, but he makes a great mistake. This type of boy always reverts. From a scientific point of view, I find him exceedingly interesting.'

As though he were about to say something specially momentous, the doctor suddenly stood still in the middle of the path, paused a moment to engage my attention, and smilingly announced:

'He has a criminal head!'

'And you think that people with criminal heads should be left to become criminals?'

'Certainly not. I believe in discipline. These boys ought to be put into labour-camps.'

'And what are you going to do with them when you've got them there? You say that they can't be altered, anyhow, so I suppose you'd keep them locked up for the rest of their lives?'

The doctor laughed delightedly, as though this were a joke against himself which he could, nevertheless, appreciate. He laid a caressing hand on my arm:

'You are an idealist! Do not imagine that I don't understand your point of view. But it is unscientific, quite unscientific. You and your friend do not understand such boys as Otto. I understand them. Every week, one or two such boys come to my clinic, and I must operate on them for adenoids, or mastoid, or poisoned tonsils. So, you see, I know them through and through!'

'I should have thought it would be more accurate to say you knew their throats and ears.'

Perhaps my German wasn't quite equal to rendering the sense of this last remark. At all events, the doctor ignored it completely. 'I know this type of boy very well,' he repeated. 'It is a bad degenerate type. You cannot make anything out of these boys. Their tonsils are almost invariably diseased.'

* * *

There are perpetual little rows going on between Peter and Otto, yet I cannot say that I find living with them actually unpleasant. Just now, I am very much taken up with my new novel. Thinking about it, I often go out for long walks, alone. Indeed, I find myself making more and more frequent excuses to leave them to themselves; and this is selfish, because, when I am with them, I can often choke off the beginnings of a quarrel by changing the subject or making a joke. Peter, I know, resents my desertions. 'You're quite an ascetic,' he said maliciously the other day, 'always withdrawing for your contemplations.' Once, when I was sitting in a café near the pier, listening to the band, Peter and Otto came past. 'So this is where you've been hiding!' Peter exclaimed. I saw that, for the moment, he really disliked me.

One evening, we were all walking up the main street, which was crowded with summer visitors. Otto said to Peter, with his most spiteful grin: 'Why must you always look in the same direction as I do?' This was surprisingly acute, for, whenever Otto turned his head to stare at a girl, Peter's eyes mechanically followed his glance with instinctive jealousy. We passed the photographer's window, in which, every day, the latest groups snapped by the beach camermen are displayed. Otto paused to examine one of the new pictures with great attention, as though its subject were particularly attractive. I saw Peter's lips contract. He was struggling with himself, but he couldn't resist his own jealous curiosity—he stopped too. The photograph was of a fat old man with a long beard, waving a Berlin flag. Otto, seeing that his trap had been successful, laughed maliciously.

Invariably, after supper, Otto goes dancing at the Kurhaus or the café by the lake. He no longer bothers to ask Peter's permission to do this; he has established the right to have his evenings to himself. Peter and I generally go out too, into the village. We lean over the rail of the pier for a long time without speaking, staring down at the cheap jewellery of the Kurhaus lights reflected in the black water, each busy with his own thoughts. Sometimes we go into the Bavarian café and Peter gets steadily drunk—his stern, Puritan mouth contracting slightly with distaste as he raises the glass to his lips. I say nothing. There is too much to say. Peter, I know, wants me to make some provocative remark about Otto which will give him the exquisite relief of losing his temper. I don't, and we drink —keeping up a desultory conversation about books and concerts and plays. Later, when we are returning home, Peter's footsteps will gradually quicken until, as we enter the house, he leaves me and runs upstairs to his bedroom. Often we don't get back till half past twelve or a quarter to one, but it is very seldom that we find Otto already there.

Down by the railway station, there is a holiday home for children from the Hamburg slums. Otto has got to know one of the teachers from this home, and they go out dancing together nearly every evening. Sometimes the girl, with her little troop of children, comes marching past the house. The children glance up at the windows and, if Otto happens to be looking out, indulge in precocious jokes. They nudge and pluck at their young teacher's arm to persuade her to look up, too.

On these occasions, the girl smiles coyly and shoots one glance at Otto from under her eyelashes, while Peter, watching behind the curtains, mutters through clenched teeth: 'Bitch . . . bitch . . . bitch . . .' This persecution annoys him more than the actual friendship itself. We always seem to be running across the children when we are out walking in the woods. The children sing as they march—patriotic songs about the Homeland—in voices as shrill as birds. From far off, we hear them approaching, and have to turn hastily in the opposite direction. It is, as Peter says, like Captain Hook and the Crocodile.

Peter has made a scene, and Otto has told his friend that she mustn't bring her troop past the house any more. But now they have begun bathing on our beach, not very far from the fort. The first morning this happened, Otto's glance kept turning in their direction. Peter was aware of this, of course, and remained plunged in gloomy silence.

'What's the matter with you to-day, Peter?' said Otto. 'Why are you so horrid to me?'

'Horrid to *you*?' Peter laughed savagely.

'Oh, very well then.' Otto jumped up. 'I see you don't want me here.' And, bounding over the rampart of our fort, he began to run along the beach towards the teacher and her children, very gracefully, displaying his figure to the best possible advantage.

Yesterday evening there was a gala dance at the Kurhaus. In a mood of unusual generosity, Otto had promised Peter not to be later than a quarter to one, so Peter sat up with a book to wait for him. I didn't feel tired, and wanted to finish a chapter, so suggested that he should come into my room and wait there.

I worked. Peter read. The hours went slowly by. Suddenly I looked at my watch and saw that it was a quarter past two. Peter had dozed off in his chair. Just as I was wondering whether I should wake him, I heard Otto coming up the stairs. His footsteps sounded drunk. Finding no one in his room, he banged open my door. Peter sat up with a start.

Otto lolled grinning against the doorpost. He made me a half-tipsy salute. 'Have you been reading all this time?' he asked Peter.

'Yes,' said Peter, very self-controlled.

'Why?' Otto smiled fatuously.

'Because I couldn't sleep.'

'Why couldn't you sleep?'

'You know quite well,' said Peter between his teeth.

Otto yawned in his most offensive manner. 'I don't know and I don't care . . . Don't make such a fuss.'

Peter rose to his feet. 'God, you little swine!' he said, smacking Otto's face hard with the flat of his hand. Otto didn't attempt to defend himself. He gave Peter an extraordinarily vindictive look out of his bright little eyes. 'Good!' He spoke rather thickly. 'To-morrow I shall go back to Berlin.' He turned unsteadily on his heel.

'Otto, come here,' said Peter. I saw that, in another moment, he would burst into tears of rage. He followed Otto out on to the landing. 'Come here,' he said again, in a sharp tone of command.

'Oh, leave me alone,' said Otto, 'I'm sick of you. I want to sleep now. To-morrow I'm going back to Berlin.'

This morning, however, peace has been restored—at a price. Otto's repentance has taken the form of a sentimental outburst over his family: 'Here I've been enjoying myself and never thinking of them . . . Poor mother has to work like a dog, and her lungs are so bad . . . Let's send her some money, shall we, Peter? Let's send her fifty marks . . .' Otto's generosity reminded him of his own needs. In addition to the money for Frau Nowak, Peter has been talked into ordering Otto a new suit, which will cost a hundred and eighty, as well as a pair of shoes, a dressing-gown, and a hat.

In return for this outlay, Otto has volunteered to break off his relations with the teacher. (We now discover that, in any case, she is leaving the island tomorrow.) After supper, she appeared, walking up and down outside the house.

'Just let her wait till she's tired,' said Otto. 'I'm not going down to her.'

Presently the girl, made bold by impatience, began to whistle. This sent Otto into a frenzy of glee. Throwing open the window, he danced up and down, waving his arms and making hideous faces at the teacher who, for her part, seemed struck dumb with amazement at this extraordinary exhibition.

'Get away from here!' Otto yelled. 'Get out!'

The girl turned, and walked slowly away, a rather pathetic figure, into the gathering darkness.

'I think you might have said goodbye to her,' said Peter, who could afford to be magnanimous, now that he saw his enemy routed.

But Otto wouldn't hear of it.

'What's the use of all those rotten girls, anyhow? Every night they came pestering me to dance with them . . . And you know how I am, Peter—I'm so easily persuaded . . . Of course, it was horrid of me to leave you alone, but what could I do? It was all their fault, really . . .'

Our life has now entered upon a new phase. Otto's resolutions were short-lived. Peter and I are alone together most of the day. The teacher has left, and with her, Otto's last inducement to bathe with us from the fort. He now goes off, every morning, to the bathing-beach by the pier, to flirt and play ball with his dancing-partners of the evening. The little doctor has also disappeared, and Peter and I are free to bathe and loll in the sun as unathletically as we wish.

After supper, the ritual of Otto's preparations for the dance begins. Sitting in my bedroom, I hear Peter's footsteps cross the landing, light and springy with relief—for now comes the only time of the day when Peter feels himself altogether excused from taking any interest in Otto's activities. When he taps on my door, I shut my book at once. I have been out already to the village to buy half-a-pound of peppermint creams. Peter says goodbye to Otto, with a vain lingering hope that, perhaps to-night, he will, after all, be punctual: 'Till half past twelve, then . . .'

'Till one,' Otto bargains.

'All right,' Peter concedes. 'Till one. But don't be late.'

'No, Peter, I won't be late.'

As we open the garden gate and cross the road into the wood, Otto waves to us from the balcony. I have to be careful to hide the peppermint creams under my coat, in case he should see them. Laughing guiltily, munching the peppermints, we take the woodland path to Baabe. We always spend our evenings in Baabe, nowadays. We like it better than our own village. Its single sandy street of low-roofed houses among the pine-trees has a romantic, colonial air; it is like a ramshackle, lost settlement somewhere in the backwoods, where people come to look for a non-existent gold mine and remain, stranded, for the rest of their lives.

In the little restaurant, we eat strawberries and cream, and talk to the young waiter. The waiter hates Germany and longs to go to America. '*Hier ist nichts los*'. During the season, he is allowed no free time at all, and in the winter he earns nothing. Most of the Baabe boys are Nazis. Two of them come into the restaurant sometimes and engage us in good-humoured political agruments. They tell us about their field-exercises and military games.

'You're preparing for war,' says Peter indignantly. On

these occasions—although he has really not the slightest interest in politics—he gets quite heated.

'Excuse me,' one of the boys contradicts, 'that's quite wrong. The Führer does not want war. Our programme stands for peace, with honour. All the same . . .' he adds wistfully, his face lighting up, 'war can be fine, you know! Think of the ancient Greeks!'

'The ancient Greeks,' I object, 'didn't use poison gas.'

The boys are rather scornful at this quibble. One of them answers loftily, 'That's a purely technical question.'

At half past ten we go down, with most of the other inhabitants, to the railway station, to watch the arrival of the last train. It is generally empty. It goes clanging away through the dark woods, sounding its harsh bell. At last it is late enough to start home; this time, we take the road. Across the meadows, you can see the illuminated entrance of the café by the lake, where Otto goes to dance.

'The lights of Hell are shining brightly this evening,' Peter is fond of remarking.

Peter's jealousy has turned into insomnia. He has begun taking sleeping-tablets, but admits that they seldom have any effect. They merely make him feel drowsy next morning, after breakfast. He often goes to sleep for an hour or two in our fort, on the shore.

This morning the weather was cool and dull, the sea oyster-grey. Peter and I hired a boat, rowed out beyond the pier, then let ourselves drift, gently, away from the land. Peter lit a cigarette. He said abruptly:

'I wonder how much longer this will go on . . .'

'As long as you let it, I suppose.'

'Yes . . . We seem to have got into a pretty static condition, don't we? I suppose there's no particular reason why Otto and I should ever stop behaving to each other as we do at present . . .' He paused, added: 'Unless, of course, I stop giving him money.'

'What do you think would happen then?'

Peter paddled idly in the water with his fingers. 'He'd leave me.'

The boat drifted on for several minutes. I asked: 'You don't think he cares for you, at all?'

'At the beginning he did, perhaps . . . Not now. There's nothing between us now but my cash.'

'Do you still care for him?'

'No . . . I don't know. Perhaps . . . I still hate him, sometimes—if that's a sign of caring.'

'It might be.'

There was a long pause. Peter dried his fingers on his handkerchief. His mouth twitched nervously.

'Well,' he said at last, 'what do you advise me to do?'

'What do you want to do?'

Peter's mouth gave another twitch.

'I suppose, really, I want to leave him.'

'Then you'd better leave him.'

'At once?'

'The sooner the better. Give him a nice present and send him back to Berlin this afternoon.'

Peter shook his head, smiled sadly:

'I can't.'

There was another long pause. Then Peter said: 'I'm sorry, Christopher . . . You're absolutely right, I know. If I were in your place, I'd say the same thing . . . But I can't. Things have got to go on as they are—until something happens. They can't last much longer, anyhow . . . Oh, I know I'm very weak . . .'

'You needn't apologize to me,' I smiled, to conceal a slight feeling of irritation: 'I'm not one of your analysts!'

I picked up the oars and began to row back towards the shore. As we reached the pier, Peter said:

'It seems funny to think of now—when I first met Otto, I thought we should live together for the rest of our lives.'

'Oh, my God!' The vision of a life with Otto opened before me, like a comic inferno. I laughed out loud. Peter laughed, too, wedging his locked hands between his knees. His face turned from pink to red, from red to purple. His veins bulged. We were still laughing when we got out of the boat.

In the garden the landlord was waiting for us. 'What a pity!' he exclaimed. 'The gentlemen are too late!' He pointed over the meadows, in the direction of the lake. We could see the smoke rising above the line of poplars, as the little train drew out of the station: 'Your friend was obliged to leave for Berlin, suddenly, on urgent business. I hoped the gentlemen might have been in time to see him off. What a pity!'

This time, both Peter and I ran upstairs. Peter's bedroom was in a terrible mess—all the drawers and cupboards were open. Propped up on the middle of the table was a note, in Otto's cramped, scrawling hand:

> *Dear Peter. Please forgive me I couldn't stand it any longer here so I am going home.*
>
> *Love from Otto.*
> *Don't be angry.*

(Otto had written it, I noticed, on a fly-leaf torn out of one of Peter's psychology books: *Beyond the Pleasure-Principle.*)

'Well . . .!' Peter's mouth began to twitch. I glanced at him nervously, expecting a violent outburst, but he seemed fairly calm. After a moment, he walked over to the cupboards and began looking through the drawers. 'He hasn't taken much,' he announced, at the end of his search. 'Only a couple of my ties, three shirts—lucky my shoes don't fit him!—and, let's see . . . about two hundred marks . . .' Peter started to laugh, rather hysterically: 'Very moderate, on the whole!'

'Do you think he decided to leave quite suddenly?' I asked, for the sake of saying something.

'Probably he did. That would be just like him . . . Now I come to think of it, I told him we were going out in that boat, this morning—and he asked me if we should be away for long . . ."

'I see . . .'

I sat down on Peter's bed—thinking, oddly enough, that Otto has at last done something which I rather respect.

Peter's hysterical high spirits kept him going for the rest of the morning; at lunch he turned gloomy, and wouldn't say a word.

'Now I must go and pack,' he told me when we had finished.

'You're off, too?'

'Of course.'

'To Berlin?'

Peter smiled. 'No, Christopher. Don't be alarmed! Only to England . . .'

'Oh . . .'

'There's a train which'll get me to Hamburg late to-night. I shall probably go straight on . . . I feel I've got to keep travelling until I'm clear of this bloody country . . .'

There was nothing to say. I helped him pack, in silence. As Peter put his shaving-mirror into the bag, he asked: 'Do you remember how Otto broke this, standing on his head?'

'Yes, I remember.'

When we had finished, Peter went out on to the balcony of his room: 'There'll be plenty of whistling outside here, to-night,' he said.

I smiled: 'I shall have to go down and console them.'

Peter laughed: 'Yes. You will!'

I went with him to the station. Luckily, the engine-driver was in a hurry. The train only waited a couple of minutes.

'What shall you do when you get to London?' I asked.

Peter's mouth curved down at the corners; he gave me a kind of inverted grin: 'Look round for another analyst, I suppose.'

'Well, mind you beat down his prices a bit!'

'I will.'

As the train moved out, he waved his hand: 'Well, good-bye, Christopher. Thank you for all your moral support!'

Peter never suggested that I should write to him, or visit him at home. I suppose he wants to forget this place, and everybody concerned with it. I can hardly blame him.

It was only this evening, turning over the pages of a book I have been reading, that I found another note from Otto, slipped between the leaves.

> *Please dear Christopher don't you be angry with me too because you aren't an idiot like Peter. When you are back in Berlin I shall come and see you because I know*

where you live; I saw the address on one of your letters and we can have a nice talk.

Your loving friend,
Otto.

I thought, somehow, that he wouldn't be got rid of quite so easily.

Actually, I am leaving for Berlin in a day or two, now. I thought I should stay on till the end of August, and perhaps finish my novel, but suddenly, the place seems so lonely. I miss Peter and Otto, and their daily quarrels, far more than I should have expected. And now even Otto's dancing-partners have stopped lingering sadly in the twilight, under my window.

EDWARD MORGAN FORSTER

THE OBELISK

Ernest was an elementary schoolmaster, and very very small; it was like marrying a doll, Hilda sometimes thought, and one with glass eyes too. She was larger herself: tall enough to make them look funny as they walked down the esplanade, but not tall enough to look dignified when she was alone. She cherished aspirations; none would have guessed it from her stumpy exterior. She yearned for a trip in a Rolls-Royce with a sheikh, but one cannot have everything or anything like it, one cannot even always be young. It is better to have a home of one's own than to always be a typist. Hilda did not talk quite as she should, and her husband had not scrupled to correct her. She had never forgotten—it was such a small thing, yet she could not forget it—she had never forgotten that night on their honeymoon when she had said something ungrammatical about the relative position of their limbs.

He was now asking her to decide whether they should sit in the shelter or walk to the obelisk. There was time to do one or the other before the bus went, but not to do both.

'Sit down will be best,' she replied. But as soon as they were in the shelter, looking at the undersized and undercoloured sea, she wished she had chosen the obelisk. 'Where is it? What's it for? Who's it to?' she asked.

'I don't know to whom it was erected—to some local worthy, one presumes. As regards its situation, it stands above the town in the direction of the landslip.'

'Would *you* like to go to it?'

'I can't honestly say that I should. My shoes are somewhat tight.'

'Yes, I suppose we're best where we are and then some tea. Do you know how far off it is?'

'I can't say that I do.'

'It may be quite near. Perhaps you could ask these people.' She lowered her voice, not to be overheard by the people in question: two sailors who were seated on the other side of the glass screen.

'I don't think I could well do that,' said Ernest timidly; a martinet at home and at school, he was terrified of anything unfamiliar.

'Why not?'

'They won't know.'

'They might.'

'There is no naval station here, Hilda, they are merely visitors like ourselves, no ships are ever stationed at a small watering-place.' He breathed on his pince-nez, and placed it between himself and the sea.

'Shall I ask them?'

'Certainly, if you wish to do so.'

Hilda opened her mouth to speak to the sailors, but no sound came out of it. 'You ask, it seems better,' she whispered.

'I don't wish to ask, I shall not ask, I have told you my reasons already, and if you are incapable of following them I really can do no more.'

'Oh, all right, dear, don't get in such a fuss, it doesn't matter, I'm sure I don't want to go to your obelisk.'

'Why, in that case, do you want to inquire how to get there? And why "my" obelisk? I was not aware that I possessed one.'

She felt cross—Ernest did tie one up so—and determined to

speak to the sailors to prove her independence. She had noticed them as she sat down, one of them particularly. 'Please excuse me,' she began. They were laughing at something, and did not hear her. 'Please could you kindly tell us—' No reply. She got up and said to her husband, 'Oh, let's go, I hate this place.'

'Certainly, certainly,' said he, and they moved off down the esplanade in an offended silence. Hilda, who had been in the wrong, soon felt ashamed of herself. What on earth had made her behave like that, she wondered; it had been almost a quarrel, and all about nothing. She determined never to mention the beastly obelisk again.

This was not to be, for it appeared on a noticeboard, 'To the Obelisk and Landslip', and an arrow pointed to a gap in the crumbly cliffs. She would have marched by, but Ernest stopped. 'I think I should—I think I *should* like to go if you don't object,' he said, in a voice that was intended to be conciliatory. 'I could talk to the class about it on Monday. I am very short of material.'

Turning back, she looked at the shelter where they had sat. She could see the long dark legs of the sailors sticking out of it; the esplanade was almost deserted otherwise. 'No, of course I shouldn't mind,' she said.

'Excellent, excellent, admirable.' He led the way. The sea, such as it was, disappeared, and they began climbing a muddly sort of gorge—not romantic, though she tried to pretend it was so. Rocks of no great size overhung them, a stream dripped through mud. The weather was stuffy and an aeroplane could be heard being sick in the distance. Hilda took a stern line with herself; whatever they did this afternoon, she wanted to be doing something else. How nice Ernest was really! How genuine! How sincere! If only his forehead wasn't quite so bulgy, and had a little more hair hanging over it, if his shoes weren't quite so small and yellow, if he had eyes like a hawk and an aquiline nose and a sinewy sunburnt throat . . . no, no, that was asking too much, she must keep within bounds, she must not hope for a sinewy throat, or for reckless arms to clasp her beyond redemption . . . That came of going to those cinemas . . .

'It's ever so lovely here, don't you think,' she exclaimed, as they rounded a corner and saw a quantity of unripe blackberries.

'I should scarcely describe it in those terms.'

'I'm ever so glad we didn't stick in that awful shelter.'

'What makes you keep on saying "ever so"?'

'Oh, I'm sorry. Did I? Ever so what oughtn't I to have said?'

'No, no, you are getting it wrong. "Ever so what" is not the question, but "ever so" itself. The phrase is never needed. I can't think why it has become so popular. It is spreading into circles where one would not expect to hear it. Curious. You try to form a sentence in which "ever so" is not redundant.'

She tried, but her thoughts went off to that disastrous night when he had pulled her up in much the same way, and had made her feel worthless, and had humiliated her, and had afterwards tried to caress her, and she couldn't stand it. That had been his fault, but it was her fault if she minded now, she wanted to be really educated, and here he was helping her. Penitent, she looked at his pink and pear-shaped face, slightly beaded with sweat and topped by too small a hat, and determined to improve her grammar and to really love him.

There was a scrambling noise behind, and the two sailors came rushing up the path like monkeys.

'What do these fellows want here? I don't like this,' cried Ernest.

Stopping dead short, they smiled, showing dazzling teeth. One of them—not the one she had noticed—said, 'We right for the Oboblisk, chum?'

Ernest was nervous. The place was deserted, the path narrow, and he wouldn't anywhere have been easy with people whose bodies were so different from his own. He replied with more than his usual primness: 'Obelisk. The notice on the esplanade says "To the Obelisk and Landslip". I fear I can tell you no more.'

'Call it the Ob and be done, eh!'

'Thank you, sir, thank you, and thank you, madam,' said the other sailor. He was a much better type—an educated voice and a gallant bearing, and when Hilda stood aside to let them stride past he saluted her. 'Excuse us, sir,' he called back, as if the path and indeed the whole gorge was Ernest's private property. 'Sorry to trouble you, but we thought we'd go a walk, make the most of our brief time on shore, sir, you know.'

'A sensible thing to do,' said Ernest, who was recovering from his alarm, and liked being called sir.

'Just a little change, anyhow. Got a fag on you, Tiny?'

The other sailor fumbled in his jumper. 'Fergot 'em again,' he replied.

'Well, of all the . . .'

'Ferget me own what d'ye call 'em next.'

'Nice person to go out with, isn't he, sir? Promised to bring along a packet, then lets us both down!'

'Have one of mine if it comes to that,' said Ernest.

'No, sir, I won't do that, but it's very good of you all the same.'

'Oh, come along, my man, take one.'

'No, sir; I don't cadge.'

'Oh!' said Ernest, rather taken aback.

'Do have one, my husband has plenty.'

'No, thank you, madam, I'd rather not.' He had pride and a will, and a throb of pleasure went through her, pleasure mixed with despair. She felt him looking at her, and turned away to inspect the blackberries. In a moment he would go on, dart up the path with his companion, and disappear as it were into heaven.

'What about you?' said Ernest to the sailor so strangely called Tiny.

Tiny had no such scruples. He thrust out his huge paw with a grin and a grunt. 'Her' sailor shook his head and looked a little disdainful. 'There's nothing Tiny wouldn't say no to, is there, Tiny?' he remarked.

'Tiny's a sensible fellow,' said Ernest. The sailors, by their civil yet cheerful demeanour, had quite reassured him. He now dominated the situation, and behaved as if he was conducting an open-air class for older boys. 'Come along, Tiny.' He stretched up a match to the expectant lips.

'Thanks ever so,' Tiny responded.

Hilda let out a cackle. It was 'ever so', the forbidden phrase.

The sailors laughed too, as did Ernest. He had become unusually genial. He astonished her by saying, 'Oh, Hilda, I'm so sorry, here I am smoking and I never asked you whether you would smoke too.' It was the first time he had invited her to smoke in public. She declined, thinking he was testing her, but he asked her again and she took one.

'I'm ever so—I'm very sorry.'

'That's quite all right, dear, might I have a match?'

'Her' sailor whipped a box out of his breast. Tiny, equally polite, blew on the tip of his cigarette and held it towards her. She felt flustered, enmeshed in blue arms, dazzled by rose-red and sunburnt flesh, intoxicated by strength, saltiness, the unknown. When she escaped it was to her husband. Her sailor still held out the lighted match which she had used. 'Sir, may I change my mind and have one of your cigarettes after all?' he said coolly.

'Of course, of course, come along all and sundry.'

He took one, used the lighted match on it, then blew the match out and placed it in his breast. The match they had shared—there it lay . . . close to him, hidden in him, safe . . . He looked at her, touched his jumper, smiled a little and looked away, puffing his cigarette. At that moment the sun blazed out and it turned into a nice afternoon.

She looked away too. There was something dangerous about the man, something of the bird of prey. He had marked her down for his fell purpose, she must be careful like any other heroine. If only he wasn't so handsome, so out-of-the-way handsome. 'Who's saying no, Stan, now?' his companion guffawed. So his name was Stan . . . Stanley perhaps. What had led such a man to join the Navy? Perhaps some trouble at home.

'Stan's sensible, don't you tease Stan,' piped Ernest. They proceeded in a safe enough formation towards the Obelisk, the two sailors in front, she behind Tiny's buttocks, from which she had nothing to fear. Gradually the order altered—Ernest's fault. He was elated with his success, and kept on pestering the men with questions about their work. Tiny fell back to deal with them, but was ill-informed. So 'Stan' joined them, and she went on ahead. It was nicer than she expected—everyone good-tempered, including her husband. But she still wished she had not come.

'It's a funny thing, a day on shore,' said the easy silky voice. He had stolen up behind her—no scrambling this time. She turned, and his eyes moved up and down her body.

'How do you mean, funny? I don't understand.'

'You hardly know what to do with yourself. You're let out of prison, as it were, the discipline stops, you find a shipmate who happens to be on leave too, you go off with him, though you have nothing in common, he wants to go to the pictures, so you go, he thinks he'd like a walk, so you go, he asks the way of strangers, with the result that you inflict yourself on them too. It's a funny life, the Navy. You're never alone, you're never independent. I don't like tacking on to people, the way that youngster I'm with does. I've told him of it before, but he turns everything into a joke.'

'Why is he called Tiny?'

'Merely because he's so large. Another joke. You know the kind of thing, and how weary one gets of it. Still, life's not a bed of roses anywhere, I suppose.'

'No, it isn't, it isn't.'

She ought not to have made such a remark, and she was glad when he ignored it and went on: 'And I've got to be called Stan although my name's really Stanhope.'

'Stanhope?'

'It was my mother's family name. We came from Cheshire. However, all that's over, and I'm Stan.' There was a tinge of melancholy in his voice which made it fatally attractive. For all his gaiety, he had suffered, suffered . . . When she threw away her cigarette he did the same and he gently touched his breast.

This frightened Hilda. She didn't want any nonsense, and she suggested that they should wait for her husband. He obeyed, and turned his profile to her as they waited. He looked even finer that way than full-face; the brow was so noble, the nose and the chin so firm, the lips so tender, the head poised so beautifully upon the sinewy neck, the colouring lovelier than imagination can depict. Here, however, was Ernest, coming round the corner like a cheerful ant. He held Tiny's cap in his hand, and was questioning him on the subject of his naval costume.

'Are we going on any further?' she called.

'I think so. Why not?'

'It seems turning out rather a climb.'

'We have plenty of time, abundance of time, before the bus goes.'

'Yes, but we must be keeping these gentlemen back, you and I walk so slowly.'

'I was not aware of walking slowly. You in a hurry, Stan?' he called familiarly.

'Not the least, not in the very least, sir, thank you.'

'You, Tiny?'

'Hurry for what?'

'Do you want to go on and leave us?'

Grateful to Hilda for calling him a gentleman, he beamed up at her and said, 'What's 'is name, please?'—pointing to Ernest as if he were some rare animal and could not answer questions.

'My husband—his name's Ernest.'

'Think his trilby'd fit me?' His hand shot out to pull it off, but he was checked by a quiet word of reproof from Stanhope. Ernest scuttled back a step. 'Chum, I won't hurt you, chum, chuck chuck, chum, chum,' as if feeding chicken.

'Certain people always go too far, they spoil things, it's a pity,' Stanhope remarked to her as they continued their walk.

How right he was—though for the moment Tiny had entertained her, also she got a wicked pleasure when Ernest's cowardice got exposed. She smiled, and felt clever herself, not realizing that Stanhope now walked behind her, which was exactly what she had not meant to happen. 'My husband and him seem getting on quite nicely,' she said.

'Tiny's always ready to play the fool, day in, day out. I'm afraid I don't understand it. Something wrong with me, I suppose.'

'One gets rather tired of anything that's always the same, I think.'

He offered no opinion, and they walked on for five minutes without saying anything. The path was well marked and not steep, and many pretty flowers, both yellow and pink, grew between the stones. Glimpses of the sea appeared, dancing blue, the aeroplane turned into a gull. The interval separating the two sailors gradually increased. 'What made you join the Navy?' she said suddenly.

He told her—it was fascinating. He was of good family—she had guessed as much!—but wanted to see the world. He had left a soft job in an office when he was eighteen. He told her the name of the office. She happened to have heard of it in her typist days, and was instantly possessed by a feeling of security. Of course she was safe with him—ridiculous. He reeled off the names of ports, known and unknown. He was not very young when you were close to him, but Hilda did not like very young men, they were not distinguished, and her dream was distinction. These well-marked features, this hair, raven-black against the snowy line of the cap, yet flecked at the temples with grey, suited her best, oh and those eyes, cruel eyes, kind eyes, kind, cruel, oh! they burnt into your shoulders, if you turned and faced them it was worse. And she so dumpy! She tried to steady herself by her modesty, which was considerable, and well-grounded. And a batch of people came downhill and passed them—it was only an extension of the esplanade. 'No, Hilda, no one like this is going to bother to seduce you,' she told herself.

'I suppose I can't persuade you,' he said. He took out of his jumper a cigarette-case, and opened it.

'But I thought you hadn't got any cigarettes,' she cried.

He snapped the case up, put it back, and said, 'Caught!'

'What do you mean? Why ever did you ask for one when you had all those?'

'I decline to answer that question,' he smiled.

'I want to know. You must answer. Tell me! Oh, go on! Do tell me.'

'No, I won't.'

'Oh, you're horrid.'

'Am I? Why?' The ravine had got wilder, almost beautiful. The path climbed above thick bushes and little trees. She knew they ought to wait again for Ernest, but her limbs drove her on. She repeated: 'You must tell me. I insist.' He drove her more rapidly before him. Then he said, 'Very well, but promise not to be angry.'

'I'm angry with you already.'

'Then I may as well tell. I pretended I'd no cigarettes on the chance of your husband offering me one.'

'But why? You said no when he did.'

'It wasn't a cigarette that I wanted. And now I suppose you're angry. I didn't want to go on, and it was my only chance of stopping. So I asked Tiny for one. I knew he'd be out of them, he always is. I wanted to—' He took the extinguished match from his pocket. 'Better throw this away now, hadn't I? Or you'll be angry again.'

'I'm not angry, but don't start being silly, please.'

'There are worse things than silliness.'

Hilda didn't speak. Her knees were trembling, her heart thumping, but she hurried on. Whether he threw the match away or not she did not know. After a pause he said in quite a different voice: 'I've done quite enough talking, you know. Now you talk.'

'I've nothing to say,' she said, her voice breaking. 'Nothing ever happens to me, nothing will, I . . . I do feel so odd.' He seemed to tug her this way and that. If only he wasn't so lovely! His hand touched her. Almost without her knowing, he guided her off the path, and got her down among the bushes.

Once there, she was lost. Under pretext of comforting he came closer. He persuaded her to sit down. She put her hand to his jersey to thrust him off, and it slid up to his throat. He was so gentle as well as so strong, that was the trouble, she did not know which way to resist him, and those eyes, appealing, devouring, appealing. He constrained her to lie down. A little slope of grass, scarcely bigger than a couch, was the scene of her inadequate resistance; beyond the dark blue of his shoulders she could see the blue of the sea, all around were thick thorny bushes covered with flowers, and she let him do what he wanted.

'Keep still,' he whispered. 'They're passing.'

From the path came the sound of feet.

'Don't talk just yet.' He continued to hold her, his chin raised, listening. 'They've gone now, but talk quietly. It's all right. He won't know. I'll fix up a story. Don't you worry. Don't you cry.'

'It's your fault, you made me . . .'

He laughed gently, not denying it. He raised her up, his arms slanting across her back unexpectedly kind. He let her say whatever she wanted to, as long as she did not say it too loud, and now and then he stroked her hair. She accused him, she exalted Ernest, repeating, 'I'm not what you think I am at all.' All he said was 'That's all right,' or 'You shan't come into any trouble, I swear it, I swear it, and you mustn't cry,' or 'I play tricks—yes. But I never let a woman down. Look at me. Do as I tell you! Look at me, Hilda.'

She obeyed. Her head fell on his shoulder, and she gave him a kiss. For the first time in her life she felt worthy. Her humiliation slipped from her, never to return. She had pleased him.

'Stanhope . . .'

'Yes, I know.'

'What do you know?'

'I'm waiting until it's absolutely safe. Yes.'

He held her against him for a time, then laid her again on the grass. She was consciously deceiving her husband, and it was heaven. She took the lead, ordered the mysterious stranger, the film-star, the sheikh, what to do, she was, for one moment, a queen, and he her slave. They came out of the depths together, confederates. He helped her up, then respectfully turned away. She hated grossness, and nothing he did jarred.

When they were back on the path, he laid his plans. 'Hilda, it's no use going on to the Obelisk,' he said, 'it's too late, they're in front of us and we shall meet them coming down. He'll want to know how they passed us without seeing us, and if you've an explanation of that I've not. No. We shall have to go back and wait for them on the esplanade.'

She patted her hair—she had good hair.

'Make up some story when they arrive. Muddle them. We shall never muddle them if we meet them face to face on this path. You leave it to me—I'll confuse them in no time.'

'But how?' she said dubiously, as they started the long descent.

'I shall see when I see them. That's how I always work.'

'Don't you think it would be better if you hid here, and I went down alone? Our bus leaves before very long, then you'll be safe.'

He shook his head, and showed his teeth, scorning her gaily. 'No, no, I'm better at telling stories than you, I don't trust you. Take your orders from me, don't ask questions, and it'll be all right. I swear it will. We shall pull through.'

Yes, he was wonderful. She would have this gallantry to look back upon, especially at night. She could think of Ernest quite kindly, she'd be able to put up with him when he made his little wrong remarks or did his other little wrong things. She'd her dream, and what people said was false and what the Pictures said was true: it was worth it, worth being clasped once in the right arms, though you never had them round you again. She had got what she longed for, and it was what she longed for, not a smack in the face, not a sell . . . She had always yearned for a lover who would be nice *afterwards*—not turn away like a satisfied brute, as handsome men are supposed to do. Stanhope was—what do you call it . . . a gentleman, a knight in armour, a real sport . . . O for words. Her eyes filled with happy tears of happiness.

Swinging ahead of her on to the esplanade, he gave her his final instructions. 'Take your line from me, remember we've done nothing we shouldn't, remember it's going to be much easier than you think, and don't lose your head. Simpler to say than to do, all the same don't do it, and if you can't think of anything else to do look surprised. Our first job is to sit down quietly on the esplanade and wait.'

But they were not to wait. As they came out of the gap in the cliffs, they saw Ernest on a bench, and Tiny leaning on the esplanade railings observing the sea. Ernest jumped up all a bunch of nerves, crying, 'Hilda, Hilda, where have you been? Why weren't you at the Obelisk? We looked and looked for you there, we hunted all the way back—'

Before she could answer, indeed before he had finished, Stanhope launched a violent counter-attack. 'What happened to you, sir? We got up to the Obelisk and waited, then we've been shouting and calling all the way back. The lady's been so worried—she thought an accident had happened. Are you all right, sir?' He bayed on, full-chested, magnificent, plausible, asking questions and allowing no time for their reply.

'Hilda, impossible, you couldn't have been, or I should have seen you.'

'There we were, sir, we had a good look at the view and waited for you, and then came down. It was not meeting you on the way back that puzzled us so.'

'Hilda, were you really . . .'

By now she had had her cue, and she heard her voice a long way off saying in fairly convincing tones, 'Oh yes, we got up to the Obelisk.'

And he believed, or three-quarters believed her. How shocking, but what a respite! It was the first lie she had ever told him, and it was unlikely she would ever tell him a worse. She felt very odd—not ashamed, but so queer, and Stanhope went on with his bluffing. The wind raised his dark forelock and his collar. He looked the very flower of the British Navy as he lied and lied. 'I can't understand it,' he repeated. 'It's a relief to know nothing's wrong, but not to run into you as we came down . . . I don't understand it, I'm what you may call stumped, well, I'm damned.'

'I'm puzzled equally, but there is nothing to be gained by a prolonged discussion. Hilda, shall we go to our bus?'

'I don't want you to go until you feel satisfied,' said she. A false step; she realized as much as soon as she had spoken.

'Not satisfied? I am perfectly satisfied. With what have I to be dissatisfied? I only fail to grasp how I failed to find you when I reached the monument.'

Hilda dared not go away with him with things as they were. She didn't know how to work out the details of the lie, it was in too much of a lump. Alarmed, she took refuge in crossness. 'You've got to grasp it some time or other, you may as well now,' she snapped. Her lover looked at her anxiously.

'Well, be that as that may be, we must go.'

'What's your explanation, Tiny?' called Stanhope, in his splendid authoritative way, to create a diversion.

Tiny cocked up one heel and replied not.

'He can scarcely solve a problem which baffles the three of us, and it is so strange that you were ahead of us on the path going up, yet a good ten minutes behind us coming down,' enunciated Ernest.

'Come along, Tiny, you've a tongue in your head, haven't you, mate? I'm asking you a question. Don't stand there like a stuck pig.'

'Ber-yutiful view,' said Tiny, turning round and extending his huge blue arms right and left along the railings of the esplanade. 'You was showing the lady the Ob, perhaps.'

'Of course we inspected the monument. You know that. You haven't answered my question.'

' 'Ope you showed it 'er properly while you was about it, Stan. Don't do to keep a thing like that all to yourself, you know. Ern, why they call that an ob?'

'Obelisk, obelisk,' winced Ernest, and was evidently more anxious to go.

'You said it, obblepiss.'

'I said nothing of the sort.'

'You said it, obblepiss.' The giant was grinning amiably, and seemed totally unaware that anything had gone wrong. But how different sailors are! How unattractive, in Tiny's case, was the sun-reddened throat and the line of broad shoulders against the sea! He was terribly common, really, and ought not to be answering people back. 'Anyone ever seed a bigger one?' he inquired. No one replied, and how should they to so foolish a question? 'Stands up, don't it?' he continued. No one spoke. 'No wonder they call that a needle, for wouldn't that just prick.'

'Stop that infernal talk at once,' exploded Stanhope, and he seemed needlessly vexed, but, oh, how handsome he looked, and how his dark eyes flashed; she was glad to see him angry and to have this extra memory.

'Stan, Stan, what's the matter, Stan?'

'If you speak again I'll brain you.'

'Ever seed a bigger one—a bigger obolokist, I mean. That's all I said. Because I'ave. Killopatra's Needle's bigger. Well? Well? What you all staring at me for? What you think I was going to say? Eh? Oh, look at little Ern, ain't he just blushing. Oh, look at Stan. Lady, look at 'em.'

Hilda did observe that the two older men were going most extraordinary colours, her lover purplish, her husband rose-pink. And she did not like the tone of the conversation herself, she scarcely knew why, and feared something awkward might come out if it went on much longer. 'We must go, or we shall miss that bus,' she announced. 'We shall never clear up why we never met, and it isn't of the least importance. Ernest, do come along, dear.'

Ernest muttered that he was willing, and the episode ended. Goodbyes were said, by Tiny tempestuously. Plunging across the esplanade, he seized the unfortunate schoolmaster's arm, and whirled it around like a windmill. 'Goo bye, Ern, take care of yerself, pleased to have met yer, termater face and all,' he bawled.

'Pleased to have met you both,' said Ernest with restraint.

'Ju-jitsu . . . now as yer neck snaps . . .'

Hilda and Stanhope profited by this noisy nonsense to say their farewells. They would not have dared otherwise. The touch of his hand was cool and dry, but he was nearly worn out, and it trembled. It had not been easy for him, returning her unreproached and unsuspected to her husband, fighting for her, using strategem after strategem, following hopeless hints . . . The perfect knight! The gangster lover who really cares, who knows . . . 'My darling . . . thank you for everything for ever,' she breathed. He dared not reply, but his lips moved, and he slipped his left hand into his breast. She knew what he meant: the match was there, the symbol of their love. He would never forget her. She had lived. She was saved.

What a contrast to the other—so boisterous, so common, so thoroughly unattractive! It was strange to think of them in the same uniform, strange to look down the esplanade and see them getting more and more like one another as the distance increased. The actual parting had gone off easily. Ernest had produced his cigarettes again. 'Have one more, both of you, before you repair to your boat,' he called. The powerfully made sailors stooped, the lean distinguished fingers and the battered clumsy ones helped themselves again to his bounty.

Perky, he had lit up himself, and now he was strutting away with his good little wife on his arm.

Of course the first few minutes alone with him were awful. Still, she drew strength from the fact that she had deceived him so completely. And somehow she did not despise him, she did not despise him at all. He seemed nicer than usual, and she was pleased when he started to discuss the relative advantages of gas and electricity. He said one thing, she another, while the cloud of her past swept gloriously out to sea. Home and its details had a new freshness. Even when the night came, she should feel differently and not mind.

They reached the bus-stop with several minutes to spare. There was a picture-postcard kiosk, and she had a good idea: she would buy a postcard of the Obelisk, so that if the topic came up again she would know what it looked like.

There was an excellent selection, and she soon visualized it from several points of view. Though not as tall as Cleopatra's Needle, it boasted a respectable height. One of the cards showed the inscription 'Erected in 1879 to the memory of Alfred Judge, one-time Mayor'. She memorized this, for Ernest often mentioned inscriptions, but she actually bought a card which brought in some of its surroundings. The monument was nobly placed. It stood on a tongue of rock overlooking the landslip.

'Well, you won't have seen that today! Will you?' said the woman in the kiosk as she took payment.

Hilda thought she would fall to the ground. 'Oh gracious, whatever do you mean?' she gasped.

'It's not there to be seen.'

'But that's the Obelisk. It says so.'

'It says so, but it's not there. It fell down last week. During all that rain. It's fallen right over into the landslip upside-down, the tip of it's gone in ever so far, rather laughable, though I suppose it'll be a loss to the town.'

'Ah, there it is,' said her husband, coming up and taking the postcard out of her hand. 'Yes, it gives quite a good idea of it, doesn't it? I'll have one displaying the inscription.'

Then the bus swept up and took them away. Hilda sank into a seat nearly fainting. Depth beneath depth seemed to open.

For if she couldn't have seen the Obelisk he couldn't have seen it either, if she had dawdled on the way up he must have dawdled too, if she was lying he must be lying, if she and a sailor —she stopped her thoughts, for they were becoming meaningless. She peeped at her husband, who was on the other side of the coach, studying the postcard. He looked handsomer than usual, and happier, and his lips were parted in a natural smile.

STANLEY KAUFFMANN

FULVOUS YELLOW

Mr. and Mrs. Sprague were a very nice middle-aged couple. They lived in Albany, New York, and they had managed to remain mentally alive. They read a lot of books, some of them not chosen by book clubs, owned a few nice paintings, and had quite a good collection of phonograph records, including "Scheherazade."

They were proudest, however, of their son Everett. He was an unusual and talented boy. In six months down in New York City he had done well. He was already top assistant to one of the most important dress designers in the business.

"Fashion stylists," Mrs. Sprague had corrected her husband once. "Ev says they don't call them dress designers any more."

"Fashion stylists," Mr. Sprague agreed quickly.

They were on their way down to New York now to visit Ev. They hadn't seen him in almost four months. When he had first got his New York job, he had come home every week end. Then his visits had slacked off to every two weeks. Then four months had gone by without his visiting them. But Mr. and Mrs. Sprague were not foolish or demanding parents. They understood that their son was in a new life, making new friends, finding new interests, and as long as his letters once a week told them that he was well and happy, they were reasonably content.

Now Mr. Sprague had managed to get Friday off from the office and they were going down for a long week end. They hadn't told Ev in advance; they wanted it to be a surprise. They sent a wire just before they got on the train.

"Make sure you send it to the new address," said Mrs. Sprague. "Remember, he moved last month."

"I know that as well as you do," Mr. Sprague replied testily. Ev was as much his son as hers.

They had lunch in the dining car. The steward put them at a table for four and then seated a big bald man next to Mr. Sprague. They fell into talk and the big bald man told them that he was on his way to his son's wedding in Brooklyn Heights. The Spragues agreed that that was fine and envied the bald man. Then they told him about Ev's progress in six short months.

"What's your son's work?" asked the bald man, impressed.

"He's a dress de—he's in fashion styling," Mr. Sprague said. "Always had an eye for color, and things like that."

"Always," agreed his mother. "Ever since he was a very little boy."

"Oh," said the man, with the hint of a wrinkle between his brows. "That's fine. Fine."

Mr. Sprague noticed the wrinkle. "You know," he said with a laugh, "lots of people have the wrong idea about the fashion field. It takes ability and business sense just like any other business."

"Oh, sure, I know," nodded the bald man quickly. "I saw an article about it in *Life*."

Ev wasn't at the station to meet them, but Mr. Sprague said that probably the wire hadn't given him time enough to get away. On an off chance, he called the apartment before he tried the office and was surprised to hear Ev answer.

Ev was glad to hear his father's voice. Yes, he'd received the wire but he hadn't been able to meet the train. He had some things he had to finish up for Ty. Ty was his roommate.

Also his boss. Why didn't they take a cab and come right over before they went to their hotel?

It was a remodeled private house in the East Fifties, not far from the river. The card for Apt. 3 said "Emmet" with "Sprague" written in below it. Mr. Sprague gave the bell two pokes.

Ev stood at the top of the stairs in a striped basque shirt and a pair of slacks. "Hello, Mother," he said. "Gosh, it's good to see you. What a wonderful surprise. Hello, Father."

He used to call Mr. Sprague "Dad." Mr. Sprague thought he looked a little pale. Working too hard, probably.

The apartment was eye-filling. The furniture was low and modern, pearl gray and coral red. There were good reproductions of Picasso and Matisse and Utrillo in wide natural-wood frames. And there were small white-enameled wrought-iron gates between the living room and the tiny kitchen.

Ev gave his parents each a glass of sherry and apologized for not having been up to Albany for so long. "But gosh, I've been busy," he said. He indicated the drawing board at the side of the room; there was a large colored sketch of a woman in a coat tacked on it. "We're doing some rush work on a new line of casual clothes and Ty's given me some of the tougher things. But I don't mind. It's pretty exciting."

"Do you always work at home, Ev?" his mother asked.

"When I've got something really tough, yes. Because that office is a madhouse." He laughed. It was Mr. Sprague's boy's laugh, all right. "That's one advantage of living with your boss."

"It's certainly a nice place to work," said Mr. Sprague. He cleared his throat. "Ev—er, you mind if I ask? This is all pretty expensive, isn't it? And—"

"Oh, I pay my share," Ev replied. "Of the rent, anyway. Ty had the place for years before I moved in, of course, so I got the use of the furnishings for nothing. But when he saw that hole I was boarding in on Forty-fifth Street, he insisted on my coming in with him."

"He sounds like a very nice man," said his mother.

"Ty?" laughed Ev. "You'll love him. He ought to be along

pretty soon. I phoned him when I got your wire and he said he'd come home early."

"By the way, Ev," said Mr. Sprague, "I've got regards for you. Or a bawling out, depending on how you look at it. Joanie Carson wants to be remembered, and she says she's not going to write to you again until you answer her last letter."

Ev laughed shortly. "Joanie Carson. That child."

"She still talks about you, Ev," said his mother.

"Does she?" said Ev.

Ty came in soon. He was a big man with a large, roundish face. He wore a beautiful gabardine suit and brown suède shoes. He had two boxes under his arm, and he gave one—a corsage box—to Mrs. Sprague.

"I'm so happy to meet Ev's parents" he said with a pleasant smile. "I hope you won't mind—I've brought you these, and I've taken the liberty of arranging things for this evening." He took a ticket envelope from his pocket. "There's a new musical—a smash—but a friend of mine did the costumes and he got tickets for me. 'Ice to the Eskimos.' Have you heard of it?"

"Oh, yes," said Mr. Sprague, who kept up on things. "I read the review of it. We'd love to see it. That's very nice of you, Mr. Emmet."

Mrs. Sprague opened her box. "Orchids!" she exclaimed. "How lovely! Oh, Mr. Emmet, you shouldn't have—really."

Ty bowed, almost from the waist. "Pleasure, I assure you. It's only once that I'll meet Ev's parents for the first time. Talented Ev." He put his hand briefly on Ev's shoulder. "Which reminds me—this other box." He opened it as he spoke. "I was passing Quentin's at lunch time today—" He explained to the Spragues. "Quentin's a friend of mine who keeps a shop. Men's accessories. Really unusual things." From the box he took a silk muffler, a beautiful tawny yellow. "There, Ev. What do you think of it?"

"It's stunning," said Ev. "But—"

Ty proceeded to wind it around Ev's neck and to knot it. "It'll go nicely with your chocolate-brown jacket."

Ev shook his head. "Ty, as Mother says, you shouldn't have—really."

"Nonsense." Ty hushed him grandly. "Anniversary present. You know," he said to the Spragues, "it's a wonderful coincidence, your coming down today. It's just a month today that Ev's been living here."

"Yes," said Mr. Sprague, "that's right, I guess it is. I remember Ev's letter telling us about it came right on my birthday."

"But just the same, Ty," said Ev, stroking the silken scarf around his neck, "you're much too extravagant and generous."

Ty shrugged. "When I saw it in the window, I thought of you at once. It seemed your color somehow. A kind of—" he hesitated for a word, "—fulvous yellow."

"What kind?" asked Mr. Sprague.

"Fulvous," said Ty. "Tawny. Smoky yellow."

"Oh," said Mr. Sprague. He nodded thoughtfully. Then he sighed and got up. "Well, I suppose we ought to go on to our hotel."

They agreed to meet in the hotel lobby to go out to dinner, and Ev put them in a cab. On the way to the hotel, which was not far, Mrs. Sprague held the flower box carefully and Mr. Sprague sat with his hands in his lap, one on each leg, palms down.

After a while, Mrs. Sprague said, "It's a lovely apartment, don't you think?"

"Very pretty," he replied.

She looked at him. "Mr. Emmet's a nice man, don't you think?"

The taxi stopped for a light. Then the light changed and they went on.

"Very nice," said Mr. Sprague.

That night Ty took the Spragues to a French restaurant where the headwaiter knew him quite well and where the specialty was little soufflé potatoes. At dinner Ty told them what a fine future he thought Ev had in designing. He said he felt no hesitancy in telling them, even at this early date, that he was training Ev for the time when they might operate a studio together.

"I think there are really great things ahead for Ev," said Ty.

Ev flushed happily and turned to his mother. "Gosh, Mother, wasn't I lucky to meet him? Some people have to struggle for years before they get a real break."

"Not the ones like you, Ev," said Ty, patting his arm. "Not the ones with real talent."

"Well, Ev," said his mother gently, "we've been bragging all over Albany about your wonderful progress."

"Yes," said his father, "we have been."

In the cab on the way to the theater Ty explained that their seats wouldn't be together; he'd had to take what he could get. But he and Ev would be sitting almost directly behind the Spragues. Mr. Sprague wanted to take the second row, but Ty insisted that his guests have the better seats.

The show was loud and fast. The audience expected it to be funny, and where the show fell short of the mark, the audience's expectation filled up the gap and they laughed anyway. There was a scene in the first act in which a girl in a tight sweater threw herself on a bashful sailor's lap and made love to him. While the audience was howling, Mr. Sprague, vaguely disinterested, glanced around at the row behind. Ev was chuckling and Ty, his arm linked with Ev's, was smiling; the smile made his face seem larger.

Later, Ty wanted to take them to a supper club for drinks, but Mr. and Mrs. Sprague asked to be excused after their long day. Ty promised to pick them up in his car next morning at ten-thirty; they would drive out to his beach club on Long Island for lunch.

The Spragues were in the lobby next morning promptly at ten-thirty. They had not wanted much breakfast, but the coffee was very good and Mr. Sprague had had a barbershop shave, complete with hot towel, which had refreshed him.

Ty came smiling through the revolving doors and behind him came Ev in his chocolate-brown jacket with the new muffler knotted about his neck. Mr. Sprague thought that Ty was right, the muffler went very well with the jacket.

"Good morning," beamed Ty. "A wonderful day. I'll get you some suits out at the club so you can take a dip."

"Goodness," laughed Mrs. Sprague, "do you think they'd have any to fit me?"

"Why, they must have," said Mr. Sprague. "Lots of fellows' mothers must come to visit them, don't they, Ev?"

"Sure, I suppose so," Ev nodded.

"It's a long time since Ev and I went swimming together," said Mr. Sprague. "Can you still do that shallow dive I taught you, Ev?"

Ty's car was a roadster and Mr. and Mrs. Sprague sat together in the little back seat. Mr. Sprague was busy most of the time keeping his hat on his head, but Ty wore a beret when he drove and Ev's hair never seemed the worse for wind. Mr. Sprague sat right behind his son and could see Ev's hair.

They got suits quickly enough at the club and Mrs. Sprague dabbled in the shallow end of the pool while the men swam. Mr. Sprague was very good for his age but he soon climbed up on the edge of the pool, puffing, and dangled his legs in the water. Ty swam over soon after and hoisted himself up next to Mr. Sprague.

"Those are nice trunks," said Mr. Sprague. Ty had Hawaiian trunks, yellow with a blue flower design.

"These?" smiled Ty. "They're Ev's idea. He picked them out for me. Said he liked them but didn't quite dare to wear them himself." Ev's trunks were a solid light blue. "Ev," he called, "let's see you dive."

Ev, swimming in toward the board, laughed and said, "Right. The professor will be happy to oblige."

"Where he did learn to dive, Mr. Sprague?" asked Ty.

"Oh, I taught him some," said Mr. Sprague, "and he was on the team at school."

Ev climbed to the board and walked to the end. He raised his arms and arched himself.

"Watch this, now," said Ty, watching.

Ev leaped into the air, then spread his arms wide in the sun and came sailing down. Just before he hit the water, he brought his hands together over his head.

Ty applauded. "Ah, perfect," he said. "That was perfect."

"Pretty good," said Mr. Sprague. "Knees might have been a little straighter."

They had lunch on the terrace overlooking the pool. Ty was dissatisfied with the salad dressing and asked the waiter to bring him oil and seasoning so that he could mix a dressing himself. "It seems a shame to invite you all the way out here and then just give you run-of-the-mill fare," he said to the Spragues.

"Wait till you taste this, Mother," said Ev. "You've never tasted anything like this salad dressing."

Mr. Sprague thought it was very good indeed, but he wasn't especially hungry. When he had finished lunch, he lit a pipe and said, "I thought maybe tonight we'd all have dinner and go up to the Stadium concert to hear Lily Pons. The ticket man in the hotel said he might get me tickets."

"Oh, I always love Lily Pons," said Mrs. Sprague. "So do you, Ev."

Ev glanced at Ty, then said, "Yes, Mother, I do. But I'm afraid I can't go tonight. I should have told you yesterday. I'm terribly sorry, but gosh, I didn't know that you were coming this week end."

"Oh," said Mrs. Sprague.

"It's my fault, Mrs. Sprague," Ty said. "You see, we were invited to this dinner party about a week ago and I accepted for us. Business friends, and some people from out of town. It's really rather important, but I suppose I could make excuses for you, Ev, if you wanted to go with your parents."

"Well—" said Ev.

"No, no," said Mr. Sprague, "I wouldn't want to interfere. I know how these things are, I'm a businessman myself. It's our fault for not letting you know far enough ahead. No, you go out to your party, Ev. Your mother and I will make out."

When they started back, Ty invited Mrs. Sprague to sit in front with him. Ev sat in back next to his father and they talked for a while of things in New York, then they talked a little about things in Albany. Then they just sat and enjoyed the ride.

Ty dropped them at their hotel and Ev apologized for not being able to see them again that night. They said they understood perfectly. They all agreed to have dinner next day at three so that the Spragues could catch the five-o'clock train, and Mrs. Sprague thanked Ty for the pleasant day. Then Ev got into the front seat next to Ty and they drove off.

Mr. Sprague watched them go. Mrs. Sprague said, "Well, do you want to see the man about Lily Pons?"

"Oh," said Mr. Sprague, "sure."

They went to the agency counter, but the man said he had only one seat left for that night and it wasn't a very good one. "I guess it's just as well that Ev went to his party," said Mrs. Sprague.

"Yes," replied Mr. Sprague thoughtfully. He said, "Anyway, that Stadium's awfully far uptown."

They rested for a while in their room, then went to an Italian restaurant which Ev had recommended. They couldn't understand most of the things on the menu and finally ordered meat balls and spaghetti.

"What would you like to do tonight?" asked Mrs. Sprague.

"Oh, I don't know," he answered. "I don't much care. What would you like to do?"

"Would you like to go to the Music Hall?" she asked. "You always like to go to the Music Hall."

"Well, it's probably pretty crowded," he said. "What's playing there?"

"That life-of-a-composer picture," she said. "They say it's very good."

Mr. Sprague moved his spoon over close to his knife and lined it up exactly parallel. Then he pushed the knife ahead gently until the bottom was precisely level with the spoon. "Well," he said, "I don't know. I suppose we can see it up home."

"Sure," said Mrs. Sprague. "Sure we can."

They bought some papers and magazines after dinner and went back to their room. Later, when he undressed for bed, Mr. Sprague took his wallet out of his pocket, as was his custom, to put it in a drawer. He remembered a picture of Ev and himself that he carried in his wallet and found it. It had been snapped on an Adirondacks fishing trip about six years before. The boy was wearing high-top shoes and breeches and a plaid shirt open at the throat. He was grinning and squinting into the sun. In his hands he held the string of bass and pickerel he had caught that day.

When Mrs. Sprague came out of the bathroom, she scolded her husband for reading in the dark; and he went in and brushed his teeth.

They waited in the lobby next day until half-past three before Mr. Sprague called the apartment. Ev answered sleepily. When he recognized his father's voice, he seemed to wake up. "Oh, gosh, Father," he said, "what time is it?"

Mr. Sprague told him.

"Good Lord," said Ev. "I had no idea. We were up terribly late. Gosh, I'm sorry, Father. I'm awfully sorry."

"Well," said Mr. Sprague, "those things happen."

"Are you still going to catch the five-o'clock?" Ev asked.

"I'm afraid we have to, Ev," answered Mr. Sprague.

"Then that spoils our dinner date," Ev said. "That's terrible."

"Oh, well," Mr. Sprague said, "we had a late breakfast. It doesn't matter."

"Well, at least we'll come over and take you to the train," Ev said. "We'll be right over."

Ty had dark circles under his eyes, but Ev looked all right. He had on a hound's-tooth jacket today, but he was still wearing the muffler.

Ty let go of Ev's arm to gesture apologetically. "A fine thing," he smiled ruefully, "a fine thing. And I wanted to make a good impression on you both. What ever are you going to think of me now?"

"Well," said Mr. Sprague, "as I told Ev, these things happen."

They drove to the station, and Ty and Ev put them aboard the train. Ty shook hands with both of them, said how happy he'd been to meet them, and hoped they'd forgive them for oversleeping. Then Ev kissed his mother's cheek and shook hands with his father.

"Ev," said Mr. Sprague calmly, "please. I know how busy you are. But try to come up next Friday, won't you? I'd like to have one of our old-fashioned week ends. Real old walk and talk. Try. Won't you, Ev?"

"All right, Father," nodded Ev, "I'll try. I really will. It was awfully nice to see you again."

Harlem, Hastings, Harmon. Change of engines. Mr. and Mrs. Sprague sat in the coach and didn't talk much. The train was really quite comfortably air-conditioned, but Mr. Sprague had buttoned his jacket to the top.

The waiter came through with the last call for dinner. Mrs. Sprague said, "We'd better have something, dear," and they went into the dining car. She ordered a sandwich and tea; he ordered a piece of pie and coffee.

The waiter brought their food. Mr. Sprague had been staring out the window, but he picked up his fork automatically and turned his attention to the pumpkin pie. He stared at it a minute, then he prodded the viscous, flabby filling with his fork. Then he dropped his fork sharply.

His wife looked up anxiously, and after a moment, he spoke.

"Fulvous yellow," he said.

WITOLD GOMBROWICZ

PUTO

Cursed be the distortions of mankind! Cursed be this dung-smeared pig! To hell with this filthy muckhole! And that one, the one WALKING along, with whom I WALKED, that was no bull, but only a poor cow!

The local people endow him with the name "Puto"—a man who as a man wishes not to be a man, but instead runs after men, pursues them giddily, adores—oh, loves them, is enflamed by them, desires them, lusts after them, flirts with them, dances attendance on them, fawns over them. When I first glimpsed these lips which, though masculine, bled with womanish rouge, I had not the shadow of a doubt but that destiny had blessed me with such a Puto. With him I had walked along in public view—walked like a pair forever paired.

And as we walked he told me in breathy tones everything about himself, and I listened. This man, a real *mestizo,* a Portuguese whose mother was a Persian Turk, was born in Libya and was named Gonzalo; he is very rich, gets out of bed in the morning around 11 or 12 and drinks coffee, then goes into the street and walks around, following boys and young men. When he has picked one out, he approaches forthwith and asks about some street or other; and after he has made his advances he begins to chatter about this and that, only to determine whether the young man can be talked into sin for two-and-a-half or even ten pesos. Most of the time, in fear and trembling, he dared not speak of it, they brushed him off, and he went away like a wet poodle. Hence, off again, after another young man, a youth or boy who caught his eye . . . And thus, my dear, once more questions about a street, talks either about games or about dances—coaxing, and all that in order to seduce him for five or ten pesos; but either such a young man gave him a sharp answer or spat at his feet. Then he takes to his heels, but strangely aroused. And so again on the track of a dark-haired lad or a blond, accosting, questioning. When he grows weary he goes home to rest, and then, after having recuperated somewhat on a chaise longue, back to the streets and to the quest, wandering, accosting, questioning—now a mechanic, then a laborer, a dishwasher or soldier or sailor. But most of the time, trembling with fear, scarcely having approached him, he turns away again; or, my dear, he even follows one who suddenly walks into a shop or otherwise disappears from his field of vision, and nothing comes of it. And so yet again he returns home limp and weary, though burning with desire, and after he has eaten a little and rested on the chaise longue, he dashes into the street to eye some handsome man or other, to chat him up. If he makes a catch and the two come to terms over two, five, or ten pesos, he immediately pilots him home and there, having locked the door, takes off jacket, tie, trousers, throws them to the floor, strips to his shirt and dims the light, sprays the air with perfume. And then the young man really lets him have it, empties the closet or snatches his money! Frightened out of his wits, Puto dares not cry out, permits him to take everything and endures the most agonizing blows. From these blows and cuffs he burns and flames even more with desire, and goes once more into the street, fired by passion, burning and flaming, enraptured, even though terrified and exhausted, and again on the track of young men, on the track of mechanics, laborers, soldiers or sailors; but scarcely has he approached one than he retreats, for even when the desire is great, fear is greater still. And it is already late at night and the streets more and more empty:

Puto thus returns home, strips to his shirt and stretches his tired, lonely bones out in bed, in order to arise again in the morning, drink coffee, and run after young men. And on the day after that, when he has gotten out of bed, into the streets once more to run after boys.

And so I think to myself: What does it all mean, where is it getting me, what am I doing? And I would have long since left him, but I was loathe to abandon my only companion. For he was a companion. But as he stood there with me under the trees, it was a little strange, for he was neither fish nor fowl. Although he had fine black hairs on the back of his hand, the hand was somehow a dainty, feminine hand, plump, white . . . and probably the foot as well . . . and albeit the cheek was dark with the stubble of a beard, this same cheek appeared fair and delicate, as if it were not dark but white after all . . . and also, though the foot was masculine, it behaved as if it wished to be a dainty feminine foot and played the coquette with wondrous flutters . . . and while the head of this man in the prime of life was becoming bald and grizzled at the temples, it seemed as though out of this head there emerged another that wished to be a dainty feminine head . . . It was as though he did not like himself, and as though he transformed himself in the nocturnal quiet, and one no longer knew whether this was He or She . . . and being neither the one nor the other, he has the semblance of a creature and not of a man.

He was waiting in ambush, the rogue, he stands there, says not a word, and only stares mutely at his boy. I think, what a devil and werewolf, and why then am I standing here with him when he is bringing me disgrace, and I have him to thank, as well, for my disgrace at the ambassador's reception. To hell with him, the devil take him—and yet I shall not leave him, for he walked with me, and now we walk together.

An older man with salt-and-pepper hair approached the young man; when Puto saw this, he was dreadfully insulted, began to signal to me, and said, "My curse and my misfortune! What an old fossil, what does he want from him, probably they have a rendezvous here, and the old man is going to buy himself a little fun! . . . Go and listen in on what they're saying to each other . . . get going, eavesdrop, I'm dying with jealousy . . . get going, go . . ."

His hot breath almost singed my ear. I stepped out from under the trees, drew near the youngster, who was of medium build, fair-haired, his foot, his hand middle-sized, and such eyes, such teeth, such a shock of hair, that—oh, rogue, oh, you rascal Gonzalo! . . . And what is that I hear! It is my own native tongue!

As if scalded I sprang away from the two and back to Gonzalo: "Do as you please, but I am leaving and want nothing to do with that, for they are my countrymen and probably father and son! I want nothing to do with it, and I'm going home!"

He seized my hand. "Oh," he cried, "God sent you to me, you—my friend, and you will not deny me your assistance! And if these are your countrymen, it will be child's play to make yourself acquainted with them. And then you will introduce me to them, and I will be your friend, a devoted friend forever, and give you 10, 20, 30 thousand or even more! Come, let's follow them, they're already entering the park!"

I would have liked to clobber him. But he draws near, presses himself against me: "Come, let's go, we're going together anyhow—come, come, let's go, let's go!" And still talking he went ahead, and I fell in behind him, stumbled, and we are walking, we are walking, we are walking! We trot into the park. And there: the rattle of miniature trains thundering round a boulder, here and there clowns or pyramids of empty bottles, there again carousels or swings or a trampoline, further on a round-about with wooden horses, target-shooting, an artificial grotto or distorting mirror, and thus, my dear, everything is revolving, flying, rocketing through the din of amusement, and in the midst of it all Japanese lanterns and the dazzling blossomings of Roman candles! And the people wander about in confusion: one stands staring at the swing, another at a clown, and then he drifts from the mirror to the bottle-game and gapes at this or that; but everything is a chaos, torn this way and that—here a monster, there a mesmerist. The pleasure-seeking boils and bubbles so, swings are swinging, carousels revolve, chasing their own tails, and the people walk and walk and walk and walk from swing to carousel, or from carousel to swing. The swings are swinging. And the people are WALKING. And only the mirrors entice the Japanese lanterns, and the bottles cry out with the ballyhooing pitchman's voice, and if it is not the bottles, then the miniature train comes rattling past, or it's the lake in the artificial grotto, or a clown; and through it all a glitter and buzz and the spinning of pleasure-seeking, and a drilling and flying of entertainment. But when the amusements only amuse each other, the people depart, and walk, walk! . . .

The young man and his father (for it was his father) were sitting at a small table and drinking beer; Gonzalo and I sat at a table nearby, and Gonzalo insisted that I introduce myself: "Go to them, drink with them as fellow-countrymen do, and I shall also drink, and then we will drink together, in company!"

The hall is large, with many lights, and the people stare so that I become ill at ease again, and I say, "It doesn't work that way, that would be too forward" . . . and rack my brain for some excuse or other to leave, for to me it is a disgrace to sit at a table with such an individual. He pleads with me. I resist. We are drinking wine, and the music is playing, and dancing couples twirl about the floor. Again Gonzalo insists I should go over to them, and as though intoxicated he stares at his chosen one and, wishing to please him and to catch his eye, he winks broadly, flutters his hands, giggles and frisks about on his chair . . . and then with a nudge in the side he asks the waiter for wine and rolls little balls out of bread and flicks them into the air, accompanying his prank with shrill peals of laughter. I feel more and more ashamed, for people are staring; and so I say that I must excuse myself and go to the toilet, but really with the intention to get out of his sight and do a vanishing act. I go to the toilet, go . . . But someone in the crowd seizes me by the arm, and who is it? . . . Pitzkal! And behind Pitzkal the Baron, and beside him Ciumkala! I am baffled. How did they get here? And I wonder if they're not looking for a fight, for perhaps that's the reason they came after me, and wanted to avenge themselves for that disgrace they had to swallow at the ambassador's reception . . . But no!

"My dear Mr. Witold, my dear sir! And so we meet again! Come, let's have something to drink! Let's have a drink together! Just one! Come, it's my treat!"

"No, it's my treat."

"No, no, it's mine."

Pitzkal at once roared, "What do you mean it's your treat, you clown! Are you the ones who spotted him?! The drinks are on me!"

But the Baron takes my arm, leads me aside, and buzzes fiercely as a bee, "Don't listen to them; my ears are already ringing with their boorishness; the two of us, we'll have a drink together, please, please, old man!"

Then Pitzkal grabs me by the sleeve and drags me away and whispers in my ear, "What does this ridiculous French lap-dog mean by boring you to death with his idiotic, cretinous snobbery? Come with me, we'll have a drink together and without all this pretense!"

And I reply, "God be praised, God be praised, there could be no greater honor for me than to have a drink with these gentlemen, my friends, but I am here with a companion."

As I say it, they nudge each other with their elbows, one after the other, and blink their eyes, nod their heads: "Companion, companion! Ah yes, with a companion! To be sure, as it appears, with Gonzalo—you devil, you! You've made friends with Gonzalo, you go around with him, and the whole world sees you! The man is worth millions! You're really not as crazy as people say. Come on, let's have one—let's have one! Let's have a drink! It's my treat!"

"No, no, it's on me!"

Ever more heartily, more chummily, they urge me, and since they dare not poke me with their elbows, they nudge each other in the ribs, showing off to each other, and one says to the next, "Let's go, let's have a drink!" I realize they pretend as though this is all happening only among themselves, but it is all directed toward me . . . And they begin to embrace and kiss each other (for with me they wouldn't have such audacity), and: "Let's go, let's get going, it's my treat, no, no, it's on me!" Pitzkal shakes his portmonnaie, the Baron his, Ciumkala takes out a banknote, each shows the other his money and holds it under his nose. And Pitzkal cries out, "Why do you want to treat me, I shall treat, and perhaps I shall give you another 100 pesos, if I so desire!"

The Baron shouts, "I'll give you 200!"

And Ciumkala: "I've got 300 here, 300 is what I've got, and another 15 in change!"

I see that, although they're so generous with each other, invite each other and show each other their money, they basically want to treat me and show me their money. But they don't dare . . . And already they suspect me of some kind of romance with the filthy-rich Puto, and for that reason they would promise me mountains of gold, and scarcely know how to regale me, how to entice me! After such a grievous offence and this insult, that they apparently take me for Puto's sweetheart, I would have liked to take a swing at them; but I only shouted that they shouldn't turn my head, for I had no time! . . . And so I quickly turned, entered the restroom, and they with me. There was a man spending a penny in a urinal. I to a urinal, they to urinals. But when the man who had already spent his penny had left, the horde pounced on me, and the Baron shouted to Pitzkal, "Here are 500 pesos for you," and Ciumkala to the Baron: "Here are 600 for you," and Pitzkal to Ciumkala: "Here are 700, 700, take it when I give it to you!" They pull their money out, wave it around under each others' noses and under mine, shove it into each others' hands. They must be insane!

I realize that, although they were giving each other money, they would much rather give it to me in order to buy my goodwill, except that it was embarrassing to them and they didn't have the courage. And so I say, "Don't get so heated-up, gentlemen, take it easy, easy." But they were only looking for a way to force the money on me, and finally the Baron clapped his hand on his head: "Oh, I have a hole in my pocket! I'd better give you the money or I might lose it!" And began to stuff the money into my pockets, and the others, seeing this, stuffed theirs in too: "Take mine as well, and mine too, because I've also got a hole in my pocket." I say, "For God's sake, gentlemen, why give it to me?" But at this instant someone else enters to make water, so they return to the urinals, unbutton their pants, whistle nonchalantly, as if nothing was up, as if they had to spend a penny . . . As soon as the one who had entered had made his departure, they sidled up to me again, and having more courage—they were off and running, stuffing the money in my pockets and crying, "Take it, take it!"—I say, "For heaven's sake, gentlemen, why are you giving me this, what should I do with your money?" In that instant someone entered to take a leak, and they returned to the urinals, whistling nonchalantly, but hardly were we alone together than they sprang at me again, and Pitzkal shouted, "Take it, take it, when somone gives, you have to take it, take it, for he has 300 or 400 million!"—"Don't take it from Pitzkal, take it from me," screamed the Baron, droning and buzzing like a wasp, "from me you should take it. God knows, he's got 400 or even 500 million!"

Ciumkala, however, wheezed and groaned, sighing, "I beg your mercy, and maybe it's even 600 million, do take my small change, most venerable gentleman!" Fired-up, flushed, they squeezed against me, waving their money, thrusting and stuffing it in my pockets, two at a time and then a third, one reaching over the other, then over the third, and so all together, all at once, until I didn't have the heart to resist any longer and gave in, let them stuff the money into my pockets. All of them dashed to the urinals, for someone had entered. With the money I ran to the door, out of the restroom and into the hall; and there the music is playing, the couples revolving. I remain standing there with the money and observe that my Gonzalo is still larking about and showing off.

Now he flutters his hand, then he darts a glance, then he flicks a bread-ball, now tinkles a melody on his glass, then crooks his little finger, and thus at the center of his own little comedy, he is like a turkey among sparrows, and greets his own jokes with peals of soprano laughter! Those sitting close to him actually think he's a little tipsy, but I know what kind of wine has intoxicated him, and to whom his larking is directed. Although, disgusted as I was, I would have liked to go home, run away and be rid of the whole lot, this instant pierced me like a dagger (and there he is, stretching his foot in the air), and he was after all my companion (and here he fluttered his handkerchief in my direction), my devotee (he claps his hands, flings his knees apart), with whom I walked (his fingers dance lightly on the air), and I simply cannot permit that he cut such capers for me before all these people (he is tooting on a paper trumpet). And thus I returned to the table.

As he caught sight of me he began to wave and nod his head playfully. Only when I had drawn near did he cry: "Ha, ha, sit down, sit down, and let's amuse ourselves! High-ho! Sweetheart, lovebird!

Hansel is a lovely lad,
But Jan's physique is not so bad!"

And he flicks a bread-ball at my nose, blows his paper trumpet, and says softly, "Traitor, where have you been, what have you done, my little campaign bores you!" And he immediately clinks his glass of wine against mine, flings shreds of paper in the air and then fills my glass with wine. "Let's drink! Let's drink!

Mama says I may not dance,
But I waltz at every chance!

Hey-ho, let us amuse ourselves, let's have a ball!" He pours more wine for me. It is hard to refuse when he makes his request so forcefully. We drink. But nearby, at another table, the Baron, Pitzkal, Ciumkala have taken their seats and are calling for wine. The devil take them! One could tell by looking at them that after having given me money they were feeling bolder, and as soon as Gonzalo drinks they grab their glasses, clinking them together, drink, draining them to the dregs, shout hoorah, heigh-ho, and let come what may! Not having sufficient courage to drink to us, they drank to each other. We, Gonzalo and I, also drank to each other.

"Little eye, why do you gleam?
Hansel comes, that's why you beam!"

And softly he said to me, "Go over to the old guy and ask them to join us. We'll get acquainted."

I say, "It doesn't work that way."

Under the table he shoves something into my hand and urges, "Take it, take it, hold onto it." And it was money. "Take it," he insists, "you need it, look on me as a friend, an admirer, you were my friend already, and I'll be a friend to you!" I don't want to take it, but he pushes it at me violently, forces it on me. I would have liked to throw the money at his feet; but as I already had the money from the others, and now this added to it, I didn't know what to do; for all in all it probably amounted to at least four thousand. Meanwhile, the Baron and his chums were drinking to each other, but they also began to drink to me. With their money in my pocket I couldn't do anything else but drink to them as well; they in turn to me; Gonzalo as well to me; I to Gonzalo; they to Gonzalo; Gonzalo to them! We all drink to each other. What fun!

And at last I get up and, approaching the old gentleman, I utter these words: "Excuse this intrusion, but I recognize my own native language, and thus would like to greet a fellow-countryman."

Immediately rising with the utmost civility, he introduced himself as Thomas Kobrzycki, a former major, now retired, and he also presented his son Ignaz. Then he requested that I take a seat. I sit, he offers beer, but one could tell that my company was not to his taste, and this because of the company I myself had kept. And above all, because there they are—shouting, guzzling, and kicking up a row! Realizing that he is an extraordinarily upright, correct kind of gentleman, I express myself in these words: "I am with a group, but they seem to be a little tipsy; and you will certainly appreciate that no one can seek his own company in such a place as this; sometimes it would be better if one's acquaintances were transformed into strangers."

And they are still roistering about. But he says, "I understand your quandary, and if you permit, please join us in our quieter amusement." So we continue with our conversation.

The man was exceptionally upright and proper, with dry, even features, salt-and-pepper hair, light grey eyes with bushy brows, a gaunt but hairy face, a hawk-nose that sprouted wooly hair, and ears that were also overgrown with bushy tufts of old grey hair. From close-up the son seemed to me quite well developed and pleasing, and had such hands, such feet, such even teeth and such a shock of hair that—oh, you rogue Gonzalo, you rogue! . . . And there the others were, screaming and shouting! The old man tells me that he is preparing his son for the military, and if he doesn't succeed in getting back to his own country, then he will register in England or in France, in order to combat the enemy. And he explains, "We went to this park so that my Ignaz could have a little diversion before his departure, and I wanted to show him the common folk amusing themselves." He speaks, and across the way they are drinking. What was remarkable about this man was the extraordinary circumspection and deliberation of his speech, his whole precise manner of behavior, and he was so circumspect and cautious in words and actions that he might have been an astronomer continuously examining the skies of his inmost self, listening and questioning. He was also extremely polite. In view of such cultivation, such circumspection, an ever greater sense of shame seized me because of my cronies and my situation and my petty intentions. But I didn't want to confess my concerns, and instead only said, "I wish you the greatest success with your splendid objective, and beg to be allowed to drink—also with your son—to the consummation of these noble, capital intentions." And so we clinked our glasses together. But as I touched glasses with the son, Gonzalo drank to me—and also the Baron, Pitzkal and Ciumkala. "Hip-hip, let's drink, let's have fun!"—I had to drink to them; and they returned the toast.

The old man says, "I see that they are drinking."

"To be sure, they are drinking."

"They are drinking to you, as well."

"They drink to me because they are acquaintances."

He was sunk in thought, inwardly agitated . . . and finally in an undertone: "Oh, it is really not the proper time for such amusements . . . not the time . . ."

I felt ashamed! Then, leaning toward him, I whispered into his ear, "For Christ's sake, get your son out of here, and I say that to you out of friendship, for they are indeed drinking to someone, but they are not drinking to me!" The old gentleman's face seemed to darken: "And to whom are they drinking then?" I reply, "They are drinking to that foreigner there, my chum, but he is drinking neither to them nor to me, but to your son."

He flared up and stiffened. "He is drinking to my little Ignaz? Whatever for?"

"Yes, he is drinking to Ignaz, and you must leave with your Ignaz, for that one over there is after him. Go on, get going, I say!"

And at this moment they all make a great uproar, draining their glasses, trumpeting and rioting continuously, emptyig glasses, mugs and tumblers. And hip, hip, tralala! A row, a racket like a country fair! The old gentleman became red as a tomato: "I have also observed him glancing at my son, but I didn't know why."

"Get out, get out of here with your son, you're only making yourself ridiculous in front of these men."

"I with Ignaz" (and still we whispered in each other's ears), "I will not take to my heels with Ignaz, for my son is no maiden! For God's sake, don't mix Ignaz up in this thing, say nothing to Ignaz! I will settle the matter myself with that man."

In the meantime the Baron and Pitzkal were vigorously toasting Gonzalo, and Gonzalo waves to us with his handkerchief and drains his glass—oh, what a fine time we are having, oh, how we are enjoying it all.

The old gentleman seized his glass as if he wanted to drink to Gonzalo, and suddenly he slammed the table with the glass and sprang to his feet! Gonzalo leapt up as well! Instantly the others began to get up, for they could see there was going to be a brawl. Only the son did not move, but he was apparently not feeling well, for he realized what was up, and the poor thing turned the color of a boiled lobster.

And so the old man stands there; and Gonzalo also stands there. The latter, in spite of his girlishness, was a portly man;

however, since the smell of a brawl was in the air, he had become very feeble; and thus Puto is afraid, and the old man merely stands there. And this continued for quite some time. Gonzalo moved the fingers of his left hand delicately and playfully, as if he were wagging his tail and imploring that the whole thing be turned into a joke, a *jeu d'esprit*. But the old man just stands there, and in shock and fear and uncertainty Gonzalo raised to his mouth the glass he held in his other hand, and drank to him. That was his misfortune! He had apparently forgotten that with just such a toast he had thrown the first stone!

One heard the old man asking, "To whom are you drinking?!"

But to whom was he drinking? He was drinking to no one. He drank out of fear, and doesn't take the glass away from his mouth, since if he were to set it down, he would have to answer! He drinks, then, only to be drinking. And there's the hitch—devil, devil—that just as he had surreptitiously drunk to the son before, the drinking is once more aimed at the son (the son sits at the table and makes not a move), and so he only stands there, this rogue, and drinks—ah, only a very, very little—to the son! Puto was becoming aware of this, and fearing the wrath of doubting Thomas, he became limp as a rag, and still he drinks out of sheer fear, only more and more he delivers himself with this drinking to the wrath of Thomas . . . And fearing ever more and more this wrath, he drinks and drinks!

Thomas bellows, "Ah, you are drinking to me!"

Puto wasn't drinking to him at all, but to the son. However, Thomas had apparently bellowed so intentionally in order to deflect this drinking away from his son. At that point Pitzkal, the Baron and Ciumkala roared with laughter! Gonzalo fixes one eye on the old man and drinks—even though he has drained the glass, drinks and drinks . . . But now he is pointedly drinking to the youngster, and through his drinking he transforms himself into a dame, seeks protection from Thomas' wrath. For, after all, he is no longer a man! He is already a woman!

Then Thomas screams, anger making him as red as a monstrous tomato, "I forbid you, sir, to drink to me, I forbid absolutely that a stranger drink to me!"

But what kind of "sir" is that? No sir, but a lady! And she is not drinking to him but to the son. Thus he drinks and drinks, and though the glass is empty, he drinks and drinks and prolongs his drinking to infinity and defends himself with his drinking, with his drinking he drinks everything away and doesn't stop drinking. Until finally, since he cannot drink any more, he lowers the glass from his mouth and flings it at the old man.

That made a racket! The glass shattered over old Thomas's eye in a thousand splinters!

Thomas didn't budge an inch, but stood there.

The son leapt to his feet, but Thomas roared, "Don't get involved in this, Ignaz!"

And then nothing: he stands there, simply stands there. And he is bleeding, and a big drop runs along his cheek. Now it is clear there will be a punch-up, that they're going to smash each others' heads in . . . Pitzkal, the Baron, Ciumkala sprang from the table and grabbed whatever they could grab, the one a beer mug, the other a bottle, the third a stake or a stool. Thomas, however, doesn't budge, but is simply standing there. They fume so that it seems to grow dark. Those who were some distance away draw closer, and Pitzkal and the Baron, who don't dare begin a scrap with anyone else, commence to slug it out with each other, smashing heads, biting ears . . . and everything seems to go dark—a buzz, a fog, for I too had been drinking. But Thomas stands there. And a second drop of blood oozes out and follows the trail of the first . . .

I see: but nothing; only Thomas is standing there, and Gonzalo is standing as well. A third drop flows slowly from Thomas and follows the trail of the first two, then drips onto his jacket. By God's most gracious majesty, what is this, why doesn't Thomas move? But he only stands there. And a new drop, a fourth one, wells out of him. From these quiet drops it grows quiet in the hall, and Thomas looks at us, and we at Thomas; and now a fifth drop ebbs forth.

It drips, drips. We all stand there. Gonzalo doesn't stir. And then he returns to his table, takes his hat, and walks slowly away, until his back disappears from view. Then, when Gonzalo had departed, each turned, took his hat, went home, and so we all dispersed—everything . . . everything was dispersed.

—Translated by
David Galloway and
Christian Sabisch

WILLIAM INGE

THE BOY IN THE BASEMENT

SCENE ONE

The setting is an old Victorian house of fussy dignity, kept in the most excellent tidiness and repair. It is in a small mining town close to Pittsburgh. Outside the house, pinned into the ground, is a small, neatly painted sign, "Rest in peace with Scranton. Mortuary." SPENCER SCRANTON, *a man nearing fifty, lives in this house with his father and mother, using the house as a funeral parlor as well as a home. Most of the action of the play takes place in the kitchen of the house—a big, clean, white room, with a table in the center. One gets the feeling that the family lives a great deal of its life here, using it as a kind of sitting room, too. At the right end of the room is a stairway leading to the second floor. At the back of the room, a doorway leading to the outside and the garage. At the left of the room, a big bay window and a door leading to the steps into the basement. A small, dark room at the left indicates the basement. It is in darkness until the action moves there. It is then dimly lighted. When the play opens,* MR. SCRANTON, SPENCER'S *invalid father, is alone onstage, sitting in a big overstuffed chair in the bay window, looking out of the window through his thick-lensed glasses that blur our vision of his eyes and give him an almost inanimate appearance. He is an ancient man, close to eighty, whose life for several years now has been confined to this chair, where he sits like a discarded bridegroom, his only activity looking out of the bay window onto the little bit of world before him. After a few moments,* SPENCER *comes up from the basement, where he has been at work. There is a troubled look on his face that one feels is there most of the time; it is the expression of a man trying to solve some problem that lies too deeply in his subconscious for him ever to see very clearly. He is a big man with long, hairy arms and big hands, yet with a kind of reluctance about him, as though his very size is an embarrassment to him. His sleeves are rolled up above his wrist, and he looks weary. He goes to the stove, finds a pot of coffee there and pours himself a cup. Then he brings his cup to his father, showing it to him. This is his way of asking his father if he wants some. His father shakes his head slowly,* and SPENCER *takes his coffee to the table at center and sits wearily, lighting a cigarette. Now* MRS. SCRANTON *comes down the stairway from above. She is a regal-looking woman in her early seventies, still very alert and active. This is a lovely spring afternoon, and she is dressed to go out. She looks very dignified with her white hair in a neat bun at the back of her head and wearing a simple navy-blue print dress and a small, queenly hat. She is putting on her white gloves as she comes into the kitchen and speaks to* SPENCER.

MRS. SCRANTON Have you finished with poor old Mrs. Herndon?

SPENCER . . Yes.

MRS. SCRANTON Were the burns real bad?

SPENCER One whole side of her, raw and purple.

MRS. SCRANTON (*Makes an ugly face*) Poor old lady. Did you fix her up to look all right?

SPENCER Yah. Covered her face with grease paint. She looks like a chorus girl now.

MRS. SCRANTON Son! You mustn't talk disrespectful of the dead.

SPENCER Well, they all get to lookin' pretty much alike. One dead body after another. That's all life gets to be.

MRS. SCRANTON The good Lord doesn't like us to complain. Well, I'm sure you've done a nice job on her. You always do. You're a regular artist in your work. Imagine—burned to death, a poor old critter like her, when her henhouse caught fire. We all have to go sometime, but I pray to the good Lord I won't have to go that way. Her family wants the most expensive funeral, you know.

SPENCER Well, they'll get it.

MRS. SCRANTON Is the organ tuned?

SPENCER Yes.

MRS. SCRANTON Elsie Featheringill is going to sing. I've got to find out what her numbers are. I hope she picks something I won't have to practice. Can the family pay?

SPENCER I guess so.

MRS. SCRANTON I hope so. You're going to need the money, aren't you?

SPENCER What do ya mean by that, exactly?

MRS. SCRANTON After last weekend in Pittsburgh. Turned out to be pretty expensive, didn't it?

SPENCER I told you, I...

MRS. SCRANTON Calling me here in the middle of the night, telling me you have to have two hundred dollars wired to you that very minute. What in God's name were you doing that you had to have two hundred dollars that very minute?

SPENCER I told you, I... I had a little trouble with the car...

MRS. SCRANTON You said it was something wrong with the power brakes, but they act just the same now as they did before. Besides, why did the man have to have the money that very minute? Any dependable garage would wait till morning, surely. And besides, you sounded like you'd been drinking.

SPENCER I . . . I'd had a beer. That's all. Just one glass of beer.

MRS. SCRANTON I still don't see what you were doing, out until three o'clock in the morning. I certainly wonder at times what goes on those weekends you spend in the city.

SPENCER What goes on when I leave this house is *my* business.

MRS. SCRANTON Were you with a woman?

SPENCER No!

MRS. SCRANTON No, you never took to women the way your brother did. Well, maybe he taught you a lesson. You see where he's ended up, don't you? A mental hospital for the rest of his life. And what sent him there? Whiskey and women. Whiskey and women.

SPENCER (*As though it were too painful for him to think about*) Stop it, Mom.

MRS. SCRANTON (*With a nod at* MR. SCRANTON) It's a wonder he didn't end up the same way, but a stroke got him instead. Something was bound to get him some day.

SPENCER A-men!

MRS. SCRANTON Well, I've done everything I can for the men in my family. Everything I can. If they choose to go on in their own godless ways, I can't help it. I don't know why you have to keep running into the city every weekend, but I'm not going to plague you about it any more.

SPENCER I just gotta have a change once in a while.

MRS. SCRANTON Lotta good the change does you. You've been jumpy and nervous ever since you got back from that last trip. Something happened there, I guess I'll never know about. Maybe the good Lord is keeping it from me, just to spare me. God knows, I've had enough to put up with in my life. Well . . . (*With a long resentful look at* MR. SCRANTON) I guess my boys didnt come by their ways from any stranger.

SPENCER Don't pick on the Old Man any more, Mom.

MRS. SCRANTON Who says I "pick" on him?

SPENCER You *do.*

MRS. SCRANTON If I hadn't picked on him once in a while, where'd we be now, I'd like to know? Did he have any ambition? No. It was me that made him go to work and earn enough money to send you to school. If it hadn't been for me, we'd be living now in a pigsty. That's the truth. You've got to admit it. (SPENCER *lowers his head in recognition of the probable truth*) Well, I'm going to my meeting now.

SPENCER Have a good time.

MRS. SCRANTON We ladies don't have these meetings to have a good time. We meet to accomplish things. To try to keep some semblance of order in this godless little mining town.

SPENCER What's the meeting about this afternoon?

MRS. SCRANTON Some of us ladies disapprove of some of the movies they've been showing down at the theater. Movies that are too insinuating for our young people to see today. We're going to see to it that these movies are not to be shown any more. We've got the churches behind us, and we're getting the businessmen behind us, too. It's no wonder our young people are making so much trouble today, if that's the kind of thing they see.

SPENCER When'll you be back?

MRS. SCRANTON In time to get your dinner. Good-bye, Son.

SPENCER Good-bye, Mom.

MRS. SCRANTON I'm going to take the Buick.

SPENCER O.K.

(*She goes to her husband's chair to speak to him*)

MRS. SCRANTON (*In a loud voice, for he is hard of hearing*) I'm going now.

MRS. SCRANTON (*He cannot speak, but only makes guttural sounds*) Uh?

MRS. SCRANTON I said I'm going to my meeting now.

MR. SCRANTON Uh?

MRS. SCRANTON Well, never mind.

(*She goes out the back door.* SPENCER *continues sitting by the table, finishes his coffee, then gets up and stretches.* MR. SCRANTON *makes a series of guttural sounds which draw* SPENCER *to his side. Apparently* SPENCER *understands him*)

SPENCER I'm sorry, Pop. There isn't any beer. Her Royal Highness won't let us keep it. (MR. SCRANTON *makes a sound of annoyance*) I'm sorry, Pop. If I bring home beer, she takes it right out of the ice box and pours it down the sink. She just won't have it lying around. (MR. SCRANTON *makes another series of sounds*) Yah. I'm sorry, too, Pop.

(*Now* JOKER EVANS *bursts in through the back door. He is a delivery boy for the supermarket. He carries a large sack of groceries under his arm and sets it on the kitchen table. He is a boy of about eighteen, handsome, husky, full of quick life and humor. There seems to be a spirit of real camaraderie between him and* SPENCER. SPENCER'S *face brightens immediately upon* JOKER'S *sudden entrance*)

JOKER (*In a voice that even stirs* MR. SCRANTON) Supermarket!

SPENCER Well, hello, Joker, ya li'l bastard!

JOKER Hi, Spence! Man, it's a great day outside. It's quit raining now, and its really spring. Man, it's great to be alive, a day like this.

SPENCER (*Laconically*) Yah! Sure!

JOKER A bunch of us cats are taking dates down to the river tonight. A wienie roast. Why don't you get a date, Spence, and join us?

SPENCER (*Chuckles warmly at the foolishness of the invita-*

tion) Me? Go on a wienie roast with a bunch of you young punks?

(*They begin boxing with each other, slapping at each other good-naturedly*)

JOKER Sure. Why not? You can be our chaperon. We'd promise not to do anything you wouldn't do. How's that?

SPENCER How do you know what I'd do and what I wouldn't do?

JOKER Jeepers! You tie one on in Pittsburgh almost every weekend, don't you? Yah, you may act respectable around here during the week, but I'll bet you really throw a ball when you get to the city.

SPENCER Mind your business, you!

JOKER Why don't you take me with you sometime, Spence? Huh? How 'bout it? Show me the city, too.

SPENCER You no-good li'l bastard, I wouldn't take you to a dog fight.

JOKER Yah? You're scared I'd steal all your women away from you, aren't ya?

SPENCER Why, you li'l bastard, you couldn't get to first base with the women I see.

JOKER (*With a total lack of self-consciousness or conceit*) Bet I could. Girls like me. (*Spencer makes a disparaging noise*) No fool, Spence! They *do*. They really like me. Ya know why? They can't boss me. Yah! I'm real independent with 'em. I just take the attitude . . . (*He strikes a pose of boyish boastfulness*) Ho-hum, girls! Here I am. If you like me, I'll see what I can do to make you happy. Now I can't keep 'em off me.

SPENCER You stuck-up little bastard!

JOKER I'm *not* stuck-up. I just hold my own, that's all. And man, if you don't learn to hold your own with a girl, she can give you real misery.

SPENCER You got yourself a girl now?

JOKER *Do* I? Sue Carmody. Best-lookin' girl in the whole school. Jeepers, I never knew I could fall so hard. We've been goin' together about three months now. She's the greatest. A real good sport, too. Know what I mean?

SPENCER You going to marry her?

JOKER I sure wish I could. She wants to get married, but I just gotta get to college if I ever wanta get outa this town. If I married her now, I'd have to stay here and maybe go to work in the mines. I wouldn't like that, and in a few years we'd both be miserable. Sue was trying to hold me at first, but I had a long talk with her and helped her see things my way. She understands how it is now.

SPENCER She going to wait for you?

JOKER We talked all that over, too. I don't know if it's fair. By the time I get outa college, I may be in love with someone else. She may be, too. You can't tell about those things. We finally agreed that after I go to college we no longer have any strings on each other, except when I come home for vacations. And while I'm gone, if either of us finds someone we like better, then . . . Well, we'll try to understand.

SPENCER You talked all this over together?

JOKER Yah. It was tough to have to face it all. But I decided we'd better be grown-up about things. I didn't wanta go around feeling someone had any strings on me. Know what I mean?

SPENCER Yah. I know what you mean.

JOKER And she shouldn't feel I have any strings on her, either.

SPENCER When did you decide to go to college for sure?

JOKER Oh, the scholarship came through.

SPENCER That's swell, Joker.

JOKER (*A little ruefully*) Yah, but it means I'll have to play football, and that's kind of a pain. I wanted to quit that jazz after I got outa high school, and really settle down and do some work. But if that's the only way I can get to college, O.K. I'll play football.

SPENCER What're ya gonna study?

JOKER Gee, I wanta go into medicine, but I don't know if I'll be able to make it. I think I can make the grades O.K. I'm pretty smart, did ya know it? Yah. I'm graduating this spring in the top five percent of the class. But I don't know if I'll have the dough. It takes about three years longer to get through medical school, and I won't be able to play football then. I'll have to manage on my own. The folks can't help me much. I might be able to get another scholarship, though. Oh well, I won't have to worry about that for a few years anyway. If I can't make it through medical school, I'll get myself a job coaching some high school football team, maybe.

SPENCER (*Deeply serious*) Gee, kid, I hope you can make it. It'd be great, you getting to be a doctor.

JOKER We'd fix us up a system, Spence. I'd kill off all my patients and send 'em to you.
(*Now they laugh again,* SPENCER *slapping* JOKER *on the shoulder with rough good nature*)

SPENCER No thanks. I got more patients now than I want.

JOKER (*Sobering up*) I sure don't envy you your job. I'd think it'd get kinda depressing being around dead people all the time.

SPENCER (*Melancholy again*) Yah. One dead body after another. That's all my life is.

JOKER How come you never got married, Spence?

SPENCER (*Wishing he could dodge the question*) Oh, I . . . I just never got around to it, Joker.

JOKER You know what? I bet in some ways you never grew

up, Spence. No fool! I can have as much fun talkin' with you as with any guy my own age. And I bet you have more fun talkin' with me than you do with all the squares you meet at the Rotary Club . . .

SPENCER That's the God's truth.

JOKER In some ways, Spence, you're like a kid, too. Know it?

SPENCER (*Reflectively*) I suppose.

JOKER (*Looking at the clock on the wall*) Gee, I gotta beat it. I gotta finish my deliveries.
(*He starts for the door as* SPENCER *thinks of something*)

SPENCER Oh, just a minute, kid, before you go off in such a hurry.
(*He digs a wallet out of his pocket*)

JOKER What is it, Spence?

SPENCER I still owe you for washing the hearse for me last Sunday.

JOKER Oh . . . yah. Gee, I'm glad you remembered.

SPENCER (*Handing him a bill*) Here!

JOKER (*Looks at the bill and whistles*) You mean . . . all this, Spence?

SPENCER Sure.

JOKER Ten bucks? For washing the carcass wagon?

SPENCER Sure. It was a hard job, all covered with mud.

JOKER Gee, Spence, you coulda got it done anywhere in town for three or four bucks.

SPENCER Shut up, ya li'l bastard. If I say it's worth ten bucks, don't bicker with me.

JOKER (*Deeply touched*) Sure. Thanks a lot, Spence.

SPENCER Forget it.

JOKER I . . . I'll *never* forget it, Spence. Gee, you've always been swell to me.

SPENCER Get outa here now before I throw you out.

JOKER Gee, Spence, if there's anything I can ever do for you, anything at all, just let me know, huh?

SPENCER Sure. Sure. Beat it now.

JOKER So long, Spence.

(*He runs out the back door now as* SPENCER *begins putting away the groceries—into the refrigerator, the bread box, and the cupboard. He turns on the kitchen radio, too, and gets a lilting, romantic Viennese waltz that starts him whistling,* MR. SCRANTON *utters a new series of unintelligible sounds*)

SPENCER What's that, Pop? (MR. SCRANTON *repeats the sounds)* Her Royal Highness is bound to find out. (MR. SCRANTON *makes new noises, somewhat angrily*) Well, I guess it wouldn't hurt either of us to have a short one.

(SPENCER *opens the basement door and brings out a large bottle of embalming fluid, which he opens; he pours a small snifter full, which he gives to his father. Then he pours one for himself. For a moment, the atmosphere is quite merry. The old man begins nodding his head in rhythm with the waltz, and* SPENCER *takes a dustmop from the cupboard, drapes an apron around it and uses it as a dancing partner. He is waltzing about the room when he hears the Buick drive into the garage. Then he returns the mop to the cupboard hurriedly, and puts the bottle of embalming fluid back behind the basement door*)

SPENCER Her Royal Highness. She's back.

(*The old man sobers up and* SPENCER *returns to the table, lighting a cigarette and looking very solemn when she comes in. The second we see her, we know she is somehow stricken. It is as though a flash of lightning had parted the skies for a moment and given her a glimpse into some far truth she had never before quite realized, and now she is dumbfounded and horror stricken. She grasps the doorway for support.* SPENCER *looks at her wonderingly*)

SPENCER Mom, you back already?

MRS. SCRANTON (*In a hoarse and halting voice*) I came back as soon as I could . . . after I heard . . . certain things.

SPENCER (*Frightened by her tone and demeanor*) Wh . . . what'd you hear, Mom?

MRS. SCRANTON I heard my dearest friends . . . some of the finest ladies in this town . . . talk about certain things that went on in the city . . . that made my blood chill . . . and made me understand things I never understood before . . .

SPENCER (*Terrified but trying to conceal it*) Wh . . . what do you mean, Mom?

MRS. SCRANTON I was presiding over the meeting, too, and I had to beg them to pardon me. I said I had one of my migraine headaches and had to go home that instant. But I just couldn't sit there and face them any longer. I . . . I don't know how I'll ever keep my head high again, when I walk down the streets of this town.

SPENCER (*Very flustered*) Mom, I . . . d-don't know wh-what you're talking about.

MRS. SCRANTON And to think . . . I raised my son, praying he'd become a great man. I raised both my sons to be great men. No one can say I didn't do my part. And *look* how destiny laughs in my face.

SPENCER Mom, t-tell me.

MRS. SCRANTON (*Spying the book of matches on the kitchen table which Spencer has been using to light cigarettes. She grabs them and forces them in his face*) Where did you get these matches?
(*Her very tone is like a condemnation to hell*)

SPENCER I . . . uh . . . I don't remember, Mom. I g-guess I just picked them up some place.

MRS. SCRANTON The Hi Ho Bar . . . in Pittsburgh. That's where they came from.

SPENCER Yah. I see, Mom. I . . . I don't know *where* I got'em.

MRS. SCRANTON You got them when you went there last Saturday night, and the place was raided, and you called me for two hundred dollars to pay the policeman to keep him from putting you in jail and to keep your name out of the paper. (*Her detective work has thoroughly shattered* SPENCER'S *nerves. He can no longer look at her. He cannot even speak. His incoherent grunts give him a moment's resemblance to his father's mumbling inarticulateness*)

MRS. SCRANTON And the police raided the place because it's a meeting place for degenerates. (SPENCER *collapses over the table, his head in his arms.* MRS. SCRANTON *now has the bearing of a tragic victor*) Dear God, my own son! My own flesh and blood! Corrupting himself in low degeneracy. Going to some disgusting saloon, where men meet other men and join together in . . . in some form of unnatural vice, in some form of . . . of lewd depravity. (*With this,* SPENCER *runs upstairs in panic.* MRS. SCRANTON *now drops to the floor, on her knees, leaning on the table in anguished prayer)* O God, why do you make me suffer so? Why do you thrust every kind of sorrow and humiliation on me to endure? Haven't I always tried to live in your holy light? And haven't I always fought to keep my family there? My loved ones? Why do you continue to punish me, O Lord? I've loved my son since the day he was born and kept him to my breast with loving care. I think I even loved him more than I loved my own husband, for my son's infant love was innocent and pure, and demanded no fleshly act to satisfy its need. O God, will you punish me forever? *I*, who have fought so hard for the *right!* Have fought so hard to keep my mind and heart and body *pure* and free from all physical craving. All my life, I've been a God-fearing woman. Maybe you punish me for sins I don't know anything about. Are you, O Lord? Are you punishing me for sins I know not of? Then tell me, so I can atone for them and be forgiven. I don't want to suffer all my life long. When was the day I did wrong? Dear God, when was the day I did wrong? (SPENCER *comes hurrying down the stairs now, wearing the jacket to his conservative blue suit, a white shirt, a dark tie and a gray hat. He carries a topcoat over one arm and a suitcase. He has made up his mind what he has to do. He heads straight for the back door,* MRS. SCRANTON *slowly rousing herself to the fact of his leaving*) Son! Where you going?

SPENCER I don't know. I'm just goin'.

MRS. SCRANTON (*Getting up, running to him and grasping his arm*) Son!

SPENCER I should have left here a long time ago, but I didn't. I just stayed on, and on, and on. But I'm going now. Never you fear. And it'll be a cold day in hell before I ever come back.

MRS. SCRANTON Son! Listen to me. Now don't do anything crazy...

SPENCER I suppose it's something crazy if I wanta be my own boss. Forty-six years old. And I stay around here and listen to your yapping. I don't have to do it. See? I'm as free as the next one. I can get a job like that. (*Snaps his fingers*) And live the way I wanta live. And to hell with you!

MRS. SCRANTON (*Breathlessly*) I'm your mother, Son. I'm your mother. You can't leave your old home. Now think a minute...

SPENCER (*Loosening her hands on his arm*) It's no use, Mom. I'm goin.' By God, I'm goin'.
(*He tears out the door*)

MRS. SCRANTON (*Crying desperately*) Son! Son! Don't do anything foolish. Come back here, Son. You'll be sorry you left this way. Now come back here and be reasonable. (*But she only hears the sound of the Buick pull out of the garage and drive away. She utters one last futile cry*) Son! (*But he is gone. She drags herself back into the kitchen and drops into the chair by the table)* Oh God, give me peace! Give me peace!
(*She sobs.* MR. SCRANTON *has not moved throughout the scene but has continued staring out the window like a piece of patient wreckage*)

Curtain

SCENE TWO

It is early the next morning. The sun is just beginning to show and bring a soft light to the interior of the house. MRS. SCRANTON *is alone onstage, sitting in her husband's chair, looking out of the window but seeing nothing. She is dressed in a long night dress and loose robe, her long, white hair down her back. Her face is stricken with emptiness and grief. She is absolutely immobile for several moments. Then she hears the Buick drive into the driveway, into the garage. A wave of relief comes over her that makes us think for a moment she might faint. But she has never fainted in her life, and she doesn't now. In a few moments* SPENCER *comes in carrying his suitcase, tossing his hat on the post at the bottom of the stairway. He is defeated and knows it. And his bearing tells us he accepts the fact, although sadly. He sets the suitcase down at the bottom of the stairs and stands there, not knowing what to say, hoping his mother will take over the situation. But she doesn't. There is something almost shy about the woman now, and her eyes are full and her chin trembles. Finally,* SPENCER *speaks.*

SPENCER That you, Mom?

MRS. SCRANTON (*Jumps up from her chair and runs to him*) My boy! My boy! My boy!
(*All the fears and resentments they have fought inside themselves during the past several hours are purged now in a fast embrace. Their need, their desperate dependence on each other, their deep love bring them together like lovers*)

SPENCER Mom!
(*They share a fast embrace. Undoubtedly, this is the only person* SPENCER *truly loves*)

MRS. SCRANTON Oh, my son! Thank God you're back. If you hadn't come back, I'd have been ready for the basement myself.

SPENCER Yah. I came back.

MRS. SCRANTON You won't ever leave me again, will you, Son?

SPENCER No, Mom.

MRS. SCRANTON Because it's like we'd made a pact together, a long time ago. If one of us breaks it, we're both destroyed.

SPENCER I know it, Mom.

MRS. SCRANTON I've just been sitting here all night. I got your father to bed and then came down here and just sat, staring out the window. It's morning now, isn't it? Where have you been, Son?

SPENCER I just drove all over, one town to another. Not stopping any place. Just driving. I'm not sure I know now where I've been.

MRS. SCRANTON Well, you're back now. That's the important thing. And we're going to try to treat each other nicer now, aren't we? To speak to each other with a little more consideration.

SPENCER Sure, Mom.

MRS. SCRANTON It's just all wrong for us to get so impatient with each other.

SPENCER Sure, Mom.

MRS. SCRANTON (*Sighing deeply*) Oh God, I'm still heaving with relief. (*Upstairs now,* MR. SCRANTON *makes some guttural noises that demand their attention*) Your father's up. You go help him downstairs and I'll get your breakfast. (*Now there is a knocking at the back door*) Oh, it's the body. I took a call for you while you were gone. Some young boy got drowned in the river last night. They said they'd bring the body over first thing this morning. I was too distracted to get the details.

SPENCER One dead body after another. That's all my life is.

MRS. SCRANTON Now, Son, let's not complain.

SPENCER How'd you know I'd be back?

MRS. SCRANTON (*A little hesitantly, with just an edge of guilt*) I . . . I thought . . . you would be. (SPENCER *accepts the minor debasement and her self-confidence, and goes wearily upstairs as* MRS. SCRANTON *opens the back door, admitting two men, dressed as miners, carrying a body on a stretcher, the body covered with a blanket*) Right this way, gentlemen. Over here to the basement door. (*The two silent men carry the body through the kitchen to the basement door, then down the stairs, as* SPENCER *brings his father down the stairs from the second floor, the old man hanging onto* SPENCER *with infant dependence, having to feel his way cautiously every step he takes. Down in the basement, the two men put the body on a long white slab, something like a kitchen sideboard, that drains into a big sink. They keep their heads down in heavy grief.* MRS. SCRANTON *is talking with them in a low voice that comes over to the audience as just a mumble. Their answers to her are monosyllables. She is a business woman now.* SPENCER *is just getting his father into the big chair as* MRS. SCRANTON *leads the two men up from the basement*) Yes, we'll take care of the dear boy. My son does the best work in town. You can ask anyone. I know what a grief it is to you, sudden death always is. But he'll have the boy looking like he could sit up and speak to you. He'll have a fine Christian burial. You may depend on that. (*She lets the two men out the back door now, and turns to* SPENCER) It's the Evans boy. (SPENCER *gasps*) Delivered groceries here for the supermarket. The one that washed your hearse for you sometimes.

SPENCER (*As though to himself*) No . . . No . . .

MRS. SCRANTON (*Busying herself at the stove, getting breakfast*) The little fool, he and a bunch of kids decided to go swimming last night in the river. Boys and girls together, going in swimming *naked*. Oh! That's what they do. Those high school kids have no shame. What are things coming to? And after all these spring rains. They might have known what to expect. Oh, that old devil river gets someone every year.

SPENCER (*Runs down the basement stairs*) Joker! Joker! (*He tears the blanket off the young, naked body and stares at it, unable to believe what has happened. Then he returns slowly back up the stairs to the kitchen*) Mom! It's Joker! It's Joker!

MRS. SCRANTON I know. That's what I was trying to tell you. The little fool went in swimming after all these spring rains we've been having. Should have known better. Oh, that old devil river gets someone every year.

SPENCER (*Can only mutter to himself with a feeling of mysterious loss*) Joker! Joker!

MRS. SCRANTON I'm afraid you'll have to get right to work on him. They want the funeral tomorrow. They just want the cheap funeral, too, so don't go to any extra pains. Remember, you've got old Mrs. Herndon's funeral this afternoon at two-thirty. I've got to practice some of Elsie Featheringill's numbers, too. (*Dazed,* SPENCER *returns to the basement and stands beside the body, just staring at it.* MRS. SCRANTON *goes over to her husband's chair and delivers an ultimatum*) There'll be no more whiskey drinking.

MR. SCRANTON Uh?

MRS. SCRANTON (*Louder*) I said there'll be no more whiskey drinking. I found where you were hiding it, in the bottle of embalming fluid.

MR. SCRANTON Uh?

MRS. SCRANTON Nothing! How do you want your eggs?

MR. SCRANTON Uh?

MRS. SCRANTON I said, how do you want your eggs?

MR. SCRANTON Uh?

MRS. SCRANTON (*Giving up*) Well, I'll poach them. They're easier on the digestion.

MR. SCRANTON Uh?

MRS. SCRANTON (*Shouting*) Nothing! (*To herself now, returning to stove*) You don't *want* to hear me. You never did want to hear me. I could holler my lungs out and you still wouldn't hear me.
(*She is busy getting breakfast.* MR. SCRANTON *looks out of his window on a sunny morning, birds twittering now in the trees.* MRS. SCRANTON, *contented as a new bride, sings "Rock of Ages" as she gets breakfast. Down in the basement,* SPENCER *finally moves from his frozen stance at* JOKER*'s side to rub one soft hand warmly over the boy's chest, as though it were precious metal*)

SPENCER (*In a tone of reverence and awe*) Joker, you little bastard! I never expected to see you down here. Why couldn't you have been more careful, boy? You were alive. Didn't you appreciate it? Most of us are just pretending, and it don't matter when we end up down here. But you were alive. You were alive. Jesus! And I wanted you to stay that way.
(MRS. SCRANTON, *a little curious as to what is going on, sticks her head in the basement door and calls down*)

MRS. SCRANTON (*Suspiciously*) What are you doing down there?

SPENCER You'd be suspicious if I was in the same room with a stuffed owl.

MRS. SCRANTON Don't be sassy. (SPENCER *has no retort*) You can eat your breakfast while he's draining, can't you?

SPENCER (*In a firm voice*) I won't want any breakfast.

MRS. SCRANTON Oh, well you'll want coffee. It's ready. Do you want me to help you down there?

SPENCER (*Most definitely*) I do *not*.

MRS. SCRANTON Well, you don't have to bite my head off.
(*She slams the door and goes back to her work.* SPENCER *now picks up one of the boy's hands and kisses it warmly*)

SPENCER Jesus Christ, Joker, I wanted you to live.

(*Now he takes his scalpel. It is the hardest thing he ever had to do in his life, and he has to steel himself to do it, but he severs the main arteries, feeling the pain of doing it to himself, and then drops to a chair, his perspiring face in his hands*)

Curtain

JEAN GENET

RITON

Let us continue the account of the events on the rooftops. Anxiety prevented the sergeant from sleeping. He got up during the night and made the rounds of the apartment. In the bedroom, the three soldiers were sleeping on the bed in a tangle that the most indulgent of men would have regarded as scandalous, but it was fatigue alone that thus entangled the soldiers at the edge of the grave. He entered the dining room, carefully directing the beam of his flashlight. At his feet he saw the sight I have depicted. Riton was sleeing with his arm out and his hand almost entirely buried in the trousers of the sleeping Erik.

At daybreak, when they were awakened, caution obliged the soldiers to remain sitting where they were lest their walking make a sound that would worry the tenants on the floor below. Nevertheless, they would have liked to explore the conquered rooms that were still warm with the life of the occupants who had fled. Apartments offer themselves to the burglar with painful immodesty. Without looking for them, we find the very personal habits of the bourgeois, and I can say for a fact that I have opened drawers in which there were underpants with shit stains, and hard, dried, crumpled socks that emitted their sad fragrance when spread out. I have even found abandoned fragments of shit in the drawers of elegant commodes. For a long time I thought that women are the dirtier, but actually men are. As for the imagination of both, it's on a par with that of the police. If they have hidden the hundred francs in a fold of the window curtain, under a pile of sheets, or behind a frame, their mind is at rest. At rest, except for the mortal anxiety that is the very stuff of their life when they are more than fifty feet away from the hoard. But who am I to talk, since I piss in the sink, I forget turds that I leave in old newspapers in the wardrobes of hotel rooms, and I don't have the guts to leave my money in my room for an hour. I walk with it, I steal with it, I sleep with it.

The soldiers did not wash themselves. Nothing came out of the taps. The lack of water made them panicky. There was hardly any left in their canteens. The sergeant allowed them to talk in an undertone, for the noises of day drowned out their murmuring. Their blond hair was in their eyes, and at the corner of their eyelids were bits of white mucus. It was a miserable awakening. The apartment seemed the domain of death to the soldiers. It was as disturbing to be there as in certain regions where the land is mined, where snakes bulge their delicate throats, where rose-laurels grow. We were afraid. Not of the danger but of the accumulation of fateful signs. At each window the sergeant posted a man who could fire on the insurgents. Then he divided the day's food into eight equal parts. Although he did not want to talk about it, he twice made smiling remarks about Riton to Erik, which showed that he knew what had happened. Erik smiled and, in the presence of his joking comrades, admitted the night's adventure. There was no scandal. They laughed a little and were silently amused as they looked at the kid whose beauty was suddenly revealed to them. He was squatting on the bed and eating bread with chocolate. Riton bit into the chocolate and took a canteen in order to drink, but Erik snatched it from his hands. The child's astonished eyes looked into his. Erik murmured with a gentle laugh as he handed the canteen back to him without having drunk:

"I'm German."

Riton smiled back. Erik pointed a finger at him:

"You're French," and he laughed a little more loudly.

And I can understand polygamy when I realize how quickly the charms of a boy-girl are exhausted and how much more slowly those of a boy-male disappear. Erik tried to act as if he were joking about that pretension, but the fact that it was already stated, even though in an ironic tone, indicated sufficiently that it was at the basis of his relations with Riton. The pride which he sensed, instead of saddening Riton, afforded him a kind of repose. Five Germans were in the room. Erik was standing behind the bed. His comment distracted the attention of the soldiers, who spoke about something else, but a soldier smilingly stroked Riton's tousled hair as he walked by him. The kid was filled with surprise and then anxiety. He tossed his head to shake off the hand, but he didn't dare make a gesture or scowl, not even frown. And immediately he realized, from the soldiers' looks and laughter, that they knew. He thought they were mocking contemptuously. He blushed. Not having been able to wash, his face shined and the blush seemed sparkling, then warm. One of the soldiers saw him in the mirror, and, without showing the kid that he had noticed the blush, revealed it smilingly to Erik, who gently went up behind Riton, took him by the neck, pulled him back a little, and kissed him very sweetly on the hair, in the presence of his comrades and the sergeant. Nobody commented on the gesture, which was natural and charming. Riton smiled, for, though he pretended not to care, he was so in love with Erik, whose sovereign person had just compelled everyone's recognition by that quiet kiss, that he was willing to announce his marriage.

Then Riton suddenly felt he was falling over a precipice. Did Erik really love him? He would have liked to tell him that at the hour of their death in each other's arms, the most human thing was to grant each other the greatest happiness. But that was hard to say. He did not know German. He felt like crying. For a moment they all looked at one another gravely, in silence. The soldiers who had been posted at the half-open windows with instructions to shoot were lying flat on their stomachs on the rug so as not to be seen from the houses opposite. When they assumed that position, the sun was hardly up. The light was gray, though the weather promised to be fine. They saw nothing on the boulevard, which was slightly blurred by a light mist. They were watching listlessly. Erik cleaned his revolver and Riton his machine gun. The others dozed off. An hour later, the sun had driven off the mist, and when Riton went to the window, behind a tulle curtain with lace designs, after a moment of amazement the strangest emotion took hold of his mind and body, twisted him, and left him in tatters. He did not cry. The whole boulevard was decked with two rows of French flags. He solemnly bade France farewell. The flags were out for his treason. He was being thrown out of his country, and upon awakening, every Frenchman waved at his window the flag of freedom regained, of purity recaptured. He was going to the realm of the dead that day, and it was a fête on earth, in the sun, in the blue air. He was in the realm of the dead. He did not cry. But he realized that he loved his country. Just as it was on the day Jean died that I knew I loved him, so it was on losing France that he knew he loved her. The English and American flags were at the windows along with the French. A tri-colored shit and spew was dripping from everywhere. Riton realized the meaning of the house's silent activity. All night long the whole city had been spinning yards of red, white, and blue cotton fabric. And that morning, the *Marseillaise*, weary of flying over Paris, had dropped to the streets, torn and exhausted. That miracle had taken place on the day of his death. For a second Riton thought he could still go down the stairs without the Boches' knowing it (the Boches—the word clearly shows that grief invents a whole symbolism whereby one hopes to act mystically: I hesitated to write the word Boche with a capital B, out of contempt, in order to make it a *common* noun—the Boches and the Militiamen killed Jean, whom I revere, and as I see it this is the finest story of Boche and Militiaman, which I offer up to his memory. Erik has my favor). Or spring from the balcony to the street. He would not hurt himself, for this was the day when to wish for a miracle sufficed for it to take place. The Fritzes would no doubt shoot, and he then thought very seriously of running the risk of death from a German bullet. A feeling of purification, of redemption, was involved in the idea, bringing to his eyelids a tear that did not flow. He had betrayed France, but he would be dying for her. He very nearly performed a heroic act, a tailspin among the three colors.

"What the hell do I care about France? They're all jerks. Fuck 'em all on foot and on horseback."

He was bound to think that. But he was still too young for his face to remain serene, and the corners of his puffy little mouth drooped painfully at the thought of what France was doing to him, at the thought of the joy he was losing, and also because, despite its force, the bitterness of losing the things of the world always accompanies the gravest joy of marvelous expeditions in forbidden lands. He made a face. It did not occur to him that he had gambled and lost and that he was paying. What he felt was not comparable to the pain caused by turning up the wrong card. It was due mainly to the decision taken by France, his friends, his family: to expel him from joy, from play, from pleasures, and to display the flags in honor of that exile. His mouth was still pasty after the bread and chocolate. It was dark in the room where the Germans were sleeping. He was not combed. Hairs from combs and brushes were strewn all over the bedroom. An untidy soldier whose belt was unbuckled and whose shirt was half out of his trousers, playing the role of a bare-headed girl getting out of bed, went from the bedroom to the living room. Riton sniffled. A drop of snot had just started dripping from his nose. He would never again wash his face. He tried to clean the corner of his somewhat rheumy eyes with his fingernail. A slight breeze stirred all the flags.

It's bright and gay!
Good morning, swallows, it's bright and gay!

He whistled a measure of the tune between his teeth. The first car that passed in the street was white and had a red cross on the roof. There were more wounded Frenchmen. He had fired. A slight pride at the thought of it cheered him. He had killed young men on the barricades. He had wounded others with the machine gun. With Mademoiselle. Girls were looking after the wounded, were kissing them. France would make speeches. France. France, France, forever. He had Erik. Then and there that love did not fill him enough. There was a place for regret in him. The Germans suddenly—for a great sorrow gives you extraordinary lucidity, things which do not go together dovetail, and others that appeared to be decked in splendid clothes look scraggy in their bony nakedness—the Germans seemed to him to be what they were: monsters. It was not because they shot Frenchmen. Riton did not regret those they had killed. He regretted not being able to be near those who sniveled for them. The Germans did their job. Everything about them was monstrous, that is, was opposed to the joy of the French. The Germans were dismal, black, but the others were green. In that room they had the gravity of people whose destiny is only pain. Riton was not good at thinking; nevertheless he ventured the following reflection to himself:

"Who are my pals now, my com-rades? It's them, it ain't my Paris pals. I'm washed up, and that's no shit, I'm washed up, Riton my boy."

The soldiers were snoring. A subterranean soul animated that exceptional tomb which had been raised to the top of a giant building from which Riton, his heart overflowing with peace, could watch the naive joy of the inhabitants of the earth. He stood stock-still, his face still ravaged. His grief lasted five to six minutes, long enough to prepare him for what follows. He squatted with his back to the window and looked at the loose-leaf calendar on the wall, the block calendar that showed August 15, Assumption Day, and he loosened his belt a bit. The sergeant was rereading his letters. Erik was gazing sadly at his harmonica, he was waiting for a screaming of sirens to be able to play a little, if only in a muted tone. Three shots shook the apartment. The soldier in the bedroom had fired at some fellows crossing the boulevard. The question of shooting had been discussed. They had decided to fire only when it was essential so as to husband ammunition, and particularly so as not to give away their hideout. The house was certainly not abandoned. They were to shoot mainly to help German comrades who were grappling in the street with insurgents. The sergeant seemed frightened by the sniper's firing. They no doubt had a plan of escape over the rooftops, but they could not have gone very far since the block of houses was only a steep rock cut out among four streets. If they were found, it was sure death. After the shots the silence became crueler. Anxiety made its way into the apartment in the form of signs revealed by the objects. It seemed impossible that a radio would be there or that the frame of a photo would be turned or that a spot on the wall would be visible if they were not to die that day, if they were not to be blasted. The seven males and the kid, who were all tired from the struggle, which had lasted perhaps a quarter of an hour, were caught in the pose in which the burst of gunfire had stopped them. An anguish had been floating in the apartment since morning, an anguish so painful that it made the air in the rooms and the look of the faces almost black. Every angle, every sharp point of a motionless gesture, a badly wrinkled fold of cloth, a hole, a finger, instantly emitted distress signals. They were extremely nervous. The anguish with which the rooms were mined increased a hundredfold in two seconds. The sergeant muttered reproaches to the sniper, who answered in a scarcely higher tone with another mutter whose meaning was conveyed chiefly by the lips. The sergeant mastered his desire to scream an order, but the impossibility of expressing his rage exasperated him. He made the unfortunate gesture of pushing the soldier away from his weapon and giving it to a comrade whom he posted in his place. The sniper's little mug, buffeted by locks of hair, contracted, the look on his face hardened. Under constraint, the anger grew. This rapid and necessarily silent scene was prolonged as the men waited anxiously. The soldier had half sprung up, with one knee barely touching the floor and his hands empty, one of them hanging at his side, the other clutching his hair, but quivering with an uncompleted movement, somewhat like that of the runner set to go waiting impatiently to continue—and already continuing by the quivering of his body—with a run or a leap. Anger contorted his mouth, turned his face pale, the accompanying hatred brought his knitted eyebrows together into a mass of darkness from which lightning flashed at regular intervals to strike the sergeant and destroy Germany. Cowed by the necessity of being submissive even at such a moment, the soldier remained in that position, stupefied and motionless. But anxiety had made its way into the apartment. Sitting at the foot of the bed, on the edge, Erik, without realizing it, kept his dry lips on the bee's nest of his harmonica. He didn't give a damn. They waited. The sergeant, who, after his short-tempered gesture, had remained still for a moment, hesitated a second and went into the living room. As he walked out, his body discovered Riton, who was crouching, gaping, as the sniper stared at him. It was nighttime. Unless it was continually day. I even think there was neither night nor day at the top of the tall building. In broad daylight they were sometimes in utter darkness, that is, every moment revealed a nighttime activity. They went through space so gently, the movement of the Earth was so slow, that the soldiers' gestures were all gentleness. A body was asleep with its head on a heap of rope. Or a boy was whispering. A boy was dreaming. The maneuver was muted. Riton got up. Suddenly he was concerned with what day it was. He went to the wall to tear off the pages of the calendar. This gesture drew him out of the tragic a little and then put him back into it more deeply.

"It's ass-headed, but I've got to see what day it is."

As he stood up, his trousers, which had no belt loops, slid completely out from under the belt, and the shirt bunched up against his chest and back. He was hardly aware of it, yet he made the gesture of pulling up his pants with his hand. In order to go to the wall, he had to push aside or disturb the sniper, who had not moved and whose eyes, which had been hostile since the sergeant had left the room, weighed on Riton. When the kid neared him, the soldier, on seeing the sloppiness of his attire, finally found an excuse for releasing his anger. He roughly grabbed the belt and pulled the kid, whose torso was delicate despite its hardness. It was also flexible, and it bent back, as if to regain its balance, or to escape, but the soldier prevented it by putting his left hand even more angrily around his waist. Riton thought he was being playful and, though he had seldom fooled around with that soldier, supported himself with both hands on the curly head which the swiftness of the whole rather brusque movement had knocked against him. Now, the soldier, despite his anger, was unable, on feeling the irony, to keep from being (in, to be sure, a very imprecise way) under the charm of the noblest posture of respect and faith. A kind of confusion ruffled his soul and made him slightly dizzy. The child, who saw in the mirror over the fireplace that Erik was watching him from behind, tried to get away. The soldier felt it and tightened his embrace, and Riton, clutching the Fritz's hair, pressed the head harder against himself. The forehead rested on his belly, in the space between the belt and the trousrs, while the mouth was crushed on the stiff blue cloth of the fly. The significance of the posture was changing. The German seemed to be clinging to the kid by the belt, as to a lifebuoy. The wounded male, who was in a rage, was on his knees before a sixteen-year-old Frenchman who seemed to be his protector and to be indulgently crowning his head with two strong clasped hands. Everyone in the room waited in silence. The soldier refused to let go of the kid, holding him firmly with his muscular arms, furious and humiliated at the fact that his face was lost in the shadow of the trousers, whose smell he breathed in with his open mouth. He tried to raise his head, but the buckle of the belt scraped his forehead. Pain made him finally make the gesture toward the performing of which everything was converging, the gesture after which the day was later named: with wild fury, the German, whose arms were tensed and whose torso had suddenly come to life on his thighs, which were buttressed by his rising motion, bent the kid under him. Ritons eyes became those of a hunted animal. He wanted to flee, but he was trapped, and his head banged against the wooden bed. The three other soldiers were silently watching his almost motionless *corps à corps*. Their attention and silence were part of the action itself. They made it perfect by making it public and publicly accepted. Their attention—their presence, at three points in the room—enveloped the action. Two men and a soldier were on guard at the sixth-floor windows of a mined building, which was menaced by a hundred rifles, so that a black pirate could bugger a young traitor at bay. Fear is a kind of element in which gestures are made without their being recognized. It could play the role of the ether. It even lightens acts that are not conditioned by what caused it. It quickens one's knowledge of them. It weighs down and blurs others. This fear that the nest would be spotted, that the house would explode, that they would be drilled, did not seem to preoccupy them. Rather, it made a kind of emptiness inside them, in which there was room only for that extraordinary fact, which was really unexpected at the hour of death. Since they were at the edge of the world, at the top of that rock posted at the outermost point of Finis Terrae, they could watch with their minds at ease, could give themselves utterly to the perfect execution of the act. Since they could view it only in its closed form, which was cut off from the future, it was the ultimate one. After it, nothing else. They had to make it as intense as possible, that is, each of them had to be as acutely conscious of it as he could be so as to concentrate as much life as possible in it. Let their moments be brief, but charged with consciousness. A faint smile played over their lips. Erik's hand, which was lying on the bed, was still holding his harmonica. He was smiling with the same smile as the others. When Riton's head banged against the wooden bed, there was a dull but weak thud, and he uttered a very faint moan of pain. The three witnesses of the struggle, who felt no pity but were very angry with the one who threatened to botch everything, made the same gestures of the arms and silently articulated, opening their mouths wide, the same threats whose meaning the kid understood from the hardness of their features and expressions. Instead of cursing the torturer, their hatred was directed toward the child who was capable of depriving them of the joy of his tortures. Finally sure that the thud would be without danger, the hatred subsided when silence was restored. The subtle smile flowered on their mouths again, but the kid, who had been knocked out by the blow on the chin, from which blood was flowing, was already lying on the bed, with his pants down, his face against the sheets, his body pounded by the husky body of the soldier, who had the self-possession to lay down his burden delicately so as not to make the spring of the mattress groan. There was only the barest creaking. For Riton it had happened. . . . Unable to imagine how far that fury would go, he nevertheless made the movements that might help calm the soldier. The militiaman on the mattress placed his legs, which had been dangling down to the floor, next to Erik, who had remained seated, with his harmonica in his fist. The other soldiers looked on.

"Good thing I cleaned my hole a little."

The sergeant, who was at the door, was also watching. Annoyed at having been too rough with a soldier who was fighting and who would probably die that day, he dared not interfere. Besides, he was under the sway of a feeling that I shall speak about presently. In the silence of the city, which was at times disturbed by the sound of a Red Cross car carrying arms, there entered through the half-open window, from a thin, cracked voice, purer for being cracked—a broken toy—the following song, composed of the tenacity of the weak, which rose up from the pavement and, passing through the foliage of the trees, reached the ear of Riton, to whom the melody seemed radiant:

They have broken my violin . . .

Riton, who had been knocked senseless by the Fritz, bit the bolster so as not to scream. The brute stopped and panted a little, letting his cheek rest against the back of Riton's neck. He snorted. A short rest, a lull in the fellow's fury, enabled the kid to make out the end of the stanza, which the fragile voice was repeating:

For its soul was French.
It fearlessly made the echoes
Sing the Marseillaise.

Riton dared not stir. He first wondered anxiously whether he should clean himself or simply suck the jissom in. And what could he clean himself with if there was not water? He could only wipe himself. With his handkerchief. The soldier, whose bearded chin Riton felt on the back of his neck, gave a shove, which made the kid groan.

. . . Sing the Marseillaise . . .

Erik had not stirred. He had to watch the kid who had been drowned by force get sawed in half.

Riton wanted the rape to be over with, and he feared the end of it.

Surely they would all take a crack at him. Erik's presence, which he still felt at the edge of the bed, kept him from moving his rump to make the soldier come more quickly.

... *made the echoes* ...

Finally the warmth of the liquid escaped in slower and slower throbs, like the blood of a cut artery. The fellow from the North was discharging into his bronze eye. . . . When he raised himself up, gently so as not to make any noise, the soldier was calm. He was smiling. He remained standing beside the bed for a moment. He looked defiantly at his smiling cronies, then, slowly, smiling more broadly and tossing back his blond hair with a flick of his head, he adjusted his trousers and little black tank driver's jacket and rebuckled his belt. He said to the soldiers:

"What are you waiting for?"

He looked Erik in the eye. Riton, relieved of the bruiser but still outstretched, had pulled up his pants and tucked in his shirttails. Turning his head, he waited with a feeble smile on his lips. One of the soldiers who was sitting in the armchair was about to follow up, but he changed his mind and, turning to the door, laughingly invited the sergeant to enjoy himself first. The sergeant looked at Erik and signaled to him. Erik whispered a word, and they all went out. Nothing happened. They had to flee by the rooftops.

The German soldiers and Riton had gone back to the roof. They felt they were being pursued less by the tenants of the building than by fear. They were fleeing from it. Slowly, in broad daylight, following the least exposed slopes of the roof, they got to a corner formed by three chimneys. The hiding place was narrow. It could hardly contain them, though they squatted together in a kind of cluster from which the notion of the individual disappeared. No thought was born of that armed mass, but rather a somnolence, a dream whose chief and mingled themes were a feeling of dizziness, the act of falling, and nostalgia for the Vaterland. No longer worried about being heard, they spoke aloud. Riton was caught in Erik's legs. They crouched against each other, and they spent the day that way, crushed by the five soldiers who at times overflowed onto the sky. There were potshots all around them, but they could see nothing, not a single patch of street, or a single window of an apartment. The heat was overpowering. Toward evening, the mass of males was loosened by a little elasticity. Numbed limbs came to life again. Erik and Riton awoke. Beneath the shelter of the chimneys, the sergeant divided the remaining food and they ate their last meal. The general idea was to get down under cover of darkness and make their way to the Bois de Vincennes. There was much less shooting. Evening was imposing its calm. There was nothing visible on the rooftops; yet they felt that every windowsill, every balcony, concealed a danger, the side of every chimney was capable of being a soldier's shield and the other side that of his enemy. The sergeant and the men crawled off to explore. Two Germans remained in the hideout with the weapons and water. They were to shoot only in case of emergency. Erik and Riton went around the chimney and sat down at the foot of that cliff, with the machine gun between Riton's legs. Erik was weary. His springy blond beard softened his face, which was hollowed by fatigue. Neither of them spoke. They were coming out of their tangled sleep. Their eyes were dim, their mouths slack. The visibility was a little better from their observatory and they could see a few housefronts and windows. Opposite them, about two hundred yards away, one of the windows lit up with a faint, shifting light. A man's silhouette stood out in the rectangle. Riton aimed and then fired a burst. The silhouette moved back into the shadow. Erik's firm, imperious hand came down on Riton's.

"Don't."

Riton pulled away impatiently and his nervous finger let loose a second burst.

"Don't," Erik repeated hoarsely in a scolding but low tone. "Don't."

Erik uttered the word more calmly, more gently, he seemed

to be roaring from a deeper, more mysterious part of the forest. His hand remained, preventing Riton from continuing to shoot.

"Not . . . (Erik hesitated, trying to find the word) not . . . now."

Riton's hand lost its will power and Erik's became more friendly. Gently, with the other hand, the German took the machine gun and put it down at his side. He had not let go of Riton, in fact he made his hug more affectionate. He drew the kid's head to him. He kissed him.

"Up. . . ."

This single word had the curtness of an order, but Riton was already used to Erik's ways. He stood up. Leaning back against the brick monument, facing a Paris that was watching and waiting, Erik buggered Riton. Their trousers were lowered over their heels where the belt buckles clinked at each movement. The group was strengthened by leaning against the wall, by being backed up, protected by it. If the two standing males had looked at each other, the quality of the pleasure would not have been the same. Mouth to mouth, chest to chest, with their knees tangled, they would have been entwined in a rapture that would have confined them in a kind of oval that excluded all light, but the bodies in the figurehead which they formed looked into the darkness, as one looks into the future, the weak sheltered by the stronger, the four eyes staring in front of them. They were projecting the frightful ray of their love to infinity. That sharp relief of darkness against the brick surface was the griffin of a coat of arms, the sacred image on a shield behind which two other German soldiers were on the lookout. Erik and Riton were not loving one in the other, they were escaping from themselves over the world, in full view of the world, in a gesture of victory. It was thus that, from his room in Berlin or Berchtesgaden, Hitler, taking a firm stand, with his stomach striking their backs and his knees in the hollows of theirs, emitted his transfigured adolescents over the humiliated world. But Erik's fatigue was already, and more obstinately, drawing him back. He was reentering himself, was recapturing his youth, his first marriage with the executioner in the shrubbery when each of his hands, which were equally skillful in wielding the ax, unbuttoned a fly, pushed aside a shirt, took out a prick, and Erik raised his frightened eyes to those of the brute and said to him sweetly:

"Don't be angry with me if I don't do it well, but it's the first time."

Standing against a tree, the executioner made Erik face him, and he put his member between the kid's thighs. Riton's arms grabbed Erik's disheveled head and pressed the strong, famous neck, which bent forward, Erik's head finally touched the pale face, which was an utter appeal, a dying concert. Riton's arms quivered around the captured neck and enclosed it in a basket of tenderness and roses, of children's frills, of lace, and the kid's voice murmured against the ear of the half-naked warrior:

"All right now. Come in, it's time."

In passing through all his flesh, the memory of the executioner obliged Erik to greater humility toward the child. All his excitement receded. The executioner's hideous but hard face and sovereign build and stature, which he could see in his mind's eye, must be feeling freer, either the thought of them gave him greater pride in buggering Riton and caused him to beat and torture him so as to be surer of his freedom and his own strength and then take revenge for having been weak, or else he had remained humiliated by past shame and finished his job with greater movements and reached the goal in a state of brotherly anguish. Riton, surprised at the respite of love, wanted to murmur a few very mild words of reproach, but the vigor of the movements gave him the full awareness that great voluptuaries always retain in love. He said, almost sobbingly: "You won't have me! No, you won't have me!" and at the same time impaled himself with a leap.

"*Einmal. . . .*"

The whole member entered in, and Riton's behind touched Erik's warm belly. The joy of both of them was great, as was their confusion, since that joy had been attained. In the kind of swing which is in the form of a closed cage, the kind you see at county fairs, two kids pool their efforts. The cage goes up. Each oscillation acquires greater amplitude, and when the cage reaches the zenith after describing a semi-circle, it hesitates before falling in order to complete its perfect curve. For two seconds it is motionless. During that moment the kids are upside down. It is then that their faces come together and their mouths kiss and their knees get entangled. Beneath them the crowd, whose heads are inverted, looks on. Riton became even more tender. He murmured as one prays:

"Say, listen, see if you can't get it all in!"

For Erik this sentence was only a graceful song. He answered with an equally lovely sentence and in an equally hoarse tongue. And Riton:

"You're right, try."

Then suddenly Erik's body arches a little.

Only white roses could emerge from Erik's member to enter the bronze eye. They flowed out slowly with each quick but regular pulsation of the prick, as round and heavy as cigar smoke rings from pursed lips. Riton felt them rising within him by a path swifter than that of the intestines all the way up to his chest, where their fragrance spread in layers, though surprisingly it did not perfume his mouth. Now that Riton is dead, killed by a Frenchman, if one perhaps opened his chest would one find, caught in the trellis of the thorax, a few of those slightly dried roses?

Erik covered the sweating face with kisses. The perforating tool so hurt the child that he longed for an increase of pain so as to be lost in it.

"Ich. . . ."

Erik's mouth was speaking, breathing on the kid's shoulder. And his back kept thrusting. His eyes, which he had kept closed, opened on those of Riton. It's banal to say: "Those eyes have beheld death." Yet such eyes do exist, and after the ghastly encounter, the gaze of the men who possess them retains an unwonted hardness and brilliance.

Erik's eyes: Erik had known the snows of Russia, the cruelty of hand-to-hand fighting, the bewilderment of being the only survivor of a company; death was familiar to his eyes. When he opened them, Riton saw their brilliance despite the darkness. Remembering all of Erik's campaigns, he also thought very quickly: "He's been face to face with death."

Erik had stopped work. His eyes kept staring; his mouth was still pressed against Riton's.

Riton murmured: "I now have the impression that I love you more than before." Erik did not understand.

No tenderness could have been expressed, for as their love was not recognized by the world, they could not feel its natural effects. Only language could have informed them that they actually loved each other. We know how they spoke to each other at the beginning. Seeing that neither understood the other and that all their phrases were useless, they finally contented themselves with grunts. This evening, for the first time in ten days, they are going to speak and to envelop their language in the most shameless passion. A happiness that was too intense made the soldier groan. With both hands clinging, one to the ear, the other to the hair, he wrenched the kid's head from the steel axis that was getting even harder.

"Stop."

Then he drew to him the mouth that pressed eagerly to his in the darkness. Riton's lips were still parted, retaining the shape and caliber of Erik's prick. The mouths crushed against each other, linked as by a hyphen, by the rod of emptiness, a rootless member that lived alone and went from one palate to the other. The evening was marvelous. The stars were calm. One imagined that the trees were alive, that France was awakening, and more intensely in the distance, above, that the Reich was watching. Riton woke up. Erik was sad. He was already thinking of faraway Germany, of the fact that his life was in danger, of how to save his skin. Riton buttoned his fly in a corner, then quietly picked up the machine gun. He fired a shot. Erik collapsed, rolled down the slope of the roof, and fell flat. The soldiers in the hideout neither heard the fall nor noticed the oddness of the shot. For ten seconds, a joyous madness was mistress of Riton. For ten seconds, he stamped on his friend's corpse. Motionless, with his back against the chimney and his eyes staring, he saw himself dancing, screaming, jumping about the body and on it and crushing it beneath his hobnailed heels. Then he quietly came to his senses and slowly made his way to other rooftops. All night long, all the morning of August 20, abandoned by his friends, by his parents, by his love, by France, by Germany, by the whole world, he fired away until he fell exhausted, not because of his wounds but with fatigue, as sweat glued desperate locks of hair to his temples. For a moment, he was so afraid of being killed that he thought of suicide. The Japanese, according to the papers, advised their soldiers to fight on even after death so that their souls could sustain and direct the living. . . . The beauty of that objurgation (which shows me a heaven bursting with a *potential* activity and full of dead men eager to shoot) impels me to make Riton utter the following words:

"Help me die."

—Translated by
Bernard Frechtmann

FRANK O'HARA

GRAND CENTRAL

The wheels are inside me thundering.
They do not churn me, they are inside.
They were not oiled, they burn
with friction and out of my eyes
comes smoke. Then the enormous bullets
streak towards me with their black tracers
and bury themselves deep in my muscles.
They won't be taken out. I can still
move. Now I am going to lie down
like an expanse of marble floor
covered with commuters and information:
it is my vocation, you believe that,
don't you? I don't have an American
body, I have an anonymous body, though
you can get to love it, if you love
the corpses of the Renaissance; I am
reconstructed from a model of poetry,
you see, and this might be a horseless
carriage, it might be but it is not,

it is riddled with bullets, am I.
And if they are not thundering into me
they are thundering across me, on
the way to some devastated island
where they will eat waffles with the
other Americans of American persuasion.
On rainy days I ache as if a train
were about to arrive, I switch my tracks.
During the noon-hour rush a friend
of mine took a letter carrier across
the catwalk underneath the dome
behind the enormous (wheels! wheels!)
windows which are the roof of the sun
and knelt inside my cathedral, mine
through pain! and the thundering went on.
He unzipped the messenger's trousers
and relieved him of his missile, hands
on the messenger's dirty buttocks,
the smoking muzzle in his soft blue mouth.
That is one way of dominating the terminal,
but I have not done that. It will be
my blood, I think, that dominates the trains.

LARRY

Watching the muddy light attack
some resemblances, you took
my letters from your drawers and said
"You were careful to me." Some look.

Outside in white trousers the night
works. A bus signals into oblivion
and is already at the boundary. If
we lower ourselves by rope down

in front over the marquee we won't
get burned by the neon and it'll be

sheer agony. The mountain kind. I wished
already some bar chirruping, aknee

with painters' molls hep to genius.
So we're great friends constant and true
to not being sure of your being sure
of my being sure of your being sure of you.

LEBANON

Perhaps he will press his warm lips
to mine in a phrase exceptionally historic,
which seemed to have lived on lips
in Galilee now that I have already felt

its sting. The sweet fetid dust
of his breath will linger upon my lips
as if my understanding were affected and a soul
of passion and arrogant surmise had my lips

for a moment and then passed through my lips
into the rendering azure of the temple.
It was coolly dawning and his lips
opened, "I'll go with you to the other country,

no matter that my all is here,
my childhood on the plains' grapelike lips,
my father's handkerchief, my mother's tomb,
my memory of games; they go up like lips

in a stadium; all that comes from my white lips
and shall ease you on the unnecessary journey."
And thus the day did blanch upon his lips
despite the dirty windowpanes and cold air.

He did go to the mountains and perhaps I
shall be daily upon those wooded sloping lips,
so that as he is fleetly hunting goats
my breath will find its altar in those lips.

my will relaxes with the fresh green reeds
which spring arrogantly though they're not sown.
Indeed, they want no wind. They are a lake,
and bend when they wish and do not invite
the sun. They flay the air and do not break;
indifferently they disappear at night,
  and just as calmly earth's of them bereft.
  They found earth mute and passionless, and left.

HOMOSEXUALITY

So we are taking off our masks, are we, and keeping
our mouths shut? as if we'd been pierced by a glance!

The song of an old cow is not more full of judgment
than the vapors which escape one's soul when one is sick;

so I pull the shadows around me like a puff
and crinkle my eyes as if at the most exquisite moment

of a very long opera, and then we are off!
without reproach and without hope that our delicate feet

will touch the earth again, let alone "very soon."
It is the law of my own voice I shall investigate.

I start like ice, my finger to my ear, my ear
to my heart, that proud cur at the garbage can

in the rain. It's wonderful to admire oneself
with complete candor, tallying up the merits of each

of the latrines. 14th Street is drunken and credulous,
53rd tries to tremble but is too at rest. The good

love a park and the inept a railway station,
and there are the divine ones who drag themselves up

and down the lengthening shadow of an Abyssinian head
in the dust, trailing their long elegant heels of hot air

crying to confuse the brave "It's a summer day,
and I want to be wanted more than anything else in the
world."

A WHITMAN'S BIRTHDAY BROADCAST WITH STATIC

Pas la jeunesse à moi,
ni delicacy, ich kann nicht, ich kann nicht, keines
Vorsprechen!
Ugly on the patio, silly on the floor, unkempt,
dans le vieux parc je m'asseois, et je ne vois pas
à droite ni à gauche.
Personne! mais des bruits, des vagues particulières,
und ich habe Kummer, es könnte ihm ein Schaden
zustossen, lacht der Kundschafter.
And then someone comes along who's sick and I say
"Tiens, ça! c'est las de l'amour, c'est okay!"
and fall.
Da, ich bin der Komponist, und ich bin komponiert.

LONNIE COLEMAN

THE THEBAN WARRIORS

The night Montgomery came aboard we were in Norfolk, Virginia, about to sail for North Africa. Starboard watch had liberty. I was port, so I was sitting around third division quarters with some of the other guys chewing the fat. There were four or five of us, and I don't remember what we were talking about. Whatever it was, we forgot it when Montgomery showed up. He clattered down the ladder with his sea bag, shouting, "Where are third division bunks?" We looked around at him. He was a big, good-looking boy with his hat pushed back on his head.

I answered. "This is third division."

He looked at me and smiled. "Thank you. Now, would you be a dear and help me with my bag? Your mother's all tired out. Such a time I had finding the ship, I thought I'd never—" I helped him get the sea bag to the deck.

"What you got in here, Mac? It's like lead."

"You're not far wrong. I take a few things around with me to keep in trim. One mustn't let down. Such a temptation in wartime, don't you think? Is there an empty bunk?"

I pointed to the only one reluctantly, for it was above mine.

"Thank you. Will we be neighbors?"

I nodded. He looked around at the others. "Cat got your tongues? All of you in third division? We'd better get acquainted. My name is William Montgomery, and I'm a bosun second."

"I'm Barney Casper," I said, and we shook hands. He had a strong grip, and he didn't seem to be putting it on.

I told him the names of the others, who were still too surprised to say anything, and they shook hands all around. They looked relieved after shaking hands. Whether his grip relieved their minds or whether just touching him made them believe he was real, I don't know, but everybody relaxed some.

Montgomery smiled. "Good, now we all know one another. It's so important to start off right. Mother says a first impression is seldom erased. Or maybe she says never. She talks such a lot, I can't always quote her precisely. Like a canary bird, chatter, chatter, chatter. I tell her it's no wonder four husbands left her, but she says never mind, it's easy to get another when you're in the theater. And didn't she ever laugh when I told her I had been assigned to the *Nellie Crocker*. She said, 'Monty, my dear, don't you ever in future let me hear you say the Navy doesn't know what it's doing!' Such a wit, mother. Now I don't suppose any of you has a bit of gin in his locker?" He sailed his hat onto his bunk, sat down beside me and unfastened his pea jacket. "That's just coffee in those?" He referred to the mugs we held in our hands. "How cosy you all look sitting there with your thick hands around those thick mugs—what fun we'll have! I can see it now—sitting around in the evenings drinking joe, or do you call it java here? Telling tales of dare-and-do, chanting sea chanties. What a lot I shall have to remember in my old age. Tell me, do any of you dance?" Noting the startled looks on our faces he went on with a laugh. "I don't mean together, of course. Unless you do. If you do, speak right up and say so; I always think it's best to be frank with one another. Surprise can be so disturbing. I meant dancing like in a show. I wondered if there were any entertainment on board, if we might get up a little show now and then to amuse ourselves. I don't do anything much. I sing a bit, though I'll never be professional, mother says. I don't care in the least, for that isn't the life for little old me. I prefer something more rugged. Powder and rouge are all very well in their place, but I mean, they make you feel like such a belle, don't you agree?"

The young freckled sailor named Walters stared at Montgomery with his mouth open.

Montgomery sighed. "Sports are more my field. I love to box. Anybody box aboard? Isn't that funny, alliterative you know, *b-b-b*, to say nothing of the *d's.*"

"When we're at sea or in foreign ports," I said, "we have boxing matches every Sunday."

"Thank you. You seem to be the spokesman for the group. Do you yourself box?"

"No."

"I'll teach you if you like. You ought to be good. You're big. You look like you've got the muscle. What's the matter, are you slow on your feet?"

"I can't think quick enough to know what the other fellow's going to do next."

"Oh, it isn't a matter of thinking. Look at the professionals. Oafs. Couldn't box a hedge if it took brains, not a one of them. Let me teach you."

"We'll see."

Sellers had been quiet all this time, but he seemed finally to have made up his mind how things stood. He said with a fishy smile and in a mincing voice, "You can teach me how to box, Monty-dear!"

Montgomery placed his hands on his thighs and leaned forward, shaking his head. "This moment always comes when I meet new people," he said to me, or anyway in my direction. Then looking at Sellers: "We'd better get this straight right off. I don't like ugly little men who snicker. You are ugly and little, and you snicker. God knows, I would be loath to touch you even in punishment, but I warn you, I make the jokes about myself. I hope you understand. Now perhaps you'd like to rephrase your request?"

Sellers flushed and looked at me. I simply looked back at him, neither supporting nor deserting. He looked at the others who, one by one, decided to play it cautious.

"Good," Montgomery said after a pause. "That's all settled. Now tell me about things. What's the captain like?"

"He's a good guy," Walters, the youngest sailor, said. "He's strict, but only about things that count. He ain't chicken."

Montgomery looked pleased. "Charming."

"The exec's the tough one," Walters went on.

"So often the case," Montgomery said. "What about the division officer? What's his name?"

"Ensign Mason," I said.

"First name?"

"Wes. Wesley, I think."

"Wesley Mason," he repeated. "He sounds terribly earnest. Is he?"

"He's the best division officer on the ship," Walters said. "All the fellows like him."

"Is he terribly butch?" Montgomery asked, and when he was again met with blank looks, expanded: "You know, rough, rugged—oh hell, where have you been all your lives? Don't people talk where you come from? I can see I'll have to teach a language course around here, so I won't have to translate every remark I make. Now let's see what we have. A good captain, a tough executive officer—both in the grand tradition. And a division officer who is popular with his men. What a spot to be in. Now the really important question. How's the chief?"

"He makes you work," I said.

"Good. I don't approve of slackness in a chief. How does he make you work? Does he curse, is he mean, or does he just tell you what to do and leave you to do it?"

"He tells you what to do," I said, "and he leaves you to do it, but if he comes back and finds you haven't done it, he's likely to curse a little, and he's been known to get mean."

"You know," he said, "you're not only nice, but you have wit and intelligence too. Are you married?"

"Look—"

"Are you?"

"No, but—"

"You've got a girl."

"Sure."

"The way you say it, I don't believe you. At least not an important one, I'll bet. You sound more and more intelligent." He slid out of his bunk. "Where's the head? I want to take a shower. Is the water on?"

"Water's almost always on, and the head's aft and starboard."

He began to undress, and we watched him silently. I'd seen a lot of guys undress in my time and never noticed them, but somehow the way Montgomery did it, he made you curious so that you had to notice. He was showing himself off like one of those women who strip in night clubs. Not that obvious maybe, but as though it were some kind of act. He was conscious of himself, never relaxed. He didn't look uncomfortable, I don't mean that. In fact, he smiled, as though at himself and us too. He was well built, with a flat belly, big muscular thighs, and a good back and good arms. The black hair started at the bottom of his neck and went down to his toenails. While he was undressing, we didn't say much. He had been talking such a streak himself that when he stopped, nobody seemed to find anything on his mind. And the way I said, we couldn't help looking at Montgomery. As he reached into his sea bag for a towel, he said with a laugh, "I don't know when I've had such a good audience. Thank you, lads. You've made me feel right at home." He slung the towel over his shoulder and went off humming.

Contrary to what all of us expected, Montgomery got along fine. Everybody in the division heard about him right off, and within a day everybody on the ship must have known about him. He seemed to enjoy causing a stir, and didn't change his way of talking much, no matter where he was. If people froze, he just kept talking, but made out like it was a joke and that he was innocent of the impression he caused. We'd come up to muster every morning after we got to sea, with nothing facing us but a long day's work and a night with a watch in it somewhere, and there Montgomery would be with his hands on his hips. "What shall it be today, girls? Let's get out the carriage and horses, put on our red dresses and high-heeled shoes, carry our sauciest parasols, and drive right by the Methodist Church like we're good as anybody!"

The thing was, Montgomery looked too much a man for anybody to take offense out loud. Some of the boys talked to one another privately, and some made fun of him behind his back, which he knew and which I don't think bothered him, but nobody came right out and said anything to his face. It got to where he was pretty well liked, or anyway, people were glad he made some kind of joke they could laugh at. I think the fact that he never tried anything made everybody believe his talk was all put on. Even the chief smiled now and then, and only once in a while, when he had something big on his mind, he'd say, "Hell, Montgomery, knock it off, so I can think."

Montgomery never shirked when there was work to be done, and sometimes his joking made the work seem easier. When a working party was called at night, he'd slide out of his bunk without a whimper, saying one time, "La, dears, I feel like a call girl."

Every afternoon after work he had a sun bath and some exercise. He did this in the gun tubs aft, out of sight of the midships house. We weren't supposed to be on deck with any of our clothes off when we were at sea, because of the possibility of attack. Montgomery worked out in regular boxer's trunks, and he had a set of dumbbells he varied the weights on. He invited me to work out with him several times, but I never took him up on it, although some of the others were eager enough. He never asked them though. They'd stand around looking at him, counting off for him. He'd smile at them once in a while or maybe say something funny, but most of the time he acted like he was off by himself.

The first Sunday we were at sea, he boxed. There had been considerable speculation up to this time about whether he just happened to be built well or whether he actually had any strength behind him. Well, we found out. He took on our best boxer for three rounds, and when he got in the ring, he didn't kid. I think it was the first time any of us had seen him without a smile on his face. Kelly, the man he was fighting, was heavier than he was and had the backing of the whole ship. You could tell that from the way the men yelled and carried on. It took Montgomery about one minute to learn everything about Kelly though: where he was weak, where he was strong, how good his breath was going to be, how quick his fists and his feet were. Montgomery fought with a serious look on his face, so most of the boys watching thought he was scared. One or two of them got brave and called out, "Kill the fairy, Kelly!" By that time Kelly probably knew he wasn't going to do anything worth watching, so he tried to make himself look good. He acted like he was mad and tried a few hard punches that looked all right and raised the boys' spirits some but didn't much more than touch Montgomery. Montgomery looked solemn for the whole first round, like he didn't even hear what the boys were yelling. When he came out for the second round, he went after Kelly. He knocked him to the mat for a slow count of seven in the first thirty seconds, and the crowd got quiet. Then he let up until just before the bell ending the second round, when he knocked him to the mat again. Kelly stayed there even after the bell rang. In the third and last round Kelly was too groggy to care what he was doing, knowing that Montgomery could have taken him any time he wanted to. The crowd didn't know anything about boxing, but they could have learned from watching Montgomery. It was as pretty a demonstration match as you'd want to see. He didn't hurt Kelly. He just made him look like a damn fool.

That stupid crowd, when they finally saw what was happening, started yelling for Kelly's hide, like they'd been rooting for Montgomery all along. Montgomery didn't pay any attention to them at all until the bout was over. Then, when the referee held up one of his hands, he cupped his crotch with the other hand and smiled at them like he knew they were crud.

After the match a lot of the guys crowded around him and followed him down to the compartment, where he started to undress to take a shower. They yelled the usual things and slapped him on the back, those who could get close enough to touch him. People always want to touch athletes after they've won, as if doing so gives them luck or lets them share in the victory. But Montgomery just went about his business. I'm a boxing fan, and I was excited about how good he was, so I stuck around when the others drifted away. He looked at me as he toweled himself down. "What do you say, Barney, was I all right?"

"You were four-o," I said, meaning perfect.

He wrinkled his face. "I was showing off. I shouldn't have. Now nobody will want to box me, and I won't have any fun."

"You'll have fun all right," I said, remembering how he had looked and how cool he had kept in the ring. "All the guys would like to work out with you; you can get a sparring mate any time you want to. That is, if you promise not to hurt them."

He blinked. "That isn't the question. The little dirty-drawers idiots can always be had for the nudging. I'm more particular." He smiled again. "I'm saving myself. I always get what I want, too."

"Good. Swell," I said uncertainly, thinking for the first time he might be talking about something else.

He looked at me steadily, draping the towel over his shoulders. "You know what I mean. Don't play dumb."

"I don't get you," I said honestly.

"I'm dead serious. I may joke, because unless I do it's all too tedious—"

"I don't know what you mean," I said, beginning to understand.

He saw my understanding. "I mean I've got my eye on you, and I'll get you sooner or later."

"Sure," I said, trying to make a joke of it. "You'll get me. Right flat on my ass on the mat, like you did Kelly today." Suddenly we were both blushing.

"Tell me about yourself, Barney. Where did you come from?"

"My old man's a cop in Baltimore. I worked on a Coca-Cola truck a couple of years after I finished high school. Then the call to the colors."

He shrugged. "It doesn't explain anything, does it? It seldom does. You know the score in all kinds of ways, but nothing in your background points to why. You could have got every bit of education you have from a cereal-box top."

"Now wait a minute," I laughed, glad to be on a safe topic.

"I studied civics and hygiene and American history. I learned to scan *Lady of the Lake* and memorized speeches from *Julius Caesar* just like everybody else."

"That isn't how you got your charm."

"You know," I said finally, "I've busted guys for saying less than you've said to me."

"Why don't you try busting me?"

"You're bigger than I am," I laughed.

"That isn't the reason." I started to go. He put his hand on my arm, not holding me, but making me pause. "I have to laugh when I hear you straight guys talk about beating up fairies. You'd be surprised how few get beat up. It's usually the plain janes no self-respecting faggot would look at twice who're always talking about what they'd do if anybody tried to lay a hand on them. Let's face it, Barney, the world of straight men is a fraud. They can all be had if anybody wants them enough to work things the right way. And wait his chance. Like I'm waiting my chance with you."

I shook his hand away. "Don't wait too long, Monty."

He laughed. "You see, you like me. You're calling me Monty already."

"I'm calling you Monty because in spite of pretending to be queer as a three-dollar bill, you're a nice guy basically."

"You don't know how nice I can be."

"Oh, hell, you're impossible."

"I'm the most possible thing you ever met up with."

"Look, Montgomery, don't make me mad. It's all right to kid the others but—"

"I kid them because they bore me, and because it's an easy way to insult them."

"So kid me too if you like, the way you've just been doing. But if I thought for a minute—"

He wasn't smiling at all. "There's no hurry. I can wait. When I get you, it's going to be for good, and nobody's going to pretend afterwards that nothing happened. When it happens, we'll both want it to happen. Understand?"

"Why me?"

"The ones I've liked come in all shapes and sizes, blonde and brunette and redhead, skinny and strong. But there's one thing they have in common that makes them stand out from everybody else around. They're men, not babies."

"Thanks," I said as sarcastically as I could manage. "What a crazy bastard you are, Montgomery!"

He scratched his thigh absently and smiled. I was suddenly aware of his nakedness, even though he had taken off his boxing trunks a long time ago and had used the towel for nothing more than to dry himself. "When you want to hear some more of my crazy talk, let me know!"

My embarrassment made me lose my temper again. "Any time you say, Monty old boy, because I want you to know one thing—I'm not afraid of you!"

"Tonight at ten-thirty by the incinerator on the fantail," he said quickly.

I walked away calling over my shoulder, "Go take a cold shower."

The trouble was, I couldn't forget the things he said. The more I thought about them, the madder I got, and I wondered why I hadn't told him to go to hell. One reason, I guess he was impossible to tell to go to hell. He could talk as well as he could box. When somebody's doing something you don't like, you can beat hell out of them, outtalk them, or walk away. I stood no chance of beating Montgomery. I couldn't outtalk him. And I hadn't walked away. I thought of things I should have said. I realized I should have told him all about my girl back in Baltimore. She's a pretty thing, and smart too. Sometimes I think she's smarter than I am, though no better educated. We both finished high school and went to work right afterwards. She doesn't let anyone outsmart her, whether in talk or deeds. Next time he got going, I'd tell him about Doris. Just thinking about her made me feel better. We were going to get married in a year or two, as soon as we'd saved something and it began to look like I might live through the war. Or maybe the war would be over.

Since it was Sunday, I didn't have much to do until midnight. Then I was to have the bosun watch on the bridge. I kept away from Monty. I was careful not to eat at the same table with him or sit near him later when they showed the movie. The movie was over before ten o'clock, and I went back to the compartment to write a letter to Doris. I got out her last one, the one I'd had just before we left Norfolk, and read it over. It was all about this girl friend of hers that worked in the blanket department of the same big store, Price and Sons, that Doris worked in. Doris was in kitchenware. This girl was getting married to a marine, and the other girls had given her a big shower. Doris wrote about the shower and all the presents, and what they'd served. She said she'd almost got tipsy. I had to smile reading that again, because Doris never drank more than a couple of beers, or one drink of regular liquor, or a little wine maybe over an entire evening, so I knew she was kidding.

Reading her letter made me feel good, but all of a sudden Montgomery was on my mind. I thought: I'll show the bastard I'm not nervous about him. I looked around the compartment. He wasn't there. "What time is it?" I asked Sellers, who was sitting on an upturned bucket on the deck writing a letter to somebody.

"Nearly ten-thirty. You got the midwatch?"

"Yes." I dropped my writing board, swung out of my bunk, and went topside.

Sure enough, he was leaning on the rail by the incinerator. I felt damn good about coming out to meet him, because I felt stronger than him, and in my mind I was daring him to say anything wise. He didn't seem surprised at seeing me at all, not surprised nor glad nor sorry.

He said, "Hello, Barney."

I didn't know what to say. I mumbled something about its being hot below deck.

He said, "Well, we're getting a little farther south every hour."

"Yeah."

I leaned on the rail alongside him. I kept expecting him to say something so I'd know what he was thinking, but damned if he didn't just look down at the water and the foam made by the propellers and not say a word for a long time.

I was about to make a crack like, "Well, here I am, you smart bastard, what are you going to do about it? You see I'm not scared of seeing you by yourself," when he said, "It's such a nice night. I almost wish I had a watch."

"Oh yeah?" Somehow that made me mad. "Well, I got one at midnight, and if you're so keen to stay up and watch the stars and the sea floating by, you can take mine," I said. "If you want to. Don't let me deprive you of any pleasures."

His head jerked around. "What's the matter, Barney?"

"Nothing's the matter," I said. "I just said if you want to stay up the whole god damn night, then you might as well take my watch and do so, that's all I said."

"You want me to take your watch?" he asked slowly.

"No! I didn't say that. I just said that if—"

"I'll take your watch if you're tired, and you can take one of mine some time. I don't mind."

I don't know why, but I got more excited. "I'm not asking you to do a god damn thing for me, not a *god damn* thing. If I had—oh hell, you're all tired out from your big boxing match. You're lucky not to have a watch."

"Barney, something's the matter," he said, innocent as you please. "Have I done anything wrong? Has anybody else done something or said something to hurt you?"

"I never asked you any favors, did I?" I shouted. "Did I?" He shook his head. "If anybody asked you did I ask you any favors, you'd say no, wouldn't you, isn't that right?"

"Barney, what the hell—"

I backed away from him. "Just keep away from me. Keep away from me, understand?"

I went below and crawled into my bunk to try to rest until time to go on watch. I didn't feel like writing a letter to Doris, but I thought about her. Usually when I thought about her I remembered the times we talked or danced, or the plans we had, the way her face looked, and her hair and eyes. Sometimes about kissing her, but we'd never gone much further than that. Now I thought of her naked, and I was shocked at myself and excited. I thought of her breasts, but I didn't know what they looked like, so I just thought about breasts. Doris used to let me feel them, but only in the dark, and I'd never seen them. Now I tried to think what they would look like, and what her body would look like. It was very important to know. I was horny for her for the first time I'd known her.

It seemed no time at all before somebody touched my shoulder and said, "It's time to go on watch, Barney." It was Montgomery, and he was looking at me seriously.

"You feel all right?"

I swung out of the bunk. "You got the messenger watch, haven't you, Walters?" I said. He nodded. "Come on, let's get up there."

All during watch I felt horny as a bull, and I made up my mind that first liberty in Algiers I was heading straight for the Sphinx Club. When the watch was over and I crawled in my bunk to go to sleep, Montgomery's arm had slipped over the side of his bunk while he was sleeping.

Next day after I'd had noon chow I was in the gun tub aft taking a sun bath. I kept my dungarees on but had my shirt off and was lying on deck face down when I heard somebody flop down beside me. I didn't turn my head or open my eyes, but I knew it was Montgomery, and I was glad. "That you, Montgomery?" I said, calm and easy.

He seemed to be himself again. "You're getting a nice tan on your upper body," he said, "but you ought to get it all over. You never know who'll see you all over."

"Yes, I do," I answered, still easy and calm.

His "Who?" was surprised and expectant, I thought.

"Rina," I said.

"Rina? Such a name, like a burlesque queen."

"Rina's a well-stacked piece in the Sphinx Club in Algiers, and that's where I'm heading the first liberty I get."

"All right, I'll go with you."

My eyes snapped open, and I raised up to look at him. He was the one who was calm and easy now, lying on his back with sun glasses on and his boxing trunks pulled tight to his body. "You don't understand, Monty old fellow," I said. "This isn't your kind of thing at all. This Sphinx Club is a house where they keep a lot of little pussy cats."

"I know what it is," he said, "and I'm coming with you."

"I don't want you to."

"Afraid?"

"Come on, I don't give a damn. I just don't see why."

"I like to keep posted on what the competition has to offer," he said. "But that isn't the real reason I'm coming. I want to be there when you change your mind. I know those cold little bitches with their ooh-la-las and pretense of passion. They couldn't fool a gorilla. If you think that's going to satisfy you, you've got something to learn. I want to be there when you learn, Barney."

"I know what it's like, and it's damn good, don't try to tell me! They make me feel like a man, not like a—"

"What, Barney?" he said, and I could feel him looking at me through the dark glasses. The sun had reddened the tips of dark hair on his chest.

We were in different watches, but Montgomery fixed things so we left the ship together on the first liberty when we hit Algiers. It was hot as hell, and we didn't talk much as we headed for the Casbah. I saw some leather pocketbooks and thought about getting one for Doris, then decided I couldn't take it with me where I was going. There was a bar with tables on the sidewalk facing the park just where the Casbah begins, and we stopped for a couple of vermouths. "You're really going through with it," I said.

"Varieties of religious experience." He finished off his wine. "Let's go."

We knocked at the door at the end of the little alley and were let in by a quiet, hard-faced old woman. Montgomery smiled. "Enchanting. The perfect porter for the house of sin." He pushed his cap back on his head. The old woman led us through the entrance room with its copy of the Sphinx that gave the place its name. It had the face of a young girl and big, tinted breasts. The next room had a lot of chairs and sofas in it. There were a couple of sailors sitting there with girls on their laps. They looked around at us. The girls smiled, and one of them called something over her shoulder in French. This was the part of coming to the place I hated, the preliminaries. I looked at Montgomery, who was taking in the room with a smile on his face that wasn't exactly a smile, though he seemed relaxed enough.

"It's a lovely place," he said. "Puts you right in the mood

for love, even if you weren't already, don't you agree? That darling sofa, a bit worn and not too clean, but who cares? Those nice muddy-rose walls, how divinely appropriate, the telling feminine touch. And over all the aura, the essence, the very smell of sin. They'd better bring out the girls before I attack you."

A door opened behind us and two girls entered. One was blonde, and the other was brunette. They wore short dresses with nothing underneath, and they had on a lot of rouge and lipstick and eye make-up. The blonde was Rina, and she remembered me. She came over with her arms open and a big smile on her face that made her look older. "*Chéri,* you have come back!"

"Hello, Rina," I said. "Yes, I'm back, and I brought a friend along this time." I hugged her and avoided her lips. She smelled a little like the disinfectant in a men's room.

Rina drew away from me to look at Montgomery. "He is very nice, your friend. Handsome," she said mockingly. "My lucky friend!" She pulled the brunette forward. "Marjane," she introduced.

Montgomery stepped toward her, smiling. "William. Willy."

"Willi!" the brunette squealed. She patted his chest. "Nice! Handsome! Rich! The Virgin smiles on me today!"

"There's nothing like being smiled on by a virgin," Montgomery laughed, putting his arms around Marjane, pulling her to him hard and kissing her full on the lips.

Rina looked at me swiftly and laughed. "He is—hot!" She nodded her head rapidly, raising her black penciled eyebrows. I sat on the sofa and pulled her down on my lap. She squealed as I unbuttoned the top of her dress. Montgomery had raised Marjane's dress until it was gathered about her waist, leaving her naked from there down. He had his hands on her behind, and she was giggling and slapping his hands.

Rina said, "Don't look at them, look at me, *chéri*! I excite you, *chéri*!"

The two girls had adjoining rooms upstairs, and we all rode together on the small slow elevator with the wrinkled old woman who had let us in. When the elevator stopped, the girls went ahead of us while we paid the old woman, who explained what I already knew, that we were to pay the girls the same we paid her, or more if we desired.

"Willi!" Marjane called.

"Barney!" Rina called.

"Isn't it all too thrilling?" Montgomery said to me as we went toward them. "The real thing, no counterfeit here."

Marjane grabbed Montgomery by the hand, bit his thumb, and pulled him into her room. I followed Rina.

After a while she drew away from me. "First time today for me," she bragged. "What is wrong, you don't want love?"

"Love?" I said.

"Love, this is love!" she exclaimed. "I am love, *chéri*!" She smiled patiently. "Tell Rina what is wrong."

"Nothing's wrong."

"You listen to them all the time you lie with me. They laugh. Come! We have good time like Willi—" She took my head in her hands to kiss me. I was about to kiss her when I heard Montgomery laugh again. I drew away. Rina shrugged and relaxed on the bed. I got up, found a cigarette in my jumper and lit it. In the next room I could hear Marjane grunting like a hog. Rina looked at the wall and began to laugh.

"Shut up," I said.

"Give me a cigarette."

I threw the pack on the bed beside her. She fished one out and put it between her lips. She was staring at me as I held the match for her. "*Chéri*, you love this Willi?"

I went cold all over. I put out my cigarette on the floor, took hers out of her mouth and put it out too. Then I jumped at her.

I waited for Montgomery on the sidewalk in front of the house. When he came out, he didn't smile, he didn't frown. He just looked at me like he knew everything there was to know about me. He lit a cigarette, cupping his hand around the match out of habit, although there was no wind in the alley. When he blew the match out, he watched it until it stopped smoking before he dropped it. He said, "Where would you like to go, *chéri*?"

I turned away and walked quickly down the alley. He came after me whistling, caught up and walked in step with me, not saying anything. I wouldn't look at him. I walked across the street into the park and down one of the paths. When I sat down on a bench, he sat down beside me. He was still whistling. Finally I looked at him. His face was relaxed. I studied his face and then his neck, and then I let my eyes follow all the way down his body. I knew just what he looked like under the white jumper and white pants, I remember thinking that. I said, "You certainly stayed with her a long time!" He turned and looked at me. He looked at my face the way I had looked at his, and then his eyes followed down my body. "Why don't you say something? What are you thinking?"

"I am thinking," he said slowly, "what an ugly thing a woman's body is, and what a beautiful thing a man's is."

"That's funny," I said. "That certainly is funny, considering the way you were going on with that French whore."

"I was being kind," he said. "She knows she's ugly, and I thought it would be nice to make her feel for a little while that she wasn't."

"Big-hearted Monty."

He shrugged.

"How many times were you kind to her?"

"Just once," he said softly.

"I guess you talked to her afterwards."

"A little."

I lit a cigarette very carefully because my hands were shaking. When it was going I said, "Did you talk to Rina too?"

"She knocked on the door when she heard us talking, and Marjane let her in. It's a friendly, informal place."

"What did she say about me?" I demanded.

After a slight hesitation he said evenly, "She and Marjane made fun of you. She told Marjane that you had been listening to us and that you couldn't do anything until you got mad. She said she thought you were queer for me."

"She's a god damn—"

"I told them, although I don't know why it should matter to you what they think, I told them you were straight as dye. I told them it was I who wanted you."

My laugh sounded ugly. "What did they say to that?"

"They didn't believe me."

"I guess the three of you had a good laugh about it. Did you kiss Rina too?"

"Oh hell, Barney."

"Well, did you?"

He didn't say anything for a long time, and when he did, it wasn't an answer to my question. "Are you ready, Barney?"

"Ready?"

"I think you are. I have to know, though. I have to be certain. Don't you understand yet what I was doing? I was showing you how empty that is, showing you it isn't what you want. I know what's in you, and I know it isn't going to be satisfied with a whore shrieking ooh-la-la. You want somebody to touch you with love. If things had happened differently, it might have been your Doris. But they didn't happen that way. She's there, I'm here, and I'm going to have you. When the war's over, you can go back to her if you want to. But I don't think you'll want to. Why didn't she let you make love to her when you were with her? Don't you know that most women hate men and use their sex to insult them and dominate them? I'm offering you something better than that, you damned fool. I'm offering you myself, and I'm promising you that I'll take you and hold you and keep you as long as—such promises last. I love you, Barney."

It was that that made me cry. My mouth was open, and I was biting my knuckles, and I couldn't see for the tears.

"Barney, this is what we're going to do. I found out about a place a few blocks from here. It's a sort of hotel where we can rent a room for a few hours, and they don't ask any questions about why two sailors want to rent it. We can take a bath, get clean again, and then we can be together until it's time to go back to the ship. Wouldn't you like that?"

It was a long time before I could answer. "I guess I'd like a bath."

He stood up.

"Are you sure this place is safe?" I said.

"Come on."

GIORGIO BASSANI

DR. FADIGATI

That summer, like the one before it, we went on holiday to Riccione, on the nearby Adriatic coast. Every year we did the same. My father had tried vainly to drag us up into the Dolomites, to places he had been to in the war, but in the end he had resigned himself to returning to Riccione, and renting the same small house beside the Grand Hotel. I remember it all very well: myself, my mother, and Fanny, my little sister, going to Riccione on August 10th, with the maid. (Ernesto, my brother, had been in England since the middle of July, living *au pair* with a family in Bath to practise the language.) As for my father, he stayed in town, and was to join us later, as soon as he could get away from his rural labours at Masi Torello.

The very day I arrived I heard at once about Fadigati and Deliliers. On the beach, which even then was crammed with families on holiday from Ferrara, people were talking of nothing but the pair of them and their scandalous "friendship".

Since the beginning of August they had been seen going from one hotel to another in various seaside towns scattered between Porto Corsini and the Punta di Pesaro. The first time they appeared was at Milano Marittima; from there they went on to the canal port of Cervia, and took a fine room at the Mare e Pineta Hotel. After a week they went on to Cesenatico, at the Britannia Hotel. And then gradually, everywhere they went arousing an enormous amount of noise and gossip, they went to Viserba, to Riccione itself, to Rimini and to Cattolica. They were making the journey by car: a red Alfa Romeo 1750 two-seater, very sporty looking.

Around August 20th they turned up unexpectedly at Riccione, staying at the Grand Hotel as they had done ten days before.

The car was brand new and its motor gave out a kind of snarl. Apart from travelling in it, the two friends went driving in it every afternoon, just at sunset when most bathers left the beach to stroll along the front. Deliliers always drove, fair and sunburnt and dazzlingly handsome in his tight shirts and cream woollen trousers (on the hands that lay negligently on the driving wheel, he wore unimaginably expensive-looking leather gloves), and obviously the car was entirely at the disposal of his every whim. Dr. Athos Fadigati, the well-known professional man from Ferrara, who for the occasion wore a flat tartan beret and a pair of mechanic's goggles, as if he was a substitute driver (goggles he never removed, even if the car had to crawl at walking pace along the road in front of the café Zanarini), merely rode up and down, stuck in the seat beside his companion.

They still slept in the same room, and ate at the same table. In the evenings, too, they sat at the same little table when the Grand Hotel orchestra, having carried its instruments from the dining-room down to the outside terrace, exposed to the sea breezes, changed abruptly from light music to jazz. The terrace soon filled up (I often went myself with new friends I had made at the seaside), and Deliliers never missed a tango or a waltz, a quickstep or a slow foxtrot. Fadigati never danced, of course. Every now and then he pressed to his lips the little stick he had taken out of his drink, and his round eyes never ceased watching, over the rim of the glass, Deliliers's perfect movements as he danced at a distance with young girls or with the smartest and most expensive-looking women. As soon as they returned from their drive, they both went punctually to put on evening dress; Fadigati's was grave and heavy and black, Deliliers wore a natty white jacket, short on the hips.

They went on the beach together too—although in the morning it was usually Fadigati who left the hotel first.

He arrived before nine o'clock, when there was still nobody about, greeted respectfully by the bathing hut assistants, whom (people said) he always tipped generously. He was dressed from head to foot in normal city clothes (only later, when it grew hotter, he left off his tie and shoes, but the white panama hat with its brim lowered over his glasses he never took off at all), and went to sit down under the solitary umbrella which he had ordered to be set farther ahead than the rest, only a few yards from the sea. Stretched out in a chaise-lounge, his hands crossed behind his neck and a detective story open on his knees, he remained for a good two hours, doing nothing and looking at the sea.

Deliliers would come along at about eleven o'clock. With his lazy, animal walk, which the slight difficulty of walking in his wooden beach shoes made even more elegant, he would cross the space of burning sand between the bathing huts and the tents unhurriedly, almost naked. The white trunks which he was still tying at his left hip, the gold chain he wore round his neck, from which a medal of the Madonna hung just above his thorax, somehow accentuated his nakedness. And although, especially during the first days, he found it something of an effort to greet even me, when he saw me there beside our tent; although, as he made his way through the spaces between the tents and umbrellas he never failed to wrinkle his forehead with annoyance; yet it was hard to believe him, for it was obvious that he felt most people there, men as well as women, in their hearts admired him, and this he enjoyed a great deal.

Everyone admired him, men and women, there was no doubt about it at all. But Fadigati had to make up for the indulgence which Deliliers was shown on the beach at Riccione by people from Ferrara.

In the tent next to us that year was Signora Lavezzoli, wife of the lawyer. Today she seems nothing but an old woman and has lost much of her old importance. But then, in the mature splendour of her forty years, surrounded by the perpetual deference of her three adolescent children, two boys and a girl, and the no less perpetual deference of her worthy husband, the distinguished expert in civil law, a university don and an ex-deputy, well, in those days she could be considered one of those who most authoritatively inspired public opinion in our town.

Pointing her eyeglasses at the umbrella Deliliers made for, Signora Lavezzoli, who was born and had grown up at Pisa, "on the banks of the Arno", and used her quick Tuscan speech with extraordinary dexterity, kept us continually informed of all that was happening over there.

With the tone of voice and almost the technique of a radio sports commentator, she would tell us how, say, the couple had got up and were now going to the nearest raft: obviously Deliliers had expressed a wish to go bathing and the "old man", so as not to wait "palpitating" under the umbrella, had got permission to go with him. Or else she would describe Deliliers's gymnastics after bathing to dry himself off in the sun, while the "beloved" stood there doing nothing with a sponge towel in his hand, so anxious to dry him and touch him, she'd swear.

Oh, that Deliliers—she would then comment from her tent to ours, though addressing my mother in particular: believing she had lowered her voice, perhaps, so as not to let the children hear, but in fact talking louder than ever—that Deliliers was nothing but a spoilt boy, a lout that military service would do a great deal of good. But Dr. Fadigati, no. A man of his class, of his age, was in no way excusable. Well, so he had special tastes? He was "like that"? What of it! No one had ever made a fuss of it before. But to come and make an exhibition of himself here at Riccione, where of course he knew people would know him; to come and make a spectacle of himself here, while everywhere in Italy there were thousands of beaches where there would be absolutely no danger of meeting a single person from Ferrara! No, really: only someone really filthy (and as she said this Signora Lavezzoli's big blue eyes would shoot great flames of authentic indignation) only a "real degenerate"—she went on—would do a thing like that.

Signora Lavezzoli went on talking, and I would have given a great deal to shut her up once and for all. I felt she was unjust. I didn't like Fadigati, of course, but it wasn't he who seemed offensive. I knew Deliliers's character perfectly well. In choosing this beach so near to Ferrara, he had shown all his beastliness, all his lack of restraint. Fadigati had had nothing to do with it, I was sure. My feeling was, he felt ashamed. If he didn't greet me, if he even pretended not to recognize me, that must be why.

Unlike Lavezzoli, who had been at the sea since the beginning of August and so like everyone else knew all about the scandal (though while his wife held court all he did was read *Anthony Adverse* in his tent; I never even heard him speak), my father arrived at Riccione only on the morning of the 25th, a Saturday: even later than he had expected to be, and not knowing a thing, of course. He came by train without warning, and not finding a soul at home, even the cook, came down to the beach at once.

He noticed Fadigati almost at once. And before my mother or the Lavezzolis could stop him he went gaily across to him.

"Just look who's here!" he cried, striding up to the doctor's big umbrella.

Fadigati jerked round. My father was already holding out his hand, and Fadigati tried to pull himself up out of his chaise-longue.

At last he managed to. After which, for at least five minutes, we saw them standing under the big umbrella, talking with their backs to us.

Both of them were gazing at the motionless strip of sea, smooth, palely luminous, completely unruffled. And my father, whose whole person expressed the joy of having "shut up shop" (this was how he put it at Riccione when he wanted to refer to all the unpleasant things he had left in town: business, the empty house, the heat of summer, melancholy lunches at the *Roveraro,* mosquitoes, etc.), raised his arm and pointed out to Fadigati the hundreds of rafts scattered at odd distances along the shore, and, a long way off, scarcely visible on the horizon and as if suspended in mid-air, the rust-coloured sails of small fishing boats. At last they came toward our tent,

Fadigati about a yard in front of my father with a strange expression on his face, at once imploring, disgusted, and guilty. It must have been eleven o'clock; Deliliers had not yet appeared. As I got up to meet them, I noticed the doctor glanced anxiously at the line of bathing huts, from where, at any minute, he hoped or feared to see his friend emerge.

He kissed my mother's hand.

"You do know Signor Lavezzoli, don't you?" my father said loudly, right away. Fadigati hesitated a moment. He looked at my father, and nodded; then turned, obviously on tenterhooks, towards the Lavezzolis' tent.

Lavezzoli seemed more than ever immersed in *Anthony Adverse.* The three children lay on the sand a couple of yards away, in a ring round a blue towel, browning their backs, as immobile as lizards. Their mother was embroidering a tablecloth, which hung in long folds from her knees. She looked like a Renaissance madonna on a throne of clouds.

My father, who was famous for his straightforwardness, had noticed nothing amiss in the situation until he found himself up to his neck in it.

"Just look who's here!" he cried.

Before her husband could answer, Signora Lavezzoli intervened. She looked quickly up from her tablecloth, and suddenly held out the back of her hand to Fadigati.

"Of course, of course," she warbled, and smiled invitingly, showing her fine mouthful of teeth.

Downcast, Fadigati crossed over to the sun, walking a little unsteadily as usual because of wearing shoes on the sand. When he reached the Lavezzolis' tent, he kissed Signora Lavezzoli's hand, shook hands with her husband, who meantime had risen, and shook hands too with the three children, one by one. Finally he came back to our tent, where my father had already prepared a chaise-longue for him beside my mother. He seemed much calmer than a while before: relieved as a student after a difficult exam.

As soon as he was sitting down he gave a sigh of satisfaction.

"How lovely it is here," he said. "How delightfully airy!"

He turned sideways to talk to me.

"Remember last month at Bologna, how terribly hot it was?" he said.

Then he explained to my parents, whom I had never told anything about our meetings on the morning train at 6.50, how for the last three months we had been "the best of friends". He talked casually, like a man of the world. Obviously he could scarcely believe that he was there with us, even with the alarming Lavezzolis, restored to what just then he regarded as *his* circle, accepted again by the cultivated, well-bred society to which he had always belonged. "Ah!" he said every now and then, throwing out his chest for a breath of balmy sea air. It was clear that he felt free and happy: and at the same time filled with gratitude (a little indiscreetly, I thought) towards everyone who allowed him to feel so.

Meantime my father had started talking about the incredible sultriness of August in Ferrara.

"You couldn't sleep at night," he said, with a grimace of discomfort, as if the memory of the heat in the city was enough to make him feel its oppressiveness. "Do believe me, doctor, you couldn't sleep a wink. Some people say the modern age began in the year when Flit was invented. I don't dispute it. But Flit means you've got to have the windows hermetically sealed. And closed windows means sheets that stick to your skin with sweat. I'm not joking; till yesterday I swear I dreaded the coming of night. Those damned mosquitoes!"

"Here it's completely different," said Fadigati enthusiastically. "Even on the hottest nights you can always breathe."

And he began to dwell on the advantages of the Adriatic compared with the whole of the rest of Italy. He was Venetian, he admitted, he had spent his childhood and adolescence on the Lido, so probably his judgement was not entirely unbiased. But he did really feel the Adriatic was a great deal more restful than the Tyrrhenian.

Signora Lavezzoli pricked up her ears. Disguising her malice with a pretence at civic pride, she began defending the Tyrrhenian warmly. If, like him, she could have chosen between a holiday at Riccione and one at Viareggio, she wouldn't have hesitated a moment, she declared.

"Look at the way it is in the evenings," she continued. "Going past the café Zanarini makes you feel you're not a single mile from Ferrara. In the summer at least, it's rather nice, quite frankly, to see new faces: just once in a way different from those you see the rest of the year. It feels like walking along the Giovecca, or along the Corsa Roma, along the arches of the caffè della Borsa, don't you think so?"

Fadigati moved uneasily on his chaise-longue. Again his eyes crept across to the bathing huts. But there was still no sign of Deliliers.

"Perhaps, perhaps," he replied with a nervous smile, and looked out to sea again.

As happened every morning between eleven and twelve, the water had quickly changed colour. It was no longer the pale oily mass it had been half an hour before. The wind from the open sea, the sun which stood almost at its zenith, had made it smooth and blue, scattered with innumerable glints of gold. The first bathers began to run across the beach. And the three Lavezzoli children, when they had asked their mother's permission, went to their bathing hut to change.

"Perhaps," repeated Fadigati. "But, dear lady, where do you find afternoons like those the sun gives us here, when it sets behind 'the blue vision of San Marino'?"

He declaimed Pascoli's line in a sing-song, slightly nasal voice, separating each syllable and accentuating the diaeresis in *vision.* An embarrassed silence followed, but the doctor went on at once.

"I know of course that the sunsets on the Levant Riviera are magnificent. All the same, you have to pay dearly for them: the price, I mean, is burning hot afternoons, with the sea turned into a kind of burning-glass, so that people have to shut themselves up at home or at best take refuge in the pine-woods. You will have noticed, too, the colour of the Adriatic after midday. It's more black than blue, it never dazzles one. The surface of the water doesn't reflect the sun's rays, it absorbs them. Or rather it does reflect them, but in the direction of . . . Yugoslavia! As for me," he continued, as if he had forgotten nothing, "I always long for lunch to be over so that I can come back to the beach at once. There's no lovelier moment to enjoy our divine Amarissimo in perfect peace than two in the afternoon."

"I imagine you come here with your . . . inseparable friend," said Signora Lavezzoli acidly.

Called rudely back to reality, Fadigati was silent and confused. Then, several hundred yards away, in the direction of Rimini, a crowd suddenly gathering attracted my father's attention.

"What's happening?" he asked, putting a hand to his forehead to see better.

Shouts of hurrah and clapping came to us on the wind.

"It's the Duce going into the water," explained Signora Lavezzoli reproachfully.

My father made a face. "Surely they don't cheer him even in the sea?" he growled between his teeth.

Romantic, patriotic, politically ingenuous and inexperienced like so many other Jews of his generation, my father had joined the fascist party when he returned from the front in 1919. So he had been a fascist from the very beginning and this in his heart he had remained, in spite of his mildness and integrity. But since Mussolini, after his early quarrels, had begun to make friends with Hitler, he had grown anxious. He thought of nothing but a possible outburst of antisemitism in Italy, too, and every now and then, though suffering for it, he let fall some bitter comment on the régime.

"He's so simple, so human," went on Signora Lavezzoli, taking no notice of him. "Such a good husband, too. Every Saturday morning he takes the car and dashes off, and he's quite capable of coming all the way from Rome to Riccione in one go."

"Marvellous!" sneered my father. "How happy Donna Rachele must be!"

He looked meaningly at Lavezzoli, trying to get him to agree. Lavezzoli was no fascist. He had even signed Croce's famous Manifesto in 1924 and for some years, at least until

1930, he was supposed to be a liberal democrat and antifascist. It was all in vain, though. Lavezzoli's eyes had at last been torn from the closely printed pages of *Anthony Adverse*, but were insensible to my father's silent pleading. Stretching out his neck, half-closing his eyes, he was staring obstinately at the water. The children had hired a boat and were going too far into the open sea . . .

"The other day," said Signora Lavezzoli, "Filippo and I were going home arm-in-arm through the Viale dei Mille. It was half-past seven or a little later. Suddenly, through the gate of a house, who d'you think I saw coming? The Duce himself, dressed in white from head to foot. Instinctively I said 'Good evening, your Excellency.' And he took off his hat and said most charmingly: 'Good evening, madam.' Isn't it true, Pippo," she went on, turning to her husband, "isn't it true he was terribly nice?" Lavezzoli nodded.

"Perhaps we should be modest enough to recognize we were mistaken," he said gravely, turning to my father. "We mustn't forget it was he who gave us our Empire."

I can remember every word spoken that far-away morning, as if everything was taken down on a tape recorder.

When he had pronounced sentence (my father's eyes opened wide as he heard it), Lavezzoli returnd to his book. But there was no stopping his wife. Encouraged by what her husband had said, and in particular by the word *Empire,* which she had probably never yet heard on her husband's austere lips, she continued to insist on the Duce's good heart and on the generous nature he had inherited from his birthplace, the Romagna.

"That reminds me," she said. "I must tell you something I saw for myself three years ago right here at Riccione. One morning the Duce was bathing with the eldest boys, Vittorio and Bruno. About one o'clock he came out of the water and what d'you think was waiting for him? A telegram had arrived a moment before with the news of the assassination of the Austrian Chancellor Dollfuss. That year our tent was very close to the Mussolinis' tent, so what I'm saying is really true. As soon as he read the telegram, the Duce came out with a tremendous swear word in dialect—oh, of course, one must realize he's a passionate man! Then he began crying, I saw the tears running down his cheeks! They were great friends, the Mussolinis and the Dollfusses. What's more, Dollfuss's wife, a tiny, thin, very pretty, unobtrusive little creature, was their guest that very summer with the children. And as he wept the Duce was obviously thinking of what he'd have to say in a few minutes to that unhappy mother, when they all got together for lunch...."

Suddenly Fadigati rose to his feet. Since Signora Lavezzoli's poisonous remarks had wounded him so deeply, he had not opened his mouth. All he did was bite his lips thoughtfully. Why was Deliliers so long? What could have happened?

"Will you excuse me?" he stammered, embarrassed.

"But it's early," protested Signora Lavezzoli. "Aren't you waiting for your friend? There are still twenty minutes to go!"

Fadigati stammered something incomprehensible. He shook hands all round and then went off in the direction of his umbrella. When he reached it he leant down to pick up the detective story and the sponge towel, and then we saw him cross the beach under the midday sun, but this time going directly to the hotel.

He walked tiredly, holding his detective story under his arm and the towel over his shoulder, his face altered with sweat and with anxiety. So much so that my father, who had been told everything right away, and was following his progress with pitying eyes, murmured softly: "Poor chap."

Straight after lunch I went back to the beach alone.

I sat in our tent. Yes, at two in the afternoon the Adriatic became dark blue, almost black. That day, though, as far as you could see, the top of every wave was crested with a tuft of foam, whiter than snow. The wind was still blowing from the open sea, but now came a little sidelong. If I raised my father's military field-glasses to take in the spur of the Punta di Pesaro which closed in the arc of the bay on my right, I could see high up the tops of the pines doubled over, and their foliage flung wildly about. Pressed on by the afternoon wind from Greece the long, ink-coloured, white-crested waves came on in serried and successive ranks. From where I was, they seemed to be hurling themselves to land like an invasion force. But, as they approached, their foamy crests gradually diminished, and vanished altogether in the last few yards. Stretched out on my chaise-longue, I could hear the dull roar of each wave against the shore.

The empty sea, from which the fishermen's sails had gradually disappeared (on the following morning, which was Sunday, I would see most of them spread out on the benches of the canal gates at Rimini and Cesenatico), was like the empty beach. In a tent not far from ours someone was playing a gramophone. I couldn't say what music it was, perhaps it was jazz. For more than three hours I stayed so, my eyes fixed on an old cockleshell fisherman dragging the bottom of the sea not far from the shore, and my ears filled with that music, which was no less sad and tireless than he was. When I got up, shortly after five, the old man was still searching, the gramophone still playing. The sun was setting and the shadows of the tents and the umbrellas had lengthened. The shadow of Fadigati's umbrella now nearly touched the water.

Outside the Grand Hotel, facing the sea, was a pavilion adjoining the beach. As soon as I set foot there, I noticed Fadigati sitting on one of the cement benches in front of the outside staircase of the hotel.

He had seen me, too. Too late to avoid him!

"Good afternoon," I said, and went up to him.

He indicated the bench. "Why don't you sit down? Do, for a moment."

I obeyed. He put his hand into the inside pocket of his jacket, took out a packet of Nazionali cigarettes, and offered them to me. There were only two cigarettes in the packet. He realized I was hesitating to accept.

"They're Nazionali!" he exclaimed, a strangely fanatical gleam in his eyes.

At last he realized the reason for my hesitation and smiled.

"Oh go on, do take one!" he said. "We'll share them like good friends, one for you and one for me."

A car whistled on the asphalt and curved into the square. Fadigati turned to look at it, but without hope. And it wasn't his Alfa: it was a Fiat 1500, a grey Berlin.

"I think I should go," I said. All the same I took one of the two cigarettes.

He noticed my beach shoes. "I see you've come from the beach. The sea must have been wonderful today."

"Yes, but not for swimming," I said.

"Don't ever think of bathing before the right time, I do beg you!" he exclaimed. "You're a boy and of course your heart's excellent, you lucky fellow, but congestion may strike in a moment, even the strongest."

He held out the lighted match to me. "And now, have you got a date?" he asked.

I answered—and it was quite true—that at six the young Lavezzolis were expecting me. We had arranged to meet on the tennis court behind the café Zanarini. It was true it was still twenty to six. But I had to go home and change and get my racket and balls; in fact I was afraid I wouldn't be in time.

"Let's hope Fanny doesn't get it into her head to come, too!" I went on. "Mummy won't let her come without doing her pigtails, and that'll mean I'll lose another good ten minutes."

While I was talking, I saw him carry out a curious ritual. He took the Nazionali from his lips so as to light it at the opposite end, where the trade mark was. Then he threw away the empty packet. Only then did I realize that the ground around us was scattered with cigarette stubs, more than a dozen.

"Have you seen how much I smoke?" he said.

"I have."

A question was burning on my lips: "What about Deliliers?" But I couldn't bring it out.

I got up and shook hands.

"Before, if I'm not mistaken, you didn't smoke at all," I said.

"I'm trying to make my modest contribution to the spread of sore throats," he retorted wretchedly. "I thought I ought to."

I moved off a few steps.

"Did you say the tennis court near the café Zanarini?" he called after me. "Maybe later I'll come along and admire you."

Afterwards we learnt that nothing serious had happened to Deliliers. Just this: instead of bathing at Riccione, he had suddenly got it into his head to bathe at Rimini, where, high up in the Hotel Vittoria, he knew some sisters from Parma. He had taken the car and vanished without even bothering to leave a note for Fadigati, and came back about eight o'clock, Signora Lavezzoli told us, when she happened to be drinking an aperitif with her husband in the hall of the Grand Hotel. Suddenly they had seen Deliliers crossing the hall in a great hurry, looking furiously angry, with Fadigati almost in tears at his heels.

It was Deliliers who came up to me that same evening on the terrace of the Grand Hotel.

I had gone there with my parents and the Lavezzolis again, the lawyer and his wife. I was still tired from the tennis, and so not dancing, but listening in silence to Signora Lavezzoli, who, though clearly she must have known how much it would wound us, had begun talking "objectively" of Hitler's Germany—just imagine!—and its "undeniable" greatness.

"You must realize, though, that your dear Dollfuss appears to have been liquidated by Hitler," I tried to make her see.

"What does that mean?" she retorted at once, with the compassionate and patient air of a school-mistress ready to justify any amount of cheating in her brightest pupil. "That's political necessity, alas. Let's leave our personal likes or dislikes out of it: the fact is that in certain circumstances the head of a government, a statesman worthy of the name, must for the good of his own people pass over the sensibilities of ordinary people . . . little people like ourselves." And she smiled proudly, completely contradicting her last words.

Horrified, my father opened his mouth to say something. But once again Signora Lavezzoli gave him no time. As if she was changing the subject, she turned directly to him, and went on to describe an "interesting" article which had appeared in the last number of *Catholic Civilization,* signed by the well-known Father Gemelli.

The theme of the article was the so-called Jewish question. According to Father Gemelli, she said, the recurrent persecutions of the "Israelites" in every part of the world for nearly two thousand years could only be explained as a sign of God's anger. The article ended with this question: May a Christian, even if in his heart he hates the idea of violence, pass judgement on historical events through which God's will is expressed?

At that point, not very politely, I got up from my cane armchair and left.

And so I was leaning against the side of the large window that separated the dining-room from the terrace, and the orchestra, if I am not mistaken, had started *Blue Moon.*

But you, pale moon, why
Are you so sad, what is . . .

the usual idiotic voice was singing, when suddenly I felt two fingers tapping me hard on the shoulder.

"Hello," said Deliliers.

It was the first time he had spoken to me at Riccione. "Hello," I answered. "How are you?"

"A bit better today," he said, winking. "What about you? What are you doing?"

"Oh reading, working," I lied. "I've got a couple of exams in October."

"Oh of course!" said Deliliers, thoughtfully scratching his hair, which shone with brilliantine, with his little finger.

But he wasn't thinking about his hair. Suddenly his expression changed. In a low voice, as if letting me into an important secret, peering back over his shoulder every now and then as if he were afraid of being surprised, he quickly told me about his bathe at Rimini with the two girls from Parma.

"Why don't you come with me tomorrow morning in the car? I'm going back. Come on, do help me! I can't go with two girls all on my own. Just leave your old work!"

At the end of the room Fadigati appeared, wearing a dinner jacket, his short-sighted eyes peering round behind his spectacles.The moonlit gloom created artificially for *Blue Moon* prevented him seeing Deliliers's white jacket straight away.

"Well," I said, "I don't know if I can."

"I'll wait for you in the hotel."

"I'll try and come. What time do we leave?"

"Half-past nine. That's all right?"

"Yes, but it's not definite."

I jerked my chin in Fadigati's direction. "You're wanted."

"Well, that's fixed then?" said Deliliers, turning on his heel and going up to Fadigati who was feverishly cleaning his spectacles with his handkerchief.

And a few seconds later the unmistakable roar of the Alfa Romeo rose from the nearby square to tell the entire hotel that the "couple", perhaps to celebrate their reconciliation, had decided to make it a very special evening.

I must confess that the following morning I was tempted for a moment to go to Rimini with Deliliers.

What attracted me most was the thought of going along the sea road by car. But afterwards?—I wondered. What did Deliliers's suggestion really mean? And who really were these sisters from Parma he had told me about? Were they two ordinary girls we could take into the pine-woods, which was all too easy; or two girls of good family we must entertain on the beach under the sharp eyes of another Signora Lavezzoli? In either case (though it wasn't quite out of the question that they might come somewhere between the two!) I didn't feel I was friendly enough with Deliliers to accept his invitation lightheartedly. If I accepted, I foresaw a day full of regrets and humiliations; and besides, why ever had Deliliers, who had never really liked me or shown any sort of regard for me, suddenly asked me, almost implored me, to go "womanizing" with him? Was it perhaps because he wanted to show me that it wasn't a matter of vice, his being with Fadigati, but just to have his holiday paid for, and that in any case he always preferred a pretty girl?

In the end I stayed behind. And when, a little later, I saw Fadigati on the beach under his big umbrella, abandoned in a solitude that suddenly appeared to me immense and incurable, I felt, deep within me, repaid for what I had given up. I at least had not deceived him, I thought; when I was asked to join someone who was deceiving him and taking advantage of him, I had managed to resist, and kept a minimum of respect for him.

Then I thought he might like a little company.

A moment before I reached his umbrella he turned.

"Oh it's you," he said, but without surprise. "How nice of you to come and see me."

Everything about him showed the weariness and the suffering caused by a recent quarrel. Although very likely he had dragged a promise to stay from Deliliers, the boy had gone to Rimini just the same.

Fadigati shut the book he was reading and laid it down on a stool there beside him, half in shadow and half in the sun. It was not the usual detective story, but a small volume with an old flowered paper cover.

"What were you reading?" I asked, with a gesture at the book. "Is it poetry?"

"Have a look."

It was a school edition of the first canto of the *Iliad,* translated line by line.

"I found it in my suitcase," he said. "Mènin aèide teà peleiadeo Achillèos," he added, with a bitter smile.

My parents arrived just then, my mother holding Fanny's hand. I waved to show them where I was, and whistled the family signature tune: the first line of a Schubert *Lied.*

Fadigati turned, half-rose from his chaise-longue, and raised his panama hat politely. My parents answered together: my mother nodding slightly, my father touching the visor of his brand-new white cloth cap with two fingers. I realized at once that they disliked seeing me with Fadigati. As soon as she saw me, Fanny had turned to ask my mother something, probably permission to join me. But clearly my mother had stopped her.

"How very sweet your sister is," said Fadigati. "How old is she?"

"Twelve: exactly eight years younger than me," I answered, embarrassed.

"But there are three of you altogether, I believe," he said.

"Yes, there are. Two boys and a girl: there are four years between each of us. Ernesto, the second, is in England. . . ."

"What an intelligent little face!" said Fadigati, still looking in Fanny's direction. "And how well that pink bathing dress suits her! She's lucky to have two big brothers, you know."

"Oh, she's still a kid," I said.

"Oh yes, so I see. I'd have thought she was ten or so. But that means nothing. Girls develop all of a sudden. You'll have such a surprise. . . . She's at high school, isn't she?"

"Yes, in the third form."

He shook his head with a kind of melancholy regret, as if he were thinking of all the effort and the pain which every human being must meet to grow, to come to maturity. But his thoughts soon changed.

"And what about Signora Lavezzoli?" he asked.

"Oh, her. I think this morning, because of Mass, we shan't see them before midday."

"Oh that's true, today's Sunday," he said, startled. "Well, in that case," he added, after another pause, as he got to his feet, "let's go and say how d'you do to your parents."

We walked side by side along the sand, already uncomfortably hot.

"I've a feeling," he said to me, "I've a feeling Signora Lavezzoli doesn't like me all that much."

"Oh no, I don't think so."

"All the same, it's not a bad idea to take advantage of her absence."

Without the Lavezzolis, my parents were unable to stick to their obvious resolution to keep him at a distance: especially my father, who was soon talking to him in the friendliest way.

A light wind was coming up from inland, the wind called the *garbino.* The sea had no sails at all on it, and though the sun had not yet reached its zenith, it already looked dark: a thick, leaden colour. Perhaps because he had just read the first canto of the *Iliad,* Fadigati spoke of the Greeks' feeling for nature, and in particular of the meaning he thought we must attribute to adjectives like *purple* and *violet,* applied by Homer to the sea. My father then spoke of Horace, and of Carducci's *Odi Barbare* which he considered—and we argued over it almost daily—his ideal in the field of modern poetry. In fact they chatted so agreeably (the fact that Deliliers was not likely to pop out from the bathing huts from one minute to the next obviously steadied the doctor's nerves), that when the Lavezzoli family, fresh from Mass, landed on us complete towards midday, Fadigati felt strong enough, protected enough, so to speak, to bear Signora Lavezzoli's inevitable remarks quite casually, and even to answer back quite successfully.

We saw no more of Deliliers on the beach: neither that day nor the days that followed. He never returned from his sorties in the car before two o'clock in the morning and Fadigati, left on his own, sought our company more than ever.

And so it was that, apart from spending the morning in our tent (it hardly seemed true to my father that he could discuss music, literature and art with him, instead of politics with Signora Lavezzoli!), he got into the habit of coming to the tennis court behind the café Zanarini in the afternoon when he heard that the Lavezzoli children and I were going there.

There was certainly nothing very exciting about our lazy games, one male couple against one mixed couple. I was a pretty poor player, but Franco and Gilberto Lavezzoli could hardly hold a racket. And as for Cristina, their blonde, rosy and delicate sister of fifteen (she emerged from a convent boarding school in Florence every now and then, and had the entire family running round her), she played even worse than her brothers. Her hair grew in a little crown round her head "like one of Melozzo's singing angels", as Fadigati put it, with fatherly admiration, one day—and rather than disarrange a single curl she would have given up walking. So there was absolutely no question of her bothering about the style of a drive or having a decent backhand!

Yet in spite of all this, Fadigati seemed to be highly interested in our game, however boring and pointless it was.

"Good shot!" "Only just out!" "Bad luck!" He was generous with his praise for all of us, and had some comment, sometimes wildly out, for every shot.

Sometimes our game languished a bit too much even for such an indulgent audience.

"Why don't you play a match?" he would suggest.

"Oh dear," Cristina would protest at once, blushing. "I just can't handle a ball!"

But he refused to listen.

"Order of the Day!" he proclaimed gaily. "Doctor Fadigati will give the winning couple a prize of two superb bottles of San Pellegrino orangeade!"

He ran to the keeper's hut and dragged out a rickety and dangerous umpire's chair at least two yards high, pulled it to one side of the tennis court himself and finally clambered up it. Gradually the air darkened; his hat appeared in the half-light aureoled by a cloud of flies. But, perched up there like a great bird, he stayed and called out the score in a metallic voice, determined to keep up his role as an impartial umpire to the end. Obviously he had no idea what else to do, or how to fill the terrible emptiness of the days.

—Translated by
Isabel Quigly

WILLIAM S. BURROUGHS

HASSAN'S RUMPUS ROOM

Gilt and red plush. Rococo bar backed by pink shell. The air is cloyed with a sweet evil substance like decayed honey. Men and women in evening dress sip pousse-cafés through alabaster tubes. A Near East Mugwump sits naked on a bar stool covered in pink silk. He licks warm honey from a crystal goblet with a long black tongue. His genitals are perfectly formed—circumcised cock, black shiny pubic hairs. His lips are thin and purple-blue like the lips of a penis, his eyes blank with insect calm. The Mugwump has no liver, maintaining himself exclusively on sweets. Mugwump push a slender blond youth to a couch and strip him expertly.

"Stand up and turn around," he orders in telepathic pictographs. He ties the boy's hands behind him with a red silk cord. "Tonight we make it all the way."

"No, no!" screams the boy.

"Yes. Yes."

Cocks ejaculate in silent "yes." Mugwump part silk curtains, reveal a teak wood gallows against lighted screen of red flint. Gallows is on a dais of Aztec mosaics.

The boy crumples to his knees with a long "OOOO-OOOOH," shitting and pissing in terror. He feels the shit warm between his thighs. A great wave of hot blood swells his lips and throat. His body contacts into a foetal position and sperm spurts hot into his face. The Mugwump dips hot perfumed water from alabaster bowl, pensively washes the boy's ass and cock, drying him with a soft blue towel. A warm wind plays over the boy's body and the hairs float free. The Mugwump puts a hand under the boy's chest and pulls him to his feet. Holding him by both pinioned elbows, propels him up the steps and under the noose. He stands in front of the boy holding the noose in both hands.

The boy looks into Mugwump eyes blank as obsidian mirrors, pools of black blood, glory holes in a toilet wall closing on the Last Erection.

An old garbage collector, face fine and yellow as Chinese ivory, blows The Blast on his dented brass horn, wakes the Spanish pimp with a hard-on. Whore staggers out through dust and shit and litter of dead kittens, carrying bales of aborted foetuses, broken condoms, bloody Kotex, shit wrapped in bright color comics.

A vast still harbor of iridescent water. Deserted gas well flares on the smoky horizon. Stink of oil and sewage. Sick sharks swim through the black water, belch sulphur from rotting livers, ignore a bloody, broken Icarus. Naked Mr. America, burning frantic with self bone love, screams out: "My asshole confounds the Louvre! I fart ambrosia and shit pure gold turds! My cock spurts soft diamonds in the morning sunlight!" He plummets from the eyeless lighthouse, kissing and jacking off in face of the black mirror, glides oblique down with cryptic condoms and mosaic of a thousand newspapers through a drowned city of red brick to settle in black mud with tin cans and beer bottles, gangsters in concrete, pistols pounded flat and meaningless to avoid short-arm inspection of prurient ballistic experts. He waits the slow striptease of erosion with fossil loins.

The Mugwump slips the noose over the boy's head and tightens the knot caressingly behind the left ear. The boy's penis is retracted, his balls tight. He looks straight ahead breathing deeply. The Mugwump sidles around the boy goosing him and caressing his genitals in hieroglyphs of mockery.

He moves in behind the boy with a series of bumps and shoves his cock up the boy's ass. He stands there moving in circular gyrations.

The guests shush each other, nudge and giggle.

Suddenly the Mugwump pushes the boy forward into space, free of his cock. He steadies the boy with hands on the hip bones, reaches up with his stylized hieroglyph hands and snaps the boy's neck. A shudder passes through the boy's body. His penis rises in three great surges pulling his pelvis up, ejaculates immediately.

Green sparks explode behind his eyes. A sweet toothache pain shoots through his neck down the spine to the groin, contracting the body in spasms of delight. His whole body squeezes out through his cock. A final spasm throws a great spurt of sperm across the red screen like a shootingstar.

The boy falls with soft gutty suction through a maze of penny arcades and dirty pictures.

A sharp turd shoots clean out of his ass. Farts shake his slender body. Skyrockets burst in green clusters across a great river. He hears the faint put-put of a motor boat in jungle twilight. . . . Under silent wings of the anopheles mosquito.

The Mugwump pulls the boy back onto his cock. The boy squirms, impaled like a speared fish. The Mugwump swings on the boy's back, his body contracting in fluid waves. Blood flows down the boy's chin from his mouth, half-open, sweet, and sulky in death. The Mugwump falls with a fluid, sated plop.

Windowless cubicle with blue walls. Dirty pink curtain cover the door. Red bugs crawl on the wall, cluster in corners. Naked boy in the middle of the room twang a two-string ouad, trace an arabesque on the floor. Another boy lean back on the bed smoking keif and blow smoke over his erect cock. They play game with tarot cards on the bed to see who fuck who. Cheat. Fight. Roll on the floor snarling and spitting like young animals. The loser sit on the floor chin on knees, licks a broken tooth. The winner curls up on the bed pretending to sleep. Whenever the other boy come near kick at him. Ali seize him by one ankle, tuck the ankle under the arm pit, lock his arm around the calf. The boy kick desperately at Ali's face. Other ankle pinioned. Ali tilt the boy back on his shoulders. The boy's cock extends along his stomach, float free pulsing. Ali put his hands over his head. Spit on his cock. The other sighs deeply as Ali slides his cock in. The mouths grind together smearing blood. Sharp musty odor of penetrated rectum. Nimun drive in like a wedge, force jism out the other cock in long hot spurts. (The author has observed that Arab cocks tend to be wide and wedge shaped.)

Satyr and naked Greek lad in aqualungs trace a ballet in pursuit in a monster vase of transparent alabaster. The Satyr catches the boy from in front and whirls him around. They move in fish jerks. The boy releases a silver stream of bubbles from his mouth. White sperm ejaculates into the green water and floats lazily around the twisting bodies.

Negro gently lifts exquisite Chinese boy into a hammock. He pushes the boy's legs up over his head and straddles the hammock. He slides his cock up the boy's slender tight ass. He rocks the hammock gently back and forth. The boy screams, a weird high wail of unendurable delight.

A Javanese dancer in ornate teak swivel chair, set in a socket of limestone buttocks, pulls an American boy—red hair, bright green eyes—down onto his cock with ritual motions. The boy sits impaled facing the dancer who propels himself in circular gyrations, lending fluid substance to the chair. "Weeeeeeeeee!" scream the boy as his sperm spurt up over the dancer's lean brown chest. One gob hit the corner of the dancer's mouth. The boy push it in with his finger and laugh: "Man, that's what I call suction!"

Two Arab women with bestial faces have pulled the shorts off a little blond French boy. They are screwing him with red rubber cocks. The boy snarls, bites, kicks, collapses in tears as his cock rises and ejaculates.

Hassan's face swells, tumescent with blood. His lips turn purple. He strip off his suit of banknotes and throw it into an open vault that closes soundless.

"Freedom Hall here, folks!" he screams in his phoney Texas accent. Ten-gallon hat and cowboy boots still on, he dances the Liquefactionist Jig, ending with a grotesque cancan to the tune of *She Started a Heat Wave*.

"Let it be! And no holes barred!!!"

Couples attached to baroque harnesses with artificial wings copulate in the air, screaming like magpies.

Aerialists ejaculate each other in space with one sure touch.

Equilibrists suck each other off deftly, balanced on perilous poles and chairs tilted over the void. A warm wind brings the smell of rivers and jungle from misty depths.

Boys by the hundred plummet through the roof, quivering and kicking at the end of ropes. The boys hang at different levels, some near the ceiling and others a few inches off the floor. Exquisite Balinese and Malays, Mexican Indians with fierce innocent faces and bright red gums. Negroes (teeth, fingers, toe nails and pubic hair gilded), Japanese boys smooth and white as China, Titian-haired Venetian lads, Americans with blond or black curls falling across the forehead (the guests tenderly shove it back), sulky blond Polacks with animal brown eyes, Arab and Spanish street boys, Austrian boys pink and delicate with a faint shadow of blond pubic hair, sneering German youths with bright eyes scream "Heil Hitler!" as the trap falls under them. Sollubis shit and whimper.

Mr. Rich-and-Vulgar chews his Havana lewd and nasty, sprawled on a Florida beach surrounded by simpering blond catamites:

"This citizen have a Latah he import from Indo-China. He figure to hang the Latah and send a Xmas TV short to his friends. So he fix up two ropes—one gimmicked to stretch, the other the real McCoy. But that Latah get up in feud state and put on his Santa Claus suit and make with the switcheroo. Come the dawning. The citizen put one rope on and the Latah, going along the way Latahs will, put on the other. When the traps are down the citizen hang for real and the Latah stand with the carny-rubber stretch rope. Well, the Latah imitate every twitch and spasm. Come three times.

"Smart young Latah keep his eye on the ball. I got him working in one of my plants as an expeditor.

"Aztec priests strip blue feather robe from the Naked Youth. They bend him back over a limestone altar, fit a crystal skull over his head, securing the two hemispheres back and front with crystal screws. A waterfall pour over the skull snapping the boy's neck. He ejaculate in a rainbow against the rising sun."

Sharp protein odor of semen fills the air. The guests run hands over twitching boys, suck their cocks, hang on their backs like vampires.

Naked lifeguards carry in iron-lungs full of paralyzed youths.

Blind boys grope out of huge pies, deteriorated schizophrenics pop from under a rubber cunt, boys with horrible skin diseases rise from a black pond (sluggish fish nibble yellow turds on the surface).

A man with white tie and dress shirt, naked from the waist down except for black garters, talks to the Queen Bee in elegant tones. (Queen Bees are old women who surround themselves with fairies to form a "swarm." It is a sinister Mexican practice.)

"But where is the statuary?" He talks out of one side of his face, the other is twisted by the Torture of a Million Mirrors. He masturbates wildly. The Queen Bee continues the conversation, notices nothing.

Couches, chairs, the whole floor begins to vibrate, shaking the guests to blurred grey ghosts shrieking in cock-bound agony.

Two boys jacking off under railroad bridge. The train shakes through their bodies, ejaculate them, fades with distant whistle. Frogs croak. The boys wash semen off lean brown stomachs.

Train compartment: two sick young junkies on their way to Lexington tear their pants down in convulsions of lust. One of them soaps his cock and works it up the other's ass with a corkscrew motion. "Jeeeeeeeeeeeeeesus!" Both ejaculate at once standing up. They move away from each other and pull up their pants.

"Old croaker in Marshall writes for tincture and sweet oil."

"The piles of an aged mother shriek out raw and bleeding for the Black Shit. . . . Doc, suppose it was your mother, rimmed by resident leeches, squirming around so nasty. . . . De-active that pelvis, mom, you disgust me already."

"Let's stop over and make him for an RX."

The train tears on through the smoky, neon-lighted June night.

Pictures of men and women, boys and girls, animals, fish, birds, the copulating rhythm of the universe flows through the room, a great blue tide of life. Vibrating, soundless hum of deep forest—sudden quiet of cities when the junky copes. A moment of stillness and wonder. Even the Commuter buzzes clogged lines of cholesterol for contact.

Hassan shrieks out: "This is your doing, A.J.! You poopa my party!"

A.J. looks at him, face remote as limestone: "Uppa your ass, you liquefying gook."

A horde of lust-mad American women rush in. Dripping cunts, from farm and dude ranch, factory, brothel, country club, penthouse and suburb, motel and yacht and cocktail bar, strip off riding clothes, ski togs, evening dresses, levis, tea gowns, print dresses, slacks, bathing suits and kimonos. They scream and yipe and howl, leap on the guests like bitch dogs in heat with rabies. They claw at the hanged boys shrieking: "You fairy! You bastard! Fuck me! Fuck me! Fuck me!" The guests flee screaming, dodge among the hanged boys, overturn iron lungs.

A.J.: "Call out my Sweitzers, God damn it! Guard me from these she-foxes!"

Mr. Hyslop, A.J.'s secretary, looks up from his comic book: "The Sweitzers liquefy already."

(Liquefaction involves protein cleavage and reduction to liquid which is absorbed into someone else's protoplasmic being. Hassan, a notorious liquefactionist, is probably the beneficiary in this case.)

A.J.: "Gold-bricking cocksuckers! Where's a man without his Sweitzers? Our backs are to the wall, gentlemen. Our very cocks at stake. Stand by to resist boarders, Mr. Hyslop, and issue short arms to the men."

A.J. whips out a cutlass and begins decapitating the American Girls. He sings lustily:

Fifteen men on the dead man's chest
Yo Ho Ho and a bottle of rum.

Drink and the devil had done for the rest
Yo Ho Ho and a bottle of rum.

Mr. Hyslop, bored and resigned: "Oh Gawd! He's at it again." He waves the Jolly Roger listlessly.

A.J., surrounded and fighting against overwhelming odds, throws back his head and makes with the hog-call. Immediately a thousand rutting Eskimos pour in grunting and squealing, faces tumescent, eyes hot and red, lips purple, fall on the American women.

(Eskimos have a rutting season when the tribes meet in short Summer to disport themselves in orgies. Their faces swell and lips turn purple.)

A House Dick with cigar two feet long sticks his head in through the wall: "Have you got a menagerie in here?"

Hassan wrings his hands: "A shambles! A filthy shambles! By Allah I never see anything so downright nasty!"

He whirls on A.J. who is sitting on a sea chest, parrot on shoulder, patch over one eye, drinking rum from a tankard. He scans the horizon with a huge brass telescope.

Hassan: "You cheap Factualist bitch! Go and never darken my rumpus room again!"

ALLEN GINSBERG

A SUPERMARKET IN CALIFORNIA

What thoughts I have of you tonight, Walt Whitman, for I walked down the sidestreets under the trees with a headache self-conscious looking at the full moon.

In my hungry fatigue, and shopping for images, I went into the neon fruit supermarket, dreaming of your enumerations!

What peaches and what penumbras! Whole families shopping at night! Aisles full of husbands! Wives in the avocados, babies in the tomatoes!—and you, Garcia Lorca, what were you doing down by the watermelons?

I saw you, Walt Whitman, childless, lonely old grubber, poking among the meats in the refrigerator and eyeing the grocery boys.

I heard you asking questions of each: Who killed the pork chops? What price bananas? Are you my Angel?

I wandered in and out of the brilliant stacks of cans following you, and followed in my imagination by the store detective.

We strode down the open corridors together in our solitary

fancy tasting artichokes, possessing every frozen delicacy, and never passing the cashier.

Where are we going, Walt Whitman? The doors close in an hour. Which way does your beard point tonight?

(I touch your book and dream of our odyssey in the supermarket and feel absurd.)

Will we walk all night through solitary streets? The trees add shade to shade, lights out in the houses, we'll both be lonely.

Will we stroll dreaming of the lost America of love past blue automobiles in driveways, home to our silent cottage?

Ah, dear father, graybeard, lonely old courage-teacher, what America did you have when Charon quit poling his ferry and you got out on a smoking bank and stood watching the boat disappear on the black waters of Lethe?

BERKELY 1955

PLEASE MASTER

Please master can I touch your cheek
please master can I kneel at your feet
please master can I loosen your blue pants
please master can I gaze at your golden haired belly
please master can I gently take down your shorts
please master can I have your thighs bare to my eyes
please master can I take off my clothes below your chair
please master can I kiss your ankles and soul
please master can I touch lips to your hard muscle hairless
 thigh
please master can I lay my ear pressed to your stomach
please master can I wrap my arms around your white ass
please master can I lick your groin curled with blond soft fur
please master can I touch my tongue to your rosy asshole

please master may I pass my face to your balls,
please master, please look into my eyes,
please master order me down on the floor,
please master tell me to lick your thick shaft
please master put your rough hands on my bald hairy skull
please master press my mouth to your prick-heart
please master press my face into your belly, pull me slowly strong thumbed
till your dumb hardness fills my throat to the base
till I swallow & taste your delicate flesh-hot prick barrel veined Please
Master push my shoulders away and stare in my eye, & make me bend over the table
please master grab my thighs and lift my ass to your waist
please master your hand's rough stroke on my neck your palm down my backside
please master push me up, my feet on chairs, till my hole feels the breath of your spit and your thumb stroke
please master make me say Please Master Fuck me now Please
Master grease my balls and hairmouth with sweet vaselines
please master stroke your shaft with white creams
please master touch your cock head to my wrinkled selfhole
please master push it in gently, your elbows enwrapped round my breast
your arms passing down to my belly, my penis you touch w/your fingers
please master shove it in me a little, a little, a little,
please master sink your droor thing down my behind
& please master make me wiggle my rear to eat up the prick trunk
till my asshalfs cuddle your thighs, my back bent over,
till I'm alone sticking out, your sword stuck throbbing in me
please master pull out and slowly roll into the bottom
please master lunge it again, and withdraw to the tip
please please master fuck me again with your self, please fuck me Please
Master drive down till it hurts me the softness the

Softness please master make love to my ass, give body to center, & fuck me for good like a girl,
tenderly clasp me please master I take me to thee,
& drive in my belly your selfsame sweet heat-rood
you fingered in solitude Denver or Brooklyn or fucked in a maiden in Paris carlots
please master drive me thy vehicle, body of love drops, sweat fuck
body of tenderness, Give me your dog fuck faster
please master make me go moan on the table
Go moan O please master do fuck me like that
in your rhythm thrill-plunge & pull-back-bounce & push down
till I loosen my asshole a dog on the table yelping with terror delight to be loved
Please master call me a dog, an ass beast, a wet asshole,
& fuck me more violent, my eyes hid with your palms round my skull
& plunge down in a brutal hard lash thru soft drip-flesh
& throb thru five seconds to spurt out your semen heat
over & over, bamming it in while I cry out your name I do love you
please Master.

MAY 1968

RAIN-WET ASPHALT

Rain-wet asphalt heat, garbage curbed cans overflowing

I hauled down lifeless mattresses to sidewalk refuse-piles,
old rugs stept on from Paterson to Lower East Side filled with bed-bugs,
grey pillows, couch seats treasured from the street laid back on the street
—out, to hear Murder-tale, 3rd Street cyclists attacked tonite—
Bopping along in rain, Chaos fallen over City roofs,

shrouds of chemical vapour drifting over building-tops—
Get the *Times,* Nixon says peace reflected from the Moon,
but I found no boy body to sleep with all night on pavements
3 AM home in sweating drizzle—
Those mattresses soggy lying by full five garbagepails—
Barbara, Maretta, Peter Steven Rosebud slept on these Pillows years ago,
forgotten names, also made love to me, I had these mattresses
four years on my floor—
Gerard, Jimmy many months, even blond Gordon later,
Paul with the beautiful big cock, that teenage boy that lived in
Pennsylvania,
forgotten numbers, young dream loves and lovers, earthly
bellies—
many strong youths with eyes closed, come sighing and helping me come—
Desires already forgotten, tender persons used and kissed
goodbye
and all the times I came to myself alone in the dark dreaming
of Neal or Billy Budd
—nameless angels of half-life—heart beating & eyes weeping
for lovely phantoms—
Back from the Gem Spa, into the hallway, a glance behind
and sudden farewell to the bedbug-ridden mattresses piled
soggy in dark rain.

AUGUST 2, 1969

YUKIO MISHIMA

ONNAGATA

Masuyama had been overwhelmed by Mangiku's artistry; that was how it happened that, after getting a degree in classical Japanese literature, he had chosen to join the kabuki theatre staff. He had been entranced by seeing Mangiku Sanokawa perform.

Masuyama's addiction to kabuki began when he was a high-school student. At the time, Mangiku, still a fledgling *onnagata,* was appearing in such minor roles as the ghost butterfly in *Kagami Jishi* or, at best, the waiting maid Chidori in *The Disowning of Genta.* Mangiku's acting was unassertive and orthodox; nobody suspected he would achieve his present eminence. But even in those days Masuyama sensed the icy flames given off by this actor's aloof beauty. The general public, needless to say, noticed nothing. For that matter, none of the drama critics had ever called attention to the peculiar quality of Mangiku, like shoots of flame visible through the snow, which illuminated his performances from very early in his career. Now everyone spoke as if Mangiku had been a personal discovery.

Mangiku Sanokawa was a true *onnagata,* a species seldom encountered nowadays. Unlike most contemporary *onnagata,* he was quite incapable of performing successfully in male roles. His stage presence was colourful, but with dark overtones; his every gesture was the essence of delicacy. Mangiku never expressed anything—not even strength, authority, endurance, or courage—except through the single medium open to him, feminine expression, but through this medium he could filter every variety of human emotion. That is the way of the true *onnagata* but in recent years this breed has become rare indeed. Their tonal colouring, produced by a particular, exquisitely refined musical instrument, cannot be achieved by playing a normal instrument in a minor key, nor, for that matter, is it produced by a mere slavish imitation of real women.

Yukihime, the Snow Princess, in *Kinkakuji* was one of Mangiku's most successful roles. Masuyama remembered having seen Mangiku perform Yukihime ten times during a single month, but no matter how often he repeated this experience, his intoxication did not diminish. Everything symbolizing Sanokawa Mangiku may be found in this play, the elements entwined, beginning with the opening words of the narrator: 'The Golden Pavilion, the mountain retreat of Lord Yoshimitsu, Prime Minister and Monk of the Deer Park, stands three stories high, its garden graced with lovely sights: the night-lodging stone, the water trickling below the rocks, the flow of the cascade heavy with spring, the willows and cherry-trees planted together; the capital now is a vast, many-hued brocade.' The dazzling brilliance of the set, depicting cherry-trees in blossom, a waterfall, and the glittering Golden Pavilion; the drums, suggesting the dark sound of the waterfall and contributing a constant agitation to the stage; the pale, sadistic face of the lecherous Daizen Matsunaga, the rebel general; the miracle of the magic sword which shines in morning sunlight with the holy image of Fudō, but shows a dragon's form when pointed at the setting sun; the radiance of the sunset glow on the waterfall and cherry-trees; the cherry blossoms scattering down petal by petal—everything in the play exists for the sake of one woman, the beautiful, aristocratic Yukihime. There is nothing unusual about Yukihime's costume, the crimson silk robe customarily worn by young princesses. But a ghostly presence of snow, befitting her name, hovers about this granddaughter of the great painter Sesshū, permeated with snow, may be sensed across the breadth of the scene; this phantom snow gives Yukihime's crimson robe its dazzling brilliance.

Masuyama loved especially the scene where the princess, bound with ropes to a cherry-tree, remembers the legend told of her grandfather, and with her toes draws in the fallen blossoms a rat, which comes to life and gnaws through the ropes binding her. It hardly needs be said that Mangiku Sanokawa did not adopt the puppetlike movements favoured by some *onnagata* in this scene. The ropes fastening him to the tree made Mangiku look lovelier than ever: all the artificial arabesques of this *onnagata*—the delicate gestures of the body, the play of the fingers, the arch of the hand—contrived though they might appear when employed for the movements of daily life, took on a strange vitality when used by Yukihime, bound to a tree. The intricate, contorted attitudes imposed by the constraint of the rope made of each instant an exquisite crisis, and the crises seemed to flow, one into the next, with the irresistible energy of successive waves.

Mangiku's performances unquestionably possessed moments of diabolic power. He used his lovely eyes so effectively that often with one flash he could create in an entire audience the illusion that the character of a scene had completely altered: when his glance embraced the stage from the *hanamichi* or the *hanamichi* from the stage, or when he darted one upward look at the bell in *Dōjōji*. In the palace scene from *Imoseyama,* Mangiku took the part of Omiwa, whose lover was stolen from her by Princess Tachibana and who has been cruelly mocked by the court ladies at the back of the stage saying, 'A groom without peer has been found for our princess! What joy for us all!' The narrator, seated at the side of the stage, declaims in powerful tones, 'Omiwa, hearing this, at once looks back.' At this moment Omiwa's character is completely transformed, and her face reveals the marks of a possessive attachment.

Masuyama felt a kind of terror every time he witnessed this moment. For an instant a diabolic shadow had swept over both the bright stage with its splendid set and beautiful costumes and over the thousands of intently watching spectators. This force clearly emanated from Mangiku's body, but at the same time transcended his flesh. Masuyama sensed in such passages something like a dark spring welling forth from this figure on the stage, this figure so imbued with softness, fragility, grace, delicacy, and feminine charms. He could not identify it, but he thought that a strange, evil presence, the final residue of the actor's fascination, a seductive evil which leads men astray and makes them drown in an instant of beauty, was the true nature of the dark spring he had detected. But one explains nothing merely by giving it a name.

Omiwa shakes her head and her hair tumbles in disarray. On the stage, to which she now returns from the *hanamichi*, Funashichi's blade is waiting to kill her.

'The house is full of music, an autumn sadness in its tone,' declaims the narrator.

There is something terrifying about the way Omiwa's feet hurry forward to her doom. The bare white feet, rushing ahead towards disaster and death, kicking the lines of her kimono askew, seem to know precisely when and where on the stage the violent emotions now urging her forward will end, and to be pressing towards the spot, rejoicing and triumphant even amidst the tortures of jealousy. The pain she reveals outwardly is backed with joy like her robe, on the outside dark and shot with gold thread, but bright with variegated silken strands within.

2

Masuyama's original decision to take employment at the theatre had been inspired by his absorption with kabuki, and especially with Mangiku; he realized also he could never escape his bondage unless he became thoroughly familiar with the world behind the scenes. He knew from what others had told him of the disenchantment to be found backstage, and he wanted to plunge into that world and taste for himself genuine disillusion.

But the disenchantment he expected somehow never came. Mangiku himself made this impossible. Mangiku faithfully maintained the injunctions of the eighteenth-century *onnagata's* manual *Ayamegusa,* 'An *onnagata,* even in the dressing-room, must preserve the attitudes of an *onnagata.* He should be careful when he eats to face away from other people, so that they cannot see him.' Whenever Mangiku was obliged to eat in the presence of visitors, not having the time to leave his dressing-room, he would turn towards his table with a word of apology and race through his meal, so skilfully that the visitors could not even guess from behind that he was eating.

Undoubtedly, the feminine beauty displayed by Mangiku on the stage had captivated Masuyama as a man. Strangely enough, however, this spell was not broken even by close observation of Mangiku in the dressing-room. Mangiku's body, when he had removed his costume, was delicate but unmistakably a man's. Masuyama, as a matter of fact, found it rather unnerving when Mangiku, seated at his dressing-table, too scantily clad to be anything but a man, directed polite, feminine greetings towards some visitor, all the while applying a heavy coating of powder to his shoulders. If even Masuyama, long a devotee of kabuki, experienced eerie sensations on his first visits to the dressing-room, what would have been the reactions of people who dislike kabuki, because the *onnagata* make them uncomfortable, if shown such a sight?

Masuyama, however, felt relief rather than disenchantment when he saw Mangiku after a performance, naked except for the gauzy underclothes he wore in order to absorb perspiration. The sight in itself may have been grotesque, but the nature of Masuyama's fascination—its intrinsic quality, one might say—did not reside in any surface illusion, and there was accordingly no danger that such a revelation would destroy it. Even after Mangiku had disrobed, it was apparent that he was still wearing several layers of splendid costumes beneath his skin; his nakedness was a passing manifestation. Something which could account for his exquisite appearance on stage surely lay concealed within him.

Masuyama enjoyed seeing Mangiku when he returned to the dressing-room after performing a major role. The flush of the emotions of the part he had been enacting still hovered over his entire body, like sunset glow or the moon in the sky at dawn. The grand emotions of classical tragedy—emotions quite unrelated to our mundane lives—may seem to be guided, at least nominally, by historical facts—the world of disputed successions, campaigns of pacification, civil warfare, and the like—but in reality they belong to no period. They are the emotions appropriate to a stylized, grotesquely tragic world, luridly coloured in the manner of a late wood-block print. Grief that goes beyond human bounds, superhuman passions, searing love, terrifying joy, the brief cries of people trapped by circumstances too tragic for human beings to endure: such were the emotions which a moment before had lodged in Mangiku's body, It was amazing that Mangiku's slender frame could hold them and that they did not break from that delicate vessel.

Be that as it may, Mangiku a moment before had been living amidst these grandiose feelings, and he had radiated light on the stage precisely because the emotions he portrayed transcended any known to his audience. Perhaps this is true of all characters on the stage, but among present-day actors none seemed to be so honestly living stage emotions so far removed from daily life.

A passage in *Ayamegusa* states, 'Charm is the essence of the *onnagata*. But even the *onnagata* who is naturally beautiful will lose his charm if he strains to impress by his movements. If he consciously attempts to appear graceful he will seem thorougly corrupt instead. For this reason, unless the *onnagata* lives as a woman in his daily life, he is unlikely ever to be considered an accomplished *onnagata*. When he appears on stage, the more he concentrates on performing this or that essentially feminine action, the more masculine he will seem. I am convinced that the essential thing is how the actor behaves in real life.'

How the actor behaves in real life . . . yes, Mangiku was utterly feminine in both the speech and bodily movements of his real life. If Mangiku had been more masculine in his daily life, those moments when the flush from the *onnagata* role he had been performing gradually dissolved like the high-water mark on a beach into the femininity of his daily life—itself an extension of the same make-believe—would have become an absolute division between sea and land, a bleak door shut between dream and reality. The make-believe of his daily life supported the make-believe of his stage performances. This, Masuyama was convinced, marked the true *onnagata.* An *onnagata* is the child born of the illicit union between dream and reality.

3

Once the celebrated veteran actors of the previous generation had all passed away, one on the heels of the other, Mangiku's authority backstage became absolute. His *onnagata* disciples waited on him like personal servants; indeed, the order of seniority they observed when following Mangiku on stage as maids in the wake of his princess or great lady was exactly the same they observed in the dressing-room.

Anyone pushing apart the door curtains dyed with the crest of the Sanokawa family and entering Mangiku's dressing-room was certain to be struck by a strange sensation: this charming sanctuary contained not a single man. Even members of the same troupe felt inside this room that they were in the presence of the opposite sex. Whenever Masuyama went to Mangiku's dressing-room on some errand, he had only to brush apart the door curtains to feel—even before setting foot inside—a curiously vivid, carnal sensation of being a male.

Sometimes Masuyama had gone on company business to the dressing-rooms of chorus girls backstage at revues. The rooms were filled with an almost suffocating femininity and the rough-skinned girls, sprawled about like animals in the zoo, threw bored glances at him, but he never felt so distinctly alien as in Mangiku's dressing-room; nothing in these real women made Masuyama feel particularly masculine.

The members of Mangiku's entourage exhibited no special friendliness towards Masuyama. On the contrary, he knew that they secretly gossiped about him, accusing him of being disrespectful or of giving himself airs merely because he had gone through some university. He knew too that sometimes they professed irritation at his pedantic insistence on historical facts. In the world of kabuki, academic learning unaccompanied by artistic talent is considered of no value.

Masuyama's work had its compensations too. It would happen when Mangiku had a favour to ask of someone—only, of course, when he was in good mood—that he twisted his body diagonally from his dressing-table and gave a little nod and a smile; the indescribable charm in his eyes at such moments made Masuyama feel that he wished for nothing more than to slave like a dog for this man. Mangiku himself never forgot his dignity: he never failed to maintain a certain distance, though he obviously was aware of his charms. If he had been a real woman, his whole body would have been filled with the allure in his eyes. The allure of an *onnagata* is only a momentary glimmer, but that is enough for it to exist independently and to display the eternal feminine.

Mangiku sat before the mirror after the performance of *The Castle of the Lord Protector of Hachijin,* the first item of the programme. He had removed the costume and wig he wore as Lady Hinaginu, and changed to a bathrobe, not being obliged to appear in the middle work of the programme. Masuyama, informed that Mangiku wanted to see him, had been waiting in the dressing-room for the curtain of *Hachijin.* The mirror suddenly burst into crimson flames as Mangiku returned to the room, filling the entrance with the rustle of his robes. Three disciples and dressers joined to remove what had to be removed and store it away. Those who were to leave departed, and now no one remained except for a few disciples around the hibachi in the next room. The dressing-room had all at once fallen still. From a loudspeaker in the corridor issued the sounds of stage assistants hammering as they dismantled the set for the play which had just ended. It was late November, and steam heat clouded the window-panes, bleak as in a hospital ward. White chrysanthemums bent gracefully in a cloisonné vase placed beside Mangiku's dressing-table. Mangiku, perhaps because his stage name meant literally 'ten thousand chrysanthemums', was fond of this flower.

Mangiku sat on a bulky cushion of purple silk, facing his dressing-table. 'I wonder if you'd mind telling the gentleman from Sakuragi Street?' (Mangiku, in the old-fashioned manner, referred to his dancing and singing teachers by the names of the streets where they lived.) 'It'd be hard for me to tell him.' He gazed directly into the mirror as he spoke. Masuyama could see from where he sat by the wall the nape of

Mangiku's neck and the reflections in the mirror of his face still made up for the part of Hinaginu. The eyes were not on Masuyama; they were squarely contemplating his own face. The flush from his exertions on the stage still glowed through the powder on his cheeks, like the morning sun through a thin sheet of ice. He was looking at Hinaginu.

Indeed, he actually saw her in the mirror—Hinaginu, whom he had just been impersonating, Hinaginu, the daughter of Mori Sanzaemon Yoshinari and the bride of the young Satō Kazuenosuke. Her marriage ties with her husband having been broken because of his feudal loyalty, Hinaginu killed herself so that she might remain faithful to a union 'whose ties were so faint we never shared the same bed'. Hinaginu had died on stage of a despair so extreme she could not bear to live any longer. The Hinaginu in the mirror was a ghost. Even that ghost, Mangiku knew, was at this very moment slipping from his body. His eyes pursued Hinaginu. But as the glow of the ardent passions of the role subsided, Hinaginu's face faded away. He bade it farewell. There were still seven performances before the final day. Tomorrow again Hinaginu's features would no doubt return to the pliant mould of Mangiku's face.

Masuyama, enjoying the sight of Mangiku in this abstracted state, all but smiled with affection. Mangiku suddenly turned towards him. He had been aware all along of Masuyama's gaze, but with the nonchalance of the actor, accustomed to the public's stares, he continued with his business. 'It's those instrumental passages. They're simply not long enough. I don't mean I can't get through the part if I hurry, but it makes everything so ugly.' Mangiku was referring to the music for the new dance-play which would be presented the following month. 'Mr. Masuyama, what do *you* think?'

'I quite agree. I'm sure you mean the passage after "How slow the day ends by the Chinese bridge at Seta." '

'Yes, that's the place. How-ow slo-ow the da-ay . . .' Mangiku sang the passage in question, beating time with his delicate fingers.

'I'll tell him. I'm sure that the gentleman from Sakuragi Street will understand.'

'Are you sure you don't mind? I feel so embarrassed about making a nuisance of myself all the time.'

Mangiku was accustomed to terminate a conversation by standing, once his business had been dealt with. 'I'm afraid I must bathe now,' he said. Masuyama drew back from the narrow entrance to the dressing-room and let Mangiku pass. Mangiku, with a slight bow of the head, went out into the corridor, accompanied by a disciple. He turned back obliquely towards Masuyama and, smiling, bowed again. The rouge at the corners of his eyes had an indefinable charm. Masuyama sensed that Mangiku was well aware of his affection.

4

The troupe to which Masuyama belonged was to remain at the same theatre through November, December, and January, and the programme for January had already become the subject of gossip. A new work by a playwright of the modern theatre was to be staged. The man, whose sense of his own importance accorded poorly with his youth, had imposed innumerable conditions, and Masuyama was kept frantically busy with complicated negotiations intended to bring together not only the dramatist and the actors but the management of the theatre as well. Masuyama was recruited for this job because the others considered him to be an intellectual.

One of the conditions laid down by the playwright was that the direction of the play be confided to a talented young man whom he trusted. The management accepted this condition. Mangiku also agreed, but without enthusiasm. He conveyed his doubts in this manner: 'I don't really know, of course, but if this young man doesn't understand kabuki very well, and makes unreasonable demands on us, it will be so hard explaining.' Mangiku was hoping for an older, more mature—by which he meant a more compliant—director.

The new play was a dramatization in modern language of the twelfth-century novel *If Only I Could Change Them!* The managing director of the company, deciding not to leave the production of this new work to the regular staff, announced it would be in Masuyama's hands. Masuyama grew tense at the thought of the work ahead of him but, convinced that the play was first-rate, he felt that it would be worth the trouble.

As soon as the scripts were ready and the parts assigned, a preliminary meeting was held one mid-December morning in the reception room adjoining the office of the theatre owner. The meeting was attended by the executive in charge of production, the playwright, the director, the stage designer, the actors, and Masuyama. The room was warmly heated and sunlight poured through the windows. Masuyama always felt happiest at preliminary meetings. It was like spreading out a map and discussing a projected outing: Where do we board the bus and where do we start walking? Is there drinking water where we're going? Where are we going to eat lunch? Where is the best view? Shall we take the train back? Or would it be better to allow enough time to return by boat?

Kawasaki, the director, was late. Masuyama had never seen a play directed by Kawasaki, but he knew of him by reputation. Kawasaki had been selected, despite his youth, to direct Ibsen and modern American plays for a repertory company, and in the course of a year had done so well, with the latter especially, that he was awarded a newspaper drama prize.

The others (except for Kawasaki) had all assembled. The designer, who could never bear waiting a minute before throwing himself into his work, was already jotting down in a large notebook especially brought for the purpose suggestions made by the others, frequently tapping the end of his pencil on the blank pages, as if bursting with ideas. Eventually the executive began to gossip about the absent director. 'He may be as talented as they say, but he's still young, after all. The actors will have to help out.'

At this moment there was a knock at the door and a secretary showed in Kawasaki. He entered the room with a dazed look, as if the light were too strong for him and, without uttering a word, stiffly bowed towards the others. He was rather tall, almost six feet, with deeply etched, masculine—but highly sensitive—features. It was a cold winter day, but Kawasaki wore a rumpled, thin raincoat. Underneath, as he presently disclosed, he had on a brick-coloured corduroy jacket. His long, straight hair hung down so far—to the tip of his nose—that he was frequently obliged to push it back. Masuyama was rather disappointed by his first impression. He had supposed that a man who had been singled out for his abilities would have attempted to distinguish himself somehow from the stereotypes of society, but this man dressed and acted exactly in the way one would expect of the typical young man of the modern theatre.

Kawasaki took the place offered him at the head of the table. He did not make the usual polite protests against the honour. He kept his eyes on the playwright, his close friend, and when introduced to each of the actors he uttered a word of greeting, only to turn back at once to the playwright. Masuyama could remember similar experiences. It is not easy for a man trained in the modern theatre, where most of the actors are young, to establish himself on easy terms with the kabuki actors, who are likely to prove to be imposing old gentlemen when encountered off stage.

The actors assembled for this preliminary meeting managed in fact to convey somehow their contempt for Kawasaki, all with a show of the greatest politeness and without an unfriendly word. Masuyama happened to glance at Mangiku's face. He modestly kept to himself, refraining from any demonstration of self-importance; he displayed no trace of the others' contempt. Masuyama felt greater admiration and affection than ever for Mangiku.

Now that everyone was present, the author described the play in outline. Mangiku, probably for the first time in his career—leaving aside parts he took as a child—was to play a male role. The plot told of a certain Grand Minister with two children, a boy and a girl. By nature they are quite unsuited to their sexes and are therefore reared accordingly: the boy (actually the girl) eventually becomes General of the Left, and the girl (actually the boy) becomes the chief lady-in-waiting in the Senyoden, the palace of the Imperial concubines. Later, when the truth is revealed, they revert to lives more appropriate to the sex of their birth; the brother marries the fourth daughter of the Minister of the Right, and sister a Middle Counsellor, and all ends happily.

Mangiku's part was that of the girl who is in reality a man. Although this was a male role, Mangiku would appear as a man only in the few moments of the final scene. Up to that point, he was to act throughout as a true *onnagata* in the part of a chief lady-in-waiting at the Senyoden. The author and director were agreed in urging Mangiku not to make any special attempt even in the last scene to suggest that he was in fact a man.

An amusing aspect of the play was that it inevitably had the effect of satirizing the kabuki convention of the *onnagata*. The lady-in-waiting was actually a man; so, in precisely the same manner, was Mangiku in the role. That was not all. In order for Mangiku, at once an *onnagata* and a man, to perform this part, he would have to unfold on two levels his actions of real life, a far cry from the simple case of the actor who assumes female costume during the course of a play so as to work some deception. The complexities of the part intrigued Mangiku.

Kawasaki's first words to Mangiku were, 'I would be glad if you played the part throughout as a woman. It doesn't make the least difference if you act like a woman even in the last scene.' His voice had a pleasant, clear ring.

'Really? If you don't mind my acting the part that way, it'll make it ever so much easier for me.'

'It won't be easy in any case. Definitely not,' said Kawasaki decisively. When he spoke in this forceful manner his cheeks glowed red as if a lamp had been lit inside. The sharpness of his tone cast something of a pall over the gathering. Masuyama's eyes wandered to Mangiku. He was giggling good-naturedly, the back of his hand pressed to his mouth. The others relaxed to see Mangiku had not been offended.

'Well, then,' said the author, 'I shall read the book.' He lowered his protruding eyes, which looked double behind his thick spectacles, and began to read the script on the table.

5

Two or three days later the rehearsal by parts began, whenever the different actors had free time. Full-scale rehearsals would only be possible during the few days in between the end of this month and the beginning of next month's programme.

Unless everything that needed tightening were attended to by then, there would be no time to pull the performance together.

Once the rehearsal of the parts began it became apparent to everyone that Kawasaki was like a foreigner strayed among them. He had not the smallest grasp of kabuki, and Masuyama found himself obliged to stand beside him and explain word by word the technical language of the kabuki theatre, making Kawasaki extremely dependent on him. The instant the first rehearsal was over Masuyama invited Kawasaki for a drink.

Masuyama knew that for someone in his position it was generally speaking a mistake to ally himself with the director, but he felt he could easily understand what Kawasaki must be experiencing. The young man's views were precisely defined, his mental attitudes were wholesome, and he threw himself into his work with boyish enthusiasm. Masuyama could see why Kawasaki's character should have so appealed to the playwright; he felt as if Kawasaki's genuine youthfulness were a somehow purifying element, a quality unknown in the world of kabuki. Masuyama justified his friendship with Kawasaki in terms of attempting to turn this quality to the advantage of kabuki.

Full-scale rehearsals began at last on the day after the final performances of the December programme. It was two days after Christmas. The year-end excitement in the streets could be sensed even through the windows in the theatre and the dressing-rooms. A battered old desk had been placed by a window in the large rehearsal room. Kawasaki and one of Masuyama's seniors on the staff—the stage manager—sat with their backs to the window. Masuyama was behind Kawasaki. The authors sat on the *tatami* along the wall. Each would go up centre when his turn came to recite his lines. The stage manager supplied forgotten lines.

Sparks flew repeatedly between Kawasaki and the actors. 'At this point,' Kawasaki would say, 'I'd like you to stand as you say, "I wish I could go to Kawachi and have done with it." Then you're to walk up to the pillar at stage right.'

'That's one place I simply can't stand up.'

'Please try doing it my way.' Kawasaki forced a smile, but his face visibly paled with wounded pride.

'You can ask me to stand up from now until next Christmas, but I still can't do it. I'm supposed at this place to be mulling over something. How can I walk across stage when I'm thinking?'

Kawasaki did not answer, but he betrayed his extreme irritation at being addressed in such terms.

But things were quite different when it came to Mangiku's turn. If Kawasaki said, 'Sit!' Mangiku would sit, and if he said 'Stand!' Managiku stood. He obeyed unresistingly every direction given by Kawasaki. It seemed to Masuyama that Mangiku's fondness for the part did not fully explain why he was so much more obliging than was his custom at rehearsals.

Masuyama was forced to leave this rehearsal on business just as Mangiku, having run through his scene in the first act, was returning to his seat by the wall. When Masuyama got back, he was met by the following sight: Kawasaki, all but sprawled over the desk, was intently following the rehearsal, not bothering even to push back the long hair falling over his eyes. He was leaning on his crossed arms, the shoulders beneath the corduroy jacket shaking with suppressed rage. To Masuyama's right was a white wall interrupted by a window, through which he could see a balloon swaying in the northerly wind, its streamer proclaiming an end-of-the-year sale. Hard, wintry clouds looked as if they had been blocked in with chalk against the pale blue of the sky. He noticed a shrine to Inari and a tiny vermilion torii on the roof of an old building near by. Farther to his right, by the wall, Mangiku sat erect in Japanese style on the *tatami*. The script lay open on his lap, and the lines of his greenish-grey kimono were perfectly straight. From where Masuyama stood at the door he could not see Mangiku's full face; but the eyes, seen in profile, were utterly tranquil, the gentle gaze fixed unwaveringly on Kawasaki.

Masuyama felt a momentary shudder of fear. He had set one foot inside the rehearsal room, but it was now almost impossible to go in.

6

Later in the day Masuyama was summoned to Mangiku's dressing-room. He felt an unaccustomed emotional block when he bent his head, as so often before, to pass through the door curtains. Mangiku greeted him, all smiles, from his perch on the purple cushion and offered Masuyama some cakes he had been given by a visitor.

'How do you think the rehearsal went today?'

'Pardon me?' Masuyama was startled by the question. It was not like Mangiku to ask his opinion on such matters.

'How did it seem?'

'If everything continues to go as well as it did today, I think the play'll be a hit.'

'Do you really think so? I feel terribly sorry for Mr. Kawasaki. It's so hard for him. The others have been treating him in such a high-handed way that it's made me quite nervous. I'm sure you could tell from the rehearsal that I've made up my mind to play the part exactly as Mr. Kawasaki says. That's the way I'd like to play it myself anyway, and I thought it might make things a little easier for Mr. Kawasaki, even if nobody else helps. I can't very well tell the others, but I'm sure they'll notice if I do exactly what I'm told. They know how difficult I usually am. That's the least I can do to protect Mr. Kawasaki. It'd be a shame, when he's trying so hard, if nobody helped.'

Masuyama felt no particular surge of emotions as he listened to Mangiku. Quite likely, he thought, Mangiku himself was unaware that he was in love: he was so accustomed to portraying love on a more heroic scale. Masuyama, for his part, considered that these sentiments—however they were to be termed—which had formed in Mangiku's heart were most inappropriate. He expected of Mangiku a far more transparent, artificial, aesthetic display of emotions.

Mangiku, most unusually for him, sat rather informally, imparting a kind of languor to his delicate figure. The mirror reflected the cluster of crimson asters arranged in the cloisonné vase and the recently shaved nape of Mangiku's neck.

Kawasaki's exasperation had become pathetic by the day before stage rehearsals began. As soon as the last private rehearsal ended, he invited Masuyama for a drink, looking as if he had reached the end of his tether. Masuyama was busy at the moment, but two hours later he found Kawasaki in the bar where they had arranged to meet, still waiting for him. The bar was crowded, though it was the night before New Year's Eve, when bars are usually deserted. Kawasaki's face looked pale as he sat drinking alone. He was the kind who only gets paler the more he has had to drink. Masuyama, catcing sight of Kawasaki's ashen face as soon as he entered the bar, felt that the young man had saddled him with an unfairly heavy spiritual burden. They lived in different worlds; there was no reason why courtesy should demand that Kawasaki's uncertainties and anguish should fall so squarely on his shoulders.

Kawasaki, as he rather expected, immediately engaged him with a good-natured taunt, accusing him of being a double agent. Masuyama took the charge with a smile. He was only five or six years older than Kawasaki, but he possessed the self-confidence of a man who had dwelt among people who 'knew the score'. At the same time, he felt a kind of envy of this man who had never known hardship, or at any rate, enough hardship. It was not exactly a lack of moral integrity which had made Masuyama indifferent to most of the backstage gossip directed against him, now that he was securely placed in the kabuki hierarchy; his indifference demonstrated that he had nothing to do with the kind of sincerity which might destroy him.

Kawasaki spoke. 'I'm fed up with the whole thing. Once the curtain goes up on opening night, I'll be only too glad to disappear from the picture. Stage rehearsals beginning tomorrow! That's more than I can take, when I'm feeling so disgusted. This is the worst assignment I've ever had. I've reached my limit. Never again will I barge into a world that's not my own.'

'But isn't that what you more or less expected from the outset? Kabuki's not the same as the modern theatre, after all.' Masuyama's voice was cold.

Kawasaki's next words came as a surprise. 'Mangiku's the hardest to take. I really dislike him. I'll never stage another play with him.' Kawasaki stared at the curling wisps of smoke under the low ceiling, as if into the face of an invisible enemy.

'I wouldn't have guessed it. It seems to me he's doing his best to be cooperative.'

'What makes you think so? What's so good about him? It doesn't bother me too much when the other actors don't listen to me during rehearsals or try to intimidate me, or even when they sabotage the whole works, but Mangiku's more than I can figure out. All he does is stare at me with that sneer on his face. At bottom he's absolutely uncompromising, and he treats me like an ignorant little squirt. That's why he does everything exactly as I say. He's the only one of them who obeys my directions, and that burns me up all the more. I can tell just what he's thinking: "If that's the way you want it, that's the way I'll do it, but don't expect me to take any responsibility for what happens in the performance." That's what he keeps flashing at me, without saying a word, and it's the worst sabotage I know. He's the nastiest of the lot.'

Masuyama listened in astonishment, but he shrank from revealing the truth to Kawasaki now. He hesitated even to let Kawasaki know that Mangiku was intending to be friendly, much less the whole truth. Kawasaki was baffled as to how he should respond to the entirely unfamiliar emotions of this world into which he had suddenly plunged; if he were informed of Mangiku's feelings, he might easily suppose they represented just one more snare laid for him. His eyes were too clear: for all his grasp of the principles of theatre, he could not detect the dark, aesthetic presence lurking behind the texts.

The New Year came and with it the first night of the new programme.

Mangiku was in love. His sharp-eyed disciples were the first to gossip about it. Masuyama, a frequent visitor to Mangiku's dressing-room, sensed it in the atmosphere almost immediately. Mangiku was wrapped in his love like a silkworm in its cocoon, soon to emerge as a butterfly. His dressing-room was the cocoon of his love. Mangiku was of a retiring disposition in any case, but the contrast with the New Year's excitement elsewhere gave his dressing-room a peculiarly solemn hush.

On the opening night, Masuyama, noticing as he passed Mangiku's dressing-room that the door was wide open, decided to take a look inside. He saw Mangiku from behind, seated before the mirror in full costume, waiting for his signal to go on. His eyes took in the pale lavender of Mangiku's robe, the gentle slope of the powdered and half-exposed shoulders, the glossy, lacquer-black wig. Mangiku at such moments in the deserted dressing-room looked like a woman absorbed in her spinning; she was spinning her love, and would continue spinning for ever, her mind elsewhere.

Masuyama intuitively understood that the mould for this *onnagata*'s love had been provided by the stage alone. The stage was present all day long, the stage where love was incessantly shouting, grieving, shedding blood. Music celebrating the sublime heights of love sounded perpetually in Mangiku's ears, and each exquisite gesture of his body was constantly employed on stage for the purpose of love. To the tips of his fingers, nothing about Mangiku was alien to love. His toes encased in white *tabi*, the seductive colours of his under kimono barely glimpsed through the openings in his sleeves, the long, swanlike nape of his neck were all in the service of love.

Masuyama did not doubt but that Mangiku would obtain guidance in pursuing his love from the grandiose emotions of his stage roles. The ordinary actor is apt to enrich his performances by infusing them with the emotions of his real life, but not Mangiku. The instant that Mangiku fell in love, the loves of Yukihime, Omiwa, Hinaginu, and the other tragic heroines came to his support.

The thought of Mangiku in love took Masuyama aback, however. Those tragic emotions for which he had yearned so fervently since his days as a high-school student, those sublime emotions which Mangiku always evoked through his corporeal presence on stage, encasing his sensual faculties in icy flames, Mangiku was now visibly nurturing in real life. But the object of these emotions—granted that he had some talent—was an ignoramus as far as kabuki was concerned; he was merely a young, commonplace-looking director whose only qualification as the object of Mangiku's love consisted in being a foreigner in this country, a young traveller who would soon depart the world of kabuki and never return.

7

If Only I Could Change Them! was well received. Kawasaki, despite his announced intention of disappearing after opening night, came to the theatre every day to complain of the performance, to rush back and forth incessantly through the subterranean passages under the stage, to finger with curiosity the mechanisms of the trap door or the *hanamichi.* Masuyama thought this man had something childish about him.

The newspaper reviews praised Mangiku. Masuyama made it a point to show them to Kawasaki, but he merely pouted, like an obstinate child, and all but spat out the words, 'They're all good at acting. But there wasn't any *direction.*' Masuyama naturally did not relay to Mangiku these harsh words, and Kawasaki himself was on his best behaviour when he actually met Mangiku. It nevertheless irritated Masuyma that Mangiku, who was utterly blind when it came to other people's feelings, should not have questioned that Kawasaki was aware of his good will. But Kawasaki was absolutely insensitive to what other people might feel. This was the one trait that Kawasaki and Mangiku had in common.

A week after the first performance Masuyama was summoned to Mangiku's dressing-room. Mangiku displayed on his table amulets and charms from the shrine where he regularly worshipped, as well as some small New Year's cakes. The cakes would no doubt be distributed later among his disciples. Mangiku pressed some sweets on Masuyama, a sign that he was in a good mood. 'Mr. Kawasaki was here a little while ago,' he said.

'Yes, I saw him out front.'

'I wonder if he's still in the theatre.'

'I imagine he'll stay until *If Only* is over.'

'Did he say anything about being busy afterwards?'

'No, nothing particular.'

'Then, I have a little favour I'd like to ask you.'

Masuyama assumed as businesslike an expression as he could muster. 'What might it be?'

'Tonight, you see, when the performance is over . . . I mean, tonight . . .' The colour had mounted in Mangiku's cheeks. His voice was clearer and higher-pitched than usual. 'Tonight, when the performance is over, I thought I'd like to have dinner with him. Would you mind asking if he's free?'

'I'll ask him.'

'It's dreadful of me, isn't it, to ask you such a thing.'

'That's quite all right.' Masuyama sensed that Mangiku's eyes at that moment had stopped roving and were trying to read his expression. He seemed to expect—and even to desire—some perturbation on Masuyama's part. 'Very well,' Masuyama said, rising at once, 'I'll inform him.'

Hardly had Masuyama gone into the lobby than he ran into Kawasaki, coming from the opposite direction; this chance meeting amidst the crowd thronging the lobby during the interval seemed like a stroke of fate. Kawasaki's manner poorly accorded with the festive air pervading the lobby. The somehow haughty airs which the young man always adopted seemed rather comic when set amidst a buzzing crowd of solid citizens dressed in holiday finery and attending the theatre merely for the pleasure of seeing a play.

Masuyama led Kawasaki to a corner of the lobby and informed him of Mangiku's request.

'I wonder what he wants with me now? Dinner together—that's funny. I have nothing else to do tonight, and there's no reason why I can't go, but I don't see why.'

'I suppose there's something he wants to discuss about the play.'

'The play! I've said all I want to on that subject.'

At this moment a gratuitous desire to do evil, an emotion always associated on the stage with minor villains, took seed within Masuyama's heart, though he did not realize it; he was not aware that he himself was now acting like a character in a play. 'Don't you see—being invited to dinner gives you a marvellous opportunity to tell him everything you've got on your mind, this time without mincing words.'

'All the same—'

'I don't suppose you've got the nerve to tell him.'

The remark wounded the young man's pride. 'All right. I'll

go. I've known all along that sooner or later I'd have my chance to have it out with him in the open. Please tell him that I'm glad to accept his invitation.'

Mangiku appeared in the last work of the programme and was not free until the entire performance was over. Once the show ends, actors normally make a quick change of clothes and rush from the theatre, but Mangiku showed no sign of haste as he completed his dressing by putting a cape and a scarf of a muted colour over his outer kimono. He waited for Kawasaki. When Kawasaki at last appeared, he curtly greeted Mangiku, not bothering to take his hands from his overcoat pockets.

The disciple who always waited on Mangiku as his 'lady's maid' rushed up, as if to announce some major calamity. 'It's started to snow,' he reported with a bow.

'A heavy snow? Mangiku touched his cape to his cheek.

'No, just a flurry.'

'We'll need an umbrella to the car.' Mangiku said. The disciple rushed off for an umbrella.

Masuyama saw them to the stage entrance. The door attendant had politely arranged Mangiku's and Kawasaki's footwear next to each other. Mangiku's disciple stood outside in the thin snow, holding an open umbrella. The snow fell so sparsely that one couldn't be sure one saw it against the dark concrete wall beyond. One or two flakes fluttered on to the doorstep at the stage entrance.

Mangiku bowed to Masuyama. 'We'll be leaving now,' he said. The smile on his lips could be seen indistinctly behind his scarf. He turned to the disciple, 'That's all right. I'll carry the umbrella. I'd like you to go instead and tell the driver we're ready.' Mangiku held the umbrella over Kawasaki's head. As Kawasaki in his overcoat and Mangiku in his cape walked off side by side under the umbrella, a few flakes suddenly flew—all but bounced—from the umbrella.

Masuyama watched them go. He felt as though a big, black wet umbrella were being noisily opened inside his heart. He could tell that the illusion, first formed when as a boy he saw Mangiku perform, an illusion which he had preserved intact even after he joined the kabuki staff, had shattered that instant in all directions, like a delicate piece of crystal dropped from a height. At last I know what disillusion means, he thought. I might as well give up the theatre.

But Masuyama knew that along with disillusion a new sensation was assaulting him, jealousy. He dreaded where this new emotion might lead him.

—Translated by
Donald Keene

LEROI JONES

THE TOILET

The *Toilet* was first presented by Leo Garen and Stan Swerdlow at the St. Marks Playhouse, New York, on December 16, 1964. It was directed by Leo Garen, designed by Larry Rivers, and the lighting was by Harold Baldridge. The cast was as follows:

ORA .... James Spruill

WILLIE LOVE .... Gary Bolling

HINES .... D'Urville Martin

JOHNNY BOY HOLMES .... Bostic Van Felton

PERRY .... Norman Bush

GEORGE DAVIS .... Antonio Fargas

SKIPPY .... Tony Hudson

KNOWLES .... Walter Jones

DONALD FARRELL .... Gary Haynes

FOOTS .... Hampton Clanton

KAROLIS .... Jaime Sanchez

CHARACTERS

ORA (Big Shot): *Short, ugly, crude, loud.*

WILLIE LOVE: *Tall, thin. Should have been sensitive. Smiles.*

HINES: *Big, husky, garrulous. He and Love are closest friends.*

JOHNNY BOY HOLMES: *Short, curly hair. Bright, fast, likable.*

PERRY: *Tall, dark, somber, cynical.*

GEORGE DAVIS: *Tall, thin, crudely elegant. Judicious.*

SKIPPY: *Quick. Rather stupid but interested. Someone to be trusted.*

KNOWLES: *Large and ridiculous. A grinning ape.*

DONALD FARRELL: *Tall, thin, blond, awkward, soft.*

FOOTS (Ray): *Short, intelligent, manic. Possessor of a threatened empire.*

KAROLIS: *Medium height. Very skinny and not essentially attractive except when he speaks.*

The scene is a large bare toilet built of gray rough cement. There are urinals along one wall and a partition separating them from the commodes which are along the same wall. The toilet must resemble the impersonal ugliness of a school toilet or a latrine of some institution. A few rolls of toilet paper are spread out on the floor, wet through. The actors should give the impression frequently that the place smells.

Ora breaks through the door grinning, then giggling. Looks around the bleak place, walks around, then with one hand on his hip takes out his joint and pees, still grinning, into one of the commodes, spraying urine over the seat.

LOVE (*sticking his head through the door*): Big Shot! Hey, Big Shot! These guys say come and help them.

ORA (*zipping his fly and wiping the one hand on the back of his pants*): Yeh? (*Turning to* LOVE.) Yeh? They got him, huh?

LOVE (*pushing door open so his arm is straight*): Naw, they don't have him yet. He's on the second floor, running back and forth and hiding in empty rooms. But Knowles said for you to come help.

ORA (*flushing all the commodes and urinals in the row as he walks past*): Sheet! I'll catch that bastid in a second. (*Ducks under* LOVE's *arm to go out.*) Why the hell don't you get up there. You supposed to be faster than me.

LOVE: I'm s'posed to stay here and keep the place clear. (*Making a face.*) Damn. This place smells like hell.

ORA (*without turning around*): Yeh (*giggling*), this must be your momma's house.

LOVE (*slipping inside the door and holding it against* ORA): Shit. At least I got one.

ORA (*thumps against the door, not really angry*): Bastid!

LOVE *waits a few seconds, then pulls the door open slightly. Then lets it shut and walks to a closed commode and noticing it's wet wipes it with some of the strewn toilet paper. He sits down and stretches his legs. Then gets up and opens the commode to pee. There are voices outside and then the door swings open and* HINES *and* HOLMES *come in.*

HINES: Hey, Willie.

LOVE (*still peeing*): What you want? (*Comes out, zipping his pants.*)

HINES (*to* HOLMES): Man, this cat's in here pulling his whatchamacallit.

HOLMES (*to* LOVE): Yeh. Damn, Love, why don't you go get Gloria to do that stuff for you.

LOVE: She-et. (*Grinning.*) Huh. I sure don't need your ol' lady to be pullin' on my joint. (*Laughs.* HOLMES *begins to spar with him.*)

HINES: They didn't even catch that skinny nose punk yet.

LOVE: No? Why in hell not?

HOLMES: He's still running up and down the damn halls. I should go up there and drag that sonofabitch down.

HOLMES *and* HINES *begin to pee also—in the commodes.* LOVE *pulls open the door a small bit and looks out.*

LOVE: Shit. Boy, all you slow ass cats. I'd catch that little skinny paddy boy in a second. Where's that little popeyed Foots?

HINES: Damn if I know. I think he's still in Miss Powell's class. You know if he missed her class she'd beat his head, and then get his ol' lady to beat his head again.

HOLMES: Shit. Skippy should've got hold of that damn Karolis by now. He ain't fast worth a bitch.

LOVE: Yeh, but he's so so goddamned scary he might just jump out a goddamn window.

HOLMES *finishes peeing and starts pushing* LOVE *and they begin to spar around.* HOLMES *is very funny, making boxer-like sounds and brushing his nose continuously with his thumbs.* LOVE *just stands straight with his left hand stiff and stabbing it out toward Holmes' face.* HINES *finishes and gets in the action too. Both he and* HOLMES *are against* LOVE, *who starts to laugh and curse good naturedly.*

LOVE: Two a' you bastids, huh? I'll take you both. (*He starts kicking at them.*)

HINES: Boy, if you kick me, you'll die just like that . . . with your skinny ass leg up. They'll have to build you a special coffin with a part for your leg.

HOLMES (*backing away, and then turning on* HINES. *Laughing*): Let's get this sum'bitch, Willie.

HINES (*backing away, now kicking and swinging . . . but just timing blows so they won't strike anyone*): Goddamn, Johnny Boy, you a crooked muthafucka. You cats think you can mess with the kid?

The two spar against HINES *and then* LOVE *turns against* HOLMES.

LOVE: Let's get this little assed cat.

HOLMES *kicks at them, then jumps up on the commodes in order to defend himself more "heroically."*

HOLMES: I'm gonna get your ass, Willie. I'm just trying to help you out and you gonna play wise. Ya' bastid.

HINES: Listen to that cat. (*Runs after* HOLMES.) I'm gonna put your damn head in one of those damn urinals.

He and LOVE *finally grab* HOLMES *and he begins struggling with them in earnest.*

Let's put this little bastard's head in the goddamn urinal!

HOLMES: You bastids! Let me go! I'm gonna cut somebody. Bastids!

The door opens and ORA *comes in. His shirt is torn. But he rushes over laughing and starts punching everyone, even* HOLMES.

HINES: Goddamn it, Big Shot, get the hell out of here.

HOLMES: Get 'em, Big Shot.

ORA (*punches* HOLMES *who's still being held by* LOVE): I'm gonna punch you, you prick. Hold the cocksucker, Love.

LOVE (*releasing* HOLMES *immediately*): I ain't gonna hold him so you can punch him.

ORA *and* HOLMES *square off, both laughing and faking professional demeanor.*

LOVE: Hey, Big Shot, what happened to your shirt?

ORA (*putting his hands down and handling the torn part of his shirt*): That muthafuckin' Karolis ripped it.

The other three yowl. HINES *puts his fingers to the hole as if to tear it again.*

Get outta here you black ass bastid. (*He squares off at* HINES, *then pushes him away.*) That paddy bastid! I had the cocksucker around the waist, and then he rips my shirt and scratches me. (*He holds up his wounded hand.*)

HINES: You let him get away?

ORA: No, hell. I punched the bastid right in his lip. But he was making so much noise we thought somebody'd come out and see us so Knowles and Skippy took him in the broom closet and I cut down the stairs. The stupid bastid was screaming and biting right outside of ol' lady Powell's room.

HOLMES: Did anybody come outta there?

ORA: You think I was gonna stay around and see? She and Miss Golden after me anyway.

LOVE: Did you see Foots in there?

ORA (*going to the door and peering out*): Yeh. And George Davis and Perry are in there too. (*He pushes door open and leans all the way out.*)

HINES: Shit. They're never gonna bring that sonofabitch down here. We ain't got all day.

ORA: (*letting the door shut*): Yeh, Perry and Foots and them ought to be down here in a few minutes. It's almost 3:00 now.

LOVE (*pretending he has a basketball in his hands, he pretends to dribble and lunges forward simulating a fake at* HINES, *then he sweeps past* HINES *and leaps in the air as if making a layup shot*): Peed on you, just then, buddy.

HINES: Sheet, Man, you what you call a self-checker. I don't even have to block that shot. I just take it off the backboard like this. (*He spins around and leaps up at the imaginary basket and scoops the imaginary ball off, landing and shaking his head as if to shake off imaginary defenders.*) Another rebound! (*Makes motion of long pass down toward opposite "court."*) Now, the fast break (*He moves in position for his own pass, receives it, makes one long stepping dribble and leaps as if dunking the ball in the basket.*) Two!

HOLMES: Boy, you guys sure play a lot of ball . . . off the court.

ORA (*opening the door again*): No shootin', cocksuckas.

LOVE (*still whirling and leaping as if he is making successful hook shots from an imaginary foul line*): Hey, what we gonna do to this cat when he gets here?

ORA (*leaning back in from the door though keeping it open with his fingers*): Damn, Love. You a stupid bastid. (*Peeks out door.*) We gonna kick that little frail bastid's ass.

HINES: In fact, you the one gonna do it, Willie.

HOLMES: Yeh, Love. (*Blocking one of Love's "shots."*)

LOVE: Shit. Karolis never bothered me. (*Faking* HOLMES *and swinging to shoot from the other side.*)

ORA (*looking back in and letting the door swing shut*): Damn, Willie (*in mocking seriousness*), Karolis is always telling everybody how he bangs the hell out of Caroline, every chance he gets. (*Begins to giggle.*)

HOLMES: Is that your mother's name, Love, Caroline?

HINES (*busy trying to lift a back window to look out on the yard*): What you mean, Johnny Boy, is that his mother's name? You the one told me.

LOVE (*swinging around as if to shoot again he suddenly punches* HOLMES *on the shoulder.* HOLMES *lets out a yelp of pain*): Uhhuh . . . I told you about messin' with me.

HOLMES (*holding his shoulder*): Shit. Why didn't you hit Big Shot, you bastard? He brought the shit up.

ORA (*has the door propped open again*): Shit. That narrow head bastid know better than to fuck with me. (*He peers out the door and as he does* LOVE *gestures as if to hit him in the back.*)

HOLMES (*to* LOVE): You scared ass bastard. Why don't you do it?

ORA (*turning around and throwing up his hands to defend himself*): Yeh, I wish you would, you bullet head sonofabitch.

HOLMES *goes and sits on a radiator next to* HINES.

LOVE: Man, nobody's thinking about you, Big Shot. (*He goes to pee.*)

ORA (*pulling the door open again*): Here come Perry and them.

HOLMES (*jumping off the radiator still holding his shoulder*): Perry and who else?

ORA: George Davis and Donald Farrell.

HINES: Donald Farrell? What the hell's he doin' down here? Where the hell is Foots?

LOVE: Yeh, what the hell is Perry doing bringing Farrell down here with 'em? Shit.

ORA *pulls the door open, and* PERRY, DAVIS *and* FARRELL *come in.*

PERRY: Hey, what's happening?

HOLMES: Shit. I should ask you. Where's Foots?

GEORGE: He had to stay upstairs for awhile. Powell wanted to talk to him . . . or something.

ORA (*to* FARRELL): Man, whatta you want down here? Nobody asked you to come.

GEORGE: I told him he could come. Why not?

ORA: Whatta you mean, why not? You know goddamn well, why not. Silly sumbitch!

PERRY: Ah, Big Shot, why don't you be cool for a change, huh?

GEORGE: Yeh, man, Big Shot. Donald's not going to hurt anything.

ORA: No? (*Taking out a much-smoked cigarette butt.*) Maybe you don't think so . . . but I do.

GEORGE: Oh, man, shit.

FARRELL: Why don't you want me here, Big Shot?

ORA (*glancing at* FARRELL): Man, don't be asking me questions.

FARRELL: Don't ask you questions? Why the hell not?

ORA (*menacingly at* FARRELL): Cause I said so, that's why. You don't like it, muthafucka?

PERRY (*stepping between them*): Goddamn it, Big Shot, why don't you sit your ass down for awhile and shut the hell up?

ORA (*turning to* PERRY): You gonna make me, muthafucka?

PERRY (*stepping to face* ORA): I can. And you better believe it, baby!

ORA: Shit. (*Disparagingly. Moving away from* FARRELL *and back to the center of the room.*) Well you damn sure got your chance right now, you black sonofabitch.

GEORGE (*moves between* PERRY *and* ORA): Oh, goddamit why don't both you guys sit down. You too, Donald.

FARRELL *moves to sit on a radiator beside* HOLMES *and* HINES.

Ora, you wrong, man, and you know it.

ORA: How come I'm wrong, huh? You know goddamn well that skinny cocksucka over there (*at* FARRELL) ain't got no business down here. He ain't gonna do a damn thing but stand around and look.

LOVE (*laughing*): That's all I'm gonna do.

HINES (*hunching* HOLMES *with his elbow*): Yeh, but that's okay for you, Willie. You so black, if you stand still nobody'll know you're standing there anyway.

All laugh. ORA *takes the opportunity to go to the door and crack it open.*

PERRY: Where's the rest of those guys?

HINES: I guess they must still be upstairs in that broom closet.

PERRY: Broom closet?

He and DAVIS *lean against one of the walls and begin to smoke.*

HINES: Yeh, Knowles and Skippy got Karolis upstairs in a

broom closet waiting till everybody leaves the floor I guess.

FARRELL: Jimmy Karolis?

HOLMES: Yeah, that's who we're waiting for. (*Giggles.*)

FARRELL: What the hell's gonna happen then?

ORA (*turning from door*): Man, what the hell you care, huh? Pee-the-bed muthafucka!

HINES: Damn, George!

GEORGE: Damn, what?

HINES: Seems to me like Big Shot's right. You bring this cat down here and he doesn't even know what's happening.

ORA: You goddamn real I'm right. Simple ass cats.

FARRELL: What're you guys gonna gang Jimmy Karolis?

ORA: We gonna break that muthafucka's back.

FARRELL: For what?

ORA: Look man, why don't you shut up and get the hell out of here, huh?

FARRELL: You mean all you guys're gonna jump on Karolis?

ORA (*walking over to* FARRELL *and grabbing him by the shirt*): You gonna stick up for him?

FARRELL *tries to push Ora's hands from his shirt, and though he is much taller than* ORA, ORA *pulls him from his seat.*

FARRELL: Goddamn it, Ora, why don't you cut the shit?

GEORGE: Yeh, Ora, cut it out.

PERRY: Goddamn; that cat's always going for bad.

GEORGE *comes over to restrain* ORA, but ORA *succeeds in punching* FARRELL *in the stomach.* FARRELL *clutches his stomach and sinks to the floor groaning.*

PERRY: (*to* ORA): You bastard.

ORA *swings around to confront him.*

ORA: You come on too, if you want to, you black sonofabitch!

GEORGE *pushes them apart again and his push sends* ORA *rattling heavily against the door.*

Goddamnit, George, why don't you stay the fuck out of this?

GEORGE: Because there wasn't a goddamn reason in the world for you to hit Donald like that. (*Going to help* FARRELL *up.*) Damn, Ora, you're a wrong sonofabitch, you know that?

FARRELL (*still doubled up and holding his stomach. He pulls his arm back when* GEORGE *tries to help him up*): No, man!

Lemme stay here. (*Still groaning.*) Ora, you dirty cocksucker.

ORA: Boy, you better shut up before I stomp mudholes in your pissy ass.

The door is suddenly pushed open and KNOWLES *and* SKIPPY *come in holding* KAROLIS *by the arms.* KAROLIS' *head is hanging, and he is crying softly and blood is on his shirt and face. His hair is mussed and standing all over his head.*

LOVE: Ga-uhd damn! What'd you cats do?

KNOWLES (*giggling stupidly*): Love, now what the hell does it look like we did? Broke this muthafucka's jaw.

HINES: Damn. I thought we were just bringing the cat down here to fight Foots. I didn't know you guys were gonna break his head first.

SKIPPY: Well, he didn't wanna come. We had to persuade him.

KNOWLES: Shit, Skippy, whatta you mean "we"? I did all the persuading.

ORA: Aw, shit, Knowles. I bloodied the cat's lip. You trying to take all the credit.

SKIPPY: Yeh, Knowles. You didn't hit the cat but once, and that was on the goddamn shoulder.

Letting KNOWLES *drag* KAROLIS *into a corner where he lets him drop.*

You know what this cat was doing all the time we was in that goddamn broom closet? Tellin' jokes. (*Laughs.*) They must not a been funny either. Karolis didn't laugh once.

KNOWLES: What should I do with this guy. I gotta drag him everywhere.

ORA: Drop him in that goddamn corner. (*Walks over to corner and nudges* KAROLIS *with his foot.*) Hey, muthafucka. Hey! Why don't you straighten up?

SKIPPPY (*noticing* FARRELL, *who is still crumpled in an opposite corner, but stirring*): Damn! What the hell happened to Donald?

PERRY: That goddamn Big Shot had to show how bad he was.

ORA (*laughing paradoxically*): He called me a nigger.

All laugh.

LOVE: Well, what the hell are you? Wha's the matter, you shamed of your people?

ORA: Fuck you! (*He still stands over* KAROLIS, *nudging him with his foot.*) Hey, man, get up! (*Laughs.*)

HINES: Damn, Ora. Why don't you leave the cat alone?

ORA (*bending over as if to talk in* KAROLIS' *ear)*: Hey, baby, why don't you get up? I gotta nice fat sausage here for you.

GEORGE: Goddamn, Big Shot . . . You really a wrong sonofabitch!

ORA: Look man. (*Now kneeling over the slumped figure.*) If you want to get in on this you line up behind me. I don't give a shit what you got to say.

LOVE: Man, George, leave the cat alone. You know that's his stick. That's what he does (*laughing*) for his kicks . . . rub up against half-dead white boys.

All laugh.

ORA (*looking over his shoulder . . . grudgingly having to smile too*): I'd rub up against your momma too. (*Leaning back to* KAROLIS.) Come on, baby . . . I got this fat ass sa-zeech for you!

LOVE: Ora, you mad cause you don't have a momma of your own to rub up against.

All laugh.

ORA (*turns again, this time less amused*): Fuck you, you bony head sonofabitch. As long as I can rub against your momma . . . or your fatha' (*laughs of his invention*) I'm doin' alright.

Door is pushed open suddenly and FOOTS *comes in. He is nervous but keeps it hidden by a natural glibness and a sharp sense of what each boy in the room expects, singularly, from him. He is the weakest physically and smallest of the bunch, but he is undoubtedly their leader. When* FOOTS *comes in* KAROLIS *looks up quickly, then slumps again.*

HINES: Man, where the hell you been?

FOOTS: That goddamn Van Ness had me in his office. He said I'm a credit to my race. (*Laughs and all follow.*) He said I'm smart-as-a-whip (*imitating Van Ness*) and should help him to keep all you unsavory (*again imitating*) elements in line.

All laugh again.

LOVE: Yeh? What's he talking about?

FOOTS: Well, he seems to think that you guys . . . particularly that goddam Big Shot and Knowles, are not good influences in this joint.

PERRY: Boy, you can say that again. Nutty muthafuckas!

ORA (*to* PERRY): Fuck you, tar baby!

FOOTS: Well, I'm supposed to make sure that you guys don't do anything bad to anybody. Especially to James Karolis. (*Laughing.*)

GEORGE: Oh yeh? He know about that?

FOOTS: Yeh, somebody told him Knowles said he was gonna kick Karolis' ass. (*Seeing* KAROLIS *in the corner for the first time. His first reaction is horror and disgust . . . but he keeps it controlled as is his style, and merely half-whistles.*) Goddamn! What the fuck happened to him? (*He goes over to* KAROLIS *and kneels near him, threatening to stay too long. He controls the impulse and gets up and walks back to where he was. He is talking throughout his action.*) Damn! What'd you guys do, kill the cat?

PERRY: Heavy handed Big Shot again.

FOOTS (*looks at* ORA *quickly with disgust but softens it immediately to comic disdain*): What the hell you hit him with, Ora, a goddamn train?

ORA (*happy at the notice of his destruction*): No, man, I just bopped him in the mouth with the back of my hand.

FOOTS: Ga-uhd damn! You a rough ass cat, Shot. He sure don't look like he's in any way to fight anybody.

ORA (*laughing*): No, but he might be able to suck you off. Hee, hee.

LOVE: Shit. You the one that look like you want that, Big Shot.

FOOTS: Oh, shit. There wasn't any need of bringing the cat down here if you guys were gonna fuck him up before I got here. He was supposed to fight me. (*Almost angry.*)

HINES: Yeh, that's what I thought. You shouldn't of sent Ora and Knowles up after him then.

FOOTS: The only person I asked to go up was Skippy.

SKIPPY: Well, the sonofabitch wouldn't come . . . so, I got Superduck over there to help me. I didn't ask Ora to come. Knowles did.

KNOWLES: Oh, man, the cat's here. Get him up on his feet

(*laughs*) then knock him down. That's all. That don't seem like no big problem to me. (*Through most of the action* KNOWLES *is drumming on the walls or the window or the door or the floor, in a kind of drum and bugle corps beat . . . also supplying the bugle parts vocally.*)

LOVE: Man, Knowles, why don't you stop being a goddamn Elk all the time. Damn. That cat's always drumming on something. Why don't you get a goddamn drum?

KNOWLES: I'm going to drum on your bony head in a little while if you don't shut up.

FOOTS: Well, I don't see any reason to keep all this shit up. Just pour water on the cat and let's get outta here.

ORA: What? You mean you made us go through all this bullshit for nothing?

FOOTS: Well, what the hell am I gonna do, beat on the guy while he's sprawled on the floor. Damn, Ora, you're a pretty lousy sonofabitch.

HINES: Man, Big Shot'd stomp anybody in any damn condition. He likes it when they're knocked out first, especially.

FOOTS: I'm pushed! There's no reason to stay here. I can't fight the guy like he is.

FARRELL (*who has pushed himself up and is leaning against the wall*): I sure am glad somebody's got some sense here.

FOOTS (*seeing* FARRELL *for the first time*): What the hell you doing here? Who asked you to come here, huh? (*Embarrassed and angry.*)

ORA: That stupid ass Perry brought him.

PERRY: That's right. I just thought there was gonna be a fight. I didn't know you guys were gonna lynch anybody.

FOOTS: Lynch, your ass. Look. Donald, why don't you leave, huh? Nobody needs you here.

FARRELL (*slowly*): Yeh, O.K., Ray. But I just want to know why you're gonna beat up on Jimmy like this. What the hell did he do to you?

FOOTS (*almost indignantly*): None of your goddamn business, Farrell. Just leave!

ORA: Yeh, man. I should've thrown your ass out when you first come in here. Pee-the-bed sonofabitch.

FARRELL: O.K. (*Stands up, still lightly holding his stomach.*) O.K. But I want to take Jimmy out of here with me. He can't fight anybody.

ORA: Man, you better shut your goddamn mouth and get outta here!

FOOTS: Look, Donald, just leave, that's all. You hear? (*Turns his back on* FARRELL *and walks toward* KAROLIS, *then thinking better of it turns toward* FARRELL *again.*)

FARRELL: Ray! You're not gonna beat the guy up when he's like that are you?

FOOTS: I don't need you to tell me what to do. (*He goes over and pulls the door open slightly.*) Just get out of here . . . now!

FARRELL (*takes a step then looks toward* KAROLIS): But look at him, he can't do anything. (*To* FOOTS.) Why do you want to do this?

FOOTS: Goddamn it, get out!

FARRELL: That's no answer.

FOOTS: Man, I'll punch you in the belly myself.

FARRELL: Shit. (*Disparagingly . . . which makes* FOOTS *madder.*)

FOOTS (*in low horrible voice*): Goddamn it. You better get the fuck outta here, right now!

FARRELL: Nobody's gonna tell me why? (*He starts to move for the door.*)

PERRY: Look, Donald, you better cool it, buddy. You heard about that letter didn't you?

FARRELL: Letter? What letter?

FOOTS: Man, I told you to leave. I'm not gonna tell you again.

PERRY (*laughing*): The letter Karolis sent Foots telling him he thought he was "beautiful" . . . and that he wanted to blow him.

All giggle.

FARRELL (*turning sharply toward* FOOTS): A letter?

ORA (*rushing at* FARRELL *from the side and punching him*): Goddamn it! Didn't you hear somebody say leave, pee ass?

FOOTS (*pushing between* FARRELL *and* ORA): Cut it out, Ora!

FARRELL (*hurt again and slumping.* ORA *tries to hit him again and the punch is blocked by* FOOTS *who glares savagely at* ORA): A letter? (*Groaning.*) Oh, Ray, come on. Why don't you come off it? (*He is looking up at* FOOTS.)

ORA (*leaps around* FOOTS *and pushes* FARRELL *into the door*): Get out of here, you dumb bastid!

KNOWLES *pulls the door open and shoves* FARRELL *through it.* Goddamn, what a stupid punk. (*He laughs, as do some of the others.*)

FOOTS (*stares at the closed door for a second, then he turns slowly to the others*): Look, let's get out of here. This stuff is finished.

KAROLIS (*has brought his head up during the preceding scuffle, and has been staring at* FOOTS *As* FOOTS *and the others look over toward him, he speaks very softly, but firmly*): No. Nobody has to leave. I'll fight you, Ray. (*He begins to pull himself up. He is unsteady on his feet, but determined to get up . . . and to fight.*) I *want* to fight you.

FOOTS *is startled and his eyes widen momentarily, but he suppresses it.*

HINES: Damn. Some guys don't know when they're well off.

ORA: Yeh. You little skinny muthafucka. You should've kept your mouth shut, and played dead.

KNOWLES: Goddamn. You mean that sonofabitch wasn' dead? Shit, Big Shot, you must hit like a girl.

ORA (*to* KNOWLES): Yeh? Well, let me hit you, you bastid.

KNOWLES (*disparagingly*): Shit.

KAROLIS (*pushing himself off the wall slightly and wiping his face with his sleeve*): No, Ray. Don't have them leave. I want to fight you.

FOOTS (*very silent and stiff, not wanting to be pushed*): Oh? (*Slowly.*) Well, that's damn fine with me.

ORA (*going behind* KAROLIS *and pushing him toward* FOOTS): You wanna fight? Well, go ahead, dick licker. (*Howls.*)

HINES: Yeh, get it on, fellas.

He lunges at FOOTS *and manages to grab him in a choke hold.*) Ray, you said your name was. You said Ray. Right here in this filthy toilet. You said Ray. (*He is choking* FOOTS *and screaming.* FOOTS *struggles and is punching* KAROLIS *in the back and stomach, but he cannot get out of the hold.*) You put your hand on me and said Ray!

SKIPPY: Goddamn, that bastid is choking the shit out of Foots.

The two still struggle, with KAROLIS *continuing to have the advantage.*

HINES: That fuck is trying to kill Foots!

HOLMES: Goddamn it!

ORA (*suddenly leaping on* KAROLIS' *back, puts the same choke hold on him*): You cocksucka . . . how's that feel, huh? (*He pulls* KAROLIS *off of* FOOTS *who falls to his knees.*) Huh?

KNOWLES: Let's kick this cocksucka's ass real good.

He rushes up to help ORA, *and the whole of the crowd surges into the center punching the fallen* KAROLIS *in the face.* KNOWLES *is screaming with laughter.*

KAROLIS: No no, his name is Ray, not Foots. You stupid bastards. I love somebody you don't even know.

He is dragged to the floor. The crowd is kicking and cursing him. ORA *in the center punching the fallen* KAROLIS *in the face.* KNOWLES *is screaming with laughter.*

FOOTS *is now on his hands and knees but his head hangs limply and he is unaware of what is happening. He slumps again.*

They have beaten KAROLIS *enough.* KAROLIS *is spread in the center of the floor and is unmoving.* ORA *drapes some of the wet toilet paper across his body and face.*

ORA: Let's stick the sonofabitch's head in the damn toilet.

PERRY: Oh, man, fuck you. The cat's completely out. What more can you do to him?

GEORGE: Yeh, let's get Foots, and get outta here before somebody comes in.

ORA: Yeh. Hee, hee. Look at ol' Foots. That fuckin' paddy boy almost kilt him.

LOVE: Yeh (*Laughing.*) I told you Karolis was probably bad! *All laugh.*

KNOWLES: Nutty sonofabitch.

LOVE (*picking up* FOOTS, *helped by* HINES *and* HOLMES): Hey, big eye! Get the hell up.

ORA (*takes a paper cup and dips it in the commode and throws it in* FOOTS' *face*) : Yeh, get up, bad ass. (*Laughs.*)

They all leave, as FOOTS *begins to come to. All making noise, laughing, cursing.* KAROLIS *lies as before in the center of the room, motionless.*

After a minute or so KAROLIS *moves his hand. Then his head moves and he tries to look up. He draws his legs up under him and pushes his head off the floor. Finally he manages to get to his hands and knees. He crawls over to one of the commodes, pulls himself up, then falls backward awkwardly and heavily. At this point, the door is pushed open slightly, then it opens completely and* FOOTS *comes in. He stares at* KAROLIS' *body for a second, looks quickly over his shoulder, then runs and kneels before the body, weeping and cradling the head in his arms.*

BLACK

LOUIS WILKINSON

THE BETTER END

[*The scene is a Gentleman's Library. A small company, select, is assembled. One gentleman, somewhat elderly, stands bending near the fire, his head parallel to his knees. Another gentleman, younger, stands behind him, unbent. The trousers of both gentlemen lie gathered about their ankles.*]

It was, the advance to that target, heralded by a preamble somewhat more deferring than he, the bender, would, we might suppose, himself have chosen, though he was not—most indubitably he was not—one to be, on any occasion even remotely imaginable, figured as betraying an eagerness that could emerge, in the least discernibly, as "vulgar". He reflected, indeed, how fine, after a manner, this choice of method—of style and mode—was: and how engaging—how really and perfectly, one might even call it, whimsical—was the way of his friend to rearward, who, while he so bristled, stiffly enough, he safely trusted, to satisfy, most admirably, their common great intent, yet with a kind of reluctant—or, it might be, even coy—patience, stretching tangents, he conceived, unexpectedly this way and unexpectedly that, held so strangely aloof, in the very aloofness none the less conveying the sense of an, at any rate not far from, almost vertiginous precipitancy. Ray Lester had, as the phrase is, the horn; but it strained, this nervous pointer, for him, under what was, in a fashion, an intellectual—could it be?—subjugation: those alert anticipatory fibres, with the quite visible quiver that they had—or indeed, if one were brought to the point of admitting it, the swelling and throbbing—hinted, and more than hinted, at some subtle variation, hardly definable, of a tragic mental tensity; while they submitted none the less—indeed, all the more—to the nicest conditions of some remoter and blander—in a way—influence: or perhaps we may conceive of them, in a more romantic view, enskied, as it were, in some far blue extraordinary recess, where vapours curl thinly, too tenuous—hardly that, though—but quite exquisitely communicative their slender—should we say?—smoke-coils and delicate films of mist. This tensity, then, held, under a certain exterior grossness of mere appearance, a quality definable, after all, as frail; something, indeed, quite undeniably shy and sweet, while with a felicity—how rare this was!—it interrelated aether with lowly matter, and revealed—almost you might believe—the secrets—some at least—of such an interrelation, so magically penetrative, and more than a little likely—in fact, "not half" as they say, "bloody likely"—to pass beyond the reach of any interpreting that one could, in the usual "set terms", express. The older man sustained his posture, cherished his—ah!—anticipations; nor did even the indifferent warmth of that slowly dying fire prove, so far as any of the little party assembled could opine, an affliction to the forbearance that he, so incomparably, guarded.

The, as some might have supposed it, dilatoriness of Ray Lester was, rather, a test to him, to the bender, of the fine endurance, the supremely extensive restraint, that he was able—how magnificently well!—to summon and to stand—how beautifully completely!—by; and it brought about, into the, so to speak, bargain, a superlative emergence, unexpected—oh, "a bit"!—of hidden values, the patency of which was quite blithely vivifying, and therefore welcome utterly, at all tangible points, for the assurance that it, in so luminous an enlightenment, conveyed.

Nor did the fact that, in the end, little would seem to have come of it all, break the real, the unquestioned—unquestionable, even—beauty of this "preparedness" that they had had between them, this perfectly outlined preoccupation, either for Lester or for—more strangely, perhaps? or less?—the other. It could not, this especial situation, this lovely little particular phase of theirs, go on, they knew, forever; and if that devolvulent blanching stain now perceivable upon the space of carpet dividing, yet, the two—Lester had "come", as they say, "off" —may have furnished a consummation that they could not too enthusiastically greet as the most appropriate and, wholly, satisfying that might have been looked for, at least they could recognize it as one worthy—and why not?—of their acceptance; one, indeed, to be—you understand?—bowed to.

"Ah, well, my dear," said the elder, turning and straightening, a little, and glancing forth, as he spoke, the most incalculable of comprehending eye-beams towards his—could one say "companion"? "—ah, well, my dear, so there, you see, we are!"

EDUARDO GUDIÑO KIEFFER

A SINNER'S GUIDE BOOK

She knows it, she knows she's the One and Only of Buenos Aires, *rara avis in terris,* she knows there's no other who can do what she does with the skill she does it; she knows she's the Phoenix, the Chosen One, the Incomparable, the heroic Joan of Arc, but no virgin, thank God;

she knows others exist, sure, she knows it because she herself belongs to that garrulous and multicolor fauna, because secret tropisms pushed her toward closed lodges, mysterious clans, guilds whose passwords are smirks, gasps, and sashaying;

she knows others exist but few of them dare to wear the bracelets, necklaces, beads, plumes, high heels, and fake eyelashes except in clandestine mystical phallic ceremonies while she, the One and Only, can strut all that in public, in front of rows and rows of seats packed with hot bodies with lascivious or jeering eyes; the All Defiant, the All Enlightened and not because of some miraculous Celestial Charity but because of Violet Spots describing a centerstage halo at the Orléans; guided not by Voices but by the Sublime Electronic Music;

and she also knows she has almost or completely magical powers; she knows how that audience shouts obscenities at

Leila (Rita Fuad in real life) while she takes off her veils to the tune of "In a Persian Market"; they stamp and whistle while Yoko (Yolanda Cardoza in real life) takes off her kimono to "Poor Butterfly"; they get worked up to fever pitch while Marilyn (Rosita Kluczinsky in real life) takes off her tight-fitting black dress to "Blues in the Night"; but they grow quiet, surprised at first, and then absolutely fascinated, stupefied, bewitched, wrapping her in an almost frightening silence when the esoteric violet aura is switched on and the choral prelude "Jesu, Joy of Man's Desiring" starts up unexpectedly, solemnly, strangely, anagogically;

that's when she comes out of the shadows to station herself under the lights, in her snow-white, floor-length tunic and her jewels like scapulars, like medallions, and her fluttering false silky eyelashes and her ceremonial high heels and the languid wig; she comes forward and hardly begins to move to the contemplative phrasing of the chords;

first raise the right arm then the left in immolation and holocaust let the hair fall forward covering the face bending the head slowly push out the hip advance the leg letting the taut muscle be seen through the furtive slit; oh anointed priestess in the androlatrous ritual of her own adoration, first take off the earrings then the necklaces then the bracelets then one shoe then the other to the beat of the holy sacrifice, and the crowd's silence getting denser moment by moment and the music more overwhelming moment by moment essentially more and more Bach moment by moment interpreted by Walter Carlos on the Moog neosynthesizer and toward the end of the two minutes and fifty-seven seconds which is exactly how long the number lasts let the white tunic drop dramatically turn away from the audience unsnap the bra turn around again facing the thousand-headed monster silenced transported hypnotized modestly covering the breasts with both arms and now without uncovering it with one arm lower the other sllloooowllly slloowlly until loosening the small rose on the panties and then with a properly miraculous precision "Jesu, Joy of Man's Desiring" ends and the spots go off and the violet halo is extinguished and the darkness covers her total nudity with mourning clothes and crepe and she runs off between the teasers and quickly puts on the raincoat she left hanging there on a nail just for that purpose;

she also knows that during those two seconds after the lights go out, those two clocked seconds, silence will reign over the orchestra of the Orléans like smoke from the cigarettes, like the echo of that already faded music; and then someone will clap and applause from those who have realized for the very first time that strip tease can be something like a solemn mass, a votive mass, a mass of purification with the body present;

she also knows (although she'd like to forget it) that the applause would roar out of a maddened beast if the light didn't go out at exactly the right moment and if the public discovered the truth, that deceitful truth or, better said, that painful reality she feels between her legs while walking toward the dressing room, oh God, dear God of my soul how mean you were to me when you put this right here, what do I want with something so lovely on men so useless on me, why do you make me feel more of a woman than any woman and you stuck a prick where I'd like to have something else, warm and loving;

sure, the applause would roar out and she would die, crushed by the cheated furious irate iconoclastic crowd and maybe it would be beautiful to die like that with all those sweaty drunken ferocious men on top, stepping on her, spitting on her, and tearing at her;

but the lights always go out on time and she goes to the dressing room (the girls, her associates, say "changing room," but she prefers to say dressing room, it's so much more elegant, so much more aristocratic, dressing room instead of changing room, maybe Sarah Bernhardt had a changing room, no, surely she had a dressing room, maybe Maria Callas has a changing room, but enough of that);

and in the dressing room the noisy chatterboxes talking complaining it's disgraceful three thousand pesos a day and on my last tour of Central America I was earning a thousand dollars a month; shut up what're you talking about Central America for if you never made it past Berazategui; it's easy to see you're blabbing out of jealousy, what's happening is if you keep getting fatter you're not going to be able to strip any more, who's going to pay to see cellulitis, and the laughing and the nasty cracks and did'ja get a load of that and, but what a thing to say;

and when she enters and sits down in front of the mirror and begins to take off her makeup with Aqualane even though Aqualane is used for other necessities, there's a very short silence having nothing to do with the great majestic silence in the theater; a short silence caused by the fact that the others, even doing what she is doing, would love to feel as feminine as she does;

and while she makes the blush and rouge and shadow disappear with a slow and circular massaging of her fingertips on her forehead, on her cheeks, on her neck, the others watch waiting for that ridiculous and sublime moment that is repeated like a sacrament every night;

that moment she waits for too, a martyr facing the lions, a sacrificial victim;

that moment which should also have some background music because it is the moment of true nudity, awesome solemn Wagnerian music that would make the last interior masks fall away:

THE MOMENT OF TAKING OFF THE WIG

now,

like this;

and what is it as if they don't know by heart, as if I haven't repeated it every night these last three years;

take it off suddenly, with a quick jerk, in a defiant gesture that exposes her skull where two or three stray hairs do not cover the miserable premature baldness, sign of a masculinity unchosen but inevitable;

that moment;

she with the wig in her hand looking at the others with a blank stare, the others lowering their eyes as if ashamed suddenly breaking the silence with small talk, something about the weather or about the fat man in the front row, anything;

and little by little the return to normality, she taking off the false eyelashes now with Johnson's Baby Oil, as good for her very delicate eyelids as for very delicate babies' rear ends;

the others beginning to ask her things and she replying as if she were the lonely-hearts column, answering Yoko (Yolanda Cardoza in real life) who consults her about whether it's worthwhile to give up the Orléans and devote herself to studying anthropology, or listening to the moaning of Leila (Rita Fuad in real life) who complains that men are all the same or ducking the innuendos of Marilyn (Rosita Kluczinsky in real life) who attacks her because she's envious, of course;

but the one sure thing is that when all is said and done they all depend on her, all revolve around her, the One and Only of Buenos Aires, *rara avis in terris,* Phoenix, Joan of Arc;

the One and Only capable of imagining that it's possible to strip to Bach put to electronic music;

the One and Only capable of dominating that dragon audience;

the One and Only whose sex is a false sex and yet more genuine than the female bearers of a genuine sex;

the only One and Only;

Corybant at the mad feast of Cybele, druid in the forest of skyscrapers, hierophant officiating at secret ceremonies;

Pope Joan on a canopied throne but on the pyre every day as well, on the sacrificial altar ready to receive a dagger in the center of her breast;

the only One and Only;

who's now entirely clean of makeup, entirely divested of wig, high heels, and false eyelashes, who now stands up, letting the raincoat slip off, who with perfect naturalness walks naked in front of the others who don't even look at her because they're so used to her by now, who walks trying to move her skimpy buns as if they were the mighty buttocks of the others, showing off what she doesn't have and embarrassing herself with what she does have, oh God my God how mean you were to me;

heading toward the locker where the striped pants pink shirt sandals are that she'll wear on the street because obviously, on the street you can't dress like a woman even if you'd like to;

listening to the little cries of the others the goodbyes of the others who and, dressed now, watching them with her head thrown back and the right eyebrow disdainfully raised like Maria Felix as an Aztec deity, sweeping them with a circular gaze, a fiery gaze that could incinerate these other poor women for no more than being just that: women;

and flinging a half languid, half scornful ciao that drops in the midst of Leila, Yoko, and Marilyn like a wilted carnation that tears out the other carnations, other flowers other ciao sweetheart see you tomorrow, good luck, hope something turns up, hope everything goes well, see ya', good night;

and going out on to the street and crossing over to the bar to dial a number on the payphone;

beep beeep beep beep busy;

then sitting down at the usual table asking Mario for the usual Mario coffee please

Mario attentive bringing her the coffee asking how're you how're things going;

sweetheart, things are always pretty good, justa little tired, you know, when a lady's an artist;

a startled customer who turns around hearing the hoarse voice refer to herself in the feminine gender, when the voice as well as the appearance indicate the masculine;

she winking an accomplice eye at Mario and another devilish eye at the customer and the customer turning red up to here and burying himself in the pages of *La Razón* and Mario's accomplice smile;

the hot coffee does her good, stimulates her stomach, awakens the gratifying memory of her strip tease, the only number of the One and Only, others would've liked to have had the idea, but what were they going to do, so few like classical music, so few who'd think of using Bach for the art of stripping in public;

ten minutes and to the telephone again, once again to dial the number engraved in her memory and now, yes, ringing, one, two, three, then the click and his sleepy voice:

hello who's it;

and she the only One and Only suddenly quaking shivering timid trembling Joan of Arc defeated, handed over letting herself be condemned, yearning for the burning flames, pronouncing just one word:

love;
oh, it's you;
love, tell me that you love me;
shit, you want to be flattered at this hour;
I'm done now, I'm coming out there, I want to see you, please let me in don't be mean;
look, you nut, I'm really tired;
please, sweetheart;
go fuck yourself;
oh cruel stab, oh another click from him when he hangs up, oh injustice, oh pain, oh broken heart;
suddenly wilted, humiliated, repentant, hurt alone
paying for the coffee while Mario looks on sympathetically
going out on to the street alone
walking to the bus stop alone
getting on the bus alone
riding alone
getting off the bus alone
entering her two-room apartment in the Abasto, right there on Gardel Street alone;
looking at the photo of Manfredi under the glass on the bedside table alone;
getting ready for bed alone;
looking at herself in the mirror, seeing herself alone;
alone alone so alone,
and to top it off bald.

—Translated by
Ronald Christ and
Gregory Kolovakos

THOM GUNN

MODES OF PLEASURE

New face, strange face, for my unrest.
I hunt your look, and lust marks time
Dark in his doubtful uniform,
Preparing once more for the test.

You do not know you are observed:
Apart, contained, you wait on chance,
Or seem to, till your callous glance
Meets mine, as callous and reserved.

And as it does we recognize
That sharing an anticipation
Amounts to a collaboration—
A warm game for a warmer prize.

Yet when I've had you once or twice
I may not want you any more:
A single night is plenty for
Every magnanimous device.

CALAMUS

Why should that matter? Why pretend
Love must accompany erection?
This is a momentary affection,
A curiosity bound to end,

Which as good-humored muscle may
Against the muscle try its strength
—Exhausted into sleep at length—
And will not last long into day.

FEVER

Impatient all the foggy day for night
  You plunged into the bar eager to loot.
A self-defeating eagerness: you're light,
  You change direction and shift from foot to foot,
Too skittish to be capable of repose
  Or of deciding what is worth pursuit.

Your mother thought you beautiful, I suppose,
  She dandled you all day and watched your sleep.
Perhaps that's half the trouble. And it grows:
  An unattended conqueror now, you keep
Getting less beautiful toward the evening's end.
  The boy's potential sours to malice, deep
Most against those who've done nothing to offend.
  They did not notice you, and only I
Have watched you much—though not as covert friend
  But picturing roles reversed, with you the spy.

The lights go up. What glittering audience
  Tier above tier notices finally
Your ragged defeat, your jovial pretence?
  You stand still, but the bar is emptying fast.
Time to go home babe, though now you feel most tense.
  These games have little content. If you've lost

It doesn't matter tomorrow. Sleep well. Heaven knows
  Feverish people need more sleep than most
And need to learn all they can about repose.

THE MIRACLE

"Right to the end, that man, he was so hot
That driving to the airport we stopped off
At some McDonald's and do you know what,
We did it there. He couldn't get enough."
—"There at the counter?"—"No, that's public stuff:

"There in the rest room. He pulled down my fly,
And through his shirt I felt him warm and trim.
I squeezed his nipples and began to cry
At losing this, my miracle, so slim
That I could grip my wrist in back of him.

"Then suddenly he dropped down on one knee
Right by the urinal in his only suit
And let it fly, saying Keep it there for me,
And smiling up. I can still see him shoot.
Look at that snail-track on the toe of my boot."

—"Snail-track?"—"Yes, there."—"That was six months ago
How can it still be there?"—"My friend, at night
I make it shine again, I love him so,
Like they renew a saint's blood out of sight.
But we're not Catholic, see, so it's all right."

SONG

SAN FRANCISCO STREETS

I've had my eye on you
  For some time now.

You're getting by it seems,
  Not quite sure how.
But as you go along
  You're finding out
What different city streets
  Are all about.

Peach country was your home.
  When you went picking
You ended every day
  With peach fuzz sticking
All over face and arms,
  Intimate, gross,
Itching like family,
  And far too close.

But when you came to town
  And when you first
Hung out on Market Street
  That was the worst:
Tough little group of boys
  Outside Flagg's shoes.
You learned to keep your cash.
  You got tattoos.

Then by degrees you rose
  Like country cream—
Hustler to towel boy,
  Bath house and steam;
Tried being kept a while—
  But felt confined,
One brass bed driving you
  Out of your mind.

Later on Castro Street
  You got new work
Selling chic jewelry.
  And as sales clerk

You have at last attained
   To middle class.
(No one on Castro Street
   Peddles his ass.)

You gaze out from the store.
   Watching you watch
All the men strolling by
   I think I catch
Half veiled uncertainty
   In your expression.
Good looks and great physique
   Pass in procession.

You've risen up this high—
   How, you're not sure.
Better remember what
   Makes you secure.
Fuzz is still on the peach,
   Peach on the stem.
Your looks looked after you.
   Look after them.

MAARTEN 'T HART

BROTHERS IN ARMS

We walk in the spacious garden. There is no wind. The summer is almost too hot. The dark-green leaves of the creeper on the wall of the house are drooping, limp and heavy. The humming of the insects sounds dull and menacing, but very summery. The woman strolling with Arthur in the summer sunlight among blooming flowers is me. What a marvelous feeling!

We sit down at the bottom of the garden in the tall grass beside a broad ditch. The grass gives way to reeds. The ditch is completely overgrown with green-brown duckweed. Flowering rush and bur reed are growing in the ditch. Further down I see arrowhead and water crowfoot. Two eyes peer at me from the surface of the water. I move. The frog vanishes. In the place where it has dived into the depths there is, for a brief moment, a small, dark opening in the duckweed that quickly closes again. On the other side of the water there is a hedge with hedge-bells growing along it. The brilliant white flowers stand out sharply against the green leaves.

"Sweet girl," Arthur says mockingly but cheerfully, tenderly. He strokes my blond hair. He puts his arm round me. I don't move. His caresses grow more intense and I submit to them without guilt. I think of the shower. When he caressed me for the first time, I found it wonderful, but I felt guilty. Men doing shameful things with other men. Even though I am not religious, the guilt feelings remain. Later, too, I always felt guilty: in bed in the dormitory when we lay next to each other while the others slept, in the tent during the field exercise. I thought I would always experience it as something wonderful that would nonetheless make you feel sinful. But not now. The more he caresses me the more I feel myself a woman. It is now easier, too, for me to overcome my fear at my own actions. Feeling guilty made me passive. I am still not as active as he is; I shall never be able to be very active because I am a woman. I know it is a myth, passive women. But in my case the myth is true. I still feel a vague kind of remorse because I cannot honestly and brutally live out my homosexuality but have to make use of this subterfuge, a subterfuge through which I place myself even further outside the world of ordinary, healthy people who are repelled by everything they do not understand. It will probably never be possible without guilt, without remorse. Maybe it would not be as good then, either.

I lie on my belly and press my face into the prickly, aromatic grass. A grasshopper is sitting on a blade of grass close to me. I gaze at the leaves of a buttercup as if I had never seen them before. Do they have feather-shaped veins, I think, are they pinnate-veined? Are the leaves crenate? It is curious that I cannot think of anything but pinnate-veined and crenate leaves when I reach the climax and Arthur's hands disappear, and I remain still and I am not tired.

We lie side by side in the grass. Arthur hums a tune. The sun is warm on my face. The clouds hang threateningly over us. Who was it who said that man is sad after an orgasm?

"Arthur, are you sad?"

"No," he says, "why should I be?" The sound of his voice is almost tender. His eyes are closed. He laughs easily.

"Were you thinking about the famous proverb that everyone is sad after coitus? But that wasn't coitus."

"No," I say, "that's true."

"That saying was probably invented by the dutifully married who went whoring."

He falls silent, I think about the future. I still have another year and a half in the army with Arthur. And after that? Why should I not be able to go on living with Arthur afterwards?

"Are we going to live together, Arthur, when we get out of the army?"

"That's still a long way off," he says.

Does my question irritate him? I get that impression from the slight wrinkling of his eyebrows. But I am dreaming of my future with Arthur, I am lost in a reverie and see him and myself in the same house, where I am living as a woman. My imagination goes no further. I dare not let it go any further even if I should like to. Other images rise up before me, images of long ago, and I notice with astonishment that even my memories are different now that I am wearing these clothes. I go far back in time, I am four years old and I am walking from our house to the Nieuwe Weg. Along the Nieuwe Weg are a great many poppies. I have often gathered flowers for my mother. I love my mother even if she is often ill-tempered and unfriendly. I had picked dandelions and daisies for her and she had said, "Thank you," but she was never really happy with the flowers. But then they had only been small flowers, weeds. Now I can pick poppies for her. How lovely she will think the poppies are! Big, red flowers, no common, everyday flowers. I gather poppies for my mother, a great bunch. I also pick buds, lots of buds. They will open at home. I run back with my bunch of flowers. I can hardly carry the big bouquet. I am very happy to be able to give my mother these poppies. How excited she will be. She will say, "What pretty flowers, Ammer, I have never seen such pretty flowers." Perhaps my mother will give me a kiss for bringing her flowers. After all, other mothers also kiss when they receive something nice from their children. I reach home. I can scarcely carry the bouquet any longer. In the corridor of our house I call, "Mother, flowers!"

My mother opens the door of the living-room. "What are those? Poppies? Nasty, poisonous flowers. They make opium from them. Dangerous flowers! Throw those flowers away at once! Throw them in the trash pit in front of the house. And the buds? What are they?"

"Poppies, too."

"Into the pit. Out with the flowers. Not in my house. Out with them!" She pushes me along the corridor. She shows me the trash pit beside the edge of the steps. A lid with small square holes lies on top of the pit. "In here," she says imperiously.

I cannot thrust many of the flowers into the trash pit at the same time. I do not want to, either. I take each flower separately in my right hand. Slowly I let it drop into the pit, first the long stem and then the red flower. With each flower that I let fall, a part of the love for my mother disappears. How I had loved my mother! But the bouquet is so big—so many flowers that they use up all my love for my mother.

I sit on the edge of the steps for a long time, looking at the flowers under the grating. They are wilting. Perhaps she would have taken the buds if I had not said that they were poppies, too.

I had never before realized that I loved my mother so much. Now I discover it, now that I am a woman myself and see such indistinct images before me. I am sitting with my mother and my aunts on a Sunday afternoon in the sunlight beside the canal. Are there other little nephews and nieces as well? My mother is wearing a white dress, white as the billowing sails of the boats that sail by, and I look at my mother, I cannot keep my eyes off my mother and I stroke the white cloth of her dress with my hands. I cannot remember any more. What a discovery! I loved my mother.

I was cured of loving her because she did not want my flowers. Could my lying here in the grass with a blond wig on my head be the result of this perverted love?

Arthur puts an end to these reminiscenses. He says, "Dressing in women's clothes goes very deep, I think. Do you know the story of the two men in Auschwitz who were missing from rollcall? They had dressed themselves as women. Of course it wasn't very difficult, everybody was naked and so thin that the breasts had gone. A few rags were enough. Terrific consternation among the camp leaders: two men were missing. When it was eventually discovered what the two men had done, everyone laughed and thought it a good joke. But the Nazi killers executed the whole group the two had belonged to. Yes, you never knew if it was in fact only for fun that the guys had dressed as women. It began as a joke but the result was to be killed. It can never be a joke, I think, it always has serious consequences. Come, let's go indoors. We'll listen to Wagner now."

"Wagner?"

"Yes, it's lacking in your education."

"Flashy, pretentious music."

"You don't know what you're talking about."

As we go back into the house we tease each other, the kind of quarreling that can exist only between people who are very fond of each other. I do not protest when he wants to listen to *Die Walküre,* and before we can begin we first have to look for the score. Searching through piles of old music is a delightful occupation, especially on a Sunday afternoon in summer when, from time to time, with a nonchalant, absentminded feminine gesture you have to tuck your hair back because it keeps falling over your eyes. When doing it you hear the clinking of the bracelet and feel the movement of the earrings.

"What a collection of music," I say.

"Not bad," Arthur says, "yes, we have quite a lot."

"But no Bach," I say.

"Boy, you and your everlasting Bach."

"I'm not a boy."

"That's true. You're a woman in a man's body that you have managed to camouflage very well. It is really crazy that now you're like this you're much more natural than in normal circumstances, you're less inhibited than normally, less turned into yourself. I should feel like saying, take them off. Now that you've done it, it's going to be harder to play your usual role. Each time you dress up makes it more impossible to live normally."

"Then there is a better solution, I must go on living as a woman, I must let my hair grow. I think it will be a success."

"Yes, I'm sure it would work very well," says Arthur, "too well. You'd have to go to the Johns Hopkins Institute in Baltimore. You can have an operation that will change you into a woman. You go to Baltimore and come back with Nobalmore. I bet you would be very good in the role of a housewife. Still, it's an idiotic idea. But tell me something, would you really want to be a woman?"

"I have never thought very deeply about it. There were always dreams of being a woman; but now that I've seen how happy I am, I have discovered how much I'd like to be a woman."

"So you see that by dressing as a woman you have made yourself conscious of a desire that scarcely existed before. With each succeeding disguise it will grow stronger, the longing to be a woman, and finally you will be a hopeless transsexual, somebody who, no matter what the cost, will want to be freed from his manhood, first from his sexual organs and then all the rest. You are still happy now, but then you will be so miserable! And supposing it succeeds, in Baltimore or Casablanca or wherever, afterwards there will be the difficulties with the registration authorities. And why would you want to be a woman now?"

"I could be married to a strong man, mentally strong, I mean, and then I could be a bit protected."

"Jesus, Ammer, what a nineteenth-century ideal: the strong man, the weak woman. Put the clock back and make everything that women are fighting for undone. That's really a sign of weakness in you, of impotence. But I accept it from you because it is real. You are simply that way, you really do have something of a helpless child that makes people like you. I truly believe it is a pity for you that you weren't born a woman. But you can also look after yourself perfectly well, you don't need the protection of a strong man at all."

"You say that, but right from the first days in the army you always stood up for me when the others were putting me down."

"Is that true? Give me an example."

"At breakfast on the second day a boy from an earlier draft

said that when I was on the assault course I lay down dead after the first obstacle. He was putting me down but you began . . ."

"Yes, I remember. Now that you mention it, situations like that cropped up later, too. And with Marijke . . . How crazy, I never realized it. But it's my fault, I'm always talking out of turn, I never give you a chance to say anything."

"I thought it was very nice of you to stand up for me like that."

"You should have protested! I'll have to think about it. Let's listen to Wagner, though."

The music of *Die Walküre* is just as pathos-laden, heavy and barbaric as I imagine Wagner to be. I don't like Wagner, I shall never like Wagner. But Arthur is sitting beside me on a low bench and he holds the score with one hand while I turn the pages and with his other hand he holds me pressed against him except when he changes a record. How long the opera is! I lose consciousness of time, I look at the staves of music but hardly listen to the music, I am lost in a reverie. I imagine things that cannot happen: I have an operation in Baltimore and come back and live in this house with Arthur and see children before me and am ashamed of these naive fantasies that rise up unhindered and easily within me; a kind of crystalline dreaming, slightly sad, slightly mournful and not intense but with a sudden affinity with the music at the point when the opera is almost finished and Arthur has said, "Now for the most beautiful part." The music is a soft whispering. A constantly repeated motif, with a horn suddenly playing a related motif, and I am completely amazed because it is so inexpressibly beautiful. It is a lyrical instrumental intermezzo, a fragment of music that conjures up lights gliding past over dark waters. Afterwards a male voice sings the motif of a moment ago and it is repeated again but faster now, more passionately, so that my dreams, too, grow more rapid and the former sadness turns to melancholy and I feel the tears welling up in my eyes. For two days now I have been living as a different person. Am I unable to bear it? I cry without making a sound. I feel the make-up mixing with the moisture from my eyes.

Arthur looks at me. "Ammer, you're crying! Why are you crying?"

"I don't know. The music . . . It's because it's so overwhelming, to be sitting here, and being a woman . . ."

But that is not it, it is not because of what I am now but because of what I have never been, because of my unhapy youth, because of all the possibilities that have never been realized and also because of the farewell to youth, because of the sudden weight of a genuine relationship with another person, an undertaking that has been so difficult for me, which is why I am wearing these clothes and have run away from my true self, not having dared simply to be myself.

I let myself fall back on the bench and cry like a child with long, racking sobs. My body is convulsed.

"Are you crazy, Ammer? Stop it!"

"Let me," I say. "I need to have a good cry, I have never had a friend with whom I could listen to music like this. Can't we stay here, Arthur, can't I stay with you always? I would like to do that so much . . ." Crying makes it difficult to speak.

"Are you as over-sensitive, too?" Arthur says.

"As who?"

"As the girl, Marijke. She also sat here one evening, in the same place, she also cried and said, 'Arthur, when are we going to get married? I want to stay with you always.' Do I have to keep on running into hysterical women who want to change a pleasant friendship into a kind of eternal marriage? You're howling as hysterically as that girl. Goddamn it, Ammer, these clothes haven't done you any good. They show you for what you are—a spineless, hysterical woman. I think it's disgusting. In my opinion you're crying because it's too much for you. You simply can't take the luxury of a simple relationship with another person; you're behaving exactly like someone who is experiencing a homosexual friendship for the first time. I believe it would be better for us to give each other more freedom. We're chained together like two love-sick fools. The others are noticing it and making fun of us. It wouldn't be so bad if you weren't always talking about the future. 'I always want to be with you.' I find that so damned boring. To tie yourself down now for more than a year and a half. Stop it, you crybaby. What is it now?"

"Why do you always say that?"

"I've had enough of it. You cling to me as if I were saving your life. You really behave just like those dumb girls."

"Dumb girls?"

"Yes. Marijke was not my first girl friend and I hope she won't be the last, either. The only thing is, from now on I must be sure they won't immediately start talking about 'for always' and adorable things like that. Do you know what I'll do with the stupid girls? I'll throw them out. I shouldn't have to do that. But between two sobs they tell you they love you. God, what a lousy kind of love. That anyone could humiliate himself like that before someone else. Love! Rubbish. People should have fun with each other and not make use of the big words and especially not want to tie each other up in a permanent relationship. I hate crying women, Ammer, and anyway I think we've been much too intimate with each other. We sit feeding each other on childhood memories like love-sick turtle doves. Do you know what we'll do? We'll give it a rest from now on, we'll both look for someone else. One of these days they're going to throw us out of the army because we . . . That's something I certainly want to prevent. You have all sorts of problems afterwards, too. I don't intend letting my life be wrecked by you, letting some homosexual or other who has never had a relationship with anyone and clings to me like a madman and sits howling like a child screw up my future. Howling like a child. But why, actually?"

Although I hear his outburst, I can barely grasp the sense of what he says, even if the words that generate new and stronger expressions engrave themselves deeply in my memory. The words do not yet have any connection with the strange, uncontrollable grief, this sudden, appallingly clear glimpse of my past. But the misery is also because of the pent-up tension of the past six weeks, it is because of Arthur, walking with Sergeant Eelwout and talking about the girl Marijke, it is because of the hopeless transformation that has taken place and through which, now that I am a woman, I am suddenly able to give expression to all my repressed feelings. Now I have a right to my jealousy, a right to my friendship with Arthur. But he does not understand it, he is shocked by the tears, he is only talking and in him, too, repressed emotions come to the surface, but of a different kind than mine. I am crying in order to express my feelings, he talks, but you don't exorcize demons with words.

He is still talking. "I am almost certain they all know already. Sergeant Eelwout made an insinuation about our friendship when we were playing billiards in the café and I think they're only waiting for a suitable opportunity to catch us. But you have never done anything to hide it, and neither have I, like the idiot I am, because somehow I felt sorry for you, you were such a damned nice fellow . . . But now I see it all differently, now I see the other side of the niceness: cowardice, pettiness. Now I see that you're just like everyone else, that you'll be damned if you'll accept that all friendship is a thing that remains free, not some kind of passion like Tristan and Isolde. We haven't swallowed a love potion. Man, pull yourself together. Take off those clothes, you have given yourself away in them."

"Arthur, don't say any more now, shut up now . . ."

"I, shut up?" My request releases new rage. He continues, "I will not shut up, I should have told you much sooner, I was only waiting for the right moment. I hadn't intended to be so hard on you but tears scare me to death. I keep on seeing the girls in front of me, especially Marijke. They throw themselves, they lie at your feet crying. 'Arthur,' they say, 'I love you, say something. Why don't you say something?' I'm expected to talk, too. They try to cage you in with their heart-rending sobbing, to tie you to them and you, you're no different with your inane whining, your jealous hysterics. I must say, it suits you, that part of the drag show is very well done."

I am not really surprised at his words. I have always sensed a menacing undertone in his speech. He had often talked about Marijke Reehorst, a sort of veiled warning. And yet, his words hurt now. He cannot take them back, they have been spoken. They will go on sinking more deeply into me, go on tormenting me more and more. Why is he saying all this? Is it due to my hysterical crying or has he, now that I've let myself go like this, seized the opportunity of ridding himself of me, something he has wanted to do for a long time but has not dared? Arthur not dare anything? Could that be true? Could he really have been afraid of hurting me? That could only be true if he had liked me. This last thought intensifies the pain caused by his words.

"Listen," he says, "you have got to stop now, enough is enough. Drink some water. Wash your face. I can't bear to look at you. I'm leaving, I'll go and fetch us something to eat at a Chinese place in Amsterdam. Meanwhile you can get hold of yourself a bit and take off those clothes, that seems the best thing to do. I'll fetch your uniform from the car and put it in the kitchen. I'll be back soon."

In the bathroom I look at my face in the mirror. A wreck. But with my puffy eyes and smeared make-up I am a real woman. I stare at the reflection. I comb the hair. I cannot take leave of myself. The tears start to flow again, now because of Arthur's monologue. An hysterical woman! I let cold water run down beside my eyes. I have a headache. My eyes sting. I walk back into the living-room. I sit down by the window. Spineless, hysterical woman. Two love-sick fools. The stupid girls. I throw them out. What a lousy sort of love! I don't intend letting my life be ruined by you, my life . . . We have already been too intimate with each other. Why not? I think, why must you not be too intimate with each other? Can you ever be too intimate? A jealous hysteric. Why has he insulted me like this? Why did he have to touch that sensitive spot? I felt so happy in this disguise, even if a little insecure, and was only waiting for some recognition of its genuineness. "Hysterical woman," he said. In this way he acknowledged its authenticity. I go to the kitchen, I pick up the uniform from a chair and walk to the bathroom. I get undressed, wash the make-up from my face and take off the wig. Slowly I transform myself into a soldier and loathe the sloppy trousers, the beige shirt, the stock and the jacket that I do not put on yet. I carry the clothes and the wig to the kitchen. I lay them carefully down on a chair. In a little while we will take them back to the Zwanenburgerstraat. I take my artificial fingernails and fake eyelashes into the garden. With my hands I make a hole in the ground next to a rosebush. I bury the nails and the eyelashes.

—Translated by
Derek Yeld

YVES NAVARRE

LUC

The bigger the city, the more the young men feel at home there. This is the biggest cradle Luc has ever known. Yet get lost in it. A cradle of corners of streets and avenues, with toy boxes all over the place and shady nooks where baby can go to sleep with his arms spreadeagled or held outstretched. Papa is there, tall as tall, with something sticking out in front of him. Everything starts again from scratch. It is raining and in a few seconds the city becomes human: it looks at its reflection and assesses its own beauty. The cradle is wet and Luc is happy. He exists.

He will take the Downtown road again, trudging through the rain. He will arrive there soaked, clammy, feverish. He will arrive behind the evening trucks ahead of all the others. He will wait there in a corner, sitting on an oil-drum with his feet on a pile of planks. He will watch the rain disturb the surface of the puddles. He will tap his fists against the palms of his hands, as though he's messed up one appointment and was sure he'd miss out on the next. What had Rasky meant when he left him? 'Go away, Luc, I don't want to see you any more . . .' Was he to come back tomorrow or the day after? Or true to their pattern of parallel affinities, should he go on alone with hands in pockets and a truant conscience, never asking any more questions, with the vague remembrance of a friend he once met on the way, his travelling companion for nearly fifteen years? The rain fell twice as hard. Luc took cover under a truck and squatted down with his hands clasped under his chin. It is Saturday. He counts up the days, then works them out again, it's Saturday night all right, a time for rendezvous of all kinds. Everyone's out. Cramp. Luc shifts his position. A handsome Negro comes and crouches next to him. He stuffs a popper up his nose, then holds it out to Luc, who contemplates the two-pronged capsule. Luc sticks it into his nose like a plug into a socket and inhales ferociously. The effect is instantaneous: the city becomes a pin-cushion spinning around in the troubled sky of the puddles. And the raindrops turn into bloodstains. Beneath the truck the ground is hard and dry: Luc lies full length. The guy crawls right up against him, opening his jacket, bare-chested. Luc pinches his nipples, two large pieces of confetti, pink against the black skin. 'Harder!' Luc bites them. The guy groans, with his left hand undoes Luc's clothing and plants one prong of the popper in Luc's nostril. 'Go on, have a good sniff!'

The truck, childhood, that gigantic piano which Luc would hide under with his special treats, a lump of cane sugar or a piece of quince cheese, on Thursday afternoons when he was bored, with all his lessons learnt and all his homework done, and it was raining and the visit to the Musée Carnavalet was off and Maman would ask Nanny where Luc was. 'I don't know, Madame.' Luc was hiding under the piano, in the drawing-room under the piano, that musical coffin on which nobody played, forsaken, out of tune, a memorial in a room for the living. Luc hid there with his afternoon snack. At school he was a good pupil. A well-behaved child. On the day of his First Holy Communion the chaplain gave him an art-book, *The Shrine of Saint Ursula,* fifteen reproductions in colour, with the following inscription on the fly-leaf: 'For Luc, who I am sure will always be as good as these pictures.' Pictures of fire, of pin-cushions, blood and martyrdom. Luc was to tear out the fly-leaf and then hide the beautiful book so that no-one should ever know what it was that he secretly refused and desired. Pictures of towns going up in flames . . .

The guy slaps Luc, 'Hey, man!' He is biting Luc's ear and Luc grasps him by the hair and twines himself round him. With concertinaed trousers masking their shoes and their clothes scattered about they lie face to face, outspread hand clamped on outspread hand, and they kiss as if kissing their own image in a mirror. Poppers again. Luc pulls himself up and bangs his head against the steel casing of this travelling piano. He is bleeding. The other guy licks the graze on his forehead. Luc is not sure whether he has hurt himself or whether it is his heart that has leapt into his head and is drumming a tattoo. He lies flat and the guy takes him like a woman, from the front, gently, very gently. Canoeing down the Mississippi. Watch out, don't rock the boat or it's going to capsize in that river of rain. This time Luc shuts his eyes, he no longer belongs anywhere. He can feel this boy on top of him, plunging. And the boy puts a yellow pill on Luc's tongue. 'Come on, swallow it, get that saliva flowing and swallow.' Silence. 'Come on, come on!' The fellow braces his back. With one fingertip he strokes the wounded brow, there under the piano that hides you and kills. And wounds. 'If the truck moved off, if the truck ran over me, I'd be a puddle.'

Caresses. Afterwards. The guy lights a cigarette. He rolls his jacket into a ball and slips it under Luc's neck. Luc opens his eyes. Crouching all round them, new arrivals are taking everything in. Motionless. Scared. Dazed. Conniving. Speechless. The great *soirée* is about to begin. Luc feels his trouser pockets. He has lost his keys, his wallet. Now he cannot even raise a smile. He lies back. His partner licks his navel, then all round it in ever-widening circles. Every now and again he moistens his tongue and then resumes. Concentric circles. Luc feels himself swept into the vortex. Hudson. Deep waters in the Port of New York. Black waters. Negro.

Negro is sitting cross-legged. Luc is sprawling in front of him, his head resting between the other fellow's legs, the back of his neck against his fly. It is still raining. The truck makes a curious canopy, which could start in New York and finish in the inner suburbs of Mexico City: the biggest truck in the world, the biggest Big Top on earth, the Lucus Sexus Circus and its whipping pricks, a new show every half-hour. It is played out on a north-south axis, in the recumbent position, the head clamped between the folded legs of the other creature, the black-jacketed scurbius with its black penis and shiny black skin. Negro, chocolate blackamoor: coarse-grained, vanilla-scented skin, lips like little cushions of tender flesh, a body veiled for a funeral. The ceremony is beginning. Crawling, on their knees, or with their legs upright but bending at the waist, arms hanging limply or jerking into action, here come the robots, the others, the voyeurs, visitors to the interminable truck, a steel umbrella which could cover the whole earth. But what was that yellow pill which grows and grows inside Luc's head, exploding into a thousand colours, distorting the world with its firework display? Luc is naked, but who has removed his trousers, his shoes and socks? Who is sucking at his toes, first one mouth, then two, then three? He wants to buck and wriggle and break the hold these mouths have on the Downtown end of his body, but the sensation is too acute, the sweetness of it too much like pain, too intense for him to take evasive action. He plays dead. Pretends that nothing is happening. Negro's knees are squeezing his shoulders, crushing him; he can hardly breathe, a fine mess, there'll be nothing left of him, he knows that, and the thought of it overwhelms him. Bye-bye to the dolly boys of Paris, the lonely gropers of the Tuileries, the gigolos of the Pincio and the tea-room trade of the Tivoli Gardens. The trucks of the United States are the biggest trucks in the world. They breed men like insects and the elite is hatched out on Saturday and Sunday nights. They lay their eggs when it's raining. And they do it on a patch of wasteland when the earth is dry, with puddles near at hand so the grubs will have something to drink. The congregation has gathered, worshippers shaking their left wrists. And they spit in your eye and all over. Downtown.

'Oh, cool it!' Negro waves them off. They move aside and make room. He puts Luc's socks on again, pulling them tight over Luc's feet, each gesture slow and deliberate, with a gleam of passion that flares up in Luc's mind and dazzles him. 'Don't move, I'll take care of you.' He pulls Luc's trousers back on. 'Fuck off, leave us alone.' His voice sounds far away, hoarse, velvety, dusky, at one and the same time rasping and caressing. Luc tries to get up but a shaft of light nails him to the ground. 'Police!' The glare of headlights, the thrill of fear, dispersal and flight. Negro flattens himself over Luc. 'Don't move.' The squad car remains facing the trucks for a long, a very long time, long enough to drive out of one's mind all memory of history books and wars and fine mornings on the way to school when you don't feel like going but you go all the same and through the classroom window gaze at the sky that is pretending to be the sea with islands of cloud and currents of wind and men drowning unseen. 'Don't move.' The squad car turns around. No-one left under the trucks but Luc and Negro. 'Help me, they'll be back.' Luc slips on his shirt and buttons it up. The wrong buttons. He undoes them and does them up again. 'O.K.?' 'O.K., hurry!' Negro ties up Luc's shoelaces. 'What got into you, wearing shoes with laces, *here*!' They crawl out behind the trucks as the others begin to creep back. 'My name's Andrew, what's yours?' 'Luc.' 'Luck?' 'No, Luc, without a K at the end, I'm French.' Luc has the feeling that someone else has answered for him, another self. 'Come on.' In places Luc's shirt is sticking to his chest. In places Luc's trousers are sticking to his legs. 'Here,' says Andrew, 'here's your keys, a good thing you've got me with you.' Luc shrugs his shoulders, takes the keys and puts them in the left pocket of his jacket. 'I saw the guy who stole your billfold. Did you have much with you?' Luc shrugs his shoulders. 'Come on, we'll get a drink in here. Gay bar.' In the restroom Luc strips to the waist. He dries his shoulders and his stomach with paper towels. He spits in the wash-basin, soaks his face, fills his mouth with water and spits again and again. Then he puts his shirt on, pushes open the door of a W.C. behind him, lowers his trousers and wipes the slime from his legs, that spittle of rain and larvae, those tears from under the trucks. There is no lock on the door. Someone pushes at it. 'Wait.' 'It's Andrew, everything O.K.?' 'O.K.' Latrines, a cul-de-sac, no exit. The wall carries a constellation of addresses and telephone numbers, a matter of discipline, lovers of bondage and leather and chains. Luc smiles. The first smile of the evening.

They are celebrating the anniversary of the bar. On a platform a coffin on which is written in large letters ONE MORE YEAR FOLKS. Flashing lights, fairground décor, sprays of flowers and, hanging from their necks from the ceiling, strangled dolls, each one bearing the name of a rival establishment. The bartenders wear leather tee-shirts with the words: 'Mrs. Nixon is expected at any moment. Do her proud.' Andrew offers Luc a tankard of beer. 'You're crazy.' 'Which of us is the crazier?' Andrew pinches Luc's ear and strokes the back of his neck. 'I felt a bit scared, those guys were beginning to do just anything.' 'What's anything?' 'Well, they'd gotten out of control. I don't trust those trucks. Still, you can trust me.' Silence. 'You do trust me, don't you?'

'My father's black, my mother's Puerto Rican. I have an Irish name, I'm a Baptist, and I work for a Jewish florist. And you're the first Frenchman I've ever met.' Andrew spoke in a dry tone. 'Listen', he says, pinching Luc's arm. The noise of steel-studded boots, the creak of leather jackets, the smell of badly tanned hide, sounds and smells battling together, bruised and battered faces, everyone waiting, lashing out at each other with their eyes. A night of brutality. 'I don't go for this dump, come on back to my place.'

80th Street, Westside. 'This is my ghetto,' Andrew admits, 'I love it and you're sure gonna love it too.' Andrew squeezes the words out through clenched teeth. 'Don't you know how to smile?' 'It makes me tired.' A ramshackle staircase with tall steps, steeply pitched. 'You go first.' 'Which floor is it?' 'Way up at the top, last door.'

The walls are leprous. Broad patches of yellowish paint have scaled off. 'I don't even sweep it, I like it like this, I like it to look neglected,' says Andrew, tossing his leather jacket on the floor. Short-sleeved tee-shirt, ebony arms: Luc remembers that book of strip cartoons which he had read and re-read as a child. *The Adventures of Chocolate,* the nice little black boy who wants to learn to read and write, gets taken up by the Missionary Priest and finally lands up in Paris where he feels cold, very cold, but where a very rich old lady offers him a pullover and has suits made for him out of old frock-coats that belonged to her husband, who died in the war. So Chocolate becomes an engineer, learns how to build dams and goes back to his own country. His own village is doomed by the very first dam he constructs (all alone?). The Missionary dies in his arms and gives him his blessing. To be continued in our next. 'Right, get moving.' 'I'd like to take a shower.' 'If you want to, but there's no hot water.'

Luc gets undressed. It is a huge room with a high ceiling and over the fireplace a picture of Louis XIV on a prancing horse. Pinned to the picture are photographs of Andrew, naked, front view, back view, sprawling, in chains, and with a sailor's cap on his head. 'Come on, move.' Socks screwed into a ball left lying on the floor, dirty briefs and threadbare shirts. 'Right, yeah, O.K., it's my mess, I like it that way.' Luc is warily folding his blue jeans, then his shirt and his socks. 'What the hell are you doing?' Andrew snatches the clothes out of Luc's hands and hurls them to the ground. Chocolate is getting cross. He grips Luc by the shoulder. 'If you want that shower, buddy, get on with it!'

Luc crosses the bedroom. The bed is unmade, ravaged, filthy, quite filthy with stains all over. It is framed between two large wardrobes, like giant strong-boxes. Instead of a canopy over the bed, a mirror slung from the ceiling. 'Bathroom's in there.' Andrew is giving orders, pushing Luc at arm's length in front of him. 'What are you gaping at? You scared?' 'Those insects . . .' 'Oh, they're all over the place, gotta get used to them, man. The bathroom belongs to them.' Standing in the bath-tub Luc turns on the hot water and hears the empty pipes shudder and croak like someone vomiting. Andrew cuts it off. 'I told you, cold water, that's all.' And he turns that on. Luc is caught in a glacial jet. 'No soap: better just scrub yourself.' The water is green and then yellow, and the stink of chlorine fills the bathroom. Luc's hair gets plastered over his face and blinds him. The cold water beats down on the top of his head like hail and re-echoes inside him. He kneels in the bath: this time the powerful jet pins him down. It's raining pebbles. It seems to Luc as if the whole building is vibrating with him. Niagara. Chocolate is getting his own back. Chocolate has learned his lesson. Luc feels he'd like to claw off the discoloured enamel of the tub, but in the five days since he arrived in New York City he has conscientiously bitten his nails right down. He clenches his fists. Andrew stops the cold water. 'O.K., move, out! No towels, so you'll have to jump around.' Andrew takes hold of him and sets him on his feet. Luc mutters: 'What was that yellow thing you gave me just now?' Nothing, man, nothing, a fun thing.' 'Tell me,' murmurs the shivering Luc, 'tell me.' Happiness, buddy, happiness, and now we're going to have a ball.' 'No.' 'What d'ya mean, no? Come on . . .' Dripping wet, Luc stretches out on the bed. Andrew dries him with the dirty sheets. Luc is thinking how the dirt will make him filthy again. He closes his eyes. Lets it happen. Andrew is whispering: 'I'm your friend, you hear me, your friend . . .' And in the mirror over the bed Luc watches Andrew bend over him and nibble at his navel. A fringe of frizzy hair tickles his stomach. The black hands take a grip on his thighs. Andrew is still wearing his trousers and tee-shirt. He is breathing heavily, and then more and more noisily. 'It's what you wanted, eh? This is what you were looking for? Tell me it's what you were looking for. Here, you see!' Andrew gets up and opens the doors of the wardrobes on either side of the bed. In each of them a strip of neon lights up: what a collection, an untidy array of whips, plastic gadgets and studded corsets. 'Which would you like? Tell me what you want.' 'But . . .' 'Come on, you know damn well what you want.' Luc shuts his eyes. Andrew leaps up, straddling him and pinches Luc's cheeks between the thumb and forefinger of both hands. 'Come on, talk, you can choose, open your eyes and look!' Luc tries to sit up. Andrew clobbers him with a good resounding slap. Luc falls back on the Missionary's lap. The Missionary blesses him. The wardrobe doors creak. Sound of metal, sound of leather. In the bathroom columns of insects were marching up the wall, insects like enormous ants with strange nightcaps on their heads and hairy legs, eight, ten, twelve hairy legs. An electric light bulb hung from the ceiling. Attracted by the light, the insects were making for it, avoiding the leprous patches of flaking paint, selecting the routes which they could best adhere to, though sometimes they fell with an unpleasant smack on the tiled floor. As he had stepped out of the bath, Luc had taken care not to tread on them, for they could still have been alive. Then he had told himself that 'he was inside Rasky's body' and that he'd really like to 'make a go of it with Rasky and pick up where they left off', but Andrew's arm was pushing him towards the bed. Ceremonial.

A whip, like a dog's lead. Andrew strikes his legs, then his thighs, harder and harder, then his stomach and his chest. Luc bites his lips. He would like to cry out, but sharp as the pain is it also seems remote, so unbearable that it can in fact be borne. Who is striking whom? Yes, this pain will save Rasky. And the insects in the bathroom will be the first to witness his recovery. The trip to New York will at least have served some purpose. Rasky will return to Paris his old self again, with his smile, and his luggage full of bits and pieces and his gilded life of vacuity and his talent for farewell letters and telephone calls in the middle of the night. 'Come to me, I need you.' With his eyes wide open Luc is watching in the mirror canopied above him the black shadow bent on hurting him: 'You're white, anyone can see that, look and you can see. When I get beaten it leaves no marks behind. Aha!' The laughter of Chocolate returning home to find his village is going to be submerged. What a lot of things he has learnt from him, thanks to him! After the whip, then the chains and the corset, Luc is hardly conscious of anything. Except, above him, the finest picture he has seen in his life, a picture which would go on being finished off forever. No longer will he see that fixed, precise, unmoving image of himself, which used to bring him comfort and despair. He no longer belongs to himself. He is emerging from a cocoon of pain and distress.

Then Luc tells himself that he has missed out on everything. Every chance of courtesy or contemplation, all the great truths. There is nothing moral about his life anyway, just one long record of misconduct. He has missed everything on the way. So that was his body, that white thing with the over-large hips and the fine-boned angular shoulders, the rather weak chin and the rather slack face, a body ready to resign. Andrew makes a bound and grips him round the throat: 'What's on your mind?' Luc is suffocating, he is going to faint. Andrew loosens his hold. Luc gets his breath back. 'What were you thinking?' Silence. 'Answer!' Again Andrew squeezes, more and more tightly. Luc gets the feeling that his eyes are going to swivel round and look into his brain. He tries to cry out. Andrew slackens his grip. Luc gets his breath back. 'Well, answer!' 'I . . .' 'Talk.' '. . . stop a moment.' 'I'll stop if you answer.' Silence. Andrew chucks on the floor all the sheets that encumber the bed, the pillows and the blankets, and shifting Luc round lengthwise on the smooth surface of the mattress, pulls out the straps level with his feet, his genitals and his neck. 'There, that'll stop you moving.' 'Let me go.' 'Where to?' 'Home.' 'Where's home?' 'To Rasky's.' 'Who's Rasky?' 'My friend.' 'He'll wait.' 'Let me alone . . .' 'What are you thinking about, what?' 'I was thinking about Tom, he's coming with his leather cushion. He'll protect me.' 'How do you expect him to get here? No-one knows where you are.' 'Tom and Bill are coming, I know they are.' Andrew smiles. 'Wait, we're gonna celebrate their arrival.' He stands up and goes to the left-hand wardrobe where he makes a choice among several knives. 'We're gonna play a little game, it's only a game, but I hope it's gonna scare you.' He sharpens a large kitchen knife, bends over Luc, bears down on Luc's stomach, and caresses Luc with the cutting edge of the blade. 'Don't move now, or you might get a little scratch.' Andrew puts down the knife, pulls a popper from his pocket and sticks it up Luc's nostrils. 'Come on, take a deep breath, come on, that's it, this'll help you take it easy, do you good, that's the way . . .'

'Wake up, so I can hit you.' That fourth article of yours, we've been waiting for your fourth article. And now, at the last moment, you think you can turn out a piece that shows you're a genius. Oh no! I'll have nothing to do with genius. I'll fling it back in your face. There's no sale for genius. We'd only get another pile of letters. And don't tell me that we only publish the readers' letters that suit us, complimentary ones if they're snappy enough and critical ones if they're stupid. Get on with that article. You have half an hour . . .

'Come on, baby, on your feet, there's plenty more for us to

do.' On the corner of a table in the editor's office Luc is scribbling away on white sheets of paper, sweeping over them with his fountain pen. He twists the nib, tries to scratch it straight, wipes it on a piece of blotting-paper and licks it with the tip of his tongue. Then he shakes the pen and attempts to write, but nothing happens. Out of ink? But he has just filled it! So he squeezes out a blob of ink and dips the nib in it, but apart from the blob the ink fails to make a mark. He tries writing the words without ink, but one by one he digs a hole in every sheet. Hurry up. Only twenty minutes left. You ought to have a moment to think. Luc picks up a pencil, a piece of wood with no lead in it. So he takes a paper-knife, makes a nick in the forefinger of his left hand, squeezes out two drops of blood and dips the nib in that: at last it writes, makes a mark, he spreads the globule out and tries to form a word, but the word refuses to take shape . . .

'On your feet, beauty, on your feet.' Andrew undoes the straps and lifts Luc up. The editor enters the office. Ah! there you are, you might have let us know you were back. That article, it's time! Luc holds out a sheet of paper with one spot of blood on it. Is that all? Yes, sir, that's all. So that's what New York means to you. You promised us a piece on the Presidential elections. Is this it? Yes, sir. Since when have you been calling me sir? Yes, sir . . . Come on, stop fooling around, give me the article. You're hiding it. No. Luc, what's got into you? Grasping him with both hands, the editor squares up to Luc, pinches his cheeks, tugs his hair and upbraids him. Come on, give me that article! What's your little game? We've no time to lose. Rasky is dead? What's that? Rasky is dead, there, he just died, I know, I can feel it. Who is Rasky? A friend, my friend. What are you going on about? My private life. I've got a private life too, old man, but I don't blurt it out. I keep it to myself. He slaps Luc. Wake up, good God, what's happened to you? It was a trap! What's that? I've been caught in a trap . . .

Andrew pushes Luc into the living-room and flings him on the floor. Rolled-up socks and dirty briefs. Luc's head is full of flashing colours, meteors that explode, meadows soaked in dew, too lush and too green, blue canopies torn asunder:

through the port-hole of a plane he stretches out his arm and snatches at the blue cloth and the clouds. The editor keeps coming back to him, holding out the blood-stained page. What do you think I'm going to do with this then, eh? What am I going to do with this mark? You're a dead duck, Luc, a dead duck. And Luc wonders how he could ever have been the friend of such a bastard. He holds out his arms to his boss. He holds out his arms to Andrew. Andrew yanks his head back by the hair. 'Here, swallow this.' Two pills, a glass of water. 'Come on, swallow.' Luc gulps. 'Again.' The water trickles down his chin, forming bubbles at the corners of his mouth. 'Good, right, that's good.' He takes a grip on the nape of Luc's neck, forces him up and drives him back into the bed-room. 'This time, we're gonna have fun, you wanna have fun?' Luc can feel a ball of fire growing in his stomach. He is dazzled by too many lights: he flies off into the infinite immensity of the palms of Andrew's black hands. The pages of the *Collected Adventures of Chocolate* are turning furiously, creating a violent wind. In a daze, Luc can neither see nor feel anything now. He makes one last effort and tries to explain to his boss that it is not his fault. He cries to Rasky for help, but on the pavement outside his school there is no-one waiting for him. Luc is sinking.

Only then does Andrew strip naked. Luc can no longer see him. An ebony totem streaming with sweat, he is rubbing his left fist and forearm all over with viscous jelly from a tube. Long minutes the ritual lasts. His forearm becomes a second member, which slowly, very slowly, twisting like a trepan, forces a passage into Luc, plunges and takes him. Luc is lying on his stomach, his face embedded in a pillow. When Andrew's foream has been lodged in its most comfortable position, without loosening his hold Andrew pulls himself up over Luc's body and with his right hand, using all his force, he presses the face of the white boy down into the white pillow. He stays that way for several long minutes, holding his breath, waiting for the other to die. Death arrives on the scene unannounced. She was concealed in the pillow. Epitaph for a life: asphyxia.

—Translated by
Donald Watson

CHRISTIAN KAMPMANN

FEELINGS

The priest said on the telephone that if I want to turn Catholic I must first attend instruction. A new class is beginning soon, and he will decide whether I'll be allowed to join the group after he has had a personal conversation with me. I can come to see him fifteen minutes before the class begins.

It's what I want to do. I'm sure of it. It's what I've always been looking for, without realizing it. I sense new meanings and connections. There is a reason for my being so depressed during the first months of this year: I needed to be forced to understand the innermost purpose of my longing.

The priest receives me in a friendly yet somewhat sceptical manner. He observes me with more than his eyes. He is wearing a black suit with a clerical collar, and there is a crucifix hanging on the wall. But that doesn't seem strange, here. He must be about ten years older than my father.

We seat ourselves one on each side of the desk. My heart is pounding. The moment is filled to the bursting point with meaning.

He asks why I don't want to continue being a Protestant. I try to describe what my childhood was like—the purely religious aspects of it—and why Confirmation classes didn't change a thing. He seems to have heard the story often.

"But what makes you think that Catholicism will be any better for you?"

My restlessness. Books. None of these things provide real proof.

"My life has been lacking something," I say, "as do the lives of most Danes, it seems to me. If you compare our lives with those of people in southern Europe . . ." I make a vague gesture which I immediately regret.

The priest wants to know what I plan to do when I've completed my military service. When I reply that I want to try to become a journalist, he makes a slight grimace.

"In that case, you'll have to be even better informed than others. It will take time."

"I'm prepared for that—now."

He smiles a little. When the doorbell rings he says, "Perhaps you'll help me set up the chairs."

In the class are three women and one other man, all much older than I. Apparently it usually takes people half their lives to begin to find their way.

The priest seems somewhat different now, more relaxed. He pays less attention to me than to the others. That's fine with me.

"Let's begin with the reason why we are here on earth," he says very calmly. "We are here to do God's will, so we can be saved and go to heaven. That is the purpose of our lives."

Aside from my grandfather, no one has ever told me that life has a purpose, or what that purpose is. I like the priest's explanation better than my grandfather's.

I guard my secret. Everything will be changed. At least, I feel that's what will happen. My perspective has been altered—or created; up to now, I haven't had any perspective. The hope of change is in itself a change.

Sometimes I'm afraid that it's all just something I'm imagining. Then I think about the millions of people on earth who profess the same faith I'll soon have, and I keep on reading.

I'm amazed by the fact that Christianity hasn't made a greater impact—true Christianity, I mean. Of course, I've always been aware of the gulf between the way everything could be and the way everything, unfortunately, is. But now I can accept this without the disgust I previously felt, because now I know there is hope.

In order for change to occur, I must help—and not just spiritually. I try to drink less without stopping completely, which might call attention to myself. I try to be more friendly toward other people, both at the office on the military base and at home. This doesn't seem to make much difference to anyone; I'm probably still so reserved that people barely notice the change in my behavior. But in time it will be noticed.

And then there's her. Here too, something has to be changed. I've always thought that, in a country like Denmark that sort of thing is permissible, especially when two people are fond of each other—but no. I've read it, and I've heard the priest say it: "When a young man marries a young woman they must both be virgins." I know what I have to do, and I want to do it. But I wish I could avoid hurting her. I'm going to have to break off our relationship. She isn't the one I eventually want to marry after all.

Until I'm ready to get married, I'll just have to get used to being alone. In a way, I'm already alone. So I'm sure I'll manage.

I arrange to meet her in town as usual. She thinks it's just an ordinary date. While we sit waiting for our drinks I wish it were she who was getting ready to say something unpleasant. I would make sure I acted surprised and unhappy, and then I would forgive her and wish her happiness and good luck.

We raise our glasses and say *skål,* then lapse into quietness. The silence is stifling.

"What's wrong?" she finally asks.

With a sense of relief, I realize that I can do what has to be done after all. She has reached out to take what's coming. I hardly need to do anything myself.

"There's nothing wrong," I reply. "I mean—yes, there is."

"What is it?"

"You know perfectly well. Don't you? I'm really sorry. But I'm sure it will be best for you too, at least in the long run."

Her look grows more and more intense, and then suddenly weakens. She leans back.

I have to explain. Try to explain. To some extent. "It doesn't have anything to do with you."

"But with someone else?"

"Not at all. No, no. Just with me. If you see what I mean?"

"Maybe I do," she says slowly. And then, a little later: "How long have you felt this way?"

"Let's not go into it."

"Since New Year's Eve?"

"Well . . . yes. Sort of. Please don't misunderstand."

"I'm trying not to," she says, as she reaches for her purse and stands up.

"Don't feel bad about it," I say. "I still like you a lot."

Fortunately, she pretends not to have heard me. After she has left I sit for a while without moving or thinking about anything at all. I finish her drink and order another. I'm free.

I go to mass each Sunday. Look forward to it all week. No one knows what I'm doing except the priest, who sometimes gives me an impassive look. The first Saturday night I sleep at the barracks, even though I've always got a weekend pass, but after that I prefer to find an excuse. I tell my parents that I'm going to a museum or, if I stay in town afterwards, that I'm going to visit her.

It's over a month since the last time I was really with her. During the first two weeks I managed to be "chaste," to use the embarrassing term the priest often uses in dead seriousness. Then I "satisfied myself," to use an expression that over-evaluates the act. From now on I'll let it happen in my sleep. ("Angel pussy," they call it in the barracks.) That's the way it will have to be for the time being. Other things are more important to me.

I want to guard my secret until my faith is even stronger. But one evening when I'm at home alone with my mother and we've had a little more than usual to drink, I suddenly feel that she will understand.

"There's something I'd like to talk to you about," I say, and regret having started with that stupid old sentence. It's generally used in order to ward off the consequences of small, painful disclosures, and I can see by my mother's face—before she assumes a neutral expression—that this is in fact what she fears.

"Something good," I hasten to add.

My mother tries to appear as though she had not expected anything different. She lights another cigarette.

Then I say it. It's out. At first my mother looks as though she is going to cry. Then she gives me a strange smile.

"I can understand very well," she says. "But whether your father will understand—that's another question. Your grandmother will be happy."

"I don't want her to know yet."

"What about other people?"

"No."

"Nobody?"

"Not yet. Don't you agree?"

My mother shakes her head, a faraway look in her eyes. Then she says, "You haven't definitely made up your mind, have you?"

"Yes," I say. And with that the decision is made.

I explain about the time it will take before I'm accepted into the Church, about all the things in my life I must get in order first.

"Danes think they know the answers to everything," she says. "Like I say to your father: Wait till you die—you'll get the surprise of your life."

Eternal life is something I'll wait to decide about until later. I'll think about it when my faith is stronger.

"That way out," says my mother," is closed to me, of course."

"Why?"

"Because of your father."

"Would *you* want to?"

Although she says nothing, my mother responds nevertheless, with one of the wordless communications I've experienced since earliest childhood, a secret look into her that we both are supposed to pretend we're not aware of.

"What's most important to me, of course," she says, "is how things are between your father and me."

I nod. I want to add that she is free to do whatever she wants in her thoughts and feelings, but I don't say it, because I know I would not be satisfied with so little either. One can't be a Catholic in secret.

"Do you know anyone who is a Catholic?" asks my mother. "Have you met any?"

"It's something that just happened inside me. I can't explain it any better."

"I really do understand. When one is a child, one has one's parents. That is, if one has both parents. Later—Yes, one gets married, but—anyway, I do understand."

"I'm glad."

"Do you love your mother?" my mother asks in English.

We hug each other and have something more to drink.

One day while running errands for the office I stop in front of a movie theater to look at the stills. The sun warms my back —it is spring—and as I'm standing there one of my old classmates from high school comes riding by on his bicycle. We talk together a while and then go our separate ways. The next time I'm at home I find a letter there from him asking if I'd like to meet him in town some evening.

If I'm going to spend an evening with another fellow I'd rather have it be my friend from the barracks; but until that happens, I can certainly sacrifice one evening. The fact that my classmate was never among the few I regarded as my friends in high school is probably all the better.

We meet in Tivoli and get drunk. Then we wander around the amusement park. I find myself in that mellow state I sometimes achieve: I seem to flow together with everything around me. A squeeze on my arm isolates me again. He wants to know what we should do now. I wish I could get rid of him so I could once again become part of the sounds and the movements. On the other hand, I certainly don't want to be rude. How about a ride on the roller coaster? Once I suggest it and he says "yes," I start to feel like doing it myself. I decide that soon I'll ask my friend at the barracks if he wants to spend an evening in town with me, and immediately it's easier to reconcile myself to the fact that he's not the one I'm walking beside now. When my classmate says something, I turn toward him and smile, and the electric lights twinkling in the trees flow into me and give a rhythm to my expectation.

We're lucky—we get the back car on the roller coaster.

"Are you scared?" he asks.

"Are you?"

"Not as much as usual."

The row of cars starts with a jolt. We slowly glide into a tunnel. The tracks curve upward, carrying us into the open air. We turn toward each other, as though impelled by a common movement, and kiss each other. For a moment everything is still, all movement stops. Then the sounds burst out again, louder than ever, and the car climbs higher, abruptly, and we ride the entire trip without reacting to it, or to the other thing.

He overtakes me at the bottom of the stairs.

"Let's go somewhere and talk."

"No. I have to get back," I say.

"Already?"

"Yes. Thanks for the nice time."

"Wait! If you think that I—that we—have done anything wrong . . ."

"There's nothing to talk about."

"Yes there is!"

"I don't think so."

"Yes, but we both—we agreed like two sparrows."

I see how confused and unhappy he is. As for me, I feel totally calm. I hurry off, grateful that each person I pass puts me farther away from him. At the heart of my calmness I feel a kernel of anger, directed only at myself. I don't feel a thing for him, and of course I won't ever have anything to do with him again.

What happened to me? It wasn't even a genuine desire that I gave in to. Had it happened in the right way, it should have been with someone else, a fellow I really like.

I catch myself with a start. What have I just admitted? Something I've known for a long time. Yes, of course. But until now I've blocked off my knowledge from the rest of me.

Outside Tivoli I discover I've got to take a piss so badly that I can't wait until I get back to the barracks, not even if I take a taxi. I know there are public toilets at Radhuspladsen —the square is just a few blocks away—and even though I prefer to avoid that type of dirty, smelly place, I'm going to have to make an exception.

The area outside the toilets, where there are telephones and a coatroom, looks relatively clean. I'm about to go inside when the door swings open and my classmate comes out.

We stop and look at each other. It appears that the situation is so unexpected he can't even react to it, rather than that he's feeling bad about things the way he was before. I myself feel nothing at all, except an even stronger need to take a piss.

I walk the whole way home. I've got to straighten out my thoughts and feelings.

I've always known something like this would happen. That much I'm quite willing to admit. I've been longing for it, at the same time as I've tried to prevent myself from having such feelings. How much it actually means, I don't know. Truly. I'm being completely honest.

I hate him for comparing us to a couple of sparrows. The next time I go home I find a letter from him. In it he asks me to forgive him if he has done anything wrong and says he can't be as strong as I am, he's tried, and if I change my mind, there's nothing he'd rather do than see me again. I tear up the letter and flush it down the toilet.

"I've told him," says my mother. "I had to tell him."

I give a slight nod, understanding what she means.

"I think he wants to talk to you," she continues. "He's your father, after all."

Of course I've known that such a conversation between my father and myself would have to take place. I've rehearsed fragments of it. Although they have varied in tone and major points, all the versions have had one thing in common: they surprise my father, and thereby prevent him from going around shaking his head disapprovingly in advance.

"Did I do anything wrong?" asks my mother.

"No, no." I would have preferred to have been even stronger in my faith. The "episode"—I see mocking quotation marks whenever my thoughts are forced back to that evening—also made it necessary to wait a little. I have to be completely sure about everything, including those things I keep secret.

"You *are* certain," says my mother, "aren't you?"

My anxiety is a false alarm. She is referring to something else after all.

"More certain than ever," I say.

My mother, who normally sits and waits for my father to come home from the office, turns her head, listens.

"That's him." She puts out her cigarette and smoothes her skirt.

My father comes in whistling. My mother runs over and gives him a hug. I greet him in my usual way. My friends who have witnessed it have been surprised to see me greet my father with a kiss on the cheek—they don't do anything like that even to their mothers—and I've felt myself to be rather lucky. But since "it" happened that stupid evening I've begun to notice that my father obviously prefers to just shake hands.

My father goes upstairs to take a bath and change his clothes. I go up to my room. I sit by the window looking out at the backyards and at the water far away; beyond the water a strip of land shines in the sunlight. Something within me is trying to burst out, but for my own sake I repress it.

While we're eating dinner I get an idea: I can refuse to discuss the subject with my father. That's my right, after all. For a while I sit relishing the idea, but then all its dangerous aspects bubble to the surface and corrode it away. When we've drunk our after-dinner coffee, when my brothers and sisters have gone upstairs to do their homework and my mother gets up and closes the glass doors to the room where my father and I are sitting, I try to pull myself together. I'm the one who has the upper hand, not he.

"Your mother told me that—"

"Yes," I say, "I know."

"Do you want to explain anything about it to me?"

"All right. But either you understand, in which case you don't need an explanation, or else—"

"I'd like you to try anyway."

"I've been looking for something. And I've found it."

"I see. How did you find it? Forgive me for asking. But that sort of thing has always seemed so foreign to me."

"And irrelevant?"

"It would be strange if it were otherwise, wouldn't it? Is it because you know some?"

"Know some . . .?"

"Some Catholics."

I shake my head. Now is when I have to be most careful if I don't want my father to think I've fallen prey to weird ideas.

"Who would that be?"

"It could be you've met somebody. You must have come in contact with it somehow or other."

"That's true, of course. But it's not exactly a small, obscure sect we're talking about after all. It's hard to overlook Catholicism if one is the least bit observant."

My father pretends to ponder this line of reasoning. Then he slowly draws in his breath and expels it with a sudden, violent puff.

"So this is something you've thought of all by yourself?" he says.

"I didn't think of it."

"Then who did?"

I'm about to reply that it's essentially a matter of feelings, and that feelings aren't something you "think of." But I let it go. He neither can nor wants to understand. He may as well direct the conversation however he wants to; I'll act like I'm still taking part in it. That way we can both feel satisfied afterwards.

"It must be self-suggestion," he says.

I give him a slight smile.

"What do you expect it to offer you?" he asks.

The true, spontaneous answer—a meaning in life and a desire to live—I keep to myself.

"Is that so hard to figure out?" I say.

He mulls that over. I wonder if he has ever before been so intensely interested in me.

"What will you do on Fridays," he asks teasingly, "you who don't like any fish except lobster?"

"Eat just potatoes. Like I already do. Actually, there are more important things than that."

"And they're even more impossible to accept."

"Who says it's supposed to be easy?"

"You've already learned something, I see."

"I don't think it will be so hard," I argue. "Besides, I'm tired of all that 'bed-hopping.' "

The final word elicits a look of mild surprise on my father's face. He wants me to think that the expression is deliberately assumed and that he's done it to deal gently with me. What kind of stupid word is that to use anyway? Does such a word even exist? Why did I blurt that out?

"I don't imagine you've tried too much of that sort of thing yet," he says.

"Enough to know I'd rather—I'd rather be serious about it."

In order to avoid the word "love" I say: "I don't want to be with someone unless it's really serious."

"And do you think you can tell when it's serious?"

"Couldn't you?"

"With your mother? Yes. But that was far from the first time. For her too. You already know that. If you want to enjoy life, why join a group that says you shouldn't do it?"

I shrug my shoulders. It's not particularly convincing, but I can't come up with anything better. I'm tired. I want the conversation to end so I can go up to my room and figure out what it meant.

"I guess you know about the Catholics' humane, up-to-date attitudes toward things like divorce and contraception."

"Yes. But what does that matter, if people really care about each other?"

My father smiles. Things have gone exactly as I figured they would. That's obvious. My father can't understand me, and therefore hopes that I can't understand myself either. Otherwise, in his opinion, I must be a little crazy.

"I've got to go to the bathroom," I explain.

"Go ahead."

I'm about to close the glass doors again. "Leave them open," my father says. "It's a bit stuffy in here."

A short time later my mother steals up to my room.

"How did it go?"

"Fine."

"I thought it would. He isn't so—what word should I use? —unreasonable after all, is he?"

"You can use that word. No, he isn't unreasonable."

"But he couldn't really understand, could he?"

I shake my head, and my mother smiles contentedly.

"Still, I love him," she says. "And you know what? The most important thing isn't what a person believes. It's got to do with something else entirely."

When, in the following days, I try to figure out where I stand now, I get a strange feeling. It seems as though most of my thoughts are already so muddled by the time they reach my consciousness that there's nothing left of the true, original impulse. But the sun is shining, there are new leaves on all the trees, and when I ride off on my bicycle in the sunshine, my movements melting into those of everything around me, I'm closer to an explanation than when I try to think.

A witty, light-hearted friend of mine from officers' training school invites me and my friend from the barracks to have dinner at his stepmother's home. She's very anxious to meet a couple of his military friends, and he can't invite just anybody. Not that his stepmother is a snob; it would just be too bad if she unintentionally made someone feel he was using his knife and fork incorrectly.

I look forward to it. I call up a girl, whom I've thought about before too—we went together for a while in high school —and ask her if she'd like to go out with me some evening. She'd like to very much. We agree to talk more about it later. Now everything is in order. In the meantime, I'm going to spend a whole long evening with my friend from the barracks and my other friend from officers' training school, toward whom I must always act equally friendly. Nobody can tell what I really feel.

We all three take the streetcar together to the stepmother's home. Each building we jolt past gleams with hidden meaning. I'm careful to pay exactly the same amount of attention to each of my companions. I see the way small dark hairs curl up over the neck of the undershirt that my friend from the barracks is wearing. Quickly, I look away.

We get off in an area I'm not familiar with. "My stepmother's mailing address is Copenhagen V.—the Vesterbro district," says my friend, "but it *is* the Frederiksberg district. At least, I know the Nørrebro district doesn't start until way over there. And the apartment itself is very nice." We all know, of course, that Frederiksberg is a better district than either Vesterbro or Nørrebro.

His stepmother is in her late thirties, but looks younger. Naturally she tries to hide the fact that she's nervous. She is from Sweden and speaks with a slight accent, and I realize this makes me feel that she's a little—what should I call it?—different. Even though I understand why she seems that way. When it's so easy to appear different without really being so, how can one ever keep from seeming different when one really is?

After we've had a couple of drinks and are seated at the dinner table I stop worrying. I become part of something light and bubbling: a cultivated atmosphere. It's impossible to say anything wrong. Each new comment binds us gently together, and I'm careful to treat everyone exactly the same.

I make a pleasant observation about a piece of furniture. Suddenly my friend's stepmother is on her guard; something has to be defended.

"We all know, of course, that when my husband died he left us nothing. I was forced to disclaim the assets and liabilities of the estate. I had to buy our furniture back at auction with my own savings. Sometimes I wonder: what is that furniture doing *here*? It would certainly fit in better somewhere else. But what would I put here instead? What *would* fit in? And besides, when I get home from the office I'm simply too tired to do anything about it."

We talk some more about various tasteless ways to furnish the living room. The fact that my friend from the barracks doesn't understand, that he thinks the rest of us are only having fun, makes my tender feelings for him break through my usual defenses. He's better than we are, finer. Which is why I—Nothing.

I'm drunk, but in a manner that my father would approve: witty, brilliant. My friend's stepmother tells about the manor house she had visited with her husband. She gets out a book about the family she married into and reads one of her favorite passages. It's something about a captain who successfully survives a dangerous situation sometime around the end of the eighteenth century, and how he thereby earns some sort of title. I try to keep my attention focused on the conversation, but the entire time I'm aware of a radiance surrounding my friend. In a little while I'm going to do something terrible: put my arm around him or something. I've got to get away.

I look at my watch several times. The thin smile on my hostess's face when I say I must leave indicates that, no matter how fortunate I'd been in making the right impression up to that point, I've now ruined everything. In my mind I take from the corner cupboard some of the antique goblets I've just been admiring and smash them through a couple of glass panes. Then I thank the hostess and say a polite goodbye.

When I get outside, my friend asks if we're heading in the same direction. I tell him I'm going to sleep overnight at my grandparents; I can't stand to be near him, and yet I hope he will insist on accompanying me. Pain is better than nothing. He says he will just be in time to catch the streetcar. I let him go.

I'm relieved. I've never been so much on the verge of revealing myself. Fortunately, he's too drunk to notice anything. And besides, he doesn't have any suspicion, of course. I've got to make sure at all costs that he keeps a good impression of me. Nobody's respect means more to me than his.

I hail a taxi and it stops at the curb. Where do I want to go? The main entrance of Tivoli. I have to tell the driver something after all. I'm so excited that my undershirt is soaked with sweat. Out in the bluish summer darkness the lights rush past and flow together into a glowing, pulsating pattern. A faint scent of lemon detaches itself from the smell of old tobacco in the taxi.

We arrive at the entrance to Tivoli. I wait until the taxi has disappeared. Then I turn and walk slowly toward the central square at Radhuspladsen. Each face I pass is so intense that I gasp for breath. Everything is trembling on the edge of transformation. In front of the townhall I decide that if someone should seem startled that I'm standing here I can just look up at the words of the "news in lights" that flash constantly outside the Politiken newspaper building. I try. The words flickering past have no meaning to me. I walk around a little. There's no law against a person doing that.

Gradually I become aware that something is going on at the other side of the square. I see how it happens. Either one stands still, or one moves around. The person who is moving passes close to the one standing still. He walks a short distance, looks back, continues a bit further, then turns and goes back and holds out a cigarette to get a light. A little later they go off together, or the one who was moving walks away alone and begins all over again with someone else.

I'm on the verge of fainting the whole time. I sit down on a bench. All around me advertisements in neon lights blink: Do it now! A clear, deep violet sky arches the entire scene, indifferent to my small actions.

It's too early, or else maybe the moment when I felt brave enough is already past. I've got to get away from the square for a while. I walk by the building where my grandfather has his office. I don't want to think about him or anyone else. As I continue walking away I know with growing certainty that I'll soon go back to the square. Nothing else has any meaning to me now.

I go into a courtyard and take a leak. Might as well get it over with. I am calm. What is supposed to happen, and will happen, is something I've been waiting for always.

On the way back, I pass a man and look directly into his eyes. At first all I can see is a haze; then his expression comes into focus. I can't understand the look at first, it seems so contradictory. But a little later, after I've walked over to some shop windows, I realize what his expression meant: first, curiosity that gives rise to an urge to do something audacious and is, in turn, penetrated by a deeper-lying despair and loneliness; then, an immediate camouflage of indifference which, in the end, turns into something roguish and noncommittal. The man must be forty years old, or even older. At the same time he seems almost boyish. If he has misunderstood my look and is on his way over here, I'll leave. Then I'll just have to come back another night. Besides, I'm so exhausted that I'm sick to my stomach. Fortunately, he seems to have understood.

Eventually I've looked at all the books in the windows. For the third or fifth time I decide to go home. Then I discover that someone has stopped a short distance away from me.

I stand motionless and stare straight ahead until I can catch my breath. I turn my head just slightly. The other fellow has done the same. He is younger than the first one, much younger —in his early twenties. His hair is dark and curly. He is good-looking. His light-colored pants and dark suede jacket are an inconspicuous outfit. There is nothing strange about him, except that no one has ever attracted me so powerfully.

He smiles a little. I try to do the same, but the muscles of my face are too stiff to smile. Nonetheless, he comes closer and stands a few steps away from me.

"Hi," he says.

I manage to make a weak, hoarse sound.

"Want to take a walk?"

I clear my throat. "O.K." I don't understand what he means. Maybe he's using code words.

He wants to go down a side street off the main shopping street. Fine with me. He asks what my name is, and how old I am. I tell him that I'm eighteen and that my name is Peter. That's my middle name too. When he hears that I'm in the military he laughs.

"I'm Tom."

I've never known anyone by that name before. I'm glad to have waited until now. Tom is exactly the right name. Nice, friendly, safe. A lot of unpleasant qualities are unthinkable in a person with that name. I want to tell him everything about myself immediately, and to hear all about him.

"What do you do?" I ask.

"Hairdresser."

I'm just about to say that he doesn't look like one. But obviously I still have to think twice before saying things, at least at the start. Later we'll be able to say everything to each other without fear of being misunderstood.

He radiates the same type of calmness as my friend at the barracks. And there's something wise about him. Suddenly I realize why he doesn't fit my idea of a hairdresser. The idea isn't my own. I've never known, or even talked with, a hairdresser; I've never been inside one of those places where women get their hair done. My impression of hairdressers hasn't had anything to do with my personal experience. And this can hardly be the only area where that is true.

As we are crossing a deserted square he touches my arm briefly. A warm feeling spreads throughout my entire body. We come to Rundetarn, the Round Tower. He stops, looks around. Not a person in sight. The only sound, other than that of his breathing next to me, is the faint hum of a car far away. The silence and the empty streets increase my sense of being in a dream, where everything is both surprising and obvious at the same time.

"Come," he says in a low voice.

I follow him through a gate and then on into a courtyard. He looks carefully all around, including upwards. The courtyard is surrounded by gray-painted buildings. All of the darkened windows are closed, except for one on the top floor which is half-open.

"Do you think anyone lives here?" I whisper.

He shakes his head. "Offices," he says, and turns toward me.

We move, in unison, into each other's arms. For the first time in my life I really feel another person's body, and my own. Stronger than the smell of either his tobacco or his suede jacket is the smell of Tom himself. It's the key to everything I've been longing for. We begin to kiss each other. This way is the right way for me. There's nothing wrong with me: I can feel what the songs and the novels praise; I can get out of myself and flow into another person. The other way was pleasant, and I felt something during it—no doubt about that—but it was always shadowed by the longing for this. I understand everything. I'm glowing inside.

We look at one another. I put my arms around his neck and curve my fingers down into his thick hair. All the caresses I've given in the sleepwalker existence of my past I can now experience in reality. I touch his forehead with the tip of a finger. We smile at each other. He takes hold of my thighs, between my legs. It's the most exciting thing I've ever felt.

He unzips my pants and puts his hand inside. I feel its warmth around my cock, which he tries to take out without success. I want to help him, but am too shy. Yet when he squats down and begins to pull at my pants I manage to get them and my undershorts pulled down around my thighs. He pulls them down even further with a caressing movement along my legs, then carefully takes hold of my cock and puts it in his mouth; suckles, sucks. I've never tried anything like this before, or ever read or heard about it, but that doesn't make it either strange or surprising. It's the most wonderful physical sensation I've ever had. The only problem is that I get more and more excited so quickly that I'm afraid I'll come before he lets go of me. I've already started—in my head too, in every part of my body. I come in a wave of light. The next thing I'm aware of is the sound of a small splash on the asphalt as he spits out my sperm, and then the feeling of the chilly air on my rear end and thighs.

For the time being it's probably best that I put on my pants. I do it hurriedly. He has lit a cigarette. He looks at his watch, shakes himself a little.

"What time do you have to be at the base tomorrow?" he asks.

"Six-thirty."

"Ugh! I don't have to be at work until nine."

"What time is it now?"

"Almost two-thirty. Should we head off together?"

I ask what direction he's going before the meaning of his words hits me.

"Vanløse. I'll take a taxi from Radhuspladsen."

"I'll walk that far with you then."

The question of why he shouldn't get to have a come too is

pushed aside, because he has put his arms around me. We kiss each other again and again. Somewhere nearby a few birds have started to sing, and when I look up I see that the panes in the half-opened window are reflecting the dawn.

The street is still deserted except for the two of us. Light filters down over it, there is a smell of salt water, and when we come out into an open square a breeze wafts over us and he puts his arm around me for a moment.

In the past I've always thought I could never be really alive, or even just be completely involved in the attempt, and, furthermore, I've accepted that. Why? I can't understand it, now that it's ended. Everything has become simple and real. And if I were holding his hand now there would be nothing left to wish for.

A shrill, foolish laughter reaches us, and two men come around the corner and walk quickly past us—mince past us, in the case of the younger one, the one who continues laughing.

Tom quickens his pace. "I can't stand people like that," he says, making some exaggerated movements with his arms and hips that look like a gross parody of a woman who considers herself extremely high-class. He abruptly becomes himself again and, after lighting another cigarette, continues talking about his dislike of that type of person. I nod, agreeing with him. Relief and pride stream through me, until suddenly I start to be afraid that he has the same opinion about me but is just hiding it carefully. In spite of everything, what we did together was pretty limited after all. Maybe he lost his desire during it, or even before.

"You feel the same way?" he asks.

I venture a slight nod.

"That's easy to see," he adds, and I hide my relief.

We have come to Radhuspladsen. It mustn't end. I nod eagerly when he says that perhaps we'll see each other again.

"Are you in town a lot?" he asks.

"What do you mean?"

"At all the places."

I'm about to explain about places that are off-limits for the military. He pats my arm.

"Stay happy," he says, and turns and walks away quickly and gets into a taxi. We wave to one another.

I walk a little further and then take a taxi. The sun is up. I ask the driver to stop a short distance from the house, out of consideration for my sleeping grandparents. The smell of the sea is stronger out here and blends with the fragrance from all the gardens. My feeling of having broken through to reality has increased; I'm even more intensely a part of it than before. Everything is incredibly obvious and, at the same time, full of secrets.

The grandfather clock in the hall shows twenty minutes after four. I've only got one hour to sleep, if I want time to eat some breakfast before I leave for the base. I tiptoe up the stairs, stepping in and out of broad bands of sunshine which I've never seen here on the stairway before. I can hear my grandfather's heavy breathing. He must have fallen asleep again after his late-night reading. On the table beside my bed is a glass and a bottle of mineral water. Next to a bottle opener are some aspirin and a piece of paper on which my grandmother has written: "Sleep well. Take one if necessary." I do that, drink some mineral water, and hear her turn in bed in the next room before sleep unites me with him.

—Translated by
Nadia Christensen

DARCY PENTEADO

THE ICE-CREAM FAIRY

Dr. Chrisóstomo Mascarenhas was mayor of Riacho Escuro in the state of São Paulo. He and his wife were a fine, upstanding couple of irreproachable moral, religious, civic and sexual principles, an honor and adornment to their town and state—in fact, to every fortunate spot they had ever chosen to grace with their illustrious presence. As a consequence, this worthy gentleman had been elected to three consecutive terms as president of the Riacho Escuro Recreation Association, fashionable gathering place for the cream of local society. That he should in due course be appointed mayor as well was only the logical culmination of a social and political career solidly based on a lifetime of perfect propriety.

Shortly after the new mayor took office, Silvio Santos, the producer of a popular weekly television series, began promoting a "Tournament of Towns" in which Riacho Escuro was invited to participate. Before replying, Dr. Chrisostomo passed on the invitation to the city councilmen, who would base their decision on how much support they thought they could expect from local industry and the Chamber of Commerce, as well as the sports clubs and cultural and social organizations. If they entered the contest at all, they would have to go the whole hog; if they tried to cut corners they would be pushed out of the running by the other towns. As it happened, money was no problem, for they were in the middle of a boom. Tax revenue was rolling in, Riacho Escuro produced all its own food supply, and there was even a labor shortage because the town was growing so rapidly.

The mayor's pride at the thought of showing off his home town on a nationwide television program proved infectious. The city council voted unanimously to participate, if the sponsors would give them a reasonable length of time to prepare. In the end it was decided that Riacho Escuro would be the eighth town to appear on the program. As soon as that point was settled the mayor called a meeting of local industrialists, prominent businessmen, sports club directors, the presidents of the Lions and Rotary Clubs (inevitably) and the vicar of the mother church, together with several members of the Marian Congregation. The meeting resulted in a finance committee, a ways and means committee on which the vicar would serve, and a committee of society matrons and debutantes to look after the finer details.

By this time most of the population of Riacho Escuro—excited, argumentative and fearful by the turns—were eagerly following the competition among the other towns. Imagine the excitement there would be when their home town joined in! The rivals were actually bringing in all the strange and improbable things they were being asked to produce, and a mere point or two might spell the difference between glory and defeat. The contenders were all doing their damnedest, and Riacho Escuro could do no less. The mayor's house became battle headquarters, where major and minor decisions were made and announced. As the working group with its friends and hangers-on grew more numerous, Dr. Chrisóstomo had a massive color television installed in the den so they could all watch the Sunday program together. During the breaks for commercials and while everyone was vigorously dissecting the show after it was over, snacks were served, with whisky for the men and tangerine cordial or soda-water for the ladies.

Riacho Escuro's turn to go into action came in the eighth week of the Tournament of Towns. That Sunday morning at six an imposing cortège set out for São Paulo. It was composed of three buses, several private cars, a moving van loaded with sports equipment, ballet costumes and miscellaneous props, and finally a cattle truck conveying the most important entry for the shows—a Brahma bull which had won prizes in five livestock competitions, to be displayed on television with all his blue ribbons and medals. That hadn't been much of a challenge since Riacho Escuro was prime cattle country; the mayor's wife had just asked her second cousin to lend them one of the fine animals from his herd.

The entire presentation had been planned to perfection; there was even a youthful cheering section waving streamers, banners and balloons stamped with "Riacho Escuro" in large letters. That part had been planned and rehearsed by the debutantes of the ladies' auxiliary. After an athletics display the real show began, with a parade of rare items and an artistic program complete with ballet, folk songs, instrumental music and a poetry recital. Thanks to the mayor and the city council —and perhaps still more to the keen discussion and thoughtful analysis of the rivals' performance by the ways and means committee and the ladies' auxiliary—Riacho Escuro scored a resounding victory in that first encounter.

The triumphal procession returned in the wee hours of the morning. The whole town had stayed up to welcome the champions, and the celebration went on until dawn. From that Sunday on Riacho Escuro thought, ate and slept "Tournament of Towns." It was the topic of conversation for every group in every social class; people thought of nothing but learning about or hunting for the curious objects required by the program's producers. The objects would become more exotic and the quest more and more arduous, they knew, particularly since every item had to be produced in a scant week's time. The rare object demanded for the second show was an antique image of a female saint which would shed tears on Corpus Christi. It wouldn't have been so hard to find one if the rules hadn't called for making it cry on cue before the cameras. Naturally, the mayor turned this problem over to the vicar, who served as chairman of the ways and means committee.

Not a single old figure remained in any of the churches in Riacho Escuro. All had been sold to antique dealers and plaster ones put in their place, but perhaps there were a few left in nearby villages or on some old *fazenda*. The priest and all the members of the sodality set out to beat the bushes. On Friday afternoon, when the committee was beginning to lose hope, a sodalist walked in triumphantly with a carved figure in his arms. The old woman who cared for the little chapel where he had found it had assured him that the saint shed tears not only on the feast of Corpus Christi but on various other holy days scattered throughout the calendar.

That Sunday morning the cortège set off again with the mayor and his lady, the vicar bearing the precious image, an honor guard of twelve men from the sodality with their sky-blue sashes and flag, plus the athletes, singers, musicians, recitalists, little girls from the ballet school, and the claque of liberated young people already high on marijuana and primed to yell their lungs out from the audience.

That Dr. Chrisóstomo's team would walk away with the prize on the second show was a foregone conclusion when Riacho Escuro's image not only wept before the cameras but smiled immediately afterwards to show its support for the town. The young fans, who by then were feeling no pain, shouted out, "It's the greatest, the greatest, the greatest!" and the audience went wild with agreement.

The main attraction Riacho Escuro was asked to contribute to the next show, the semi-final round, was a pair of adult Siamese twins, preferably a male and a female. (Really, the imagination of Silvio Santos and his team knew no bounds!) Luckily, a member of the finance committee recalled having read in a magazine, years before, a feature article about two babies who were born together in a village 150 miles away, off near the border of Minas Gerais. This time the mayor and his wife went to search for the hidden treasure themselves and found a pair of black Siamese twins living in a decrepit shack. They were seventeen and could therefore be considered adult. The only difficulty was that both of them were girls. What to do? The mayor thought a few minutes, consulted his wife, and with one accord, thinking of the difficulty of finding any more suitable Siamese twins in the short time remaining, took the pair away with them.

Because the Siamese twins were the same sex, Riacho Escuro came within an inch of losing, but led by two points in the final voting because the singing toad from the rival town forgot the words to the second verse of "Bésame Mucho" and was booed.

This time the celebration in Riacho Escuro was more restrained. On the way home the mayor admitted to his wife and to the vicar that he had misgivings about the finals, for which they were required to present a transvestite who had been born and raised in Riacho Escuro (a firm stipulation) and could do a perfect imitation of Carmen Miranda. In any other town this would have presented no problem, but it was an impossibility in Riacho Escuro because the mayor himself, immediately after taking office, had ordered the police chief to make a clean sweep of all public places suspected of harboring vice and to throw all unsavory characters out of town in the name of decency and morality. In one fell swoop the police closed down the whore houses, the motels on the edge of town, and a nightclub that alternated a timid drag show with the routine strip-tease numbers. Now it looked as if the mayor's impulsive cleanup campaign would ruin the town's chances of winning the contest. But they *had* to win, or the civic pride of Riacho Escuro would be dragged in the dust.

When he started out for City Hall on Monday morning the mayor was deeply troubled. Passing the Two Fatherlands Bar and Ice Cream Parlor on the courthouse square, he decided a cup of coffee might help him collect his thoughts. A few minutes later, as he raised the steaming cup to his lips, he noticed a young man behind the counter stirring sherbet in a mixer with a wooden paddle. While he distractedly stirred the thick mass of sherbert, the youth sang to himself in time with the mixer, "*You say I've come back an American, that I'm rich and got money to burn?* . . ." Leaning on the paddle, the youth swayed seductively, making sinuous movements with his free arm. Dr. Chrisóstomo could hardly believe his eyes. When the ice-cream maker noticed the mayor watching him he turned up his eyes, waved coquettishly and finished the verse: ". . . *now don't talk so bad about me.*" Then he smiled, a dazzling white smile that narrowed his mischievous eyes into almond-shaped slits. It was as though Carmen Miranda herself had come to life again!

"Hey, young fellow, were you born around here?"

The youth put his hands on his hips and flung the mayor a scornful look and a saucy retort: "Yes I was, if you want to know. Do the authorities think they can shut me up? This is a democracy!"

Without thinking twice, a jubilant Dr. Chrisóstomo seized the young man by the arm, dragged him down the street to City Hall and showed him off to all the municipal employees and city councilmen he could find. The verdict was unanimous: tart him up a little and he'd be the spitting image of the great entertainer. The mayor phoned his wife and told her to call a meeting of the ladies' auxiliary without delay. Then he gave orders that every last detail should be settled then and there in the conference room in City Hall, so that Claudinho (that was the young man's name) would be ready for Sunday's grand finale.

Everyone scurried around being helpful. The mayor's wife insisted on taking Claudinho to São Paulo that very afternoon to be fitted for a frilly Bahiana costume and start being coached by a choreographer, a music arranger, a voice teacher and an expert in bodily expression. (They could have managed without the last, but just to be on the safe side, they thought their new star ought to be drilled in the fine points of walking on platform shoes and holding his wrists a little limper.) Dr. Chrisóstomo, pleased as punch at having unearthed such a treasure on his own, called in the reporter and photographer from the Riacho Escuro *Post* to have his picture taken with Claudinho. He also contributed the headline for the story that appeared the following day: "Thanks to Dr. Chrisóstomo Mascarenhas, His Honor the Mayor, the Next Carmen Miranda Makes His Debut in Riacho Escuro and Will Soon Belong to Brazil and the World."

The next five days were the most hectic Claudinho had ever spent in his life. He was rushed from choreographer to voice coach, from there to the dressmaker, next to the hairdresser, then to the makeup artist, and back to the choreographer without a break. At night he fell into his hotel bed and slept like a log until the next morning, when the same dizzy round began again. By Saturday, though, he was perfectly primed and sure of himself, belting out his songs with verve and pizazz, gyrating expertly on his platform shoes, swinging his hips saucily, moving his arms with incredible grace and rolling his eyes in a way that provoked enthusiastic applause from the soberest citizen. The grand finale was a triumph. Riacho Escuro easily surged ahead of its last rival and was awarded top honors in the Tournament of Towns.

That night Claudinho, still in his makeup and gorgeous costume, rode home in the mayor's car between that dignitary and the vicar, the mayor's wife having gone in the other car with the police chief and his wife. They were welcomed in glory at dawn in the courthouse square by a brass band, ovations, applause, confetti and streamers. (The young cheering section, thoroughly stoned, even risked a sniff of illegal ether spray.) The owner of the Two Fatherlands treated everyone to ice cream and Claudinho, borne aloft on the shoulders of the cheering crowd, had to repeat his triumphal number on top of the mayor's car.

The award ceremony, with the handing over of countless medals, trophies and a scroll with gold letters commemorating the victory, took place the following Sunday at the end of Silvio's program. It was a bang-up show. A special stage set had been designed with circular platforms and elaborate lamps that blinked on and off. On the first platform stood the prize Brahma bull who had won the first competition for Riacho Escuro, nobly bedecked with all his ribbons and medals, with the girls from the ballet class poised like sylphs in a semi-circle around him. On the second platform were the Siamese twins, dressed as Princess Isabel the emancipator and José do Patrocínio the abolitionist, and behind them the athletes forming an allegorical frieze of the freeing of the slaves. On the ramps leading up to the platforms were grouped the authorities of Riacho Escuro—the mayor and his wife, the vicar, the chief of police, the district judge, the presidents of the Lions and Rotary Clubs and the city councilmen. At the apex, rising from the second platform and ending in an imposing metallic curtain, was a huge open fan with its ribs illuminated by more blinking lights. Framed in each section of the fan was a member of the Marian Sodality and at the very top, in a blaze of light from slowly revolving mirrored globes and a shower of glittering tinsel, Claudinho struck a pose in his magnificent Carmen Miranda garb, holding in his arms the image that shed tears on Corpus Christi and on other, less sanctified days.

But that was only the beginning of Claudinho's brilliant career. No sooner had he stepped down from the fan at the end of the show than he was offered a contract by Waldemar Issa as the star of a musical revue at São Paulo's Medieval Theater. And it looks as if it will be Claudinho and not a famous television actress (as had been rumored), who will get the title role in the million-dollar film Luiz Carlos Barreto is currently negotiating with an American producer: "The Life and Loves of Carmen Miranda."

—Translated by
Barbara Shelby Morello

ANNA RHEINSBERG

VISITING

Ruth stands in the bathroom before the mirror and scrubs the lilac lipstick from her mouth. "Johannes comes tomorrow," she says, then turns her head and gives Thomas a quizzical glance. "We won't have much time for each other!" Thomas, with one foot on the floor and the other on the side of the bath, is drying his thighs with a towel. She loves it when his legs are slightly spread and his body bent forward so that she can see the twin spheres sway to and fro as he dries himself. In that position he has firm buttocks, like milk and honey, and his hips are wide. Thomas has hips like a woman, and a slender waist.

Ruth adores being in the bathroom: here it is damp and warm, and after a shower they stand rubbing cream into each other until the skin becomes silken and fragrant. She always wants to stand behind him, and at the moment he stoops forward she bends her head and sinks her white teeth into his bottom. Each time he jerks up, flinging his damp hair across his shoulders, then whirls about, and they kiss until both are gasping for breath.

But tomorrow Johannes is coming.

She senses, even though he makes a dismissing gesture with his hand, how pleased he really is. Johannes has been a friend for many years, but now has time to visit them only every couple of months. Johannes is his lover.

She still remembers vividly how it all began three years before. How Johannes sat on the old plush sofa in the kitchen with weary eyes and slightly trembling hands and finally, finally had to tell them something about himself, something they could have no idea of, could never have guessed for themselves. He had remained silent for such a long time. Out of fear, as he later admitted, that they might turn away from him, leave him alone forever.

It took a long while before the whole thing was out. Ruth had become impatient. She had no love for such endless wrestling with words, always wanted to have everything stated quickly and straightforwardly, and without the long, oppressive silences. A strange atmosphere surrounded the kitchen sofa that day. Johannes with his soft lips that seemed unable to speak, even though she already knew what they wanted to say. It had caught her attention the instant he entered the apartment.

He moved differently, he spoke softly to her as he took off his jacket, and he wore his hair longer than before. But it wasn't merely the external clues that caught her attention, it was more the feeling that this man whom she had known for so many years and who was her friend had altered in some way or other.

And then Thomas. He was restless the whole afternoon, smoked too much and had a look in his eyes which always gave her delight when she saw it. But this time it was not meant for her.

That evening Thomas was agitated, he stared greedily and had the same expression around his mouth as when he was about to kiss her after spending an hour together in the bath. But he did not take her in his arms.

He sat fumbling with his tobacco and gazed at Johannes, gazed at his slender face, at the full, sensuous lips, which sometimes gave him the appearance of a fretful sleepy child about to burst into tears; he stared at Johannes's slanting eyes, at the brown page-boy hair, the ring in his right earlobe, and Ruth realized that Thomas was randy.

That night she observed him carefully. The way he looked up when Johannes went to the stove to put on more water for tea. The way he sized up the long legs, mesmerized by the way Johannes's tight jeans parted his buttocks and outlined their firm shape.

Thomas's constant staring escaped neither her nor the friend. "So you're a fag," she said suddenly, to give a name to the unspoken. Thomas and Johannes both recoiled at the same instant. "And Thomas is randy," she said with a laugh, sprang to her feet, embraced the friend and kissed him lightly on the mouth. "You can't fool Ruth!"

They sat for a long time then and discussed it, though no one referred to Thomas's desire with even a single sentence. Later, as Ruth lay in bed beside him, with Johannes in the adjoining room, she cuddled against him and he kissed her, stroking her with his hands, until she told him he should go to his friend.

"I can't do that!" Thomas shook his head, but the idea haunted him; his entire body desired it, and yet he dared not. He was afraid. "What would you say to that," he asked her, sitting up in the bed. "I find you so desirable—your breasts, your cunt, your legs . . ."

Thus he sought to justify himself in a way that was completely unnecessary. "If you want it," she said to him, "then go. He may already be asleep. Don't miss your chance."

"And you?" he asked, his eyes seeking her face in the darkness.

"I'll come with you!" she said. "I'll sit with my back to the wall and watch!"

And that was precisely what happened. Ruth pulled on her socks, dragged her quilt and Thomas behind her; he held back timidly, protesting each time she was about to knock on Johannes's door. "No, no, we can't do that," he whispered. "Pssst—don't be so loud." Finally her patience was worn out. She rapped her knuckles briskly on the door, pressed down on the handle even before Johannes could answer, and pushed the resisting Thomas into the room.

A streetlamp that glowed outside the window cast its light over the friend; his bluntly cut hair flowed softly across his shoulders, and he had thrown aside the sheet so that he lay naked before them, a dream.

Ruth sat on the floor, drew her legs up, and wrapped herself in the quilt. Come what may, she was prepared! She snuggled the quilt about her shoulders. Suddenly Thomas was left standing alone in the room, and his first thought was to rush to her, to crawl under the quilt. But it couldn't be done. She stared stubbornly ahead, as she always did when there was a decision to be reached that he didn't feel confident to make.

Johannes, not quite understanding the charade, but guessing whose idea it was, took a deep breath, and after that resistance faded quickly.

Ruth sat in her corner, fascinated, while the two men reached for each other, first uncertainly, with erratic movements, then more and more sure of themselves. Confidently they stroked each other's bodies, exploring, touching, running their hands wherever pleasure led them. When they finally rolled apart and lay still, not knowing where to look, Ruth shuffled across to them. She pulled the quilt behind her like a child, stumbled over it, and sprawled across the naked pair.

They all laughed with relief and each of the men kissed her on the mouth and on the neck, tickled her behind the ears and pulled her between them. Thomas put his arms around her, cradled her so that her rump pressed against his stomach, while Johannes buried his head in her hair. They slept.

"Johannes is coming today," she says, but Thomas's eyes are still tightly shut, and she presses her lips against his forehead. She points at his penis, which has raised itself as it always does after sleep, standing boldly upright and quivering. Quickly he turns on his side and grumbles something incomprehensible, but once she is awake there is no more dreaming for him, either.

He finally gets up and begins to paint his eyes with kohl.

Carefully he pulls the skin taut and skillfully outlines the lids in black. He had had to practice often before he succeeded in doing it without tears flowing and smearing everything. Then he shaves with great care, letting no single hair escape; all fall to the merciless blade. He wants to be beautiful. Wants to smell of cinnamon and to be as supple as a young cat.

"You're a goose," says Ruth, who perches on the toilet seat and watches him. "What a vain, silly goose!"

"You're jealous—envious is what you are. I do just the same for you." And Thomas squares his shoulders, so that he seems taller than usual.

"I'll put a book on your head," she nags, "and until he comes you can spend your time walking up and down the hall —straight as a candle, head up. It improves the posture." She stands on her toes and gives him a demonstration. "That's the way young ladies learn how to walk properly," she says, and snorts contemptuously. But he splashes so much water that she shrieks in protest. Today no one can spoil his mood. Let the woman across the way stick her twentieth note of the week into the mailbox about finally cleaning the stairs! He also declines to fetch the breakfast-rolls; his hair is wet, he says, and getting the sniffles is unthinkable.

Silently Ruth curses Johannes for turning everything upside down. When the bell rings she at first doesn't want to open the door. That can't be him yet, they think, and who knows what sort of nuisance it could mean. They want to have a cozy breakfast together, taking their time, and afterwards go back to bed to read and make love.

When she opens the door, someone is standing there. In the first instant she thinks it is a woman, but then she recognizes Johannes. He is wearing a dress covered with ruffles and frills, a yellow dress with a beaded collar, and he has painted his mouth scarlet. "How fabulous you look," he warbles as he enters. "There was almost an accident in the street, *chérie,*" he says, and extends her a cheek so that she can give him a peck—but very carefully, so as not to spoil his make-up. "How do I look?" It sounds like three question marks, and while they float through the air he arches his eyebrows. They stand there in the hall, Ruth with her hands on her hips and staring critically, Johannes in high drag and with rouged cheeks, his hair teased into a bouffant cloud.

"Well?" he asks, and minces toward her, a complete parody. He wiggles his fanny, swings an imaginary purse. "I'm Johannes," he says with a nasal twang, sugar-sweet and twittering, "don't you know me any more?"

Then she gives a joyful yelp, takes a running start, as she always did when he returned—takes a running start and leaps into his arms. Johannes has strong arms. Now, as he catches her, holds her, they protrude from the wide sleeves of his dress. Arms downed with pale hair, blue veins lacing the backs of his hands. They contract as he holds her, bulging, and she can see that the little fingernail of his right hand is lacquered black.

Johannes is beautiful. Like a child she clings to him and gazes into his face. The sloping eyes are as full of expression as before. They gleam beneath lids dusted with golden powder. Then the nose, so firmly aquiline, and the full bottom lip which once so gently caressed her. He is half man, half woman, with strong arms and a flat chest, wearing a brilliant yellow dress and the face of a primadonna.

"What have you got under your dress? Show me, Johannes!" As he lowers her to her feet, she reaches under and raises the skirt. "You're wearing underpants? Goodness gracious! You're not supposed to be wearing anything underneath," she teases. "How's anybody supposed to get a hand in if you've got panties on?"

Johannes pretends to be embarrassed, as if the whole thing were frightfully distressing. "But you mustn't," he pipes. "Don't touch me there, don't you dare!"

Thomas enters from the kitchen. His mouth, that had curved in an impish smile when Ruth asked him how he had enjoyed himself with Johannes, is now clamped firmly shut.

"Hell." He stands there stiff as a poker, his legs welded together.

"He's here." Ruth, enjoying herself thoroughly, draws the friend forward. "Johannes is finally here." She is delighted, but Thomas only raises the corners of his mouth disdainfully.

"What a sight you are!" He gestures at the dress. "Like a scarecrow. You really dare to go out on the street like that?"

Ruth drops the friend's hand, bites her lip. Why is he saying such things?

"Don't you like it?" Johannes conceals his bewilderment. "Look!" Again he waggles his fanny and swings an imaginary purse. "Just look, sweetie. I'm beautiful!" He parades around Thomas, and pauses to give him a quick kiss on the nose.

Thomas shrinks back. "You look like a . . . woman . . . like a real faggot. I always thought you didn't go in for that kind of thing. I thought you were a . . . man! And now you look like something out of the comics. A real freak!"

He doesn't want a friend like that—or so he tells himself, and tries to look cold, imperious. But that isn't honest. For Johnnes is indeed beautiful, and this combination of penis and woman, the lure of manly arms with their faint down, and the long skirt trapping the powerful legs and preventing them from striding out—it is all exciting, arousing.

Thomas knows that. Like Ruth, he has the desire to see what Johannes is wearing under his skirt, but he controls himself. Instead, he heats water for tea, arranges cups and saucers on the flowered tablecloth, takes out spoons and sugar. He has forgotten the penciled lines on his own lids, the scent of cinnamon and the morning shave. He is doing this for her as well, he thinks to himself, and that is nothing out of the ordinary.

They sit around the table in silence. Ruth wants somehow to break through the barrier, and begins to question Johannes about everything that can possibly be questioned. About the life he leads, about the clothes he wears—the why and wherefore, the method of it all. Johannes at first replies only in monosyllables, but the old familiarity between them is still there, though Thomas broods gloomily and wrinkles his forehead.

They sit through the whole morning, the afternoon. Toward evening Thomas prepares something to eat. He remains silent, ignores Johannes's appearance, refuses to acknowledge that there is anything his timid heart cannot tolerate or comprehend.

Ruth suffers. She fails in her efforts to lead Thomas back to his friend. Well, that's that, she thinks. Let him sulk, but he'll get a hard-on anyhow.

That, of course, is up to her. She coos and flirts and finally brings in her make-up so that she can paint Johannes's face to her own liking, with heavy black circles around his eyes, high cheekbones and lilac lips. Lilac is her own color. The whole thing is a wonderful game between them, and it takes her breath away. She drags in the most outrageous things—a picture-hat with a veil, yards of colored tulle, her great-grandmother's mink collar, spike-heeled shoes.

Johannes must try everything on. Let's play dress-up is her motto, and she adores seeing him slipping into the most wildly different roles. At one moment he is the *grande dame,* then the dandy with top-hat and cane. Johannes gives everything a touch of the bizarre: he is a gentleman who menaces her even as he gallantly tips his hat, he is a villainess who purrs and entices her.

Ruth sits with her legs spread, her arms resting on the back of the chair, and holds first one hand and then the other over her mouth as she plunges into renewed fits of laughter.

Thomas can't tear himself away. There is something fascinating about Johannes: he takes on a thousand different personalities—is simultaneously conqueror and conquered, is hustler, ladies' man, clod.

They no longer take any notice of Thomas. He kneels on the sofa and lets the film unreel. They don't look toward him. Or? Ruth watches him from the corner of her eye, knowing he is not unaffected by their presentation. Indeed, she knows he is randy and can't comprehend Johannes, can't fit him into the pigeonholes of man or woman. And there should be nothing in between. Far from it, Thomas. The show goes on.

Ruth brings wine from a shop on the corner. They sip from mother-of-pearl cups and play their game. Indefatigably.

They continue to drink. Ruth has put on a negligee of rose-colored silk, so deeply cut in the front that the tops of her small breasts are visible. She smells of some heavy perfume, has dabbed musk behind her ears and her wrists. She has also drawn up her long dark dair, and a few stray locks curl down her neck.

She is wearing a fine gold chain at her throat. The rose-colored negligee reaches to her feet, cut voluptuously narrow in the hips and slit in the center up to the knee. What is further up one must imagine. And so she sits again on her chair, legs spread, but from the waist up a lady.

Johannes is naked; his chest is almost hairless and his nipples small as the heads of pins. His deeply tanned skin is stretched taut across his biceps, his stomach, and Ruth wants to bury her head there. She wants to do it at once, and she spends little time considering whether he might dislike it. She is already there, slips onto his knees and presses her cheek beneath his left nipple, where she hears the heart pounding. Thomas now accepts Johannes's glances. Relaxed, he sprawls on the sofa, his hands folded over his crotch. He has stretched out his legs, and he shifts them slightly to draw Johannes's attention. And so they exchange glances. Ruth, with her arms flung around the friend's neck, feels his penis stirring. Although she knows it is not meant for her, she is excited by it. Johannes rocks her without taking his eyes from Thomas. Or Thomas from him. The make-up is beginning to flake away; Johannes's eyelids are no longer so golden as in the morning, the kohl has gathered in the corners of Thomas's eyes, and he wipes it with the back of his hand.

The three stand up. They seem to proceed in slow-motion into the next room, approach the wide wooden bed that Thomas built for Ruth when she was away from him for a few days and telephoned almost every hour, desperate with yearning for him.

It is her bed. Thomas pulls off his linen shirt and overalls. He stands before them with his wide, womanly hips. Johannes is already naked. Now it is Ruth's turn. The friends draw her to the bed and she sits between them as they run their hands up her arms, press their mouths first against her right breast, then the left. They kiss the flesh around her brown nipples, suck at them until her thighs begin to spread, she feels her body opening and a hand probing her fleece. But to whom does she belong—Thomas or Johannes? Johannes kisses Thomas on the lips, and Thomas does the same to Ruth. Is that him kissing her on the mouth, between the legs?

Burrowing in Ruth's hair, Thomas nibbles at her ear lobes while a hand tenderly strokes her belly, then slides down to massage her where she has grown firm and moist with passion. She seizes Thomas vigorously by the hips, pulls him up and into her, while Johannes braces her back. He runs his fingers along her neck, braces her so that she can sit firmly and hold Thomas inside her.

She cries out slightly, groans loudly, arches her body until her head is so far back that she sees Johannes. His penis is close to her, she can feel the silken skin and rub her cheek against it, and still he is the one who holds her so that she doesn't sink back against the pillows.

Even when they change positions, Ruth on top of Thomas now, locking him tightly with her thighs, the friend kneels behind her, runs his hands down her back and then along Thomas's legs. Ruth knows that Johannes does not desire her, even though he fondles her; it is only a way of showing his affection. Then she lies still. Johannes kisses her fingers. Suddenly needing to feel his mouth against her once more, she pulls him to her, flings her arms around him, and offers him her lips. She holds him tightly, rumples his hair, tastes his salt. And yet it can last only a second, it must be over before the spark jumps once more and he turns away from her, disappointed that she refuses to acknowledge the real direction of his lust.

Then she rolls into a corner against the wall and remains still. Thomas has laid his head on Johannes's chest. His mouth makes a damp trail across his skin and burrows beneath Johannes's arm while with one hand he strokes the damp tip of the friend's penis until his entire body begins to tremble. There is no longer anything here for Ruth, and she makes no use of the position Johannes had taken before. Masculine arms grasp each other, legs are buried in pillows, and mouths grind together; their tongues dart and lick between the thighs, on the ass, along the spine. Thomas's hair gives off a sweet smell, and Johannes moans softly.

They rock together, rub and bite each other's nipples, their bodies gliding up and down. For Thomas it is all as it was then, a long while ago.

As morning dawns they wearily raise their heads. Golden make-up shimmers from the pillows, and some corner of the sheet has long since wiped the last traces of lilac lipstick from Johannes's mouth.

—Translated by
David Galloway and
Christian Sabisch

NOTES ON AUTHORS

SHERWOOD ANDERSON, born in the town of Camden, Ohio, in 1876, was strongly shaped by his midwestern boyhood, which supplied the major themes and settings and strongly influenced the language of his writings. Like many American authors of the period, he was largely self-educated, and was forty at the time his first novel appeared. After a series of odd jobs and military service in Cuba during the Spanish-American War, Anderson married and settled down in Elyria, Ohio, as the manager of a paint factory. When he walked out one day, left his family behind and headed for Chicago to pursue a literary career, he created for numerous writers and intellectuals a symbol for the plight of the artist in materialistic America. Anderson first attracted wide attention with the collection of interlocked short stories entitled *Winesburg, Ohio* (1919), a kind of *Bildüngsroman* in which a young reporter peers behind the polite, ordered facades of small-town America. In a series of epiphanies he encounters the loneliness, yearning and sexual frustration that make up the secret life of Winesburg. The book's critical success assured Anderson's reception by the literati of New York and Paris, where for a time he joined the celebrated circle of Gertrude Stein, who strongly influenced his novel of Negro life, *Dark Laughter* (1925). In his last years Anderson lived with his fourth wife in a simple cottage in rural Virginia; he died in 1941 during an unofficial goodwill tour of South America. Anderson once enjoyed a kind of notoriety as a writer on sex, the focal theme of many of his stories, and his name was frequently linked to that of D.H. Lawrence. It is true that he viewed sexual experience as an opportunity to escape the ruthless standardization of the modern age, the confinement of the regulated life; and he believed that the primal, instinctive forces of human behavior must not be denied. On the other hand, sexuality ultimately has a mystical rather than an erotic dimension in Anderson's work, and properly viewed is only one aspect of the struggle for identity and personal dignity chronicled in his writings.

GIORGIO BASSANI was born in Bologna, Italy, in 1916, and educated at the University of Bologna, but his most famous writings are set in the medieval town of Ferrara. In a series of interlocking short stories and novels, including *The Gold-Rimmed Spectacles* (1958) and *The Garden of the Finzi-Continis* (1963), he has recorded the destinies of dozens of families, from the working class to the faded aristocracy, focusing on the period from 1930 to 1945. Characters appear and reappear, threading the works together into a dense and vivid tapestry as noteworthy for its refined social and political observations as for its elegantly spare, lyric style. The figure of the homosexual Doctor Athos Fadigati plays a central role in *The Gold-Rimmed Spectacles*, not only because of his influence on the young narrator's vision of life, but also because his double existence is a key to other characters in the novel who are compelled to mask their inner feelings and desires. Revealing his true nature to his fellow citizens eventually leads to Dr. Fadigati's suicide; similarly, opening up their enchanted garden leads to the death of the Finzi-Continis in a Nazi concentration camp. In addition to novels and short stories, Giorgio Bassani has also published several volumes of poetry, lectured on drama, and served as vice-president of Italian Radio and Television.

WILLIAM BURROUGHS was born in St. Louis in 1914, the grandson of the inventor of the famous Burroughs adding-machine. After graduation from Harvard College, he studied medicine in Vienna, worked at a variety of odd jobs, and served briefly in the U.S. Army. While living in Mexico shortly after World War II, Burroughs killed his wife in a game of "William Tell," attempting to shoot a champagne glass balanced on her head. In the following years he became legendary as a haunted, drug-addicted homosexual who wandered between Tangiers, London and Paris. His highly autobiographical first novel, *Junkie* (1953), is a painful, straightforward account of the tormented underground life of an addict, but incorporates vignettes of sexuality and police action that anticipate the themes of his later, more experimental work. *The Naked Lunch* (1959) also begins as a first-person narrative by an addict, but quickly breaks with linear discourse in favor of a kind of hallucinatory continuum where the viewpoint is in continuous flux. The book blends fragmentary narratives, violent images, satirical effects and raw sexual encounters—usually of a sensationally homosexual nature. In the works that followed, including *Nova Express* (1964), Burroughs developed "cut-up" and "fold-up" techniques of random composition that sometimes resemble surrealist collages; he also showed a growing interest in science fiction. An admirer of de Sade, Kafka and Genet, he is by turns fiendishly comic, coldly surreal; he has repeatedly attacked technological power groups, corporate capitalism and medical tyranny. William Burroughs is often seen as the "Guru" of the Beat Generation, and his extreme formal experimentation has been a major influence on contemporary American writing.

MATEI CARAGIALE was born in Bucharest, Rumania, in 1885, and died there in 1936. He was the son of Ion Luca Caragiale, a brilliant and eccentric dramatist whose comic plays mocked bourgeois pretension and political rhetoric. Ion Caragiale had a deep and passionate love for Germany, and he exiled himself in Berlin in 1904. His impressionable son Matei was deeply influenced by his own stay in the German capital as a young man; when he returned to Bucharest he worked as a miniature painter, heraldist and civil servant. Although Caragiale produced relatively little in his lifetime, he is remembered as a consummate stylist whose meticulous language evoked a submerged world hovering between reality and dream. His models included Poe, Oscar Wilde and Baudelaire, but the exotic lessons he learned from them were given his own distinctive stamp. In his most famous work, *The Four from the Old Court* (1929), he explored the city of Bucharest from the mud of unpaved alleys to the airy drawing-rooms of the nobility. He began the novel in 1910 and worked at it, meticulously revising and rewriting, for nearly two decades. Other than sonnets, a few sketches and an extensive diary, Caragiale published only one other work—the remarkable novella *Remember* (1924), which drew heavily in mood and atmosphere on his own stay in Berlin.

CONSTANTIN CAVAFY was born to a prosperous Greek merchant family in 1863 in Alexandria, where he lived for most of his life and died in 1933. At school he developed such a deep love for ancient Greek civilization that he eventually became a Greek citizen. When anti-European, anti-Christian riots broke out in Alexandria in 1882, Cavafy went to Constantinople to live for three years in the home of his grandfather; there he discovered the delights of modern, demotic Greek, and composed his first poems. His linguistic gifts were a prime recommendation for the clerical post he received in Egypt's Ministry of Irrigation in 1892, and held for the next thirty years. Cavafy was a rigorous aesthetician, whose work underwent continuous revision; he wrote as many as seventy poems a year, but usually destroyed all but four or five. His first book of verse, published in 1904, contained a mere fourteen titles, and a later edition added only twelve more; though various poems appeared in periodicals in Greece and Egypt, these were the sole book-length publications in Cavafy's lifetime. The poet once identified the three principal modes of his verse as the erotic, the philosophical and the historical; the first two are frequently interwoven, and all three sometimes come together in a single work. The erotic poems are almost all frankly homosexual. These frequently set up a dialogue between the imagination of the artist-speaker and the realities—often sordid or disillusioning—of the flesh; yet Cavafy insists that the imagination must always be rooted in physical reality. In the original Greek, Cavafy's poems were revolutionary in their mingling of classical and modern voices—an aspect lost in any translation. Nonetheless, his work has had a profound impact on other writers, including E.M. Forster, who introduced Cavafy's poems to T.S. Eliot and D.H. Lawrence, among others; W.H. Auden also acknowledged that many of his own poems were shaped by his reading of Cavafy.

JEAN COCTEAU was born in 1891 into a social milieu whose members presumed the arts to be an essential part of the good life, and as a child he formed a life-long passion for the theater, which he described as "the fever of crimson and gold." A sense for theatrical illusion and flair is one of the elements uniting his amazingly versatile work. Shortly after his seventeenth birthday Cocteau published his first volume of poems, *Aladin's Lamp*, and for more than half a century would explore not only every existing literary genre but the cinema, ballet, the circus and jazz. He made his debut as a novelist with *Thomas the Impostor* in 1923, and perfected his fictional expressionism with *The Grand Ecart* (1923) and *Enfants Terribles* (1929). Cocteau made a firm distinction between his "sleeping books" and his "waking books," the latter composed after the new self-awareness he learned through contact with friends like André Gide. Thus, he dated his own literary beginnings from the publication of the prose fantasy *Le Potomak,* which became even more imaginative, more baroque, in the revised edition that appeared in 1919. The same spirit would inform films like *Blood of a Poet* and *Beauty and the Beast,* his most successful plays, his paintings and drawings, and the sensuous little novella—a kind of prose poem—which Cocteau published anonymously in 1928 under the title *Le livre blanc.* It has been said that of the artistic generation whose daring vision gave birth to twentieth-century art, Cocteau came closest to being a Renaissance man. As his own posthumous tribute to that phenomenal range of talent, following his death in 1963 he was buried in the garden of the chapel of Saint-Blaise-des-Simples which he had designed himself.

LONNIE COLEMAN was born in 1920 in Barstow, Georgia, which provided him with much of the setting for his most popular work, the trilogy of novels entitled *Beulah Land.* This complex saga of the destinies of a nineteenth-century plantation family became a television mini-series, and established the author's international reputation. Following work as an editor for *Collier's* magazine, Coleman lived for seven years in England and Ireland, and since 1979 has made his home in Savannah. He is the author of more than a dozen novels, and has frankly explored homosexual themes in *Ship's Company* (1955), *Sam* (1959) and *Mark* (1981). *Sam* was a pioneering work in its conscious opposition to the formula whereby homosexual experience inevitably ends in suicide or murder; the portrayal of a successful relationship between two men is saved from sentimentality by the author's restrained style and his flair for dry, witty dialogue.

OTTO VILHELM EKELUND, the son of a blacksmith, was born in 1880 in Scania, the southernmost province of Sweden, and died in 1949. His first book of verse, *Varbris* (*Spring Breeze*), appeared in 1900, and from that year he devoted himself exclusively to a literary career. Ekelund's early collections were lyrical and impressionistic, drawing chiefly on the experiences of his own country childhood. With *Elegier* (*Elegies,* 1903), his mature style was formed—a distinctive amalgam of influences from classical Greek poetry, Expressionism, and Swedish and German Romanticism—most notably, the free verse of Hölderlin and Platen. The links with Platen were not only formal but thematic, for the subject of homosexual love was important to them both. Largely because of his frank treatment of this subject, Ekelund soon found himself without either a publisher or an audience, and almost entirely abandoned the writing of verse. In 1908 he was sentenced to a month in prison for obstructing justice. Rather than serve the sentence, he spent the next twelve years in exile in Germany and Denmark. Ekelund married in 1914, and his daughter was born in the same year; in 1921 he returned to Sweden, and the last collection of his poetry was released. Ekelund's marriage and his abandonment of homosexual subjects was not a recantation, but a deliberate remaking of the self. The choice facing him, as his letters show, was either a heterosexual "transformation" or destruction both as a writer and as an individual. A few aphorisms from his later years testify to a continuing sympathy for the dilemmas facing homosexuals in a hostile society.

JAMES (THOMAS) FARRELL was born in 1904 on the South Side of Chicago, where he lived until he moved to New York in 1931; the city would provide the setting for his most important fiction, which in an urgent, naturalistic style exposes the boredom, violence and isolation of modern urban life. While a student at Chicago University, Farrell wrote a sketch that would eventually grow into a trilogy of novels about Studs Lonigan. For *Young Lonigan* (1932) the author drew heavily on his own experiences as a pupil in a Catholic school and the numerous odd jobs he held as a young man —including that of a newspaper reporter. *The Young Manhood of Studs Lonigan* (1934) and *Judgment Day* (1935) continue the dispassionate record of the brutalized life and pathetic death of the inarticulate hero. Farrell's vision was shaped by the Great Depression, and he never lost a sense of indignation at social and economic inequalities. In a tetralogy of novels about Danny O'Neill, Farrell holds out hope that the hero can escape the destructive forces of his environment, and in a trilogy focused on novelist Bernard Carr, the author seems to have vicariously fulfilled some of his own aesthetic ambitions. But Farrell's most characteristic writings show man caught in a trap formed by the familiar naturalistic forces of heredity and environment. Though he remained incredibly prolific, producing essays, novels and more than 200 short stories, most critics agree that Farrell's work shows little real development, and that his proletarian-naturalistic aesthetic tends to produce a flat, self-conscious prose. The work of the 1930's, however, made a substantial contribution to the school of urban fiction in America.

EDWARD MORGAN FORSTER was born in London in 1879 and educated at King's College, Cambridge, where he was appointed honorary fellow in 1946. His years in Italy provided background for his earliest novels, *Where Angels Fear to Tread* (1905) and *A Room with a View* (1908). In 1910 Forster published *Howards End*, which dramatizes his ideal of effecting harmony between the discordant elements within man himself and between man and the universe. During World War I the author served as a Red Cross volunteer, visiting both India and Egypt, where he met Constantin Cavafy. His most celebrated novel, *A Passage to India* (1924), masterfully blends symbolic suggestion, psychological insight and social realism. Forster borrowed his title from the famous poem of the same name by Walt Whitman, and like Whitman he stressed the need to combine the technical triumphs of Western civilization with a new exploration of man's spiritual resources. The novel documents the struggles of individuals to reach out across barriers of race, culture and social convention. Figuratively, the predicament of the isolated individual analyzed in *A Passage to India* offers a key to understanding the situation of the homosexual in British society of the same period. E.M. Forster suppressed his own homosexual novel *Maurice,* composed in 1913, and the seven explicitly homosexual short stories he wrote between 1922 and 1958; it was only after his death in 1970 that what the author called his ''indecent writings'' first appeared in print. Perhaps it was in part his reluctance to explore the sexual manifestations of his philosophical vision that blocked Forster in his later years; he produced essays and occasional writings and collaborated on the libretto for Benjamin Britten's opera *Billy Budd*, but there was no more major fiction, though Forster lived for nearly a half-century after the publication of *A Passage to India.*

JEAN GENET, born in Paris as an illegitimate child in 1910, only learned the name of his mother when he was issued a birth certificate at the age of twenty-one. As a ward of the *Assistance Publique* he developed a precocious sympathy for the outcast and the criminal, and was himself first sentenced to a reformatory at the age of ten; he would spend the next thirty years in and out of the most notorious prisons in Europe. It was in the Fresnes prison is 1942 that he completed his first book, *Our Lady of the Flowers,* composed on the sheets of coarse brown paper with which prisoners produced paper bags. The novel described the life of a young man who, like the author, had spent his childhood in the provinces and became a male prostitute in Paris, changing his name to Divine and his identity from masculine to feminine. Such inversions are typical of Genet's work, which repeatedly mocks the values and assumptions of bourgeois society; the homosexual, the murderer and the thief become the ''angels'' of this underworld, their lives startlingly transformed by the incantatory power of Genet's narrative voice. By 1948 Genet had published three novels, two plays and two long poems when he was sent to prison for the tenth time and thus received an automatic life-sentence. France's leading intellectuals —including Gide, Sartre and Jean Cocteau—successfully petitioned the government for his release. Particularly for the Existentialists, Genet's life and his writings seemed symbolic of the condition of modern man, and Sartre made him the subject of a mammoth biography entitled *Saint Genet.* Genet's most characteristic work—including the highly autobiographical *Thief's Journal* (1949)—blends motifs of eroticism, religious ecstasy and anarchy, fused in a poetic language of startling vividness and inventiveness.

ALLEN GINSBERG was born in 1926 in Newark, New Jersey, the son of the poet and teacher Louis Ginsberg; his mother Naomi was a Russian Jewish immigrant active in the politics of the Left. After school in Paterson and study at Columbia University, Ginsberg worked at a variety of odd jobs, began to experiment with drugs, to explore Zen Buddhism, and intensely absorbed the inspiration of other poets—including Blake, Whitman and Pound. He exploded onto the literary scene in 1956 with a collection of poems entitled *Howl,* apocalyptically chanting the alienation of "the best minds of my generation." The slim volume, with an introduction by another New Jersey poet, William Carlos Williams, was indicted in California for obscenity and thus won the author instant notoriety. Together with Jack Kerouac and William Burroughs, Ginsberg would be celebrated as a pioneer of the Beat Generation; both his work and his life—including his exuberant proclamation of homosexuality—were a protest against the conformity of the Eisenhower decade, and a herald of the youth revolution of the 1960's. In *Kaddish* (1960) he produced a painfully frank autobiographical elegy on the illness and death of his mother, in which her recurrent madness becomes a metaphor for the fall of Western civilization. Most of his later volumes are part of a single long, discursive, socially critical work based on his own travels and composed with the assistance of a tape-recorder. Ginsberg's characteristic poems are either short, intensely personal lyrics or long, rhapsodic discourses blending personal confession, social criticism, prophetic utterance and quasi-religious rituals. Above all, this egocentric and visionary poetry celebrates individual experience, pacifism and the need for human tenderness; its appeal is personal and immediate, and much of it only achieves its full effect through the poet's energetic public performances.

WITOLD GOMBROWICZ, born in Poland in 1904 to a prominent noble family, studied in Warsaw and Paris, and as a young man became a celebrated member of the Polish avant-garde. He made his literary debut with a collection of seven short stories entitled *Memoirs of Immaturity* (1933). When war broke out in Europe, Gombrowicz was visiting Buenos Aires, and he remained in Argentina for the next twenty-four years, isolated and unknown, but continuing to write. In 1958 his satirical novel *Ferdydurke,* originally published in 1937, appeared in a French translation and immediately established the author's European reputation. Gombrowicz described the book, which parodied in form the popular Polish novel of an earlier time, as "the struggle for maturity by a man in love with immaturity." The "myth of immaturity" also informs the grotesque satire on Polish nationalism, *Trans-Atlantyk* (1950), and *Pornografia* (1960), his best-known novel. In the latter two old men, intrigued and then indecently excited by the innocence of an adolescent boy and girl, conspire to bring about the consummation of the young people's imagined love. In seeking to make their fantasies real, the conspirators are figuratively participating in an elaborate homoerotic charade. Here, as in most of his writings, Gombrowicz demonstrated his fascination with the fusion of contraries. Like Gide, he felt the diary to be the form best suited to contemporary narration; his own diaries, which he began to publish in 1953, describe Proust as ineffectual, praise Genet as the greatest French writer, and acknowledge his close ties to the Existentialists. In 1963 Gombrowicz returned to Europe, settling in Vence in the South of France, where he died in 1969.

THOM(SON) GUNN, born in Gravesend, England, in 1929, studied at Cambridge University and at Stanford, and has for many years made his home in California. His first book of poems appeared in 1953, and he was early recognized as a gifted proponent of the "new" poetry in Britain. Unlike his English contemporaries, however, he did not cultivate a distanced, neutral poetic tone, but experimented widely with poetic forms and frequently explored violent themes, praising action over sensibility. In a poem on the bomb plot against Hitler, he stressed that violence may often be both rational and necessary; he has given heroic status to the black-jacketed motorcyclist, and bestowed his blessing on "all the toughs through history." But Gunn is also capable of immense tenderness, subtlety and intellectual complexity; his powerful images and compelling rhythms can vivify even the banal and commonplace subject. Among his most influential collections of verse are *The Sense of Movement* (1957), *My Sad Captains* (1961), *Touch* (1967) and *Jack Straw's Castle* (1976). *Touch* contains a remarkable sequence of poems entitled "Misanthropos" which deals with the plight of the last man alive after an atomic holocaust, and which richly illustrates the poet's tough humanism. Homosexual allusion has often played a role in Gunn's verse, but it has become more overt and more central in recent years.

MAARTEN 'T HART was born in 1944 in the small Dutch town of Maassluis, and presently teaches ethnology at the University of Leiden. While still studying biology at the university, he published his first novels—*Steenen voor een ransuil* (*Stones for a Horned Owl,* 1971) and *Ik had een wapenbroeder* (*I Had a Brother in Arms,* 1973); in these penetrating studies of psychological development, he focused on a working-class milieu indelibly stamped by the Reformed Church of Holland. The poverty, obsessive religiosity and sexual prudery he records were elements he knew well from his own childhood. In addition to various scholarly papers, Maarten 't Hart has written essays on music, feminism and the behavioral sciences; his short-story collection *Mammoet op Zondag* (*Mammoth on Sunday*) received the Dutch Literary Award for 1977.

ERNEST HEMINGWAY was born in upper-middle-class Oak Park, Illinois, in 1899, but his boyhood and youth were strongly influenced by the northern Michigan woods, where his doctor father introduced him to the rituals of the sportsman. After working briefly for the famous *Kansas City Star* as a cub reporter, Hemingway served in France and Italy as honorary lieutenant in the Red Cross ambulance corps. The wound he received on the Italian front became a central metaphor in his work, and he went on to become the leading spokesman for the so-called "lost generation." Hemingway's work as a newspaper reporter had a profound impact on his lean, understated prose; Sherwood Anderson, Gertrude Stein and Ezra Pound also helped shape his early style. In 1921 Hemingway and the first of his four wives settled in Paris, and in 1923 his first book, *Three Stories & Ten Poems,* appeared there, followed in 1925 by the American publication of *In Our Time.* These early stories record a midwestern boy's initiation into the duplicities of the adult world; they also show Hemingway's sympathy for the soldier, hunter and professional athlete. Later the bullfighter would be added to the galaxy of Hemingway heroes faced with elemental tests of dignity and courage; in the famous Hemingway "code," the hero was a stoic who never flinched at danger, never falsified his emotions, and always observed the rules of the game. In 1926 Hemingway published *The Sun Also Rises,* the definitive portrait of the lost generation, and in 1929 *A Farewell to Arms.* In the decades that followed, the legends of his escapades as drinker, lover and daredevil sportsman often overshadowed the work he produced. Though Hemingway sometimes aggressively projected the supermasculine "macho" image in both his prose and his life, many of his heroes reveal a surprising tenderness and emotional vulnerability. Homosexual characters are central to four of his stories: both "The Light of the World" and "The Mother of a Queen" are savage in their indictments, extending the negative tones with which a giddy crowd of homosexuals is presented in *The Sun Also Rises;* "Homage to Switzerland," though archly condescending, takes a somewhat more objective view; and "A Simple Enquiry" shows genuine compassion for the confused, sexually frustrated young officer. Ernest Hemingway was awarded the Nobel Prize for Literature in 1954, and in 1961 committed suicide at his ranch near Ketchum, Idaho.

WILLIAM INGE, born in Independence, Kansas, in 1913, was fascinated by the theater from childhood. While majoring in drama at the University of Kansas, he also acted with stock companies; though he then became a schoolteacher, he yearned for some connection with the theater, and in 1943 became drama and film critic for the St. Louis *Star Times.* The job gave Inge a life-long respect for the well-made play, and his own full-length dramas show a careful sense of craftsmanship, though his themes are conventional and his essentially realistic style can verge toward melodrama. Encouraged by Tennessee Williams, whom he greatly admired, Inge produced his first play in 1947, but his first real success was *Come Back, Little Sheba* (1950); it was rapidly followed by three other box-office hits —*Picnic* (1953), which received the Pulitzer Prize, *Bus Stop* (1955) and *The Dark at the Top of the Stairs* (1957). Inge's most important plays are psychodramas focusing on the lives of seemingly ordinary midwestern characters who, in the author's own words, suddenly reveal "surprising depths of feeling that lie far below the public surface of human personality." Inge's later works tend to be rather flat and repetitious, with an unhappy inclination toward platitudinous self-analysis; their seriousness is too often stated rather than demonstrated. The one-act plays—including *The Boy in the Basement*—are less polished and their dramatic mechanisms are sometimes clumsy, but they often reveal a raw power obscured in the realistic dramas critics praised so highly in the 1950's. William Inge died in 1973.

CHRISTOPHER ISHERWOOD was born in Cheshire, England, in 1904, and educated at Cambridge University. After a year of medical study in London, he went to Berlin in 1929 and remained there for the next four years—until "Hitler's coming to power made me an honorary refugee." Though his first novel, *All the Conspirators,* had appeared in 1928, it was with the publication of two impressionistic, highly episodic novels of the Berlin years—*Mr. Norris Changes Trains* (1935) and *Goodbye to Berlin* (1939)—that Isherwood established his reputation as a subtle, gifted social observer. In the 1930's Isherwood collaborated with W.H. Auden, his friend since boarding-school days, to produce three plays and a travel book describing their visit to China. In 1939 he went to California to work for the film industry and eventually became an American citizen. In his earlier writings Isherwood showed a pronounced fascination for eccentrics; his narrators take mischievous delight in depicting characters whom polite society would shun—including a series of older men obsessed by heterosexual youths. In later works the homosexual becomes more central and is far more complexly portrayed—as in *Down There on a Visit* (1962) and *A Single Man* (1964). In the autobiographical volume *Christopher and His Kind* (1976), Isherwood analyzed the period from his departure for Berlin to his arrival in America and acknowledged the deep conflict then existing between his sexual and social selves; his youthful homosexual existence was, he reasoned, one way of expressing his reaction against the stuffy Puritanism of his own class. His perennial themes of the multiplicity of self, loneliness and separation, and the search for a homeland can all be related to a fundamental rebellion against the "Others"—above all, against what Isherwood labels "the heterosexual dictatorship."

LEROI JONES was born in Newark, New Jersey, in 1934, and studied at Rutgers, Howard and Columbia universities, as well as the New School for Social Research, where he earned an M.A. in German literature. In 1964 three of his plays were produced in New York; one of them, *Dutchman,* spoke fiercely but lucidly to black Americans about the merciless destruction of their cultural identity. The works that followed—plays, poetry, short stories, essays and novels—became increasingly revolutionary, and Jones was the acknowledged new leader of the black cultural awakening. His semi-autobiographical novel, *The System of Dante's Hell* (1965), impressionistically equated the Newark slums with Dante's Inferno. To create a showcase for black theatrical talent, Jones founded the Black Arts Repertory Theater, but economic problems and his own continuing difficulties with the law forced its closing; in 1968 he formed the Black Community Development and Defense Organization, dedicated to the creation of new values for Afro-Americans. The organization encouraged the adoption of the Muslim faith and Arabic names; Jones himself assumed the name Amiri Baraka, preceded by the title "Imamu" for spiritual leader. His more recent writings continue to urge Afro-Americans to root out white values from their hearts, including the hypocrisy of Christianity. Rite and ritual play important roles here, and the voice is one of fierce, lyric urgency. Homosexual themes are present in several of Jones's works, including *Experimental Death Unit # 1* (1965), in which two homosexuals are beheaded by a black liberation army. In *The Toilet* Jones hints that the races may someday come together, but only after the black has earned his manhood by defeating the white.

CHRISTIAN KAMPMANN was born in Hellerup, Denmark, in 1939, and trained as a journalist. His novelistic career began in 1962 with *Blandt venner* (*Among Strangers*), but he first achieved major critical recognition with a complex tetraology of novels on the Gregersen family, published between 1973 and 1975. Beginning in the 1950's and continuing through the early 1970's, this chronicle traces the way in which a prosperous bourgeois family copes with the decay of older traditions, of the family as a self-contained and self-defining unit. Although neurosis often results from the new "freedom" of the post-war decades, Kampmann implies in the conclusion of the fourth volume that there is now hope for the individual's discovery of more fulfilling modes of self-expression. One of the central characters of the tetralogy is a homosexual who acts as spokesman for the novelist—thus anticipating the homosexual focus of Kampmann's autobiographical novel *Fornemmelser* (*Feelings,* 1978), which explores the conflicts aroused by the narrator's awakening recognition of his homosexual impulses. *Fornemmelser* is the first of a trilogy of novels that includes *Videre Trods Alt* (*Proceed in Spite of All,* 1979) and *I Glimt* (*In Flashes,* 1980). Kampmann himself has been an outspoken advocate for the social rights of homosexuals in Denmark.

STANLEY KAUFFMANN is the quintessential New Yorker. He was born in the city in 1916, studied at New York University, and has pursued a remarkably versatile career there in publishing, journalism and the theater. His early love for the theater led to work as actor, stage-manager and director, chiefly with the Washington Square Players. Following World War II he held editorial positions with several major publishers, and meanwhile began to write both plays and novels; most of the latter were concerned with the world of artists, writers and musicians he knew so well. *The Philanderer* (1954) became the subject of a famous obscenity case in the

English courts. As film critic for the *New Republic* and a member of the board of *Film Quarterly*, Kauffmann made an important contribution to the development of a new critical aesthetics for the motion picture, but he became best known as drama critic for the *New York Times;* his uncompromising standards and urbane style have made him one of the most feared and influential critics in America.

EDUARDO GUDIÑO KIEFFER, born in 1935 in Esperanza, Argentina, is a novelist and journalist distinguished by his passionate social engagement. For many years he served as foreign correspondent for numerous magazines and newspapers in Argentina. Newspaper headlines and captions frequently play a role in the collage-like structure of his novels, which seek to reveal the absurdity and grotesqueness, the quality of dread which he sees as a continuous element of contemporary experience. After the sensational *Para comerte mejor* (*The Better to Eat,* 1968), Kieffer published a picaresque novel in 1972 that explored the lives of the poor and the oppressed living in the underworld of Buenos Aires. It is from this work, *Guía de pecadores* (*Handbook for Sinners*), that the startling monologue of "Rara avis in terra" is extracted.

MIKHAIL ALEKSEYEVICH KUZMIN was born in St. Petersburg, Russia, in 1875. Little is known about his childhood, but as a young man he toured Italy and visited Alexandria—events that made a deep impression on his literary imagination. His first sonnets were published in 1905, and in 1906 he scandalized the literary *beau monde* of Russia by publishing a novel entitled *Wings,* clearly autobiographical in content and forthright in its portrayal of homosexual experience. Several of his "Alexandrian Songs" also explored homosexual themes; like *Wings,* the poems first appeared in *The Scales,* a symbolist journal, but were collected in a separate edition in 1921. In 1920 Kuzmin privately printed a collection of homoerotic poems, together with drawings by his friend Vladimir Milashevski. Strongly influenced by both the *fin-de-siècle* Aesthetes and the theories of Walter Pater, Kuzmin created a resonant poetic mythology focused on Alexandria. Mingling eroticism, an exquisite artificiality and the quest for Gnostic wisdom, the city of his poems has numerous parallels to the writings of Constantin Cavafy. Though later officially suppressed as "bourgeois-decadent," Kuzmin's *Alexandrian Songs* had an immense impact on his contemporaries. His uncanny sense for the avant-garde persists in the later poetry collections, *Parabolas* (1923) and *The Trout Breaks the Ice* (1929). During the Stalinist purges of the 1930's, Kuzmin's lover was executed, and he himself was reportedly on the list of those to be eliminated when he died in 1936.

DAVID HERBERT LAWRENCE was born in 1885 in the coal-mining village of Eastwood in Nottinghamshire, one of five children of a miner and a former schoolteacher. The conflict of sensibilities between his parents, the poverty and boredom and alcoholism that surrounded the family, would be documented in Lawrence's first mature novel, *Sons and Lovers* (1913). Lawrence nearly died of pneumonia in childhood, and his weakened lungs disqualified him for service in World War I; they also accounted for numerous later illnesses and his death from tuberculosis in 1930. Encouraged by his mother, Lawrence developed a deep love for books and a determination to receive a good education; he attended Nottingham University and after graduation worked as a schoolteacher. Meanwhile, he had already begun to write poetry, and in 1911 published his first novel, *The White Peacock.* Lawrence and his German wife Frieda spent most of their tempestuous married life abroad, chiefly in Italy and New Mexico. In one of his most famous novels, *Women in Love* (1920), the author described his central concern as "the passionate struggle into conscious being." Repeatedly, he showed men and women grappling with their inmost needs—often against the restrictions and conventions of society—and struggling to give them both emotional and intellectual fulfillment. Frequently, he contrasted a passionate, instinctive, "southern" temperament with an intellectual, icily controlled "northern" one. In Lawrence's ideal, the better qualities of the two were fused. The full articulation of the inner self also included sexual expression, and Lawrence's direct treatment of the theme often caused problems with the authorities. The entire first edition of *The Rainbow* (1915) was seized and destroyed, and *Lady Chatterley's Lover* (1928) was not legally published in England until 1960. In Lawrence's fiction and poetry there are often strong homoerotic implications, but his frankest treatment of homosexual yearning, the "Prologue" to *Women in Love,* seems to have been suppressed by the author himself.

FEDERICO GARCÍA LORCA spent most of his childhood on the farm outside Granada, Spain, where he was born in 1899; his most characteristic poetry and plays were deeply rooted in Spanish landscape and folklore. Lorca published his first book at the age of nineteen, and after a brief stay at the university devoted himself entirely to his literary endeavors, which included the transcription of Castilian folksongs, public readings of his own verse, and the organization of an annual folksong festival at the Alhambra. In

1929 Lorca departed for New York, where he lived at Columbia University for a year, though never formally attending classes. He spent hours each day wandering the streets, gathering images of the great city plagued by the Depression; in particular, he was drawn to Harlem, finding in the rhythms of Negro street life and music something that recalled the gypsy traditions of Spain. The isolated poems Lorca began to compose in his dormitory room gradually fitted together into the complex mosaic of *Poet in New York,* the visionary work first published four years after his death. The poem's imagery and tone differ considerably from those made familiar by *Gypsy Ballads* (1928), *Lament for the Death of a Bullfighter* (1937) and his plays, so frequently concerned with the tragic lot of women in rural Spain. Yet Lorca's obsession with primitive passions, earthy emotions and the omnipresence of death are central elements in the New York poems as well. Many have a feeling of hallucination, of a world in permanent metamorphosis—in part, at least, the result of recent exposure to the tenets of Surrealism. But Lorca's vision was also reshaped by the work of Walt Whitman, by a sense of the betrayal of Whitman's democratic faith. The year in America was clearly a period of emotional crisis for Lorca, and he may also have turned to Whitman as a fellow-poet who had successfully come to terms with his own homosexuality. In 1933 Lorca's most famous play, the stark rural tragedy of *Blood Wedding,* was first produced in Madrid. Shortly after the outbreak of the Civil War in 1936, Lorca was murdered by Franquist soldiers, and his books were burned in Granada's Plaza del Carmen.

WILLEM DE MERODE was born Willem Eduard Keuning in 1887, in the village of Groningen, Holland. In the orthodox Calvinistic household where he grew up, pleasure of every sort was regarded as sinful. De Merode began to teach in the village school in 1906, and nourished a deep love for literature—particularly the writings of the Decadents; Aestheticism, with its stress on individuality and "l'art pour l'art," had an immense appeal, and inspired his own youthful, pseudonymous writings. The early poems he published in literary reviews brought him new contacts and acquaintances, as well as the courage to live more openly with his own homosexuality. In 1924 he was sentenced to eight months in prison for allegedly seducing a minor; after serving the sentence he officially withdrew from the church and retired to a small farm, where he lived obscurely until his death in 1939. De Merode's writings are shaped by his own long spiritual conflict with religious dogma and by the seemingly antagonistic demands of the flesh and the spirit. Only in recent years has he been given proper critical recognition as a writer of poetry distinguished both by its rich contemplative mood and its refined lyricism.

YUKIO MISHIMA was the pen-name of the brilliant Japanese novelist, dramatist and short-story writer born in Tokyo in 1925. His real name was Kimitake Hiraoka, and he adopted his pseudonym at the age of sixteen, when his first fiction was published; so successful was he in promoting the dynamic popular image of warrior-writer that the Japanese public was unaware of his true identity until after his death. Mishima was a sickly, delicate child, dominated by a severe grandmother who instilled in him a fanatical reverence for the family's ancient Samurai tradition. One of his obsessions was the beauty of the violent or painful death of a handsome youth; later he himself posed for photographs as St. Sebastian, and his writings were frequently preoccupied with blood, death and suicide. Rejected as physically unfit for service in World War II, he worked in a munitions factory and later studied at the University of Tokyo. After a brief career in banking, he devoted himself completely to literature, producing both serious novels and popular romances, plays for the No and Kabuki theaters, film scenarios, short stories and essays. Though influenced by European writers and devoted to Greek culture, he deplored the corruption of Japanese tradition by the introduction of Western values. Soon after his marriage in 1959 Mishima began a rigorous campaign of kendo and bodybuilding, seeking to make his physique conform to the Samurai ideal. Eventually he founded a private army, the *Tate no kai* (Shield Society), dedicated to the military arts and defense of the Emperor. In 1970 the *Tate no kai* stormed the military headquarters near downtown Tokyo; after a ten-minute speech from the balcony, Yukio Mishima committed harakiri and was decapitated by one of his followers.

ROBERT MUSIL was born in 1880 in the small but prosperous city of Klagenfurth, Austria. As a boy he was trained for a military career and spent some time in the same grim academy where the poet Rilke had been so desperately unhappy. While Musil adapted well to such rigors, he quit the military academy in Vienna shortly before being commissioned in favor of studying civil engineering. Ultimately, mathematics and machines failed to satisfy him, and he enrolled as a student of philosophy at the University of Berlin, earning his Ph.D. in 1908. Meanwhile, Musil had completed *Young Törless,* whose publication in 1906 won wide acclaim as a sensitive, complex study of the psychology of puberty. Through an adolescent's painful initiation into the mechanisms of sexuality and power, Musil examined the thin tissues of convention separating the rational world from the dangerous but alluring world of the irrational. Musil rejected a promising academic career to pursue his literary ambitions, and in 1911 published *Vereinigungen,* a pair of stories minutely scrutinizing the emotional and psychological consequences of adultery. From 1914 to 1918 he served as an officer in the Austrian Army, first at the front and later as a military journalist. From 1922 he lived in Vienna as a free-lance novelist, playwright and critic, devoting his most intense energies to a vast novel entitled *The Man without Qualities,* which established his international reputation. The first volume appeared in 1930, the second in 1933, but the work was still unfinished in 1942 when Musil died in Geneva, where he lived in exile after the affiliation of Austria with Nazi Germany. Some critics see the ambitious novel as a product of German Expressionism; others liken its unhurried sweep and bristling detail, its wit and verbal dexterity, to the work of James Joyce. It offers a breathtaking, constantly shifting panorama of a culture and shows a continuous refinement of the concern with psychology that characterized all Musil's writings.

YVES NAVARRE, born in Gascogne, France, in 1940, made a spectacular novelistic debut in 1971 with *Lady Black*, the memoirs of a transvestite. He soon established himself as one of the most prolific writers of his generation, as well as an articulate advocate of homosexual experience. *Evolène* (1972), the story of the solitude of a seven-year-old child, confirmed his talent, but the book most enthusiastically received by the critics was *Sweet Tooth* (1973). Set in New York, the novel's fragmented narrative presents the bizarre, interlocking stories of three characters doomed by obsession and disease. Like most of Navarre's fiction—including *Killer* (1975)—the novel blended tender intimacy with raw candor; the city itself is seen as predatory, and the scenes in New York's sexual underground are brutally explicit. Yves Navarre has not only produced a novel a year since *Lady Black,* but numerous pieces for the theater; he has been actively involved in the homosexual rights movement, and took a leading part in creating the *Syndicat des Ecrivains de la Langue Française* in 1976. His most recent novel, *Le jardin d'acclimatation,* received the Prix Goncourt in 1980.

FRANK O'HARA was born in 1926 in Baltimore, Maryland, and the following year his family moved to Massachusetts, where he attended school. At the precocious age of fifteen he was admitted to the New England Conservatory as a piano student. After two years in the Navy, O'Hara entered Harvard College; there he majored in music and began to compose poetry. He had already developed a passionate interest in American painting, and when he moved to New York in 1951, was employed at the Museum of Modern Art; his first collection of poems, *A City Winter* (1952), was published by the Tibor de Nagy Gallery. At the Club of New York Painters he met Franz Kline, Willem de Kooning and Jackson Pollock, and also cultivated a broad circle of friendship in the musical and literary worlds of New York. Among the most influential volumes of poetry published during his lifetime were *Lunch Poems* (1964) and *Love Poems* (1965), the latter including several of the remarkable love poems written to Vincent Warren from 1959 to 1961. O'Hara's verse had little in common with American literary traditions; it was influenced by Rimbaud, Mallarmé and Mayakovsky, but even more fundamentally shaped by the poet's love for music and painting. The Abstract Expressionists helped him develop a concept of art as process, of the poem as living chronicle of the creative act. Most of his subjects were provided by New York, with its surrealistic accumulations of imagery, its nightmares and delights and paradoxes; the poems have a consistent visual precision, though their moods range from exuberance to melancholy. O'Hara also produced verse dramas, incidental music and distinguished art criticism—including *Jackson Pollock* (1959) and *Robert Motherwell* (1965). He died as a result of a beach accident in 1966.

DARCY PENTEADO was born in São Roque (São Paulo), Brazil, in 1926, and started to work as a commercial artist at the age of eighteen. In 1945 he began to illustrate books, and later would design costumes for both the theater and television. Penteado's lyrically romantic paintings, which often have a clear homosexual content, have been exhibited not only throughout Brazil, but also in Europe and the United States. The sense of delicate fantasy that characterizes his visual art is also a prominent element in Penteado's three collections of short stories—*The Goal* (1976), *Crescilda and the Spartans* (1977) and *Theoremambo* (1979). In the form of contemporary fables and inverted fairy-tales, they frequently employ motifs of transformation: a married homosexual permanently altered by an affair with a transvestite, a transsexual couple who have sex changes before their marriage, a naive fairy godmother who punishes her beautiful godson by turning him into a heterosexual, a leading intellectual revealed as a transvestite rhumba-dancer. Penteado repeatedly seeks to demystify sexual, religious and social taboos; his comic inventiveness and incisive irony have led Brazilian critics to compare Penteado to Mark Twain.

ANNA RHEINSBERG was born in Berlin in 1956 and spent her childhood in a small town in Niedersachsen. At the University of Marburg she studied folklore and German literature, and continues to live in Marburg as a free-lance writer. Her first book, a collection of poems entitled *Marlene in den Gassen* (*Marlene in the Alleys*) appeared in 1979, the same year in which she helped found a new feminist journal in Germany. Rheinsberg's recent novel, *Die Reise nach Jerusalem* (*The Journey to Jerusalem,* 1981), is the story of a pregnant fourteen-year-old as related by an objective narrator, the girl herself, and a diary covering the months of her pregnancy. Anna Rheinsberg worked for a time for *Don,* one of Germany's most successful magazines for male homosexuals, and there she published numerous erotic stories, as well as critical articles. "Visiting" originally appeared in a volume entitled *Wo die Nacht den Tag umarmt* (*Where the Night Embraces the Day,* 1980), a collection of stories in which women were invited to explore their own sexual fantasies.

H.H. VON W. was the pseudonym of an author who contributed to Adolf Brand's *Der Eigene* (*The Special*), a periodical of "masculine art and culture" that first appeared in 1896. Adolf Brand, its founder, was a member of the so-called "Community of the Special," a homosexual rights organization active in the campaign to repeal discriminatory legislation, but equally concerned with the promotion of cultural achievements. In 1907 Brand himself wrote a courageous attack on the notorious "Paragraph 175," but his claim that Chancellor von Bülow was a homosexual brought him a prison sentence. Following World War I *Der Eigene* became an important literary forum, and began to publish its own books. Among them was a collection of stories entitled *Armer Junge!* (*Poor Boy!*), edited by German author Hanns Heinz Ewers in 1927. That volume provides the source for the anonymous "Marquis de Saint-Brissac." Publication of *Der Eigene* was suppressed by the National Socialists, and Brand himself was killed during an air-raid on Berlin in 1945.

LOUIS WILKINSON was born in Aldeburgh, Suffolk, in 1881, the son of a clergyman who afterwards kept a school in the town. According to Frank Harris, Wilkinson "sucked in rebellion with his mother's milk," and throughout his life remained highly critical of convention. Expelled from Pembroke College, Oxford, for what the authorities described as blasphemy, he completed his education at the more liberal St. John's College, Cambridge. A small inheritance gave him the freedom to travel widely, supplementing his income by lecturing and writing. Married four times, he had three daughters and a son, and as one of the last great cosmopolitans was equally at home in London, Berlin, New York and Rome. In addition to numerous shorter pieces, he published ten novels, three biographical works and two volumes of autobiography. Some of these, including "The Better End," appeared under the nom-de-plume of Louis Marlow. Wilkinson died on September 13, 1966.

WILLIAM CARLOS WILLIAMS attended preparatory schools in Geneva and Paris and did postgraduate study in pediatrics at the University of Leipzig, but his name is permanently linked with the town of Rutherford, New Jersey, where he was born in 1883 and spent all his professional life. As a student at the University of Pennsylvania, Williams came to know Ezra Pound, and his earliest poems show a clear debt to the Imagist school, which stressed the need for a new poetry that relied on clear, precise and concentrated images to express its meaning, much in the manner of Japanese Haiku. The tenets of Imagism were clearly etched in Williams's first books, *Poems* (1909) and *The Tempers* (1913). As his own poetic voice matured, Williams found the Imagist formula restricting, and developed the thesis of "Objectivism," in which the poem itself was regarded as an object projecting its meaning primarily through form. His technique became freer and more vernacular, but was still characterized by vivid observation restricted almost entirely to sensory experience—in such volumes as *Collected Poems* (1934), *Pictures from Brueghel* (1963) and the four parts of an ambitious, structureless epic entitled *Paterson* published between 1946 and 1951. Williams practiced medicine until a few years before his death in 1963; seen in terms of his demanding career as a pediatrician, his literary output was truly prodigious—embracing not only more than twenty volumes of poetry, but essays, novels, plays and autobiographical works. Among them is a collection of impressionistic essays, *In the American Grain*, widely regarded as one of the most remarkable prose works in modern English. Williams's particular gift for reducing experience to its essence and holding emotion at arm's length is also richly evident in short stories like "The Sailor's Son," collected in *The Knife of the Times* in 1932.